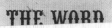

THE WORD

D0628611

A HUNDRED YEARS.

★★★

It brings to mind a campfire on a starry night, riding the range with the wind in your face or conquering a ton of bucking bull for an eight-second ride.

Whether that's you getting down on that bronc in the chute, backing in the roping box, or a working cowboy making a living,

watching your favorite western movie, on vacation enjoying a trail ride or just pulling on your boots and hat to go to a rodeo, you've felt the cowboy spirit.

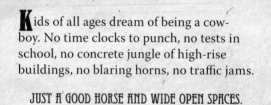

Kids of all ages dream of being a cowboy. No time clocks to punch, no tests in school, no concrete jungle of high-rise buildings, no blaring horns, no traffic jams.

JUST A GOOD HORSE AND WIDE OPEN SPACES.

★ ★ ★

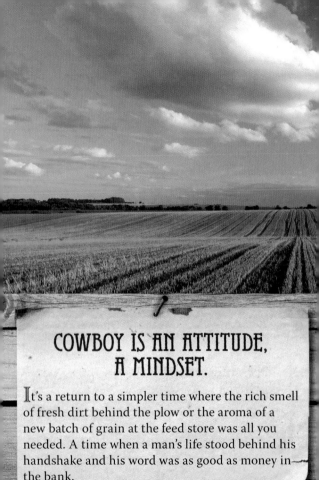

COWBOY IS AN ATTITUDE, A MINDSET.

It's a return to a simpler time where the rich smell of fresh dirt behind the plow or the aroma of a new batch of grain at the feed store was all you needed. A time when a man's life stood behind his handshake and his word was as good as money in the bank.

LOOKING FOR THE WAY...

★★★

A favorite pastime for cowboys is telling stories. Whether it's around a campfire or on tailgates at a rodeo, there's nothing better than a good story.

Have you ever noticed that your group of friends has a favorite story? You can tell it over and over again, and no one gets tired of it.

Stories are what give us meaning. They give us identity. The sharing of a story makes us feel included. The more stories we share, the more we bond together.

A similar thing happens with this book you hold in your hand. The Bible tells the story of the Creator making everything, of the world going astray and then of the Creator working to restore it. The interesting part is that the work of restoration is going on right now, continuing the big story that's told in these pages. You have the opportunity to become a character in the story. You can begin telling others how God is active in your life as you sit on the tailgate telling stories.

It's very important to dive deep into the story of the Bible. Grabbing a small phrase here and there gives you a little glimpse, but it doesn't get you into the story. It's like a city slicker who comes to a rodeo saying, "I like broncs and spurs." You know he's not a cowboy, but you can encourage him to learn more and grow into that life.

The best way to read the Bible is to read whole books or big sections. That's how you'll get to know the real Bible.

HOW TO READ THIS BOOK

★ ★ ★

This deep story of the Bible tells us of a God who loves us so much that he gave what was most precious to him—his only Son, Jesus—to redeem us of our selfish ways.

Reading the Bible will help you learn who Jesus is, and how he came to bring God's rule back to earth. He showed us the Way that God always wanted us to live. The Bible will challenge you to come into God's kingdom by following Jesus.

Try the following reading plan for 28 days. Here are some steps to get you started:

1. Pick a regular time to read. It may be early in the day or late at night, but try to keep it the same. Plan on a minimum of 10 minutes.

2. Choose a quiet place where you can be alone. This can be tough, but getting away from phones, computers and the TV really pays off.

3. Make sure you have a pen and notebook with you to write down questions or thoughts you have as you read.

Some days you just won't want to go through the discipline. But remember, as in other areas of life, it is the consistency that results in steady progress.

28 DAYS TO START THE WAY

WHAT SHOULD I READ WHEN...?

The Scriptures were written by God's people a long time ago. But God is the same, and God's word speaks powerfully to us today:

So, what should I read when...

I feel **alone**? Psalm 13 (p 358); Psalm 22 (p 365)
I'm **anxious**? Philippians 4 (p 265)
I'm **angry**? James 1:19-27 (p 305)
I **can't sleep**? Psalm 4 (p 352)
I'm in **danger**? Psalm 91 (p 423)
I'm **depressed**? Psalm 34 (p 374)
I'm **discouraged**? Psalm 42 (p 382);
    2 Corinthians 4 (p 240)
Everything's **going right**? Psalm 103 (p 430);
    Psalm 150 (p 466)
I need **forgiveness**? Psalm 51 (p 389)
God seems **distant**? Psalm 139 (p 458)
I'm **grieving**? Psalm 88 (p 419); Psalm 70 (p 403)
I'm **lonely**? Psalm 23 (p 366)
I feel **lost**? Romans 8:18-39 (p 209)
I can't find **peace**? John 14 (p 144)
I need **hope** for the future? 1 Corinthians 15 (p 234)
I'm in a **struggle**? Ephesians 6:10-20 (p 261)
I want to know about **God's love**? John 13–17 (p 143)
I'm **tempted**? James 1:12-16 (p 305)
I'm **thankful**? Psalm 100 (p 428)
I'm **worried**? Matthew 6:19-34 (p 8)

THE DRAMA OF THE BIBLE

INTRODUCTION

The heart and soul of the Bible is its story. It is God's story; he is the Storyteller and it's about God. It is the real saga of a particular people, how God called them and dealt with them. He intended for them to be the means by which he would bring his redemption—restoration and liberation from sin—to the world. The Bible really is The Greatest Story Ever Told.

To understand the Bible you must get to know its characters, understand its setting and follow its plot. The climax and ultimate resolution will make sense only if you've followed the earlier parts of the story.

Here is an abbreviated version of the story of the Bible as a drama in five acts. In the end this story can't be put safely back on the shelf. This is a dangerous story—it's risky to read—because it eventually claims to be your story. It is not merely relevant to your life. It doesn't just have lessons that apply to your life. In one way or another, it is your life's story. The question, of course, is Where do you fit in? Or, what part will you play?

ACT I: INTENTION

The drama begins with God on stage at work. He is creating the world. He makes a man, Adam, out of the ground and places him in the Garden of Eden to work in it and take care of it. (Adamah is the word for ground in the original Hebrew language, in which this part of the Bible was written.)

One of the fundamental teachings of the Bible is that God is the Creator. The creation is completely dependent on him. Any beauty, strength or order found in the creation is there only because God put it there. The creation itself is not divine, but it reflects the power of God and his own delight in beauty. It points us toward the true God.

Act I reveals God's desire for humans and provides the setting for all the action that follows. God's intention is for humanity to be in close, intimate relationship with him and in harmony with the rest of creation around them. God is described in these early chapters of the Bible as dwelling in the garden with the first human beings, Adam and Eve. At the end of the first chapter of Genesis, God gives his own assessment of his work: *God saw all that he had made, and it was very good.*

ACT II: EXILE

Tension is introduced in the story almost immediately when Adam and Eve decide to figure things out on their own. They listen to the beguiling voice of God's enemy, Satan, and doubt the word that God has given them. The disobedience of Adam and Eve—the first instance of sin—is presented in the Bible as having devastating consequences for all of the human race and all of creation:

> *The earth dries up and withers,*
> *the world languishes and withers,*
> *the exalted of the earth languish.*
> *The earth is defiled by its people;*
> *they have disobeyed the laws,*
> *violated the statutes*
> *and broken the everlasting covenant.*
> *Therefore a curse consumes the earth.*
> —the prophet Isaiah

The first exile in the story takes place as a result of this rebellion: *The LORD God banished him [Adam] from the Garden of Eden to work the ground from which he had been taken. After he drove them out, he placed on the east side of the Garden of Eden cherubim and a flaming sword flashing back and forth to guard the way to the tree of life.*

The story of humanity in the Bible is a tale of greatness and tragedy. Created as a unity, body and soul together, we are unique in God's creation. We alone are made in God's likeness. Yet at times we behave in ways that are barely higher than the beasts. This paradox is explained within the story of the Bible. Placed in a special role over the rest of creation, humans squandered this unique status and rebelled against God.

So the gifts of reason, language and creativity, intended to be used in service to God and others, are turned to destructive and selfish ends. The question is then raised: Can God regain his relationship with humanity and remove the curse from the creation, or did God's enemy effectively end the plan and subvert the story?

Act I and Act II only take up the first few pages in the Bible. Yet they introduce the struggle that dominates the rest of the story. From this point on God will be working to end the rebellion of the people he created and lift the curse on the earth.

ACT III: CALLING ISRAEL TO A MISSION

The LORD had said to Abram, "Leave your country, your people and your father's household and go to the land I will show you.

> *"I will make you into a great nation,*
> *and I will bless you;*
> *I will make your name great,*
> *and you will be a blessing.*
> *I will bless those who bless you,*
> *and whoever curses you I will curse;*
> *and all peoples on earth*
> *will be blessed through you."*
>
> —from the Book of Genesis

Abraham (called Abram here) is the beginning of the divine answer to the trouble Adam caused. In calling Abraham and promising to make him into a great nation, God is narrowing his focus and concentrating on one group of people for a period of time. But the ultimate goal remains the same: to bless every group of people on earth, to remove the curse and to restore the original relationship.

When Abraham's descendants are enslaved in Egypt, a central pattern in the upcoming story is set: God returns to his people, frees them and restores them to the land he'd promised them. God makes a covenant with this new nation of Israel at Mt. Sinai, having appointed Moses to be their leader during their liberation from Egypt—the Exodus. As part of the covenant, God makes it clear that if Israel remains true to him and faithfully follows his ways, he will bless them in their new land. This land is compared to the Garden of Eden in beauty and abundance, making it clear that Israel is being used by God to restore the human race.

However, if Israel isn't faithful to the covenant, God warns them that he will have to send them out of the land into exile, just as he did with Adam and Eve. In spite of God's repeated warnings, pleadings and even cajoling, Israel breaks the covenant, follows the false gods and brings the judgment of God on itself.

So God faces a two-fold difficulty. Adam has fallen and taken the world down with him. Israel, whom God has chosen to help set this problem right, has now become part of the problem.

As the story progresses however, God plants the seeds of a better outcome. When Israel asks for a human king, God appoints one, even while he protests. The monarchy brings Israel no closer to keeping the covenant with God. In fact, the kings often lead the way into sin. But one king, David, is noted for being "a man after God's own heart." So God promises to send a new king to Israel, a son of David, who will lead Israel wisely and bring the nation back to God.

Act III—and the Old Testament—ends with Israel in shambles and God apparently absent. But the hope of a promise remains. Since God has done it before, perhaps he will rescue Israel once more. Perhaps there will be a new Moses, or a new David, who will lead Israel out of its self-inflicted misery. The fate not just of Israel, but of the whole world, rests on this possibility.

ACT IV: THE SURPRISING VICTORY OF JESUS

Centuries later, the people of Israel are groaning under Roman occupation and waiting for God to return. An angel of God comes to a young woman named Mary and announces, *"You will be with child and give birth to a son, and you are to give him the name Jesus. He will be great and will be called the Son of the Most High. The Lord God will give him the throne of his father David, and he will reign over the house of Jacob forever; his kingdom will never end"* (from the Gospel of Luke). The seeds God planted in the first three acts are now bearing fruit with his own Son coming as the Messiah, the promised deliverer, to make things right for Israel.

Jesus' arrival is introduced with the claim that at long last God is keeping his promise. (One important aid to understanding the New Testament is to realize that it repeatedly claims to be the fulfillment of Old Testament promises.) From the beginning God planned for Christ to become the key to the story. When God promised Abraham that the whole world would be blessed through his offspring, he kept this promise in Jesus. Without Christ the story is incomplete, with problems introduced but no viable solution offered. Christ fulfills all that God has said he will do for his people.

Jesus heals sickness and disease among the people—those things that are signs of the curse on the creation. He confronts God's enemies in the spiritual realm—the demons—and forcefully orders them to leave the people they torment. Jesus forgives the sins of those who humbly come to him. The heart of Jesus' message is the good news of the coming of God's reign: God is coming back to dwell with his people. This is why Jesus is called Immanuel, which means "God with us." The Old Testament hope that God would dwell with his people and set things right has been fulfilled.

But Jesus receives mixed responses. Many people watch him with amazement, not knowing quite what to make of him. Some believe, and out of these Jesus chooses twelve followers. (Twelve is a symbolic number showing that Jesus was claiming to build a new nation of Israel around himself, based on the twelve tribes of Israel.) But the religious leaders, the scribes and Pharisees, quickly become hostile toward him. This conflict escalates to the breaking point when the religious leaders conspire to have Jesus arrested and killed by the Romans.

So the story of the Bible has come to this: The Creator sends his own Son to defeat evil and call his people back home into relationship with him—but his very own people turn on his Son and hand him over to be crucified. It would appear that all of God's attempts to reverse the downward spiral of the history of the world are coming to nothing. First Adam fails and all his offspring are polluted. Then Abraham's children, who were chosen to bring blessing and reverse Adam's fall, fail repeatedly themselves. Now God's ultimate effort, sending his own Son, seemingly fails. Whatever it is that mars the hearts of human beings seems to be beyond repair.

But the thing about stories (the good ones anyway) is that there is always a surprise somewhere, a twist that shows that things aren't what they seem. And that's what happens here.

God's ultimate defeat, the failure of his final plan, is actually, miraculously, his greatest victory. The death of Jesus is not a defeat after all. The death of Jesus turns the tables on God's enemy and turns the world upside down. By willingly sacrificing his life, Jesus takes onto himself God's judgment for our wrongdoing. As the early Christian leader Paul later wrote: *God made you alive with Christ. He forgave us all our sins, having canceled the written code, with its regulations, that was against us and that stood opposed to us; he took it away, nailing it to the cross. And having disarmed the powers and authorities, he made a public spectacle of them, triumphing over them by the cross* (from the Letter to the Colossians).

God publicly declares this victory by raising Jesus from the dead. The resurrection shows Jesus to be who he claimed: the promised one who is bringing the rule of God back to our world.

Jesus speaks the message of God as Israel's true prophet. He defeats the very power behind all evil as Israel's true king, the son of David. He gives up his own life as a sacrifice for his people as Israel's true priest. He leads his people to a new exodus, through death to a new life, as a new Moses. In all of this Jesus shows himself to be the true Israel, the promised child of Abraham who reconciles humanity with God. It is through Jesus, the faithful and obedient one, that Israel can finally fulfill its role, the purpose God called Abraham for.

Because he is the true Israel, Jesus is also a new Adam. Jesus is a new start for the entire human race: *Since death came through a man, the resurrection of the dead comes also through a man. For as in Adam all die, so in Christ all will be made alive* (from the Letter of 1 Corinthians).

God's intention for humanity has been reclaimed.

ACT V: THE NEW PEOPLE OF GOD

If the key victory has already been won, why is there another Act? The answer is that God wants the victory of Jesus to spread to all the nations of the world. The risen Jesus says to his disciples, *"Peace be with you! As the Father has sent me, I am sending you"* (from the Gospel of John).

God is gathering people from all around the world and forming them into his church. These Messiah-followers are being built into God's new temple, the place where his Spirit lives. They are the community of those who have pledged their allegiance to Jesus as the true Lord of the world. They are the ones who have already crossed from death into new life, through the power of the Spirit of God. They demonstrate God's love across the usual boundaries of race, class, tribe and nation.

According to the New Testament, all those who belong to the Messiah are children of Abraham, heirs of both the ancient promises and the ancient mission. The task of bringing blessing to the peoples of the world has been given again to Abraham's family. Their mission is to live out the liberating message of the good news of God's kingdom.

Forgiveness of sins and reconciliation with God can now be announced to all. Following in the steps of Jesus, his followers are to proclaim this gospel of the kingdom in both word and deed. The power of this new, God-given life breaking into the world is to be demonstrated by the real-world actions of the Christian community. The message also has a warning, however. When the Messiah returns, he will come as the rightful judge of the world.

The Bible is the story of the central struggle winding its way through the history of the world. And now the story moves right up to our own time, enveloping us into its drama.

So the challenge of a decision confronts us. What will we do? How will we fit into this story? What role will we play? God is inviting us to be a part of his mission of re-creation—of bringing restoration, healing, justice and forgiveness. We are to join in the task of making things new.

ACT VI: REUNION

For now, we live in the time of the overlap of the ages. God's future has already begun because of the work of Jesus the Messiah. Yet the present evil age continues. The final Act is coming, but it has not yet arrived.

We live in the time of invitation, and the call of the gospel goes out to every creature. Of course, many still live as though God did not exist. They do not acknowledge the rule of the Messiah. But the day is coming when Jesus will return and the reign of God will become an uncontested reality throughout the world. Those who have rejected God's rule will be judged.

God's plan of redemption will reach its goal. The creation will experience its own Exodus, finding freedom from its bondage to decay. The curse will be removed. Pain and tears, regret and shame, suffering and death will be no more.

When the day of resurrection arrives God's people will find that their hope has been realized. The dynamic force of an indestructible life will course through their bodies. Empowered by the Spirit, and unhindered by sin and death, a renewed humanity will pursue their original vocation. They will be culture-makers, under God but over the world. Having been remade in the image of Christ, they will share in bringing his wise, caring rule to the earth.

But at the center of it all will be God himself. He will return and make his home with us, this time in a new heavens and a new earth. We, along with the rest of creation, will worship him perfectly and fulfill our true calling. God will be all in all, and the whole world will be full of his glory.

KNOWING HOW TO LIVE THE STORY

The story of Jesus offers a new beginning for humanity and confronts each of us with a personal choice. If you haven't begun to follow the way that Jesus provided for restoring your relationship with God, this section will help you to understand what this means. If you are following Jesus, these ideas are valuable in helping you realize what you have been given through the Messiah.

Soon after Jesus had given his mission to his followers and returned to God's realm, Peter (who was a disciple of Jesus and a leader in the early church) was speaking to a gathering of Jews. He recounts the story of Jesus' life, death and resurrection, then challenges them to make the right response to what God has done for them:

"Repent, then, and turn to God, so that your sins may be wiped out, that times of refreshing may come from the Lord, and that he may send the Christ, who has been appointed for you—even Jesus. He must remain in heaven until the time comes for God to restore everything, as he promised long ago through his holy prophets. For Moses said, 'The Lord your God will raise up for you a prophet like me from among your own people; you must listen to everything he tells you. Anyone who does not listen to him will be completely cut off from among his people.'

"Indeed, all the prophets from Samuel on, as many as have spoken, have foretold these days. And you are heirs of the prophets and of the covenant God made with your fathers. He said to Abraham, 'Through your offspring all peoples on earth will be blessed.' When God raised up his servant, he sent him first to you to bless you by turning each of you from your wicked ways" (from the Book of Acts).

Peter connects Jesus' sacrifice to the ancient promise made to Abraham. He makes clear that now is the time for the blessing to occur. God has made a way for you to turn away from your wrong-doing and return to him.

As a son or daughter of Adam, you were born separated from God and the close, trusting relationship he desires to have with you. Jesus is the one who can bring you back to God. Your sins can be forgiven and your life can be renewed when you personally accept Christ's sacrifice on your behalf. As John's account of the story of Jesus puts it:

"For God so loved the world that he gave his one and only Son, that whoever believes in him shall not perish but have eternal life" (from the Gospel of John).

Your life's story can be rewritten within the storyline of the Bible. You can join with God's people from all over the world who are living out Act V today. For this to happen, though, you must turn away from your sins and commit to trust and follow Jesus.

THE

NEW TESTAMENT
PSALMS AND PROVERBS

NEW INTERNATIONAL VERSION®

Biblica™

COLORADO SPRINGS · HYDERABAD · LONDON · MANILA · MIAMI · NAIROBI

Call us today or visit us online to receive a free catalog featuring hundreds
of Scripture products priced for ministry.

Website: BiblicaDirect.com   **Phone:** 800-524-1588
E-mail: BiblicaService@Biblica.com   **Mail:** 1820 Jet Stream Drive
                                     Colorado Springs, CO 80921-3696

Transforming lives through God's Word
1820 Jet Stream Drive, Colorado Springs, CO 80921-3696

Eng. NT NIV 1914/1918/1955/1956/1957/1958/1959/1969/BB064/CC183   12/09
45000/18000/65000/77000/120000/45000/20000/20000/30000/20000   Printed in U.S.A.
1914: ISBN 978-1-56320-603-0   1918: ISBN 978-1-56320-604-7
1955: ISBN 978-1-56320-606-1   1956: ISBN 978-1-56320-605-4
1957: ISBN 978-1-56320-601-6   1958: ISBN 978-1-56320-607-8
1959: ISBN 978-1-56320-608-5   1969: ISBN 978-1-56320-581-1

Contents

Contents

The Drama of the Bible 1A

The New Testament

A Word about the NIV ....

THE
NEW TESTAMENT

Matthew

The Genealogy of Jesus

1 1 A record of the genealogy of Jesus Christ the son of David, the son of Abraham:

2 Abraham was the father of Isaac,
Isaac the father of Jacob,
Jacob the father of Judah and his brothers,
3 Judah the father of Perez and Zerah, whose mother was Tamar,
Perez the father of Hezron,
Hezron the father of Ram,
4 Ram the father of Amminadab,
Amminadab the father of Nahshon,
Nahshon the father of Salmon,
5 Salmon the father of Boaz, whose mother was Rahab,
Boaz the father of Obed, whose mother was Ruth,
Obed the father of Jesse,
6 and Jesse the father of King David.

David was the father of Solomon, whose mother had been Uriah's wife,
7 Solomon the father of Rehoboam,
Rehoboam the father of Abijah,
Abijah the father of Asa,
8 Asa the father of Jehoshaphat,
Jehoshaphat the father of Jehoram,
Jehoram the father of Uzziah,
9 Uzziah the father of Jotham,
Jotham the father of Ahaz,
Ahaz the father of Hezekiah,
10 Hezekiah the father of Manasseh,
Manasseh the father of Amon,
Amon the father of Josiah,
11 and Josiah the father of Jeconiah[a] and his brothers at the time of the exile to Babylon.

12 After the exile to Babylon:
Jeconiah was the father of Shealtiel,
Shealtiel the father of Zerubbabel,
13 Zerubbabel the father of Abiud,
Abiud the father of Eliakim,
Eliakim the father of Azor,
14 Azor the father of Zadok,
Zadok the father of Akim,
Akim the father of Eliud,
15 Eliud the father of Eleazar,
Eleazar the father of Matthan,
Matthan the father of Jacob,
16 and Jacob the father of Joseph, the husband of Mary, of whom was born Jesus, who is called Christ.

17 Thus there were fourteen generations in all from Abraham to David, fourteen from David to the exile to Babylon, and fourteen from the exile to the Christ.[b]

The Birth of Jesus Christ

18 This is how the birth of Jesus Christ came about: His mother Mary was pledged to be married to Joseph, but before they came together, she was found to be with child through the Holy Spirit. 19 Because Joseph her husband was a righteous man and did not want to expose her to

---

a 11 That is, Jehoiachin; also in verse 12   *b* 17 Or *Messiah*. "The Christ" (Greek) and "the Messiah" (Hebrew) both mean "the Anointed One."

1

public disgrace, he had in mind to divorce her quietly.

20 But after he had considered this, an angel of the Lord appeared to him in a dream and said, "Joseph son of David, do not be afraid to take Mary home as your wife, because what is conceived in her is from the Holy Spirit. **21** She will give birth to a son, and you are to give him the name Jesus,[c] because he will save his people from their sins."

22 All this took place to fulfill what the Lord had said through the prophet: **23** "The virgin will be with child and will give birth to a son, and they will call him Immanuel"[d] — which means, "God with us."

24 When Joseph woke up, he did what the angel of the Lord had commanded him and took Mary home as his wife. **25** But he had no union with her until she gave birth to a son. And he gave him the name Jesus.

The Visit of the Magi

2 **1** After Jesus was born in Bethlehem in Judea, during the time of King Herod, Magi[e] from the east came to Jerusalem **2** and asked, "Where is the one who has been born king of the Jews? We saw his star in the east[f] and have come to worship him."

3 When King Herod heard this he was disturbed, and all Jerusalem with him. **4** When he had called together all the people's chief priests and teachers of the law, he asked them where the Christ[g] was to be born. **5** "In Bethlehem in Judea," they replied, "for this is what the prophet has written:

6 "'But you, Bethlehem, in the
   land of Judah,
are by no means least among
   the rulers of Judah;
for out of you will come a ruler
   who will be the shepherd of
   my people Israel.'[h]"

7 Then Herod called the Magi secretly and found out from them the exact time the star had appeared. **8** He sent them to Bethlehem and said, "Go and make a careful search for the child. As soon as you find him, report to me, so that I too may go and worship him."

9 After they had heard the king, they went on their way, and the star they had seen in the east[i] went ahead of them until it stopped over the place where the child was. **10** When they saw the star, they were overjoyed. **11** On coming to the house, they saw the child with his mother Mary, and they bowed down and worshiped him. Then they opened their treasures and presented him with gifts of gold and of incense and of myrrh. **12** And having been warned in a dream not to go back to Herod, they returned to their country by another route.

The Escape to Egypt

13 When they had gone, an angel of the Lord appeared to Joseph in a dream. "Get up," he said, "take the child and his mother and escape to Egypt. Stay there until I tell you, for Herod is going to search for the child to kill him." **14** So he got up, took the child and his mother during the night and left for Egypt, **15** where he stayed until the death of Herod. And so was fulfilled what the Lord had

---

c *21* Jesus is the Greek form of Joshua, which means the Lord saves.   d *23* Isaiah 7:14
e *1* Traditionally Wise Men   f *2* Or star when it rose   g *4* Or Messiah   h *6* Micah 5:2
i *9* Or seen when it rose

said through the prophet: "Out of Egypt I called my son."[j]

16 When Herod realized that he had been outwitted by the Magi, he was furious, and he gave orders to kill all the boys in Bethlehem and its vicinity who were two years old and under, in accordance with the time he had learned from the Magi. **17** Then what was said through the prophet Jeremiah was fulfilled:

18 "A voice is heard in Ramah,
    weeping and great mourning,
Rachel weeping for her children
    and refusing to be comforted,
    because they are no more."[k]

The Return to Nazareth

19 After Herod died, an angel of the Lord appeared in a dream to Joseph in Egypt **20** and said, "Get up, take the child and his mother and go to the land of Israel, for those who were trying to take the child's life are dead."

21 So he got up, took the child and his mother and went to the land of Israel. **22** But when he heard that Archelaus was reigning in Judea in place of his father Herod, he was afraid to go there. Having been warned in a dream, he withdrew to the district of Galilee, **23** and he went and lived in a town called Nazareth. So was fulfilled what was said through the prophets: "He will be called a Nazarene."

John the Baptist Prepares the Way

3 **1** In those days John the Baptist came, preaching in the Desert of Judea **2** and saying, "Repent, for the kingdom of heaven is near." **3** This is he who was spoken of through the prophet Isaiah:

"A voice of one calling in the desert,
'Prepare the way for the Lord,
    make straight paths for him.'"[l]

4 John's clothes were made of camel's hair, and he had a leather belt around his waist. His food was locusts and wild honey. **5** People went out to him from Jerusalem and all Judea and the whole region of the Jordan. **6** Confessing their sins, they were baptized by him in the Jordan River.

7 But when he saw many of the Pharisees and Sadducees coming to where he was baptizing, he said to them: "You brood of vipers! Who warned you to flee from the coming wrath? **8** Produce fruit in keeping with repentance. **9** And do not think you can say to yourselves, 'We have Abraham as our father.' I tell you that out of these stones God can raise up children for Abraham. **10** The ax is already at the root of the trees, and every tree that does not produce good fruit will be cut down and thrown into the fire.

11 "I baptize you with[m] water for repentance. But after me will come one who is more powerful than I, whose sandals I am not fit to carry. He will baptize you with the Holy Spirit and with fire. **12** His winnowing fork is in his hand, and he will clear his threshing floor, gathering his wheat into the barn and burning up the chaff with unquenchable fire."

The Baptism of Jesus

13 Then Jesus came from Galilee to the Jordan to be baptized by John. **14** But John tried to deter him, saying, "I need to be baptized by you, and do you come to me?"

j 15 Hosea 11:1   *k 18* Jer. 31:15   *l 3* Isaiah 40:3   *m 11* Or *in*

15 Jesus replied, "Let it be so now; it is proper for us to do this to fulfill all righteousness." Then John consented.

16 As soon as Jesus was baptized, he went up out of the water. At that moment heaven was opened, and he saw the Spirit of God descending like a dove and lighting on him. **17** And a voice from heaven said, "This is my Son, whom I love; with him I am well pleased."

The Temptation of Jesus

4 **1** Then Jesus was led by the Spirit into the desert to be tempted by the devil. **2** After fasting forty days and forty nights, he was hungry. **3** The tempter came to him and said, "If you are the Son of God, tell these stones to become bread."

4 Jesus answered, "It is written: 'Man does not live on bread alone, but on every word that comes from the mouth of God.'"[n]

5 Then the devil took him to the holy city and had him stand on the highest point of the temple. **6** "If you are the Son of God," he said, "throw yourself down. For it is written:

"'He will command his angels concerning you,
   and they will lift you up in their hands,
so that you will not strike your foot against a stone.'"[o]

7 Jesus answered him, "It is also written: 'Do not put the Lord your God to the test.'"[p]

8 Again, the devil took him to a very high mountain and showed him all the kingdoms of the world and their splendor. **9** "All this I will give

you," he said, "if you will bow down and worship me."

10 Jesus said to him, "Away from me, Satan! For it is written: 'Worship the Lord your God, and serve him only.'"[q]

11 Then the devil left him, and angels came and attended him.

Jesus Begins to Preach

12 When Jesus heard that John had been put in prison, he returned to Galilee. **13** Leaving Nazareth, he went and lived in Capernaum, which was by the lake in the area of Zebulun and Naphtali— **14** to fulfill what was said through the prophet Isaiah:

15 "Land of Zebulun and land of Naphtali,
   the way to the sea, along the Jordan,
   Galilee of the Gentiles—
16 the people living in darkness have seen a great light;
   on those living in the land of the shadow of death
   a light has dawned."[r]

17 From that time on Jesus began to preach, "Repent, for the kingdom of heaven is near."

The Calling of the First Disciples

18 As Jesus was walking beside the Sea of Galilee, he saw two brothers, Simon called Peter and his brother Andrew. They were casting a net into the lake, for they were fishermen. **19** "Come, follow me," Jesus said, "and I will make you fishers of men." **20** At once they left their nets and followed him.

21 Going on from there, he saw two other brothers, James son of

---

[n] *4* Deut. 8:3   [o] *6* Psalm 91:11,12   [p] *7* Deut. 6:16   [q] *10* Deut. 6:13   [r] *16* Isaiah 9:1,2

Zebedee and his brother John. They were in a boat with their father Zebedee, preparing their nets. Jesus called them, **22** and immediately they left the boat and their father and followed him.

Jesus Heals the Sick

23 Jesus went throughout Galilee, teaching in their synagogues, preaching the good news of the kingdom, and healing every disease and sickness among the people. **24** News about him spread all over Syria, and people brought to him all who were ill with various diseases, those suffering severe pain, the demon-possessed, those having seizures, and the paralyzed, and he healed them. **25** Large crowds from Galilee, the Decapolis,⁵ Jerusalem, Judea and the region across the Jordan followed him.

The Beatitudes

5 **1** Now when he saw the crowds, he went up on a mountainside and sat down. His disciples came to him, **2** and he began to teach them saying:

3 "Blessed are the poor in spirit,
    for theirs is the kingdom of
       heaven.
4 Blessed are those who mourn,
    for they will be comforted.
5 Blessed are the meek,
    for they will inherit the earth.
6 Blessed are those who hunger
       and thirst for
       righteousness,
    for they will be filled.
7 Blessed are the merciful,
    for they will be shown mercy.
8 Blessed are the pure in heart,
    for they will see God.

9 Blessed are the peacemakers,
    for they will be called sons of
       God.
10 Blessed are those who are
       persecuted because of
       righteousness,
    for theirs is the kingdom of
       heaven.

11 "Blessed are you when people insult you, persecute you and falsely say all kinds of evil against you because of me. **12** Rejoice and be glad, because great is your reward in heaven, for in the same way they persecuted the prophets who were before you.

Salt and Light

13 "You are the salt of the earth. But if the salt loses its saltiness, how can it be made salty again? It is no longer good for anything, except to be thrown out and trampled by men.

14 "You are the light of the world. A city on a hill cannot be hidden. **15** Neither do people light a lamp and put it under a bowl. Instead they put it on its stand, and it gives light to everyone in the house. **16** In the same way, let your light shine before men, that they may see your good deeds and praise your Father in heaven.

The Fulfillment of the Law

17 "Do not think that I have come to abolish the Law or the Prophets; I have not come to abolish them but to fulfill them. **18** I tell you the truth, until heaven and earth disappear, not the smallest letter, not the least stroke of a pen, will by any means disappear from the Law until everything is accomplished. **19** Anyone who breaks one of the least of these

⁵ **25** That is, the Ten Cities

commandments and teaches others to do the same will be called least in the kingdom of heaven, but whoever practices and teaches these commands will be called great in the kingdom of heaven. **20** For I tell you that unless your righteousness surpasses that of the Pharisees and the teachers of the law, you will certainly not enter the kingdom of heaven.

Murder

21 "You have heard that it was said to the people long ago, 'Do not murder,*t* and anyone who murders will be subject to judgment.' **22** But I tell you that anyone who is angry with his brother*u* will be subject to judgment. Again, anyone who says to his brother, 'Raca,*v*' is answerable to the Sanhedrin. But anyone who says, 'You fool!' will be in danger of the fire of hell.

23 "Therefore, if you are offering your gift at the altar and there remember that your brother has something against you, **24** leave your gift there in front of the altar. First go and be reconciled to your brother; then come and offer your gift.

25 "Settle matters quickly with your adversary who is taking you to court. Do it while you are still with him on the way, or he may hand you over to the judge, and the judge may hand you over to the officer, and you may be thrown into prison. **26** I tell you the truth, you will not get out until you have paid the last penny.*w*

Adultery

27 "You have heard that it was said, 'Do not commit adultery.'*x*

28 But I tell you that anyone who looks at a woman lustfully has already committed adultery with her in his heart. **29** If your right eye causes you to sin, gouge it out and throw it away. It is better for you to lose one part of your body than for your whole body to be thrown into hell. **30** And if your right hand causes you to sin, cut it off and throw it away. It is better for you to lose one part of your body than for your whole body to go into hell.

Divorce

31 "It has been said, 'Anyone who divorces his wife must give her a certificate of divorce.'*y* **32** But I tell you that anyone who divorces his wife, except for marital unfaithfulness, causes her to become an adulteress, and anyone who marries the divorced woman commits adultery.

Oaths

33 "Again, you have heard that it was said to the people long ago, 'Do not break your oath, but keep the oaths you have made to the Lord.' **34** But I tell you, Do not swear at all: either by heaven, for it is God's throne; **35** or by the earth, for it is his footstool; or by Jerusalem, for it is the city of the Great King. **36** And do not swear by your head, for you cannot make even one hair white or black. **37** Simply let your 'Yes' be 'Yes,' and your 'No,' 'No'; anything beyond this comes from the evil one.

An Eye for an Eye

38 "You have heard that it was said, 'Eye for eye, and tooth for tooth.'*z*

---

t 21 Exodus 20:13   *u 22* Some manuscripts *brother without cause*   *v 22* An Aramaic term of contempt   *w 26* Greek *kodrantes*   *x 27* Exodus 20:14   *y 31* Deut. 24:1   *z 38* Exodus 21:24; Lev. 24:20; Deut. 19:21

39 But I tell you, Do not resist an evil person. If someone strikes you on the right cheek, turn to him the other also. **40** And if someone wants to sue you and take your tunic, let him have your cloak as well. **41** If someone forces you to go one mile, go with him two miles. **42** Give to the one who asks you, and do not turn away from the one who wants to borrow from you.

Love for Enemies

43 "You have heard that it was said, 'Love your neighbor[a] and hate your enemy.' **44** But I tell you: Love your enemies[b] and pray for those who persecute you, **45** that you may be sons of your Father in heaven. He causes his sun to rise on the evil and the good, and sends rain on the righteous and the unrighteous. **46** If you love those who love you, what reward will you get? Are not even the tax collectors doing that? **47** And if you greet only your brothers, what are you doing more than others? Do not even pagans do that? **48** Be perfect, therefore, as your heavenly Father is perfect.

Giving to the Needy

6 **1** "Be careful not to do your 'acts of righteousness' before men, to be seen by them. If you do, you will have no reward from your Father in heaven.

2 "So when you give to the needy, do not announce it with trumpets, as the hypocrites do in the synagogues and on the streets, to be honored by men. I tell you the truth, they have received their reward in full. **3** But when you give to the needy, do not let your left

hand know what your right hand is doing, **4** so that your giving may be in secret. Then your Father, who sees what is done in secret, will reward you.

Prayer

5 "And when you pray, do not be like the hypocrites, for they love to pray standing in the synagogues and on the street corners to be seen by men. I tell you the truth, they have received their reward in full. **6** But when you pray, go into your room, close the door and pray to your Father, who is unseen. Then your Father, who sees what is done in secret, will reward you. **7** And when you pray, do not keep on babbling like pagans, for they think they will be heard because of their many words. **8** Do not be like them, for your Father knows what you need before you ask him.

9 "This, then, is how you should pray:

> "'Our Father in heaven,
> hallowed be your name,
> **10** your kingdom come,
> your will be done
> on earth as it is in heaven.
> **11** Give us today our daily bread.
> **12** Forgive us our debts,
> as we also have forgiven our
> debtors.
> **13** And lead us not into
> temptation,
> but deliver us from the evil one.[c]'

14 For if you forgive men when they sin against you, your heavenly Father will also forgive you. **15** But if you do not forgive men their sins, your Father will not forgive your sins.

---

a 43 Lev. 19:18　　*b* 44 Some late manuscripts *enemies, bless those who curse you, do good to those who hate you*　　*c* 13 Or *from evil;* some late manuscripts *one, / for yours is the kingdom and the power and the glory forever. Amen.*

Fasting

16 "When you fast, do not look somber as the hypocrites do, for they disfigure their faces to show men they are fasting. I tell you the truth, they have received their reward in full. 17 But when you fast, put oil on your head and wash your face, 18 so that it will not be obvious to men that you are fasting, but only to your Father, who is unseen; and your Father, who sees what is done in secret, will reward you.

Treasures in Heaven

19 "Do not store up for yourselves treasures on earth, where moth and rust destroy, and where thieves break in and steal. 20 But store up for yourselves treasures in heaven, where moth and rust do not destroy, and where thieves do not break in and steal. 21 For where your treasure is, there your heart will be also.

22 "The eye is the lamp of the body. If your eyes are good, your whole body will be full of light. 23 But if your eyes are bad, your whole body will be full of darkness. If then the light within you is darkness, how great is that darkness!

24 "No one can serve two masters. Either he will hate the one and love the other, or he will be devoted to the one and despise the other. You cannot serve both God and Money.

Do Not Worry

25 "Therefore I tell you, do not worry about your life, what you will eat or drink; or about your body, what you will wear. Is not life more important than food, and the body more important than clothes?

26 Look at the birds of the air; they do not sow or reap or store away in barns, and yet your heavenly Father feeds them. Are you not much more valuable than they? 27 Who of you by worrying can add a single hour to his life*d*?

28 "And why do you worry about clothes? See how the lilies of the field grow. They do not labor or spin. 29 Yet I tell you that not even Solomon in all his splendor was dressed like one of these. 30 If that is how God clothes the grass of the field, which is here today and tomorrow is thrown into the fire, will he not much more clothe you, O you of little faith? 31 So do not worry, saying, 'What shall we eat?' or 'What shall we drink?' or 'What shall we wear?' 32 For the pagans run after all these things, and your heavenly Father knows that you need them. 33 But seek first his kingdom and his righteousness, and all these things will be given to you as well. 34 Therefore do not worry about tomorrow, for tomorrow will worry about itself. Each day has enough trouble of its own.

Judging Others

7 1 "Do not judge, or you too will be judged. 2 For in the same way you judge others, you will be judged, and with the measure you use, it will be measured to you.

3 "Why do you look at the speck of sawdust in your brother's eye and pay no attention to the plank in your own eye? 4 How can you say to your brother, 'Let me take the speck out of your eye,' when all the time there is a plank in your own eye? 5 You hypocrite, first take the plank out of

---

d 27 Or *single cubit to his height*

your own eye, and then you will see clearly to remove the speck from your brother's eye.

6 "Do not give dogs what is sacred; do not throw your pearls to pigs. If you do, they may trample them under their feet, and then turn and tear you to pieces.

Ask, Seek, Knock

7 "Ask and it will be given to you; seek and you will find; knock and the door will be opened to you. 8 For everyone who asks receives; he who seeks finds; and to him who knocks, the door will be opened.

9 "Which of you, if his son asks for bread, will give him a stone? 10 Or if he asks for a fish, will give him a snake? 11 If you, then, though you are evil, know how to give good gifts to your children, how much more will your Father in heaven give good gifts to those who ask him! 12 So in everything, do to others what you would have them do to you, for this sums up the Law and the Prophets.

The Narrow and Wide Gates

13 "Enter through the narrow gate. For wide is the gate and broad is the road that leads to destruction, and many enter through it. 14 But small is the gate and narrow the road that leads to life, and only a few find it.

A Tree and Its Fruit

15 "Watch out for false prophets. They come to you in sheep's clothing, but inwardly they are ferocious wolves. 16 By their fruit you will recognize them. Do people pick grapes from thornbushes, or figs from thistles? 17 Likewise every good tree bears good fruit, but a bad tree bears

bad fruit. 18 A good tree cannot bear bad fruit, and a bad tree cannot bear good fruit. 19 Every tree that does not bear good fruit is cut down and thrown into the fire. 20 Thus, by their fruit you will recognize them.

21 "Not everyone who says to me, 'Lord, Lord,' will enter the kingdom of heaven, but only he who does the will of my Father who is in heaven. 22 Many will say to me on that day, 'Lord, Lord, did we not prophesy in your name, and in your name drive out demons and perform many miracles?' 23 Then I will tell them plainly, 'I never knew you. Away from me, you evildoers!'

The Wise and Foolish Builders

24 "Therefore everyone who hears these words of mine and puts them into practice is like a wise man who built his house on the rock. 25 The rain came down, the streams rose, and the winds blew and beat against that house; yet it did not fall, because it had its foundation on the rock. 26 But everyone who hears these words of mine and does not put them into practice is like a foolish man who built his house on sand. 27 The rain came down, the streams rose, and the winds blew and beat against that house, and it fell with a great crash."

28 When Jesus had finished saying these things, the crowds were amazed at his teaching, 29 because he taught as one who had authority, and not as their teachers of the law.

The Man With Leprosy

8 1 When he came down from the mountainside, large crowds followed him. 2 A man with leprosy[e]

---

e 2 The Greek word was used for various diseases affecting the skin — not necessarily leprosy.

came and knelt before him and said, "Lord, if you are willing, you can make me clean."

3 Jesus reached out his hand and touched the man. "I am willing," he said. "Be clean!" Immediately he was cured*f* of his leprosy. **4** Then Jesus said to him, "See that you don't tell anyone. But go, show yourself to the priest and offer the gift Moses commanded, as a testimony to them."

The Faith of the Centurion

5 When Jesus had entered Capernaum, a centurion came to him, asking for help. **6** "Lord," he said, "my servant lies at home paralyzed and in terrible suffering."

7 Jesus said to him, "I will go and heal him."

8 The centurion replied, "Lord, I do not deserve to have you come under my roof. But just say the word, and my servant will be healed. **9** For I myself am a man under authority, with soldiers under me. I tell this one, 'Go,' and he goes; and that one, 'Come,' and he comes. I say to my servant, 'Do this,' and he does it."

10 When Jesus heard this, he was astonished and said to those following him, "I tell you the truth, I have not found anyone in Israel with such great faith. **11** I say to you that many will come from the east and the west, and will take their places at the feast with Abraham, Isaac and Jacob in the kingdom of heaven. **12** But the subjects of the kingdom will be thrown outside, into the darkness, where there will be weeping and gnashing of teeth."

13 Then Jesus said to the centurion, "Go! It will be done just as you believed it would." And his servant was healed at that very hour.

Jesus Heals Many

14 When Jesus came into Peter's house, he saw Peter's mother-in-law lying in bed with a fever. **15** He touched her hand and the fever left her, and she got up and began to wait on him.

16 When evening came, many who were demon-possessed were brought to him, and he drove out the spirits with a word and healed all the sick. **17** This was to fulfill what was spoken through the prophet Isaiah:

"He took up our infirmities
    and carried our diseases."*g*

The Cost of Following Jesus

18 When Jesus saw the crowd around him, he gave orders to cross to the other side of the lake. **19** Then a teacher of the law came to him and said, "Teacher, I will follow you wherever you go."

20 Jesus replied, "Foxes have holes and birds of the air have nests, but the Son of Man has no place to lay his head."

21 Another disciple said to him, "Lord, first let me go and bury my father."

22 But Jesus told him, "Follow me, and let the dead bury their own dead."

Jesus Calms the Storm

23 Then he got into the boat and his disciples followed him. **24** Without warning, a furious storm came up on the lake, so that the waves swept over the boat. But Jesus was sleeping. **25** The disciples went and woke him, saying, "Lord, save us! We're going to drown!"

f 3 Greek made clean   *g 17* Isaiah 53:4

26 He replied, "You of little faith, why are you so afraid?" Then he got up and rebuked the winds and the waves, and it was completely calm.

27 The men were amazed and asked, "What kind of man is this? Even the winds and the waves obey him!"

The Healing of Two Demon-possessed Men

28 When he arrived at the other side in the region of the Gadarenes,[h] two demon-possessed men coming from the tombs met him. They were so violent that no one could pass that way. 29 "What do you want with us, Son of God?" they shouted. "Have you come here to torture us before the appointed time?"

30 Some distance from them a large herd of pigs was feeding. 31 The demons begged Jesus, "If you drive us out, send us into the herd of pigs."

32 He said to them, "Go!" So they came out and went into the pigs, and the whole herd rushed down the steep bank into the lake and died in the water. 33 Those tending the pigs ran off, went into the town and reported all this, including what had happened to the demon-possessed men. 34 Then the whole town went out to meet Jesus. And when they saw him, they pleaded with him to leave their region.

Jesus Heals a Paralytic

9 1 Jesus stepped into a boat, crossed over and came to his own town. 2 Some men brought to him a paralytic, lying on a mat. When Jesus saw their faith, he said to the paralytic, "Take heart, son; your sins are forgiven."

3 At this, some of the teachers of the law said to themselves, "This fellow is blaspheming!"

4 Knowing their thoughts, Jesus said, "Why do you entertain evil thoughts in your hearts? 5 Which is easier: to say, 'Your sins are forgiven,' or to say, 'Get up and walk'? 6 But so that you may know that the Son of Man has authority on earth to forgive sins...." Then he said to the paralytic, "Get up, take your mat and go home." 7 And the man got up and went home. 8 When the crowd saw this, they were filled with awe; and they praised God, who had given such authority to men.

The Calling of Matthew

9 As Jesus went on from there, he saw a man named Matthew sitting at the tax collector's booth. "Follow me," he told him, and Matthew got up and followed him.

10 While Jesus was having dinner at Matthew's house, many tax collectors and "sinners" came and ate with him and his disciples. 11 When the Pharisees saw this, they asked his disciples, "Why does your teacher eat with tax collectors and 'sinners'?"

12 On hearing this, Jesus said, "It is not the healthy who need a doctor, but the sick. 13 But go and learn what this means: 'I desire mercy, not sacrifice.'[i] For I have not come to call the righteous, but sinners."

Jesus Questioned About Fasting

14 Then John's disciples came and asked him, "How is it that we and the Pharisees fast, but your disciples do not fast?"

15 Jesus answered, "How can the guests of the bridegroom mourn while he is with them? The time will

---

h 28 Some manuscripts Gergesenes; others Gerasenes   i 13 Hosea 6:6

come when the bridegroom will be taken from them; then they will fast.

16 "No one sews a patch of unshrunk cloth on an old garment, for the patch will pull away from the garment, making the tear worse. 17 Neither do men pour new wine into old wineskins. If they do, the skins will burst, the wine will run out and the wineskins will be ruined. No, they pour new wine into new wineskins, and both are preserved."

A Dead Girl and a Sick Woman

18 While he was saying this, a ruler came and knelt before him and said, "My daughter has just died. But come and put your hand on her, and she will live." 19 Jesus got up and went with him, and so did his disciples.

20 Just then a woman who had been subject to bleeding for twelve years came up behind him and touched the edge of his cloak. 21 She said to herself, "If I only touch his cloak, I will be healed."

22 Jesus turned and saw her. "Take heart, daughter," he said, "your faith has healed you." And the woman was healed from that moment.

23 When Jesus entered the ruler's house and saw the flute players and the noisy crowd, 24 he said, "Go away. The girl is not dead but asleep." But they laughed at him. 25 After the crowd had been put outside, he went in and took the girl by the hand, and she got up. 26 News of this spread through all that region.

Jesus Heals the Blind and Mute

27 As Jesus went on from there, two blind men followed him, calling out, "Have mercy on us, Son of David!"

28 When he had gone indoors, the blind men came to him, and he asked them, "Do you believe that I am able to do this?"

"Yes, Lord," they replied.

29 Then he touched their eyes and said, "According to your faith will it be done to you"; 30 and their sight was restored. Jesus warned them sternly, "See that no one knows about this." 31 But they went out and spread the news about him all over that region.

32 While they were going out, a man who was demon-possessed and could not talk was brought to Jesus. 33 And when the demon was driven out, the man who had been mute spoke. The crowd was amazed and said, "Nothing like this has ever been seen in Israel."

34 But the Pharisees said, "It is by the prince of demons that he drives out demons."

The Workers Are Few

35 Jesus went through all the towns and villages, teaching in their synagogues, preaching the good news of the kingdom and healing every disease and sickness. 36 When he saw the crowds, he had compassion on them, because they were harassed and helpless, like sheep without a shepherd. 37 Then he said to his disciples, "The harvest is plentiful but the workers are few. 38 Ask the Lord of the harvest, therefore, to send out workers into his harvest field."

Jesus Sends Out the Twelve

10 1 He called his twelve disciples to him and gave them authority to drive out evil spirits and to heal every disease and sickness.

---

j 1 Greek unclean

2 These are the names of the twelve apostles: first, Simon (who is called Peter) and his brother Andrew; James son of Zebedee, and his brother John; 3 Philip and Bartholomew; Thomas and Matthew the tax collector; James son of Alphaeus, and Thaddaeus; 4 Simon the Zealot and Judas Iscariot, who betrayed him.

5 These twelve Jesus sent out with the following instructions: "Do not go among the Gentiles or enter any town of the Samaritans. 6 Go rather to the lost sheep of Israel. 7 As you go, preach this message: 'The kingdom of heaven is near.' 8 Heal the sick, raise the dead, cleanse those who have leprosy,k drive out demons. Freely you have received, freely give. 9 Do not take along any gold or silver or copper in your belts; 10 take no bag for the journey, or extra tunic, or sandals or a staff; for the worker is worth his keep.

11 "Whatever town or village you enter, search for some worthy person there and stay at his house until you leave. 12 As you enter the home, give it your greeting. 13 If the home is deserving, let your peace rest on it; if it is not, let your peace return to you. 14 If anyone will not welcome you or listen to your words, shake the dust off your feet when you leave that home or town. 15 I tell you the truth, it will be more bearable for Sodom and Gomorrah on the day of judgment than for that town. 16 I am sending you out like sheep among wolves. Therefore be as shrewd as snakes and as innocent as doves.

17 "Be on your guard against men; they will hand you over to the local councils and flog you in their synagogues. 18 On my account you will be brought before governors and kings as witnesses to them and to the Gentiles. 19 But when they arrest you, do not worry about what to say or how to say it. At that time you will be given what to say, 20 for it will not be you speaking, but the Spirit of your Father speaking through you.

21 "Brother will betray brother to death, and a father his child; children will rebel against their parents and have them put to death. 22 All men will hate you because of me, but he who stands firm to the end will be saved. 23 When you are persecuted in one place, flee to another. I tell you the truth, you will not finish going through the cities of Israel before the Son of Man comes.

24 "A student is not above his teacher, nor a servant above his master. 25 It is enough for the student to be like his teacher, and the servant like his master. If the head of the house has been called Beelzebub,l how much more the members of his household!

26 "So do not be afraid of them. There is nothing concealed that will not be disclosed, or hidden that will not be made known. 27 What I tell you in the dark, speak in the daylight; what is whispered in your ear, proclaim from the roofs. 28 Do not be afraid of those who kill the body but cannot kill the soul. Rather, be afraid of the One who can destroy both soul and body in hell. 29 Are not two sparrows sold for a pennym? Yet not one of them will fall to the ground apart from the will of your Father. 30 And even the very hairs of

---

k 8 The Greek word was used for various diseases affecting the skin—not necessarily leprosy.
l 25 Greek Beezeboul or Beelzeboul   m 29 Greek an assarion

your head are all numbered. **31** So don't be afraid; you are worth more than many sparrows.

32 "Whoever acknowledges me before men, I will also acknowledge him before my Father in heaven. **33** But whoever disowns me before men, I will disown him before my Father in heaven.

34 "Do not suppose that I have come to bring peace to the earth. I did not come to bring peace, but a sword. **35** For I have come to turn

> " 'a man against his father,
>   a daughter against her mother,
> a daughter-in-law against her
>   mother-in-law —
> **36**   a man's enemies will be the
>   members of his own
>   household.'[n]

37 "Anyone who loves his father or mother more than me is not worthy of me; anyone who loves his son or daughter more than me is not worthy of me; **38** and anyone who does not take his cross and follow me is not worthy of me. **39** Whoever finds his life will lose it, and whoever loses his life for my sake will find it.

40 "He who receives you receives me, and he who receives me receives the one who sent me. **41** Anyone who receives a prophet because he is a prophet will receive a prophet's reward, and anyone who receives a righteous man because he is a righteous man will receive a righteous man's reward. **42** And if anyone gives even a cup of cold water to one of these little ones because he is my disciple, I tell you the truth, he will certainly not lose his reward."

Jesus and John the Baptist

11 **1** After Jesus had finished instructing his twelve disciples, he went on from there to teach and preach in the towns of Galilee.[o]

2 When John heard in prison what Christ was doing, he sent his disciples **3** to ask him, "Are you the one who was to come, or should we expect someone else?"

4 Jesus replied, "Go back and report to John what you hear and see: **5** The blind receive sight, the lame walk, those who have leprosy[p] are cured, the deaf hear, the dead are raised, and the good news is preached to the poor. **6** Blessed is the man who does not fall away on account of me."

7 As John's disciples were leaving, Jesus began to speak to the crowd about John: "What did you go out into the desert to see? A reed swayed by the wind? **8** If not, what did you go out to see? A man dressed in fine clothes? No, those who wear fine clothes are in kings' palaces. **9** Then what did you go out to see? A prophet? Yes, I tell you, and more than a prophet. **10** This is the one about whom it is written:

> " 'I will send my messenger ahead
>   of you,
>   who will prepare your way
>   before you.'[q]

11 I tell you the truth: Among those born of women there has not risen anyone greater than John the Baptist; yet he who is least in the kingdom of heaven is greater than he. **12** From the days of John the Baptist until now, the kingdom of

---

n 36 Micah 7:6   *o 1* Greek *in their towns*   *p 5* The Greek word was used for various diseases affecting the skin — not necessarily leprosy.   *q 10* Mal. 3:1

heaven has been forcefully advancing, and forceful men lay hold of it. 13 For all the Prophets and the Law prophesied until John. 14 And if you are willing to accept it, he is the Elijah who was to come. 15 He who has ears, let him hear.

16 "To what can I compare this generation? They are like children sitting in the marketplaces and calling out to others:

17 " 'We played the flute for you,
      and you did not dance;
   we sang a dirge
      and you did not mourn.'

18 For John came neither eating nor drinking, and they say, 'He has a demon.' 19 The Son of Man came eating and drinking, and they say, 'Here is a glutton and a drunkard, a friend of tax collectors and "sinners." ' But wisdom is proved right by her actions."

Woe on Unrepentant Cities

20 Then Jesus began to denounce the cities in which most of his miracles had been performed, because they did not repent. 21 "Woe to you, Korazin! Woe to you, Bethsaida! If the miracles that were performed in you had been performed in Tyre and Sidon, they would have repented long ago in sackcloth and ashes. 22 But I tell you, it will be more bearable for Tyre and Sidon on the day of judgment than for you. 23 And you, Capernaum, will you be lifted up to the skies? No, you will go down to the depths.*r* If the miracles that were performed in you had been performed in Sodom, it would have remained to this day. 24 But I tell you that it will be more bearable for

Sodom on the day of judgment than for you."

Rest for the Weary

25 At that time Jesus said, "I praise you, Father, Lord of heaven and earth, because you have hidden these things from the wise and learned, and revealed them to little children. 26 Yes, Father, for this was your good pleasure.

27 "All things have been committed to me by my Father. No one knows the Son except the Father, and no one knows the Father except the Son and those to whom the Son chooses to reveal him.

28 "Come to me, all you who are weary and burdened, and I will give you rest. 29 Take my yoke upon you and learn from me, for I am gentle and humble in heart, and you will find rest for your souls. 30 For my yoke is easy and my burden is light."

Lord of the Sabbath

12 1 At that time Jesus went through the grainfields on the Sabbath. His disciples were hungry and began to pick some heads of grain and eat them. 2 When the Pharisees saw this, they said to him, "Look! Your disciples are doing what is unlawful on the Sabbath."

3 He answered, "Haven't you read what David did when he and his companions were hungry? 4 He entered the house of God, and he and his companions ate the consecrated bread—which was not lawful for them to do, but only for the priests. 5 Or haven't you read in the Law that on the Sabbath the priests in the temple desecrate the day and yet are innocent? 6 I tell you that one*s*

_____

r 23 Greek *Hades*   *s* 6 Or *something*; also in verses 41 and 42

greater than the temple is here. **7** If you had known what these words mean, 'I desire mercy, not sacrifice,'[t] you would not have condemned the innocent. **8** For the Son of Man is Lord of the Sabbath."

9 Going on from that place, he went into their synagogue, **10** and a man with a shriveled hand was there. Looking for a reason to accuse Jesus, they asked him, "Is it lawful to heal on the Sabbath?"

11 He said to them, "If any of you has a sheep and it falls into a pit on the Sabbath, will you not take hold of it and lift it out? **12** How much more valuable is a man than a sheep! Therefore it is lawful to do good on the Sabbath."

13 Then he said to the man, "Stretch out your hand." So he stretched it out and it was completely restored, just as sound as the other. **14** But the Pharisees went out and plotted how they might kill Jesus.

God's Chosen Servant

15 Aware of this, Jesus withdrew from that place. Many followed him, and he healed all their sick, **16** warning them not to tell who he was. **17** This was to fulfill what was spoken through the prophet Isaiah:

18 "Here is my servant whom I
        have chosen,
    the one I love, in whom I
        delight;
    I will put my Spirit on him,
        and he will proclaim justice to
        the nations.
19 He will not quarrel or cry out;
    no one will hear his voice in
        the streets.
20 A bruised reed he will not
    break,

and a smoldering wick he will
    not snuff out,
    till he leads justice to victory.
21   In his name the nations will
        put their hope."[u]

Jesus and Beelzebub

22 Then they brought him a demon-possessed man who was blind and mute, and Jesus healed him, so that he could both talk and see. **23** All the people were astonished and said, "Could this be the Son of David?"

24 But when the Pharisees heard this, they said, "It is only by Beelzebub,[v] the prince of demons, that this fellow drives out demons."

25 Jesus knew their thoughts and said to them, "Every kingdom divided against itself will be ruined, and every city or household divided against itself will not stand. **26** If Satan drives out Satan, he is divided against himself. How then can his kingdom stand? **27** And if I drive out demons by Beelzebub, by whom do your people drive them out? So then, they will be your judges. **28** But if I drive out demons by the Spirit of God, then the kingdom of God has come upon you.

29 "Or again, how can anyone enter a strong man's house and carry off his possessions unless he first ties up the strong man? Then he can rob his house.

30 "He who is not with me is against me, and he who does not gather with me scatters. **31** And so I tell you, every sin and blasphemy will be forgiven men, but the blasphemy against the Spirit will not be forgiven. **32** Anyone who speaks a word against the Son of Man will be for-

---

[t] 7 Hosea 6:6   [u] 21 Isaiah 42:1-4   [v] 24 Greek *Beezeboul* or *Beelzeboul*; also in verse 27

given, but anyone who speaks against the Holy Spirit will not be forgiven, either in this age or in the age to come.

33 "Make a tree good and its fruit will be good, or make a tree bad and its fruit will be bad, for a tree is recognized by its fruit. **34** You brood of vipers, how can you who are evil say anything good? For out of the overflow of the heart the mouth speaks. **35** The good man brings good things out of the good stored up in him, and the evil man brings evil things out of the evil stored up in him. **36** But I tell you that men will have to give account on the day of judgment for every careless word they have spoken. **37** For by your words you will be acquitted, and by your words you will be condemned."

The Sign of Jonah

38 Then some of the Pharisees and teachers of the law said to him, "Teacher, we want to see a miraculous sign from you."

39 He answered, "A wicked and adulterous generation asks for a miraculous sign! But none will be given it except the sign of the prophet Jonah. **40** For as Jonah was three days and three nights in the belly of a huge fish, so the Son of Man will be three days and three nights in the heart of the earth. **41** The men of Nineveh will stand up at the judgment with this generation and condemn it; for they repented at the preaching of Jonah, and now one*w* greater than Jonah is here. **42** The Queen of the South will rise at the judgment with this generation and condemn it; for she came from the

ends of the earth to listen to Solomon's wisdom, and now one greater than Solomon is here.

43 "When an evil*x* spirit comes out of a man, it goes through arid places seeking rest and does not find it. **44** Then it says, 'I will return to the house I left.' When it arrives, it finds the house unoccupied, swept clean and put in order. **45** Then it goes and takes with it seven other spirits more wicked than itself, and they go in and live there. And the final condition of that man is worse than the first. That is how it will be with this wicked generation."

Jesus' Mother and Brothers

46 While Jesus was still talking to the crowd, his mother and brothers stood outside, wanting to speak to him. **47** Someone told him, "Your mother and brothers are standing outside, wanting to speak to you."*y*

48 He replied to him, "Who is my mother, and who are my brothers?" **49** Pointing to his disciples, he said, "Here are my mother and my brothers. **50** For whoever does the will of my Father in heaven is my brother and sister and mother."

The Parable of the Sower

13 **1** That same day Jesus went out of the house and sat by the lake. **2** Such large crowds gathered around him that he got into a boat and sat in it, while all the people stood on the shore. **3** Then he told them many things in parables, saying: "A farmer went out to sow his seed. **4** As he was scattering the seed, some fell along the path, and the birds came and ate it up. **5** Some fell

---

w 41 Or *something; also in verse* 42   *x* 43 Greek *unclean*   *y* 47 Some manuscripts do not have verse 47.

on rocky places, where it did not have much soil. It sprang up quickly, because the soil was shallow. **6** But when the sun came up, the plants were scorched, and they withered because they had no root. **7** Other seed fell among thorns, which grew up and choked the plants. **8** Still other seed fell on good soil, where it produced a crop—a hundred, sixty or thirty times what was sown. **9** He who has ears, let him hear."

10 The disciples came to him and asked, "Why do you speak to the people in parables?"

11 He replied, "The knowledge of the secrets of the kingdom of heaven has been given to you, but not to them. **12** Whoever has will be given more, and he will have an abundance. Whoever does not have, even what he has will be taken from him. **13** This is why I speak to them in parables:

"Though seeing, they do not see;
    though hearing, they do not
        hear or understand.

14 In them is fulfilled the prophecy of Isaiah:

" 'You will be ever hearing but
        never understanding;
    you will be ever seeing but
        never perceiving.
15 For this people's heart has
        become calloused;
    they hardly hear with their
        ears,
    and they have closed their
        eyes.
Otherwise they might see with
        their eyes,
    hear with their ears,
    understand with their hearts
    and turn, and I would heal
        them.'z

z 15 Isaiah 6:9,10

16 But blessed are your eyes because they see, and your ears because they hear. **17** For I tell you the truth, many prophets and righteous men longed to see what you see but did not see it, and to hear what you hear but did not hear it.

18 "Listen then to what the parable of the sower means: **19** When anyone hears the message about the kingdom and does not understand it, the evil one comes and snatches away what was sown in his heart. This is the seed sown along the path. **20** The one who received the seed that fell on rocky places is the man who hears the word and at once receives it with joy. **21** But since he has no root, he lasts only a short time. When trouble or persecution comes because of the word, he quickly falls away. **22** The one who received the seed that fell among the thorns is the man who hears the word, but the worries of this life and the deceitfulness of wealth choke it, making it unfruitful. **23** But the one who received the seed that fell on good soil is the man who hears the word and understands it. He produces a crop, yielding a hundred, sixty or thirty times what was sown."

The Parable of the Weeds

24 Jesus told them another parable: "The kingdom of heaven is like a man who sowed good seed in his field. **25** But while everyone was sleeping, his enemy came and sowed weeds among the wheat, and went away. **26** When the wheat sprouted and formed heads, then the weeds also appeared.

27 "The owner's servants came to him and said, 'Sir, didn't you sow good seed in your field? Where then did the weeds come from?'

28 " 'An enemy did this,' he replied.

"The servants asked him, 'Do you want us to go and pull them up?'

29 " 'No,' he answered, 'because while you are pulling the weeds, you may root up the wheat with them. **30** Let both grow together until the harvest. At that time I will tell the harvesters: First collect the weeds and tie them in bundles to be burned; then gather the wheat and bring it into my barn.' "

The Parables of the Mustard Seed and the Yeast

31 He told them another parable: "The kingdom of heaven is like a mustard seed, which a man took and planted in his field. **32** Though it is the smallest of all your seeds, yet when it grows, it is the largest of garden plants and becomes a tree, so that the birds of the air come and perch in its branches."

33 He told them still another parable: "The kingdom of heaven is like yeast that a woman took and mixed into a large amount*a* of flour until it worked all through the dough."

34 Jesus spoke all these things to the crowd in parables; he did not say anything to them without using a parable. **35** So was fulfilled what was spoken through the prophet:

> "I will open my mouth in parables,
> I will utter things hidden since the creation of the world."*b*

The Parable of the Weeds Explained

36 Then he left the crowd and went into the house. His disciples came to him and said, "Explain to us the parable of the weeds in the field."

37 He answered, "The one who sowed the good seed is the Son of Man. **38** The field is the world, and the good seed stands for the sons of the kingdom. The weeds are the sons of the evil one, **39** and the enemy who sows them is the devil. The harvest is the end of the age, and the harvesters are angels.

40 "As the weeds are pulled up and burned in the fire, so it will be at the end of the age. **41** The Son of Man will send out his angels, and they will weed out of his kingdom everything that causes sin and all who do evil. **42** They will throw them into the fiery furnace, where there will be weeping and gnashing of teeth. **43** Then the righteous will shine like the sun in the kingdom of their Father. He who has ears, let him hear.

The Parables of the Hidden Treasure and the Pearl

44 "The kingdom of heaven is like treasure hidden in a field. When a man found it, he hid it again, and then in his joy went and sold all he had and bought that field.

45 "Again, the kingdom of heaven is like a merchant looking for fine pearls. **46** When he found one of great value, he went away and sold everything he had and bought it.

The Parable of the Net

47 "Once again, the kingdom of heaven is like a net that was let down into the lake and caught all kinds of fish. **48** When it was full, the fishermen pulled it up on the shore. Then they sat down and collected the good fish in baskets, but threw the bad

---

a 33 Greek *three satas* (probably about 1/2 bushel or 22 liters)　　*b* 35 Psalm 78:2

away. 49 This is how it will be at the end of the age. The angels will come and separate the wicked from the righteous 50 and throw them into the fiery furnace, where there will be weeping and gnashing of teeth.

51 "Have you understood all these things?" Jesus asked.

"Yes," they replied.

52 He said to them, "Therefore every teacher of the law who has been instructed about the kingdom of heaven is like the owner of a house who brings out of his storeroom new treasures as well as old."

A Prophet Without Honor

53 When Jesus had finished these parables, he moved on from there. 54 Coming to his hometown, he began teaching the people in their synagogue, and they were amazed. "Where did this man get this wisdom and these miraculous powers?" they asked. 55 "Isn't this the carpenter's son? Isn't his mother's name Mary, and aren't his brothers James, Joseph, Simon and Judas? 56 Aren't all his sisters with us? Where then did this man get all these things?" 57 And they took offense at him.

But Jesus said to them, "Only in his hometown and in his own house is a prophet without honor."

58 And he did not do many miracles there because of their lack of faith.

John the Baptist Beheaded

14 1 At that time Herod the tetrarch heard the reports about Jesus, 2 and he said to his attendants, "This is John the Baptist; he has risen from the dead! That is why miraculous powers are at work in him."

3 Now Herod had arrested John and bound him and put him in prison because of Herodias, his brother Philip's wife, 4 for John had been saying to him: "It is not lawful for you to have her." 5 Herod wanted to kill John, but he was afraid of the people, because they considered him a prophet.

6 On Herod's birthday the daughter of Herodias danced for them and pleased Herod so much 7 that he promised with an oath to give her whatever she asked. 8 Prompted by her mother, she said, "Give me here on a platter the head of John the Baptist." 9 The king was distressed, but because of his oaths and his dinner guests, he ordered that her request be granted 10 and had John beheaded in the prison. 11 His head was brought in on a platter and given to the girl, who carried it to her mother. 12 John's disciples came and took his body and buried it. Then they went and told Jesus.

Jesus Feeds the Five Thousand

13 When Jesus heard what had happened, he withdrew by boat privately to a solitary place. Hearing of this, the crowds followed him on foot from the towns. 14 When Jesus landed and saw a large crowd, he had compassion on them and healed their sick.

15 As evening approached, the disciples came to him and said, "This is a remote place, and it's already getting late. Send the crowds away, so they can go to the villages and buy themselves some food."

16 Jesus replied, "They do not need to go away. You give them something to eat."

17 "We have here only five loaves of bread and two fish," they answered.

18 "Bring them here to me," he said. 19 And he directed the people

to sit down on the grass. Taking the five loaves and the two fish and looking up to heaven, he gave thanks and broke the loaves. Then he gave them to the disciples, and the disciples gave them to the people. **20** They all ate and were satisfied, and the disciples picked up twelve basketfuls of broken pieces that were left over. **21** The number of those who ate was about five thousand men, besides women and children.

Jesus Walks on the Water

22 Immediately Jesus made the disciples get into the boat and go on ahead of him to the other side, while he dismissed the crowd. **23** After he had dismissed them, he went up on a mountainside by himself to pray. When evening came, he was there alone, **24** but the boat was already a considerable distance[c] from land, buffeted by the waves because the wind was against it.

25 During the fourth watch of the night Jesus went out to them, walking on the lake. **26** When the disciples saw him walking on the lake, they were terrified. "It's a ghost," they said, and cried out in fear.

27 But Jesus immediately said to them: "Take courage! It is I. Don't be afraid."

28 "Lord, if it's you," Peter replied, "tell me to come to you on the water."

29 "Come," he said.

Then Peter got down out of the boat, walked on the water and came toward Jesus. **30** But when he saw the wind, he was afraid and, beginning to sink, cried out, "Lord, save me!"

31 Immediately Jesus reached out his hand and caught him. "You of little faith," he said, "why did you doubt?"

32 And when they climbed into the boat, the wind died down. **33** Then those who were in the boat worshiped him, saying, "Truly you are the Son of God."

34 When they had crossed over, they landed at Gennesaret. **35** And when the men of that place recognized Jesus, they sent word to all the surrounding country. People brought all their sick to him **36** and begged him to let the sick just touch the edge of his cloak, and all who touched him were healed.

Clean and Unclean

15 **1** Then some Pharisees and teachers of the law came to Jesus from Jerusalem and asked, **2** "Why do your disciples break the tradition of the elders? They don't wash their hands before they eat!"

3 Jesus replied, "And why do you break the command of God for the sake of your tradition? **4** For God said, 'Honor your father and mother'[d] and 'Anyone who curses his father or mother must be put to death.'[e] **5** But you say that if a man says to his father or mother, 'Whatever help you might otherwise have received from me is a gift devoted to God,' **6** he is not to 'honor his father[f]' with it. Thus you nullify the word of God for the sake of your tradition. **7** You hypocrites! Isaiah was right when he prophesied about you:

8 " 'These people honor me with
their lips,
but their hearts are far from
me.

---

c 24 Greek *many stadia*   **d** 4 Exodus 20:12; Deut. 5:16   **e** 4 Exodus 21:17; Lev. 20:9
f 6 Some manuscripts *father or his mother*

9 They worship me in vain;
    their teachings are but rules
        taught by men.'ᵍ"

10 Jesus called the crowd to him and said, "Listen and understand. 11 What goes into a man's mouth does not make him 'unclean,' but what comes out of his mouth, that is what makes him 'unclean.'"

12 Then the disciples came to him and asked, "Do you know that the Pharisees were offended when they heard this?"

13 He replied, "Every plant that my heavenly Father has not planted will be pulled up by the roots. 14 Leave them; they are blind guides.ʰ If a blind man leads a blind man, both will fall into a pit."

15 Peter said, "Explain the parable to us."

16 "Are you still so dull?" Jesus asked them. 17 "Don't you see that whatever enters the mouth goes into the stomach and then out of the body? 18 But the things that come out of the mouth come from the heart, and these make a man 'unclean.' 19 For out of the heart come evil thoughts, murder, adultery, sexual immorality, theft, false testimony, slander. 20 These are what make a man 'unclean'; but eating with unwashed hands does not make him 'unclean.'"

21 Leaving that place, Jesus withdrew to the region of Tyre and Sidon. 22 A Canaanite woman from that vicinity came to him, crying out, "Lord, Son of David, have mercy on me! My daughter is suffering terribly from demon-possession."

23 Jesus did not answer a word. So his disciples came to him and urged him, "Send her away, for she keeps crying out after us."

24 He answered, "I was sent only to the lost sheep of Israel."

25 The woman came and knelt before him. "Lord, help me!" she said.

26 He replied, "It is not right to take the children's bread and toss it to their dogs."

27 "Yes, Lord," she said, "but even the dogs eat the crumbs that fall from their masters' table."

28 Then Jesus answered, "Woman, you have great faith! Your request is granted." And her daughter was healed from that very hour.

Jesus Feeds the Four Thousand

29 Jesus left there and went along the Sea of Galilee. Then he went up on a mountainside and sat down. 30 Great crowds came to him, bringing the lame, the blind, the crippled, the mute and many others, and laid them at his feet; and he healed them. 31 The people were amazed when they saw the mute speaking, the crippled made well, the lame walking and the blind seeing. And they praised the God of Israel.

32 Jesus called his disciples to him and said, "I have compassion for these people; they have already been with me three days and have nothing to eat. I do not want to send them away hungry, or they may collapse on the way."

33 His disciples answered, "Where could we get enough bread in this remote place to feed such a crowd?"

34 "How many loaves do you have?" Jesus asked.

"Seven," they replied, "and a few small fish."

35 He told the crowd to sit down on the ground. 36 Then he took the seven loaves and the fish, and when

g 9 Isaiah 29:13   *h* 14 Some manuscripts *guides of the blind*

he had given thanks, he broke them and gave them to the disciples, and they in turn to the people. **37** They all ate and were satisfied. Afterward the disciples picked up seven basketfuls of broken pieces that were left over. **38** The number of those who ate was four thousand, besides women and children. **39** After Jesus had sent the crowd away, he got into the boat and went to the vicinity of Magadan.

The Demand for a Sign

16 **1** The Pharisees and Sadducees came to Jesus and tested him by asking him to show them a sign from heaven.

2 He replied,[i] "When evening comes, you say, 'It will be fair weather, for the sky is red,' **3** and in the morning, 'Today it will be stormy, for the sky is red and overcast.' You know how to interpret the appearance of the sky, but you cannot interpret the signs of the times. **4** A wicked and adulterous generation looks for a miraculous sign, but none will be given it except the sign of Jonah." Jesus then left them and went away.

The Yeast of the Pharisees and Sadducees

5 When they went across the lake, the disciples forgot to take bread. **6** "Be careful," Jesus said to them. "Be on your guard against the yeast of the Pharisees and Sadducees."

7 They discussed this among themselves and said, "It is because we didn't bring any bread."

8 Aware of their discussion, Jesus asked, "You of little faith, why are you talking among yourselves about having no bread? **9** Do you still not understand? Don't you remember the five loaves for the five thousand, and how many basketfuls you gathered? **10** Or the seven loaves for the four thousand, and how many basketfuls you gathered? **11** How is it you don't understand that I was not talking to you about bread? But be on your guard against the yeast of the Pharisees and Sadducees." **12** Then they understood that he was not telling them to guard against the yeast used in bread, but against the teaching of the Pharisees and Sadducees.

Peter's Confession of Christ

13 When Jesus came to the region of Caesarea Philippi, he asked his disciples, "Who do people say the Son of Man is?"

14 They replied, "Some say John the Baptist; others say Elijah; and still others, Jeremiah or one of the prophets."

15 "But what about you?" he asked. "Who do you say I am?"

16 Simon Peter answered, "You are the Christ,[j] the Son of the living God."

17 Jesus replied, "Blessed are you, Simon son of Jonah, for this was not revealed to you by man, but by my Father in heaven. **18** And I tell you that you are Peter,[k] and on this rock I will build my church, and the gates of Hades[l] will not overcome it.[m] **19** I will give you the keys of the kingdom of heaven; whatever you bind on earth will be[n] bound in heaven, and whatever you loose on earth will be[o] loosed in heaven." **20** Then he warned his disciples not to tell anyone that he was the Christ.

---

i 2 Some early manuscripts do not have the rest of verse 2 and all of verse 3.   *j* 16 Or Messiah; also in verse 20   *k* 18 Peter means rock.   *l* 18 Or hell   *m* 18 Or not prove stronger than it   *n* 19 Or have been   *o* 19 Or have been

Jesus Predicts His Death

21 From that time on Jesus began to explain to his disciples that he must go to Jerusalem and suffer many things at the hands of the elders, chief priests and teachers of the law, and that he must be killed and on the third day be raised to life.

22 Peter took him aside and began to rebuke him. "Never, Lord!" he said. "This shall never happen to you!"

23 Jesus turned and said to Peter, "Get behind me, Satan! You are a stumbling block to me; you do not have in mind the things of God, but the things of men."

24 Then Jesus said to his disciples, "If anyone would come after me, he must deny himself and take up his cross and follow me. **25** For whoever wants to save his life*ᵖ* will lose it, but whoever loses his life for me will find it. **26** What good will it be for a man if he gains the whole world, yet forfeits his soul? Or what can a man give in exchange for his soul? **27** For the Son of Man is going to come in his Father's glory with his angels, and then he will reward each person according to what he has done. **28** I tell you the truth, some who are standing here will not taste death before they see the Son of Man coming in his kingdom."

The Transfiguration

17 **1** After six days Jesus took with him Peter, James and John the brother of James, and led them up a high mountain by themselves. **2** There he was transfigured before them. His face shone like the sun, and his clothes became as white as the light. **3** Just then there appeared before them Moses and Elijah, talking with Jesus.

4 Peter said to Jesus, "Lord, it is good for us to be here. If you wish, I will put up three shelters—one for you, one for Moses and one for Elijah."

5 While he was still speaking, a bright cloud enveloped them, and a voice from the cloud said, "This is my Son, whom I love; with him I am well pleased. Listen to him!"

6 When the disciples heard this, they fell facedown to the ground, terrified. **7** But Jesus came and touched them. "Get up," he said. "Don't be afraid." **8** When they looked up, they saw no one except Jesus.

9 As they were coming down the mountain, Jesus instructed them, "Don't tell anyone what you have seen, until the Son of Man has been raised from the dead."

10 The disciples asked him, "Why then do the teachers of the law say that Elijah must come first?"

11 Jesus replied, "To be sure, Elijah comes and will restore all things. **12** But I tell you, Elijah has already come, and they did not recognize him, but have done to him everything they wished. In the same way the Son of Man is going to suffer at their hands." **13** Then the disciples understood that he was talking to them about John the Baptist.

The Healing of a Boy With a Demon

14 When they came to the crowd, a man approached Jesus and knelt before him. **15** "Lord, have mercy on my son," he said. "He has seizures and is suffering greatly. He often falls

ᵖ 25 The Greek word means either life or soul; also in verse 26.

into the fire or into the water. 16 I brought him to your disciples, but they could not heal him."

17 "O unbelieving and perverse generation," Jesus replied, "how long shall I stay with you? How long shall I put up with you? Bring the boy here to me." 18 Jesus rebuked the demon, and it came out of the boy, and he was healed from that moment.

19 Then the disciples came to Jesus in private and asked, "Why couldn't we drive it out?"

20 He replied, "Because you have so little faith. I tell you the truth, if you have faith as small as a mustard seed, you can say to this mountain, 'Move from here to there' and it will move. Nothing will be impossible for you."q

22 When they came together in Galilee, he said to them, "The Son of Man is going to be betrayed into the hands of men. 23 They will kill him, and on the third day he will be raised to life." And the disciples were filled with grief.

The Temple Tax

24 After Jesus and his disciples arrived in Capernaum, the collectors of the two-drachma tax came to Peter and asked, "Doesn't your teacher pay the temple taxr?"

25 "Yes, he does," he replied.

When Peter came into the house, Jesus was the first to speak. "What do you think, Simon?" he asked. "From whom do the kings of the earth collect duty and taxes — from their own sons or from others?"

26 "From others," Peter answered.

"Then the sons are exempt," Jesus said to him. 27 "But so that we may

not offend them, go to the lake and throw out your line. Take the first fish you catch; open its mouth and you will find a four-drachma coin. Take it and give it to them for my tax and yours."

The Greatest in the Kingdom of Heaven

18 1 At that time the disciples came to Jesus and asked, "Who is the greatest in the kingdom of heaven?"

2 He called a little child and had him stand among them. 3 And he said: "I tell you the truth, unless you change and become like little children, you will never enter the kingdom of heaven. 4 Therefore, whoever humbles himself like this child is the greatest in the kingdom of heaven.

5 "And whoever welcomes a little child like this in my name welcomes me. 6 But if anyone causes one of these little ones who believe in me to sin, it would be better for him to have a large millstone hung around his neck and to be drowned in the depths of the sea.

7 "Woe to the world because of the things that cause people to sin! Such things must come, but woe to the man through whom they come! 8 If your hand or your foot causes you to sin, cut it off and throw it away. It is better for you to enter life maimed or crippled than to have two hands or two feet and be thrown into eternal fire. 9 And if your eye causes you to sin, gouge it out and throw it away. It is better for you to enter life with one eye than to have two eyes and be thrown into the fire of hell.

q 20 Some manuscripts you. 21 But this kind does not go out except by prayer and fasting.
r 24 Greek the two drachmas

The Parable of the Lost Sheep

10 "See that you do not look down on one of these little ones. For I tell you that their angels in heaven always see the face of my Father in heaven.*s*

12 "What do you think? If a man owns a hundred sheep, and one of them wanders away, will he not leave the ninety-nine on the hills and go to look for the one that wandered off? **13** And if he finds it, I tell you the truth, he is happier about that one sheep than about the ninety-nine that did not wander off. **14** In the same way your Father in heaven is not willing that any of these little ones should be lost.

A Brother Who Sins Against You

15 "If your brother sins against you,*t* go and show him his fault, just between the two of you. If he listens to you, you have won your brother over. **16** But if he will not listen, take one or two others along, so that 'every matter may be established by the testimony of two or three witnesses.'*u* **17** If he refuses to listen to them, tell it to the church; and if he refuses to listen even to the church, treat him as you would a pagan or a tax collector.

18 "I tell you the truth, whatever you bind on earth will be*v* bound in heaven, and whatever you loose on earth will be*w* loosed in heaven.

19 "Again, I tell you that if two of you on earth agree about anything you ask for, it will be done for you by my Father in heaven. **20** For where two or three come together in my name, there am I with them."

The Parable of the Unmerciful Servant

21 Then Peter came to Jesus and asked, "Lord, how many times shall I forgive my brother when he sins against me? Up to seven times?"

22 Jesus answered, "I tell you, not seven times, but seventy-seven times.*x*

23 "Therefore, the kingdom of heaven is like a king who wanted to settle accounts with his servants. **24** As he began the settlement, a man who owed him ten thousand talents*y* was brought to him. **25** Since he was not able to pay, the master ordered that he and his wife and his children and all that he had be sold to repay the debt.

26 "The servant fell on his knees before him. 'Be patient with me,' he begged, 'and I will pay back everything.' **27** The servant's master took pity on him, canceled the debt and let him go.

28 "But when that servant went out, he found one of his fellow servants who owed him a hundred denarii.*z* He grabbed him and began to choke him. 'Pay back what you owe me!' he demanded.

29 "His fellow servant fell to his knees and begged him, 'Be patient with me, and I will pay you back.'

30 "But he refused. Instead, he went off and had the man thrown into prison until he could pay the debt. **31** When the other servants saw what had happened, they were greatly distressed and went and told their master everything that had happened.

---

s 10 Some manuscripts *heaven.* 11 *The Son of Man came to save what was lost.*
t 15 Some manuscripts do not have *against you.*   *u* 16 Deut. 19:15   *v* 18 Or *have been*
w 18 Or *have been*   *x* 22 Or *seventy times seven*   *y* 24 That is, millions of dollars
z 28 That is, a few dollars

32 "Then the master called the servant in. 'You wicked servant,' he said, 'I canceled all that debt of yours because you begged me to. **33** Shouldn't you have had mercy on your fellow servant just as I had on you?' **34** In anger his master turned him over to the jailers to be tortured, until he should pay back all he owed.

35 "This is how my heavenly Father will treat each of you unless you forgive your brother from your heart."

Divorce

19 **1** When Jesus had finished saying these things, he left Galilee and went into the region of Judea to the other side of the Jordan. **2** Large crowds followed him, and he healed them there.

3 Some Pharisees came to him to test him. They asked, "Is it lawful for a man to divorce his wife for any and every reason?"

4 "Haven't you read," he replied, "that at the beginning the Creator 'made them male and female,'ᵃ **5** and said, 'For this reason a man will leave his father and mother and be united to his wife, and the two will become one flesh'ᵇ? **6** So they are no longer two, but one. Therefore what God has joined together, let man not separate."

7 "Why then," they asked, "did Moses command that a man give his wife a certificate of divorce and send her away?"

8 Jesus replied, "Moses permitted you to divorce your wives because your hearts were hard. But it was not this way from the beginning. **9** I tell you that anyone who divorces his wife, except for marital unfaithful-

ness, and marries another woman commits adultery."

10 The disciples said to him, "If this is the situation between a husband and wife, it is better not to marry."

11 Jesus replied, "Not everyone can accept this word, but only those to whom it has been given. **12** For some are eunuchs because they were born that way; others were made that way by men; and others have renounced marriageᶜ because of the kingdom of heaven. The one who can accept this should accept it."

13 Then little children were brought to Jesus for him to place his hands on them and pray for them. But the disciples rebuked those who brought them.

14 Jesus said, "Let the little children come to me, and do not hinder them, for the kingdom of heaven belongs to such as these." **15** When he had placed his hands on them, he went on from there.

The Rich Young Man

16 Now a man came up to Jesus and asked, "Teacher, what good thing must I do to get eternal life?"

17 "Why do you ask me about what is good?" Jesus replied. "There is only One who is good. If you want to enter life, obey the commandments."

18 "Which ones?" the man inquired.

Jesus replied, " 'Do not murder, do not commit adultery, do not steal, do not give false testimony, **19** honor your father and mother,'ᵈ and 'love your neighbor as yourself.'ᵉ"

20 "All these I have kept," the young man said. "What do I still lack?"

ᵃ 4 Gen. 1:27   ᵇ 5 Gen. 2:24   ᶜ 12 Or have made themselves eunuchs
ᵈ 19 Exodus 20:12-16; Deut. 5:16-20   ᵉ 19 Lev. 19:18

21 Jesus answered, "If you want to be perfect, go, sell your possessions and give to the poor, and you will have treasure in heaven. Then come, follow me."

22 When the young man heard this, he went away sad, because he had great wealth.

23 Then Jesus said to his disciples, "I tell you the truth, it is hard for a rich man to enter the kingdom of heaven. **24** Again I tell you, it is easier for a camel to go through the eye of a needle than for a rich man to enter the kingdom of God."

25 When the disciples heard this, they were greatly astonished and asked, "Who then can be saved?"

26 Jesus looked at them and said, "With man this is impossible, but with God all things are possible."

27 Peter answered him, "We have left everything to follow you! What then will there be for us?"

28 Jesus said to them, "I tell you the truth, at the renewal of all things, when the Son of Man sits on his glorious throne, you who have followed me will also sit on twelve thrones, judging the twelve tribes of Israel. **29** And everyone who has left houses or brothers or sisters or father or mother*f* or children or fields for my sake will receive a hundred times as much and will inherit eternal life. **30** But many who are first will be last, and many who are last will be first.

The Parable of the Workers in the Vineyard

20 **1** "For the kingdom of heaven is like a landowner who went out early in the morning to hire men to work in his vineyard. **2** He agreed to pay them a denarius for the day and sent them into his vineyard. **3** "About the third hour he went out and saw others standing in the marketplace doing nothing. **4** He told them, 'You also go and work in my vineyard, and I will pay you whatever is right.' **5** So they went.

"He went out again about the sixth hour and the ninth hour and did the same thing. **6** About the eleventh hour he went out and found still others standing around. He asked them, 'Why have you been standing here all day long doing nothing?'

7 " 'Because no one has hired us,' they answered.

"He said to them, 'You also go and work in my vineyard.'

8 "When evening came, the owner of the vineyard said to his foreman, 'Call the workers and pay them their wages, beginning with the last ones hired and going on to the first.'

9 "The workers who were hired about the eleventh hour came and each received a denarius. **10** So when those came who were hired first, they expected to receive more. But each one of them also received a denarius. **11** When they received it, they began to grumble against the landowner. **12** 'These men who were hired last worked only one hour,' they said, 'and you have made them equal to us who have borne the burden of the work and the heat of the day.'

13 "But he answered one of them, 'Friend, I am not being unfair to you. Didn't you agree to work for a denarius? **14** Take your pay and go. I want to give the man who was

f 29 Some manuscripts mother or wife

hired last the same as I gave you. 15 Don't I have the right to do what I want with my own money? Or are you envious because I am generous?'

16 "So the last will be first, and the first will be last."

Jesus Again Predicts His Death

17 Now as Jesus was going up to Jerusalem, he took the twelve disciples aside and said to them, 18 "We are going up to Jerusalem, and the Son of Man will be betrayed to the chief priests and the teachers of the law. They will condemn him to death 19 and will turn him over to the Gentiles to be mocked and flogged and crucified. On the third day he will be raised to life!"

A Mother's Request

20 Then the mother of Zebedee's sons came to Jesus with her sons and, kneeling down, asked a favor of him.

21 "What is it you want?" he asked.

She said, "Grant that one of these two sons of mine may sit at your right and the other at your left in your kingdom."

22 "You don't know what you are asking," Jesus said to them. "Can you drink the cup I am going to drink?"

"We can," they answered.

23 Jesus said to them, "You will indeed drink from my cup, but to sit at my right or left is not for me to grant. These places belong to those for whom they have been prepared by my Father."

24 When the ten heard about this, they were indignant with the two brothers. 25 Jesus called them together and said, "You know that the rulers of the Gentiles lord it over them, and their high officials exercise authority over them.

26 Not so with you. Instead, whoever wants to become great among you must be your servant, 27 and whoever wants to be first must be your slave— 28 just as the Son of Man did not come to be served, but to serve, and to give his life as a ransom for many."

Two Blind Men Receive Sight

29 As Jesus and his disciples were leaving Jericho, a large crowd followed him. 30 Two blind men were sitting by the roadside, and when they heard that Jesus was going by, they shouted, "Lord, Son of David, have mercy on us!"

31 The crowd rebuked them and told them to be quiet, but they shouted all the louder, "Lord, Son of David, have mercy on us!"

32 Jesus stopped and called them. "What do you want me to do for you?" he asked.

33 "Lord," they answered, "we want our sight."

34 Jesus had compassion on them and touched their eyes. Immediately they received their sight and followed him.

The Triumphal Entry

21 1 As they approached Jerusalem and came to Bethphage on the Mount of Olives, Jesus sent two disciples, 2 saying to them, "Go to the village ahead of you, and at once you will find a donkey tied there, with her colt by her. Untie them and bring them to me. 3 If anyone says anything to you, tell him that the Lord needs them, and he will send them right away."

4 This took place to fulfill what was spoken through the prophet:

5 "Say to the Daughter of Zion,
    'See, your king comes to you,

gentle and riding on a donkey,
on a colt, the foal of a
donkey.' "g

6 The disciples went and did as
Jesus had instructed them. 7 They
brought the donkey and the colt,
placed their cloaks on them, and
Jesus sat on them. 8 A very large
crowd spread their cloaks on the
road, while others cut branches from
the trees and spread them on the
road. 9 The crowds that went ahead
of him and those that followed
shouted,

"Hosannah to the Son of David!"

"Blessed is he who comes in the
name of the Lord!"i

"Hosannaj in the highest!"

10 When Jesus entered Jerusalem,
the whole city was stirred and asked,
"Who is this?"

11 The crowds answered, "This is
Jesus, the prophet from Nazareth in
Galilee."

Jesus at the Temple

12 Jesus entered the temple area
and drove out all who were buying
and selling there. He overturned the
tables of the money changers and the
benches of those selling doves. 13 "It
is written," he said to them, " 'My
house will be called a house of
prayer,'k but you are making it a 'den
of robbers.'"l

14 The blind and the lame came to
him at the temple, and he healed
them. 15 But when the chief priests
and the teachers of the law saw the
wonderful things he did and the

children shouting in the temple area,
"Hosanna to the Son of David," they
were indignant.

16 "Do you hear what these
children are saying?" they asked him.

"Yes," replied Jesus, "have you
never read,

" 'From the lips of children and
infants
you have ordained praise'm?"

17 And he left them and went out
of the city to Bethany, where he spent
the night.

The Fig Tree Withers

18 Early in the morning, as he
was on his way back to the city, he
was hungry. 19 Seeing a fig tree by
the road, he went up to it but found
nothing on it except leaves. Then
he said to it, "May you never bear
fruit again!" Immediately the tree
withered.

20 When the disciples saw this,
they were amazed. "How did the fig
tree wither so quickly?" they asked.

21 Jesus replied, "I tell you the
truth, if you have faith and do not
doubt, not only can you do what was
done to the fig tree, but also you can
say to this mountain, 'Go, throw
yourself into the sea,' and it will be
done. 22 If you believe, you will
receive whatever you ask for in
prayer."

The Authority of Jesus Questioned

23 Jesus entered the temple
courts, and, while he was teaching,
the chief priests and the elders of the
people came to him. "By what

---

g 5 Zech. 9:9   h 9 A Hebrew expression meaning "Save!" which became an exclamation of
praise; also in verse 15   i 9 Psalm 118:26   j 9 A Hebrew expression meaning "Save!"
which became an exclamation of praise; also in verse 15   k 13 Isaiah 56:7   l 13 Jer. 7:11
m 16 Psalm 8:2

authority are you doing these things?" they asked. "And who gave you this authority?"

24 Jesus replied, "I will also ask you one question. If you answer me, I will tell you by what authority I am doing these things. 25 John's baptism—where did it come from? Was it from heaven, or from men?"

They discussed it among themselves and said, "If we say, 'From heaven,' he will ask, 'Then why didn't you believe him?' 26 But if we say, 'From men'—we are afraid of the people, for they all hold that John was a prophet."

27 So they answered Jesus, "We don't know."

Then he said, "Neither will I tell you by what authority I am doing these things.

The Parable of the Two Sons

28 "What do you think? There was a man who had two sons. He went to the first and said, 'Son, go and work today in the vineyard.'

29 " 'I will not,' he answered, but later he changed his mind and went.

30 "Then the father went to the other son and said the same thing. He answered, 'I will, sir,' but he did not go.

31 "Which of the two did what his father wanted?"

"The first," they answered.

Jesus said to them, "I tell you the truth, the tax collectors and the prostitutes are entering the kingdom of God ahead of you. 32 For John came to you to show you the way of righteousness, and you did not believe him, but the tax collectors and the prostitutes did. And even

after you saw this, you did not repent and believe him.

The Parable of the Tenants

33 "Listen to another parable: There was a landowner who planted a vineyard. He put a wall around it, dug a winepress in it and built a watchtower. Then he rented the vineyard to some farmers and went away on a journey. 34 When the harvest time approached, he sent his servants to the tenants to collect his fruit.

35 "The tenants seized his servants; they beat one, killed another, and stoned a third. 36 Then he sent other servants to them, more than the first time, and the tenants treated them the same way. 37 Last of all, he sent his son to them. 'They will respect my son,' he said.

38 "But when the tenants saw the son, they said to each other, 'This is the heir. Come, let's kill him and take his inheritance.' 39 So they took him and threw him out of the vineyard and killed him.

40 "Therefore, when the owner of the vineyard comes, what will he do to those tenants?"

41 "He will bring those wretches to a wretched end," they replied, "and he will rent the vineyard to other tenants, who will give him his share of the crop at harvest time."

42 Jesus said to them, "Have you never read in the Scriptures:

" 'The stone the builders rejected
   has become the capstone[n];
the Lord has done this,
   and it is marvelous in our
       eyes'[o]?

43 "Therefore I tell you that the kingdom of God will be taken away

---

n 42 Or *cornerstone*   o 42 Psalm 118:22,23

from you and given to a people who will produce its fruit. **44** He who falls on this stone will be broken to pieces, but he on whom it falls will be crushed."ᴾ

45 When the chief priests and the Pharisees heard Jesus' parables, they knew he was talking about them. **46** They looked for a way to arrest him, but they were afraid of the crowd because the people held that he was a prophet.

The Parable of the Wedding Banquet

22 **1** Jesus spoke to them again in parables, saying: **2** "The kingdom of heaven is like a king who prepared a wedding banquet for his son. **3** He sent his servants to those who had been invited to the banquet to tell them to come, but they refused to come.

4 "Then he sent some more servants and said, 'Tell those who have been invited that I have prepared my dinner: My oxen and fattened cattle have been butchered, and everything is ready. Come to the wedding banquet.'

5 "But they paid no attention and went off—one to his field, another to his business. **6** The rest seized his servants, mistreated them and killed them. **7** The king was enraged. He sent his army and destroyed those murderers and burned their city.

8 "Then he said to his servants, 'The wedding banquet is ready, but those I invited did not deserve to come. **9** Go to the street corners and invite to the banquet anyone you find.' **10** So the servants went out into the streets and gathered all the people they could find, both good and bad, and the wedding hall was filled with guests.

11 "But when the king came in to see the guests, he noticed a man there who was not wearing wedding clothes. **12** 'Friend,' he asked, 'how did you get in here without wedding clothes?' The man was speechless.

13 "Then the king told the attendants, 'Tie him hand and foot, and throw him outside, into the darkness, where there will be weeping and gnashing of teeth.'

14 "For many are invited, but few are chosen."

Paying Taxes to Caesar

15 Then the Pharisees went out and laid plans to trap him in his words. **16** They sent their disciples to him along with the Herodians. "Teacher," they said, "we know you are a man of integrity and that you teach the way of God in accordance with the truth. You aren't swayed by men, because you pay no attention to who they are. **17** Tell us then, what is your opinion? Is it right to pay taxes to Caesar or not?"

18 But Jesus, knowing their evil intent, said, "You hypocrites, why are you trying to trap me? **19** Show me the coin used for paying the tax." They brought him a denarius, **20** and he asked them, "Whose portrait is this? And whose inscription?"

21 "Caesar's," they replied.

Then he said to them, "Give to Caesar what is Caesar's, and to God what is God's."

22 When they heard this, they were amazed. So they left him and went away.

Marriage at the Resurrection

23 That same day the Sadducees, who say there is no resurrection,

---

ᴾ **44** Some manuscripts do not have verse 44.

came to him with a question. **24** "Teacher," they said, "Moses told us that if a man dies without having children, his brother must marry the widow and have children for him. **25** Now there were seven brothers among us. The first one married and died, and since he had no children, he left his wife to his brother. **26** The same thing happened to the second and third brother, right on down to the seventh. **27** Finally, the woman died. **28** Now then, at the resurrection, whose wife will she be of the seven, since all of them were married to her?"

29 Jesus replied, "You are in error because you do not know the Scriptures or the power of God. **30** At the resurrection people will neither marry nor be given in marriage; they will be like the angels in heaven. **31** But about the resurrection of the dead—have you not read what God said to you, **32** 'I am the God of Abraham, the God of Isaac, and the God of Jacob'*q*? He is not the God of the dead but of the living."

33 When the crowds heard this, they were astonished at his teaching.

The Greatest Commandment

34 Hearing that Jesus had silenced the Sadducees, the Pharisees got together. **35** One of them, an expert in the law, tested him with this question: **36** "Teacher, which is the greatest commandment in the Law?" **37** Jesus replied: "'Love the Lord your God with all your heart and with all your soul and with all your mind.'*r* **38** This is the first and greatest commandment. **39** And the second is like it: 'Love your neighbor as yourself.'*s*

40 All the Law and the Prophets hang on these two commandments."

Whose Son Is the Christ

41 While the Pharisees were gathered together, Jesus asked them, **42** "What do you think about the Christ*t*? Whose son is he?"

"The son of David," they replied.

43 He said to them, "How is it that David, speaking by the Spirit, calls him 'Lord'? For he says,

44 "'The Lord said to my Lord:
    "Sit at my right hand
    until I put your enemies
    under your feet."'*u*

45 If then David calls him 'Lord,' how can he be his son?" **46** No one could say a word in reply, and from that day on no one dared to ask him any more questions.

Seven Woes

23 **1** Then Jesus said to the crowds and to his disciples: **2** "The teachers of the law and the Pharisees sit in Moses' seat. **3** So you must obey them and do everything they tell you. But do not do what they do, for they do not practice what they preach. **4** They tie up heavy loads and put them on men's shoulders, but they themselves are not willing to lift a finger to move them.

5 "Everything they do is done for men to see: They make their phylacteries*v* wide and the tassels on their garments long; **6** they love the place of honor at banquets and the most important seats in the synagogues; **7** they love to be greeted in the marketplaces and to have men call them 'Rabbi.'

q 32 Exodus 3:6   *r 37* Deut. 6:5   *s 39* Lev. 19:18   *t 42* Or *Messiah*   *u 44* Psalm 110:1   *v 5* That is, boxes containing Scripture verses, worn on forehead and arm

8 "But you are not to be called 'Rabbi,' for you have only one Master and you are all brothers. 9 And do not call anyone on earth 'father,' for you have one Father, and he is in heaven. 10 Nor are you to be called 'teacher,' for you have one Teacher, the Christ.w 11 The greatest among you will be your servant. 12 For whoever exalts himself will be humbled, and whoever humbles himself will be exalted.

13 "Woe to you, teachers of the law and Pharisees, you hypocrites! You shut the kingdom of heaven in men's faces. You yourselves do not enter, nor will you let those enter who are trying to.x

15 "Woe to you, teachers of the law and Pharisees, you hypocrites! You travel over land and sea to win a single convert, and when he becomes one, you make him twice as much a son of hell as you are.

16 "Woe to you, blind guides! You say, 'If anyone swears by the temple, it means nothing; but if anyone swears by the gold of the temple, he is bound by his oath.' 17 You blind fools! Which is greater: the gold, or the temple that makes the gold sacred? 18 You also say, 'If anyone swears by the altar, it means nothing; but if anyone swears by the gift on it, he is bound by his oath.' 19 You blind men! Which is greater: the gift, or the altar that makes the gift sacred? 20 Therefore, he who swears by the altar swears by it and by everything on it. 21 And he who swears by the temple swears by it and by the one who dwells in it. 22 And he who swears by heaven swears by God's throne and by the one who sits on it.

23 "Woe to you, teachers of the law and Pharisees, you hypocrites! You give a tenth of your spices — mint, dill and cummin. But you have neglected the more important matters of the law — justice, mercy and faithfulness. You should have practiced the latter, without neglecting the former. 24 You blind guides! You strain out a gnat but swallow a camel.

25 "Woe to you, teachers of the law and Pharisees, you hypocrites! You clean the outside of the cup and dish, but inside they are full of greed and self-indulgence. 26 Blind Pharisee! First clean the inside of the cup and dish, and then the outside also will be clean.

27 "Woe to you, teachers of the law and Pharisees, you hypocrites! You are like whitewashed tombs, which look beautiful on the outside but on the inside are full of dead men's bones and everything unclean. 28 In the same way, on the outside you appear to people as righteous but on the inside you are full of hypocrisy and wickedness.

29 "Woe to you, teachers of the law and Pharisees, you hypocrites! You build tombs for the prophets and decorate the graves of the righteous. 30 And you say, 'If we had lived in the days of our forefathers, we would not have taken part with them in shedding the blood of the prophets.' 31 So you testify against yourselves that you are the descendants of those who murdered the prophets. 32 Fill up, then, the measure of the sin of your forefathers!

33 "You snakes! You brood of vipers! How will you escape being condemned to hell? 34 Therefore I

w 10 Or Messiah   x 13 Some manuscripts to. 14 Woe to you, teachers of the law and Pharisees, you hypocrites! You devour widows' houses and for a show make lengthy prayers. Therefore you will be punished more severely.

am sending you prophets and wise men and teachers. Some of them you will kill and crucify; others you will flog in your synagogues and pursue from town to town. **35** And so upon you will come all the righteous blood that has been shed on earth, from the blood of righteous Abel to the blood of Zechariah son of Berekiah, whom you murdered between the temple and the altar. **36** I tell you the truth, all this will come upon this generation.

37 "O Jerusalem, Jerusalem, you who kill the prophets and stone those sent to you, how often I have longed to gather your children together, as a hen gathers her chicks under her wings, but you were not willing. **38** Look, your house is left to you desolate. **39** For I tell you, you will not see me again until you say, 'Blessed is he who comes in the name of the Lord.'*y*"

Signs of the End of the Age

24 **1** Jesus left the temple and was walking away when his disciples came up to him to call his attention to its buildings. **2** "Do you see all these things?" he asked. "I tell you the truth, not one stone here will be left on another; every one will be thrown down."

3 As Jesus was sitting on the Mount of Olives, the disciples came to him privately. "Tell us," they said, "when will this happen, and what will be the sign of your coming and of the end of the age?"

4 Jesus answered: "Watch out that no one deceives you. **5** For many will come in my name, claiming, 'I am the Christ,'*z* and will deceive many. **6** You will hear of wars and rumors of wars,

but see to it that you are not alarmed. Such things must happen, but the end is still to come. **7** Nation will rise against nation, and kingdom against kingdom. There will be famines and earthquakes in various places. **8** All these are the beginning of birth pains.

9 "Then you will be handed over to be persecuted and put to death, and you will be hated by all nations because of me. **10** At that time many will turn away from the faith and will betray and hate each other, **11** and many false prophets will appear and deceive many people. **12** Because of the increase of wickedness, the love of most will grow cold, **13** but he who stands firm to the end will be saved. **14** And this gospel of the kingdom will be preached in the whole world as a testimony to all nations, and then the end will come.

15 "So when you see standing in the holy place 'the abomination that causes desolation,'*a* spoken of through the prophet Daniel—let the reader understand— **16** then let those who are in Judea flee to the mountains. **17** Let no one on the roof of his house go down to take anything out of the house. **18** Let no one in the field go back to get his cloak. **19** How dreadful it will be in those days for pregnant women and nursing mothers! **20** Pray that your flight will not take place in winter or on the Sabbath. **21** For then there will be great distress, unequaled from the beginning of the world until now—and never to be equaled again. **22** If those days had not been cut short, no one would survive, but for the sake of the elect those days will be shortened. **23** At that time if anyone says

y **39** Psalm 118:26   *z* **5** Or *Messiah*; also in verse 23   *a* **15** Daniel 9:27; 11:31; 12:11

to you, 'Look, here is the Christ!' or, 'There he is!' do not believe it. 24 For false Christs and false prophets will appear and perform great signs and miracles to deceive even the elect—if that were possible. 25 See, I have told you ahead of time.

26 "So if anyone tells you, 'There he is, out in the desert,' do not go out; or, 'Here he is, in the inner rooms,' do not believe it. 27 For as lightning that comes from the east is visible even in the west, so will be the coming of the Son of Man. 28 Wherever there is a carcass, there the vultures will gather.

29 "Immediately after the distress of those days

> " 'the sun will be darkened,
>> and the moon will not give its
>> light;
> the stars will fall from the sky,
>> and the heavenly bodies will
>> be shaken.'[b]

30 "At that time the sign of the Son of Man will appear in the sky, and all the nations of the earth will mourn. They will see the Son of Man coming on the clouds of the sky, with power and great glory. 31 And he will send his angels with a loud trumpet call, and they will gather his elect from the four winds, from one end of the heavens to the other.

32 "Now learn this lesson from the fig tree: As soon as its twigs get tender and its leaves come out, you know that summer is near. 33 Even so, when you see all these things, you know that it[c] is near, right at the door. 34 I tell you the truth, this generation[d] will certainly not pass away until all these things have happened.

35 Heaven and earth will pass away, but my words will never pass away.

The Day and Hour Unknown

36 "No one knows about that day or hour, not even the angels in heaven, nor the Son,[e] but only the Father. 37 As it was in the days of Noah, so it will be at the coming of the Son of Man. 38 For in the days before the flood, people were eating and drinking, marrying and giving in marriage, up to the day Noah entered the ark; 39 and they knew nothing about what would happen until the flood came and took them all away. That is how it will be at the coming of the Son of Man. 40 Two men will be in the field; one will be taken and the other left. 41 Two women will be grinding with a hand mill; one will be taken and the other left.

42 "Therefore keep watch, because you do not know on what day your Lord will come. 43 But understand this: If the owner of the house had known at what time of night the thief was coming, he would have kept watch and would not have let his house be broken into. 44 So you also must be ready, because the Son of Man will come at an hour when you do not expect him.

45 "Who then is the faithful and wise servant, whom the master has put in charge of the servants in his household to give them their food at the proper time? 46 It will be good for that servant whose master finds him doing so when he returns. 47 I tell you the truth, he will put him in charge of all his possessions. 48 But suppose that servant is wicked and

---

b 29 Isaiah 13:10; 34:4   *c* 33 Or he   *d* 34 Or race   *e* 36 Some manuscripts do not have *nor the Son*.

says to himself, 'My master is staying away a long time,' **49** and he then begins to beat his fellow servants and to eat and drink with drunkards. **50** The master of that servant will come on a day when he does not expect him and at an hour he is not aware of. **51** He will cut him to pieces and assign him a place with the hypocrites, where there will be weeping and gnashing of teeth.

The Parable of the Ten Virgins

25 ¹ "At that time the kingdom of heaven will be like ten virgins who took their lamps and went out to meet the bridegroom. **2** Five of them were foolish and five were wise. **3** The foolish ones took their lamps but did not take any oil with them. **4** The wise, however, took oil in jars along with their lamps. **5** The bridegroom was a long time in coming, and they all became drowsy and fell asleep.

6 "At midnight the cry rang out: 'Here's the bridegroom! Come out to meet him!'

7 "Then all the virgins woke up and trimmed their lamps. **8** The foolish ones said to the wise, 'Give us some of your oil; our lamps are going out.'

9 " 'No,' they replied, 'there may not be enough for both us and you. Instead, go to those who sell oil and buy some for yourselves.'

10 "But while they were on their way to buy the oil, the bridegroom arrived. The virgins who were ready went in with him to the wedding banquet. And the door was shut.

11 "Later the others also came. 'Sir! Sir!' they said. 'Open the door for us!'

12 "But he replied, 'I tell you the truth, I don't know you.'

13 "Therefore keep watch, because you do not know the day or the hour.

The Parable of the Talents

14 "Again, it will be like a man going on a journey, who called his servants and entrusted his property to them. **15** To one he gave five talents*f* of money, to another two talents, and to another one talent, each according to his ability. Then he went on his journey. **16** The man who had received the five talents went at once and put his money to work and gained five more. **17** So also, the one with the two talents gained two more. **18** But the man who had received the one talent went off, dug a hole in the ground and hid his master's money.

19 "After a long time the master of those servants returned and settled accounts with them. **20** The man who had received the five talents brought the other five. 'Master,' he said, 'you entrusted me with five talents. See, I have gained five more.'

21 "His master replied, 'Well done, good and faithful servant! You have been faithful with a few things; I will put you in charge of many things. Come and share your master's happiness!'

22 "The man with the two talents also came. 'Master,' he said, 'you entrusted me with two talents; see, I have gained two more.'

23 "His master replied, 'Well done, good and faithful servant! You have been faithful with a few things; I will put you in charge of many things. Come and share your master's happiness!'

f 15 A talent was worth more than a thousand dollars.

24 "Then the man who had received the one talent came. 'Master,' he said, 'I knew that you are a hard man, harvesting where you have not sown and gathering where you have not scattered seed. 25 So I was afraid and went out and hid your talent in the ground. See, here is what belongs to you.'

26 "His master replied, 'You wicked, lazy servant! So you knew that I harvest where I have not sown and gather where I have not scattered seed? 27 Well then, you should have put my money on deposit with the bankers, so that when I returned I would have received it back with interest.

28 " 'Take the talent from him and give it to the one who has the ten talents. 29 For everyone who has will be given more, and he will have an abundance. Whoever does not have, even what he has will be taken from him. 30 And throw that worthless servant outside, into the darkness, where there will be weeping and gnashing of teeth.'

The Sheep and the Goats

31 "When the Son of Man comes in his glory, and all the angels with him, he will sit on his throne in heavenly glory. 32 All the nations will be gathered before him, and he will separate the people one from another as a shepherd separates the sheep from the goats. 33 He will put the sheep on his right and the goats on his left.

34 "Then the King will say to those on his right, 'Come, you who are blessed by my Father; take your inheritance, the kingdom prepared for you since the creation of the world. 35 For I was hungry and you gave me something to eat, I was thirsty and you gave me something to drink, I was a stranger and you invited me in, 36 I needed clothes and you clothed me, I was sick and you looked after me, I was in prison and you came to visit me.'

37 "Then the righteous will answer him, 'Lord, when did we see you hungry and feed you, or thirsty and give you something to drink? 38 When did we see you a stranger and invite you in, or needing clothes and clothe you? 39 When did we see you sick or in prison and go to visit you?'

40 "The King will reply, 'I tell you the truth, whatever you did for one of the least of these brothers of mine, you did for me.'

41 "Then he will say to those on his left, 'Depart from me, you who are cursed, into the eternal fire prepared for the devil and his angels. 42 For I was hungry and you gave me nothing to eat, I was thirsty and you gave me nothing to drink, 43 I was a stranger and you did not invite me in, I needed clothes and you did not clothe me, I was sick and in prison and you did not look after me.'

44 "They also will answer, 'Lord, when did we see you hungry or thirsty or a stranger or needing clothes or sick or in prison, and did not help you?'

45 "He will reply, 'I tell you the truth, whatever you did not do for one of the least of these, you did not do for me.'

46 "Then they will go away to eternal punishment, but the righteous to eternal life."

The Plot Against Jesus

26 1 When Jesus had finished saying all these things, he said to his disciples, 2 "As you know, the Passover is two days away—and the Son of Man will be handed over to be crucified."

3 Then the chief priests and the elders of the people assembled in the palace of the high priest, whose name was Caiaphas, **4** and they plotted to arrest Jesus in some sly way and kill him. **5** "But not during the Feast," they said, "or there may be a riot among the people."

Jesus Anointed at Bethany

6 While Jesus was in Bethany in the home of a man known as Simon the Leper, **7** a woman came to him with an alabaster jar of very expensive perfume, which she poured on his head as he was reclining at the table.

8 When the disciples saw this, they were indignant. "Why this waste?" they asked. **9** "This perfume could have been sold at a high price and the money given to the poor."

10 Aware of this, Jesus said to them, "Why are you bothering this woman? She has done a beautiful thing to me. **11** The poor you will always have with you, but you will not always have me. **12** When she poured this perfume on my body, she did it to prepare me for burial. **13** I tell you the truth, wherever this gospel is preached throughout the world, what she has done will also be told, in memory of her."

Judas Agrees to Betray Jesus

14 Then one of the Twelve—the one called Judas Iscariot—went to the chief priests **15** and asked, "What are you willing to give me if I hand him over to you?" So they counted out for him thirty silver coins. **16** From then on Judas watched for an opportunity to hand him over.

The Lord's Supper

17 On the first day of the Feast of Unleavened Bread, the disciples came to Jesus and asked, "Where do you want us to make preparations for you to eat the Passover?"

18 He replied, "Go into the city to a certain man and tell him, 'The Teacher says: My appointed time is near. I am going to celebrate the Passover with my disciples at your house.' " **19** So the disciples did as Jesus had directed them and prepared the Passover.

20 When evening came, Jesus was reclining at the table with the Twelve. **21** And while they were eating, he said, "I tell you the truth, one of you will betray me."

22 They were very sad and began to say to him one after the other, "Surely not I, Lord?"

23 Jesus replied, "The one who has dipped his hand into the bowl with me will betray me. **24** The Son of Man will go just as it is written about him. But woe to that man who betrays the Son of Man! It would be better for him if he had not been born."

25 Then Judas, the one who would betray him, said, "Surely not I, Rabbi?"

Jesus answered, "Yes, it is you."*g*

26 While they were eating, Jesus took bread, gave thanks and broke it, and gave it to his disciples, saying, "Take and eat; this is my body."

27 Then he took the cup, gave thanks and offered it to them, saying, "Drink from it, all of you. **28** This is my blood of the*h* covenant, which is poured out for many for the forgiveness of sins. **29** I tell you, I will not

---

g 25 Or *"You yourself have said it"*   *h* 28 Some manuscripts *the new*

drink of this fruit of the vine from now on until that day when I drink it anew with you in my Father's kingdom."

30 When they had sung a hymn, they went out to the Mount of Olives.

Jesus Predicts Peter's Denial

31 Then Jesus told them, "This very night you will all fall away on account of me, for it is written:

" 'I will strike the shepherd,
   and the sheep of the flock will
   be scattered.'i

32 But after I have risen, I will go ahead of you into Galilee."

33 Peter replied, "Even if all fall away on account of you, I never will."

34 "I tell you the truth," Jesus answered, "this very night, before the rooster crows, you will disown me three times."

35 But Peter declared, "Even if I have to die with you, I will never disown you." And all the other disciples said the same.

Gethsemane

36 Then Jesus went with his disciples to a place called Gethsemane, and he said to them, "Sit here while I go over there and pray." **37** He took Peter and the two sons of Zebedee along with him, and he began to be sorrowful and troubled. **38** Then he said to them, "My soul is overwhelmed with sorrow to the point of death. Stay here and keep watch with me."

39 Going a little farther, he fell with his face to the ground and prayed, "My Father, if it is possible, may this cup be taken from me. Yet not as I will, but as you will."

40 Then he returned to his disciples and found them sleeping. "Could you men not keep watch with me for one hour?" he asked Peter. **41** "Watch and pray so that you will not fall into temptation. The spirit is willing, but the body is weak."

42 He went away a second time and prayed, "My Father, if it is not possible for this cup to be taken away unless I drink it, may your will be done."

43 When he came back, he again found them sleeping, because their eyes were heavy. **44** So he left them and went away once more and prayed the third time, saying the same thing.

45 Then he returned to the disciples and said to them, "Are you still sleeping and resting? Look, the hour is near, and the Son of Man is betrayed into the hands of sinners. **46** Rise, let us go! Here comes my betrayer!"

Jesus Arrested

47 While he was still speaking, Judas, one of the Twelve, arrived. With him was a large crowd armed with swords and clubs, sent from the chief priests and the elders of the people. **48** Now the betrayer had arranged a signal with them: "The one I kiss is the man; arrest him." **49** Going at once to Jesus, Judas said, "Greetings, Rabbi!" and kissed him.

50 Jesus replied, "Friend, do what you came for."j

Then the men stepped forward, seized Jesus and arrested him. **51** With that, one of Jesus' companions reached for his sword, drew it out and struck the servant of the high priest, cutting off his ear.

---

i *31* Zech. 13:7   j *50* Or *"Friend, why have you come?"*

52 "Put your sword back in its place," Jesus said to him, "for all who draw the sword will die by the sword. **53** Do you think I cannot call on my Father, and he will at once put at my disposal more than twelve legions of angels? **54** But how then would the Scriptures be fulfilled that say it must happen in this way?"

55 At that time Jesus said to the crowd, "Am I leading a rebellion, that you have come out with swords and clubs to capture me? Every day I sat in the temple courts teaching, and you did not arrest me. **56** But this has all taken place that the writings of the prophets might be fulfilled." Then all the disciples deserted him and fled.

Before the Sanhedrin

57 Those who had arrested Jesus took him to Caiaphas, the high priest, where the teachers of the law and the elders had assembled. **58** But Peter followed him at a distance, right up to the courtyard of the high priest. He entered and sat down with the guards to see the outcome.

59 The chief priests and the whole Sanhedrin were looking for false evidence against Jesus so that they could put him to death. **60** But they did not find any, though many false witnesses came forward.

Finally two came forward **61** and declared, "This fellow said, 'I am able to destroy the temple of God and rebuild it in three days.' "

62 Then the high priest stood up and said to Jesus, "Are you not going to answer? What is this testimony that these men are bringing against you?" **63** But Jesus remained silent.

The high priest said to him, "I charge you under oath by the living God: Tell us if you are the Christ,*k* the Son of God."

64 "Yes, it is as you say," Jesus replied. "But I say to all of you: In the future you will see the Son of Man sitting at the right hand of the Mighty One and coming on the clouds of heaven."

65 Then the high priest tore his clothes and said, "He has spoken blasphemy! Why do we need any more witnesses? Look, now you have heard the blasphemy. **66** What do you think?"

"He is worthy of death," they answered.

67 Then they spit in his face and struck him with their fists. Others slapped him **68** and said, "Prophesy to us, Christ. Who hit you?"

Peter Disowns Jesus

69 Now Peter was sitting out in the courtyard, and a servant girl came to him. "You also were with Jesus of Galilee," she said.

70 But he denied it before them all. "I don't know what you're talking about," he said.

71 Then he went out to the gateway, where another girl saw him and said to the people there, "This fellow was with Jesus of Nazareth."

72 He denied it again, with an oath: "I don't know the man!"

73 After a little while, those standing there went up to Peter and said, "Surely you are one of them, for your accent gives you away."

74 Then he began to call down curses on himself and he swore to them, "I don't know the man!"

Immediately a rooster crowed. **75** Then Peter remembered the word Jesus had spoken: "Before the

---

k 63 Or *Messiah*; also in verse 68

rooster crows, you will disown me three times." And he went outside and wept bitterly.

Judas Hangs Himself

27 ¹ Early in the morning, all the chief priests and the elders of the people came to the decision to put Jesus to death. ² They bound him, led him away and handed him over to Pilate, the governor.

³ When Judas, who had betrayed him, saw that Jesus was condemned, he was seized with remorse and returned the thirty silver coins to the chief priests and the elders. ⁴ "I have sinned," he said, "for I have betrayed innocent blood."

"What is that to us?" they replied. "That's your responsibility."

⁵ So Judas threw the money into the temple and left. Then he went away and hanged himself.

⁶ The chief priests picked up the coins and said, "It is against the law to put this into the treasury, since it is blood money." ⁷ So they decided to use the money to buy the potter's field as a burial place for foreigners. ⁸ That is why it has been called the Field of Blood to this day. ⁹ Then what was spoken by Jeremiah the prophet was fulfilled: "They took the thirty silver coins, the price set on him by the people of Israel, ¹⁰ and they used them to buy the potter's field, as the Lord commanded me."[l]

Jesus Before Pilate

¹¹ Meanwhile Jesus stood before the governor, and the governor asked him, "Are you the king of the Jews?"

"Yes, it is as you say," Jesus replied.

¹² When he was accused by the chief priests and the elders, he gave no answer. ¹³ Then Pilate asked him, "Don't you hear the testimony they are bringing against you?" ¹⁴ But Jesus made no reply, not even to a single charge—to the great amazement of the governor.

¹⁵ Now it was the governor's custom at the Feast to release a prisoner chosen by the crowd. ¹⁶ At that time they had a notorious prisoner, called Barabbas. ¹⁷ So when the crowd had gathered, Pilate asked them, "Which one do you want me to release to you: Barabbas, or Jesus who is called Christ?" ¹⁸ For he knew it was out of envy that they had handed Jesus over to him.

¹⁹ While Pilate was sitting on the judge's seat, his wife sent him this message: "Don't have anything to do with that innocent man, for I have suffered a great deal today in a dream because of him."

²⁰ But the chief priests and the elders persuaded the crowd to ask for Barabbas and to have Jesus executed.

²¹ "Which of the two do you want me to release to you?" asked the governor.

"Barabbas," they answered.

²² "What shall I do, then, with Jesus who is called Christ?" Pilate asked.

They all answered, "Crucify him!"

²³ "Why? What crime has he committed?" asked Pilate.

But they shouted all the louder, "Crucify him!"

²⁴ When Pilate saw that he was getting nowhere, but that instead an uproar was starting, he took water and washed his hands in front of the crowd. "I am innocent of this man's blood," he said. "It is your responsibility!"

[l] *10* See Zech. 11:12,13; Jer. 19:1-13; 32:6-9.

25 All the people answered, "Let his blood be on us and on our children!"

26 Then he released Barabbas to them. But he had Jesus flogged, and handed him over to be crucified.

The Soldiers Mock Jesus

27 Then the governor's soldiers took Jesus into the Praetorium and gathered the whole company of soldiers around him. 28 They stripped him and put a scarlet robe on him, 29 and then twisted together a crown of thorns and set it on his head. They put a staff in his right hand and knelt in front of him and mocked him. "Hail, king of the Jews!" they said. 30 They spit on him, and took the staff and struck him on the head again and again. 31 After they had mocked him, they took off the robe and put his own clothes on him. Then they led him away to crucify him.

The Crucifixion

32 As they were going out, they met a man from Cyrene, named Simon, and they forced him to carry the cross. 33 They came to a place called Golgotha (which means The Place of the Skull). 34 There they offered Jesus wine to drink, mixed with gall; but after tasting it, he refused to drink it. 35 When they had crucified him, they divided up his clothes by casting lots.[m] 36 And sitting down, they kept watch over him there. 37 Above his head they placed the written charge against him: THIS IS JESUS, THE KING OF THE JEWS. 38 Two robbers were crucified with him, one on his right and one on his left. 39 Those who passed by hurled insults at him, shaking their heads 40 and saying, "You who are going to destroy the temple and build it in three days, save yourself! Come down from the cross, if you are the Son of God!"

41 In the same way the chief priests, the teachers of the law and the elders mocked him. 42 "He saved others," they said, "but he can't save himself! He's the King of Israel! Let him come down now from the cross, and we will believe in him. 43 He trusts in God. Let God rescue him now if he wants him, for he said, 'I am the Son of God.' " 44 In the same way the robbers who were crucified with him also heaped insults on him.

The Death of Jesus

45 From the sixth hour until the ninth hour darkness came over all the land. 46 About the ninth hour Jesus cried out in a loud voice, "Eloi, Eloi,[n] lama sabachthani?" —which means, "My God, my God, why have you forsaken me?"[o]

47 When some of those standing there heard this, they said, "He's calling Elijah."

48 Immediately one of them ran and got a sponge. He filled it with wine vinegar, put it on a stick, and offered it to Jesus to drink. 49 The rest said, "Now leave him alone. Let's see if Elijah comes to save him."

50 And when Jesus had cried out again in a loud voice, he gave up his spirit.

51 At that moment the curtain of the temple was torn in two from top to bottom. The earth shook and the rocks split. 52 The tombs broke open and the bodies of many holy people

---

m 35 A few late manuscripts *lots that the word spoken by the prophet might be fulfilled: "They divided my garments among themselves and cast lots for my clothing"* (Psalm 22:18)
n 46 Some manuscripts *Eli, Eli*   *o* 46 Psalm 22:1

who had died were raised to life.
53 They came out of the tombs, and
after Jesus' resurrection they went
into the holy city and appeared to
many people.

54 When the centurion and those
with him who were guarding Jesus
saw the earthquake and all that had
happened, they were terrified, and
exclaimed, "Surely he was the Son[P]
of God!"

55 Many women were there,
watching from a distance. They had
followed Jesus from Galilee to care
for his needs. **56** Among them were
Mary Magdalene, Mary the mother
of James and Joses, and the mother
of Zebedee's sons.

The Burial of Jesus

57 As evening approached, there
came a rich man from Arimathea,
named Joseph, who had himself become a disciple of Jesus. **58** Going
to Pilate, he asked for Jesus' body,
and Pilate ordered that it be given
to him. **59** Joseph took the body,
wrapped it in a clean linen cloth,
60 and placed it in his own new
tomb that he had cut out of the
rock. He rolled a big stone in front
of the entrance to the tomb and
went away. **61** Mary Magdalene and
the other Mary were sitting there
opposite the tomb.

The Guard at the Tomb

62 The next day, the one after
Preparation Day, the chief priests
and the Pharisees went to Pilate.
63 "Sir," they said, "we remember
that while he was still alive that
deceiver said, 'After three days I will
rise again.' **64** So give the order for
the tomb to be made secure until the

third day. Otherwise, his disciples
may come and steal the body and tell
the people that he has been raised
from the dead. This last deception
will be worse than the first."

65 "Take a guard," Pilate
answered. "Go, make the tomb as
secure as you know how." **66** So they
went and made the tomb secure by
putting a seal on the stone and post-
ing the guard.

The Resurrection

28 **1** After the Sabbath, at dawn
on the first day of the week,
Mary Magdalene and the other Mary
went to look at the tomb.

2 There was a violent earthquake,
for an angel of the Lord came down
from heaven and, going to the tomb,
rolled back the stone and sat on it.
3 His appearance was like lightning,
and his clothes were white as snow.
4 The guards were so afraid of him
that they shook and became like
dead men.

5 The angel said to the women,
"Do not be afraid, for I know that
you are looking for Jesus, who was
crucified. **6** He is not here; he has
risen, just as he said. Come and see
the place where he lay. **7** Then go
quickly and tell his disciples: 'He
has risen from the dead and is
going ahead of you into Galilee.
There you will see him.' Now I have
told you."

8 So the women hurried away
from the tomb, afraid yet filled with
joy, and ran to tell his disciples.
9 Suddenly Jesus met them. "Greetings," he said. They came to him,
clasped his feet and worshiped him.
10 Then Jesus said to them, "Do not
be afraid. Go and tell my brothers

to go to Galilee; there they will see me."

The Guards' Report

11 While the women were on their way, some of the guards went into the city and reported to the chief priests everything that had happened. **12** When the chief priests had met with the elders and devised a plan, they gave the soldiers a large sum of money, **13** telling them, "You are to say, 'His disciples came during the night and stole him away while we were asleep.' **14** If this report gets to the governor, we will satisfy him and keep you out of trouble.' **15** So the soldiers took the money and did as they were instructed. And this story has been widely circulated among the Jews to this very day.

The Great Commission

16 Then the eleven disciples went to Galilee, to the mountain where Jesus had told them to go. **17** When they saw him, they worshiped him; but some doubted. **18** Then Jesus came to them and said, "All authority in heaven and on earth has been given to me. **19** Therefore go and make disciples of all nations, baptizing them in*q* the name of the Father and of the Son and of the Holy Spirit, **20** and teaching them to obey everything I have commanded you. And surely I am with you always, to the very end of the age."

---

q 19 Or into; see Acts 8:16; 19:5; Romans 6:3; 1 Cor. 1:13; 10:2 and Gal. 3:27.

Mark

John the Baptist Prepares the Way

1 **1** The beginning of the gospel about Jesus Christ, the Son of God.[a]

2 It is written in Isaiah the prophet:

> "I will send my messenger ahead of you,
> who will prepare your way"[b] —
> **3** "a voice of one calling in the desert,
> 'Prepare the way for the Lord,
> make straight paths for him.' "[c]

4 And so John came, baptizing in the desert region and preaching a baptism of repentance for the forgiveness of sins. **5** The whole Judean countryside and all the people of Jerusalem went out to him. Confessing their sins, they were baptized by him in the Jordan River. **6** John wore clothing made of camel's hair, with a leather belt around his waist, and he ate locusts and wild honey. **7** And this was his message: "After me will come one more powerful than I, the thongs of whose sandals I am not worthy to stoop down and untie. **8** I baptize you with[d] water, but he will baptize you with the Holy Spirit."

The Baptism and Temptation of Jesus

9 At that time Jesus came from Nazareth in Galilee and was baptized by John in the Jordan. **10** As Jesus was coming up out of the water, he saw heaven being torn open and the Spirit descending on him like a dove. **11** And a voice came from heaven: "You are my Son, whom I love; with you I am well pleased."

12 At once the Spirit sent him out into the desert, **13** and he was in the desert forty days, being tempted by Satan. He was with the wild animals, and angels attended him.

The Calling of the First Disciples

14 After John was put in prison, Jesus went into Galilee, proclaiming the good news of God. **15** "The time has come," he said. "The kingdom of God is near. Repent and believe the good news!"

16 As Jesus walked beside the Sea of Galilee, he saw Simon and his brother Andrew casting a net into the lake, for they were fishermen. **17** "Come, follow me," Jesus said, "and I will make you fishers of men." **18** At once they left their nets and followed him.

19 When he had gone a little farther, he saw James son of Zebedee and his brother John in a boat, preparing their nets. **20** Without delay he called them, and they left their father Zebedee in the boat with the hired men and followed him.

Jesus Drives Out an Evil Spirit

21 They went to Capernaum, and when the Sabbath came, Jesus went into the synagogue and began to teach. **22** The people were amazed at

---

a 1 Some manuscripts do not have *the Son of God.*   *b* 2 Mal. 3:1   *c* 3 Isaiah 40:3
d 8 Or *in*

his teaching, because he taught them as one who had authority, not as the teachers of the law. 23 Just then a man in their synagogue who was possessed by an evil[e] spirit cried out, 24 "What do you want with us, Jesus of Nazareth? Have you come to destroy us? I know who you are—the Holy One of God!"

25 "Be quiet!" said Jesus sternly. "Come out of him!" 26 The evil spirit shook the man violently and came out of him with a shriek.

27 The people were all so amazed that they asked each other, "What is this? A new teaching—and with authority! He even gives orders to evil spirits and they obey him." 28 News about him spread quickly over the whole region of Galilee.

Jesus Heals Many

29 As soon as they left the synagogue, they went with James and John to the home of Simon and Andrew. 30 Simon's mother-in-law was in bed with a fever, and they told Jesus about her. 31 So he went to her, took her hand and helped her up. The fever left her and she began to wait on them.

32 That evening after sunset the people brought to Jesus all the sick and demon-possessed. 33 The whole town gathered at the door, 34 and Jesus healed many who had various diseases. He also drove out many demons, but he would not let the demons speak because they knew who he was.

Jesus Prays in a Solitary Place

35 Very early in the morning, while it was still dark, Jesus got up, left the house and went off to a solitary place, where he prayed. 36 Simon and his companions went to look for him, 37 and when they found him, they exclaimed: "Everyone is looking for you!"

38 Jesus replied, "Let us go somewhere else—to the nearby villages—so I can preach there also. That is why I have come." 39 So he traveled throughout Galilee, preaching in their synagogues and driving out demons.

A Man With Leprosy

40 A man with leprosy[f] came to him and begged him on his knees, "If you are willing, you can make me clean."

41 Filled with compassion, Jesus reached out his hand and touched the man. "I am willing," he said. "Be clean!" 42 Immediately the leprosy left him and he was cured.

43 Jesus sent him away at once with a strong warning: 44 "See that you don't tell this to anyone. But go, show yourself to the priest and offer the sacrifices that Moses commanded for your cleansing, as a testimony to them." 45 Instead he went out and began to talk freely, spreading the news. As a result, Jesus could no longer enter a town openly but stayed outside in lonely places. Yet the people still came to him from everywhere.

Jesus Heals a Paralytic

2 1 A few days later, when Jesus again entered Capernaum, the people heard that he had come home. 2 So many gathered that there was no room left, not even outside

---

e 23 Greek unclean; also in verses 26 and 27 diseases affecting the skin—not necessarily leprosy. f 40 The Greek word was used for various

the door, and he preached the word to them. **3** Some men came, bringing to him a paralytic, carried by four of them. **4** Since they could not get him to Jesus because of the crowd, they made an opening in the roof above Jesus and, after digging through it, lowered the mat the paralyzed man was lying on. **5** When Jesus saw their faith, he said to the paralytic, "Son, your sins are forgiven."

6 Now some teachers of the law were sitting there, thinking to themselves, **7** "Why does this fellow talk like that? He's blaspheming! Who can forgive sins but God alone?"

8 Immediately Jesus knew in his spirit that this was what they were thinking in their hearts, and he said to them, "Why are you thinking these things? **9** Which is easier: to say to the paralytic, 'Your sins are forgiven,' or to say, 'Get up, take your mat and walk'? **10** But that you may know that the Son of Man has authority on earth to forgive sins . . . ." He said to the paralytic, **11** "I tell you, get up, take your mat and go home." **12** He got up, took his mat and walked out in full view of them all. This amazed everyone and they praised God, saying, "We have never seen anything like this!"

The Calling of Levi

13 Once again Jesus went out beside the lake. A large crowd came to him, and he began to teach them. **14** As he walked along, he saw Levi son of Alphaeus sitting at the tax collector's booth. "Follow me," Jesus told him, and Levi got up and followed him.

15 While Jesus was having dinner at Levi's house, many tax collectors and "sinners" were eating with him and his disciples, for there were many who followed him. **16** When the teachers of the law who were Pharisees saw him eating with the "sinners" and tax collectors, they asked his disciples: "Why does he eat with tax collectors and 'sinners'?"

17 On hearing this, Jesus said to them, "It is not the healthy who need a doctor, but the sick. I have not come to call the righteous, but sinners."

Jesus Questioned About Fasting

18 Now John's disciples and the Pharisees were fasting. Some people came and asked Jesus, "How is it that John's disciples and the disciples of the Pharisees are fasting, but yours are not?"

19 Jesus answered, "How can the guests of the bridegroom fast while he is with them? They cannot, so long as they have him with them. **20** But the time will come when the bridegroom will be taken from them, and on that day they will fast.

21 "No one sews a patch of unshrunk cloth on an old garment. If he does, the new piece will pull away from the old, making the tear worse. **22** And no one pours new wine into old wineskins. If he does, the wine will burst the skins, and both the wine and the wineskins will be ruined. No, he pours new wine into new wineskins."

Lord of the Sabbath

23 One Sabbath Jesus was going through the grainfields, and as his disciples walked along, they began to pick some heads of grain. **24** The Pharisees said to him, "Look, why are they doing what is unlawful on the Sabbath?"

25 He answered, "Have you never read what David did when he and his companions were hungry and in need? **26** In the days of Abiathar the high priest, he entered the house of

God and ate the consecrated bread, which is lawful only for priests to eat. And he also gave some to his companions."

27 Then he said to them, "The Sabbath was made for man, not man for the Sabbath. **28** So the Son of Man is Lord even of the Sabbath."

3 **1** Another time he went into the synagogue, and a man with a shriveled hand was there. **2** Some of them were looking for a reason to accuse Jesus, so they watched him closely to see if he would heal him on the Sabbath. **3** Jesus said to the man with the shriveled hand, "Stand up in front of everyone."

4 Then Jesus asked them, "Which is lawful on the Sabbath: to do good or to do evil, to save life or to kill?" But they remained silent.

5 He looked around at them in anger and, deeply distressed at their stubborn hearts, said to the man, "Stretch out your hand." He stretched it out, and his hand was completely restored. **6** Then the Pharisees went out and began to plot with the Herodians how they might kill Jesus.

Crowds Follow Jesus

7 Jesus withdrew with his disciples to the lake, and a large crowd from Galilee followed. **8** When they heard all he was doing, many people came to him from Judea, Jerusalem, Idumea, and the regions across the Jordan and around Tyre and Sidon. **9** Because of the crowd he told his disciples to have a small boat ready for him, to keep the people from crowding him. **10** For he had healed many, so that those with diseases were pushing forward to touch him.

11 Whenever the evil¹ spirits saw him, they fell down before him and cried out, "You are the Son of God." **12** But he gave them strict orders not to tell who he was.

The Appointing of the Twelve Apostles

13 Jesus went up on a mountainside and called to him those he wanted, and they came to him. **14** He appointed twelve—designating them apostlesʰ—that they might be with him and that he might send them out to preach **15** and to have authority to drive out demons. **16** These are the twelve he appointed: Simon (to whom he gave the name Peter); **17** James son of Zebedee and his brother John (to them he gave the name Boanerges, which means Sons of Thunder); **18** Andrew, Philip, Bartholomew, Matthew, Thomas, James son of Alphaeus, Thaddaeus, Simon the Zealot **19** and Judas Iscariot, who betrayed him.

Jesus and Beelzebub

20 Then Jesus entered a house, and again a crowd gathered, so that he and his disciples were not even able to eat. **21** When his family heard about this, they went to take charge of him, for they said, "He is out of his mind."

22 And the teachers of the law who came down from Jerusalem said, "He is possessed by Beelzebub!ⁱ By the prince of demons he is driving out demons."

23 So Jesus called them and spoke to them in parables: "How can Satan drive out Satan? **24** If a kingdom is divided against itself, that kingdom cannot stand. **25** If a house is divided against itself, that house cannot stand. 26 And if Satan opposes himself and is divided, he cannot stand; his end has come. 27 In fact, no one can enter a strong man's house and carry off his possessions unless he first ties up the strong man. Then he can rob his house. 28 I tell you the truth, all the sins and blasphemies of men will be forgiven them. 29 But whoever blasphemes against the Holy Spirit will never be forgiven; he is guilty of an eternal sin."

30 He said this because they were saying, "He has an evil spirit."

Jesus' Mother and Brothers

31 Then Jesus' mother and brothers arrived. Standing outside, they sent someone in to call him. 32 A crowd was sitting around him, and they told him, "Your mother and brothers are outside looking for you."

33 "Who are my mother and my brothers?" he asked.

34 Then he looked at those seated in a circle around him and said, "Here are my mother and my brothers! 35 Whoever does God's will is my brother and sister and mother."

The Parable of the Sower

4 1 Again Jesus began to teach by the lake. The crowd that gathered around him was so large that he got into a boat and sat in it out on the lake, while all the people were along the shore at the water's edge. 2 He taught them many things by parables, and in his teaching said: 3 "Listen! A farmer went out to sow his seed. 4 As he was scattering the seed, some fell along the path, and the birds came and ate it up. 5 Some fell on rocky places, where it did not have much soil. It sprang up

quickly, because the soil was shallow 6 But when the sun came up, the plants were scorched, and they withered because they had no roo 7 Other seed fell among thorns, which grew up and choked the plants, se that they did not bear grain. 8 Stil other seed fell on good soil. It came up, grew and produced a crop, multi plying thirty, sixty, or even a hundre times."

9 Then Jesus said, "He who ha ears to hear, let him hear."

10 When he was alone, the Twelve and the others around him asked him about the parables. 11 He told them "The secret of the kingdom of Goo has been given to you. But to those on the outside everything is said is parables 12 so that,

"'they may be ever seeing bu never perceiving,
and ever hearing but never understanding;
otherwise they might turn and be forgiven!'"

13 Then Jesus said to them, "Don' you understand this parable? How then will you understand any parable? 14 The farmer sows the word. 15 Some people are like seed along the path, where the word is sown. As soon as they hear it, Satar comes and takes away the word that was sown in them. 16 Others, like seed sown on rocky places, hear the word and at once receive it with joy 17 But since they have no root, the last only a short time. When trouble or persecution comes because of the word, they quickly fall away. 18 Stil others, like seed sown among thorns hear the word; 19 but the worries o this life, the deceitfulness of wealth

j 12 Isaiah 6:9,10

and the desires for other things come in and choke the word, making it unfruitful. **20** Others, like seed sown on good soil, hear the word, accept it, and produce a crop—thirty, sixty or even a hundred times what was sown."

A Lamp on a Stand

21 He said to them, "Do you bring in a lamp to put it under a bowl or a bed? Instead, don't you put it on its stand? **22** For whatever is hidden is meant to be disclosed, and whatever is concealed is meant to be brought out into the open. **23** If anyone has ears to hear, let him hear."

24 "Consider carefully what you hear," he continued. "With the measure you use, it will be measured to you—and even more. **25** Whoever has will be given more; whoever does not have, even what he has will be taken from him."

The Parable of the Growing Seed

26 He also said, "This is what the kingdom of God is like. A man scatters seed on the ground. **27** Night and day, whether he sleeps or gets up, the seed sprouts and grows, though he does not know how. **28** All by itself the soil produces grain—first the stalk, then the head, then the full kernel in the head. **29** As soon as the grain is ripe, he puts the sickle to it, because the harvest has come."

The Parable of the Mustard Seed

30 Again he said, "What shall we say the kingdom of God is like, or what parable shall we use to describe it? **31** It is like a mustard seed, which is the smallest seed you plant in the

ground. **32** Yet when planted, it grows and becomes the largest of all garden plants, with such big branches that the birds of the air can perch in its shade."

33 With many similar parables Jesus spoke the word to them, as much as they could understand. **34** He did not say anything to them without using a parable. But when he was alone with his own disciples, he explained everything.

Jesus Calms the Storm

35 That day when evening came, he said to his disciples, "Let us go over to the other side." **36** Leaving the crowd behind, they took him along, just as he was, in the boat. There were also other boats with him. **37** A furious squall came up, and the waves broke over the boat, so that it was nearly swamped. **38** Jesus was in the stern, sleeping on a cushion. The disciples woke him and said to him, "Teacher, don't you care if we drown?"

39 He got up, rebuked the wind and said to the waves, "Quiet! Be still!" Then the wind died down and it was completely calm.

40 He said to his disciples, "Why are you so afraid? Do you still have no faith?"

41 They were terrified and asked each other, "Who is this? Even the wind and the waves obey him!"

The Healing of a Demon-possessed Man

5 **1** They went across the lake to the region of the Gerasenes.[k] **2** When Jesus got out of the boat, a man with an evil[l] spirit came from

---

[k] 1 Some manuscripts *Gadarenes*; other manuscripts *Gergesenes*   [l] 2 Greek *unclean*; also in verses 8 and 13

the tombs to meet him. **3** This man lived in the tombs, and no one could bind him any more, not even with a chain. **4** For he had often been chained hand and foot, but he tore the chains apart and broke the irons on his feet. No one was strong enough to subdue him. **5** Night and day among the tombs and in the hills he would cry out and cut himself with stones.

6 When he saw Jesus from a distance, he ran and fell on his knees in front of him. **7** He shouted at the top of his voice, "What do you want with me, Jesus, Son of the Most High God? Swear to God that you won't torture me!" **8** For Jesus had said to him, "Come out of this man, you evil spirit!"

9 Then Jesus asked him, "What is your name?"

"My name is Legion," he replied, "for we are many." **10** And he begged Jesus again and again not to send them out of the area.

11 A large herd of pigs was feeding on the nearby hillside. **12** The demons begged Jesus, "Send us among the pigs; allow us to go into them." **13** He gave them permission, and the evil spirits came out and went into the pigs. The herd, about two thousand in number, rushed down the steep bank into the lake and were drowned.

14 Those tending the pigs ran off and reported this in the town and countryside, and the people went out to see what had happened. **15** When they came to Jesus, they saw the man who had been possessed by the legion of demons, sitting there, dressed and in his right mind; and they were afraid. **16** Those who had

seen it told the people what had happened to the demon-possessed man—and told about the pigs as well. **17** Then the people began to plead with Jesus to leave their region.

18 As Jesus was getting into the boat, the man who had been demon-possessed begged to go with him. **19** Jesus did not let him, but said, "Go home to your family and tell them how much the Lord has done for you, and how he has had mercy on you." **20** So the man went away and began to tell in the Decapolis[m] how much Jesus had done for him. And all the people were amazed.

A Dead Girl and a Sick Woman

21 When Jesus had again crossed over by boat to the other side of the lake, a large crowd gathered around him while he was by the lake. **22** Then one of the synagogue rulers, named Jairus, came there. Seeing Jesus, he fell at his feet **23** and pleaded earnestly with him, "My little daughter is dying. Please come and put your hands on her so that she will be healed and live." **24** So Jesus went with him.

A large crowd followed and pressed around him. **25** And a woman was there who had been subject to bleeding for twelve years. **26** She had suffered a great deal under the care of many doctors and had spent all she had, yet instead of getting better she grew worse. **27** When she heard about Jesus, she came up behind him in the crowd and touched his cloak, **28** because she thought, "If I just touch his clothes, I will be healed." **29** Immediately her bleeding stopped and she

---

m 20 That is, the Ten Cities

elt in her body that she was freed rom her suffering.

30 At once Jesus realized that ower had gone out from him. He urned around in the crowd and asked, "Who touched my clothes?"

31 "You see the people crowding against you," his disciples answered, "and yet you can ask, 'Who touched me?' "

32 But Jesus kept looking around to see who had done it. **33** Then the woman, knowing what had happened to her, came and fell at his feet and, trembling with fear, told him the whole truth. **34** He said to her, "Daughter, your faith has healed you. Go in peace and be freed from your suffering."

35 While Jesus was still speaking, some men came from the house of Jairus, the synagogue ruler. "Your daughter is dead," they said. "Why bother the teacher any more?"

36 Ignoring what they said, Jesus told the synagogue ruler, "Don't be afraid; just believe."

37 He did not let anyone follow him except Peter, James and John the brother of James. **38** When they came to the home of the synagogue ruler, Jesus saw a commotion, with people crying and wailing loudly. **39** He went in and said to them, "Why all this commotion and wailing? The child is not dead but asleep." **40** But they laughed at him.

After he put them all out, he took the child's father and mother and the disciples who were with him, and went in where the child was. **41** He took her by the hand and said to her, "Talitha koum!" (which means, "Little girl, I say to you, get up!"). **42** Immediately the girl stood up and walked around (she was twelve years old). At this they were completely astonished. **43** He gave strict orders not to let anyone know about this, and told them to give her something to eat.

A Prophet Without Honor

6 **1** Jesus left there and went to his hometown, accompanied by his disciples. **2** When the Sabbath came, he began to teach in the synagogue, and many who heard him were amazed.

"Where did this man get these things?" they asked. "What's this wisdom that has been given him, that he even does miracles! **3** Isn't this the carpenter? Isn't this Mary's son and the brother of James, Joseph,[n] Judas and Simon? Aren't his sisters here with us?" And they took offense at him.

4 Jesus said to them, "Only in his hometown, among his relatives and in his own house is a prophet without honor." **5** He could not do any miracles there, except lay his hands on a few sick people and heal them. **6** And he was amazed at their lack of faith.

Jesus Sends Out the Twelve

Then Jesus went around teaching from village to village. **7** Calling the Twelve to him, he sent them out two by two and gave them authority over evil[o] spirits.

8 These were his instructions: "Take nothing for the journey except a staff—no bread, no bag, no money in your belts. **9** Wear sandals but not an extra tunic. **10** Whenever you enter a house, stay there until you leave that town. **11** And if any place

---

[n] 3 Greek *Joses,* a variant of *Joseph*   [o] 7 Greek *unclean*

will not welcome you or listen to you, shake the dust off your feet when you leave, as a testimony against them."

12 They went out and preached that people should repent. **13** They drove out many demons and anointed many sick people with oil and healed them.

John the Baptist Beheaded

14 King Herod heard about this, for Jesus' name had become well known. Some were saying,*p* "John the Baptist has been raised from the dead, and that is why miraculous powers are at work in him."

15 Others said, "He is Elijah."

And still others claimed, "He is a prophet, like one of the prophets of long ago."

16 But when Herod heard this, he said, "John, the man I beheaded, has been raised from the dead!"

17 For Herod himself had given orders to have John arrested, and he had him bound and put in prison. He did this because of Herodias, his brother Philip's wife, whom he had married. **18** For John had been saying to Herod, "It is not lawful for you to have your brother's wife." **19** So Herodias nursed a grudge against John and wanted to kill him. But she was not able to, **20** because Herod feared John and protected him, knowing him to be a righteous and holy man. When Herod heard John, he was greatly puzzled*q*; yet he liked to listen to him.

21 Finally the opportune time came. On his birthday Herod gave a banquet for his high officials and military commanders and the leading men of Galilee. **22** When the

daughter of Herodias came in and danced, she pleased Herod and his dinner guests.

The king said to the girl, "Ask me for anything you want, and I'll give it to you." **23** And he promised her with an oath, "Whatever you ask I will give you, up to half my kingdom."

24 She went out and said to her mother, "What shall I ask for?"

"The head of John the Baptist," she answered.

25 At once the girl hurried in to the king with the request: "I want you to give me right now the head of John the Baptist on a platter."

26 The king was greatly distressed, but because of his oaths and his dinner guests, he did not want to refuse her. **27** So he immediately sent an executioner with orders to bring John's head. The man went, beheaded John in the prison, **28** and brought back his head on a platter. He presented it to the girl, and she gave it to her mother. **29** On hearing of this, John's disciples came and took his body and laid it in a tomb.

Jesus Feeds the Five Thousand

30 The apostles gathered around Jesus and reported to him all they had done and taught. **31** Then, because so many people were coming and going that they did not even have a chance to eat, he said to them, "Come with me by yourselves to a quiet place and get some rest."

32 So they went away by themselves in a boat to a solitary place. **33** But many who saw them leaving recognized them and ran on foot from all the towns and got there ahead of them. **34** When Jesus

P **14** Some early manuscripts *He was saying things*   *q* **20** Some early manuscripts *he did many*

landed and saw a large crowd, he had compassion on them, because they were like sheep without a shepherd. So he began teaching them many things.

35 By this time it was late in the day, so his disciples came to him. "This is a remote place," they said, "and it's already very late. **36** Send the people away so they can go to the surrounding countryside and villages and buy themselves something to eat."

37 But he answered, "You give them something to eat."

They said to him, "That would take eight months of a man's wages[r]! Are we to go and spend that much on bread and give it to them to eat?"

38 "How many loaves do you have?" he asked. "Go and see."

When they found out, they said, "Five—and two fish."

39 Then Jesus directed them to have all the people sit down in groups on the green grass. **40** So they sat down in groups of hundreds and fifties. **41** Taking the five loaves and the two fish and looking up to heaven, he gave thanks and broke the loaves. He then gave them to his disciples to set before the people. He also divided the two fish among them all. **42** They all ate and were satisfied, **43** and the disciples picked up twelve basketfuls of broken pieces of bread and fish. **44** The number of the men who had eaten was five thousand.

Jesus Walks on the Water

45 Immediately Jesus made his disciples get into the boat and go on ahead of him to Bethsaida, while he dismissed the crowd. **46** After leaving them, he went up on a mountainside to pray.

47 When evening came, the boat was in the middle of the lake, and he was alone on land. **48** He saw the disciples straining at the oars, because the wind was against them. About the fourth watch of the night he went out to them, walking on the lake. He was about to pass by them, **49** but when they saw him walking on the lake, they thought he was a ghost. They cried out, **50** because they all saw him and were terrified.

Immediately he spoke to them and said, "Take courage! It is I. Don't be afraid." **51** Then he climbed into the boat with them, and the wind died down. They were completely amazed, **52** for they had not understood about the loaves; their hearts were hardened.

53 When they had crossed over, they landed at Gennesaret and anchored there. **54** As soon as they got out of the boat, people recognized Jesus. **55** They ran throughout that whole region and carried the sick on mats to wherever they heard he was. **56** And wherever he went—into villages, towns or countryside—they placed the sick in the marketplaces. They begged him to let them touch even the edge of his cloak, and all who touched him were healed.

Clean and Unclean

7 **1** The Pharisees and some of the teachers of the law who had come from Jerusalem gathered around Jesus and **2** saw some of his disciples eating food with hands that were "unclean," that is, unwashed. **3** (The Pharisees and all the Jews do not eat unless they give their hands a ceremonial washing, holding to the

---

r 37 Greek take two hundred denarii

tradition of the elders. 4 When they come from the marketplace they do not eat unless they wash. And they observe many other traditions, such as the washing of cups, pitchers and kettles.ˢ)

5 So the Pharisees and teachers of the law asked Jesus, "Why don't your disciples live according to the tradition of the elders instead of eating their food with 'unclean' hands?"

6 He replied, "Isaiah was right when he prophesied about you hypocrites; as it is written:

" 'These people honor me with
      their lips,
   but their hearts are far from me.
7 They worship me in vain;
   their teachings are but rules
      taught by men.'ᵗ

8 You have let go of the commands of God and are holding on to the traditions of men."

9 And he said to them: "You have a fine way of setting aside the commands of God in order to observeᵘ your own traditions! 10 For Moses said, 'Honor your father and your mother,'ᵛ and, 'Anyone who curses his father or mother must be put to death.'ʷ 11 But you say that if a man says to his father or mother: 'Whatever help you might otherwise have received from me is Corban' (that is, a gift devoted to God), 12 then you no longer let him do anything for his father or mother. 13 Thus you nullify the word of God by your tradition that you have handed down. And you do many things like that."

14 Again Jesus called the crowd to him and said, "Listen to me, everyone, and understand this. 15 Nothing outside a man can make him 'unclean' by going into him. Rather, it is what comes out of a man that makes him 'unclean.' "ˣ

17 After he had left the crowd and entered the house, his disciples asked him about this parable. 18 "Are you so dull?" he asked. "Don't you see that nothing that enters a man from the outside can make him 'unclean'? 19 For it doesn't go into his heart but into his stomach, and then out of his body." (In saying this, Jesus declared all foods "clean.")

20 He went on: "What comes out of a man is what makes him 'unclean.' 21 For from within, out of men's hearts, come evil thoughts, sexual immorality, theft, murder, adultery, 22 greed, malice, deceit, lewdness, envy, slander, arrogance and folly. 23 All these evils come from inside and make a man 'unclean.' "

The Faith of a Syrophoenician Woman

24 Jesus left that place and went to the vicinity of Tyre.ʸ He entered a house and did not want anyone to know it; yet he could not keep his presence secret. 25 In fact, as soon as she heard about him, a woman whose little daughter was possessed by an evilᶻ spirit came and fell at his feet. 26 The woman was a Greek, born in Syrian Phoenicia. She begged Jesus to drive the demon out of her daughter.

27 "First let the children eat all they want," he told her, "for it is not right to take the children's bread and toss it to their dogs."

ˢ 4 Some early manuscripts *pitchers, kettles and dining couches*   ᵗ 7 Isaiah 29:13
ᵘ 9 Some manuscripts *set up*   ᵛ 10 Exodus 20:12; Deut. 5:16   ʷ 10 Exodus 21:17;
Lev. 20:9   ˣ 15 Some early manuscripts *'unclean.'* 16 *If anyone has ears to hear, let him hear.*
ʸ 24 Many early manuscripts *Tyre and Sidon*   ᶻ 25 Greek *unclean*

28 "Yes, Lord," she replied, "but even the dogs under the table eat the children's crumbs."

29 Then he told her, "For such a reply, you may go; the demon has left your daughter."

30 She went home and found her child lying on the bed, and the demon gone.

The Healing of a Deaf and Mute Man

31 Then Jesus left the vicinity of Tyre and went through Sidon, down to the Sea of Galilee and into the region of the Decapolis.[a] 32 There some people brought to him a man who was deaf and could hardly talk, and they begged him to place his hand on the man.

33 After he took him aside, away from the crowd, Jesus put his fingers into the man's ears. Then he spit and touched the man's tongue. 34 He looked up to heaven and with a deep sigh said to him, "Ephphatha!" (which means, "Be opened!"). 35 At this, the man's ears were opened, his tongue was loosened and he began to speak plainly.

36 Jesus commanded them not to tell anyone. But the more he did so, the more they kept talking about it. 37 People were overwhelmed with amazement. "He has done everything well," they said. "He even makes the deaf hear and the mute speak."

Jesus Feeds the Four Thousand

8 1 During those days another large crowd gathered. Since they had nothing to eat, Jesus called his disciples to him and said, 2 "I have compassion for these people; they have already been with me three days and have nothing to eat. 3 If I send them home hungry, they will collapse on the way, because some of them have come a long distance."

4 His disciples answered, "But where in this remote place can anyone get enough bread to feed them?"

5 "How many loaves do you have?" Jesus asked.

"Seven," they replied.

6 He told the crowd to sit down on the ground. When he had taken the seven loaves and given thanks, he broke them and gave them to his disciples to set before the people, and they did so. 7 They had a few small fish as well; he gave thanks for them also and told the disciples to distribute them. 8 The people ate and were satisfied. Afterward the disciples picked up seven basketfuls of broken pieces that were left over. 9 About four thousand men were present. And having sent them away, 10 he got into the boat with his disciples and went to the region of Dalmanutha.

11 The Pharisees came and began to question Jesus. To test him, they asked him for a sign from heaven. 12 He sighed deeply and said, "Why does this generation ask for a miraculous sign? I tell you the truth, no sign will be given to it." 13 Then he left them, got back into the boat and crossed to the other side.

The Yeast of the Pharisees and Herod

14 The disciples had forgotten to bring bread, except for one loaf they had with them in the boat. 15 "Be careful," Jesus warned them. "Watch out for the yeast of the Pharisees and that of Herod."

16 They discussed this with one another and said, "It is because we have no bread."

a 31 That is, the Ten Cities

17 Aware of their discussion, Jesus asked them: "Why are you talking about having no bread? Do you still not see or understand? Are your hearts hardened? **18** Do you have eyes but fail to see, and ears but fail to hear? And don't you remember? **19** When I broke the five loaves for the five thousand, how many basketfuls of pieces did you pick up?"

"Twelve," they replied.

20 "And when I broke the seven loaves for the four thousand, how many basketfuls of pieces did you pick up?"

They answered, "Seven."

21 He said to them, "Do you still not understand?"

The Healing of a Blind Man at Bethsaida

22 They came to Bethsaida, and some people brought a blind man and begged Jesus to touch him. **23** He took the blind man by the hand and led him outside the village. When he had spit on the man's eyes and put his hands on him, Jesus asked, "Do you see anything?"

24 He looked up and said, "I see people; they look like trees walking around."

25 Once more Jesus put his hands on the man's eyes. Then his eyes were opened, his sight was restored, and he saw everything clearly. **26** Jesus sent him home, saying, "Don't go into the village.*b*"

Peter's Confession of Christ

27 Jesus and his disciples went on to the villages around Caesarea Philippi. On the way he asked them, "Who do people say I am?"

28 They replied, "Some say John the Baptist; others say Elijah; and still others, one of the prophets."

29 "But what about you?" he asked. "Who do you say I am?"

Peter answered, "You are the Christ.*c*"

30 Jesus warned them not to tell anyone about him.

Jesus Predicts His Death

31 He then began to teach them that the Son of Man must suffer many things and be rejected by the elders, chief priests and teachers of the law, and that he must be killed and after three days rise again. **32** He spoke plainly about this, and Peter took him aside and began to rebuke him.

33 But when Jesus turned and looked at his disciples, he rebuked Peter. "Get behind me, Satan!" he said. "You do not have in mind the things of God, but the things of men."

34 Then he called the crowd to him along with his disciples and said: "If anyone would come after me, he must deny himself and take up his cross and follow me. **35** For whoever wants to save his life*d* will lose it, but whoever loses his life for me and for the gospel will save it. **36** What good is it for a man to gain the whole world, yet forfeit his soul? **37** Or what can a man give in exchange for his soul? **38** If anyone is ashamed of me and my words in this adulterous and sinful generation, the Son of Man will be ashamed of him when he comes in his Father's glory with the holy angels."

---

b 26 Some manuscripts *Don't go and tell anyone in the village*   *c* 29 Or *Messiah.* "The Christ" (Greek) and "the Messiah" (Hebrew) both mean "the Anointed One."
d 35 The Greek word means either *life* or *soul*; also in verse 36.

9 1 And he said to them, "I tell you the truth, some who are standing here will not taste death before they see the kingdom of God come with power."

The Transfiguration

2 After six days Jesus took Peter, James and John with him and led them up a high mountain, where they were all alone. There he was transfigured before them. 3 His clothes became dazzling white, whiter than anyone in the world could bleach them. 4 And there appeared before them Elijah and Moses, who were talking with Jesus.

5 Peter said to Jesus, "Rabbi, it is good for us to be here. Let us put up three shelters — one for you, one for Moses and one for Elijah." 6 (He did not know what to say, they were so frightened.)

7 Then a cloud appeared and enveloped them, and a voice came from the cloud: "This is my Son, whom I love. Listen to him!"

8 Suddenly, when they looked around, they no longer saw anyone with them except Jesus.

9 As they were coming down the mountain, Jesus gave them orders not to tell anyone what they had seen until the Son of Man had risen from the dead. 10 They kept the matter to themselves, discussing what "rising from the dead" meant.

11 And they asked him, "Why do the teachers of the law say that Elijah must come first?"

12 Jesus replied, "To be sure, Elijah does come first, and restores all things. Why then is it written that the Son of Man must suffer much and be rejected? 13 But I tell you, Elijah has come, and they have done to him everything they wished, just as it is written about him."

The Healing of a Boy with an Evil Spirit

14 When they came to the other disciples, they saw a large crowd around them and the teachers of the law arguing with them. 15 As soon as all the people saw Jesus, they were overwhelmed with wonder and ran to greet him.

16 "What are you arguing with them about?" he asked.

17 A man in the crowd answered, "Teacher, I brought you my son, who is possessed by a spirit that has robbed him of speech. 18 Whenever it seizes him, it throws him to the ground. He foams at the mouth, gnashes his teeth and becomes rigid. I asked your disciples to drive out the spirit, but they could not."

19 "O unbelieving generation," Jesus replied, "how long shall I stay with you? How long shall I put up with you? Bring the boy to me."

20 So they brought him. When the spirit saw Jesus, it immediately threw the boy into a convulsion. He fell to the ground and rolled around, foaming at the mouth.

21 Jesus asked the boy's father, "How long has he been like this?"

"From childhood," he answered. 22 "It has often thrown him into fire or water to kill him. But if you can do anything, take pity on us and help us."

23 "'If you can'?" said Jesus. "Everything is possible for him who believes."

24 Immediately the boy's father exclaimed, "I do believe; help me overcome my unbelief!"

25 When Jesus saw that a crowd was running to the scene, he rebuked

the evil[e] spirit. "You deaf and mute spirit," he said, "I command you, come out of him and never enter him again."

26 The spirit shrieked, convulsed him violently and came out. The boy looked so much like a corpse that many said, "He's dead." 27 But Jesus took him by the hand and lifted him to his feet, and he stood up.

28 After Jesus had gone indoors, his disciples asked him privately, "Why couldn't we drive it out?"

29 He replied, "This kind can come out only by prayer.[f]"

30 They left that place and passed through Galilee. Jesus did not want anyone to know where they were, 31 because he was teaching his disciples. He said to them, "The Son of Man is going to be betrayed into the hands of men. They will kill him, and after three days he will rise." 32 But they did not understand what he meant and were afraid to ask him about it.

Who is Greatest?

33 They came to Capernaum. When he was in the house, he asked them, "What were you arguing about on the road?" 34 But they kept quiet because on the way they had argued about who was the greatest.

35 Sitting down, Jesus called the Twelve and said, "If anyone wants to be first, he must be the very last, and the servant of all."

36 He took a little child and had him stand among them. Taking him in his arms, he said to them, 37 "Whoever welcomes one of these little children in my name welcomes

me; and whoever welcomes me does not welcome me but the one who sent me."

Whoever Is Not Against Us Is for Us

38 "Teacher," said John, "we saw a man driving out demons in your name and we told him to stop, because he was not one of us."

39 "Do not stop him," Jesus said. "No one who does a miracle in my name can in the next moment say anything bad about me, 40 for whoever is not against us is for us. 41 I tell you the truth, anyone who gives you a cup of water in my name because you belong to Christ will certainly not lose his reward.

Causing to Sin

42 "And if anyone causes one of these little ones who believe in me to sin, it would be better for him to be thrown into the sea with a large millstone tied around his neck. 43 If your hand causes you to sin, cut it off. It is better for you to enter life maimed than with two hands to go into hell, where the fire never goes out.[g] 45 And if your foot causes you to sin, cut it off. It is better for you to enter life crippled than to have two feet and be thrown into hell.[h] 47 And if your eye causes you to sin, pluck it out. It is better for you to enter the kingdom of God with one eye than to have two eyes and be thrown into hell, 48 where

" 'their worm does not die,
    and the fire is not quenched.'[i]

49 Everyone will be salted with fire. 50 "Salt is good, but if it loses its saltiness, how can you make it salty

---

e 25 Greek *unclean*   f 29 Some manuscripts *prayer and fasting*   g 43 Some manuscripts *out,* 44 *where / " 'their worm does not die, / and the fire is not quenched.'*   h 45 Some manuscripts *hell,* 46 *where / " 'their worm does not die, / and the fire is not quenched.'*   i 48 Isaiah 66:24

again? Have salt in yourselves, and be at peace with each other."

Divorce

10 1 Jesus then left that place and went into the region of Judea and across the Jordan. Again crowds of people came to him, and as was his custom, he taught them.

2 Some Pharisees came and tested him by asking, "Is it lawful for a man to divorce his wife?"

3 "What did Moses command you?" he replied.

4 They said, "Moses permitted a man to write a certificate of divorce and send her away."

5 "It was because your hearts were hard that Moses wrote you this law," Jesus replied. 6 "But at the beginning of creation God 'made them male and female.'[j] 7 'For this reason a man will leave his father and mother and be united to his wife,[k] 8 and the two will become one flesh.'[l] So they are no longer two, but one. 9 Therefore what God has joined together, let man not separate."

10 When they were in the house again, the disciples asked Jesus about this. 11 He answered, "Anyone who divorces his wife and marries another woman commits adultery against her. 12 And if she divorces her husband and marries another man, she commits adultery."

The Little Children and Jesus

13 People were bringing little children to Jesus to have him touch them, but the disciples rebuked them. 14 When Jesus saw this, he was indignant. He said to them, "Let the little children come to me, and do not hinder them, for the kingdom of God belongs to such as these. 15 I tell you the truth, anyone who will not receive the kingdom of God like a little child will never enter it." 16 And he took the children in his arms, put his hands on them and blessed them.

The Rich Young Man

17 As Jesus started on his way, a man ran up to him and fell on his knees before him. "Good teacher," he asked, "what must I do to inherit eternal life?"

18 "Why do you call me good?" Jesus answered. "No one is good — except God alone. 19 You know the commandments: 'Do not murder, do not commit adultery, do not steal, do not give false testimony, do not defraud, honor your father and mother.'[m]"

20 "Teacher," he declared, "all these I have kept since I was a boy."

21 Jesus looked at him and loved him. "One thing you lack," he said. "Go, sell everything you have and give to the poor, and you will have treasure in heaven. Then come, follow me."

22 At this the man's face fell. He went away sad, because he had great wealth.

23 Jesus looked around and said to his disciples, "How hard it is for the rich to enter the kingdom of God!"

24 The disciples were amazed at his words. But Jesus said again, "Children, how hard it is[n] to enter the kingdom of God! 25 It is easier for a camel to go through the eye of a needle than for a rich man to enter the kingdom of God."

26 The disciples were even more amazed, and said to each other, "Who then can be saved?"

---

j 6 Gen. 1:27   *k* 7 Some early manuscripts do not have *and be united to his wife.*
l 8 Gen. 2:24   *m* 19 Exodus 20:12-16; Deut. 5:16-20   *n* 24 Some manuscripts *is for those who trust in riches*

27 Jesus looked at them and said, "With man this is impossible, but not with God; all things are possible with God."

28 Peter said to him, "We have left everything to follow you!"

29 "I tell you the truth," Jesus replied, "no one who has left home or brothers or sisters or mother or father or children or fields for me and the gospel 30 will fail to receive a hundred times as much in this present age (homes, brothers, sisters, mothers, children and fields—and with them, persecutions) and in the age to come, eternal life. 31 But many who are first will be last, and the last first."

Jesus Again Predicts His Death

32 They were on their way up to Jerusalem, with Jesus leading the way, and the disciples were astonished, while those who followed were afraid. Again he took the Twelve aside and told them what was going to happen to him. 33 "We are going up to Jerusalem," he said, "and the Son of Man will be betrayed to the chief priests and teachers of the law. They will condemn him to death and will hand him over to the Gentiles, 34 who will mock him and spit on him, flog him and kill him. Three days later he will rise."

The Request of James and John

35 Then James and John, the sons of Zebedee, came to him. "Teacher," they said, "we want you to do for us whatever we ask."

36 "What do you want me to do for you?" he asked.

37 They replied, "Let one of us sit at your right and the other at your left in your glory."

38 "You don't know what you are asking," Jesus said. "Can you drink the cup I drink or be baptized with the baptism I am baptized with?"

39 "We can," they answered. Jesus said to them, "You will drink the cup I drink and be baptized with the baptism I am baptized with, 40 but to sit at my right or left is not for me to grant. These places belong to those for whom they have been prepared."

41 When the ten heard about this, they became indignant with James and John. 42 Jesus called them together and said, "You know that those who are regarded as rulers of the Gentiles lord it over them, and their high officials exercise authority over them. 43 Not so with you. Instead, whoever wants to become great among you must be your servant, 44 and whoever wants to be first must be slave of all. 45 For even the Son of Man did not come to be served, but to serve, and to give his life as a ransom for many."

Blind Bartimaeus Receives His Sight

46 Then they came to Jericho. As Jesus and his disciples, together with a large crowd, were leaving the city, a blind man, Bartimaeus (that is, the Son of Timaeus), was sitting by the roadside begging. 47 When he heard that it was Jesus of Nazareth, he began to shout, "Jesus, Son of David, have mercy on me!"

48 Many rebuked him and told him to be quiet, but he shouted all the more, "Son of David, have mercy on me!"

49 Jesus stopped and said, "Call him." So they called to the blind man, "Cheer up! On your feet! He's calling you." 50 Throwing his cloak aside, he jumped to his feet and came to Jesus.

51 "What do you want me to do for you?" Jesus asked him.

The blind man said, "Rabbi, I want to see."

52 "Go," said Jesus, "your faith has healed you." Immediately he received his sight and followed Jesus along the road.

The Triumphal Entry

11 1 As they approached Jerusalem and came to Bethphage and Bethany at the Mount of Olives, Jesus sent two of his disciples, 2 saying to them, "Go to the village ahead of you, and just as you enter it, you will find a colt tied there, which no one has ever ridden. Untie it and bring it here. 3 If anyone asks you, 'Why are you doing this?' tell him, 'The Lord needs it and will send it back here shortly.'"

4 They went and found a colt outside in the street, tied at a doorway. As they untied it, 5 some people standing there asked, "What are you doing, untying that colt?" 6 They answered as Jesus had told them to, and the people let them go. 7 When they brought the colt to Jesus and threw their cloaks over it, he sat on it. 8 Many people spread their cloaks on the road, while others spread branches they had cut in the fields. 9 Those who went ahead and those who followed shouted,

"Hosanna!o"

"Blessed is he who comes in the name of the Lord!"p

10 "Blessed is the coming kingdom of our father David!"

"Hosanna in the highest!"

11 Jesus entered Jerusalem and went to the temple. He looked around at everything, but since it was already late, he went out to Bethany with the Twelve.

Jesus Clears the Temple

12 The next day as they were leaving Bethany, Jesus was hungry. 13 Seeing in the distance a fig tree in leaf, he went to find out if it had any fruit. When he reached it, he found nothing but leaves, because it was not the season for figs. 14 Then he said to the tree, "May no one ever eat fruit from you again." And his disciples heard him say it.

15 On reaching Jerusalem, Jesus entered the temple area and began driving out those who were buying and selling there. He overturned the tables of the money changers and the benches of those selling doves, 16 and would not allow anyone to carry merchandise through the temple courts. 17 And as he taught them, he said, "Is it not written:

"'My house will be called
    a house of prayer for all
        nations'q?

But you have made it 'a den of robbers.'r"

18 The chief priests and the teachers of the law heard this and began looking for a way to kill him, for they feared him, because the whole crowd was amazed at his teaching.

19 When evening came, theys went out of the city.

The Withered Fig Tree

20 In the morning, as they went along, they saw the fig tree withered

---

o 9 A Hebrew expression meaning "Save!" which became an exclamation of praise; also in verse 10   p 9 Psalm 118:25,26   q 17 Isaiah 56:7   r 17 Jer. 7:11   s 19 Some early manuscripts he from the roots. 21 Peter remembered and said to Jesus, "Rabbi, look! The fig tree you cursed has withered!"

22 "Have[t] faith in God," Jesus answered. 23 "I tell you the truth, if anyone says to this mountain, 'Go, throw yourself into the sea,' and does not doubt in his heart but believes that what he says will happen, it will be done for him. 24 Therefore I tell you, whatever you ask for in prayer, believe that you have received it, and it will be yours. 25 And when you stand praying, if you hold anything against anyone, forgive him, so that your Father in heaven may forgive you your sins."[u]

The Authority of Jesus Questioned

27 They arrived again in Jerusalem, and while Jesus was walking in the temple courts, the chief priests, the teachers of the law and the elders came to him. 28 "By what authority are you doing these things?" they asked. "And who gave you authority to do this?"

29 Jesus replied, "I will ask you one question. Answer me, and I will tell you by what authority I am doing these things. 30 John's baptism—was it from heaven, or from men? Tell me!"

31 They discussed it among themselves and said, "If we say, 'From heaven,' he will ask, 'Then why didn't you believe him?' 32 But if we say, 'From men'...." (They feared the people, for everyone held that John really was a prophet.)

33 So they answered Jesus, "We don't know."

Jesus said, "Neither will I tell you by what authority I am doing these things."

The Parable of the Tenants

12 1 He then began to speak to them in parables: "A man planted a vineyard. He put a wall around it, dug a pit for the winepress and built a watchtower. Then he rented the vineyard to some farmers and went away on a journey. 2 At harvest time he sent a servant to the tenants to collect from them some of the fruit of the vineyard. 3 But they seized him, beat him and sent him away empty-handed. 4 Then he sent another servant to them; they struck this man on the head and treated him shamefully. 5 He sent still another, and that one they killed. He sent many others; some of them they beat, others they killed.

6 "He had one left to send, a son, whom he loved. He sent him last of all, saying, 'They will respect my son.'

7 "But the tenants said to one another, 'This is the heir. Come, let's kill him, and the inheritance will be ours.' 8 So they took him and killed him, and threw him out of the vineyard.

9 "What then will the owner of the vineyard do? He will come and kill those tenants and give the vineyard to others. 10 Haven't you read this scripture:

" 'The stone the builders rejected
    has become the capstone[v];
11 the Lord has done this,
    and it is marvelous in our
        eyes'[w]?"

12 Then they looked for a way to arrest him because they knew he had spoken the parable against them. But

---

[t] 22 Some early manuscripts *If you have*   [u] 25 Some manuscripts *sins. 26 But if you do not forgive, neither will your Father who is in heaven forgive your sins.*   [v] 10 Or *cornerstone*   [w] 11 Psalm 118:22,23

they were afraid of the crowd; so they left him and went away.

Paying Taxes to Caesar

13 Later they sent some of the Pharisees and Herodians to Jesus to catch him in his words. **14** They came to him and said, "Teacher, we know you are a man of integrity. You aren't swayed by men, because you pay no attention to who they are; but you teach the way of God in accordance with the truth. Is it right to pay taxes to Caesar or not? **15** Should we pay or shouldn't we?"

But Jesus knew their hypocrisy. "Why are you trying to trap me?" he asked. "Bring me a denarius and let me look at it." **16** They brought the coin, and he asked them, "Whose portrait is this? And whose inscription?"

"Caesar's," they replied.

17 Then Jesus said to them, "Give to Caesar what is Caesar's and to God what is God's."

And they were amazed at him.

Marriage at the Resurrection

18 Then the Sadducees, who say there is no resurrection, came to him with a question. **19** "Teacher," they said, "Moses wrote for us that if a man's brother dies and leaves a wife but no children, the man must marry the widow and have children for his brother. **20** Now there were seven brothers. The first one married and died without leaving any children. **21** The second one married the widow, but he also died, leaving no child. It was the same with the third. **22** In fact, none of the seven left any children. Last of all, the woman died too. **23** At the resurrection[x] whose wife will she be, since the seven were married to her?"

24 Jesus replied, "Are you not in error because you do not know the Scriptures or the power of God? **25** When the dead rise, they will neither marry nor be given in marriage; they will be like the angels in heaven. **26** Now about the dead rising—have you not read in the book of Moses, in the account of the bush, how God said to him, 'I am the God of Abraham, the God of Isaac, and the God of Jacob'[y]? **27** He is not the God of the dead, but of the living. You are badly mistaken!"

The Greatest Commandment

28 One of the teachers of the law came and heard them debating. Noticing that Jesus had given them a good answer, he asked him, "Of all the commandments, which is the most important?"

29 "The most important one," answered Jesus, "is this: 'Hear, O Israel, the Lord our God, the Lord is one.[z] **30** Love the Lord your God with all your heart and with all your soul and with all your mind and with all your strength.'[a] **31** The second is this: 'Love your neighbor as yourself.'[b] There is no commandment greater than these."

32 "Well said, teacher," the man replied. "You are right in saying that God is one and there is no other but him. **33** To love him with all your heart, with all your understanding and with all your strength, and to love your neighbor as yourself is more important than all burnt offerings and sacrifices."

---

x 23 Some manuscripts *resurrection, when men rise from the dead,*   y 26 Exodus 3:6
z 29 Or *the Lord our God is one Lord*   a 30 Deut. 6:4,5   b 31 Lev. 19:18

34 When Jesus saw that he had answered wisely, he said to him, "You are not far from the kingdom of God." And from then on no one dared ask him any more questions.

Whose Son Is the Christ

35 While Jesus was teaching in the temple courts, he asked, "How is it that the teachers of the law say that the Christ[c] is the son of David? 36 David himself, speaking by the Holy Spirit, declared:

" 'The Lord said to my Lord:
    "Sit at my right hand
    until I put your enemies
        under your feet.' "[d]

37 David himself calls him 'Lord.' How then can he be his son?"

The large crowd listened to him with delight.

38 As he taught, Jesus said, "Watch out for the teachers of the law. They like to walk around in flowing robes and be greeted in the marketplaces, 39 and have the most important seats in the synagogues and the places of honor at banquets. 40 They devour widows' houses and for a show make lengthy prayers. Such men will be punished most severely."

The Widow's Offering

41 Jesus sat down opposite the place where the offerings were put and watched the crowd putting their money into the temple treasury. Many rich people threw in large amounts. 42 But a poor widow came and put in two very small copper coins,[e] worth only a fraction of a penny.[f]

43 Calling his disciples to him, Jesus said, "I tell you the truth, this poor widow has put more into the treasury than all the others. 44 They all gave out of their wealth; but she, out of her poverty, put in everything—all she had to live on."

Signs of the End of the Age

13 ¹ As he was leaving the temple, one of his disciples said to him, "Look, Teacher! What massive stones! What magnificent buildings!"

2 "Do you see all these great buildings?" replied Jesus. "Not one stone here will be left on another; every one will be thrown down."

3 As Jesus was sitting on the Mount of Olives opposite the temple, Peter, James, John and Andrew asked him privately, 4 "Tell us, when will these things happen? And what will be the sign that they are all about to be fulfilled?"

5 Jesus said to them: "Watch out that no one deceives you. 6 Many will come in my name, claiming, 'I am he,' and will deceive many. 7 When you hear of wars and rumors of wars, do not be alarmed. Such things must happen, but the end is still to come. 8 Nation will rise against nation, and kingdom against kingdom. There will be earthquakes in various places, and famines. These are the beginning of birth pains.

9 "You must be on your guard. You will be handed over to the local councils and flogged in the synagogues. On account of me you will stand before governors and kings as witnesses to them. 10 And the gospel must first be preached to all nations. 11 Whenever you are arrested and brought to trial, do not worry beforehand about what to say. Just

---

c 35 Or Messiah   d 36 Psalm 110:1   e 42 Greek two lepta   f 42 Greek kodrantes

say whatever is given you at the time, for it is not you speaking, but the Holy Spirit.

12 "Brother will betray brother to death, and a father his child. Children will rebel against their parents and have them put to death. **13** All men will hate you because of me, but he who stands firm to the end will be saved.

14 "When you see 'the abomination that causes desolation'ᵍ standing where itʰ does not belong—let the reader understand—then let those who are in Judea flee to the mountains. **15** Let no one on the roof of his house go down or enter the house to take anything out. **16** Let no one in the field go back to get his cloak. **17** How dreadful it will be in those days for pregnant women and nursing mothers! **18** Pray that this will not take place in winter, **19** because those will be days of distress unequaled from the beginning, when God created the world, until now—and never to be equaled again. **20** If the Lord had not cut short those days, no one would survive. But for the sake of the elect, whom he has chosen, he has shortened them. **21** At that time if anyone says to you, 'Look, here is the Christ!' or, 'Look, there he is!' do not believe it. **22** For false Christs and false prophets will appear and perform signs and miracles to deceive the elect—if that were possible. **23** So be on your guard; I have told you everything ahead of time.

24 "But in those days, following that distress,

" 'the sun will be darkened,
    and the moon will not give its
       light;

25 the stars will fall from the sky,
    and the heavenly bodies will
       be shaken.'ⁱʲ

26 "At that time men will see the Son of Man coming in clouds with great power and glory. **27** And he will send his angels and gather his elect from the four winds, from the ends of the earth to the ends of the heavens.

28 "Now learn this lesson from the fig tree: As soon as its twigs get tender and its leaves come out, you know that summer is near. **29** Even so, when you see these things happening, you know that it is near, right at the door. **30** I tell you the truth, this generationᵏ will certainly not pass away until all these things have happened. **31** Heaven and earth will pass away, but my words will never pass away.

The Day and Hour Unknown

32 "No one knows about that day or hour, not even the angels in heaven, nor the Son, but only the Father. **33** Be on guard! Be alert!ˡ You do not know when that time will come. **34** It's like a man going away: He leaves his house and puts his servants in charge, each with his assigned task, and tells the one at the door to keep watch.

35 "Therefore keep watch because you do not know when the owner of the house will come back—whether in the evening, or at midnight, or when the rooster crows, or at dawn. **36** If he comes suddenly, do not let him find you sleeping. **37** What I say to you, I say to everyone: 'Watch!' "

---

g 14 Daniel 9:27; 11:31; 12:11   *h* 14 Or *he*; also in verse 29   *i* 21 Or *Messiah*
j 25 Isaiah 13:10; 34:4   *k* 30 Or *race*   *l* 33 Some manuscripts *alert and pray*

Jesus Anointed at Bethany

14 ¹ Now the Passover and the Feast of Unleavened Bread were only two days away, and the chief priests and the teachers of the law were looking for some sly way to arrest Jesus and kill him. ² "But not during the Feast," they said, "or the people may riot."

³ While he was in Bethany, reclining at the table in the home of a man known as Simon the Leper, a woman came with an alabaster jar of very expensive perfume, made of pure nard. She broke the jar and poured the perfume on his head.

⁴ Some of those present were saying indignantly to one another, "Why this waste of perfume? ⁵ It could have been sold for more than a year's wagesᵐ and the money given to the poor." And they rebuked her harshly.

⁶ "Leave her alone," said Jesus. "Why are you bothering her? She has done a beautiful thing to me. ⁷ The poor you will always have with you, and you can help them any time you want. But you will not always have me. ⁸ She did what she could. She poured perfume on my body beforehand to prepare for my burial. ⁹ I tell you the truth, wherever the gospel is preached throughout the world, what she has done will also be told, in memory of her."

¹⁰ Then Judas Iscariot, one of the Twelve, went to the chief priests to betray Jesus to them. ¹¹ They were delighted to hear this and promised to give him money. So he watched for an opportunity to hand him over.

The Lord's Supper

¹² On the first day of the Feast of Unleavened Bread, when it was customary to sacrifice the Passover lamb, Jesus' disciples asked him, "Where do you want us to go and make preparations for you to eat the Passover?"

¹³ So he sent two of his disciples, telling them, "Go into the city, and a man carrying a jar of water will meet you. Follow him. ¹⁴ Say to the owner of the house he enters, 'The Teacher asks: Where is my guest room, where I may eat the Passover with my disciples?' ¹⁵ He will show you a large upper room, furnished and ready. Make preparations for us there."

¹⁶ The disciples left, went into the city and found things just as Jesus had told them. So they prepared the Passover.

¹⁷ When evening came, Jesus arrived with the Twelve. ¹⁸ While they were reclining at the table eating, he said, "I tell you the truth, one of you will betray me—one who is eating with me."

¹⁹ They were saddened, and one by one they said to him, "Surely not I?"

²⁰ "It is one of the Twelve," he replied, "one who dips bread into the bowl with me. ²¹ The Son of Man will go just as it is written about him. But woe to that man who betrays the Son of Man! It would be better for him if he had not been born."

²² While they were eating, Jesus took bread, gave thanks and broke it, and gave it to his disciples, saying, "Take it; this is my body."

²³ Then he took the cup, gave thanks and offered it to them, and they all drank from it.

ᵐ *5 Greek than three hundred denarii*

24 "This is my blood of the[n] covenant, which is poured out for many," he said to them. 25 "I tell you the truth, I will not drink again of the fruit of the vine until that day when I drink it anew in the kingdom of God."

26 When they had sung a hymn, they went out to the Mount of Olives.

Jesus Predicts Peter's Denial

27 "You will all fall away," Jesus told them, "for it is written:

" 'I will strike the shepherd,
    and the sheep will be
    scattered.'[o]

28 But after I have risen, I will go ahead of you into Galilee."

29 Peter declared, "Even if all fall away, I will not."

30 "I tell you the truth," Jesus answered, "today—yes, tonight—before the rooster crows twice[p] you yourself will disown me three times."

31 But Peter insisted emphatically, "Even if I have to die with you, I will never disown you." And all the others said the same.

Gethsemane

32 They went to a place called Gethsemane, and Jesus said to his disciples, "Sit here while I pray." 33 He took Peter, James and John along with him, and he began to be deeply distressed and troubled. 34 "My soul is overwhelmed with sorrow to the point of death," he said to them. "Stay here and keep watch." 35 Going a little farther, he fell to the ground and prayed that if possible the hour might pass from him. 36 "Abba,[q] Father," he said, "every-

thing is possible for you. Take this cup from me. Yet not what I will, but what you will."

37 Then he returned to his disciples and found them sleeping. "Simon," he said to Peter, "are you asleep? Could you not keep watch for one hour? 38 Watch and pray so that you will not fall into temptation. The spirit is willing, but the body is weak."

39 Once more he went away and prayed the same thing. 40 When he came back, he again found them sleeping, because their eyes were heavy. They did not know what to say to him.

41 Returning the third time, he said to them, "Are you still sleeping and resting? Enough! The hour has come. Look, the Son of Man is betrayed into the hands of sinners. 42 Rise! Let us go! Here comes my betrayer!"

Jesus Arrested

43 Just as he was speaking, Judas, one of the Twelve, appeared. With him was a crowd armed with swords and clubs, sent from the chief priests, the teachers of the law, and the elders. 44 Now the betrayer had arranged a signal with them: "The one I kiss is the man; arrest him and lead him away under guard." 45 Going at once to Jesus, Judas said, "Rabbi!" and kissed him. 46 The men seized Jesus and arrested him. 47 Then one of those standing near drew his sword and struck the servant of the high priest, cutting off his ear.

48 "Am I leading a rebellion," said Jesus, "that you have come out with

n 24 Some manuscripts the new   o 27 Zech. 13:7   p 30 Some early manuscripts do not have twice.   q 36 Aramaic for Father

swords and clubs to capture me? **49** Every day I was with you, teaching in the temple courts, and you did not arrest me. But the Scriptures must be fulfilled." **50** Then everyone deserted him and fled.

51 A young man, wearing nothing but a linen garment, was following Jesus. When they seized him, **52** he fled naked, leaving his garment behind.

Before the Sanhedrin

53 They took Jesus to the high priest, and all the chief priests, elders and teachers of the law came together. **54** Peter followed him at a distance, right into the courtyard of the high priest. There he sat with the guards and warmed himself at the fire.

55 The chief priests and the whole Sanhedrin were looking for evidence against Jesus so that they could put him to death, but they did not find any. **56** Many testified falsely against him, but their statements did not agree.

57 Then some stood up and gave this false testimony against him: **58** "We heard him say, 'I will destroy this man-made temple and in three days will build another, not made by man.' " **59** Yet even then their testimony did not agree.

60 Then the high priest stood up before them and asked Jesus, "Are you not going to answer? What is this testimony that these men are bringing against you?" **61** But Jesus remained silent and gave no answer.

Again the high priest asked him, "Are you the Christ,*r* the Son of the Blessed One?"

62 "I am," said Jesus. "And you will see the Son of Man sitting at the right

hand of the Mighty One and coming on the clouds of heaven."

63 The high priest tore his clothes. "Why do we need any more witnesses?" he asked. **64** "You have heard the blasphemy. What do you think?"

They all condemned him as worthy of death. **65** Then some began to spit at him; they blindfolded him, struck him with their fists, and said, "Prophesy!" And the guards took him and beat him.

Peter Disowns Jesus

66 While Peter was below in the courtyard, one of the servant girls of the high priest came by. **67** When she saw Peter warming himself, she looked closely at him.

"You also were with that Nazarene, Jesus," she said.

68 But he denied it. "I don't know or understand what you're talking about," he said, and went out into the entryway.*s*

69 When the servant girl saw him there, she said again to those standing around, "This fellow is one of them." **70** Again he denied it.

After a little while, those standing near said to Peter, "Surely you are one of them, for you are a Galilean."

71 He began to call down curses on himself, and he swore to them, "I don't know this man you're talking about."

72 Immediately the rooster crowed the second time.*t* Then Peter remembered the word Jesus had spoken to him: "Before the rooster crows twice*u* you will disown me three times." And he broke down and wept.

---

r 61 Or *Messiah*   *s* 68 Some early manuscripts *entryway and the rooster crowed*
t 72 Some early manuscripts do not have *the second time*.   *u* 72 Some early manuscripts do not have *twice*.

Jesus Before Pilate

15 **1** Very early in the morning, the chief priests, with the elders, the teachers of the law and the whole Sanhedrin, reached a decision. They bound Jesus, led him away and handed him over to Pilate.

2 "Are you the king of the Jews?" asked Pilate.

"Yes, it is as you say," Jesus replied.

3 The chief priests accused him of many things. **4** So again Pilate asked him, "Aren't you going to answer? See how many things they are accusing you of."

5 But Jesus still made no reply, and Pilate was amazed.

6 Now it was the custom at the Feast to release a prisoner whom the people requested. **7** A man called Barabbas was in prison with the insurrectionists who had committed murder in the uprising. **8** The crowd came up and asked Pilate to do for them what he usually did.

9 "Do you want me to release to you the king of the Jews?" asked Pilate, **10** knowing it was out of envy that the chief priests had handed Jesus over to him. **11** But the chief priests stirred up the crowd to have Pilate release Barabbas instead.

12 "What shall I do, then, with the one you call the king of the Jews?" Pilate asked them.

13 "Crucify him!" they shouted.

14 "Why? What crime has he committed?" asked Pilate.

But they shouted all the louder, "Crucify him!"

15 Wanting to satisfy the crowd, Pilate released Barabbas to them. He had Jesus flogged, and handed him over to be crucified.

The Soldiers Mock Jesus

16 The soldiers led Jesus away into the palace (that is, the Praetorium) and called together the whole company of soldiers. **17** They put a purple robe on him, then twisted together a crown of thorns and set it on him. **18** And they began to call out to him, "Hail, king of the Jews!" **19** Again and again they struck him on the head with a staff and spit on him. Falling on their knees, they paid homage to him. **20** And when they had mocked him, they took off the purple robe and put his own clothes on him. Then they led him out to crucify him.

The Crucifixion

21 A certain man from Cyrene, Simon, the father of Alexander and Rufus, was passing by on his way in from the country, and they forced him to carry the cross. **22** They brought Jesus to the place called Golgotha (which means The Place of the Skull). **23** Then they offered him wine mixed with myrrh, but he did not take it. **24** And they crucified him. Dividing up his clothes, they cast lots to see what each would get.

25 It was the third hour when they crucified him. **26** The written notice of the charge against him read: THE KING OF THE JEWS. **27** They crucified two robbers with him, one on his right and one on his left.[v] **29** Those who passed by hurled insults at him, shaking their heads and saying, "So! You who are going to destroy the temple and build it in three days,

---

v 27 Some manuscripts *left,* 28 *and the scripture was fulfilled which says, "He was counted with the lawless ones"* (Isaiah 53:12)

30 come down from the cross and save yourself!"

31 In the same way the chief priests and the teachers of the law mocked him among themselves. "He saved others," they said, "but he can't save himself! 32 Let this Christ,ʷ this King of Israel, come down now from the cross, that we may see and believe." Those crucified with him also heaped insults on him.

The Death of Jesus

33 At the sixth hour darkness came over the whole land until the ninth hour. 34 And at the ninth hour Jesus cried out in a loud voice, "Eloi, Eloi, lama sabachthani?" — which means, "My God, my God, why have you forsaken me?"ˣ

35 When some of those standing near heard this, they said, "Listen, he's calling Elijah."

36 One man ran, filled a sponge with wine vinegar, put it on a stick, and offered it to Jesus to drink. "Now leave him alone. Let's see if Elijah comes to take him down," he said.

37 With a loud cry, Jesus breathed his last.

38 The curtain of the temple was torn in two from top to bottom. 39 And when the centurion, who stood there in front of Jesus, heard his cryʸ saw how he died, he said, "Surely this man was the Sonᶻ of God!"

40 Some women were watching from a distance. Among them were Mary Magdalene, Mary the mother of James the younger and of Joses, and Salome. 41 In Galilee these women had followed him and cared for his needs. Many other women who had come up with him to Jerusalem were also there.

The Burial of Jesus

42 It was Preparation Day (that is, the day before the Sabbath). So as evening approached, 43 Joseph of Arimathea, a prominent member of the Council, who was himself waiting for the kingdom of God, went boldly to Pilate and asked for Jesus' body. 44 Pilate was surprised to hear that he was already dead. Summoning the centurion, he asked him if Jesus had already died. 45 When he learned from the centurion that it was so, he gave the body to Joseph. 46 So Joseph bought some linen cloth, took down the body, wrapped it in the linen, and placed it in a tomb cut out of rock. Then he rolled a stone against the entrance of the tomb. 47 Mary Magdalene and Mary the mother of Joses saw where he was laid.

The Resurrection

16 ¹ When the Sabbath was over, Mary Magdalene, Mary the mother of James, and Salome bought spices so that they might go to anoint Jesus' body. 2 Very early on the first day of the week, just after sunrise, they were on their way to the tomb 3 and they asked each other, "Who will roll the stone away from the entrance of the tomb?"

4 But when they looked up, they saw that the stone, which was very large, had been rolled away. 5 As they entered the tomb, they saw a young man dressed in a white robe sitting on the right side, and they were alarmed.

ʷ 32 Or *Messiah*   ˣ 34 Psalm 22:1   ʸ 39 Some manuscripts do not have *heard his cry and.*   ᶻ 39 Or *a son*

6 "Don't be alarmed," he said. "You are looking for Jesus the Nazarene, who was crucified. He has risen! He is not here. See the place where they laid him. 7 But go, tell his disciples and Peter, 'He is going ahead of you into Galilee. There you will see him, just as he told you.'"

8 Trembling and bewildered, the women went out and fled from the tomb. They said nothing to anyone, because they were afraid.

[The most reliable early manuscripts and other ancient witnesses do not have Mark 16:9-20.]

---

9 When Jesus rose early on the first day of the week, he appeared first to Mary Magdalene, out of whom he had driven seven demons. 10 She went and told those who had been with him and who were mourning and weeping. 11 When they heard that Jesus was alive and that she had seen him, they did not believe it.

12 Afterward Jesus appeared in a different form to two of them while they were walking in the country. 13 These returned and reported it to the rest; but they did not believe them either.

14 Later Jesus appeared to the Eleven as they were eating; he rebuked them for their lack of faith and their stubborn refusal to believe those who had seen him after he had risen.

15 He said to them, "Go into all the world and preach the good news to all creation. 16 Whoever believes and is baptized will be saved, but whoever does not believe will be condemned. 17 And these signs will accompany those who believe: In my name they will drive out demons; they will speak in new tongues; 18 they will pick up snakes with their hands; and when they drink deadly poison, it will not hurt them at all; they will place their hands on sick people, and they will get well."

19 After the Lord Jesus had spoken to them, he was taken up into heaven and he sat at the right hand of God. 20 Then the disciples went out and preached everywhere, and the Lord worked with them and confirmed his word by the signs that accompanied it.

Luke

Introduction

1 1 Many have undertaken to draw up an account of the things that have been fulfilled[a] among us, **2** just as they were handed down to us by those who from the first were eyewitnesses and servants of the word. **3** Therefore, since I myself have carefully investigated everything from the beginning, it seemed good also to me to write an orderly account for you, most excellent Theophilus, **4** so that you may know the certainty of the things you have been taught.

The Birth of John the Baptist Foretold

5 In the time of Herod king of Judea there was a priest named Zechariah, who belonged to the priestly division of Abijah; his wife Elizabeth was also a descendant of Aaron. **6** Both of them were upright in the sight of God, observing all the Lord's commandments and regulations blamelessly. **7** But they had no children, because Elizabeth was barren; and they were both well along in years.

8 Once when Zechariah's division was on duty and he was serving as priest before God, **9** he was chosen by lot, according to the custom of the priesthood, to go into the temple of the Lord and burn incense. **10** And when the time for the burning of incense came, all the assembled worshipers were praying outside.

11 Then an angel of the Lord appeared to him, standing at the right side of the altar of incense. **12** When Zechariah saw him, he was startled and was gripped with fear. **13** But the angel said to him: "Do not be afraid, Zechariah; your prayer has been heard. Your wife Elizabeth will bear you a son, and you are to give him the name John. **14** He will be a joy and delight to you, and many will rejoice because of his birth, **15** for he will be great in the sight of the Lord. He is never to take wine or other fermented drink, and he will be filled with the Holy Spirit even from birth.[b] **16** Many of the people of Israel will he bring back to the Lord their God. **17** And he will go on before the Lord, in the spirit and power of Elijah, to turn the hearts of the fathers to their children and the disobedient to the wisdom of the righteous—to make ready a people prepared for the Lord."

18 Zechariah asked the angel, "How can I be sure of this? I am an old man and my wife is well along in years."

19 The angel answered, "I am Gabriel. I stand in the presence of God, and I have been sent to speak to you and to tell you this good news. **20** And now you will be silent and not able to speak until the day this happens, because you did not believe my words, which will come true at their proper time."

21 Meanwhile, the people were waiting for Zechariah and wondering why he stayed so long in the temple. **22** When he came out, he

---

a 1 Or *been surely believed* b 15 Or *from his mother's womb*

could not speak to them. They realized he had seen a vision in the temple, for he kept making signs to them but remained unable to speak.

23 When his time of service was completed, he returned home. 24 After this his wife Elizabeth became pregnant and for five months remained in seclusion. 25 "The Lord has done this for me," she said. "In these days he has shown his favor and taken away my disgrace among the people."

The Birth of Jesus Foretold

26 In the sixth month, God sent the angel Gabriel to Nazareth, a town in Galilee, 27 to a virgin pledged to be married to a man named Joseph, a descendant of David. The virgin's name was Mary. 28 The angel went to her and said, "Greetings, you who are highly favored! The Lord is with you."

29 Mary was greatly troubled at his words and wondered what kind of greeting this might be. 30 But the angel said to her, "Do not be afraid, Mary, you have found favor with God. 31 You will be with child and give birth to a son, and you are to give him the name Jesus. 32 He will be great and will be called the Son of the Most High. The Lord God will give him the throne of his father David, 33 and he will reign over the house of Jacob forever; his kingdom will never end."

34 "How will this be," Mary asked the angel, "since I am a virgin?"

35 The angel answered, "The Holy Spirit will come upon you, and the power of the Most High will overshadow you. So the holy one to be born will be called[c] the Son of God. 36 Even Elizabeth your relative is going to have a child in her old age, and she who was said to be barren is in her sixth month. 37 For nothing is impossible with God."

38 "I am the Lord's servant," Mary answered. "May it be to me as you have said." Then the angel left her.

Mary Visits Elizabeth

39 At that time Mary got ready and hurried to a town in the hill country of Judea, 40 where she entered Zechariah's home and greeted Elizabeth. 41 When Elizabeth heard Mary's greeting, the baby leaped in her womb, and Elizabeth was filled with the Holy Spirit. 42 In a loud voice she exclaimed: "Blessed are you among women, and blessed is the child you will bear! 43 But why am I so favored, that the mother of my Lord should come to me? 44 As soon as the sound of your greeting reached my ears, the baby in my womb leaped for joy. 45 Blessed is she who has believed that what the Lord has said to her will be accomplished!"

Mary's Song

46 And Mary said:

"My soul glorifies the Lord
47 and my spirit rejoices in God
        my Savior,
48 for he has been mindful
        of the humble state of his
        servant.
   From now on all generations
        will call me blessed,
49 for the Mighty One has done
        great things for me—
        holy is his name.
50 His mercy extends to those who
        fear him,
   from generation to generation.

c 35 Or So the child to be born will be called holy,

51 He has performed mighty
      deeds with his arm;
   he has scattered those who
      are proud in their inmost
      thoughts.
52 He has brought down rulers
      from their thrones
   but has lifted up the humble.
53 He has filled the hungry with
      good things
   but has sent the rich away
      empty.
54 He has helped his servant Israel,
      remembering to be merciful
55 to Abraham and his
      descendants forever,
   even as he said to our fathers."

56 Mary stayed with Elizabeth for about three months and then returned home.

The Birth of John the Baptist

57 When it was time for Elizabeth to have her baby, she gave birth to a son. 58 Her neighbors and relatives heard that the Lord had shown her great mercy, and they shared her joy.
59 On the eighth day they came to circumcise the child, and they were going to name him after his father Zechariah, 60 but his mother spoke up and said, "No! He is to be called John."
61 They said to her, "There is no one among your relatives who has that name."
62 Then they made signs to his father, to find out what he would like to name the child. 63 He asked for a writing tablet, and to everyone's astonishment he wrote, "His name is John." 64 Immediately his mouth was opened and his tongue was loosed, and he began to speak, praising God. 65 The neighbors were all filled with awe, and throughout the

hill country of Judea people were talking about all these things.
66 Everyone who heard this wondered about it, asking, "What then is this child going to be?" For the Lord's hand was with him.

Zechariah's Song

67 His father Zechariah was filled with the Holy Spirit and prophesied:

68 "Praise be to the Lord, the God
      of Israel,
   because he has come and has
      redeemed his people.
69 He has raised up a horn[d] of
      salvation for us
   in the house of his servant
      David
70 (as he said through his holy
      prophets of long ago),
71 salvation from our enemies
   and from the hand of all who
      hate us—
72 to show mercy to our fathers
   and to remember his holy
      covenant,
73 the oath he swore to our father
      Abraham:
74 to rescue us from the hand of
      our enemies,
   and to enable us to serve him
      without fear
75 in holiness and righteousness
      before him all our days.
76 And you, my child, will be
      called a prophet of the
      Most High;
   for you will go on before the
      Lord to prepare the way
      for him,
77 to give his people the
      knowledge of salvation
   through the forgiveness of
      their sins,

d 69 Horn here symbolizes strength.

78 because of the tender mercy of
    our God,
  by which the rising sun will
    come to us from heaven
79 to shine on those living in
    darkness
  and in the shadow of death,
  to guide our feet into the path
    of peace."

80 And the child grew and became
strong in spirit; and he lived in the
desert until he appeared publicly to
Israel.

The Birth of Jesus

2 ¹ In those days Caesar Augustus
    issued a decree that a census
should be taken of the entire Roman
world. 2 (This was the first census
that took place while Quirinius was
governor of Syria.) 3 And everyone
went to his own town to register.

4 So Joseph also went up from the
town of Nazareth in Galilee to Judea,
to Bethlehem the town of David, because he belonged to the house and
line of David. 5 He went there to
register with Mary, who was pledged
to be married to him and was expecting a child. 6 While they were there,
the time came for the baby to be
born, 7 and she gave birth to her
firstborn, a son. She wrapped him in
cloths and placed him in a manger,
because there was no room for them
in the inn.

The Shepherds and the Angels

8 And there were shepherds living
out in the fields nearby, keeping
watch over their flocks at night. 9 An
angel of the Lord appeared to them,
and the glory of the Lord shone

around them, and they were terrified. 10 But the angel said to them,
"Do not be afraid. I bring you good
news of great joy that will be for all
the people. 11 Today in the town of
David a Savior has been born to you;
he is Christᵉ the Lord. 12 This will be
a sign to you: You will find a baby
wrapped in cloths and lying in a
manger."

13 Suddenly a great company of
the heavenly host appeared with the
angel, praising God and saying,

14 "Glory to God in the highest,
  and on earth peace to men on
    whom his favor rests."

15 When the angels had left them
and gone into heaven, the shepherds
said to one another, "Let's go to Bethlehem and see this thing that has
happened, which the Lord has told us
about."

16 So they hurried off and found
Mary and Joseph, and the baby, who
was lying in the manger. 17 When
they had seen him, they spread the
word concerning what had been told
them about this child, 18 and all who
heard it were amazed at what the
shepherds said to them. 19 But Mary
treasured up all these things and
pondered them in her heart. 20 The
shepherds returned, glorifying and
praising God for all the things they
had heard and seen, which were just
as they had been told.

Jesus Presented in the Temple

21 On the eighth day, when it was
time to circumcise him, he was
named Jesus, the name the angel had
given him before he had been conceived.

ᵉ 11 Or *Messiah*. "The Christ" (Greek) and "the Messiah" (Hebrew) both mean "the Anointed
One"; also in verse 26.

22 When the time of their purification according to the Law of Moses had been completed, Joseph and Mary took him to Jerusalem to present him to the Lord **23** (as it is written in the Law of the Lord, "Every firstborn male is to be consecrated to the Lord"*f*), **24** and to offer a sacrifice in keeping with what is said in the Law of the Lord: "a pair of doves or two young pigeons."*g*

25 Now there was a man in Jerusalem called Simeon, who was righteous and devout. He was waiting for the consolation of Israel, and the Holy Spirit was upon him. **26** It had been revealed to him by the Holy Spirit that he would not die before he had seen the Lord's Christ. **27** Moved by the Spirit, he went into the temple courts. When the parents brought in the child Jesus to do for him what the custom of the Law required, **28** Simeon took him in his arms and praised God, saying:

29 "Sovereign Lord, as you have
      promised,
   you now dismiss*h* your
      servant in peace.
30 For my eyes have seen your
      salvation,
31   which you have prepared in
      the sight of all people,
32 a light for revelation to the
      Gentiles
   and for glory to your people
      Israel."

33 The child's father and mother marveled at what was said about him. **34** Then Simeon blessed them and said to Mary, his mother: "This child is destined to cause the falling and rising of many in Israel, and to be a sign that will be spoken against, **35** so that the thoughts of many hearts will be revealed. And a sword will pierce your own soul too."

36 There was also a prophetess, Anna, the daughter of Phanuel, of the tribe of Asher. She was very old; she had lived with her husband seven years after her marriage, **37** and then was a widow until she was eighty-four.*i* She never left the temple but worshiped night and day, fasting and praying. **38** Coming up to them at that very moment, she gave thanks to God and spoke about the child to all who were looking forward to the redemption of Jerusalem.

39 When Joseph and Mary had done everything required by the Law of the Lord, they returned to Galilee to their own town of Nazareth. **40** And the child grew and became strong; he was filled with wisdom, and the grace of God was upon him.

The Boy Jesus at the Temple

41 Every year his parents went to Jerusalem for the Feast of the Passover. **42** When he was twelve years old, they went up to the Feast, according to the custom. **43** After the Feast was over, while his parents were returning home, the boy Jesus stayed behind in Jerusalem, but they were unaware of it. **44** Thinking he was in their company, they traveled on for a day. Then they began looking for him among their relatives and friends. **45** When they did not find him, they went back to Jerusalem to look for him. **46** After three days they found him in the temple courts, sitting among the teachers, listening to them and asking them questions.

---

f 23 Exodus 13:2,12   *g* 24 Lev. 12:8   *h* 29 Or promised, / now dismiss   *i* 37 Or widow
for eighty-four years

47 Everyone who heard him was amazed at his understanding and his answers. 48 When his parents saw him, they were astonished. His mother said to him, "Son, why have you treated us like this? Your father and I have been anxiously searching for you."

49 "Why were you searching for me?" he asked. "Didn't you know I had to be in my Father's house?" 50 But they did not understand what he was saying to them.

51 Then he went down to Nazareth with them and was obedient to them. But his mother treasured all these things in her heart. 52 And Jesus grew in wisdom and stature, and in favor with God and men.

John the Baptist Prepares the Way

3 ¹ In the fifteenth year of the reign of Tiberius Caesar—when Pontius Pilate was governor of Judea, Herod tetrarch of Galilee, his brother Philip tetrarch of Iturea and Traconitis, and Lysanias tetrarch of Abilene— 2 during the high priesthood of Annas and Caiaphas, the word of God came to John son of Zechariah in the desert. 3 He went into all the country around the Jordan, preaching a baptism of repentance for the forgiveness of sins. 4 As is written in the book of the words of Isaiah the prophet:

"A voice of one calling in the desert,
'Prepare the way for the Lord,
   make straight paths for him.
5 Every valley shall be filled in,
   every mountain and hill made low.
The crooked roads shall become straight,

the rough ways smooth.
6 And all mankind will see God's salvation.'"ʲ

7 John said to the crowds coming out to be baptized by him, "You brood of vipers! Who warned you to flee from the coming wrath? 8 Produce fruit in keeping with repentance. And do not begin to say to yourselves, 'We have Abraham as our father.' For I tell you that out of these stones God can raise up children for Abraham. 9 The ax is already at the root of the trees, and every tree that does not produce good fruit will be cut down and thrown into the fire."

10 "What should we do then?" the crowd asked.

11 John answered, "The man with two tunics should share with him who has none, and the one who has food should do the same."

12 Tax collectors also came to be baptized. "Teacher," they asked, "what should we do?"

13 "Don't collect any more than you are required to," he told them. 14 Then some soldiers asked him, "And what should we do?"

He replied, "Don't extort money and don't accuse falsely—be content with your pay."

15 The people were waiting expectantly and were all wondering in their hearts if John might possibly be the Christ.ᵏ 16 John answered them all, "I baptize you withˡ water. But one more powerful than I will come, the thongs of whose sandals I am not worthy to untie. He will baptize you with the Holy Spirit and with fire. 17 His winnowing fork is in his hand to clear his threshing floor and to gather the wheat into his barn, but

j 6 Isaiah 40:3-5   k 15 Or Messiah   l 16 Or in

he will burn up the chaff with unquenchable fire." **18** And with many other words John exhorted the people and preached the good news to them.

19 But when John rebuked Herod the tetrarch because of Herodias, his brother's wife, and all the other evil things he had done, **20** Herod added this to them all: He locked John up in prison.

The Baptism and Genealogy of Jesus

21 When all the people were being baptized, Jesus was baptized too. And as he was praying, heaven was opened **22** and the Holy Spirit descended on him in bodily form like a dove. And a voice came from heaven: "You are my Son, whom I love; with you I am well pleased."

23 Now Jesus himself was about thirty years old when he began his ministry. He was the son, so it was thought, of Joseph,

the son of Heli, **24** the son of Matthat,
the son of Levi, the son of Melki,
the son of Jannai, the son of Joseph,
25 the son of Mattathias, the son of Amos,
the son of Nahum, the son of Esli,
the son of Naggai, **26** the son of Maath,
the son of Mattathias, the son of Semein,
the son of Josech, the son of Joda,
27 the son of Joanan, the son of Rhesa,

the son of Zerubbabel, the son of Shealtiel,
the son of Neri, **28** the son of Melki,
the son of Addi, the son of Cosam,
the son of Elmadam, the son of Er,
29 the son of Joshua, the son of Eliezer,
the son of Jorim, the son of Matthat,
the son of Levi, **30** the son of Simeon,
the son of Judah, the son of Joseph,
the son of Jonam, the son of Eliakim,
31 the son of Melea, the son of Menna,
the son of Mattatha, the son of Nathan,
the son of David, **32** the son of Jesse,
the son of Obed, the son of Boaz,
the son of Salmon,*m* the son of Nahshon,
33 the son of Amminadab, the son of Ram,*n*
the son of Hezron, the son of Perez,
the son of Judah, **34** the son of Jacob,
the son of Isaac, the son of Abraham,
the son of Terah, the son of Nahor,
35 the son of Serug, the son of Reu,
the son of Peleg, the son of Eber,
the son of Shelah, **36** the son of Cainan,
the son of Arphaxad, the son of Shem,

---

m 32 Some early manuscripts *Sala*   *n 33* Some manuscripts *Amminadab, the son of Admin, the son of Arni;* other manuscripts vary widely.

MATT AUSTIN
★ ★ ★

I was brought up in a Christian home. I was always taught about God, and I accepted the Lord in my heart when I was a little kid. But only in the past three years have I come to know the Lord in ways I never would have thought of. In dealing with every-day experiences down the road of life, my relation-ship with God has grown tremendously. I used to never read my Bible and didn't go to church much. Now I try to go to church whenever it's possible—it's kind of tough on the road. But we got cowboy church at the rodeos, which I think is a great thing.

I'm thankful everyday for the opportunities I've been given and the chances that I've had. I've met kids and people that have never had the opportunity I have. I'm thankful that I can get out of bed and walk and talk. That to me is a miracle, amazing! You want to get mad because you get bucked off a bull, what's the sense in that? There is always something to be thankful for.

I'm thankful everyday because I know I'm so blessed and everything I've ever done I credit to the Lord. The Bible says we can do all things through Christ; not just this and that, but all things. That's one of my favorite promises and if I feel myself getting tensed up, I just say it over and over. Have faith, go out there and seek the Lord, talk to him and read the Bible. When you talk to him, he listens.

Keep your faith, no matter what happens. You're going to have trials and tribulations through your life. Problems will come and go, but if you just keep your faith and heart with God, you can come through anything. Seek God because with him you can do all things, without him you can do nothing.

★ ★ ★

GRANT ADKISSON

It's hard to believe it's been so many years since the idea for *The Way for Cowboys* first came up and after a year long "labor of love," it came together! God has blessed it—world-wide—beyond any of our expectations. Now I pray our Lord blesses you through his wonderful Word in this new edition. I know God will use the fresh presentations and testimonies in your life. But I'm also praying you will let him draw you into reading full passages and entire books of his life-changing New Testament! Nothing else in this whole world will bring a greater benefit in your life and future than immersing yourself in God's Word!

Our family has been part of the Cowboy world for four generations. My mom's dad homesteaded a ranch in Colorado in 1888 and often sold beef to the Gold Rush miners. Later, in the 20s, he ranched and was sheriff in Greeley. Then, with the cattle crash of the 1930s, he moved to Gunnison, Colorado, to start a new ranch. My dad's family homesteaded in Cañon City, Colorado, in the 1920s and married into a ranching family that settled in the area after making the cattle drives with Charles Goodnight.

I began riding when I was a year old and began working horseback on a rough mountain ranch when I was five. Even today there's not much work from pickup trucks in this country—it takes good, tough horses to get it done.

It was through working with one of the other old ranch families that brought me into a personal relationship with Jesus Christ. The Canterbury family and our family have chased wild horses, cowboyed, rode and hunted together for generations. And for the last four decades we have worshiped and ministered to cowboys together!

Even with all the great horses I've ridden, and all the places I've seen, none of the memories of my lifetime are greater than the ministry we've had the privilege being part of! Whether it was pastoring, sharing Christ in 50 states and 40 foreign countries, preaching at churches, conferences and rodeos, helping to lead the Fellowship of Christian Cowboys, doing TV and radio ministry with Dale Evans, James Dobson and many others: nothing compares to the joy of seeing God redeem a person to himself and Heaven!

God has done so much in the rodeo and western world since the FCC started around 40 years ago. There are hundreds of cowboy ministries and churches around the country and many of the world champions are Christ-followers. But a lot of wild cowboys still need a Savior, that's why we go and why *The Way for Cowboys* is printed.

THE WAY FOR COWBOYS IS THE WAY, THE TRUTH AND THE LIFE... HE'S THE LORD JESUS CHRIST! IF HE ISN'T YOUR LORD ALREADY, HE CAN BE TODAY!
★ ★ ★

LAYNA KIGHT

I've been rodeoing my whole life, and I asked Jesus into my life when I was young. We went to church, and I knew that if I died I would be with God. But I didn't really bring God into my rodeoing like I do now.

One day, I felt in my heart that the reason I was rodeoing was to be able to make a difference in the lives of some of the girls out here. God prompted me to start trying to get to the NFR, which I did in 2006. I've built a lot of relationships with women that don't have the opportunity to get to a church. It opens up a door to be there and show them how much God cares about them.

The rodeo means nothing without God. It's pointless if you are doing it just for the winning. Rodeo is an avenue to make a difference in people's lives. I pray for wisdom about which rodeos to enter. It's amazing how God can help. For example, I had no intention of getting the horse that I ride, but God provided for me.

My goal had been to get to the pros. It's an honor to even be there, to be among all those other women. I keep a headset on, and I keep Scripture flowing in my head before I ride so that none of the pressure will get to me. The more attention I get, the more opportunity it gives me to show that it really is God doing it in me. I know it's not me, but he has put me more and more in the limelight to give me an opportunity to be a blessing to other people. I want to tell them who is doing it.

★ ★ ★

the son of Noah, the son of
  Lamech,
37 the son of Methuselah, the son
  of Enoch,
the son of Jared, the son of
  Mahalalel,
the son of Kenan, 38 the son of
  Enosh,
the son of Seth, the son of
  Adam,
the son of God.

The Temptation of Jesus

4 1 Jesus, full of the Holy Spirit,
returned from the Jordan and
was led by the Spirit in the desert,
where for forty days he was
tempted by the devil. He ate nothing
during those days, and at the end of
them he was hungry.

3 The devil said to him, "If you are
the Son of God, tell this stone to
become bread."

4 Jesus answered, "It is written:
'Man does not live on bread alone.'ᵒ"

5 The devil led him up to a high
place and showed him in an instant
all the kingdoms of the world. 6 And
he said to him, "I will give you all
their authority and splendor, for it
has been given to me, and I can give
it to anyone I want to. 7 So if you
worship me, it will all be yours."

8 Jesus answered, "It is written:
'Worship the Lord your God and
serve him only.'ᵖ"

9 The devil led him to Jerusalem
and had him stand on the highest
point of the temple. "If you are the
Son of God," he said, "throw yourself
down from here. 10 For it is written:

"'He will command his angels
  concerning you
to guard you carefully;

11 they will lift you up in their
  hands,
so that you will not strike
  your foot against a stone.'q"

12 Jesus answered, "It says: 'Do
not put the Lord your God to the test.'ʳ"

13 When the devil had finished all
this tempting, he left him until an
opportune time.

Jesus Rejected at Nazareth

14 Jesus returned to Galilee in the
power of the Spirit, and news about
him spread through the whole
countryside. 15 He taught in their
synagogues, and everyone praised
him.

16 He went to Nazareth, where he
had been brought up, and on the
Sabbath day he went into the
synagogue, as was his custom. And
he stood up to read. 17 The scroll of
the prophet Isaiah was handed to
him. Unrolling it, he found the place
where it is written:

18 "The Spirit of the Lord is on me,
  because he has anointed me
    to preach good news to the
    poor.
He has sent me to proclaim
    freedom for the prisoners
  and recovery of sight for the
    blind,
to release the oppressed,
19   to proclaim the year of the
    Lord's favor."ˢ

20 Then he rolled up the scroll,
gave it back to the attendant and sat
down. The eyes of everyone in the
synagogue were fastened on him,
21 and he began by saying to them,
"Today this scripture is fulfilled in
your hearing."

---

4 Deut. 8:3   ᵖ 8 Deut. 6:13   q 11 Psalm 91:11,12   ʳ 12 Deut. 6:16   ˢ 19 Isaiah
1:1,2

22 All spoke well of him and were amazed at the gracious words that came from his lips. "Isn't this Joseph's son?" they asked.

23 Jesus said to them, "Surely you will quote this proverb to me: 'Physician, heal yourself! Do here in your hometown what we have heard that you did in Capernaum.'"

24 "I tell you the truth," he continued, "no prophet is accepted in his hometown. **25** I assure you that there were many widows in Israel in Elijah's time, when the sky was shut for three and a half years and there was a severe famine throughout the land. **26** Yet Elijah was not sent to any of them, but to a widow in Zarephath in the region of Sidon. **27** And there were many in Israel with leprosy[t] in the time of Elisha the prophet, yet not one of them was cleansed — only Naaman the Syrian."

28 All the people in the synagogue were furious when they heard this. **29** They got up, drove him out of the town, and took him to the brow of the hill on which the town was built, in order to throw him down the cliff. **30** But he walked right through the crowd and went on his way.

Jesus Drives Out an Evil Spirit

31 Then he went down to Capernaum, a town in Galilee, and on the Sabbath began to teach the people. **32** They were amazed at his teaching, because his message had authority.

33 In the synagogue there was a man possessed by a demon, an evil[u] spirit. He cried out at the top of his voice, **34** "Ha! What do you want with us, Jesus of Nazareth? Have you come to destroy us? I know who you are — the Holy One of God!"

35 "Be quiet!" Jesus said sternly. "Come out of him!" Then the demon threw the man down before them all and came out without injuring him.

36 All the people were amazed and said to each other, "What is this teaching? With authority and power he gives orders to evil spirits and they come out!" **37** And the news about him spread throughout the surrounding area.

Jesus Heals Many

38 Jesus left the synagogue and went to the home of Simon. Now Simon's mother-in-law was suffering from a high fever, and they asked Jesus to help her. **39** So he bent over her and rebuked the fever, and it left her. She got up at once and began to wait on them.

40 When the sun was setting, the people brought to Jesus all who had various kinds of sickness, and laying his hands on each one, he healed them. **41** Moreover, demons came out of many people, shouting, "You are the Son of God!" But he rebuked them and would not allow them to speak, because they knew he was the Christ.[v]

42 At daybreak Jesus went out to a solitary place. The people were looking for him and when they came to where he was, they tried to keep him from leaving them. **43** But he said, "I must preach the good news of the kingdom of God to the other towns also, because that is why I was sent." **44** And he kept on preaching in the synagogues of Judea.[w]

---

[t] 27 The Greek word was used for various diseases affecting the skin — not necessarily leprosy. [u] 33 Greek *unclean*; also in verse 36 [v] 41 Or *Messiah* [w] 44 Or *the land of the Jews*; some manuscripts *Galilee*

The Calling of the First Disciples

5 1 One day as Jesus was standing by the Lake of Gennesaret,ˣ with the people crowding around him and listening to the word of God, 2 he saw at the water's edge two boats, left there by the fishermen, who were washing their nets.

He got into one of the boats, the one belonging to Simon, and asked him to put out a little from shore. Then he sat down and taught the people from the boat.

4 When he had finished speaking, he said to Simon, "Put out into deep water, and let downʸ the nets for a catch."

5 Simon answered, "Master, we've worked hard all night and haven't caught anything. But because you say so, I will let down the nets."

6 When they had done so, they caught such a large number of fish that their nets began to break. 7 So they signaled their partners in the other boat to come and help them, and they came and filled both boats so full that they began to sink.

8 When Simon Peter saw this, he fell at Jesus' knees and said, "Go away from me, Lord; I am a sinful man!" 9 For he and all his companions were astonished at the catch of fish they had taken, 10 and so were James and John, the sons of Zebedee, Simon's partners.

Then Jesus said to Simon, "Don't be afraid; from now on you will catch men." 11 So they pulled their boats up on shore, left everything and followed him.

The Man With Leprosy

12 While Jesus was in one of the towns, a man came along who was covered with leprosy.ᶻ When he saw Jesus, he fell with his face to the ground and begged him, "Lord, if you are willing, you can make me clean."

13 Jesus reached out his hand and touched the man. "I am willing," he said. "Be clean!" And immediately the leprosy left him.

14 Then Jesus ordered him, "Don't tell anyone, but go, show yourself to the priest and offer the sacrifices that Moses commanded for your cleansing, as a testimony to them."

15 Yet the news about him spread all the more, so that crowds of people came to hear him and to be healed of their sicknesses. 16 But Jesus often withdrew to lonely places and prayed.

Jesus Heals a Paralytic

17 One day as he was teaching, Pharisees and teachers of the law, who had come from every village of Galilee and from Judea and Jerusalem, were sitting there. And the power of the Lord was present for him to heal the sick. 18 Some men came carrying a paralytic on a mat and tried to take him into the house to lay him before Jesus. 19 When they could not find a way to do this because of the crowd, they went up on the roof and lowered him on his mat through the tiles into the middle of the crowd, right in front of Jesus.

20 When Jesus saw their faith, he said, "Friend, your sins are forgiven."

21 The Pharisees and the teachers of the law began thinking to themsel-

---

ˣ 1 That is, Sea of Galilee   *ʸ 4* The Greek verb is plural.   *ᶻ 12* The Greek word was used for various diseases affecting the skin — not necessarily leprosy.

ves, "Who is this fellow who speaks blasphemy? Who can forgive sins but God alone?"

22 Jesus knew what they were thinking and asked, "Why are you thinking these things in your hearts? **23** Which is easier: to say, 'Your sins are forgiven,' or to say, 'Get up and walk'? **24** But that you may know that the Son of Man has authority on earth to forgive sins...." He said to the paralyzed man, "I tell you, get up, take your mat and go home." **25** Immediately he stood up in front of them, took what he had been lying on and went home praising God. **26** Everyone was amazed and gave praise to God. They were filled with awe and said, "We have seen remarkable things today."

The Calling of Levi

27 After this, Jesus went out and saw a tax collector by the name of Levi sitting at his tax booth. "Follow me," Jesus said to him, **28** and Levi got up, left everything and followed him.

29 Then Levi held a great banquet for Jesus at his house, and a large crowd of tax collectors and others were eating with them. **30** But the Pharisees and the teachers of the law who belonged to their sect complained to his disciples, "Why do you eat and drink with tax collectors and 'sinners'?"

31 Jesus answered them, "It is not the healthy who need a doctor, but the sick. **32** I have not come to call the righteous, but sinners to repentance."

Jesus Questioned About Fasting

33 They said to him, "John's disciples often fast and pray, and so do the disciples of the Pharisees, but yours go on eating and drinking."

34 Jesus answered, "Can you make the guests of the bridegroom fast while he is with them? **35** But the time will come when the bridegroom will be taken from them; in those days they will fast."

36 He told them this parable: "No one tears a patch from a new garment and sews it on an old one. If he does, he will have torn the new garment, and the patch from the new will not match the old. **37** And no one pours new wine into old wineskins If he does, the new wine will burst the skins, the wine will run out and the wineskins will be ruined. **38** No new wine must be poured into new wineskins. **39** And no one after drinking old wine wants the new, for he says, 'The old is better.'"

Lord of the Sabbath

6 **1** One Sabbath Jesus was going through the grainfields, and his disciples began to pick some heads of grain, rub them in their hands and eat the kernels. **2** Some of the Pharisees asked, "Why are you doing what is unlawful on the Sabbath?"

3 Jesus answered them, "Have you never read what David did when he and his companions were hungry? **4** He entered the house of God, and taking the consecrated bread, he ate what is lawful only for priests to eat. And he also gave some to his companions." **5** Then Jesus said to them, "The Son of Man is Lord of the Sabbath."

6 On another Sabbath he went into the synagogue and was teaching and a man was there whose right hand was shriveled. **7** The Pharisee and the teachers of the law were looking for a reason to accuse Jesus so they watched him closely to see if he would heal on the Sabbath. **8** But Jesus knew what they were thinkin and said to the man with the shriveled hand, "Get up and stand in front of everyone." So he got up and stood there.

9 Then Jesus said to them, "I ask you, which is lawful on the Sabbath: to do good or to do evil, to save life or to destroy it?"

10 He looked around at them all, and then said to the man, "Stretch out your hand." He did so, and his hand was completely restored. **11** But they were furious and began to discuss with one another what they might do to Jesus.

The Twelve Apostles

12 One of those days Jesus went out to a mountainside to pray, and spent the night praying to God. **13** When morning came, he called his disciples to him and chose twelve of them, whom he also designated apostles: **14** Simon (whom he named Peter), his brother Andrew, James, John, Philip, Bartholomew, **15** Matthew, Thomas, James son of Alphaeus, Simon who was called the Zealot, **16** Judas son of James, and Judas Iscariot, who became a traitor.

Blessings and Woes

17 He went down with them and stood on a level place. A large crowd of his disciples was there and a great number of people from all over Judea, from Jerusalem, and from the coast of Tyre and Sidon, **18** who had come to hear him and to be healed of their diseases. Those troubled by evil*a* spirits were cured, **19** and the people all tried to touch him, because power was coming from him and healing them all.

20 Looking at his disciples, he said:

"Blessed are you who are poor,
for yours is the kingdom of God.
21 Blessed are you who hunger now,
for you will be satisfied.
Blessed are you who weep now,
for you will laugh.
22 Blessed are you when men hate you,
when they exclude you and insult you
and reject your name as evil,
because of the Son of Man.

23 "Rejoice in that day and leap for joy, because great is your reward in heaven. For that is how their fathers treated the prophets.

24 "But woe to you who are rich,
for you have already received your comfort.
25 Woe to you who are well fed now,
for you will go hungry.
Woe to you who laugh now,
for you will mourn and weep.
26 Woe to you when all men speak well of you,
for that is how their fathers treated the false prophets.

Love for Enemies

27 "But I tell you who hear me: Love your enemies, do good to those who hate you, **28** bless those who curse you, pray for those who mistreat you. **29** If someone strikes you on one cheek, turn to him the other also. If someone takes your cloak, do not stop him from taking your tunic. **30** Give to everyone who asks you, and if anyone takes what belongs to you, do not demand it

a 18 Greek *unclean*

back. 31 Do to others as you would have them do to you.

32 "If you love those who love you, what credit is that to you? Even 'sinners' love those who love them. 33 And if you do good to those who are good to you, what credit is that to you? Even 'sinners' do that. 34 And if you lend to those from whom you expect repayment, what credit is that to you? Even 'sinners' lend to 'sinners,' expecting to be repaid in full. 35 But love your enemies, do good to them, and lend to them without expecting to get anything back. Then your reward will be great, and you will be sons of the Most High, because he is kind to the ungrateful and wicked. 36 Be merciful, just as your Father is merciful.

Judging Others

37 "Do not judge, and you will not be judged. Do not condemn, and you will not be condemned. Forgive, and you will be forgiven. 38 Give, and it will be given to you. A good measure, pressed down, shaken together and running over, will be poured into your lap. For with the measure you use, it will be measured to you."

39 He also told them this parable: "Can a blind man lead a blind man? Will they not both fall into a pit? 40 A student is not above his teacher, but everyone who is fully trained will be like his teacher.

41 "Why do you look at the speck of sawdust in your brother's eye and pay no attention to the plank in your own eye? 42 How can you say to your brother, 'Brother, let me take the speck out of your eye,' when you yourself fail to see the plank in your own eye? You hypocrite, first take the plank out of your eye, and then you will see clearly to remove the speck from your brother's eye.

A Tree and Its Fruit

43 "No good tree bears bad fruit, nor does a bad tree bear good fruit. 44 Each tree is recognized by its own fruit. People do not pick figs from thornbushes, or grapes from briers. 45 The good man brings good thing out of the good stored up in his heart and the evil man brings evil thing out of the evil stored up in his heart. For out of the overflow of his hear his mouth speaks.

The Wise and Foolish Builders

46 "Why do you call me, 'Lord, Lord,' and do not do what I say? 47 I will show you what he is like who comes to me and hears my words and puts them into practice. 48 He is like a man building a house, who dug down deep and laid the foundation on rock. When a flood came, the torrent struck that house but could not shake it, because it was well built. 49 But the one who hears my words and does not put them into practice is like a man who built a house on the ground without a foundation. The moment the torrent struck that house, it collapsed and its destruction was complete.

The Faith of the Centurion

7 1 When Jesus had finished saying all this in the hearing of the people, he entered Capernaum. 2 There a centurion's servant, whom his master valued highly, was sick and about to die. 3 The centurion heard of Jesus and sent some elders of the Jew to him, asking him to come and heal his servant. 4 When they came to Jesus, they pleaded earnestly with him, "This man deserves to have you do this, 5 because he loves our nation and has built our synagogue." 6 So Jesus went with them.

He was not far from the house when the centurion sent friends to say to him: "Lord, don't trouble yourself, for I do not deserve to have you come under my roof. 7 That is why I did not even consider myself worthy to come to you. But say the word, and my servant will be healed. 8 For I myself am a man under authority, with soldiers under me. I tell this one, 'Go,' and he goes; and that one, 'Come,' and he comes. I say to my servant, 'Do this,' and he does it."

9 When Jesus heard this, he was amazed at him, and turning to the crowd following him, he said, "I tell you, I have not found such great faith even in Israel." 10 Then the men who had been sent returned to the house and found the servant well.

Jesus Raises a Widow's Son

11 Soon afterward, Jesus went to a town called Nain, and his disciples and a large crowd went along with him. 12 As he approached the town gate, a dead person was being carried out—the only son of his mother, and she was a widow. And a large crowd from the town was with her. 13 When the Lord saw her, his heart went out to her and he said, "Don't cry."

14 Then he went up and touched the coffin, and those carrying it stood still. He said, "Young man, I say to you, get up!" 15 The dead man sat up and began to talk, and Jesus gave him back to his mother.

16 They were all filled with awe and praised God. "A great prophet has appeared among us," they said. "God has come to help his people."

17 This news about Jesus spread throughout Judea[b] and the surrounding country.

Jesus and John the Baptist

18 John's disciples told him about all these things. Calling two of them, 19 he sent them to the Lord to ask, "Are you the one who was to come, or should we expect someone else?"

20 When the men came to Jesus, they said, "John the Baptist sent us to you to ask, 'Are you the one who was to come, or should we expect someone else?'"

21 At that very time Jesus cured many who had diseases, sicknesses and evil spirits, and gave sight to many who were blind. 22 So he replied to the messengers, "Go back and report to John what you have seen and heard: The blind receive sight, the lame walk, those who have leprosy[c] are cured, the deaf hear, the dead are raised, and the good news is preached to the poor. 23 Blessed is the man who does not fall away on account of me."

24 After John's messengers left, Jesus began to speak to the crowd about John: "What did you go out into the desert to see? A reed swayed by the wind? 25 If not, what did you go out to see? A man dressed in fine clothes? No, those who wear expensive clothes and indulge in luxury are in palaces. 26 But what did you go out to see? A prophet? Yes, I tell you, and more than a prophet. 27 This is the one about whom it is written:

" 'I will send my messenger ahead
        of you,
    who will prepare your way
        before you.'[d]

---

b 17 Or the land of the Jews   c 22 The Greek word was used for various diseases affecting the skin—not necessarily leprosy.   d 27 Mal. 3:1

28 I tell you, among those born of women there is no one greater than John; yet the one who is least in the kingdom of God is greater than he."

29 (All the people, even the tax collectors, when they heard Jesus' words, acknowledged that God's way was right, because they had been baptized by John. 30 But the Pharisees and experts in the law rejected God's purpose for themselves, because they had not been baptized by John.)

31 "To what, then, can I compare the people of this generation? What are they like? 32 They are like children sitting in the marketplace and calling out to each other:

" 'We played the flute for you,
    and you did not dance;
we sang a dirge,
    and you did not cry.'

33 For John the Baptist came neither eating bread nor drinking wine, and you say, 'He has a demon.' 34 The Son of Man came eating and drinking, and you say, 'Here is a glutton and a drunkard, a friend of tax collectors and "sinners." ' 35 But wisdom is proved right by all her children."

Jesus Anointed by a Sinful Woman

36 Now one of the Pharisees invited Jesus to have dinner with him, so he went to the Pharisee's house and reclined at the table. 37 When a woman who had lived a sinful life in that town learned that Jesus was eating at the Pharisee's house, she brought an alabaster jar of perfume, 38 and as she stood behind him at his feet weeping, she began to wet his feet with her tears. Then she wiped them with her hair,

kissed them and poured perfume on them.

39 When the Pharisee who had invited him saw this, he said to himself, "If this man were a prophet, he would know who is touching him and what kind of woman she is — that she is a sinner."

40 Jesus answered him, "Simon, I have something to tell you."

"Tell me, teacher," he said.

41 "Two men owed money to a certain moneylender. One owed him five hundred denarii,[e] and the other fifty. 42 Neither of them had the money to pay him back, so he canceled the debts of both. Now which of them will love him more?"

43 Simon replied, "I suppose the one who had the bigger debt canceled."

"You have judged correctly," Jesus said.

44 Then he turned toward the woman and said to Simon, "Do you see this woman? I came into your house. You did not give me any water for my feet, but she wet my feet with her tears and wiped them with her hair. 45 You did not give me a kiss, but this woman, from the time I entered, has not stopped kissing my feet. 46 You did not put oil on my head, but she has poured perfume on my feet. 47 Therefore, I tell you, her many sins have been forgiven — for she loved much. But he who has been forgiven little loves little."

48 Then Jesus said to her, "Your sins are forgiven."

49 The other guests began to say among themselves, "Who is this who even forgives sins?"

50 Jesus said to the woman, "Your faith has saved you; go in peace."

e 41 A denarius was a coin worth about a day's wages.

The Parable of the Sower

8 ¹ After this, Jesus traveled about from one town and village to another, proclaiming the good news of the kingdom of God. The Twelve were with him, ² and also some women who had been cured of evil spirits and diseases: Mary (called Magdalene) from whom seven demons had come out; ³ Joanna the wife of Cuza, the manager of Herod's household; Susanna; and many others. These women were helping to support them out of their own means.

⁴ While a large crowd was gathering and people were coming to Jesus from town after town, he told this parable: ⁵ "A farmer went out to sow his seed. As he was scattering the seed, some fell along the path; it was trampled on, and the birds of the air ate it up. ⁶ Some fell on rock, and when it came up, the plants withered because they had no moisture. ⁷ Other seed fell among thorns, which grew up with it and choked the plants. ⁸ Still other seed fell on good soil. It came up and yielded a crop, a hundred times more than was sown."

When he said this, he called out, "He who has ears to hear, let him hear."

⁹ His disciples asked him what this parable meant. ¹⁰ He said, "The knowledge of the secrets of the kingdom of God has been given to you, but to others I speak in parables, so that,

"'though seeing, they may not
        see;
    though hearing, they may not
        understand.'ᶠ

¹¹ "This is the meaning of the parable: The seed is the word of God. ¹² Those along the path are the ones who hear, and then the devil comes and takes away the word from their hearts, so that they may not believe and be saved. ¹³ Those on the rock are the ones who receive the word with joy when they hear it, but they have no root. They believe for a while, but in the time of testing they fall away. ¹⁴ The seed that fell among thorns stands for those who hear, but as they go on their way they are choked by life's worries, riches and pleasures, and they do not mature. ¹⁵ But the seed on good soil stands for those with a noble and good heart, who hear the word, retain it, and by persevering produce a crop.

A Lamp on a Stand

¹⁶ "No one lights a lamp and hides it in a jar or puts it under a bed. Instead, he puts it on a stand, so that those who come in can see the light. ¹⁷ For there is nothing hidden that will not be disclosed, and nothing concealed that will not be known or brought out into the open. ¹⁸ Therefore consider carefully how you listen. Whoever has will be given more; whoever does not have, even what he thinks he has will be taken from him."

Jesus' Mother and Brother

¹⁹ Now Jesus' mother and brothers came to see him, but they were not able to get near him because of the crowd. ²⁰ Someone told him, "Your mother and brothers are standing outside, wanting to see you."

²¹ He replied, "My mother and brothers are those who hear God's word and put it into practice."

ᶠ 10 Isaiah 6:9

Jesus Calms the Storm

22 One day Jesus said to his disciples, "Let's go over to the other side of the lake." So they got into a boat and set out. **23** As they sailed, he fell asleep. A squall came down on the lake, so that the boat was being swamped, and they were in great danger.

24 The disciples went and woke him, saying, "Master, Master, we're going to drown!"

He got up and rebuked the wind and the raging waters; the storm subsided, and all was calm. **25** "Where is your faith?" he asked his disciples.

In fear and amazement they asked one another, "Who is this? He commands even the winds and the water, and they obey him."

The Healing of a Demon-possessed Man

26 They sailed to the region of the Gerasenes,*g* which is across the lake from Galilee. **27** When Jesus stepped ashore, he was met by a demon-possessed man from the town. For a long time this man had not worn clothes or lived in a house, but had lived in the tombs. **28** When he saw Jesus, he cried out and fell at his feet, shouting at the top of his voice, "What do you want with me, Jesus, Son of the Most High God? I beg you, don't torture me!" **29** For Jesus had commanded the evil*h* spirit to come out of the man. Many times it had seized him, and though he was chained hand and foot and kept under guard, he had broken his chains and had been driven by the demon into solitary places.

30 Jesus asked him, "What is your name?"

"Legion," he replied, because many demons had gone into him. **31** And they begged him repeatedly not to order them to go into the Abyss.

32 A large herd of pigs was feeding there on the hillside. The demons begged Jesus to let them go into them, and he gave them permission. **33** When the demons came out of the man, they went into the pigs, and the herd rushed down the steep bank into the lake and was drowned.

34 When those tending the pigs saw what had happened, they ran off and reported this in the town and countryside, **35** and the people went out to see what had happened. When they came to Jesus, they found the man from whom the demons had gone out, sitting at Jesus' feet, dressed and in his right mind; and they were afraid. **36** Those who had seen it told the people how the demon-possessed man had been cured. **37** Then all the people of the region of the Gerasenes asked Jesus to leave them, because they were overcome with fear. So he got into the boat and left.

38 The man from whom the demons had gone out begged to go with him, but Jesus sent him away, saying, **39** "Return home and tell how much God has done for you." So the man went away and told all over town how much Jesus had done for him.

A Dead Girl and a Sick Woman

40 Now when Jesus returned, a crowd welcomed him, for they were

---

g 26 Some manuscripts *Gadarenes*; other manuscripts *Gergesenes*; also in verse 37
h 29 Greek *unclean*

all expecting him. **41** Then a man named Jairus, a ruler of the synagogue, came and fell at Jesus' feet, pleading with him to come to his house **42** because his only daughter, a girl of about twelve, was dying.

As Jesus was on his way, the crowds almost crushed him. **43** And a woman was there who had been subject to bleeding for twelve years,*ⁱ* but no one could heal her. **44** She came up behind him and touched the edge of his cloak, and immediately her bleeding stopped.

45 "Who touched me?" Jesus asked.

When they all denied it, Peter said, "Master, the people are crowding and pressing against you."

46 But Jesus said, "Someone touched me; I know that power has gone out from me."

47 Then the woman, seeing that she could not go unnoticed, came trembling and fell at his feet. In the presence of all the people, she told why she had touched him and how she had been instantly healed. **48** Then he said to her, "Daughter, your faith has healed you. Go in peace."

49 While Jesus was still speaking, someone came from the house of Jairus, the synagogue ruler. "Your daughter is dead," he said. "Don't bother the teacher any more."

50 Hearing this, Jesus said to Jairus, "Don't be afraid; just believe, and she will be healed."

51 When he arrived at the house of Jairus, he did not let anyone go in with him except Peter, John and James, and the child's father and mother. **52** Meanwhile, all the people were wailing and mourning for her.

"Stop wailing," Jesus said. "She is not dead but asleep."

53 They laughed at him, knowing that she was dead. **54** But he took her by the hand and said, "My child, get up!" **55** Her spirit returned, and at once she stood up. Then Jesus told them to give her something to eat. **56** Her parents were astonished, but he ordered them not to tell anyone what had happened.

Jesus Sends Out the Twelve

9 **1** When Jesus had called the Twelve together, he gave them power and authority to drive out all demons and to cure diseases, **2** and he sent them out to preach the kingdom of God and to heal the sick. **3** He told them: "Take nothing for the journey—no staff, no bag, no bread, no money, no extra tunic. **4** Whatever house you enter, stay there until you leave that town. **5** If people do not welcome you, shake the dust off your feet when you leave their town, as a testimony against them." **6** So they set out and went from village to village, preaching the gospel and healing people everywhere.

7 Now Herod the tetrarch heard about all that was going on. And he was perplexed, because some were saying that John had been raised from the dead, **8** others that Elijah had appeared, and still others that one of the prophets of long ago had come back to life. **9** But Herod said, "I beheaded John. Who, then, is this I hear such things about?" And he tried to see him.

Jesus Feeds the Five Thousand

10 When the apostles returned, they reported to Jesus what they had

---

i **43** Many manuscripts *years, and she had spent all she had on doctors*

done. Then he took them with him and they withdrew by themselves to a town called Bethsaida, 11 but the crowds learned about it and followed him. He welcomed them and spoke to them about the kingdom of God, and healed those who needed healing.

12 Late in the afternoon the Twelve came to him and said, "Send the crowd away so they can go to the surrounding villages and countryside and find food and lodging, because we are in a remote place here."

13 He replied, "You give them something to eat."

They answered, "We have only five loaves of bread and two fish—unless we go and buy food for all this crowd." 14 (About five thousand men were there.)

But he said to his disciples, "Have them sit down in groups of about fifty each." 15 The disciples did so, and everybody sat down. 16 Taking the five loaves and the two fish and looking up to heaven, he gave thanks and broke them. Then he gave them to the disciples to set before the people. 17 They all ate and were satisfied, and the disciples picked up twelve basketfuls of broken pieces that were left over.

Peter's Confession of Christ

18 Once when Jesus was praying in private and his disciples were with him, he asked them, "Who do the crowds say I am?"

19 They replied, "Some say John the Baptist; others say Elijah; and still others, that one of the prophets of long ago has come back to life."

20 "But what about you?" he asked. "Who do you say I am?"

Peter answered, "The Christ⍳ of God."

21 Jesus strictly warned them not to tell this to anyone. 22 And he said, "The Son of Man must suffer many things and be rejected by the elders, chief priests and teachers of the law, and he must be killed and on the third day be raised to life."

23 Then he said to them all: "If anyone would come after me, he must deny himself and take up his cross daily and follow me. 24 For whoever wants to save his life will lose it, but whoever loses his life for me will save it. 25 What good is it for a man to gain the whole world, and yet lose or forfeit his very self? 26 If anyone is ashamed of me and my words, the Son of Man will be ashamed of him when he comes in his glory and in the glory of the Father and of the holy angels. 27 I tell you the truth, some who are standing here will not taste death before they see the kingdom of God."

The Transfiguration

28 About eight days after Jesus said this, he took Peter, John and James with him and went up onto a mountain to pray. 29 As he was praying, the appearance of his face changed, and his clothes became as bright as a flash of lightning. 30 Two men, Moses and Elijah, 31 appeared in glorious splendor, talking with Jesus. They spoke about his departure, which he was about to bring to fulfillment at Jerusalem. 32 Peter and his companions were very sleepy, but when they became fully awake, they saw his glory and the two men standing with him. 33 As the men were leaving Jesus, Peter

said to him, "Master, it is good for us to be here. Let us put up three shelters—one for you, one for Moses and one for Elijah." (He did not know what he was saying.)

34 While he was speaking, a cloud appeared and enveloped them, and they were afraid as they entered the cloud. 35 A voice came from the cloud, saying, "This is my Son, whom I have chosen; listen to him." 36 When the voice had spoken, they found that Jesus was alone. The disciples kept this to themselves, and told no one at that time what they had seen.

The Healing of a Boy With an Evil Spirit

37 The next day, when they came down from the mountain, a large crowd met him. 38 A man in the crowd called out, "Teacher, I beg you to look at my son, for he is my only child. 39 A spirit seizes him and he suddenly screams; it throws him into convulsions so that he foams at the mouth. It scarcely ever leaves him and is destroying him. 40 I begged your disciples to drive it out, but they could not."

41 "O unbelieving and perverse generation," Jesus replied, "how long shall I stay with you and put up with you? Bring your son here."

42 Even while the boy was coming, the demon threw him to the ground in a convulsion. But Jesus rebuked the evil[k] spirit, healed the boy and gave him back to his father. 43 And they were all amazed at the greatness of God.

While everyone was marveling at all that Jesus did, he said to his disciples, 44 "Listen carefully to what I am about to tell you: The Son of Man is going to be betrayed into the hands of men." 45 But they did not understand what this meant. It was hidden from them, so that they did not grasp it, and they were afraid to ask him about it.

Who Will Be the Greatest

46 An argument started among the disciples as to which of them would be the greatest. 47 Jesus, knowing their thoughts, took a little child and had him stand beside him. 48 Then he said to them, "Whoever welcomes this little child in my name welcomes me; and whoever welcomes me welcomes the one who sent me. For he who is least among you all—he is the greatest."

49 "Master," said John, "we saw a man driving out demons in your name and we tried to stop him, because he is not one of us."

50 "Do not stop him," Jesus said, "for whoever is not against you is for you."

Samaritan Opposition

51 As the time approached for him to be taken up to heaven, Jesus resolutely set out for Jerusalem. 52 And he sent messengers on ahead, who went into a Samaritan village to get things ready for him; 53 but the people there did not welcome him, because he was heading for Jerusalem. 54 When the disciples James and John saw this, they asked, "Lord, do you want us to call fire down from heaven to destroy them[l]?" 55 But Jesus turned and rebuked them, 56 and[m] they went to another village.

---

k 42 Greek unclean   l 54 Some manuscripts them, even as Elijah did   m 55,56 Some manuscripts them. And he said, "You do not know what kind of spirit you are of, for the Son of Man did not come to destroy men's lives, but to save them." 56 And

The Cost of Following Jesus

57 As they were walking along the road, a man said to him, "I will follow you wherever you go."

58 Jesus replied, "Foxes have holes and birds of the air have nests, but the Son of Man has no place to lay his head."

59 He said to another man, "Follow me."

But the man replied, "Lord, first let me go and bury my father."

60 Jesus said to him, "Let the dead bury their own dead, but you go and proclaim the kingdom of God."

61 Still another said, "I will follow you, Lord; but first let me go back and say good-by to my family."

62 Jesus replied, "No one who puts his hand to the plow and looks back is fit for service in the kingdom of God."

Jesus Sends Out the Seventy-two

10 **1** After this the Lord appointed seventy-two[n] others and sent them two by two ahead of him to every town and place where he was about to go. **2** He told them, "The harvest is plentiful, but the workers are few. Ask the Lord of the harvest, therefore, to send out workers into his harvest field. **3** Go! I am sending you out like lambs among wolves. **4** Do not take a purse or bag or sandals; and do not greet anyone on the road.

5 "When you enter a house, first say, 'Peace to this house.' **6** If a man of peace is there, your peace will rest on him; if not, it will return to you. **7** Stay in that house, eating and drinking whatever they give you, for the worker deserves his wages. Do not move around from house to house.

8 "When you enter a town and are welcomed, eat what is set before you. **9** Heal the sick who are there and tell them, 'The kingdom of God is near you.' **10** But when you enter a town and are not welcomed, go into its streets and say, **11** 'Even the dust of your town that sticks to our feet we wipe off against you. Yet be sure of this: The kingdom of God is near.' **12** I tell you, it will be more bearable on that day for Sodom than for that town.

13 "Woe to you, Korazin! Woe to you, Bethsaida! For if the miracles that were performed in you had been performed in Tyre and Sidon, they would have repented long ago, sitting in sackcloth and ashes. **14** But it will be more bearable for Tyre and Sidon at the judgment than for you. **15** And you, Capernaum, will you be lifted up to the skies? No, you will go down to the depths.[o]

16 "He who listens to you listens to me; he who rejects you rejects me; but he who rejects me rejects him who sent me."

17 The seventy-two returned with joy and said, "Lord, even the demons submit to us in your name."

18 He replied, "I saw Satan fall like lightning from heaven. **19** I have given you authority to trample on snakes and scorpions and to overcome all the power of the enemy; nothing will harm you. **20** However, do not rejoice that the spirits submit to you, but rejoice that your names are written in heaven."

21 At that time Jesus, full of joy through the Holy Spirit, said, "I praise you, Father, Lord of heaven

---

[n] *1* Some manuscripts *seventy*; also in verse 17   [o] *15* Greek *Hades*

and earth, because you have hidden these things from the wise and learned, and revealed them to little children. Yes, Father, for this was your good pleasure.

22 "All things have been committed to me by my Father. No one knows who the Son is except the Father, and no one knows who the Father is except the Son and those to whom the Son chooses to reveal him."

23 Then he turned to his disciples and said privately, "Blessed are the eyes that see what you see. 24 For I tell you that many prophets and kings wanted to see what you see but did not see it, and to hear what you hear but did not hear it."

The Parable of the Good Samaritan

25 On one occasion an expert in the law stood up to test Jesus. "Teacher," he asked, "what must I do to inherit eternal life?"

26 "What is written in the Law?" he replied. "How do you read it?"

27 He answered: " 'Love the Lord your God with all your heart and with all your soul and with all your strength and with all your mind'ᵖ; and, 'Love your neighbor as yourself.'ᵠ"

28 "You have answered correctly," Jesus replied. "Do this and you will live."

29 But he wanted to justify himself, so he asked Jesus, "And who is my neighbor?"

30 In reply Jesus said: "A man was going down from Jerusalem to Jericho, when he fell into the hands of robbers. They stripped him of his clothes, beat him and went away, leaving him half dead. 31 A priest happened to be going down the same road, and when he saw the man, he passed by on the other side. 32 So too, a Levite, when he came to the place and saw him, passed by on the other side. 33 But a Samaritan, as he traveled, came where the man was; and when he saw him, he took pity on him. 34 He went to him and bandaged his wounds, pouring on oil and wine. Then he put the man on his own donkey, took him to an inn and took care of him. 35 The next day he took out two silver coinsʳ and gave them to the innkeeper. 'Look after him,' he said, 'and when I return, I will reimburse you for any extra expense you may have.'

36 "Which of these three do you think was a neighbor to the man who fell into the hands of robbers?"

37 The expert in the law replied, "The one who had mercy on him."

Jesus told him, "Go and do likewise."

At the Home of Martha and Mary

38 As Jesus and his disciples were on their way, he came to a village where a woman named Martha opened her home to him. 39 She had a sister called Mary, who sat at the Lord's feet listening to what he said. 40 But Martha was distracted by all the preparations that had to be made. She came to him and asked, "Lord, don't you care that my sister has left me to do the work by myself? Tell her to help me!"

41 "Martha, Martha," the Lord answered, "you are worried and upset about many things, 42 but only one thing is needed.ˢ Mary has chosen what is better, and it will not be taken away from her."

ᵖ 27 Deut. 6:5   ᵠ 27 Lev. 19:18   ʳ 35 Greek *two denarii*   ˢ 42 Some manuscripts *but few things are needed—or only one*

Jesus' Teaching on Prayer

11 1 One day Jesus was praying in a certain place. When he finished, one of his disciples said to him, "Lord, teach us to pray, just as John taught his disciples."

2 He said to them, "When you pray, say:

" 'Father,[t]
hallowed be your name,
    your kingdom come.[u]
3 Give us each day our daily bread.
4 Forgive us our sins,
    for we also forgive everyone
        who sins against us.[v]
And lead us not into
        temptation.[w] ' "

5 Then he said to them, "Suppose one of you has a friend, and he goes to him at midnight and says, 'Friend, lend me three loaves of bread, 6 because a friend of mine on a journey has come to me, and I have nothing to set before him.'

7 "Then the one inside answers, 'Don't bother me. The door is already locked, and my children are with me in bed. I can't get up and give you anything.' 8 I tell you, though he will not get up and give him the bread because he is his friend, yet because of the man's boldness[x] he will get up and give him as much as he needs.

9 "So I say to you: Ask and it will be given to you; seek and you will find; knock and the door will be opened to you. 10 For everyone who asks receives; he who seeks finds; and to him who knocks, the door will be opened.

11 "Which of you fathers, if your son asks for a fish, will give him a snake instead? 12 Or if he asks for an egg, will give him a scorpion? 13 If you then, though you are evil, know how to give good gifts to your children, how much more will your Father in heaven give the Holy Spirit to those who ask him!"

Jesus and Beelzebub

14 Jesus was driving out a demon that was mute. When the demon left, the man who had been mute spoke, and the crowd was amazed. 15 But some of them said, "By Beelzebub,[z] the prince of demons, he is driving out demons." 16 Others tested him by asking for a sign from heaven.

17 Jesus knew their thoughts and said to them: "Any kingdom divided against itself will be ruined, and a house divided against itself will fall. 18 If Satan is divided against himself, how can his kingdom stand? I say this because you claim that I drive out demons by Beelzebub. 19 Now if I drive out demons by Beelzebub, by whom do your followers drive them out? So then, they will be your judges. 20 But if I drive out demons by the finger of God, then the kingdom of God has come to you.

21 "When a strong man, fully armed, guards his own house, his possessions are safe. 22 But when someone stronger attacks and overpowers him, he takes away the armor in which the man trusted and divides up the spoils.

---

t 2 Some manuscripts *Our Father in heaven*   u 2 Some manuscripts *come. May your will be done on earth as it is in heaven.*   v 4 Greek *everyone who is indebted to us*   w 4 Some manuscripts *temptation but deliver us from the evil one*   x 8 Or *persistence*   y 11 Some manuscripts *for bread, will give him a stone; or if he asks for*   z 15 Greek *Beezeboul* or *Beelzeboul*; also in verses 18 and 19

23 "He who is not with me is against me, and he who does not gather with me, scatters.

24 "When an evil[a] spirit comes out of a man, it goes through arid places seeking rest and does not find it. Then it says, 'I will return to the house I left.' 25 When it arrives, it finds the house swept clean and put in order. 26 Then it goes and takes seven other spirits more wicked than itself, and they go in and live there. And the final condition of that man is worse than the first."

27 As Jesus was saying these things, a woman in the crowd called out, "Blessed is the mother who gave you birth and nursed you."

28 He replied, "Blessed rather are those who hear the word of God and obey it."

The Sign of Jonah

29 As the crowds increased, Jesus said, "This is a wicked generation. It asks for a miraculous sign, but none will be given it except the sign of Jonah. 30 For as Jonah was a sign to the Ninevites, so also will the Son of Man be to this generation. 31 The Queen of the South will rise at the judgment with the men of this generation and condemn them; for she came from the ends of the earth to listen to Solomon's wisdom, and now one[b] greater than Solomon is here. 32 The men of Nineveh will stand up at the judgment with this generation and condemn it; for they repented at the preaching of Jonah, and now one greater than Jonah is here.

The Lamp of the Body

33 "No one lights a lamp and puts it in a place where it will be hidden, or under a bowl. Instead he puts it on its stand, so that those who come in may see the light. 34 Your eye is the lamp of your body. When your eyes are good, your whole body also is full of light. But when they are bad, your body also is full of darkness. 35 See to it, then, that the light within you is not darkness. 36 Therefore, if your whole body is full of light, and no part of it dark, it will be completely lighted, as when the light of a lamp shines on you."

Six Woes

37 When Jesus had finished speaking, a Pharisee invited him to eat with him; so he went in and reclined at the table. 38 But the Pharisee, noticing that Jesus did not first wash before the meal, was surprised.

39 Then the Lord said to him, "Now then, you Pharisees clean the outside of the cup and dish, but inside you are full of greed and wickedness. 40 You foolish people! Did not the one who made the outside make the inside also? 41 But give what is inside the dish[c] to the poor, and everything will be clean for you.

42 "Woe to you Pharisees, because you give God a tenth of your mint, rue and all other kinds of garden herbs, but you neglect justice and the love of God. You should have practiced the latter without leaving the former undone.

43 "Woe to you Pharisees, because you love the most important seats in the synagogues and greetings in the marketplaces.

44 "Woe to you, because you are like unmarked graves, which men walk over without knowing it."

---

a 24 Greek unclean   b 31 Or something; also in verse 32   c 41 Or what you have

45 One of the experts in the law answered him, "Teacher, when you say these things, you insult us also."

46 Jesus replied, "And you experts in the law, woe to you, because you load people down with burdens they can hardly carry, and you yourselves will not lift one finger to help them.

47 "Woe to you, because you build tombs for the prophets, and it was your forefathers who killed them. 48 So you testify that you approve of what your forefathers did; they killed the prophets, and you build their tombs. 49 Because of this, God in his wisdom said, 'I will send them prophets and apostles, some of whom they will kill and others they will persecute.' 50 Therefore this generation will be held responsible for the blood of all the prophets that has been shed since the beginning of the world, 51 from the blood of Abel to the blood of Zechariah, who was killed between the altar and the sanctuary. Yes, I tell you, this generation will be held responsible for it all.

52 "Woe to you experts in the law, because you have taken away the key to knowledge. You yourselves have not entered, and you have hindered those who were entering."

53 When Jesus left there, the Pharisees and the teachers of the law began to oppose him fiercely and to besiege him with questions, 54 waiting to catch him in something he might say.

Warnings and Encouragements

12 1 Meanwhile, when a crowd of many thousands had gathered, so that they were trampling on one another, Jesus began to speak first to his disciples, saying:

"Be on your guard against the yeast of the Pharisees, which is hypocrisy. 2 There is nothing concealed that will not be disclosed, or hidden that will not be made known. 3 What you have said in the dark will be heard in the daylight, and what you have whispered in the ear in the inner rooms will be proclaimed from the roofs.

4 "I tell you, my friends, do not be afraid of those who kill the body and after that can do no more. 5 But I will show you whom you should fear: Fear him who, after the killing of the body, has power to throw you into hell. Yes, I tell you, fear him. 6 Are not five sparrows sold for two penniesᵈ? Yet not one of them is forgotten by God. 7 Indeed, the very hairs of your head are all numbered. Don't be afraid; you are worth more than many sparrows.

8 "I tell you, whoever acknowledges me before men, the Son of Man will also acknowledge him before the angels of God. 9 But he who disowns me before men will be disowned before the angels of God. 10 And everyone who speaks a word against the Son of Man will be forgiven, but anyone who blasphemes against the Holy Spirit will not be forgiven.

11 "When you are brought before synagogues, rulers and authorities, do not worry about how you will defend yourselves or what you will say, 12 for the Holy Spirit will teach you at that time what you should say."

The Parable of the Rich Fool

13 Someone in the crowd said to him, "Teacher, tell my brother to divide the inheritance with me."

ᵈ 6 Greek two assaria

14 Jesus replied, "Man, who appointed me a judge or an arbiter between you?" 15 Then he said to them, "Watch out! Be on your guard against all kinds of greed; a man's life does not consist in the abundance of his possessions."

16 And he told them this parable: "The ground of a certain rich man produced a good crop. 17 He thought to himself, 'What shall I do? I have no place to store my crops.'

18 "Then he said, 'This is what I'll do. I will tear down my barns and build bigger ones, and there I will store all my grain and my goods. 19 And I'll say to myself, "You have plenty of good things laid up for many years. Take life easy; eat, drink and be merry."'

20 "But God said to him, 'You fool! This very night your life will be demanded from you. Then who will get what you have prepared for yourself?'

21 "This is how it will be with anyone who stores up things for himself but is not rich toward God."

Do Not Worry

22 Then Jesus said to his disciples: "Therefore I tell you, do not worry about your life, what you will eat; or about your body, what you will wear. 23 Life is more than food, and the body more than clothes. 24 Consider the ravens: They do not sow or reap, they have no storeroom or barn; yet God feeds them. And how much more valuable you are than birds! 25 Who of you by worrying can add a single hour to his life^e? 26 Since you cannot do this very little thing, why do you worry about the rest?

27 "Consider how the lilies grow. They do not labor or spin. Yet I tell you, not even Solomon in all his splendor was dressed like one of these. 28 If that is how God clothes the grass of the field, which is here today, and tomorrow is thrown into the fire, how much more will he clothe you, O you of little faith! 29 And do not set your heart on what you will eat or drink; do not worry about it. 30 For the pagan world runs after all such things, and your Father knows that you need them. 31 But seek his kingdom, and these things will be given to you as well.

32 "Do not be afraid, little flock, for your Father has been pleased to give you the kingdom. 33 Sell your possessions and give to the poor. Provide purses for yourselves that will not wear out, a treasure in heaven that will not be exhausted, where no thief comes near and no moth destroys. 34 For where your treasure is, there your heart will be also.

Watchfulness

35 "Be dressed ready for service and keep your lamps burning, 36 like men waiting for their master to return from a wedding banquet, so that when he comes and knocks they can immediately open the door for him. 37 It will be good for those servants whose master finds them watching when he comes. I tell you the truth, he will dress himself to serve, will have them recline at the table and will come and wait on them. 38 It will be good for those servants whose master finds them ready, even if he comes in the second or third watch of the night. 39 But understand this: If the owner of the

---

^{e} 25 Or single cubit to his height

house had known at what hour the thief was coming, he would not have let his house be broken into. **40** You also must be ready, because the Son of Man will come at an hour when you do not expect him."

41 Peter asked, "Lord, are you telling this parable to us, or to everyone?"

42 The Lord answered, "Who then is the faithful and wise manager, whom the master puts in charge of his servants to give them their food allowance at the proper time? **43** It will be good for that servant whom the master finds doing so when he returns. **44** I tell you the truth, he will put him in charge of all his possessions. **45** But suppose the servant says to himself, 'My master is taking a long time in coming,' and he then begins to beat the menservants and maidservants and to eat and drink and get drunk. **46** The master of that servant will come on a day when he does not expect him and at an hour he is not aware of. He will cut him to pieces and assign him a place with the unbelievers.

47 "That servant who knows his master's will and does not get ready or does not do what his master wants will be beaten with many blows. **48** But the one who does not know and does things deserving punishment will be beaten with few blows. From everyone who has been given much, much will be demanded; and from the one who has been entrusted with much, much more will be asked.

Not Peace but Division

49 "I have come to bring fire on the earth, and how I wish it were already kindled! **50** But I have a baptism to undergo, and how distressed I am until it is completed! **51** Do you think I came to bring peace on earth? No, I tell you, but division. **52** From now on there will be five in one family divided against each other, three against two and two against three. **53** They will be divided, father against son and son against father, mother against daughter and daughter against mother, mother-in-law against daughter-in-law and daughter-in-law against mother-in-law."

Interpreting the Times

54 He said to the crowd: "When you see a cloud rising in the west, immediately you say, 'It's going to rain,' and it does. **55** And when the south wind blows, you say, 'It's going to be hot,' and it is. **56** Hypocrites! You know how to interpret the appearance of the earth and the sky. How is it that you don't know how to interpret this present time?

57 "Why don't you judge for yourselves what is right? **58** As you are going with your adversary to the magistrate, try hard to be reconciled to him on the way, or he may drag you off to the judge, and the judge turn you over to the officer, and the officer throw you into prison. **59** I tell you, you will not get out until you have paid the last penny.*f* "

Repent or Perish

13

1 Now there were some present at that time who told Jesus about the Galileans whose blood Pilate had mixed with their sacrifices. **2** Jesus answered, "Do you think that these Galileans were worse sinners than all the other

---

f 59 Greek *lepton*

Galileans because they suffered this way? **3** I tell you, no! But unless you repent, you too will all perish. **4** Or those eighteen who died when the tower in Siloam fell on them — do you think they were more guilty than all the others living in Jerusalem? **5** I tell you, no! But unless you repent, you too will all perish."

6 Then he told this parable: "A man had a fig tree, planted in his vineyard, and he went to look for fruit on it, but did not find any. **7** So he said to the man who took care of the vineyard, 'For three years now I've been coming to look for fruit on this fig tree and haven't found any. Cut it down! Why should it use up the soil?'

8 "'Sir,' the man replied, 'leave it alone for one more year, and I'll dig around it and fertilize it. **9** If it bears fruit next year, fine! If not, then cut it down.'"

A Crippled Woman Healed on the Sabbath

10 On a Sabbath Jesus was teaching in one of the synagogues, **11** and a woman was there who had been crippled by a spirit for eighteen years. She was bent over and could not straighten up at all. **12** When Jesus saw her, he called her forward and said to her, "Woman, you are set free from your infirmity." **13** Then he put his hands on her, and immediately she straightened up and praised God.

14 Indignant because Jesus had healed on the Sabbath, the synagogue ruler said to the people, "There are six days for work. So come and be healed on those days, not on the Sabbath."

15 The Lord answered him, "You hypocrites! Doesn't each of you on the Sabbath untie his ox or donkey from the stall and lead it out to give it water? **16** Then should not this woman, a daughter of Abraham, whom Satan has kept bound for eighteen long years, be set free on the Sabbath day from what bound her?"

17 When he said this, all his opponents were humiliated, but the people were delighted with all the wonderful things he was doing.

The Parables of the Mustard Seed and the Yeast

18 Then Jesus asked, "What is the kingdom of God like? What shall I compare it to? **19** It is like a mustard seed, which a man took and planted in his garden. It grew and became a tree, and the birds of the air perched in its branches."

20 Again he asked, "What shall I compare the kingdom of God to? **21** It is like yeast that a woman took and mixed into a large amount*g* of flour until it worked all through the dough."

The Narrow Door

22 Then Jesus went through the towns and villages, teaching as he made his way to Jerusalem. **23** Someone asked him, "Lord, are only a few people going to be saved?"

He said to them, **24** "Make every effort to enter through the narrow door, because many, I tell you, will try to enter and will not be able to. **25** Once the owner of the house gets up and closes the door, you will stand outside knocking and pleading, 'Sir, open the door for us.'

---

g 21 Greek *three satas* (probably about 1/2 bushel or 22 liters)

"But he will answer, 'I don't know you or where you come from.'

26 "Then you will say, 'We ate and drank with you, and you taught in our streets.'

27 "But he will reply, 'I don't know you or where you come from. Away from me, all you evildoers!'

28 "There will be weeping there, and gnashing of teeth, when you see Abraham, Isaac and Jacob and all the prophets in the kingdom of God, but you yourselves thrown out. 29 People will come from east and west and north and south, and will take their places at the feast in the kingdom of God. 30 Indeed there are those who are last who will be first, and first who will be last."

Jesus' Sorrow for Jerusalem

31 At that time some Pharisees came to Jesus and said to him, "Leave this place and go somewhere else. Herod wants to kill you."

32 He replied, "Go tell that fox, 'I will drive out demons and heal people today and tomorrow, and on the third day I will reach my goal.' 33 In any case, I must keep going today and tomorrow and the next day—for surely no prophet can die outside Jerusalem!

34 "O Jerusalem, Jerusalem, you who kill the prophets and stone those sent to you, how often I have longed to gather your children together, as a hen gathers her chicks under her wings, but you were not willing! 35 Look, your house is left to you desolate. I tell you, you will not see me again until you say, 'Blessed is he who comes in the name of the Lord.'*h*"

Jesus at a Pharisee's House

14 1 One Sabbath, when Jesus went to eat in the house of a prominent Pharisee, he was being carefully watched. 2 There in front of him was a man suffering from dropsy. 3 Jesus asked the Pharisees and experts in the law, "Is it lawful to heal on the Sabbath or not?" 4 But they remained silent. So taking hold of the man, he healed him and sent him away.

5 Then he asked them, "If one of you has a son*i* or an ox that falls into a well on the Sabbath day, will you not immediately pull him out?" 6 And they had nothing to say.

7 When he noticed how the guests picked the places of honor at the table, he told them this parable: 8 "When someone invites you to a wedding feast, do not take the place of honor, for a person more distinguished than you may have been invited. 9 If so, the host who invited both of you will come and say to you, 'Give this man your seat.' Then, humiliated, you will have to take the least important place. 10 But when you are invited, take the lowest place, so that when your host comes, he will say to you, 'Friend, move up to a better place.' Then you will be honored in the presence of all your fellow guests. 11 For everyone who exalts himself will be humbled, and he who humbles himself will be exalted."

12 Then Jesus said to his host, "When you give a luncheon or dinner, do not invite your friends, your brothers or relatives, or your rich neighbors; if you do, they may invite you back and so you will be repaid.

---

h 35 Psalm 118:26   *i* 5 Some manuscripts *donkey*

13 But when you give a banquet, invite the poor, the crippled, the lame, the blind, **14** and you will be blessed. Although they cannot repay you, you will be repaid at the resurrection of the righteous."

The Parable of the Great Banquet

15 When one of those at the table with him heard this, he said to Jesus, "Blessed is the man who will eat at the feast in the kingdom of God."

16 Jesus replied: "A certain man was preparing a great banquet and invited many guests. **17** At the time of the banquet he sent his servant to tell those who had been invited, 'Come, for everything is now ready.'

18 "But they all alike began to make excuses. The first said, 'I have just bought a field, and I must go and see it. Please excuse me.'

19 "Another said, 'I have just bought five yoke of oxen, and I'm on my way to try them out. Please excuse me.'

20 "Still another said, 'I just got married, so I can't come.'

21 "The servant came back and reported this to his master. Then the owner of the house became angry and ordered his servant, 'Go out quickly into the streets and alleys of the town and bring in the poor, the crippled, the blind and the lame.'

22 "'Sir,' the servant said, 'what you ordered has been done, but there is still room.'

23 "Then the master told his servant, 'Go out to the roads and country lanes and make them come in, so that my house will be full. **24** I tell you, not one of those men who were invited will get a taste of my banquet.'"

The Cost of Being a Disciple

25 Large crowds were traveling with Jesus, and turning to them he said: **26** "If anyone comes to me and does not hate his father and mother, his wife and children, his brothers and sisters — yes, even his own life — he cannot be my disciple. **27** And anyone who does not carry his cross and follow me cannot be my disciple.

28 "Suppose one of you wants to build a tower. Will he not first sit down and estimate the cost to see if he has enough money to complete it? **29** For if he lays the foundation and is not able to finish it, everyone who sees it will ridicule him, **30** saying, 'This fellow began to build and was not able to finish.'

31 "Or suppose a king is about to go to war against another king. Will he not first sit down and consider whether he is able with ten thousand men to oppose the one coming against him with twenty thousand? **32** If he is not able, he will send a delegation while the other is still a long way off and will ask for terms of peace. **33** In the same way, any of you who does not give up everything he has cannot be my disciple.

34 "Salt is good, but if it loses its saltiness, how can it be made salty again? **35** It is fit neither for the soil nor for the manure pile; it is thrown out.

"He who has ears to hear, let him hear."

The Parable of the Lost Sheep

15 **1** Now the tax collectors and "sinners" were all gathering around to hear him. **2** But the Pharisees and the teachers of the law muttered, "This man welcomes sinners and eats with them."

3 Then Jesus told them this parable: **4** "Suppose one of you has a hundred sheep and loses one of them. Does he not leave the ninety-nine in the open country and go after the lost sheep until he finds it? **5** And when he finds it, he joyfully puts it on his shoulders **6** and goes home. Then he calls his friends and neighbors together and says, 'Rejoice with me; I have found my lost sheep.' **7** I tell you that in the same way there will be more rejoicing in heaven over one sinner who repents than over ninety-nine righteous persons who do not need to repent.

The Parable of the Lost Coin

8 "Or suppose a woman has ten silver coins*j* and loses one. Does she not light a lamp, sweep the house and search carefully until she finds it? **9** And when she finds it, she calls her friends and neighbors together and says, 'Rejoice with me; I have found my lost coin.' **10** In the same way, I tell you, there is rejoicing in the presence of the angels of God over one sinner who repents."

The Parable of the Lost Son

11 Jesus continued: "There was a man who had two sons. **12** The younger one said to his father, 'Father, give me my share of the estate.' So he divided his property between them.

13 "Not long after that, the younger son got together all he had, set off for a distant country and there squandered his wealth in wild living. **14** After he had spent everything, there was a severe famine in that whole country, and he began to be in need. **15** So he went and hired himself out to a citizen of that country, who sent him to his fields to feed pigs. **16** He longed to fill his stomach with the pods that the pigs were

eating, but no one gave him anything.

17 "When he came to his senses, he said, 'How many of my father's hired men have food to spare, and here I am starving to death! **18** I will set out and go back to my father and say to him: Father, I have sinned against heaven and against you. **19** I am no longer worthy to be called your son; make me like one of your hired men.' **20** So he got up and went to his father.

"But while he was still a long way off, his father saw him and was filled with compassion for him; he ran to his son, threw his arms around him and kissed him.

21 "The son said to him, 'Father, I have sinned against heaven and against you. I am no longer worthy to be called your son.'*k* **22** "But the father said to his servants, 'Quick! Bring the best robe and put it on him. Put a ring on his finger and sandals on his feet. **23** Bring the fattened calf and kill it. Let's have a feast and celebrate. **24** For this son of mine was dead and is alive again; he was lost and is found.' So they began to celebrate.

25 "Meanwhile, the older son was in the field. When he came near the house, he heard music and dancing. **26** So he called one of the servants and asked him what was going on. **27** 'Your brother has come,' he replied, 'and your father has killed the fattened calf because he has him back safe and sound.'

28 "The older brother became angry and refused to go in. So his father went out and pleaded with him. **29** But he answered his father,

---

j **8** Greek *ten drachmas*, each worth about a day's wages   *k* **21** Some early manuscripts *son. Make me like one of your hired men.*

'Look! All these years I've been slaving for you and never disobeyed your orders. Yet you never gave me even a young goat so I could celebrate with my friends. 30 But when this son of yours who has squandered your property with prostitutes comes home, you kill the fattened calf for him!'

31 " 'My son,' the father said, 'you are always with me, and everything I have is yours. 32 But we had to celebrate and be glad, because this brother of yours was dead and is alive again; he was lost and is found.' "

The Parable of the Shrewd Manager

16 1 Jesus told his disciples: "There was a rich man whose manager was accused of wasting his possessions. 2 So he called him in and asked him, 'What is this I hear about you? Give an account of your management, because you cannot be manager any longer.'

3 "The manager said to himself, 'What shall I do now? My master is taking away my job. I'm not strong enough to dig, and I'm ashamed to beg— 4 I know what I'll do so that, when I lose my job here, people will welcome me into their houses.'

5 "So he called in each one of his master's debtors. He asked the first, 'How much do you owe my master?'

6 " 'Eight hundred gallons[l] of olive oil,' he replied.

"The manager told him, 'Take your bill, sit down quickly, and make it four hundred.'

7 "Then he asked the second, 'And how much do you owe?'

" 'A thousand bushels[m] of wheat,' he replied.

"He told him, 'Take your bill and make it eight hundred.'

8 "The master commended the dishonest manager because he had acted shrewdly. For the people of this world are more shrewd in dealing with their own kind than are the people of the light. 9 I tell you, use worldly wealth to gain friends for yourselves, so that when it is gone, you will be welcomed into eternal dwellings.

10 "Whoever can be trusted with very little can also be trusted with much, and whoever is dishonest with very little will also be dishonest with much. 11 So if you have not been trustworthy in handling worldly wealth, who will trust you with true riches? 12 And if you have not been trustworthy with someone else's property, who will give you property of your own?

13 "No servant can serve two masters. Either he will hate the one and love the other, or he will be devoted to the one and despise the other. You cannot serve both God and Money."

14 The Pharisees, who loved money, heard all this and were sneering at Jesus. 15 He said to them, "You are the ones who justify yourselves in the eyes of men, but God knows your hearts. What is highly valued among men is detestable in God's sight.

Additional Teachings

16 "The Law and the Prophets were proclaimed until John. Since that time, the good news of the kingdom of God is being preached, and everyone is forcing his way into

---

l 6 Greek *one hundred batous* (probably about 3 kiloliters)   *m 7* Greek *one hundred korous* (probably about 35 kiloliters)

it. **17** It is easier for heaven and earth to disappear than for the least stroke of a pen to drop out of the Law.

18 "Anyone who divorces his wife and marries another woman commits adultery, and the man who marries a divorced woman commits adultery.

The Rich Man and Lazarus

19 "There was a rich man who was dressed in purple and fine linen and lived in luxury every day. **20** At his gate was laid a beggar named Lazarus, covered with sores **21** and longing to eat what fell from the rich man's table. Even the dogs came and licked his sores.

22 "The time came when the beggar died and the angels carried him to Abraham's side. The rich man also died and was buried. **23** In hell,[n] where he was in torment, he looked up and saw Abraham far away, with Lazarus by his side. **24** So he called to him, 'Father Abraham, have pity on me and send Lazarus to dip the tip of his finger in water and cool my tongue, because I am in agony in this fire.'

25 "But Abraham replied, 'Son, remember that in your lifetime you received your good things, while Lazarus received bad things, but now he is comforted here and you are in agony. **26** And besides all this, between us and you a great chasm has been fixed, so that those who want to go from here to you cannot, nor can anyone cross over from there to us.'

27 "He answered, 'Then I beg you, father, send Lazarus to my father's house, **28** for I have five brothers. Let him warn them, so that they will not also come to this place of torment.'

29 "Abraham replied, 'They have Moses and the Prophets; let them listen to them.'

30 " 'No, father Abraham,' he said, 'but if someone goes from the dead to them, they will repent.'

31 "He said to him, 'If they do not listen to Moses and the Prophets, they will not be convinced even if someone rises from the dead.' "

Sin, Faith, Duty

17 **1** Jesus said to his disciples: "Things that cause people to sin are bound to come, but woe to that person through whom they come. **2** It would be better for him to be thrown into the sea with a millstone tied around his neck than for him to cause one of these little ones to sin. **3** So watch yourselves.

"If your brother sins, rebuke him, and if he repents, forgive him. **4** If he sins against you seven times in a day, and seven times comes back to you and says, 'I repent,' forgive him."

5 The apostles said to the Lord, "Increase our faith!"

6 He replied, "If you have faith as small as a mustard seed, you can say to this mulberry tree, 'Be uprooted and planted in the sea,' and it will obey you.

7 "Suppose one of you had a servant plowing or looking after the sheep. Would he say to the servant when he comes in from the field, 'Come along now and sit down to eat'? **8** Would he not rather say, 'Prepare my supper, get yourself ready and wait on me while I eat and drink; after that you may eat and drink'? **9** Would he thank the servant because he did what he was told to do? **10** So you also, when you have done everything you were told to do, should say, 'We are unworthy servants; we have only done our duty.'"

Ten Healed of Leprosy

11 Now on his way to Jerusalem, Jesus traveled along the border between Samaria and Galilee. **12** As he was going into a village, ten men who had leprosy[o] met him. They stood at a distance **13** and called out in a loud voice, "Jesus, Master, have pity on us!"

14 When he saw them, he said, "Go, show yourselves to the priests." And as they went, they were cleansed.

15 One of them, when he saw he was healed, came back, praising God in a loud voice. **16** He threw himself at Jesus' feet and thanked him—and he was a Samaritan.

17 Jesus asked, "Were not all ten cleansed? Where are the other nine? **18** Was no one found to return and give praise to God except this foreigner?" **19** Then he said to him, "Rise and go; your faith has made you well."

The Coming of the Kingdom of God

20 Once, having been asked by the Pharisees when the kingdom of God would come, Jesus replied, "The kingdom of God does not come with your careful observation, **21** nor will people say, 'Here it is,' or 'There it is,' because the kingdom of God is within[p] you."

22 Then he said to his disciples, "The time is coming when you will long to see one of the days of the Son of Man, but you will not see it. **23** Men will tell you, 'There he is!' or

'Here he is!' Do not go running off after them. **24** For the Son of Man in his day[q] will be like the lightning, which flashes and lights up the sky from one end to the other. **25** But first he must suffer many things and be rejected by this generation.

26 "Just as it was in the days of Noah, so also will it be in the days of the Son of Man. **27** People were eating, drinking, marrying and being given in marriage up to the day Noah entered the ark. Then the flood came and destroyed them all.

28 "It was the same in the days of Lot. People were eating and drinking, buying and selling, planting and building. **29** But the day Lot left Sodom, fire and sulfur rained down from heaven and destroyed them all.

30 "It will be just like this on the day the Son of Man is revealed. **31** On that day no one who is on the roof of his house, with his goods inside, should go down to get them. Likewise, no one in the field should go back for anything. **32** Remember Lot's wife! **33** Whoever tries to keep his life will lose it, and whoever loses his life will preserve it. **34** I tell you, on that night two people will be in one bed; one will be taken and the other left. **35** Two women will be grinding grain together; one will be taken and the other left."[r]

37 "Where, Lord?" they asked.

He replied, "Where there is a dead body, there the vultures will gather."

The Parable of the Persistent Widow

18 **1** Then Jesus told his disciples a parable to show them that they should always pray and not give up. **2** He said: "In a certain town

---

[o] 12 The Greek word was used for various diseases affecting the skin—not necessarily leprosy. [p] 21 Or *among* [q] 24 Some manuscripts do not have *in his day.* [r] 35 Some manuscripts *left.* 36 *Two men will be in the field; one will be taken and the other left.*

there was a judge who neither feared God nor cared about men. **3** And there was a widow in that town who kept coming to him with the plea, 'Grant me justice against my adversary.'

4 "For some time he refused. But finally he said to himself, 'Even though I don't fear God or care about men, **5** yet because this widow keeps bothering me, I will see that she gets justice, so that she won't eventually wear me out with her coming!' "

6 And the Lord said, "Listen to what the unjust judge says. **7** And will not God bring about justice for his chosen ones, who cry out to him day and night? Will he keep putting them off? **8** I tell you, he will see that they get justice, and quickly. However, when the Son of Man comes, will he find faith on the earth?"

The Parable of the Pharisee and the Tax Collector

9 To some who were confident of their own righteousness and looked down on everybody else, Jesus told this parable: **10** "Two men went up to the temple to pray, one a Pharisee and the other a tax collector. **11** The Pharisee stood up and prayed about[s] himself: 'God, I thank you that I am not like other men—robbers, evildoers, adulterers—or even like this tax collector. **12** I fast twice a week and give a tenth of all I get.'

13 "But the tax collector stood at a distance. He would not even look up to heaven, but beat his breast and said, 'God, have mercy on me, a sinner.'

14 "I tell you that this man, rather than the other, went home justified before God. For everyone who exalts

himself will be humbled, and he who humbles himself will be exalted."

The Little Children and Jesus

15 People were also bringing babies to Jesus to have him touch them. When the disciples saw this, they rebuked them. **16** But Jesus called the children to him and said, "Let the little children come to me, and do not hinder them, for the kingdom of God belongs to such as these. **17** I tell you the truth, anyone who will not receive the kingdom of God like a little child will never enter it."

The Rich Ruler

18 A certain ruler asked him, "Good teacher, what must I do to inherit eternal life?"

19 "Why do you call me good?" Jesus answered. "No one is good—except God alone. **20** You know the commandments: 'Do not commit adultery, do not murder, do not steal, do not give false testimony, honor your father and mother.'[t]"

21 "All these I have kept since I was a boy," he said.

22 When Jesus heard this, he said to him, "You still lack one thing. Sell everything you have and give to the poor, and you will have treasure in heaven. Then come, follow me."

23 When he heard this, he became very sad, because he was a man of great wealth. **24** Jesus looked at him and said, "How hard it is for the rich to enter the kingdom of God! **25** Indeed, it is easier for a camel to go through the eye of a needle than for a rich man to enter the kingdom of God."

26 Those who heard this asked, "Who then can be saved?"

---

s 11 Or to   *t* 20 Exodus 20:12-16; Deut. 5:16-20

27 Jesus replied, "What is impossible with men is possible with God."

28 Peter said to him, "We have left all we had to follow you!"

29 "I tell you the truth," Jesus said to them, "no one who has left home or wife or brothers or parents or children for the sake of the kingdom of God 30 will fail to receive many times as much in this age and, in the age to come, eternal life."

Jesus Again Predicts His Death

31 Jesus took the Twelve aside and told them, "We are going up to Jerusalem, and everything that is written by the prophets about the Son of Man will be fulfilled. 32 He will be handed over to the Gentiles. They will mock him, insult him, spit on him, flog him and kill him. 33 On the third day he will rise again."

34 The disciples did not understand any of this. Its meaning was hidden from them, and they did not know what he was talking about.

A Blind Beggar Receives His Sight

35 As Jesus approached Jericho, a blind man was sitting by the roadside begging. 36 When he heard the crowd going by, he asked what was happening. 37 They told him, "Jesus of Nazareth is passing by."

38 He called out, "Jesus, Son of David, have mercy on me!"

39 Those who led the way rebuked him and told him to be quiet, but he shouted all the more, "Son of David, have mercy on me!"

40 Jesus stopped and ordered the man to be brought to him. When he came near, Jesus asked him, 41 "What do you want me to do for you?"

"Lord, I want to see," he replied.

42 Jesus said to him, "Receive your sight; your faith has healed you."

43 Immediately he received his sight and followed Jesus, praising God. When all the people saw it, they also praised God.

Zacchaeus the Tax Collector

19 1 Jesus entered Jericho and was passing through. 2 A man was there by the name of Zacchaeus; he was a chief tax collector and was wealthy. 3 He wanted to see who Jesus was, but being a short man he could not, because of the crowd. 4 So he ran ahead and climbed a sycamore-fig tree to see him, since Jesus was coming that way.

5 When Jesus reached the spot, he looked up and said to him, "Zacchaeus, come down immediately. I must stay at your house today." 6 So he came down at once and welcomed him gladly.

7 All the people saw this and began to mutter, "He has gone to be the guest of a 'sinner.'"

8 But Zacchaeus stood up and said to the Lord, "Look, Lord! Here and now I give half of my possessions to the poor, and if I have cheated anybody out of anything, I will pay back four times the amount."

9 Jesus said to him, "Today salvation has come to this house, because this man, too, is a son of Abraham. 10 For the Son of Man came to seek and to save what was lost."

The Parable of the Ten Minas

11 While they were listening to this, he went on to tell them a parable, because he was near Jerusalem and the people thought that the kingdom of God was going to appear at once. 12 He said: "A man of noble birth went to a distant country to have himself appointed king and then to return. 13 So he called ten of his servants and gave

them ten minas.ᵘ 'Put this money to work,' he said, 'until I come back.'

14 "But his subjects hated him and sent a delegation after him to say, 'We don't want this man to be our king.'

15 "He was made king, however, and returned home. Then he sent for the servants to whom he had given the money, in order to find out what they had gained with it.

16 "The first one came and said, 'Sir, your mina has earned ten more.'

17 " 'Well done, my good servant!' his master replied. 'Because you have been trustworthy in a very small matter, take charge of ten cities.'

18 "The second came and said, 'Sir, your mina has earned five more.'

19 "His master answered, 'You take charge of five cities.'

20 "Then another servant came and said, 'Sir, here is your mina; I have kept it laid away in a piece of cloth. **21** I was afraid of you, because you are a hard man. You take out what you did not put in and reap what you did not sow.'

22 "His master replied, 'I will judge you by your own words, you wicked servant! You knew, did you, that I am a hard man, taking out what I did not put in, and reaping what I did not sow? **23** Why then didn't you put my money on deposit, so that when I came back, I could have collected it with interest?'

24 "Then he said to those standing by, 'Take his mina away from him and give it to the one who has ten minas.'

25 " 'Sir,' they said, 'he already has ten!'

26 "He replied, 'I tell you that to everyone who has, more will be given, but as for the one who has nothing, even what he has will be taken away. **27** But those enemies of mine who did not want me to be king over them—bring them here and kill them in front of me.' "

The Triumphal Entry

28 After Jesus had said this, he went on ahead, going up to Jerusalem. **29** As he approached Bethphage and Bethany at the hill called the Mount of Olives, he sent two of his disciples, saying to them, **30** "Go to the village ahead of you, and as you enter it, you will find a colt tied there, which no one has ever ridden. Untie it and bring it here. **31** If anyone asks you, 'Why are you untying it?' tell him, 'The Lord needs it.' "

32 Those who were sent ahead went and found it just as he had told them. **33** As they were untying the colt, its owners asked them, "Why are you untying the colt?"

34 They replied, "The Lord needs it."

35 They brought it to Jesus, threw their cloaks on the colt and put Jesus on it. **36** As he went along, people spread their cloaks on the road.

37 When he came near the place where the road goes down the Mount of Olives, the whole crowd of disciples began joyfully to praise God in loud voices for all the miracles they had seen:

38 "Blessed is the king who comes
        in the name of the Lord!"ᵛ
    "Peace in heaven and glory in
        the highest!"

39 Some of the Pharisees in the crowd said to Jesus, "Teacher, rebuke your disciples!"

40 "I tell you," he replied, "if they keep quiet, the stones will cry out."

ᵘ **13** A mina was about three months' wages.   ᵛ **38** Psalm 118:26

41 As he approached Jerusalem and saw the city, he wept over it 42 and said, "If you, even you, had only known on this day what would bring you peace—but now it is hidden from your eyes. 43 The days will come upon you when your enemies will build an embankment against you and encircle you and hem you in on every side. 44 They will dash you to the ground, you and the children within your walls. They will not leave one stone on another, because you did not recognize the time of God's coming to you."

Jesus at the Temple

45 Then he entered the temple area and began driving out those who were selling. 46 "It is written," he said to them, " 'My house will be a house of prayer'ʷ; but you have made it 'a den of robbers.'ˣ"

47 Every day he was teaching at the temple. But the chief priests, the teachers of the law and the leaders among the people were trying to kill him. 48 Yet they could not find any way to do it, because all the people hung on his words.

The Authority of Jesus Questioned

20 1 One day as he was teaching the people in the temple courts and preaching the gospel, the chief priests and the teachers of the law, together with the elders, came up to him. 2 "Tell us by what authority you are doing these things," they said. "Who gave you this authority?"

3 He replied, "I will also ask you a question. Tell me, 4 John's baptism—was it from heaven, or from men?"

5 They discussed it among themselves and said, "If we say, 'From heaven,' he will ask, 'Why didn't you believe him?' 6 But if we say, 'From men,' all the people will stone us, because they are persuaded that John was a prophet."

7 So they answered, "We don't know where it was from."

8 Jesus said, "Neither will I tell you by what authority I am doing these things."

The Parable of the Tenants

9 He went on to tell the people this parable: "A man planted a vineyard, rented it to some farmers and went away for a long time. 10 At harvest time he sent a servant to the tenants so they would give him some of the fruit of the vineyard. But the tenants beat him and sent him away empty-handed. 11 He sent another servant, but that one also they beat and treated shamefully and sent away empty-handed. 12 He sent still a third, and they wounded him and threw him out.

13 "Then the owner of the vineyard said, 'What shall I do? I will send my son, whom I love; perhaps they will respect him.'

14 "But when the tenants saw him, they talked the matter over. 'This is the heir,' they said. 'Let's kill him, and the inheritance will be ours.' 15 So they threw him out of the vineyard and killed him.

"What then will the owner of the vineyard do to them? 16 He will come and kill those tenants and give the vineyard to others." When the people heard this, they said, "May this never be!"

17 Jesus looked directly at them and asked, "Then what is the meaning of that which is written:

ʷ 46 Isaiah 56:7   ˣ 46 Jer. 7:11

" 'The stone the builders rejected
has become the capstone'$^{y\,z}$?

18 Everyone who falls on that stone
will be broken to pieces, but he on
whom it falls will be crushed."

19 The teachers of the law and the
chief priests looked for a way to arrest him immediately, because they
knew he had spoken this parable
against them. But they were afraid of
the people.

Paying Taxes to Caesar

20 Keeping a close watch on him,
they sent spies, who pretended to be
honest. They hoped to catch Jesus in
something he said so that they might
hand him over to the power and
authority of the governor. **21** So the
spies questioned him: "Teacher, we
know that you speak and teach what
is right, and that you do not show
partiality but teach the way of God
in accordance with the truth. **22** Is it
right for us to pay taxes to Caesar or
not?"

23 He saw through their duplicity
and said to them, **24** "Show me a
denarius. Whose portrait and inscription are on it?"

25 "Caesar's," they replied.

He said to them, "Then give to
Caesar what is Caesar's, and to God
what is God's."

26 They were unable to trap him in
what he had said there in public. And
astonished by his answer, they became silent.

The Resurrection and Marriage

27 Some of the Sadducees, who
say there is no resurrection, came to
Jesus with a question. **28** "Teacher,"
they said, "Moses wrote for us that if
a man's brother dies and leaves a
wife but no children, the man must
marry the widow and have children
for his brother. **29** Now there were
seven brothers. The first one married
a woman and died childless. **30** The
second **31** and then the third married
her, and in the same way the seven
died, leaving no children. **32** Finally,
the woman died too. **33** Now then, at
the resurrection whose wife will she
be, since the seven were married to
her?"

34 Jesus replied, "The people of
this age marry and are given in marriage. **35** But those who are considered worthy of taking part in that
age and in the resurrection from the
dead will neither marry nor be given
in marriage, **36** and they can no
longer die; for they are like the angels. They are God's children, since
they are children of the resurrection.
37 But in the account of the bush,
even Moses showed that the dead
rise, for he calls the Lord 'the God of
Abraham, and the God of Isaac, and
the God of Jacob.'^{a} **38** He is not the
God of the dead, but of the living, for
to him all are alive."

39 Some of the teachers of the law
responded, "Well said, teacher!"
40 And no one dared to ask him any
more questions.

Whose Son Is the Christ?

41 Then Jesus said to them, "How
is it that they say the Christ^{b} is the
Son of David? **42** David himself
declares in the Book of Psalms:

" 'The Lord said to my Lord:
  "Sit at my right hand
43 until I make your enemies
  a footstool for your feet." '^{c}

---

^{y} 17 Or cornerstone ^{z} 17 Psalm 118:22 ^{a} 37 Exodus 3:6 ^{b} 41 Or Messiah
^{c} 43 Psalm 110:1

44 David calls him 'Lord.' How then can he be his son?"

45 While all the people were listening, Jesus said to his disciples, **46** "Beware of the teachers of the law. They like to walk around in flowing robes and love to be greeted in the marketplaces and have the most important seats in the synagogues and the places of honor at banquets. **47** They devour widows' houses and for a show make lengthy prayers. Such men will be punished most severely."

The Widow's Offering

21 **1** As he looked up, Jesus saw the rich putting their gifts into the temple treasury. **2** He also saw a poor widow put in two very small copper coins.[d] **3** "I tell you the truth," he said, "this poor widow has put in more than all the others. **4** All these people gave their gifts out of their wealth; but she out of her poverty put in all she had to live on."

Signs of the End of the Age

5 Some of his disciples were remarking about how the temple was adorned with beautiful stones and with gifts dedicated to God. But Jesus said, **6** "As for what you see here, the time will come when not one stone will be left on another; every one of them will be thrown down."

7 "Teacher," they asked, "when will these things happen? And what will be the sign that they are about to take place?"

8 He replied: "Watch out that you are not deceived. For many will come in my name, claiming, 'I am he,' and, 'The time is near.' Do not follow them. **9** When you hear of wars and revolutions, do not be frightened. These things must happen first, but the end will not come right away."

10 Then he said to them: "Nation will rise against nation, and kingdom against kingdom. **11** There will be great earthquakes, famines and pestilences in various places, and fearful events and great signs from heaven.

12 "But before all this, they will lay hands on you and persecute you. They will deliver you to synagogues and prisons, and you will be brought before kings and governors, and all on account of my name. **13** This will result in your being witnesses to them. **14** But make up your mind not to worry beforehand how you will defend yourselves. **15** For I will give you words and wisdom that none of your adversaries will be able to resist or contradict. **16** You will be betrayed even by parents, brothers, relatives and friends, and they will put some of you to death. **17** All men will hate you because of me. **18** But not a hair of your head will perish. **19** By standing firm you will gain life.

20 "When you see Jerusalem being surrounded by armies, you will know that its desolation is near. **21** Then let those who are in Judea flee to the mountains, let those in the city get out, and let those in the country not enter the city. **22** For this is the time of punishment in fulfillment of all that has been written. **23** How dreadful it will be in those days for pregnant women and nursing mothers! There will be great distress in the land and wrath against this people. **24** They will fall by the sword and will be taken as prisoners to all the nations. Jerusalem will be trampled

d 2 Greek *two lepta*

on by the Gentiles until the times of the Gentiles are fulfilled.

25 "There will be signs in the sun, moon and stars. On the earth, nations will be in anguish and perplexity at the roaring and tossing of the sea. **26** Men will faint from terror, apprehensive of what is coming on the world, for the heavenly bodies will be shaken. **27** At that time they will see the Son of Man coming in a cloud with power and great glory. **28** When these things begin to take place, stand up and lift up your heads, because your redemption is drawing near."

29 He told them this parable: "Look at the fig tree and all the trees. **30** When they sprout leaves, you can see for yourselves and know that summer is near. **31** Even so, when you see these things happening, you know that the kingdom of God is near.

32 "I tell you the truth, this generationᵉ will certainly not pass away until all these things have happened. **33** Heaven and earth will pass away, but my words will never pass away.

34 "Be careful, or your hearts will be weighed down with dissipation, drunkenness and the anxieties of life, and that day will close on you unexpectedly like a trap. **35** For it will come upon all those who live on the face of the whole earth. **36** Be always on the watch, and pray that you may be able to escape all that is about to happen, and that you may be able to stand before the Son of Man."

37 Each day Jesus was teaching at the temple, and each evening he went out to spend the night on the hill called the Mount of Olives, **38** and all the people came early in the morning to hear him at the temple.

Judas Agrees to Betray Jesus

22 **1** Now the Feast of Unleavened Bread, called the Passover, was approaching, **2** and the chief priests and the teachers of the law were looking for some way to get rid of Jesus, for they were afraid of the people. **3** Then Satan entered Judas, called Iscariot, one of the Twelve. **4** And Judas went to the chief priests and the officers of the temple guard and discussed with them how he might betray Jesus. **5** They were delighted and agreed to give him money. **6** He consented, and watched for an opportunity to hand Jesus over to them when no crowd was present.

The Last Supper

7 Then came the day of Unleavened Bread on which the Passover lamb had to be sacrificed. **8** Jesus sent Peter and John, saying, "Go and make preparations for us to eat the Passover."

9 "Where do you want us to prepare for it?" they asked.

10 He replied, "As you enter the city, a man carrying a jar of water will meet you. Follow him to the house that he enters, **11** and say to the owner of the house, 'The Teacher asks: Where is the guest room, where I may eat the Passover with my disciples?' **12** He will show you a large upper room, all furnished. Make preparations there."

13 They left and found things just as Jesus had told them. So they prepared the Passover.

14 When the hour came, Jesus and his apostles reclined at the table. **15** And he said to them, "I have

---

ᵉ 32 Or *race*

eagerly desired to eat this Passover with you before I suffer. 16 For I tell you, I will not eat it again until it finds fulfillment in the kingdom of God."

17 After taking the cup, he gave thanks and said, "Take this and divide it among you. 18 For I tell you I will not drink again of the fruit of the vine until the kingdom of God comes."

19 And he took bread, gave thanks and broke it, and gave it to them, saying, "This is my body given for you; do this in remembrance of me."

20 In the same way, after the supper he took the cup, saying, "This cup is the new covenant in my blood, which is poured out for you. 21 But the hand of him who is going to betray me is with mine on the table. 22 The Son of Man will go as it has been decreed, but woe to that man who betrays him." 23 They began to question among themselves which of them it might be who would do this.

24 Also a dispute arose among them as to which of them was considered to be greatest. 25 Jesus said to them, "The kings of the Gentiles lord it over them; and those who exercise authority over them call themselves Benefactors. 26 But you are not to be like that. Instead, the greatest among you should be like the youngest, and the one who rules like the one who serves. 27 For who is greater, the one who is at the table or the one who serves? Is it not the one who is at the table? But I am among you as one who serves. 28 You are those who have stood by me in my trials. 29 And I confer on you a kingdom, just as my Father conferred one on me, 30 so that you may eat and drink at my table in my kingdom and sit on thrones, judging the twelve tribes of Israel.

31 "Simon, Simon, Satan has asked to sift you*f* as wheat. 32 But I have prayed for you, Simon, that your faith may not fail. And when you have turned back, strengthen your brothers."

33 But he replied, "Lord, I am ready to go with you to prison and to death."

34 Jesus answered, "I tell you, Peter, before the rooster crows today, you will deny three times that you know me."

35 Then Jesus asked them, "When I sent you without purse, bag or sandals, did you lack anything?"

"Nothing," they answered.

36 He said to them, "But now if you have a purse, take it, and also a bag; and if you don't have a sword, sell your cloak and buy one. 37 It is written: 'And he was numbered with the transgressors'*g*; and I tell you that this must be fulfilled in me. Yes, what is written about me is reaching its fulfillment."

38 The disciples said, "See, Lord, here are two swords."

"That is enough," he replied.

Jesus Prays on the Mount of Olives

39 Jesus went out as usual to the Mount of Olives, and his disciples followed him. 40 On reaching the place, he said to them, "Pray that you will not fall into temptation." 41 He withdrew about a stone's throw beyond them, knelt down and prayed, 42 "Father, if you are willing, take this cup from me; yet not my will, but yours be done." 43 An angel from heaven appeared to him and

f 31 The Greek is plural.   *g 37* Isaiah 53:12

strengthened him. **44** And being in anguish, he prayed more earnestly, and his sweat was like drops of blood falling to the ground.*h*

45 When he rose from prayer and went back to the disciples, he found them asleep, exhausted from sorrow. **46** "Why are you sleeping?" he asked them. "Get up and pray so that you will not fall into temptation."

Jesus Arrested

47 While he was still speaking a crowd came up, and the man who was called Judas, one of the Twelve, was leading them. He approached Jesus to kiss him, **48** but Jesus asked him, "Judas, are you betraying the Son of Man with a kiss?"

49 When Jesus' followers saw what was going to happen, they said, "Lord, should we strike with our swords?" **50** And one of them struck the servant of the high priest, cutting off his right ear.

51 But Jesus answered, "No more of this!" And he touched the man's ear and healed him.

52 Then Jesus said to the chief priests, the officers of the temple guard, and the elders, who had come for him, "Am I leading a rebellion, that you have come with swords and clubs? **53** Every day I was with you in the temple courts, and you did not lay a hand on me. But this is your hour—when darkness reigns."

Peter Disowns Jesus

54 Then seizing him, they led him away and took him into the house of the high priest. Peter followed at a distance. **55** But when they had kindled a fire in the middle of the courtyard and had sat down together,

Peter sat down with them. **56** A servant girl saw him seated there in the firelight. She looked closely at him and said, "This man was with him."

57 But he denied it. "Woman, I don't know him," he said.

58 A little later someone else saw him and said, "You also are one of them."

"Man, I am not!" Peter replied.

59 About an hour later another asserted, "Certainly this fellow was with him, for he is a Galilean."

60 Peter replied, "Man, I don't know what you're talking about!" Just as he was speaking, the rooster crowed. **61** The Lord turned and looked straight at Peter. Then Peter remembered the word the Lord had spoken to him: "Before the rooster crows today, you will disown me three times." **62** And he went outside and wept bitterly.

The Guards Mock Jesus

63 The men who were guarding Jesus began mocking and beating him. **64** They blindfolded him and demanded, "Prophesy! Who hit you?" **65** And they said many other insulting things to him.

Jesus Before Pilate and Herod

66 At daybreak the council of the elders of the people, both the chief priests and teachers of the law, met together, and Jesus was led before them. **67** "If you are the Christ,*i*" they said, "tell us."

Jesus answered, "If I tell you, you will not believe me, **68** and if I asked you, you would not answer. **69** But from now on, the Son of Man will be seated at the right hand of the mighty God."

---

h 44 Some early manuscripts do not have verses 43 and 44.   *i* 67 Or *Messiah*

70 They all asked, "Are you then the Son of God?"

He replied, "You are right in saying I am."

71 Then they said, "Why do we need any more testimony? We have heard it from his own lips."

23

1 Then the whole assembly rose and led him off to Pilate. **2** And they began to accuse him, saying, "We have found this man subverting our nation. He opposes payment of taxes to Caesar and claims to be Christ,[j] a king."

3 So Pilate asked Jesus, "Are you the king of the Jews?"

"Yes, it is as you say," Jesus replied.

4 Then Pilate announced to the chief priests and the crowd, "I find no basis for a charge against this man."

5 But they insisted, "He stirs up the people all over Judea[k] by his teaching. He started in Galilee and has come all the way here."

6 On hearing this, Pilate asked if the man was a Galilean. **7** When he learned that Jesus was under Herod's jurisdiction, he sent him to Herod, who was also in Jerusalem at that time.

8 When Herod saw Jesus, he was greatly pleased, because for a long time he had been wanting to see him. From what he had heard about him, he hoped to see him perform some miracle. **9** He plied him with many questions, but Jesus gave him no answer. **10** The chief priests and the teachers of the law were standing there, vehemently accusing him. **11** Then Herod and his soldiers ridiculed and mocked him. Dressing him in an elegant robe, they sent him

back to Pilate. **12** That day Herod and Pilate became friends—before this they had been enemies.

13 Pilate called together the chief priests, the rulers and the people, **14** and said to them, "You brought me this man as one who was inciting the people to rebellion. I have examined him in your presence and have found no basis for your charges against him. **15** Neither has Herod, for he sent him back to us; as you can see, he has done nothing to deserve death. **16** Therefore, I will punish him and then release him."[l]

18 With one voice they cried out, "Away with this man! Release Barabbas to us!" **19** (Barabbas had been thrown into prison for an insurrection in the city, and for murder.)

20 Wanting to release Jesus, Pilate appealed to them again. **21** But they kept shouting, "Crucify him! Crucify him!"

22 For the third time he spoke to them: "Why? What crime has this man committed? I have found in him no grounds for the death penalty. Therefore I will have him punished and then release him."

23 But with loud shouts they insistently demanded that he be crucified, and their shouts prevailed. **24** So Pilate decided to grant their demand. **25** He released the man who had been thrown into prison for insurrection and murder, the one they asked for, and surrendered Jesus to their will.

The Crucifixion

26 As they led him away, they seized Simon from Cyrene, who was on his way in from the country, and

---

j 2 Or *Messiah*; also in verses 35 and 39   *k 5* Or *over the land of the Jews*   *l 16* Some manuscripts *him.* *17* Now he was obliged to release one man to them at the Feast.

put the cross on him and made him carry it behind Jesus. **27** A large number of people followed him, including women who mourned and wailed for him. **28** Jesus turned and said to them, "Daughters of Jerusalem, do not weep for me; weep for yourselves and for your children. **29** For the time will come when you will say, 'Blessed are the barren women, the wombs that never bore and the breasts that never nursed!' **30** Then

> " 'they will say to the mountains,
>   "Fall on us!"
>   and to the hills, "Cover us!" '*m*

31 For if men do these things when the tree is green, what will happen when it is dry?"

32 Two other men, both criminals, were also led out with him to be executed. **33** When they came to the place called the Skull, there they crucified him, along with the criminals — one on his right, the other on his left. **34** Jesus said, "Father, forgive them, for they do not know what they are doing."*n* And they divided up his clothes by casting lots.

35 The people stood watching, and the rulers even sneered at him. They said, "He saved others; let him save himself if he is the Christ of God, the Chosen One."

36 The soldiers also came up and mocked him. They offered him wine vinegar **37** and said, "If you are the king of the Jews, save yourself."

38 There was a written notice above him, which read: THIS IS THE KING OF THE JEWS.

39 One of the criminals who hung there hurled insults at him: "Aren't you the Christ? Save yourself and us!"

40 But the other criminal rebuked him. "Don't you fear God," he said, "since you are under the same sentence? **41** We are punished justly, for we are getting what our deeds deserve. But this man has done nothing wrong." **42** Then he said, "Jesus, remember me when you come into your kingdom."*o* **43** Jesus answered him, "I tell you the truth, today you will be with me in paradise."

Jesus' Death

44 It was now about the sixth hour, and darkness came over the whole land until the ninth hour, **45** for the sun stopped shining. And the curtain of the temple was torn in two. **46** Jesus called out with a loud voice, "Father, into your hands I commit my spirit." When he had said this, he breathed his last.

47 The centurion, seeing what had happened, praised God and said, "Surely this was a righteous man." **48** When all the people who had gathered to witness this sight saw what took place, they beat their breasts and went away. **49** But all those who knew him, including the women who had followed him from Galilee, stood at a distance, watching these things.

Jesus' Burial

50 Now there was a man named Joseph, a member of the Council, a good and upright man, **51** who had not consented to their decision and action. He came from the Judean town of Arimathea and he was waiting for the kingdom of God. **52** Going

---

m 30 Hosea 10:8   *n* 34 Some early manuscripts do not have this sentence.   *o* 42 Some manuscripts *come with your kingly power*

to Pilate, he asked for Jesus' body.
53 Then he took it down, wrapped it
in linen cloth and placed it in a tomb
cut in the rock, one in which no one
had yet been laid. 54 It was Preparation Day, and the Sabbath was about
to begin.

55 The women who had come with
Jesus from Galilee followed Joseph
and saw the tomb and how his body
was laid in it. 56 Then they went home
and prepared spices and perfumes.
But they rested on the Sabbath in
obedience to the commandment.

The Resurrection

24 1 On the first day of the week,
very early in the morning, the
women took the spices they had
prepared and went to the tomb.
2 They found the stone rolled away
from the tomb, 3 but when they
entered, they did not find the body of
the Lord Jesus. 4 While they were
wondering about this, suddenly two
men in clothes that gleamed like
lightning stood beside them. 5 In their
fright the women bowed down with
their faces to the ground, but the men
said to them, "Why do you look for the
living among the dead? 6 He is not
here; he has risen! Remember how he
told you, while he was still with you in
Galilee: 7 'The Son of Man must be
delivered into the hands of sinful
men, be crucified and on the third day
be raised again.'" 8 Then they remembered his words.

9 When they came back from the
tomb, they told all these things to the
Eleven and to all the others. 10 It was
Mary Magdalene, Joanna, Mary the
mother of James, and the others with
them who told this to the apostles.
11 But they did not believe the

women, because their words seemed
to them like nonsense. 12 Peter, however, got up and ran to the tomb.
Bending over, he saw the strips of
linen lying by themselves, and he
went away, wondering to himself
what had happened.

On the Road to Emmaus

13 Now that same day two of them
were going to a village called Em-
maus, about seven miles*p* from
Jerusalem. 14 They were talking with
each other about everything that had
happened. 15 As they talked and discussed these things with each other,
Jesus himself came up and walked
along with them; 16 but they were
kept from recognizing him.

17 He asked them, "What are you
discussing together as you walk
along?"

They stood still, their faces
downcast. 18 One of them, named
Cleopas, asked him, "Are you only a
visitor to Jerusalem and do not know
the things that have happened there
in these days?"

19 "What things?" he asked.

"About Jesus of Nazareth," they
replied. "He was a prophet, powerful
in word and deed before God and all
the people. 20 The chief priests and
our rulers handed him over to be
sentenced to death, and they
crucified him; 21 but we had hoped
that he was the one who was going
to redeem Israel. And what is more,
it is the third day since all this took
place. 22 In addition, some of our
women amazed us. They went to the
tomb early this morning 23 but didn't
find his body. They came and told us
that they had seen a vision of angels,
who said he was alive. 24 Then some

P 13 Greek sixty stadia (about 11 kilometers)

of our companions went to the tomb and found it just as the women had said, but him they did not see."

25 He said to them, "How foolish you are, and how slow of heart to believe all that the prophets have spoken! 26 Did not the Christ^q have to suffer these things and then enter his glory?" 27 And beginning with Moses and all the Prophets, he explained to them what was said in all the Scriptures concerning himself.

28 As they approached the village to which they were going, Jesus acted as if he were going farther. 29 But they urged him strongly, "Stay with us, for it is nearly evening; the day is almost over." So he went in to stay with them.

30 When he was at the table with them, he took bread, gave thanks, broke it and began to give it to them. 31 Then their eyes were opened and they recognized him, and he disappeared from their sight. 32 They asked each other, "Were not our hearts burning within us while he talked with us on the road and opened the Scriptures to us?"

33 They got up and returned at once to Jerusalem. There they found the Eleven and those with them, assembled together 34 and saying, "It is true! The Lord has risen and has appeared to Simon." 35 Then the two told what had happened on the way, and how Jesus was recognized by them when he broke the bread.

Jesus Appears to the Disciples

36 While they were still talking about this, Jesus himself stood among them and said to them, "Peace be with you."

37 They were startled and frightened, thinking they saw a ghost. 38 He said to them, "Why are you troubled, and why do doubts rise in your minds? 39 Look at my hands and my feet. It is I myself! Touch me and see; a ghost does not have flesh and bones, as you see I have."

40 When he had said this, he showed them his hands and feet. 41 And while they still did not believe it because of joy and amazement, he asked them, "Do you have anything here to eat?" 42 They gave him a piece of broiled fish, 43 and he took it and ate it in their presence.

44 He said to them, "This is what I told you while I was still with you: Everything must be fulfilled that is written about me in the Law of Moses, the Prophets and the Psalms."

45 Then he opened their minds so they could understand the Scriptures. 46 He told them, "This is what is written: The Christ will suffer and rise from the dead on the third day, 47 and repentance and forgiveness of sins will be preached in his name to all nations, beginning at Jerusalem. 48 You are witnesses of these things. 49 I am going to send you what my Father has promised; but stay in the city until you have been clothed with power from on high."

The Ascension

50 When he had led them out to the vicinity of Bethany, he lifted up his hands and blessed them. 51 While he was blessing them, he left them and was taken up into heaven. 52 Then they worshiped him and returned to Jerusalem with great joy. 53 And they stayed continually at the temple, praising God.

John

The Word Became Flesh

1 ¹ In the beginning was the Word, and the Word was with God, and the Word was God. ² He was with God in the beginning.

³ Through him all things were made; without him nothing was made that has been made. ⁴ In him was life, and that life was the light of men. ⁵ The light shines in the darkness, but the darkness has not understood*a* it.

⁶ There came a man who was sent from God; his name was John. ⁷ He came as a witness to testify concerning that light, so that through him all men might believe. ⁸ He himself was not the light; he came only as a witness to the light. ⁹ The true light that gives light to every man was coming into the world.*b*

¹⁰ He was in the world, and though the world was made through him, the world did not recognize him. ¹¹ He came to that which was his own, but his own did not receive him. ¹² Yet to all who received him, to those who believed in his name, he gave the right to become children of God— ¹³ children born not of natural descent,*c* nor of human decision or a husband's will, but born of God.

¹⁴ The Word became flesh and made his dwelling among us. We have seen his glory, the glory of the One and Only,*d* who came from the Father, full of grace and truth.

¹⁵ John testifies concerning him. He cries out, saying, "This was he of whom I said, 'He who comes after me has surpassed me because he was before me.'" ¹⁶ From the fullness of his grace we have all received one blessing after another. ¹⁷ For the law was given through Moses; grace and truth came through Jesus Christ. ¹⁸ No one has ever seen God, but God the One and Only,*e,f* who is at the Father's side, has made him known.

John the Baptist Denies Being the Christ

¹⁹ Now this was John's testimony when the Jews of Jerusalem sent priests and Levites to ask him who he was. ²⁰ He did not fail to confess, but confessed freely, "I am not the Christ.*g*"

²¹ They asked him, "Then who are you? Are you Elijah?"

He said, "I am not."

"Are you the Prophet?"

He answered, "No."

²² Finally they said, "Who are you? Give us an answer to take back to those who sent us. What do you say about yourself?"

²³ John replied in the words of Isaiah the prophet, "I am the voice of one calling in the desert, 'Make straight the way for the Lord.'"*h*

---

a 5 Or *darkness, and the darkness has not overcome*   *b* 9 Or *This was the true light that gives light to every man who comes into the world*   *c* 13 Greek *of bloods*   *d* 14 Or *the Only Begotten*   *e* 18 Or *the Only Begotten*   *f* 18 Some manuscripts *but the only* (or *only begotten*) *Son*   *g* 20 Or *Messiah*. "The Christ" (Greek) and "the Messiah" (Hebrew) both mean "the Anointed One"; also in verse 25.   *h* 23 Isaiah 40:3

24 Now some Pharisees who had been sent 25 questioned him, "Why then do you baptize if you are not the Christ, nor Elijah, nor the Prophet?"

26 "I baptize with[i] water," John replied, "but among you stands one you do not know. 27 He is the one who comes after me, the thongs of whose sandals I am not worthy to untie."

28 This all happened at Bethany on the other side of the Jordan, where John was baptizing.

Jesus the Lamb of God

29 The next day John saw Jesus coming toward him and said, "Look, the Lamb of God, who takes away the sin of the world! 30 This is the one I meant when I said, 'A man who comes after me has surpassed me because he was before me.' 31 I myself did not know him, but the reason I came baptizing with water was that he might be revealed to Israel."

32 Then John gave this testimony: "I saw the Spirit come down from heaven as a dove and remain on him. 33 I would not have known him, except that the one who sent me to baptize with water told me, 'The man on whom you see the Spirit come down and remain is he who will baptize with the Holy Spirit.' 34 I have seen and I testify that this is the Son of God."

Jesus' First Disciples

35 The next day John was there again with two of his disciples. 36 When he saw Jesus passing by, he said, "Look, the Lamb of God!"

37 When the two disciples heard him say this, they followed Jesus. 38 Turning around, Jesus saw them following and asked, "What do you want?"

They said, "Rabbi" (which means Teacher), "where are you staying?"

39 "Come," he replied, "and you will see."

So they went and saw where he was staying, and spent that day with him. It was about the tenth hour.

40 Andrew, Simon Peter's brother, was one of the two who heard what John had said and who had followed Jesus. 41 The first thing Andrew did was to find his brother Simon and tell him, "We have found the Messiah" (that is, the Christ). 42 And he brought him to Jesus.

Jesus looked at him and said, "You are Simon son of John. You will be called Cephas" (which, when translated, is Peter[j]).

Jesus Calls Philip and Nathanael

43 The next day Jesus decided to leave for Galilee. Finding Philip, he said to him, "Follow me."

44 Philip, like Andrew and Peter, was from the town of Bethsaida. 45 Philip found Nathanael and told him, "We have found the one Moses wrote about in the Law, and about whom the prophets also wrote—Jesus of Nazareth, the son of Joseph."

46 "Nazareth! Can anything good come from there?" Nathanael asked.

"Come and see," said Philip.

47 When Jesus saw Nathanael approaching, he said of him, "Here is a true Israelite, in whom there is nothing false."

i 26 Or in; also in verses 31 and 33   j 42 Both Cephas (Aramaic) and Peter (Greek) mean rock.

48 "How do you know me?" Nathanael asked.

Jesus answered, "I saw you while you were still under the fig tree before Philip called you."

49 Then Nathanael declared, "Rabbi, you are the Son of God; you are the King of Israel."

50 Jesus said, "You believe[k] because I told you I saw you under the fig tree. You shall see greater things than that." 51 He then added, "I tell you[l] the truth, you[m] shall see heaven open, and the angels of God ascending and descending on the Son of Man."

Jesus Changes Water to Wine

2 ¹ On the third day a wedding took place at Cana in Galilee. Jesus' mother was there, 2 and Jesus and his disciples had also been invited to the wedding. 3 When the wine was gone, Jesus' mother said to him, "They have no more wine."

4 "Dear woman, why do you involve me?" Jesus replied, "My time has not yet come."

5 His mother said to the servants, "Do whatever he tells you."

6 Nearby stood six stone water jars, the kind used by the Jews for ceremonial washing, each holding from twenty to thirty gallons.[n]

7 Jesus said to the servants, "Fill the jars with water"; so they filled them to the brim.

8 Then he told them, "Now draw some out and take it to the master of the banquet."

They did so, 9 and the master of the banquet tasted the water that had been turned into wine. He did not realize where it had come from, though the servants who had drawn the water knew. Then he called the bridegroom aside 10 and said, "Everyone brings out the choice wine first and then the cheaper wine after the guests have had too much to drink; but you have saved the best till now."

11 This, the first of his miraculous signs, Jesus performed in Cana of Galilee. He thus revealed his glory, and his disciples put their faith in him.

Jesus Clears the Temple

12 After this he went down to Capernaum with his mother and brothers and his disciples. There they stayed for a few days.

13 When it was almost time for the Jewish Passover, Jesus went up to Jerusalem. 14 In the temple courts he found men selling cattle, sheep and doves, and others sitting at tables exchanging money. 15 So he made a whip out of cords, and drove all from the temple area, both sheep and cattle; he scattered the coins of the money changers and overturned their tables. 16 To those who sold doves he said, "Get these out of here! How dare you turn my Father's house into a market!"

17 His disciples remembered that it is written: "Zeal for your house will consume me."[o]

18 Then the Jews demanded of him, "What miraculous sign can you show us to prove your authority to do all this?"

19 Jesus answered them, "Destroy this temple, and I will raise it again in three days."

20 The Jews replied, "It has taken forty-six years to build this temple,

and you are going to raise it in three days?" **21** But the temple he had spoken of was his body. **22** After he was raised from the dead, his disciples recalled what he had said. Then they believed the Scripture and the words that Jesus had spoken.

23 Now while he was in Jerusalem at the Passover Feast, many people saw the miraculous signs he was doing and believed in his name.*p* **24** But Jesus would not entrust himself to them, for he knew all men. **25** He did not need man's testimony about man, for he knew what was in a man.

Jesus Teaches Nicodemus

3 **1** Now there was a man of the Pharisees named Nicodemus, a member of the Jewish ruling council. **2** He came to Jesus at night and said, "Rabbi, we know you are a teacher who has come from God. For no one could perform the miraculous signs you are doing if God were not with him."

3 In reply Jesus declared, "I tell you the truth, no one can see the kingdom of God unless he is born again.*q*"

4 "How can a man be born when he is old?" Nicodemus asked. "Surely he cannot enter a second time into his mother's womb to be born!"

5 Jesus answered, "I tell you the truth, no one can enter the kingdom of God unless he is born of water and the Spirit. **6** Flesh gives birth to flesh, but the Spirit*r* gives birth to spirit. **7** You should not be surprised at my saying, 'You*s* must be born again.' **8** The wind blows wherever it pleases. You hear its sound, but you

cannot tell where it comes from or where it is going. So it is with everyone born of the Spirit."

9 "How can this be?" Nicodemus asked.

10 "You are Israel's teacher," said Jesus, "and do you not understand these things? **11** I tell you the truth, we speak of what we know, and we testify to what we have seen, but still you people do not accept our testimony. **12** I have spoken to you of earthly things and you do not believe; how then will you believe if I speak of heavenly things? **13** No one has ever gone into heaven except the one who came from heaven—the Son of Man.*t* **14** Just as Moses lifted up the snake in the desert, so the Son of Man must be lifted up, **15** that everyone who believes in him may have eternal life.*u*

16 "For God so loved the world that he gave his one and only Son,*v* that whoever believes in him shall not perish but have eternal life. **17** For God did not send his Son into the world to condemn the world, but to save the world through him. **18** Whoever believes in him is not condemned, but whoever does not believe stands condemned already because he has not believed in the name of God's one and only Son.*w* **19** This is the verdict: Light has come into the world, but men loved darkness instead of light because their deeds were evil. **20** Everyone who does evil hates the light, and will not come into the light for fear that his deeds will be exposed. **21** But whoever lives by the truth comes into the light, so that it may be seen plain-

---

p 23 Or *and believed in him*   *q 3* Or *born from above; also in verse 7*   *r 6* Or *but spirit*
s 7 The Greek is plural.   *t 13* Some manuscripts *Man, who is in heaven*   *u 15* Or *believes may have eternal life in him*   *v 16* Or *his only begotten Son*   *w 18* Or *God's only begotten Son*

ly that what he has done has been done through God."[x]

John the Baptist's Testimony About Jesus

22 After this, Jesus and his disciples went out into the Judean countryside, where he spent some time with them, and baptized. **23** Now John also was baptizing at Aenon near Salim, because there was plenty of water, and people were constantly coming to be baptized. **24** (This was before John was put in prison.) **25** An argument developed between some of John's disciples and a certain Jew over the matter of ceremonial washing. **26** They came to John and said to him, "Rabbi, that man who was with you on the other side of the Jordan—the one you testified about—well, he is baptizing, and everyone is going to him."

27 To this John replied, "A man can receive only what is given him from heaven. **28** You yourselves can testify that I said, 'I am not the Christ[z] but am sent ahead of him.' **29** The bride belongs to the bridegroom. The friend who attends the bridegroom waits and listens for him, and is full of joy when he hears the bridegroom's voice. That joy is mine, and it is now complete. **30** He must become greater; I must become less.

31 "The one who comes from above is above all; the one who is from the earth belongs to the earth, and speaks as one from the earth. The one who comes from heaven is above all. **32** He testifies to what he has seen and heard, but no one accepts his testimony. **33** The man who has accepted it has certified that God

is truthful. **34** For the one whom God has sent speaks the words of God, for God[a] gives the Spirit without limit. **35** The Father loves the Son and has placed everything in his hands. **36** Whoever believes in the Son has eternal life, but whoever rejects the Son will not see life, for God's wrath remains on him."[b]

Jesus Talks With a Samaritan Woman

4 **1** The Pharisees heard that Jesus was gaining and baptizing more disciples than John, **2** although in fact it was not Jesus who baptized, but his disciples. **3** When the Lord learned of this, he left Judea and went back once more to Galilee.

4 Now he had to go through Samaria. **5** So he came to a town in Samaria called Sychar, near the plot of ground Jacob had given to his son Joseph. **6** Jacob's well was there, and Jesus, tired as he was from the journey, sat down by the well. It was about the sixth hour.

7 When a Samaritan woman came to draw water, Jesus said to her, "Will you give me a drink?" **8** (His disciples had gone into the town to buy food.)

9 The Samaritan woman said to him, "You are a Jew and I am a Samaritan woman. How can you ask me for a drink?" (For Jews do not associate with Samaritans.[c])

10 Jesus answered her, "If you knew the gift of God and who it is that asks you for a drink, you would have asked him and he would have given you living water."

11 "Sir," the woman said, "you have nothing to draw with and the well is deep. Where can you get this

---

[x] *21* Some interpreters end the quotation after verse 15.   [y] *25* Some manuscripts *and certain Jews*   [z] *28* Or *Messiah*   [a] *34* Greek *he*   [b] *36* Some interpreters end the quotation after verse 30.   [c] *9* Or *do not use dishes Samaritans have used*

living water? 12 Are you greater than our father Jacob, who gave us the well and drank from it himself, as did also his sons and his flocks and herds?"

13 Jesus answered, "Everyone who drinks this water will be thirsty again, 14 but whoever drinks the water I give him will never thirst. Indeed, the water I give him will become in him a spring of water welling up to eternal life."

15 The woman said to him, "Sir, give me this water so that I won't get thirsty and have to keep coming here to draw water."

16 He told her, "Go, call your husband and come back."

17 "I have no husband," she replied.

Jesus said to her, "You are right when you say you have no husband. 18 The fact is, you have had five husbands, and the man you now have is not your husband. What you have just said is quite true."

19 "Sir," the woman said, "I can see that you are a prophet. 20 Our fathers worshiped on this mountain, but you Jews claim that the place where we must worship is in Jerusalem."

21 Jesus declared, "Believe me, woman, a time is coming when you will worship the Father neither on this mountain nor in Jerusalem. 22 You Samaritans worship what you do not know; we worship what we do know, for salvation is from the Jews. 23 Yet a time is coming and has now come when the true worshipers will worship the Father in spirit and truth, for they are the kind of worshipers the Father seeks. 24 God is spirit, and his worshipers must worship in spirit and in truth."

25 The woman said, "I know that Messiah" (called Christ) "is coming. When he comes, he will explain everything to us."

26 Then Jesus declared, "I who speak to you am he."

The Disciples Rejoin Jesus

27 Just then his disciples returned and were surprised to find him talking with a woman. But no one asked, "What do you want?" or "Why are you talking with her?"

28 Then, leaving her water jar, the woman went back to the town and said to the people, 29 "Come, see a man who told me everything I ever did. Could this be the Christ[d]?" 30 They came out of the town and made their way toward him.

31 Meanwhile his disciples urged him, "Rabbi, eat something."

32 But he said to them, "I have food to eat that you know nothing about."

33 Then his disciples said to each other, "Could someone have brought him food?"

34 "My food," said Jesus, "is to do the will of him who sent me and to finish his work. 35 Do you not say, 'Four months more and then the harvest'? I tell you, open your eyes and look at the fields! They are ripe for harvest. 36 Even now the reaper draws his wages, even now he harvests the crop for eternal life, so that the sower and the reaper may be glad together. 37 Thus the saying 'One sows and another reaps' is true. 38 I sent you to reap what you have not worked for. Others have done the hard work, and you have reaped the benefits of their labor."

d 29 Or Messiah

Many Samaritans Believe

39 Many of the Samaritans from that town believed in him because of the woman's testimony, "He told me everything I ever did." **40** So when the Samaritans came to him, they urged him to stay with them, and he stayed two days. **41** And because of his words many more became believers.

42 They said to the woman, "We no longer believe just because of what you said; now we have heard for ourselves, and we know that this man really is the Savior of the world."

Jesus Heals the Official's Son

43 After the two days he left for Galilee. **44** (Now Jesus himself had pointed out that a prophet has no honor in his own country.) **45** When he arrived in Galilee, the Galileans welcomed him. They had seen all that he had done in Jerusalem at the Passover Feast, for they also had been there.

46 Once more he visited Cana in Galilee, where he had turned the water into wine. And there was a certain royal official whose son lay sick at Capernaum. **47** When this man heard that Jesus had arrived in Galilee from Judea, he went to him and begged him to come and heal his son, who was close to death.

48 "Unless you people see miraculous signs and wonders," Jesus told him, "you will never believe."

49 The royal official said, "Sir, come down before my child dies."

50 Jesus replied, "You may go. Your son will live."

The man took Jesus at his word and departed. **51** While he was still on the way, his servants met him with the news that his boy was living. **52** When he inquired as to the time when his son got better, they said to him, "The fever left him yesterday at the seventh hour."

53 Then the father realized that this was the exact time at which Jesus had said to him, "Your son will live." So he and all his household believed.

54 This was the second miraculous sign that Jesus performed, having come from Judea to Galilee.

The Healing at the Pool

5 **1** Some time later, Jesus went up to Jerusalem for a feast of the Jews. **2** Now there is in Jerusalem near the Sheep Gate a pool, which in Aramaic is called Bethesda[e] and which is surrounded by five covered colonnades. **3** Here a great number of disabled people used to lie — the blind, the lame, the paralyzed.[f] **5** One who was there had been an invalid for thirty-eight years. **6** When Jesus saw him lying there and learned that he had been in this condition for a long time, he asked him, "Do you want to get well?"

7 "Sir," the invalid replied, "I have no one to help me into the pool when the water is stirred. While I am trying to get in, someone else goes down ahead of me."

8 Then Jesus said to him, "Get up! Pick up your mat and walk." **9** At once the man was cured; he picked up his mat and walked.

The day on which this took place was a Sabbath, **10** and so the Jews

---

e 2 Some manuscripts *Bethzatha;* other manuscripts *Bethsaida*   *f* 3 Some less important manuscripts *paralyzed — and they waited for the moving of the waters.* *4 From time to time an angel of the Lord would come down and stir up the waters. The first one into the pool after each such disturbance would be cured of whatever disease he had.*

said to the man who had been healed, "It is the Sabbath; the law forbids you to carry your mat."

11 But he replied, "The man who made me well said to me, 'Pick up your mat and walk.'"

12 So they asked him, "Who is this fellow who told you to pick it up and walk?"

13 The man who was healed had no idea who it was, for Jesus had slipped away into the crowd that was there.

14 Later Jesus found him at the temple and said to him, "See, you are well again. Stop sinning or something worse may happen to you." **15** The man went away and told the Jews that it was Jesus who had made him well.

Life Through the Son

16 So, because Jesus was doing these things on the Sabbath, the Jews persecuted him. **17** Jesus said to them, "My Father is always at his work to this very day, and I, too, am working." **18** For this reason the Jews tried all the harder to kill him; not only was he breaking the Sabbath, but he was even calling God his own Father, making himself equal with God.

19 Jesus gave them this answer: "I tell you the truth, the Son can do nothing by himself; he can do only what he sees his Father doing, because whatever the Father does the Son also does. **20** For the Father loves the Son and shows him all he does. Yes, to your amazement he will show him even greater things than these. **21** For just as the Father raises the dead and gives them life, even so the Son gives life to whom he is pleased to give it. **22** Moreover, the Father judges no one, but has entrusted all judgment to the Son, **23** that all may honor the Son just as they honor the Father. He who does not honor the Son does not honor the Father, who sent him.

24 "I tell you the truth, whoever hears my word and believes him who sent me has eternal life and will not be condemned; he has crossed over from death to life. **25** I tell you the truth, a time is coming and has now come when the dead will hear the voice of the Son of God and those who hear will live. **26** For as the Father has life in himself, so he has granted the Son to have life in himself. **27** And he has given him authority to judge because he is the Son of Man.

28 "Do not be amazed at this, for a time is coming when all who are in their graves will hear his voice **29** and come out—those who have done good will rise to live, and those who have done evil will rise to be condemned. **30** By myself I can do nothing; I judge only as I hear, and my judgment is just, for I seek not to please myself but him who sent me.

Testimonies About Jesus

31 "If I testify about myself, my testimony is not valid. **32** There is another who testifies in my favor, and I know that his testimony about me is valid.

33 "You have sent to John and he has testified to the truth. **34** Not that I accept human testimony; but I mention it that you may be saved. **35** John was a lamp that burned and gave light, and you chose for a time to enjoy his light.

36 "I have testimony weightier than that of John. For the very work that the Father has given me to finish, and which I am doing, testifies that the Father has sent me. **37** And the Father who sent me has himself testified concerning me. You have never heard his voice nor seen his form,

38 nor does his word dwell in you, for you do not believe the one he sent. **39** You diligently study[g] the Scriptures because you think that by them you possess eternal life. These are the Scriptures that testify about me, **40** yet you refuse to come to me to have life.

41 "I do not accept praise from men, **42** but I know you. I know that you do not have the love of God in your hearts. **43** I have come in my Father's name, and you do not accept me; but if someone else comes in his own name, you will accept him. **44** How can you believe if you accept praise from one another, yet make no effort to obtain the praise that comes from the only God[h]?

45 "But do not think I will accuse you before the Father. Your accuser is Moses, on whom your hopes are set. **46** If you believed Moses, you would believe me, for he wrote about me. **47** But since you do not believe what he wrote, how are you going to believe what I say?"

Jesus Feeds the Five Thousand

6 **1** Some time after this, Jesus crossed to the far shore of the Sea of Galilee (that is, the Sea of Tiberias), **2** and a great crowd of people followed him because they saw the miraculous signs he had performed on the sick. **3** Then Jesus went up on a mountainside and sat down with his disciples. **4** The Jewish Passover Feast was near.

5 When Jesus looked up and saw a great crowd coming toward him, he said to Philip, "Where shall we buy bread for these people to eat?" **6** He asked this only to test him, for he already had in mind what he was going to do.

7 Philip answered him, "Eight months' wages[i] would not buy enough bread for each one to have a bite!"

8 Another of his disciples, Andrew, Simon Peter's brother, spoke up, **9** "Here is a boy with five small barley loaves and two small fish, but how far will they go among so many?"

10 Jesus said, "Have the people sit down." There was plenty of grass in that place, and the men sat down, about five thousand of them. **11** Jesus then took the loaves, gave thanks, and distributed to those who were seated as much as they wanted. He did the same with the fish.

12 When they had all had enough to eat, he said to his disciples, "Gather the pieces that are left over. Let nothing be wasted." **13** So they gathered them and filled twelve baskets with the pieces of the five barley loaves left over by those who had eaten.

14 After the people saw the miraculous sign that Jesus did, they began to say, "Surely this is the Prophet who is to come into the world." **15** Jesus, knowing that they intended to come and make him king by force, withdrew again to a mountain by himself.

Jesus Walks on the Water

16 When evening came, his disciples went down to the lake, **17** where they got into a boat and set off across the lake for Capernaum. By now it was dark, and Jesus had not yet joined them. **18** A strong wind was blowing and the waters grew rough. **19** When they had rowed three or three and a half miles,[j] they saw Jesus

---

g 39 Or *Study diligently* (the imperative)   *h 44* Some early manuscripts *the Only One*
i 7 Greek *two hundred denarii*   *j 19* Greek *rowed twenty-five or thirty stadia* (about 5 or 6 kilometers)

approaching the boat, walking on the water; and they were terrified. **20** But he said to them, "It is I; don't be afraid." **21** Then they were willing to take him into the boat, and immediately the boat reached the shore where they were heading.

22 The next day the crowd that had stayed on the opposite shore of the lake realized that only one boat had been there, and that Jesus had not entered it with his disciples, but that they had gone away alone. **23** Then some boats from Tiberias landed near the place where the people had eaten the bread after the Lord had given thanks. **24** Once the crowd realized that neither Jesus nor his disciples were there, they got into the boats and went to Capernaum in search of Jesus.

Jesus the Bread of Life

25 When they found him on the other side of the lake, they asked him, "Rabbi, when did you get here?"

26 Jesus answered, "I tell you the truth, you are looking for me, not because you saw miraculous signs but because you ate the loaves and had your fill. **27** Do not work for food that spoils, but for food that endures to eternal life, which the Son of Man will give you. On him God the Father has placed his seal of approval."

28 Then they asked him, "What must we do to do the works God requires?"

29 Jesus answered, "The work of God is this: to believe in the one he has sent."

30 So they asked him, "What miraculous sign then will you give that we may see it and believe you? What will you do? **31** Our forefathers ate the manna in the desert; as it is

written: 'He gave them bread from heaven to eat.'[k]"

32 Jesus said to them, "I tell you the truth, it is not Moses who has given you the bread from heaven, but it is my Father who gives you the true bread from heaven. **33** For the bread of God is he who comes down from heaven and gives life to the world."

34 "Sir," they said, "from now on give us this bread."

35 Then Jesus declared, "I am the bread of life. He who comes to me will never go hungry, and he who believes in me will never be thirsty. **36** But as I told you, you have seen me and still you do not believe. **37** All that the Father gives me will come to me, and whoever comes to me I will never drive away. **38** For I have come down from heaven not to do my will but to do the will of him who sent me. **39** And this is the will of him who sent me, that I shall lose none of all that he has given me, but raise them up at the last day. **40** For my Father's will is that everyone who looks to the Son and believes in him shall have eternal life, and I will raise him up at the last day."

41 At this the Jews began to grumble about him because he said, "I am the bread that came down from heaven." **42** They said, "Is this not Jesus, the son of Joseph, whose father and mother we know? How can he now say, 'I came down from heaven'?"

43 "Stop grumbling among yourselves," Jesus answered. **44** "No one can come to me unless the Father who sent me draws him, and I will raise him up at the last day. **45** It is written in the Prophets: 'They will all be taught by God.'[l] Everyone who listens to the Father and learns from him comes to me. **46** No one has seen the

k 31 Exodus 16:4; Neh. 9:15; Psalm 78:24,25   *l* 45 Isaiah 54:13

Father except the one who is from God; only he has seen the Father. **47** I tell you the truth, he who believes has everlasting life. **48** I am the bread of life. **49** Your forefathers ate the manna in the desert, yet they died. **50** But here is the bread that comes down from heaven, which a man may eat and not die. **51** I am the living bread that came down from heaven. If anyone eats of this bread, he will live forever. This bread is my flesh, which I will give for the life of the world."

52 Then the Jews began to argue sharply among themselves, "How can this man give us his flesh to eat?"

53 Jesus said to them, "I tell you the truth, unless you eat the flesh of the Son of Man and drink his blood, you have no life in you. **54** Whoever eats my flesh and drinks my blood has eternal life, and I will raise him up at the last day. **55** For my flesh is real food and my blood is real drink. **56** Whoever eats my flesh and drinks my blood remains in me, and I in him. **57** Just as the living Father sent me and I live because of the Father, so the one who feeds on me will live because of me. **58** This is the bread that came down from heaven. Your forefathers ate manna and died, but he who feeds on this bread will live forever. **59** He said this while teaching in the synagogue in Capernaum.

Many Disciples Desert Jesus

60 On hearing it, many of his disciples said, "This is a hard teaching. Who can accept it?"

61 Aware that his disciples were grumbling about this, Jesus said to them, "Does this offend you? **62** What if you see the Son of Man ascend to where he was before! **63** The Spirit gives life; the flesh counts for nothing. The words I have spoken to you are spirit^m and they are life. **64** Yet there are some of you who do not believe." For Jesus had known from the beginning which of them did not believe and who would betray him. **65** He went on to say, "This is why I told you that no one can come to me unless the Father has enabled him."

66 From this time many of his disciples turned back and no longer followed him.

67 "You do not want to leave too, do you?" Jesus asked the Twelve.

68 Simon Peter answered him, "Lord, to whom shall we go? You have the words of eternal life. **69** We believe and know that you are the Holy One of God."

70 Then Jesus replied, "Have I not chosen you, the Twelve? Yet one of you is a devil!" **71** (He meant Judas, the son of Simon Iscariot, who, though one of the Twelve, was later to betray him.)

Jesus Goes to the Feast of Tabernacles

7 **1** After this, Jesus went around in Galilee, purposely staying away from Judea because the Jews there were waiting to take his life. **2** But when the Jewish Feast of Tabernacles was near, **3** Jesus' brothers said to him, "You ought to leave here and go to Judea, so that your disciples may see the miracles you do. **4** No one who wants to become a public figure acts in secret. Since you are doing these things, show yourself to the world." **5** For even his own brothers did not believe in him.

6 Therefore Jesus told them, "The right time for me has not yet come; for you any time is right. **7** The world

---

m 63 Or Spirit

cannot hate you, but it hates me because I testify that what it does is evil. 8 You go to the Feast. I am not yet[n] going up to this Feast, because for me the right time has not yet come." 9 Having said this, he stayed in Galilee.

10 However, after his brothers had left for the Feast, he went also, not publicly, but in secret. 11 Now at the Feast the Jews were watching for him and asking, "Where is that man?"

12 Among the crowds there was widespread whispering about him. Some said, "He is a good man."

Others replied, "No, he deceives the people." 13 But no one would say anything publicly about him for fear of the Jews.

Jesus Teaches at the Feast

14 Not until halfway through the Feast did Jesus go up to the temple courts and begin to teach. 15 The Jews were amazed and asked, "How did this man get such learning without having studied?"

16 Jesus answered, "My teaching is not my own. It comes from him who sent me. 17 If anyone chooses to do God's will, he will find out whether my teaching comes from God or whether I speak on my own. 18 He who speaks on his own does so to gain honor for himself, but he who works for the honor of the one who sent him is a man of truth; there is nothing false about him. 19 Has not Moses given you the law? Yet not one of you keeps the law. Why are you trying to kill me?"

20 "You are demon-possessed," the crowd answered. "Who is trying to kill you?"

21 Jesus said to them, "I did one miracle, and you are all astonished. 22 Yet, because Moses gave you circumcision (though actually it did not come from Moses, but from the patriarchs), you circumcise a child on the Sabbath. 23 Now if a child can be circumcised on the Sabbath so that the law of Moses may not be broken, why are you angry with me for healing the whole man on the Sabbath? 24 Stop judging by mere appearances, and make a right judgment."

Is Jesus the Christ?

25 At that point some of the people of Jerusalem began to ask, "Isn't this the man they are trying to kill? 26 Here he is, speaking publicly, and they are not saying a word to him. Have the authorities really concluded that he is the Christ?[o] 27 But we know where this man is from; when the Christ comes, no one will know where he is from."

28 Then Jesus, still teaching in the temple courts, cried out, "Yes, you know me, and you know where I am from. I am not here on my own, but he who sent me is true. You do not know him, 29 but I know him because I am from him and he sent me."

30 At this they tried to seize him, but no one laid a hand on him, because his time had not yet come. 31 Still, many in the crowd put their faith in him. They said, "When the Christ comes, will he do more miraculous signs than this man?"

32 The Pharisees heard the crowd whispering such things about him. Then the chief priests and the Pharisees sent temple guards to arrest him.

---

n 8 Some early manuscripts do not have *yet*.   *o* 26 Or *Messiah;* also in verses 27, 31, 41
and 42

33 Jesus said, "I am with you for
only a short time, and then I go to the
one who sent me. 34 You will look for
me, but you will not find me; and
where I am, you cannot come."
35 The Jews said to one another,
"Where does this man intend to go
that we cannot find him? Will he go
where our people live scattered
among the Greeks, and teach the
Greeks? 36 What did he mean when
he said, 'You will look for me, but you
will not find me,' and 'Where I am,
you cannot come'?"
37 On the last and greatest day of
the Feast, Jesus stood and said in a
loud voice, "If anyone is thirsty, let him
come to me and drink. 38 Whoever
believes in me, as[p] the Scripture has
said, streams of living water will flow
from within him." 39 By this he meant
the Spirit, whom those who believed
in him were later to receive. Up to that
time the Spirit had not been given,
since Jesus had not yet been glorified.
40 On hearing his words, some of
the people said, "Surely this man is
the Prophet."
41 Others said, "He is the Christ."
Still others asked, "How can the
Christ come from Galilee? 42 Does
not the Scripture say that the Christ
will come from David's family[q] and
from Bethlehem, the town where
David lived?" 43 Thus the people
were divided because of Jesus.
44 Some wanted to seize him, but no
one laid a hand on him.

Unbelief of the Jewish Leaders

45 Finally the temple guards went
back to the chief priests and
Pharisees, who asked them, "Why
didn't you bring him in?"
46 "No one ever spoke the way this
man does," the guards declared.
47 "You mean he has deceived you
also?" the Pharisees retorted.
48 "Has any of the rulers or of the
Pharisees believed in him? 49 No!
But this mob that knows nothing of
the law—there is a curse on them."
50 Nicodemus, who had gone to
Jesus earlier and who was one of
their own number, asked, 51 "Does
our law condemn anyone without
first hearing him to find out what he
is doing?"
52 They replied, "Are you from
Galilee, too? Look into it, and you
will find that a prophet[r] does not
come out of Galilee."

[The earliest and most reliable
manuscripts and other ancient witnesses do not have John 7:53-8:11.]

53 Then each went to his own
home.
8 1 But Jesus went to the Mount of
Olives. 2 At dawn he appeared
again in the temple courts, where all
the people gathered around him, and
he sat down to teach them. 3 The
teachers of the law and the Pharisees
brought in a woman caught in adultery. They made her stand before the
group 4 and said to Jesus, "Teacher,
this woman was caught in the act of
adultery. 5 In the Law Moses commanded us to stone such women.
Now what do you say?" 6 They were
using this question as a trap, in order
to have a basis for accusing him.
But Jesus bent down and started
to write on the ground with his
finger. 7 When they kept on questioning him, he straightened up and said
to them, "If any one of you is without

p 38 Or / *If anyone is thirsty, let him come to me. / And let him drink,* 38 *who believes in me. / As* q 42 Greek *seed* r 52 Two early manuscripts *the Prophet*

sin, let him be the first to throw a stone at her." 8 Again he stooped down and wrote on the ground.

9 At this, those who heard began to go away one at a time, the older ones first, until only Jesus was left, with the woman still standing there. 10 Jesus straightened up and asked her, "Woman, where are they? Has no one condemned you?"

11 "No one, sir," she said.

"Then neither do I condemn you," Jesus declared. "Go now and leave your life of sin."

The Validity of Jesus' Testimony

12 When Jesus spoke again to the people, he said, "I am the light of the world. Whoever follows me will never walk in darkness, but will have the light of life."

13 The Pharisees challenged him, "Here you are, appearing as your own witness; your testimony is not valid."

14 Jesus answered, "Even if I testify on my own behalf, my testimony is valid, for I know where I came from and where I am going. But you have no idea where I come from or where I am going. 15 You judge by human standards; I pass judgment on no one. 16 But if I do judge, my decisions are right, because I am not alone. I stand with the Father, who sent me. 17 In your own Law it is written that the testimony of two men is valid. 18 I am one who testifies for myself; my other witness is the Father, who sent me."

19 Then they asked him, "Where is your father?"

"You do not know me or my Father," Jesus replied. "If you knew me, you would know my Father

also." 20 He spoke these words while teaching in the temple area near the place where the offerings were put. Yet no one seized him, because his time had not yet come.

21 Once more Jesus said to them, "I am going away, and you will look for me, and you will die in your sin. Where I go, you cannot come."

22 This made the Jews ask, "Will he kill himself? Is that why he says, 'Where I go, you cannot come'?"

23 But he continued, "You are from below; I am from above. You are of this world; I am not of this world. 24 I told you that you would die in your sins; if you do not believe that I am the one I claim to be,⁵ you will indeed die in your sins."

25 "Who are you?" they asked.

"Just what I have been claiming all along," Jesus replied. 26 "I have much to say in judgment of you. But he who sent me is reliable, and what I have heard from him I tell the world."

27 They did not understand that he was telling them about his Father. 28 So Jesus said, "When you have lifted up the Son of Man, then you will know that I am the one I claim to be and that I do nothing on my own but speak just what the Father has taught me. 29 The one who sent me is with me; he has not left me alone, for I always do what pleases him." 30 Even as he spoke, many put their faith in him.

The Children of Abraham

31 To the Jews who had believed him, Jesus said, "If you hold to my teaching, you are really my disciples. 32 Then you will know the truth, and the truth will set you free."

---

⁵ 24 Or *I am he;* also in verse 28

33 They answered him, "We are Abraham's descendants[t] and have never been slaves of anyone. How can you say that we shall be set free?"

34 Jesus replied, "I tell you the truth, everyone who sins is a slave to sin. 35 Now a slave has no permanent place in the family, but a son belongs to it forever. 36 So if the Son sets you free, you will be free indeed. 37 I know you are Abraham's descendants. Yet you are ready to kill me, because you have no room for my word. 38 I am telling you what I have seen in the Father's presence, and you do what you have heard from your father.[u]

39 "Abraham is our father," they answered.

"If you were Abraham's children," said Jesus, "then you would[v] do the things Abraham did. 40 As it is, you are determined to kill me, a man who has told you the truth that I heard from God. Abraham did not do such things. 41 You are doing the things your own father does."

"We are not illegitimate children," they protested. "The only Father we have is God himself."

The Children of the Devil

42 Jesus said to them, "If God were your Father, you would love me, for I came from God and now am here. I have not come on my own; but he sent me. 43 Why is my language not clear to you? Because you are unable to hear what I say. 44 You belong to your father, the devil, and you want to carry out your father's desire. He was a murderer from the beginning, not holding to the truth, for there is no truth in him. When he lies, he speaks his native language, for he is a liar and the father of lies. 45 Yet because I tell the truth, you do not believe me! 46 Can any of you prove me guilty of sin? If I am telling the truth, why don't you believe me? 47 He who belongs to God hears what God says. The reason you do not hear is that you do not belong to God."

The Claims of Jesus About Himself

48 The Jews answered him, "Aren't we right in saying that you are a Samaritan and demon-possessed?"

49 "I am not possessed by a demon," said Jesus, "but I honor my Father and you dishonor me. 50 I am not seeking glory for myself; but there is one who seeks it, and he is the judge. 51 I tell you the truth, if anyone keeps my word, he will never see death."

52 At this the Jews exclaimed, "Now we know that you are demon-possessed! Abraham died and so did the prophets, yet you say that if anyone keeps your word, he will never taste death. 53 Are you greater than our father Abraham? He died, and so did the prophets. Who do you think you are?"

54 Jesus replied, "If I glorify myself, my glory means nothing. My Father, whom you claim as your God, is the one who glorifies me. 55 Though you do not know him, I know him. If I said I did not, I would be a liar like you, but I do know him and keep his word. 56 Your father Abraham rejoiced at the thought of seeing my day; he saw it and was glad."

57 "You are not yet fifty years old," the Jews said to him, "and you have seen Abraham!"

---

[t] 33 Greek *seed*; also in verse 37   [u] 38 Or *presence. Therefore do what you have heard from the Father.*   [v] 39 Some early manuscripts *"If you are Abraham's children," said Jesus, "then*

58 "I tell you the truth," Jesus answered, "before Abraham was born, I am!" **59** At this, they picked up stones to stone him, but Jesus hid himself, slipping away from the temple grounds.

Jesus Heals a Man Born Blind

9 **1** As he went along, he saw a man blind from birth. **2** His disciples asked him, "Rabbi, who sinned, this man or his parents, that he was born blind?"

3 "Neither this man nor his parents sinned," said Jesus, "but this happened so that the work of God might be displayed in his life. **4** As long as it is day, we must do the work of him who sent me. Night is coming, when no one can work. **5** While I am in the world, I am the light of the world."

6 Having said this, he spit on the ground, made some mud with the saliva, and put it on the man's eyes. **7** "Go," he told him, "wash in the Pool of Siloam" (this word means Sent). So the man went and washed, and came home seeing.

8 His neighbors and those who had formerly seen him begging asked, "Isn't this the same man who used to sit and beg?" **9** Some claimed that he was.

Others said, "No, he only looks like him."

But he himself insisted, "I am the man."

10 "How then were your eyes opened?" they demanded.

11 He replied, "The man they call Jesus made some mud and put it on my eyes. He told me to go to Siloam and wash. So I went and washed, and then I could see."

12 "Where is this man?" they asked him.

"I don't know," he said.

The Pharisees Investigate the Healing

13 They brought to the Pharisees the man who had been blind. **14** Now the day on which Jesus had made the mud and opened the man's eyes was a Sabbath. **15** Therefore the Pharisees also asked him how he had received his sight. "He put mud on my eyes," the man replied, "and I washed, and now I see."

16 Some of the Pharisees said, "This man is not from God, for he does not keep the Sabbath."

But others asked, "How can a sinner do such miraculous signs?" So they were divided.

17 Finally they turned again to the blind man, "What have you to say about him? It was your eyes he opened."

The man replied, "He is a prophet."

18 The Jews still did not believe that he had been blind and had received his sight until they sent for the man's parents. **19** "Is this your son?" they asked. "Is this the one you say was born blind? How is it that now he can see?"

20 "We know he is our son," the parents answered, "and we know he was born blind. **21** But how he can see now, or who opened his eyes, we don't know. Ask him. He is of age; he will speak for himself." **22** His parents said this because they were afraid of the Jews, for already the Jews had decided that anyone who acknowledged that Jesus was the Christ[w] would be put out of the synagogue. **23** That was

---

[w] 22 Or *Messiah*

why his parents said, "He is of age; ask him."

24 A second time they summoned the man who had been blind. "Give glory to God," they said. "We know this man is a sinner."

25 He replied, "Whether he is a sinner or not, I don't know. One thing I do know. I was blind but now I see!"

26 Then they asked him, "What did he do to you? How did he open your eyes?"

27 He answered, "I have told you already and you did not listen. Why do you want to hear it again? Do you want to become his disciples, too?"

28 Then they hurled insults at him and said, "You are this fellow's disciple! We are disciples of Moses! **29** We know that God spoke to Moses, but as for this fellow, we don't even know where he comes from."

30 The man answered, "Now that is remarkable! You don't know where he comes from, yet he opened my eyes. **31** We know that God does not listen to sinners. He listens to the godly man who does his will. **32** Nobody has ever heard of opening the eyes of a man born blind. **33** If this man were not from God, he could do nothing."

34 To this they replied, "You were steeped in sin at birth; how dare you lecture us!" And they threw him out.

Spiritual Blindness

35 Jesus heard that they had thrown him out, and when he found him, he said, "Do you believe in the Son of Man?"

36 "Who is he, sir?" the man asked. "Tell me so that I may believe in him."

37 Jesus said, "You have now seen him; in fact, he is the one speaking with you."

38 Then the man said, "Lord, I believe," and he worshiped him.

39 Jesus said, "For judgment I have come into this world, so that the blind will see and those who see will become blind."

40 Some Pharisees who were with him heard him say this and asked, "What? Are we blind too?"

41 Jesus said, "If you were blind, you would not be guilty of sin; but now that you claim you can see, your guilt remains.

The Shepherd and His Flock

10 **1** "I tell you the truth, the man who does not enter the sheep pen by the gate, but climbs in by some other way, is a thief and a robber. **2** The man who enters by the gate is the shepherd of his sheep. **3** The watchman opens the gate for him, and the sheep listen to his voice. He calls his own sheep by name and leads them out. **4** When he has brought out all his own, he goes on ahead of them, and his sheep follow him because they know his voice. **5** But they will never follow a stranger; in fact, they will run away from him because they do not recognize a stranger's voice." **6** Jesus used this figure of speech, but they did not understand what he was telling them.

7 Therefore Jesus said again, "I tell you the truth, I am the gate for the sheep. **8** All who ever came before me were thieves and robbers, but the sheep did not listen to them. **9** I am the gate; whoever enters through me will be saved.*y* He will come in and go out, and find pasture. **10** The thief comes only to steal and kill and destroy; I have come that they may have life, and have it to the full.

11 "I am the good shepherd. The good shepherd lays down his life for the sheep. **12** The hired hand is not the shepherd who owns the sheep. So when he sees the wolf coming, he abandons the sheep and runs away. Then the wolf attacks the flock and scatters it. **13** The man runs away because he is a hired hand and cares nothing for the sheep.

14 "I am the good shepherd; I know my sheep and my sheep know me— **15** just as the Father knows me and I know the Father—and I lay down my life for the sheep. **16** I have other sheep that are not of this sheep pen. I must bring them also. They too will listen to my voice, and there shall be one flock and one shepherd. **17** The reason my Father loves me is that I lay down my life—only to take it up again. **18** No one takes it from me, but I lay it down of my own accord. I have authority to lay it down and authority to take it up again. This command I received from my Father."

19 At these words the Jews were again divided. **20** Many of them said, "He is demon-possessed and raving mad. Why listen to him?"

21 But others said, "These are not the sayings of a man possessed by a demon. Can a demon open the eyes of the blind?"

The Unbelief of the Jews

22 Then came the Feast of Dedication[z] at Jerusalem. It was winter, **23** and Jesus was in the temple area walking in Solomon's Colonnade. **24** The Jews gathered around him, saying, "How long will you keep us in suspense? If you are the Christ,[a] tell us plainly."

25 Jesus answered, "I did tell you, but you do not believe. The miracles I do in my Father's name speak for me, **26** but you do not believe because you are not my sheep. **27** My sheep listen to my voice; I know them, and they follow me. **28** I give them eternal life, and they shall never perish; no one can snatch them out of my hand. **29** My Father, who has given them to me, is greater than all[b]; no one can snatch them out of my Father's hand. **30** I and the Father are one."

31 Again the Jews picked up stones to stone him, **32** but Jesus said to them, "I have shown you many great miracles from the Father. For which of these do you stone me?"

33 "We are not stoning you for any of these," replied the Jews, "but for blasphemy, because you, a mere man, claim to be God."

34 Jesus answered them, "Is it not written in your Law, 'I have said you are gods'[c]? **35** If he called them 'gods,' to whom the word of God came—and the Scripture cannot be broken— **36** what about the one whom the Father set apart as his very own and sent into the world? Why then do you accuse me of blasphemy because I said, 'I am God's Son'? **37** Do not believe me unless I do what my Father does. **38** But if I do it, even though you do not believe me, believe the miracles, that you may know and understand that the Father is in me, and I in the Father." **39** Again

---

z 22 That is, Hanukkah   a 24 Or *Messiah*   b 29 Many early manuscripts *What my Father has given me is greater than all*   c 34 Psalm 82:6

they tried to seize him, but he escaped their grasp.

40 Then Jesus went back across the Jordan to the place where John had been baptizing in the early days. Here he stayed **41** and many people came to him. They said, "Though John never performed a miraculous sign, all that John said about this man was true." **42** And in that place many believed in Jesus.

The Death of Lazarus

11 **1** Now a man named Lazarus was sick. He was from Bethany, the village of Mary and her sister Martha. **2** This Mary, whose brother Lazarus now lay sick, was the same one who poured perfume on the Lord and wiped his feet with her hair. **3** So the sisters sent word to Jesus, "Lord, the one you love is sick."

4 When he heard this, Jesus said, "This sickness will not end in death. No, it is for God's glory so that God's Son may be glorified through it." **5** Jesus loved Martha and her sister and Lazarus. **6** Yet when he heard that Lazarus was sick, he stayed where he was two more days.

7 Then he said to his disciples, "Let us go back to Judea."

8 "But Rabbi," they said, "a short while ago the Jews tried to stone you, and yet you are going back there?"

9 Jesus answered, "Are there not twelve hours of daylight? A man who walks by day will not stumble, for he sees by this world's light. **10** It is when he walks by night that he stumbles, for he has no light."

11 After he had said this, he went on to tell them, "Our friend Lazarus has fallen asleep; but I am going there to wake him up."

12 His disciples replied, "Lord, if he sleeps, he will get better." **13** Jesus had been speaking of his death, but his disciples thought he meant natural sleep.

14 So then he told them plainly, "Lazarus is dead, **15** and for your sake I am glad I was not there, so that you may believe. But let us go to him."

16 Then Thomas (called Didymus) said to the rest of the disciples, "Let us also go, that we may die with him."

Jesus Comforts the Sisters

17 On his arrival, Jesus found that Lazarus had already been in the tomb for four days. **18** Bethany was less than two milesd from Jerusalem, **19** and many Jews had come to Martha and Mary to comfort them in the loss of their brother. **20** When Martha heard that Jesus was coming, she went out to meet him, but Mary stayed at home.

21 "Lord," Martha said to Jesus, "if you had been here, my brother would not have died. **22** But I know that even now God will give you whatever you ask."

23 Jesus said to her, "Your brother will rise again."

24 Martha answered, "I know he will rise again in the resurrection at the last day."

25 Jesus said to her, "I am the resurrection and the life. He who believes in me will live, even though he dies; **26** and whoever lives and believes in me will never die. Do you believe this?"

27 "Yes, Lord," she told him, "I believe that you are the Christ,e the Son of God, who was to come into the world."

---

d 18 Greek *fifteen stadia* (about 3 kilometers)   e 27 Or Messiah

28 And after she had said this, she went back and called her sister Mary aside. "The Teacher is here," she said, "and is asking for you." **29** When Mary heard this, she got up quickly and went to him. **30** Now Jesus had not yet entered the village, but was still at the place where Martha had met him. **31** When the Jews who had been with Mary in the house, comforting her, noticed how quickly she got up and went out, they followed her, supposing she was going to the tomb to mourn there.

32 When Mary reached the place where Jesus was and saw him, she fell at his feet and said, "Lord, if you had been here, my brother would not have died."

33 When Jesus saw her weeping, and the Jews who had come along with her also weeping, he was deeply moved in spirit and troubled. **34** "Where have you laid him?" he asked.

"Come and see, Lord," they replied.

35 Jesus wept.

36 Then the Jews said, "See how he loved him!"

37 But some of them said, "Could not he who opened the eyes of the blind man have kept this man from dying?"

Jesus Raises Lazarus From the Dead

38 Jesus, once more deeply moved, came to the tomb. It was a cave with a stone laid across the entrance. **39** "Take away the stone," he said.

"But, Lord," said Martha, the sister of the dead man, "by this time there is a bad odor, for he has been there four days."

40 Then Jesus said, "Did I not tell you that if you believed, you would see the glory of God?"

41 So they took away the stone. Then Jesus looked up and said, "Father, I thank you that you have heard me. **42** I knew that you always hear me, but I said this for the benefit of the people standing here, that they may believe that you sent me."

43 When he had said this, Jesus called in a loud voice, "Lazarus, come out!" **44** The dead man came out, his hands and feet wrapped with strips of linen, and a cloth around his face.

Jesus said to them, "Take off the grave clothes and let him go."

The Plot to Kill Jesus

45 Therefore many of the Jews who had come to visit Mary, and had seen what Jesus did, put their faith in him. **46** But some of them went to the Pharisees and told them what Jesus had done. **47** Then the chief priests and the Pharisees called a meeting of the Sanhedrin.

"What are we accomplishing?" they asked. "Here is this man performing many miraculous signs. **48** If we let him go on like this, everyone will believe in him, and then the Romans will come and take away both our place[f] and our nation."

49 Then one of them, named Caiaphas, who was high priest that year, spoke up, "You know nothing at all! **50** You do not realize that it is better for you that one man die for the people than that the whole nation perish."

51 He did not say this on his own, but as high priest that year he prophesied that Jesus would die for the Jewish nation, **52** and not only

f 48 Or temple

for that nation but also for the scattered children of God, to bring them together and make them one. **53** So from that day on they plotted to take his life.

54 Therefore Jesus no longer moved about publicly among the Jews. Instead he withdrew to a region near the desert, to a village called Ephraim, where he stayed with his disciples.

55 When it was almost time for the Jewish Passover, many went up from the country to Jerusalem for their ceremonial cleansing before the Passover. **56** They kept looking for Jesus, and as they stood in the temple area they asked one another, "What do you think? Isn't he coming to the Feast at all?" **57** But the chief priests and Pharisees had given orders that if anyone found out where Jesus was, he should report it so that they might arrest him.

Jesus Anointed at Bethany

12 **1** Six days before the Passover, Jesus arrived at Bethany, where Lazarus lived, whom Jesus had raised from the dead. **2** Here a dinner was given in Jesus' honor. Martha served, while Lazarus was among those reclining at the table with him. **3** Then Mary took about a pint*g* of pure nard, an expensive perfume; she poured it on Jesus' feet and wiped his feet with her hair. And the house was filled with the fragrance of the perfume.

4 But one of his disciples, Judas Iscariot, who was later to betray him, objected, **5** "Why wasn't this perfume sold and the money given to the

poor? It was worth a year's wages.*h* " **6** He did not say this because he cared about the poor but because he was a thief; as keeper of the money bag, he used to help himself to what was put into it.

7 "Leave her alone," Jesus replied. " It was intended that she should save this perfume for the day of my burial. **8** You will always have the poor among you, but you will not always have me."

9 Meanwhile a large crowd of Jews found out that Jesus was there and came, not only because of him but also to see Lazarus, whom he had raised from the dead. **10** So the chief priests made plans to kill Lazarus as well, **11** for on account of him many of the Jews were going over to Jesus and putting their faith in him.

The Triumphal Entry

12 The next day the great crowd that had come for the Feast heard that Jesus was on his way to Jerusalem. **13** They took palm branches and went out to meet him, shouting,

"Hosanna!*i* "

"Blessed is he who comes in the name of the Lord!"*j*

"Blessed is the King of Israel!"

14 Jesus found a young donkey and sat upon it, as it is written,

15 "Do not be afraid, O Daughter of Zion;
    see, your king is coming,
    seated on a donkey's colt."*k*

16 At first his disciples did not understand all this. Only after Jesus

---

g 3 Greek *a litra* (probably about 0.5 liter)   *h* 5 Greek *three hundred denarii*
i 13 A Hebrew expression meaning "Save!" which became an exclamation of praise
j 13 Psalm 118:25, 26   *k* 15 Zech. 9:9

was glorified did they realize that these things had been written about him and that they had done these things to him.

17 Now the crowd that was with him when he called Lazarus from the tomb and raised him from the dead continued to spread the word. **18** Many people, because they had heard that he had given this miraculous sign, went out to meet him. **19** So the Pharisees said to one another, "See, this is getting us nowhere. Look how the whole world has gone after him!"

Jesus Predicts His Death

20 Now there were some Greeks among those who went up to worship at the Feast. **21** They came to Philip, who was from Bethsaida in Galilee, with a request. "Sir," they said, "we would like to see Jesus." **22** Philip went to tell Andrew; Andrew and Philip in turn told Jesus.

23 Jesus replied, "The hour has come for the Son of Man to be glorified. **24** I tell you the truth, unless a kernel of wheat falls to the ground and dies, it remains only a single seed. But if it dies, it produces many seeds. **25** The man who loves his life will lose it, while the man who hates his life in this world will keep it for eternal life. **26** Whoever serves me must follow me; and where I am, my servant also will be. My Father will honor the one who serves me.

27 "Now my heart is troubled, and what shall I say? 'Father, save me from this hour'? No, it was for this very reason I came to this hour. **28** Father, glorify your name!"

Then a voice came from heaven, "I have glorified it, and will glorify it

again." **29** The crowd that was there and heard it said it had thundered; others said an angel had spoken to him.

30 Jesus said, "This voice was for your benefit, not mine. **31** Now is the time for judgment on this world; now the prince of this world will be driven out. **32** But I, when I am lifted up from the earth, will draw all men to myself." **33** He said this to show the kind of death he was going to die.

34 The crowd spoke up, "We have heard from the Law that the Christ[l] will remain forever, so how can you say, 'The Son of Man must be lifted up'? Who is this 'Son of Man'?"

35 Then Jesus told them, "You are going to have the light just a little while longer. Walk while you have the light, before darkness overtakes you. The man who walks in the dark does not know where he is going. **36** Put your trust in the light while you have it, so that you may become sons of light." When he had finished speaking, Jesus left and hid himself from them.

The Jews Continue in Their Unbelief

37 Even after Jesus had done all these miraculous signs in their presence, they still would not believe in him. **38** This was to fulfill the word of Isaiah the prophet:

> "Lord, who has believed our
> message
> and to whom has the arm of
> the Lord been revealed?"[m]

39 For this reason they could not believe, because, as Isaiah says elsewhere:

40 "He has blinded their eyes
and deadened their hearts,

---

l 34 Or Messiah   *m 38* Isaiah 53:1

so they can neither see with
      their eyes,
   nor understand with their
      hearts,
   nor turn — and I would heal
      them."[n]

41 Isaiah said this because he saw Jesus' glory and spoke about him.

42 Yet at the same time many even among the leaders believed in him. But because of the Pharisees they would not confess their faith for fear they would be put out of the synagogue; 43 for they loved praise from men more than praise from God.

44 Then Jesus cried out, "When a man believes in me, he does not believe in me only, but in the one who sent me. 45 When he looks at me, he sees the one who sent me. 46 I have come into the world as a light, so that no one who believes in me should stay in darkness.

47 "As for the person who hears my words but does not keep them, I do not judge him. For I did not come to judge the world, but to save it. 48 There is a judge for the one who rejects me and does not accept my words; that very word which I spoke will condemn him at the last day. 49 For I did not speak of my own accord, but the Father who sent me commanded me what to say and how to say it. 50 I know that his command leads to eternal life. So whatever I say is just what the Father has told me to say."

Jesus Washes His Disciples' Feet

13 1 It was just before the Passover Feast. Jesus knew that the time had come for him to leave this world and go to the Father. Having loved his own who were in the world, he now showed them the full extent of his love.[o]

2 The evening meal was being served, and the devil had already prompted Judas Iscariot, son of Simon, to betray Jesus. 3 Jesus knew that the Father had put all things under his power, and that he had come from God and was returning to God; 4 so he got up from the meal, took off his outer clothing, and wrapped a towel around his waist. 5 After that, he poured water into a basin and began to wash his disciples' feet, drying them with the towel that was wrapped around him.

6 He came to Simon Peter, who said to him, "Lord, are you going to wash my feet?"

7 Jesus replied, "You do not realize now what I am doing, but later you will understand."

8 "No," said Peter, "you shall never wash my feet."

Jesus answered, "Unless I wash you, you have no part with me."

9 "Then, Lord," Simon Peter replied, "not just my feet but my hands and my head as well!"

10 Jesus answered, "A person who has had a bath needs only to wash his feet; his whole body is clean. And you are clean, though not every one of you." 11 For he knew who was going to betray him, and that was why he said not every one was clean.

12 When he had finished washing their feet, he put on his clothes and returned to his place. "Do you understand what I have done for you?" he asked them. 13 "You call me 'Teacher' and 'Lord,' and rightly so, for that is what I am. 14 Now that I, your Lord and Teacher, have washed your feet, you also should wash one another's

---

n 40 Isaiah 6:10   o 1 Or he loved them to the last

feet. 15 I have set you an example that you should do as I have done for you. 16 I tell you the truth, no servant is greater than his master, nor is a messenger greater than the one who sent him. 17 Now that you know these things, you will be blessed if you do them.

Jesus Predicts His Betrayal

18 "I am not referring to all of you; I know those I have chosen. But this is to fulfill the scripture: 'He who shares my bread has lifted up his heel against me.'p

19 "I am telling you now before it happens, so that when it does happen you will believe that I am He. 20 I tell you the truth, whoever accepts anyone I send accepts me; and whoever accepts me accepts the one who sent me."

21 After he had said this, Jesus was troubled in spirit and testified, "I tell you the truth, one of you is going to betray me."

22 His disciples stared at one another, at a loss to know which of them he meant. 23 One of them, the disciple whom Jesus loved, was reclining next to him. 24 Simon Peter motioned to this disciple and said, "Ask him which one he means."

25 Leaning back against Jesus, he asked him, "Lord, who is it?"

26 Jesus answered, "It is the one to whom I will give this piece of bread when I have dipped it in the dish." Then, dipping the piece of bread, he gave it to Judas Iscariot, son of Simon. 27 As soon as Judas took the bread, Satan entered into him.

"What you are about to do, do quickly," Jesus told him, 28 but no one at the meal understood why Jesus said this to him. 29 Since Judas had charge of the money, some thought Jesus was telling him to buy what was needed for the Feast, or to give something to the poor. 30 As soon as Judas had taken the bread, he went out. And it was night.

Jesus Predicts Peter's Denial

31 When he was gone, Jesus said, "Now is the Son of Man glorified and God is glorified in him. 32 If God is glorified in him,q God will glorify the Son in himself, and will glorify him at once.

33 "My children, I will be with you only a little longer. You will look for me, and just as I told the Jews, so I tell you now: Where I am going, you cannot come.

34 "A new command I give you: Love one another. As I have loved you, so you must love one another. 35 By this all men will know that you are my disciples, if you love one another."

36 Simon Peter asked him, "Lord, where are you going?"

Jesus replied, "Where I am going, you cannot follow now, but you will follow later."

37 Peter asked, "Lord, why can't I follow you now? I will lay down my life for you."

38 Then Jesus answered, "Will you really lay down your life for me? I tell you the truth, before the rooster crows, you will disown me three times!

Jesus Comforts His Disciples

14 1 "Do not let your hearts be troubled. Trust in God;r trust also in me. 2 In my Father's house are

---

p 18 Psalm 41:9   q 32 Many early manuscripts do not have *If God is glorified in him.*
r 1 Or *You trust in God*

any rooms; if it were not so, I would have told you. I am going there to prepare a place for you. And if I go and prepare a place for you, I will come back and take you to be with me that you also may be where I am. 4 You know the way to the place where I am going."

Jesus the Way to the Father

5 Thomas said to him, "Lord, we don't know where you are going, so how can we know the way?"

6 Jesus answered, "I am the way and the truth and the life. No one comes to the Father except through me. 7 If you really knew me, you would know my Father as well. From now on, you do know him and have seen him."

8 Philip said, "Lord, show us the Father and that will be enough for us."

9 Jesus answered: "Don't you know me, Philip, even after I have been among you such a long time? Anyone who has seen me has seen the Father. How can you say, 'Show us the Father'? 10 Don't you believe that I am in the Father, and that the Father is in me? The words I say to you are not just my own. Rather, it is the Father, living in me, who is doing his work. 11 Believe me when I say that I am in the Father and the Father is in me; or at least believe on the evidence of the miracles themselves. 12 I tell you the truth, anyone who has faith in me will do what I have been doing. He will do even greater things than these, because I am going to the Father. 13 And I will do whatever you ask in my name, so that the Son may bring glory to the

Father. 14 You may ask me for anything in my name, and I will do it.

Jesus Promises the Holy Spirit

15 "If you love me, you will obey what I command. 16 And I will ask the Father, and he will give you another Counselor to be with you forever— 17 the Spirit of truth. The world cannot accept him, because it neither sees him nor knows him. But you know him, for he lives with you and will be[t] in you. 18 I will not leave you as orphans; I will come to you. 19 Before long, the world will not see me anymore, but you will see me. Because I live, you also will live. 20 On that day you will realize that I am in my Father, and you are in me, and I am in you. 21 Whoever has my commands and obeys them, he is the one who loves me. He who loves me will be loved by my Father, and I too will love him and show myself to him."

22 Then Judas (not Judas Iscariot) said, "But, Lord, why do you intend to show yourself to us and not to the world?"

23 Jesus replied, "If anyone loves me, he will obey my teaching. My Father will love him, and we will come to him and make our home with him. 24 He who does not love me will not obey my teaching. These words you hear are not my own; they belong to the Father who sent me. 25 "All this I have spoken while still with you. 26 But the Counselor, the Holy Spirit, whom the Father will send in my name, will teach you all things and will remind you of everything I have said to you. 27 Peace I leave with you; my peace I give you.

---

7 Some early manuscripts *If you really have known me, you will know*   t 17 Some early manuscripts *and is*

I do not give to you as the world gives. Do not let your hearts be troubled and do not be afraid.

28 "You heard me say, 'I am going away and I am coming back to you.' If you loved me, you would be glad that I am going to the Father, for the Father is greater than I. **29** I have told you now before it happens, so that when it does happen you will believe. **30** I will not speak with you much longer, for the prince of this world is coming. He has no hold on me, **31** but the world must learn that I love the Father and that I do exactly what my Father has commanded me.

"Come now; let us leave.

The Vine and the Branches

15 **1** "I am the true vine, and my Father is the gardener. **2** He cuts off every branch in me that bears no fruit, while every branch that does bear fruit he prunes[u] so that it will be even more fruitful. **3** You are already clean because of the word I have spoken to you. **4** Remain in me, and I will remain in you. No branch can bear fruit by itself; it must remain in the vine. Neither can you bear fruit unless you remain in me.

5 "I am the vine; you are the branches. If a man remains in me and I in him, he will bear much fruit; apart from me you can do nothing. **6** If anyone does not remain in me, he is like a branch that is thrown away and withers; such branches are picked up, thrown into the fire and burned. **7** If you remain in me and my words remain in you, ask whatever you wish, and it will be given you. **8** This is to my Father's glory, that you bear much fruit, showing yourselves to be my disciples.

9 "As the Father has loved me, s have I loved you. Now remain in m love. **10** If you obey my command you will remain in my love, just as have obeyed my Father's command and remain in his love. **11** I have tol you this so that my joy may be in yo and that your joy may be complete **12** My command is this: Love eac other as I have loved you. **13** Greate love has no one than this, that he la down his life for his friends. **14** Yo are my friends if you do what I com mand. **15** I no longer call you ser vants, because a servant does no know his master's business. Instead I have called you friends, for every thing that I learned from my Father have made known to you. **16** You di not choose me, but I chose you an appointed you to go and bear fruit – fruit that will last. Then the Fathe will give you whatever you ask in m name. **17** This is my command: Lov each other.

The World Hates the Disciples

18 "If the world hates you, keep i mind that it hated me first. **19** If yo belonged to the world, it would lov you as its own. As it is, you do no belong to the world, but I hav chosen you out of the world. That i why the world hates you. **20** Remem ber the words I spoke to you: 'N servant is greater than his master.'[v] I they persecuted me, they will per secute you also. If they obeyed m teaching, they will obey yours als **21** They will treat you this way be cause of my name, for they do no know the One who sent me. **22** If had not come and spoken to them they would not be guilty of sin. Now however, they have no excuse fo

---

u   2 The Greek for *prunes* also means *cleans*.   v 20 John 13:16

heir sin. **23** He who hates me hates
ny Father as well. **24** If I had not
lone among them what no one else
lid, they would not be guilty of sin.
But now they have seen these
miracles, and yet they have hated
both me and my Father. **25** But this is
to fulfill what is written in their Law:
They hated me without reason.'ʷ

26 "When the Counselor comes,
whom I will send to you from the
Father, the Spirit of truth who goes
out from the Father, he will testify
about me. **27** And you also must tes-
ify, for you have been with me from
he beginning.

16 **1** "All this I have told you so
that you will not go astray.
2 They will put you out of the
synagogue; in fact, a time is coming
when anyone who kills you will think
he is offering a service to God. **3** They
will do such things because they have
not known the Father or me. **4** I have
old you this, so that when the time
comes you will remember that I
warned you. I did not tell you this at
first because I was with you.

The Work of the Holy Spirit

5 "Now I am going to him who sent
me, yet none of you asks me, 'Where
are you going?' **6** Because I have said
these things, you are filled with grief.
7 But I tell you the truth: It is for your
good that I am going away. Unless I
go away, the Counselor will not come
to you; but if I go, I will send him to
you. **8** When he comes, he will convict the world of guiltˣ in regard to
sin and righteousness and judgment:
9 in regard to sin, because men do
not believe in me; **10** in regard to
righteousness, because I am going to
the Father, where you can see me no

longer; **11** and in regard to judgment,
because the prince of this world now
stands condemned.

12 "I have much more to say to
you, more than you can now bear.
13 But when he, the Spirit of truth,
comes, he will guide you into all
truth. He will not speak on his own;
he will speak only what he hears, and
he will tell you what is yet to come.
14 He will bring glory to me by taking
from what is mine and making it
known to you. **15** All that belongs to
the Father is mine. That is why I said
the Spirit will take from what is mine
and make it known to you.

16 "In a little while you will see me
no more, and then after a little while
you will see me."

The Disciples' Grief Will Turn to Joy

17 Some of his disciples said to one
another, "What does he mean by
saying, 'In a little while you will see
me no more, and then after a little
while you will see me,' and 'Because
I am going to the Father'?" **18** They
kept asking, "What does he mean by
'a little while'? Wᵤ don't understand
what he is saying.

19 Jesus saw that they wanted to
ask him about this, so he said to them,
"Are you asking one another what I
meant when I said, 'In a little while
you will see me no more, and then
after a little while you will see me'?
20 I tell you the truth, you will weep
and mourn while the world rejoices.
You will grieve, but your grief will
turn to joy. **21** A woman giving birth to
a child has pain because her time has
come; but when her baby is born she
forgets the anguish because of her joy
that a child is born into the world.
22 So with you: Now is your time of

ʷ **25** Psalms 35:19; 69:4   ˣ **8** Or *will expose the guilt of the world*

grief, but I will see you again and you will rejoice, and no one will take away your joy. 23 In that day you will no longer ask me anything. I tell you the truth, my Father will give you whatever you ask in my name. 24 Until now you have not asked for anything in my name. Ask and you will receive, and your joy will be complete.

25 "Though I have been speaking figuratively, a time is coming when I will no longer use this kind of language but will tell you plainly about my Father. 26 In that day you will ask in my name. I am not saying that I will ask the Father on your behalf. 27 No, the Father himself loves you because you have loved me and have believed that I came from God. 28 I came from the Father and entered the world; now I am leaving the world and going back to the Father."

29 Then Jesus' disciples said, "Now you are speaking clearly and without figures of speech. 30 Now we can see that you know all things and that you do not even need to have anyone ask you questions. This makes us believe that you came from God."

31 "You believe at last!"y Jesus answered. 32 "But a time is coming, and has come, when you will be scattered, each to his own home. You will leave me all alone. Yet I am not alone, for my Father is with me.

33 "I have told you these things, so that in me you may have peace. In this world you will have trouble. But take heart! I have overcome the world."

Jesus Prays for Himself

17 1 After Jesus said this, he looked toward heaven and prayed:

"Father, the time has come. Glorify your Son, that your Son may glorify you. 2 For you granted him authority over all people that he might give eternal life to all those you have given him. 3 Now this is eternal life: that they may know you, the only true God, and Jesus Christ, whom you have sent. 4 I have brought you glory on earth by completing the work you gave me to do. 5 And now, Father, glorify me in your presence with the glory I had with you before the world began.

Jesus Prays for His Disciples

6 "I have revealed youz to those whom you gave me out of the world. They were yours; you gave them to me and they have obeyed your word. 7 Now they know that everything you have given me comes from you. 8 For I gave them the words you gave me and they accepted them. They knew with certainty that I came from you, and they believed that you sent me. 9 I pray for them. I am not praying for the world, but for those you have given me, for they are yours. 10 All I have is yours, and all you have is mine. And glory has come to me through them. 11 I will remain in the world no longer, but they are still in the world, and I am coming to you. Holy Father, protect them by the power of your name—the name you gave me—so that they may be one as we are one. 12 While I was with them, I protected them and kept them safe by that name you gave me. None has been lost except the one doomed to destruction so that Scripture would be fulfilled.

y 31 Or "Do you now believe?"   z 6 Greek your name; also in verse 26

13 "I am coming to you now, but I say these things while I am still in the world, so that they may have the full measure of my joy within them. 14 I have given them your word and the world has hated them, for they are not of the world any more than I am of the world. 15 My prayer is not that you take them out of the world but that you protect them from the evil one. 16 They are not of the world, even as I am not of it. 17 Sanctify[a] them by the truth; your word is truth. 18 As you sent me into the world, I have sent them into the world. 19 For them I sanctify myself, that they too may be truly sanctified.

Jesus Prays for All Believers

20 "My prayer is not for them alone. I pray also for those who will believe in me through their message, 21 that all of them may be one, Father, just as you are in me and I am in you. May they also be in us so that the world may believe that you have sent me. 22 I have given them the glory that you gave me, that they may be one as we are one: 23 I in them and you in me. May they be brought to complete unity to let the world know that you sent me and have loved them even as you have loved me.

24 "Father, I want those you have given me to be with me where I am, and to see my glory, the glory you have given me because you loved me before the creation of the world.

25 "Righteous Father, though the world does not know you, I know you, and they know that you have sent me. 26 I have made you known to them, and will continue to make you known in order that the love you have for me may be in them and that I myself may be in them."

Jesus Arrested

18 1 When he had finished praying, Jesus left with his disciples and crossed the Kidron Valley. On the other side there was an olive grove, and he and his disciples went into it.

2 Now Judas, who betrayed him, knew the place, because Jesus had often met there with his disciples. 3 So Judas came to the grove, guiding a detachment of soldiers and some officials from the chief priests and Pharisees. They were carrying torches, lanterns and weapons.

4 Jesus, knowing all that was going to happen to him, went out and asked them, "Who is it you want?"

5 "Jesus of Nazareth," they replied.

"I am he," Jesus said. (And Judas the traitor was standing there with them.) 6 When Jesus said, "I am he," they drew back and fell to the ground.

7 Again he asked them, "Who is it you want?"

And they said, "Jesus of Nazareth."

8 "I told you that I am he," Jesus answered. "If you are looking for me, then let these men go." 9 This happened so that the words he had spoken would be fulfilled: "I have not lost one of those you gave me."[b]

10 Then Simon Peter, who had a sword, drew it and struck the high priest's servant, cutting off his right ear. (The servant's name was Malchus.)

---

a 17 Greek *hagiazo* (set apart for sacred use or make holy); also in verse 19   *b* 9 John 6:39

11 Jesus commanded Peter, "Put your sword away! Shall I not drink the cup the Father has given me?"

Jesus Taken to Annas

12 Then the detachment of soldiers with its commander and the Jewish officials arrested Jesus. They bound him 13 and brought him first to Annas, who was the father-in-law of Caiaphas, the high priest that year. 14 Caiaphas was the one who had advised the Jews that it would be good if one man died for the people.

Peter's First Denial

15 Simon Peter and another disciple were following Jesus. Because this disciple was known to the high priest, he went with Jesus into the high priest's courtyard, 16 but Peter had to wait outside at the door. The other disciple, who was known to the high priest, came back, spoke to the girl on duty there and brought Peter in.

17 "You are not one of his disciples, are you?" the girl at the door asked Peter.

He replied, "I am not."

18 It was cold, and the servants and officials stood around a fire they had made to keep warm. Peter also was standing with them, warming himself.

The High Priest Questions Jesus

19 Meanwhile, the high priest questioned Jesus about his disciples and his teaching.

20 "I have spoken openly to the world," Jesus replied. "I always taught in synagogues or at the temple, where all the Jews come together. I said nothing in secret.

21 Why question me? Ask those who heard me. Surely they know what I said."

22 When Jesus said this, one of the officials nearby struck him in the face. "Is this the way you answer the high priest?" he demanded.

23 "If I said something wrong," Jesus replied, "testify as to what is wrong. But if I spoke the truth, why did you strike me?" 24 Then Annas sent him, still bound, to Caiaphas the high priest.[c]

Peter's Second and Third Denials

25 As Simon Peter stood warming himself, he was asked, "You are not one of his disciples, are you?"

He denied it, saying, "I am not."

26 One of the high priest's servants, a relative of the man whose ear Peter had cut off, challenged him, "Didn't see you with him in the olive grove?" 27 Again Peter denied it, and at that moment a rooster began to crow.

Jesus Before Pilate

28 Then the Jews led Jesus from Caiaphas to the palace of the Roman governor. By now it was early morning, and to avoid ceremonial uncleanness the Jews did not enter the palace; they wanted to be able to eat the Passover. 29 So Pilate came out to them and asked, "What charges are you bringing against this man?"

30 "If he were not a criminal," they replied, "we would not have handed him over to you."

31 Pilate said, "Take him yourselves and judge him by your own law."

"But we have no right to execute anyone," the Jews objected. 32 This happened so that the words Jesus had spoken indicating the kind of

c 24 Or (Now Annas had sent him, still bound, to Caiaphas the high priest.)

death he was going to die would be fulfilled.

33 Pilate then went back inside the palace, summoned Jesus and asked him, "Are you the king of the Jews?"

34 "Is that your own idea," Jesus asked, "or did others talk to you about me?"

35 "Am I a Jew?" Pilate replied. "It was your people and your chief priests who handed you over to me. What is it you have done?"

36 Jesus said, "My kingdom is not of this world. If it were, my servants would fight to prevent my arrest by the Jews. But now my kingdom is from another place."

37 "You are a king, then!" said Pilate.

Jesus answered, "You are right in saying I am a king. In fact, for this reason I was born, and for this I came into the world, to testify to the truth. Everyone on the side of truth listens to me."

38 "What is truth?" Pilate asked. With this he went out again to the Jews and said, "I find no basis for a charge against him. **39** But it is your custom for me to release to you one prisoner at the time of the Passover. Do you want me to release 'the king of the Jews'?"

40 They shouted back, "No, not him! Give us Barabbas!" Now Barabbas had taken part in a rebellion.

Jesus Sentenced to be Crucified

19 **1** Then Pilate took Jesus and had him flogged. **2** The soldiers twisted together a crown of thorns and put it on his head. They clothed him in a purple robe **3** and went up to him again and again, saying, "Hail, king of the Jews!" And they struck him in the face.

4 Once more Pilate came out and said to the Jews, "Look, I am bringing him out to you to let you know that I find no basis for a charge against him." **5** When Jesus came out wearing the crown of thorns and the purple robe, Pilate said to them, "Here is the man!"

6 As soon as the chief priests and their officials saw him, they shouted, "Crucify! Crucify!"

But Pilate answered, "You take him and crucify him. As for me, I find no basis for a charge against him."

7 The Jews insisted, "We have a law, and according to that law he must die, because he claimed to be the Son of God."

8 When Pilate heard this, he was even more afraid, **9** and he went back inside the palace. "Where do you come from?" he asked Jesus, but Jesus gave him no answer. **10** "Do you refuse to speak to me?" Pilate said. "Don't you realize I have power either to free you or to crucify you?"

11 Jesus answered, "You would have no power over me if it were not given to you from above. Therefore the one who handed me over to you is guilty of a greater sin."

12 From then on, Pilate tried to set Jesus free, but the Jews kept shouting, "If you let this man go, you are no friend of Caesar. Anyone who claims to be a king opposes Caesar."

13 When Pilate heard this, he brought Jesus out and sat down on the judge's seat at a place known as the Stone Pavement (which in Aramaic is Gabbatha). **14** It was the day of Preparation of Passover Week, about the sixth hour.

"Here is your king," Pilate said to the Jews.

15 But they shouted, "Take him away! Take him away! Crucify him!"

"Shall I crucify your king?" Pilate asked.

"We have no king but Caesar," the chief priests answered.

16 Finally Pilate handed him over to them to be crucified.

The Crucifixion

So the soldiers took charge of Jesus. 17 Carrying his own cross, he went out to the place of the Skull (which in Aramaic is called Golgotha). 18 Here they crucified him, and with him two others—one on each side and Jesus in the middle.

19 Pilate had a notice prepared and fastened to the cross. It read: JESUS OF NAZARETH, THE KING OF THE JEWS. 20 Many of the Jews read this sign, for the place where Jesus was crucified was near the city, and the sign was written in Aramaic, Latin and Greek. 21 The chief priests of the Jews protested to Pilate, "Do not write 'The King of the Jews,' but that this man claimed to be king of the Jews."

22 Pilate answered, "What I have written, I have written."

23 When the soldiers crucified Jesus, they took his clothes, dividing them into four shares, one for each of them, with the undergarment remaining. This garment was seamless, woven in one piece from top to bottom.

24 "Let's not tear it," they said to one another. "Let's decide by lot who will get it."

This happened that the scripture might be fulfilled which said,

"They divided my garments among them
and cast lots for my clothing."[d]

So this is what the soldiers did.

25 Near the cross of Jesus stood his mother, his mother's sister, Mary the wife of Clopas, and Mary Magdalene. 26 When Jesus saw his mother there and the disciple whom he loved standing nearby, he said to his mother, "Dear woman, here is your son," 27 and to the disciple, "Here is your mother." From that time on, this disciple took her into his home.

The Death of Jesus

28 Later, knowing that all was now completed, and so that the Scripture would be fulfilled, Jesus said, "I am thirsty." 29 A jar of wine vinegar was there, so they soaked a sponge in it, put the sponge on a stalk of the hyssop plant, and lifted it to Jesus' lips. 30 When he had received the drink, Jesus said, "It is finished." With that he bowed his head and gave up his spirit.

31 Now it was the day of Preparation, and the next day was to be a special Sabbath. Because the Jews did not want the bodies left on the crosses during the Sabbath, they asked Pilate to have the legs broken and the bodies taken down. 32 The soldiers therefore came and broke the legs of the first man who had been crucified with Jesus, and then those of the other. 33 But when they came to Jesus and found that he was already dead, they did not break his legs. 34 Instead, one of the soldiers pierced Jesus' side with a spear, bringing a sudden flow of blood and water. 35 The man who saw it has given testimony, and his testimony is true. He knows that he tells the truth, and he testifies so that you also may believe. 36 These things happened so that the scripture would be fulfilled: "Not one of his bones will be broken,"[e] 37 and, as another scrip-

d 24 Psalm 22:18   e 36 Exodus 12:46; Num. 9:12; Psalm 34:20

ture says, "They will look on the one they have pierced."*f*

The Burial of Jesus

38 Later, Joseph of Arimathea asked Pilate for the body of Jesus. Now Joseph was a disciple of Jesus, but secretly because he feared the Jews. With Pilate's permission, he came and took the body away. **39** He was accompanied by Nicodemus, the man who earlier had visited Jesus at night. Nicodemus brought a mixture of myrrh and aloes, about seventy-five pounds.*g* **40** Taking Jesus' body, the two of them wrapped it, with the spices, in strips of linen. This was in accordance with Jewish burial customs. **41** At the place where Jesus was crucified, there was a garden, and in the garden a new tomb, in which no one had ever been laid. **42** Because it was the Jewish day of Preparation and since the tomb was nearby, they laid Jesus there.

The Empty Tomb

20 **1** Early on the first day of the week, while it was still dark, Mary Magdalene went to the tomb and saw that the stone had been removed from the entrance. **2** So she came running to Simon Peter and the other disciple, the one Jesus loved, and said, "They have taken the Lord out of the tomb, and we don't know where they have put him!"

3 So Peter and the other disciple started for the tomb. **4** Both were running, but the other disciple outran Peter and reached the tomb first. **5** He bent over and looked in at the strips of linen lying there but did not go in. **6** Then Simon Peter, who was behind him, arrived and went into

the tomb. He saw the strips of linen lying there, **7** as well as the burial cloth that had been around Jesus' head. The cloth was folded up by itself, separate from the linen. **8** Finally the other disciple, who had reached the tomb first, also went inside. He saw and believed. **9** (They still did not understand from Scripture that Jesus had to rise from the dead.)

Jesus Appears to Mary Magdalene

10 Then the disciples went back to their homes, **11** but Mary stood outside the tomb crying. As she wept, she bent over to look into the tomb **12** and saw two angels in white, seated where Jesus' body had been, one at the head and the other at the foot.

13 They asked her, "Woman, why are you crying?"

"They have taken my Lord away," she said, "and I don't know where they have put him." **14** At this, she turned around and saw Jesus standing there, but she did not realize that it was Jesus.

15 "Woman," he said, "why are you crying? Who is it you are looking for?"

Thinking he was the gardener, she said, "Sir, if you have carried him away, tell me where you have put him, and I will get him."

16 Jesus said to her, "Mary."

She turned toward him and cried out in Aramaic, "Rabboni!" (which means Teacher).

17 Jesus said, "Do not hold on to me, for I have not yet returned to the Father. Go instead to my brothers and tell them, 'I am returning to my Father and your Father, to my God and your God.'"

f 37 Zech. 12:10   *g 39* Greek *a hundred litrai* (about 34 kilograms)

18 Mary Magdalene went to the disciples with the news: "I have seen the Lord!" And she told them that he had said these things to her.

Jesus Appears to His Disciples

19 On the evening of that first day of the week, when the disciples were together, with the doors locked for fear of the Jews, Jesus came and stood among them and said, "Peace be with you!" **20** After he said this, he showed them his hands and side. The disciples were overjoyed when they saw the Lord.

21 Again Jesus said, "Peace be with you! As the Father has sent me, I am sending you." **22** And with that he breathed on them and said, "Receive the Holy Spirit. **23** If you forgive anyone his sins, they are forgiven; if you do not forgive them, they are not forgiven."

Jesus Appears to Thomas

24 Now Thomas (called Didymus), one of the Twelve, was not with the disciples when Jesus came. **25** So the other disciples told him, "We have seen the Lord!"

But he said to them, "Unless I see the nail marks in his hands and put my finger where the nails were, and put my hand into his side, I will not believe it."

26 A week later his disciples were in the house again, and Thomas was with them. Though the doors were locked, Jesus came and stood among them and said, "Peace be with you!" **27** Then he said to Thomas, "Put your finger here; see my hands. Reach out your hand and put it into my side. Stop doubting and believe."

28 Thomas said to him, "My Lord and my God!"

29 Then Jesus told him, "Because you have seen me, you have believed; blessed are those who have not seen and yet have believed."

30 Jesus did many other miraculous signs in the presence of his disciples, which are not recorded in this book. **31** But these are written that you may[h] believe that Jesus is the Christ, the Son of God, and that by believing you may have life in his name.

Jesus and the Miraculous Catch of Fish

21 **1** Afterward Jesus appeared again to his disciples, by the Sea of Tiberias.[i] It happened this way: **2** Simon Peter, Thomas (called Didymus), Nathanael from Cana in Galilee, the sons of Zebedee, and two other disciples were together. **3** "I'm going out to fish," Simon Peter told them, and they said, "We'll go with you." So they went out and got into the boat, but that night they caught nothing.

4 Early in the morning, Jesus stood on the shore, but the disciples did not realize that it was Jesus.

5 He called out to them, "Friends, haven't you any fish?"

"No," they answered.

6 He said, "Throw your net on the right side of the boat and you will find some." When they did, they were unable to haul the net in because of the large number of fish.

7 Then the disciple whom Jesus loved said to Peter, "It is the Lord!" As soon as Simon Peter heard him say, "It is the Lord," he wrapped his outer garment around him (for he

---

h 31 Some manuscripts *may continue to*   i 1 That is, Sea of Galilee

had taken it off) and jumped into the water. 8 The other disciples followed in the boat, towing the net full of fish, for they were not far from shore, about a hundred yards.j 9 When they landed, they saw a fire of burning coals there with fish on it, and some bread.

10 Jesus said to them, "Bring some of the fish you have just caught."

11 Simon Peter climbed aboard and dragged the net ashore. It was full of large fish, 153, but even with so many the net was not torn. 12 Jesus said to them, "Come and have breakfast." None of the disciples dared ask him, "Who are you?" They knew it was the Lord. 13 Jesus came, took the bread and gave it to them, and did the same with the fish. 14 This was now the third time Jesus appeared to his disciples after he was raised from the dead.

Jesus Reinstates Peter

15 When they had finished eating, Jesus said to Simon Peter, "Simon son of John, do you truly love me more than these?"

"Yes, Lord," he said, "you know that I love you."

Jesus said, "Feed my lambs."

16 Again Jesus said, "Simon son of John, do you truly love me?"

He answered, "Yes, Lord, you know that I love you."

Jesus said, "Take care of my sheep."

17 The third time he said to him, "Simon son of John, do you love me?"

Peter was hurt because Jesus asked him the third time, "Do you love me?" He said, "Lord, you know all things; you know that I love you."

Jesus said, "Feed my sheep. 18 I tell you the truth, when you were younger you dressed yourself and went where you wanted; but when you are old you will stretch out your hands, and someone else will dress you and lead you where you do not want to go." 19 Jesus said this to indicate the kind of death by which Peter would glorify God. Then he said to him, "Follow me!"

20 Peter turned and saw that the disciple whom Jesus loved was following them. (This was the one who had leaned back against Jesus at the supper and had said, "Lord, who is going to betray you?") 21 When Peter saw him, he asked, "Lord, what about him?"

22 Jesus answered, "If I want him to remain alive until I return, what is that to you? You must follow me." 23 Because of this, the rumor spread among the brothers that this disciple would not die. But Jesus did not say that he would not die; he only said, "If I want him to remain alive until I return, what is that to you?"

24 This is the disciple who testifies to these things and who wrote them down. We know that his testimony is true.

25 Jesus did many other things as well. If every one of them were written down, I suppose that even the whole world would not have room for the books that would be written.

j 8 Greek *about two hundred cubits* (about 90 meters)

Acts

Jesus Taken Up Into Heaven

1 **1** In my former book, Theophilus, I wrote about all that Jesus began to do and to teach **2** until the day he was taken up to heaven, after giving instructions through the Holy Spirit to the apostles he had chosen. **3** After his suffering, he showed himself to these men and gave many convincing proofs that he was alive. He appeared to them over a period of forty days and spoke about the kingdom of God. **4** On one occasion, while he was eating with them, he gave them this command: "Do not leave Jerusalem, but wait for the gift my Father promised, which you have heard me speak about. **5** For John baptized with*a* water, but in a few days you will be baptized with the Holy Spirit."

6 So when they met together, they asked him, "Lord, are you at this time going to restore the kingdom to Israel?"

7 He said to them: "It is not for you to know the times or dates the Father has set by his own authority. **8** But you will receive power when the Holy Spirit comes on you; and you will be my witnesses in Jerusalem, and in all Judea and Samaria, and to the ends of the earth."

9 After he said this, he was taken up before their very eyes, and a cloud hid him from their sight.

10 They were looking intently up into the sky as he was going, when suddenly two men dressed in white stood beside them. **11** "Men of Galilee," they said, "why do you stand here looking into the sky? This same Jesus, who has been taken from you into heaven, will come back in the same way you have seen him go into heaven."

Matthias Chosen to Replace Judas

12 Then they returned to Jerusalem from the hill called the Mount of Olives, a Sabbath day's walk*b* from the city. **13** When they arrived, they went upstairs to the room where they were staying. Those present were Peter, John, James and Andrew; Philip and Thomas, Bartholomew and Matthew; James son of Alphaeus and Simon the Zealot, and Judas son of James. **14** They all joined together constantly in prayer, along with the women and Mary the mother of Jesus, and with his brothers.

15 In those days Peter stood up among the believers*c* (a group numbering about a hundred and twenty) **16** and said, "Brothers, the Scripture had to be fulfilled which the Holy Spirit spoke long ago through the mouth of David concerning Judas, who served as guide for those who arrested Jesus— **17** he was one of our number and shared in this ministry."

18 (With the reward he got for his wickedness, Judas bought a field; there he fell headlong, his body burst open and all his intestines spilled out. **19** Everyone in Jerusalem heard

---

a 5 Or *in*   *b* 12 That is, about 3/4 mile (about 1,100 meters)   *c* 15 Greek *brothers*

about this, so they called that field in their language Akeldama, that is, Field of Blood.)

20 "For," said Peter, "it is written in the book of Psalms,

> " 'May his place be deserted;
> let there be no one to dwell in it,'d

and,

> " 'May another take his place of leadership.'e

21 Therefore it is necessary to choose one of the men who have been with us the whole time the Lord Jesus went in and out among us, 22 beginning from John's baptism to the time when Jesus was taken up from us. For one of these must become a witness with us of his resurrection."

23 So they proposed two men: Joseph called Barsabbas (also known as Justus) and Matthias. 24 Then they prayed, "Lord, you know everyone's heart. Show us which of these two you have chosen 25 to take over this apostolic ministry, which Judas left to go where he belongs." 26 Then they cast lots, and the lot fell to Matthias; so he was added to the eleven apostles.

The Holy Spirit Comes at Pentecost

2 1 When the day of Pentecost came, they were all together in one place. 2 Suddenly a sound like the blowing of a violent wind came from heaven and filled the whole house where they were sitting. 3 They saw what seemed to be tongues of fire that separated and came to rest on each of them. 4 All of them

were filled with the Holy Spirit and began to speak in other tonguesf as the Spirit enabled them.

5 Now there were staying in Jerusalem God-fearing Jews from every nation under heaven. 6 When they heard this sound, a crowd came together in bewilderment, because each one heard them speaking in his own language. 7 Utterly amazed, they asked: "Are not all these men who are speaking Galileans? 8 Then how is it that each of us hears them in his own native language? 9 Parthians, Medes and Elamites; residents of Mesopotamia, Judea and Cappadocia, Pontus and Asia, 10 Phrygia and Pamphylia, Egypt and the parts of Libya near Cyrene; visitors from Rome 11 (both Jews and converts to Judaism); Cretans and Arabs—we hear them declaring the wonders of God in our own tongues!" 12 Amazed and perplexed, they asked one another, "What does this mean?"

13 Some, however, made fun of them and said, "They have had too much wine.g "

Peter Addresses the Crowd

14 Then Peter stood up with the Eleven, raised his voice and addressed the crowd: "Fellow Jews and all of you who live in Jerusalem, let me explain this to you; listen carefully to what I say. 15 These men are not drunk, as you suppose. It's only nine in the morning! 16 No, this is what was spoken by the prophet Joel:

17 " 'In the last days, God says,
  I will pour out my Spirit on all people.
  Your sons and daughters will prophesy,

---

d 20 Psalm 69:25   e 20 Psalm 109:8   f 4 Or languages; also in verse 11
g 13 Or sweet wine

your young men will see
visions,
your old men will dream
dreams.
18 Even on my servants, both men
and women,
I will pour out my Spirit in
those days,
and they will prophesy.
19 I will show wonders in the
heaven above
and signs on the earth below,
blood and fire and billows of
smoke.
20 The sun will be turned to
darkness
and the moon to blood
before the coming of the great
and glorious day of the Lord.
21 And everyone who calls
on the name of the Lord will
be saved.'h

22 "Men of Israel, listen to this:
Jesus of Nazareth was a man ac-
credited by God to you by miracles,
wonders and signs, which God did
among you through him, as you
yourselves know. 23 This man was
handed over to you by God's set purpose and foreknowledge; and you,
with the help of wicked men,i put
him to death by nailing him to the
cross. 24 But God raised him from the
dead, freeing him from the agony of
death, because it was impossible for
death to keep its hold on him.
25 David said about him:

" 'I saw the Lord always before
me.
Because he is at my right
hand,
I will not be shaken.

26 Therefore my heart is glad and
my tongue rejoices;
my body also will live in hope,
27 because you will not abandon
me to the grave,
nor will you let your Holy
One see decay.
28 You have made known to me
the paths of life;
you will fill me with joy in
your presence.'j

29 "Brothers, I can tell you confidently that the patriarch David died
and was buried, and his tomb is here
to this day. 30 But he was a prophet
and knew that God had promised
him on oath that he would place one
of his descendants on his throne.
31 Seeing what was ahead, he spoke
of the resurrection of the Christ,k that
he was not abandoned to the grave,
nor did his body see decay. 32 God
has raised this Jesus to life, and we
are all witnesses of the fact. 33 Exalted to the right hand of God, he has
received from the Father the
promised Holy Spirit and has poured
out what you now see and hear.
34 For David did not ascend to
heaven, and yet he said,

" 'The Lord said to my Lord:
"Sit at my right hand
35 until I make your enemies
a footstool for your feet." 'l

36 "Therefore let all Israel be assured of this: God has made this
Jesus, whom you crucified, both Lord
and Christ."

37 When the people heard this,
they were cut to the heart and said
to Peter and the other apostles,
"Brothers, what shall we do?"

---

h 21 Joel 2:28-32   i 23 Or of those not having the law (that is, Gentiles)   j 28 Psalm
16:8-11   k 31 Or Messiah. "The Christ" (Greek) and "the Messiah" (Hebrew) both mean
"the Anointed One"; also in verse 36.   l 35 Psalm 110:1

38 Peter replied, "Repent and be baptized, every one of you, in the name of Jesus Christ for the forgiveness of your sins. And you will receive the gift of the Holy Spirit. **39** The promise is for you and your children and for all who are far off — for all whom the Lord our God will call."

40 With many other words he warned them; and he pleaded with them, "Save yourselves from this corrupt generation." **41** Those who accepted his message were baptized, and about three thousand were added to their number that day.

The Fellowship of the Believers

42 They devoted themselves to the apostles' teaching and to the fellowship, to the breaking of bread and to prayer. **43** Everyone was filled with awe, and many wonders and miraculous signs were done by the apostles. **44** All the believers were together and had everything in common. **45** Selling their possessions and goods, they gave to anyone as he had need. **46** Every day they continued to meet together in the temple courts. They broke bread in their homes and ate together with glad and sincere hearts, **47** praising God and enjoying the favor of all the people. And the Lord added to their number daily those who were being saved.

Peter Heals the Crippled Beggar

3 **1** One day Peter and John were going up to the temple at the time of prayer — at three in the afternoon. **2** Now a man crippled from birth was being carried to the temple gate called Beautiful, where he was put every day to beg from those going into the temple courts. **3** When he saw Peter and John about to enter, he asked them for money. **4** Peter looked straight at him, as did John. Then Peter said, "Look at us!" **5** So the man gave them his attention, expecting to get something from them.

6 Then Peter said, "Silver or gold I do not have, but what I have I give you. In the name of Jesus Christ of Nazareth, walk." **7** Taking him by the right hand, he helped him up, and instantly the man's feet and ankles became strong. **8** He jumped to his feet and began to walk. Then he went with them into the temple courts, walking and jumping, and praising God. **9** When all the people saw him walking and praising God, **10** they recognized him as the same man who used to sit begging at the temple gate called Beautiful, and they were filled with wonder and amazement at what had happened to him.

Peter Speaks to the Onlookers

11 While the beggar held on to Peter and John, all the people were astonished and came running to them in the place called Solomon's Colonnade. **12** When Peter saw this, he said to them: "Men of Israel, why does this surprise you? Why do you stare at us as if by our own power or godliness we had made this man walk? **13** The God of Abraham, Isaac and Jacob, the God of our fathers, has glorified his servant Jesus. You handed him over to be killed, and you disowned him before Pilate, though he had decided to let him go. **14** You disowned the Holy and Righteous One and asked that a murderer be released to you. **15** You killed the author of life, but God raised him from the dead. We are witnesses of this. **16** By faith in the name of Jesus, this man whom you see and know was made strong. It is Jesus' name and the faith that comes through him that has given this complete healing to him, as you can all see.

17 "Now, brothers, I know that you acted in ignorance, as did your leaders. 18 But this is how God fulfilled what he had foretold through all the prophets, saying that his Christ[m] would suffer. 19 Repent, then, and turn to God, so that your sins may be wiped out, that times of refreshing may come from the Lord, 20 and that he may send the Christ, who has been appointed for you— even Jesus. 21 He must remain in heaven until the time comes for God to restore everything, as he promised long ago through his holy prophets. 22 For Moses said, 'The Lord your God will raise up for you a prophet like me from among your own people; you must listen to everything he tells you. 23 Anyone who does not listen to him will be completely cut off from among his people.'[n]

24 "Indeed, all the prophets from Samuel on, as many as have spoken, have foretold these days. 25 And you are heirs of the prophets and of the covenant God made with your fathers. He said to Abraham, 'Through your offspring all peoples on earth will be blessed.'[o] 26 When God raised up his servant, he sent him first to you to bless you by turning each of you from your wicked ways."

Peter and John Before the Sanhedrin

4 1 The priests and the captain of the temple guard and the Sadducees came up to Peter and John while they were speaking to the people. 2 They were greatly disturbed because the apostles were teaching the people and proclaiming in Jesus the resurrection of the dead. 3 They seized Peter and John, and because it was evening, they put them in jail until the next day. 4 But many who heard the message believed, and the number of men grew to about five thousand.

5 The next day the rulers, elders and teachers of the law met in Jerusalem. 6 Annas the high priest was there, and so were Caiaphas, John, Alexander and the other men of the high priest's family. 7 They had Peter and John brought before them and began to question them: "By what power or what name did you do this?"

8 Then Peter, filled with the Holy Spirit, said to them: "Rulers and elders of the people! 9 If we are being called to account today for an act of kindness shown to a cripple and are asked how he was healed, 10 then know this, you and all the people of Israel: It is by the name of Jesus Christ of Nazareth, whom you crucified but whom God raised from the dead, that this man stands before you healed. 11 He is

> "'the stone you builders rejected,
>   which has become the
>   capstone.'[p]'[q]

12 Salvation is found in no one else, for there is no other name under heaven given to men by which we must be saved."

13 When they saw the courage of Peter and John and realized that they were unschooled, ordinary men, they were astonished and they took note that these men had been with

---

m 18 Or Messiah; also in verse 20   n 23 Deut. 18:15,18,19   o 25 Gen. 22:18; 26:4
p 11 Or cornerstone   q 11 Psalm 118:22

Jesus. **14** But since they could see the man who had been healed standing there with them, there was nothing they could say. **15** So they ordered them to withdraw from the Sanhedrin and then conferred together. **16** "What are we going to do with these men?" they asked. "Everybody living in Jerusalem knows they have done an outstanding miracle, and we cannot deny it. **17** But to stop this thing from spreading any further among the people, we must warn these men to speak no longer to anyone in this name."

18 Then they called them in again and commanded them not to speak or teach at all in the name of Jesus. **19** But Peter and John replied, "Judge for yourselves whether it is right in God's sight to obey you rather than God. **20** For we cannot help speaking about what we have seen and heard."

21 After further threats they let them go. They could not decide how to punish them, because all the people were praising God for what had happened. **22** For the man who was miraculously healed was over forty years old.

The Believers' Prayer

23 On their release, Peter and John went back to their own people and reported all that the chief priests and elders had said to them. **24** When they heard this, they raised their voices together in prayer to God. "Sovereign Lord," they said, "you made the heaven and the earth and the sea, and everything in them. **25** You spoke by the Holy Spirit through the mouth of your servant, our father David:

" 'Why do the nations rage
   and the peoples plot in vain?
26 The kings of the earth take
   their stand
and the rulers gather together
   against the Lord
and against his Anointed
   One.'[r][s]

27 Indeed Herod and Pontius Pilate met together with the Gentiles and the people[t] of Israel in this city to conspire against your holy servant Jesus, whom you anointed. **28** They did what your power and will had decided beforehand should happen. **29** Now, Lord, consider their threats and enable your servants to speak your word with great boldness. **30** Stretch out your hand to heal and perform miraculous signs and wonders through the name of your holy servant Jesus."

31 After they prayed, the place where they were meeting was shaken. And they were all filled with the Holy Spirit and spoke the word of God boldly.

The Believers Share Their Possessions

32 All the believers were one in heart and mind. No one claimed that any of his possessions was his own, but they shared everything they had. **33** With great power the apostles continued to testify to the resurrection of the Lord Jesus, and much grace was upon them all. **34** There were no needy persons among them. For from time to time those who owned lands or houses sold them, brought the money from the sales **35** and put it at the apostles' feet, and it was distributed to anyone as he had need.

---

r 26 That is, Christ or Messiah   *s 26* Psalm 2:1,2   *t 27* The Greek is plural.

36 Joseph, a Levite from Cyprus, whom the apostles called Barnabas (which means Son of Encouragement), **37** sold a field he owned and brought the money and put it at the apostles' feet.

Ananias and Sapphira

5 **1** Now a man named Ananias, together with his wife Sapphira, also sold a piece of property. **2** With his wife's full knowledge he kept back part of the money for himself, but brought the rest and put it at the apostles' feet.

3 Then Peter said, "Ananias, how is it that Satan has so filled your heart that you have lied to the Holy Spirit and have kept for yourself some of the money you received for the land? **4** Didn't it belong to you before it was sold? And after it was sold, wasn't the money at your disposal? What made you think of doing such a thing? You have not lied to men but to God."

5 When Ananias heard this, he fell down and died. And great fear seized all who heard what had happened. **6** Then the young men came forward, wrapped up his body, and carried him out and buried him.

7 About three hours later his wife came in, not knowing what had happened. **8** Peter asked her, "Tell me, is this the price you and Ananias got for the land?"

"Yes," she said, "that is the price."

9 Peter said to her, "How could you agree to test the Spirit of the Lord? Look! The feet of the men who buried your husband are at the door, and they will carry you out also."

10 At that moment she fell down at his feet and died. Then the young men came in and, finding her dead,

carried her out and buried her beside her husband. **11** Great fear seized the whole church and all who heard about these events.

The Apostles Heal Many

12 The apostles performed many miraculous signs and wonders among the people. And all the believers used to meet together in Solomon's Colonnade. **13** No one else dared join them, even though they were highly regarded by the people. **14** Nevertheless, more and more men and women believed in the Lord and were added to their number. **15** As a result, people brought the sick into the streets and laid them on beds and mats so that at least Peter's shadow might fall on some of them as he passed by. **16** Crowds gathered also from the towns around Jerusalem, bringing their sick and those tormented by evil[u] spirits, and all of them were healed.

The Apostles Persecuted

17 Then the high priest and all his associates, who were members of the party of the Sadducees, were filled with jealousy. **18** They arrested the apostles and put them in the public jail. **19** But during the night an angel of the Lord opened the doors of the jail and brought them out. **20** "Go, stand in the temple courts," he said, "and tell the people the full message of this new life."

21 At daybreak they entered the temple courts, as they had been told, and began to teach the people.

When the high priest and his associates arrived, they called together the Sanhedrin—the full assembly of the elders of Israel—and sent to the jail for the apostles. **22** But on arriving at the jail, the officers did not find them there. So they went back and reported, **23** "We found the jail securely locked, with the guards standing at the doors; but when we opened them, we found no one inside." **24** On hearing this report, the captain of the temple guard and the chief priests were puzzled, wondering what would come of this.

25 Then someone came and said, "Look! The men you put in jail are standing in the temple courts teaching the people." **26** At that, the captain went with his officers and brought the apostles. They did not use force, because they feared that the people would stone them.

27 Having brought the apostles, they made them appear before the Sanhedrin to be questioned by the high priest. **28** "We gave you strict orders not to teach in this name," he said. "Yet you have filled Jerusalem with your teaching and are determined to make us guilty of this man's blood."

29 Peter and the other apostles replied: "We must obey God rather than men! **30** The God of our fathers raised Jesus from the dead—whom you had killed by hanging him on a tree. **31** God exalted him to his own right hand as Prince and Savior that he might give repentance and forgiveness of sins to Israel. **32** We are witnesses of these things, and so is the Holy Spirit, whom God has given to those who obey him."

33 When they heard this, they were furious and wanted to put them to death. **34** But a Pharisee named Gamaliel, a teacher of the law, who was honored by all the people, stood up in the Sanhedrin and ordered that the men be put outside for a little while. **35** Then he addressed them: "Men of Israel, consider carefully what you intend to do to these men. **36** Some time ago Theudas appeared, claiming to be somebody, and about four hundred men rallied to him. He was killed, all his followers were dispersed, and it all came to nothing. **37** After him, Judas the Galilean appeared in the days of the census and led a band of people in revolt. He too was killed, and all his followers were scattered. **38** Therefore, in the present case I advise you: Leave these men alone! Let them go! For if their purpose or activity is of human origin, it will fail. **39** But if it is from God, you will not be able to stop these men; you will only find yourselves fighting against God."

40 His speech persuaded them. They called the apostles in and had them flogged. Then they ordered them not to speak in the name of Jesus, and let them go.

41 The apostles left the Sanhedrin, rejoicing because they had been counted worthy of suffering disgrace for the Name. **42** Day after day, in the temple courts and from house to house, they never stopped teaching and proclaiming the good news that Jesus is the Christ.^{v}

The Choosing of the Seven

6 **1** In those days when the number of disciples was increasing, the Grecian Jews among them complained against the Hebraic Jews because their widows were being overlooked in the daily distribution of

^{v} 42 Or *Messiah*

food. 2 So the Twelve gathered all the disciples together and said, "It would not be right for us to neglect the ministry of the word of God in order to wait on tables. 3 Brothers, choose seven men from among you who are known to be full of the Spirit and wisdom. We will turn this responsibility over to them 4 and will give our attention to prayer and the ministry of the word."

5 This proposal pleased the whole group. They chose Stephen, a man full of faith and of the Holy Spirit; also Philip, Procorus, Nicanor, Timon, Parmenas, and Nicolas from Antioch, a convert to Judaism. 6 They presented these men to the apostles, who prayed and laid their hands on them.

7 So the word of God spread. The number of disciples in Jerusalem increased rapidly, and a large number of priests became obedient to the faith.

Stephen Seized

8 Now Stephen, a man full of God's grace and power, did great wonders and miraculous signs among the people. 9 Opposition arose, however, from members of the Synagogue of the Freedmen (as it was called)—Jews of Cyrene and Alexandria as well as the provinces of Cilicia and Asia. These men began to argue with Stephen, 10 but they could not stand up against his wisdom or the Spirit by whom he spoke.

11 Then they secretly persuaded some men to say, "We have heard Stephen speak words of blasphemy against Moses and against God."

12 So they stirred up the people and the elders and the teachers of the law. They seized Stephen and brought him before the Sanhedrin. 13 They produced false witnesses, who testified, "This fellow never stops speaking against this holy place and against the law. 14 For we have heard him say that this Jesus of Nazareth will destroy this place and change the customs Moses handed down to us."

15 All who were sitting in the Sanhedrin looked intently at Stephen, and they saw that his face was like the face of an angel.

Stephen's Speech to the Sanhedrin

7 1 Then the high priest asked him, "Are these charges true?"

2 To this he replied: "Brothers and fathers, listen to me! The God of glory appeared to our father Abraham while he was still in Mesopotamia, before he lived in Haran. 3 'Leave your country and your people,' God said, 'and go to the land I will show you.'ʷ

4 "So he left the land of the Chaldeans and settled in Haran. After the death of his father, God sent him to this land where you are now living. 5 He gave him no inheritance here, not even a foot of ground. But God promised him that he and his descendants after him would possess the land, even though at that time Abraham had no child. 6 God spoke to him in this way: 'Your descendants will be strangers in a country not their own, and they will be enslaved and mistreated four hundred years. 7 But I will punish the nation they serve as slaves,' God said, 'and afterward they will come out of that country and worship me in this place.'ˣ 8 Then he gave Abraham the

---

w 3 Gen. 12:1   x 7 Gen. 15:13,14

covenant of circumcision. And Abraham became the father of Isaac and circumcised him eight days after his birth. Later Isaac became the father of Jacob, and Jacob became the father of the twelve patriarchs.

9 "Because the patriarchs were jealous of Joseph, they sold him as a slave into Egypt. But God was with him 10 and rescued him from all his troubles. He gave Joseph wisdom and enabled him to gain the goodwill of Pharaoh king of Egypt; so he made him ruler over Egypt and all his palace.

11 "Then a famine struck all Egypt and Canaan, bringing great suffering, and our fathers could not find food. 12 When Jacob heard that there was grain in Egypt, he sent our fathers on their first visit. 13 On their second visit, Joseph told his brothers who he was, and Pharaoh learned about Joseph's family. 14 After this, Joseph sent for his father Jacob and his whole family, seventy-five in all. 15 Then Jacob went down to Egypt, where he and our fathers died. 16 Their bodies were brought back to Shechem and placed in the tomb that Abraham had bought from the sons of Hamor at Shechem for a certain sum of money.

17 "As the time drew near for God to fulfill his promise to Abraham, the number of our people in Egypt greatly increased. 18 Then another king, who knew nothing about Joseph, became ruler of Egypt. 19 He dealt treacherously with our people and oppressed our forefathers by forcing them to throw out their newborn babies so that they would die.

20 "At that time Moses was born, and he was no ordinary child.*y* For three months he was cared for in his father's house. 21 When he was placed outside, Pharaoh's daughter took him and brought him up as her own son. 22 Moses was educated in all the wisdom of the Egyptians and was powerful in speech and action.

23 "When Moses was forty years old, he decided to visit his fellow Israelites. 24 He saw one of them being mistreated by an Egyptian, so he went to his defense and avenged him by killing the Egyptian. 25 Moses thought that his own people would realize that God was using him to rescue them, but they did not. 26 The next day Moses came upon two Israelites who were fighting. He tried to reconcile them by saying, 'Men, you are brothers; why do you want to hurt each other?'

27 "But the man who was mistreating the other pushed Moses aside and said, 'Who made you ruler and judge over us? 28 Do you want to kill me as you killed the Egyptian yesterday?'*z* 29 When Moses heard this, he fled to Midian, where he settled as a foreigner and had two sons.

30 "After forty years had passed, an angel appeared to Moses in the flames of a burning bush in the desert near Mount Sinai. 31 When he saw this, he was amazed at the sight. As he went over to look more closely, he heard the Lord's voice: 32 'I am the God of your fathers, the God of Abraham, Isaac and Jacob.'*a* Moses trembled with fear and did not dare to look.

33 "Then the Lord said to him, 'Take off your sandals; the place where you are standing is holy ground. 34 I have indeed seen the oppression of my people in Egypt. I

y 20 Or *was fair in the sight of God*   *z 28* Exodus 2:14   *a 32* Exodus 3:6

have heard their groaning and have come down to set them free. Now come, I will send you back to Egypt.'[b]

35 "This is the same Moses whom they had rejected with the words, 'Who made you ruler and judge?' He was sent to be their ruler and deliverer by God himself, through the angel who appeared to him in the bush. 36 He led them out of Egypt and did wonders and miraculous signs in Egypt, at the Red Sea[c] and for forty years in the desert.

37 "This is that Moses who told the Israelites, 'God will send you a prophet like me from your own people.'[d] 38 He was in the assembly in the desert, with the angel who spoke to him on Mount Sinai, and with our fathers; and he received living words to pass on to us.

39 "But our fathers refused to obey him. Instead, they rejected him and in their hearts turned back to Egypt. 40 They told Aaron, 'Make us gods who will go before us. As for this fellow Moses who led us out of Egypt—we don't know what has happened to him!'[e] 41 That was the time they made an idol in the form of a calf. They brought sacrifices to it and held a celebration in honor of what their hands had made. 42 But God turned away and gave them over to the worship of the heavenly bodies. This agrees with what is written in the book of the prophets:

" 'Did you bring me sacrifices and offerings
　　forty years in the desert, O
　　　　house of Israel?
43 You have lifted up the shrine of
　　Molech

and the star of your god Rephan,
　the idols you made to worship.
Therefore I will send you into
　exile'[f] beyond Babylon.

44 "Our forefathers had the tabernacle of the Testimony with them in the desert. It had been made as God directed Moses, according to the pattern he had seen. 45 Having received the tabernacle, our fathers under Joshua brought it with them when they took the land from the nations God drove out before them. It remained in the land until the time of David, 46 who enjoyed God's favor and asked that he might provide a dwelling place for the God of Jacob.[g] 47 But it was Solomon who built the house for him.

48 "However, the Most High does not live in houses made by men. As the prophet says:

49 " 'Heaven is my throne,
　　and the earth is my footstool.
　What kind of house will you
　　　build for me?
　　　　　　　says the Lord.
　Or where will my resting
　　　place be?
50 Has not my hand made all
　　these things?'[h]

51 "You stiff-necked people, with uncircumcised hearts and ears! You are just like your fathers: You always resist the Holy Spirit! 52 Was there ever a prophet your fathers did not persecute? They even killed those who predicted the coming of the Righteous One. And now you have betrayed and murdered him— 53 you who have received the law that was put into effect through angels but have not obeyed it."

---

b 34 Exodus 3:5,7,8,10　c 36 That is, Sea of Reeds　d 37 Deut. 18:15　e 40 Exodus 32:1
f 43 Amos 5:25-27　g 46 Some early manuscripts the house of Jacob　h 50 Isaiah 66:1,2

The Stoning of Stephen

54 When they heard this, they were furious and gnashed their teeth at him. **55** But Stephen, full of the Holy Spirit, looked up to heaven and saw the glory of God, and Jesus standing at the right hand of God. **56** "Look," he said, "I see heaven open and the Son of Man standing at the right hand of God."

57 At this they covered their ears and, yelling at the top of their voices, they all rushed at him, **58** dragged him out of the city and began to stone him. Meanwhile, the witnesses laid their clothes at the feet of a young man named Saul.

59 While they were stoning him, Stephen prayed, "Lord Jesus, receive my spirit." **60** Then he fell on his knees and cried out, "Lord, do not hold this sin against them." When he had said this, he fell asleep.

8 **1** And Saul was there, giving approval to his death.

The Church Persecuted and Scattered

On that day a great persecution broke out against the church at Jerusalem, and all except the apostles were scattered throughout Judea and Samaria. **2** Godly men buried Stephen and mourned deeply for him. **3** But Saul began to destroy the church. Going from house to house, he dragged off men and women and put them in prison.

Philip in Samaria

4 Those who had been scattered preached the word wherever they went. **5** Philip went down to a city in Samaria and proclaimed the Christ[i] there. **6** When the crowds heard Philip and saw the miraculous signs he did, they all paid close attention to what he said. **7** With shrieks, evil[j] spirits came out of many, and many paralytics and cripples were healed. **8** So there was great joy in that city.

Simon the Sorcerer

9 Now for some time a man named Simon had practiced sorcery in the city and amazed all the people of Samaria. He boasted that he was someone great, **10** and all the people, both high and low, gave him their attention and exclaimed, "This man is the divine power known as the Great Power." **11** They followed him because he had amazed them for a long time with his magic. **12** But when they believed Philip as he preached the good news of the kingdom of God and the name of Jesus Christ, they were baptized, both men and women. **13** Simon himself believed and was baptized. And he followed Philip everywhere, astonished by the great signs and miracles he saw.

14 When the apostles in Jerusalem heard that Samaria had accepted the word of God, they sent Peter and John to them. **15** When they arrived, they prayed for them that they might receive the Holy Spirit, **16** because the Holy Spirit had not yet come upon any of them; they had simply been baptized into[k] the name of the Lord Jesus. **17** Then Peter and John placed their hands on them, and they received the Holy Spirit.

18 When Simon saw that the Spirit was given at the laying on of the apostles' hands, he offered them money **19** and said, "Give me also this ability so that everyone on whom

---

i 5 Or *Messiah*   *j* 7 Greek *unclean*   *k* 16 Or *in*

I lay my hands may receive the Holy Spirit."

20 Peter answered: "May your money perish with you, because you thought you could buy the gift of God with money! 21 You have no part or share in this ministry, because your heart is not right before God. 22 Repent of this wickedness and pray to the Lord. Perhaps he will forgive you for having such a thought in your heart. 23 For I see that you are full of bitterness and captive to sin."

24 Then Simon answered, "Pray to the Lord for me so that nothing you have said may happen to me."

25 When they had testified and proclaimed the word of the Lord, Peter and John returned to Jerusalem, preaching the gospel in many Samaritan villages.

Philip and the Ethiopian

26 Now an angel of the Lord said to Philip, "Go south to the road — the desert road — that goes down from Jerusalem to Gaza." 27 So he started out, and on his way he met an Ethiopian*l* eunuch, an important official in charge of all the treasury of Candace, queen of the Ethiopians. This man had gone to Jerusalem to worship, 28 and on his way home was sitting in his chariot reading the book of Isaiah the prophet. 29 The Spirit told Philip, "Go to that chariot and stay near it."

30 Then Philip ran up to the chariot and heard the man reading Isaiah the prophet. "Do you understand what you are reading?" Philip asked.

31 "How can I," he said, "unless someone explains it to me?" So he invited Philip to come up and sit with him.

32 The eunuch was reading this passage of Scripture:

"He was led like a sheep to the slaughter,
and as a lamb before the shearer is silent,
so he did not open his mouth.
33 In his humiliation he was deprived of justice.
Who can speak of his descendants?
For his life was taken from the earth."*m*

34 The eunuch asked Philip, "Tell me, please, who is the prophet talking about, himself or someone else?" 35 Then Philip began with that very passage of Scripture and told him the good news about Jesus.

36 As they traveled along the road, they came to some water and the eunuch said, "Look, here is water. Why shouldn't I be baptized?"*n* 38 And he gave orders to stop the chariot. Then both Philip and the eunuch went down into the water and Philip baptized him. 39 When they came up out of the water, the Spirit of the Lord suddenly took Philip away, and the eunuch did not see him again, but went on his way rejoicing. 40 Philip, however, appeared at Azotus and traveled about, preaching the gospel in all the towns until he reached Caesarea.

Saul's Conversion

9 1 Meanwhile, Saul was still breathing out murderous threats against the Lord's disciples. He went to the high priest 2 and asked him for

---

l 27 That is, from the upper Nile region   *m* 33 Isaiah 53:7,8   *n* 36 Some late manuscripts baptized?" 37 Philip said, "If you believe with all your heart, you may." The eunuch answered, "I believe that Jesus Christ is the Son of God."

letters to the synagogues in Damascus, so that if he found any there who belonged to the Way, whether men or women, he might take them as prisoners to Jerusalem. 3 As he neared Damascus on his journey, suddenly a light from heaven flashed around him. 4 He fell to the ground and heard a voice say to him, "Saul, Saul, why do you persecute me?"

5 "Who are you, Lord?" Saul asked.

"I am Jesus, whom you are persecuting," he replied. 6 "Now get up and go into the city, and you will be told what you must do."

7 The men traveling with Saul stood there speechless; they heard the sound but did not see anyone. 8 Saul got up from the ground, but when he opened his eyes he could see nothing. So they led him by the hand into Damascus. 9 For three days he was blind, and did not eat or drink anything.

10 In Damascus there was a disciple named Ananias. The Lord called to him in a vision, "Ananias!"

"Yes, Lord," he answered.

11 The Lord told him, "Go to the house of Judas on Straight Street and ask for a man from Tarsus named Saul, for he is praying. 12 In a vision he has seen a man named Ananias come and place his hands on him to restore his sight."

13 "Lord," Ananias answered, "I have heard many reports about this man and all the harm he has done to your saints in Jerusalem. 14 And he has come here with authority from the chief priests to arrest all who call on your name."

15 But the Lord said to Ananias, "Go! This man is my chosen instrument to carry my name before the Gentiles and their kings and before the people of Israel. 16 I will show him how much he must suffer for my name."

17 Then Ananias went to the house and entered it. Placing his hands on Saul, he said, "Brother Saul, the Lord — Jesus, who appeared to you on the road as you were coming here — has sent me so that you may see again and be filled with the Holy Spirit." 18 Immediately, something like scales fell from Saul's eyes, and he could see again. He got up and was baptized, 19 and after taking some food, he regained his strength.

Saul in Damascus and Jerusalem

Saul spent several days with the disciples in Damascus. 20 At once he began to preach in the synagogues that Jesus is the Son of God. 21 All those who heard him were astonished and asked, "Isn't he the man who raised havoc in Jerusalem among those who call on this name? And hasn't he come here to take them as prisoners to the chief priests?" 22 Yet Saul grew more and more powerful and baffled the Jews living in Damascus by proving that Jesus is the Christ.°

23 After many days had gone by, the Jews conspired to kill him, 24 but Saul learned of their plan. Day and night they kept close watch on the city gates in order to kill him. 25 But his followers took him by night and lowered him in a basket through an opening in the wall.

26 When he came to Jerusalem, he tried to join the disciples, but they were all afraid of him, not believing that he really was a disciple. 27 But

° 22 Or *Messiah*

Barnabas took him and brought him to the apostles. He told them how Saul on his journey had seen the Lord and that the Lord had spoken to him, and how in Damascus he had preached fearlessly in the name of Jesus. 28 So Saul stayed with them and moved about freely in Jerusalem, speaking boldly in the name of the Lord. 29 He talked and debated with the Grecian Jews, but they tried to kill him. 30 When the brothers learned of this, they took him down to Caesarea and sent him off to Tarsus.

31 Then the church throughout Judea, Galilee and Samaria enjoyed a time of peace. It was strengthened; and encouraged by the Holy Spirit, it grew in numbers, living in the fear of the Lord.

Aeneas and Dorcas

32 As Peter traveled about the country, he went to visit the saints in Lydda. 33 There he found a man named Aeneas, a paralytic who had been bedridden for eight years. 34 "Aeneas," Peter said to him, "Jesus Christ heals you. Get up and take care of your mat." Immediately Aeneas got up. 35 All those who lived in Lydda and Sharon saw him and turned to the Lord.

36 In Joppa there was a disciple named Tabitha (which, when translated, is Dorcas*P*), who was always doing good and helping the poor. 37 About that time she became sick and died, and her body was washed and placed in an upstairs room. 38 Lydda was near Joppa; so when the disciples heard that Peter was in Lydda, they sent two men to him and urged him, "Please come at once!"

39 Peter went with them, and when he arrived he was taken upstairs to the room. All the widows stood around him, crying and showing him the robes and other clothing that Dorcas had made while she was still with them.

40 Peter sent them all out of the room; then he got down on his knees and prayed. Turning toward the dead woman, he said, "Tabitha, get up." She opened her eyes, and seeing Peter she sat up. 41 He took her by the hand and helped her to her feet. Then he called the believers and the widows and presented her to them alive. 42 This became known all over Joppa, and many people believed in the Lord. 43 Peter stayed in Joppa for some time with a tanner named Simon.

Cornelius Calls for Peter

10 1 At Caesarea there was a man named Cornelius, a centurion in what was known as the Italian Regiment. 2 He and all his family were devout and God-fearing; he gave generously to those in need and prayed to God regularly. 3 One day at about three in the afternoon he had a vision. He distinctly saw an angel of God, who came to him and said, "Cornelius!"

4 Cornelius stared at him in fear. "What is it, Lord?" he asked.

The angel answered, "Your prayers and gifts to the poor have come up as a memorial offering before God. 5 Now send men to Joppa to bring back a man named Simon who is called Peter. 6 He is staying with Simon the tanner, whose house is by the sea."

7 When the angel who spoke to him had gone, Cornelius called two

---

P 36 Both *Tabitha* (Aramaic) and *Dorcas* (Greek) mean *gazelle.*

of his servants and a devout soldier who was one of his attendants. **8** He told them everything that had happened and sent them to Joppa.

Peter's Vision

9 About noon the following day as they were on their journey and approaching the city, Peter went up on the roof to pray. **10** He became hungry and wanted something to eat, and while the meal was being prepared, he fell into a trance. **11** He saw heaven opened and something like a large sheet being let down to earth by its four corners. **12** It contained all kinds of four-footed animals, as well as reptiles of the earth and birds of the air. **13** Then a voice told him, "Get up, Peter. Kill and eat."

14 "Surely not, Lord!" Peter replied. "I have never eaten anything impure or unclean."

15 The voice spoke to him a second time, "Do not call anything impure that God has made clean."

16 This happened three times, and immediately the sheet was taken back to heaven.

17 While Peter was wondering about the meaning of the vision, the men sent by Cornelius found out where Simon's house was and stopped at the gate. **18** They called out, asking if Simon who was known as Peter was staying there.

19 While Peter was still thinking about the vision, the Spirit said to him, "Simon, three*q* men are looking for you. **20** So get up and go downstairs. Do not hesitate to go with them, for I have sent them."

21 Peter went down and said to the men, "I'm the one you're looking for. Why have you come?"

22 The men replied, "We have come from Cornelius the centurion. He is a righteous and God-fearing man, who is respected by all the Jewish people. A holy angel told him to have you come to his house so that he could hear what you have to say." **23** Then Peter invited the men into the house to be his guests.

Peter at Cornelius' House

The next day Peter started out with them, and some of the brothers from Joppa went along. **24** The following day he arrived in Caesarea. Cornelius was expecting them and had called together his relatives and close friends. **25** As Peter entered the house, Cornelius met him and fell at his feet in reverence. **26** But Peter made him get up. "Stand up," he said, "I am only a man myself."

27 Talking with him, Peter went inside and found a large gathering of people. **28** He said to them: "You are well aware that it is against our law for a Jew to associate with a Gentile or visit him. But God has shown me that I should not call any man impure or unclean. **29** So when I was sent for, I came without raising any objection. May I ask why you sent for me?"

30 Cornelius answered: "Four days ago I was in my house praying at this hour, at three in the afternoon. Suddenly a man in shining clothes stood before me **31** and said, 'Cornelius, God has heard your prayer and remembered your gifts to the poor. **32** Send to Joppa for Simon who is called Peter. He is a guest in the home of Simon the tanner, who lives by the sea.' **33** So I sent for you immediately, and it was good of you to come. Now we are all here in the presence of God

---

q 19 One early manuscript *two*; other manuscripts do not have the number.

to listen to everything the Lord has commanded you to tell us."

34 Then Peter began to speak: "I now realize how true it is that God does not show favoritism 35 but accepts men from every nation who fear him and do what is right. 36 You know the message God sent to the people of Israel, telling the good news of peace through Jesus Christ, who is Lord of all. 37 You know what has happened throughout Judea, beginning in Galilee after the baptism that John preached — 38 how God anointed Jesus of Nazareth with the Holy Spirit and power, and how he went around doing good and healing all who were under the power of the devil, because God was with him.

39 "We are witnesses of everything he did in the country of the Jews and in Jerusalem. They killed him by hanging him on a tree, 40 but God raised him from the dead on the third day and caused him to be seen. 41 He was not seen by all the people, but by witnesses whom God had already chosen — by us who ate and drank with him after he rose from the dead. 42 He commanded us to preach to the people and to testify that he is the one whom God appointed as judge of the living and the dead. 43 All the prophets testify about him that everyone who believes in him receives forgiveness of sins through his name."

44 While Peter was still speaking these words, the Holy Spirit came on all who heard the message. 45 The circumcised believers who had come with Peter were astonished that the gift of the Holy Spirit had been poured out even on the Gentiles. 46 For they heard them speaking in tongues[r] and praising God.

Then Peter said, 47 "Can anyone keep these people from being baptized with water? They have received the Holy Spirit just as we have." 48 So he ordered that they be baptized in the name of Jesus Christ. Then they asked Peter to stay with them for a few days.

Peter Explains His Actions

11 1 The apostles and the brothers throughout Judea heard that the Gentiles also had received the word of God. 2 So when Peter went up to Jerusalem, the circumcised believers criticized him 3 and said, "You went into the house of uncircumcised men and ate with them."

4 Peter began and explained everything to them precisely as it had happened: 5 "I was in the city of Joppa praying, and in a trance I saw a vision. I saw something like a large sheet being let down from heaven by its four corners, and it came down to where I was. 6 I looked into it and saw four-footed animals of the earth, wild beasts, reptiles, and birds of the air. 7 Then I heard a voice telling me, 'Get up, Peter. Kill and eat.'

8 "I replied, 'Surely not, Lord! Nothing impure or unclean has ever entered my mouth.'

9 "The voice spoke from heaven a second time, 'Do not call anything impure that God has made clean.' 10 This happened three times, and then it was all pulled up to heaven again.

11 "Right then three men who had been sent to me from Caesarea stopped at the house where I was staying. 12 The Spirit told me to have no hesitation about going with them.

r 46 Or other languages

These six brothers also went with me, and we entered the man's house. 13 He told us how he had seen an angel appear in his house and say, 'Send to Joppa for Simon who is called Peter. 14 He will bring you a message through which you and all your household will be saved.'

15 "As I began to speak, the Holy Spirit came on them as he had come on us at the beginning. 16 Then I remembered what the Lord had said: 'John baptized with^s water, but you will be baptized with the Holy Spirit.' 17 So if God gave them the same gift as he gave us, who believed in the Lord Jesus Christ, who was I to think that I could oppose God?"

18 When they heard this, they had no further objections and praised God, saying, "So then, God has granted even the Gentiles repentance unto life."

The Church in Antioch

19 Now those who had been scattered by the persecution in connection with Stephen traveled as far as Phoenicia, Cyprus and Antioch, telling the message only to Jews. 20 Some of them, however, men from Cyprus and Cyrene, went to Antioch and began to speak to Greeks also, telling them the good news about the Lord Jesus. 21 The Lord's hand was with them, and a great number of people believed and turned to the Lord.

22 News of this reached the ears of the church at Jerusalem, and they sent Barnabas to Antioch. 23 When he arrived and saw the evidence of the grace of God, he was glad and encouraged them all to remain true to the Lord with all their hearts. 24 He was a good man, full of the Holy Spirit and faith, and a great number of people were brought to the Lord.

25 Then Barnabas went to Tarsus to look for Saul, 26 and when he found him, he brought him to Antioch. So for a whole year Barnabas and Saul met with the church and taught great numbers of people. The disciples were called Christians first at Antioch.

27 During this time some prophets came down from Jerusalem to Antioch. 28 One of them, named Agabus, stood up and through the Spirit predicted that a severe famine would spread over the entire Roman world. (This happened during the reign of Claudius.) 29 The disciples, each according to his ability, decided to provide help for the brothers living in Judea. 30 This they did, sending their gift to the elders by Barnabas and Saul.

Peter's Miraculous Escape From Prison

12 1 It was about this time that King Herod arrested some who belonged to the church, intending to persecute them. 2 He had James, the brother of John, put to death with the sword. 3 When he saw that this pleased the Jews, he proceeded to seize Peter also. This happened during the Feast of Unleavened Bread. 4 After arresting him, he put him in prison, handing him over to be guarded by four squads of four soldiers each. Herod intended to bring him out for public trial after the Passover.

5 So Peter was kept in prison, but the church was earnestly praying to God for him.

---

^{s} 16 Or *in*

6 The night before Herod was to bring him to trial, Peter was sleeping between two soldiers, bound with two chains, and sentries stood guard at the entrance. **7** Suddenly an angel of the Lord appeared and a light shone in the cell. He struck Peter on the side and woke him up. "Quick, get up!" he said, and the chains fell off Peter's wrists.

8 Then the angel said to him, "Put on your clothes and sandals." And Peter did so. "Wrap your cloak around you and follow me," the angel told him. **9** Peter followed him out of the prison, but he had no idea that what the angel was doing was really happening; he thought he was seeing a vision. **10** They passed the first and second guards and came to the iron gate leading to the city. It opened for them by itself, and they went through it. When they had walked the length of one street, suddenly the angel left him.

11 Then Peter came to himself and said, "Now I know without a doubt that the Lord sent his angel and rescued me from Herod's clutches and from everything the Jewish people were anticipating."

12 When this had dawned on him, he went to the house of Mary the mother of John, also called Mark, where many people had gathered and were praying. **13** Peter knocked at the outer entrance, and a servant girl named Rhoda came to answer the door. **14** When she recognized Peter's voice, she was so overjoyed she ran back without opening it and exclaimed, "Peter is at the door!"

15 "You're out of your mind," they told her. When she kept insisting that it was so, they said, "It must be his angel."

16 But Peter kept on knocking, and when they opened the door and saw him, they were astonished. **17** Peter motioned with his hand for them to be quiet and described how the Lord had brought him out of prison. "Tell James and the brothers about this," he said, and then he left for another place.

18 In the morning, there was no small commotion among the soldiers as to what had become of Peter. **19** After Herod had a thorough search made for him and did not find him, he cross-examined the guards and ordered that they be executed.

Herod's Death

Then Herod went from Judea to Caesarea and stayed there a while. **20** He had been quarreling with the people of Tyre and Sidon; they now joined together and sought an audience with him. Having secured the support of Blastus, a trusted personal servant of the king, they asked for peace, because they depended on the king's country for their food supply.

21 On the appointed day Herod, wearing his royal robes, sat on his throne and delivered a public address to the people. **22** They shouted, "This is the voice of a god, not of a man." **23** Immediately, because Herod did not give praise to God, an angel of the Lord struck him down, and he was eaten by worms and died.

24 But the word of God continued to increase and spread.

25 When Barnabas and Saul had finished their mission, they returned from[t] Jerusalem, taking with them John, also called Mark.

---

t 25 Some manuscripts to

Barnabas and Saul Sent Off

13 ¹ In the church at Antioch there were prophets and teachers: Barnabas, Simeon called Niger, Lucius of Cyrene, Manaen (who had been brought up with Herod the tetrarch) and Saul. ² While they were worshiping the Lord and fasting, the Holy Spirit said, "Set apart for me Barnabas and Saul for the work to which I have called them." ³ So after they had fasted and prayed, they placed their hands on them and sent them off.

On Cyprus

⁴ The two of them, sent on their way by the Holy Spirit, went down to Seleucia and sailed from there to Cyprus. ⁵ When they arrived at Salamis, they proclaimed the word of God in the Jewish synagogues. John was with them as their helper.

⁶ They traveled through the whole island until they came to Paphos. There they met a Jewish sorcerer and false prophet named Bar-Jesus, ⁷ who was an attendant of the proconsul, Sergius Paulus. The proconsul, an intelligent man, sent for Barnabas and Saul because he wanted to hear the word of God. ⁸ But Elymas the sorcerer (for that is what his name means) opposed them and tried to turn the proconsul from the faith. ⁹ Then Saul, who was also called Paul, filled with the Holy Spirit, looked straight at Elymas and said, "You are a child of the devil and an enemy of everything that is right! You are full of all kinds of deceit and trickery. Will you never stop perverting the right ways of the Lord? ¹¹ Now the hand of the Lord is

against you. You are going to be blind, and for a time you will be unable to see the light of the sun."

Immediately mist and darkness came over him, and he groped about, seeking someone to lead him by the hand. ¹² When the proconsul saw what had happened, he believed, for he was amazed at the teaching about the Lord.

In Pisidian Antioch

¹³ From Paphos, Paul and his companions sailed to Perga in Pamphylia, where John left them to return to Jerusalem. ¹⁴ From Perga they went on to Pisidian Antioch. On the Sabbath they entered the synagogue and sat down. ¹⁵ After the reading from the Law and the Prophets, the synagogue rulers sent word to them, saying, "Brothers, if you have a message of encouragement for the people, please speak."

¹⁶ Standing up, Paul motioned with his hand and said: "Men of Israel and you Gentiles who worship God, listen to me! ¹⁷ The God of the people of Israel chose our fathers; he made the people prosper during their stay in Egypt, with mighty power he led them out of that country, ¹⁸ he endured their conduct^u for about forty years in the desert, ¹⁹ he overthrew seven nations in Canaan and gave their land to his people as their inheritance. ²⁰ All this took about 450 years.

"After this, God gave them judges until the time of Samuel the prophet. ²¹ Then the people asked for a king, and he gave them Saul son of Kish, of the tribe of Benjamin, who ruled forty years. ²² After removing Saul, he made David their king. He tes-

---

u 18 Some manuscripts *and cared for them*

tified concerning him: 'I have found David son of Jesse a man after my own heart; he will do everything I want him to do.'

23 "From this man's descendants God has brought to Israel the Savior Jesus, as he promised. **24** Before the coming of Jesus, John preached repentance and baptism to all the people of Israel. **25** As John was completing his work, he said: 'Who do you think I am? I am not that one. No, but he is coming after me, whose sandals I am not worthy to untie.'

26 "Brothers, children of Abraham, and you God-fearing Gentiles, it is to us that this message of salvation has been sent. **27** The people of Jerusalem and their rulers did not recognize Jesus, yet in condemning him they fulfilled the words of the prophets that are read every Sabbath. **28** Though they found no proper ground for a death sentence, they asked Pilate to have him executed. **29** When they had carried out all that was written about him, they took him down from the tree and laid him in a tomb. **30** But God raised him from the dead, **31** and for many days he was seen by those who had traveled with him from Galilee to Jerusalem. They are now his witnesses to our people.

32 "We tell you the good news: What God promised our fathers **33** he has fulfilled for us, their children, by raising up Jesus. As it is written in the second Psalm:

" 'You are my Son;
today I have become your
Father.'*v*w*

34 The fact that God raised him from the dead, never to decay, is stated in these words:

" 'I will give you the holy and sure
blessings promised to
David.'*x*

35 So it is stated elsewhere:

" 'You will not let your Holy One
see decay.'*y*

36 "For when David had served God's purpose in his own generation, he fell asleep; he was buried with his fathers and his body decayed. **37** But the one whom God raised from the dead did not see decay.

38 "Therefore, my brothers, I want you to know that through Jesus the forgiveness of sins is proclaimed to you. **39** Through him everyone who believes is justified from everything you could not be justified from by the law of Moses. **40** Take care that what the prophets have said does not happen to you:

41 " 'Look, you scoffers,
wonder and perish,
for I am going to do something
in your days
that you would never believe,
even if someone told you.'*z*

42 As Paul and Barnabas were leaving the synagogue, the people invited them to speak further about these things on the next Sabbath. **43** When the congregation was dismissed, many of the Jews and devout converts to Judaism followed Paul and Barnabas, who talked with them and urged them to continue in the grace of God.

v 33 Or *have begotten you*   *w 33* Psalm 2:7   *x 34* Isaiah 55:3   *y 35* Psalm 16:10   *z 41* Hab. 1:5

44 On the next Sabbath almost the whole city gathered to hear the word of the Lord. **45** When the Jews saw the crowds, they were filled with jealousy and talked abusively against what Paul was saying.

46 Then Paul and Barnabas answered them boldly: "We had to speak the word of God to you first. Since you reject it and do not consider yourselves worthy of eternal life, we now turn to the Gentiles. **47** For this is what the Lord has commanded us:

> " 'I have made you[a] a light for the
>   Gentiles,
> that you[b] may bring salvation
>   to the ends of the earth.'[c] "

48 When the Gentiles heard this, they were glad and honored the word of the Lord; and all who were appointed for eternal life believed.

49 The word of the Lord spread through the whole region. **50** But the Jews incited the God-fearing women of high standing and the leading men of the city. They stirred up persecution against Paul and Barnabas, and expelled them from their region. **51** So they shook the dust from their feet in protest against them and went to Iconium. **52** And the disciples were filled with joy and with the Holy Spirit.

In Iconium

14 **1** At Iconium Paul and Barnabas went as usual into the Jewish synagogue. There they spoke so effectively that a great number of Jews and Gentiles believed. **2** But the Jews who refused to believe stirred up the Gentiles and poisoned their minds against the brothers. **3** So Paul and Barnabas spent considerable time there, speaking boldly for the Lord, who confirmed the message of his grace by enabling them to do miraculous signs and wonders. **4** The people of the city were divided; some sided with the Jews, others with the apostles. **5** There was a plot afoot among the Gentiles and Jews, together with their leaders, to mistreat them and stone them. **6** But they found out about it and fled to the Lycaonian cities of Lystra and Derbe and to the surrounding country, **7** where they continued to preach the good news.

In Lystra and Derbe

8 In Lystra there sat a man crippled in his feet, who was lame from birth and had never walked. **9** He listened to Paul as he was speaking. Paul looked directly at him, saw that he had faith to be healed **10** and called out, "Stand up on your feet!" At that, the man jumped up and began to walk.

11 When the crowd saw what Paul had done, they shouted in the Lycaonian language, "The gods have come down to us in human form!" **12** Barnabas they called Zeus, and Paul they called Hermes because he was the chief speaker. **13** The priest of Zeus, whose temple was just outside the city, brought bulls and wreaths to the city gates because he and the crowd wanted to offer sacrifices to them.

14 But when the apostles Barnabas and Paul heard of this, they tore their clothes and rushed out into the crowd, shouting: **15** "Men, why are you doing this? We too are only men, human like you. We are bringing you good news, telling you to turn from

---

47 The Greek is singular.   *b 47* The Greek is singular.   *c 47* Isaiah 49:6

these worthless things to the living God, who made heaven and earth and sea and everything in them. **16** In the past, he let all nations go their own way. **17** Yet he has not left himself without testimony: He has shown kindness by giving you rain from heaven and crops in their seasons; he provides you with plenty of food and fills your hearts with joy. **18** Even with these words, they had difficulty keeping the crowd from sacrificing to them.

19 Then some Jews came from Antioch and Iconium and won the crowd over. They stoned Paul and dragged him outside the city, thinking he was dead. **20** But after the disciples had gathered around him, he got up and went back into the city. The next day he and Barnabas left for Derbe.

The Return to Antioch in Syria

21 They preached the good news in that city and won a large number of disciples. Then they returned to Lystra, Iconium and Antioch, **22** strengthening the disciples and encouraging them to remain true to the faith. "We must go through many hardships to enter the kingdom of God," they said. **23** Paul and Barnabas appointed elders*d* for them in each church and, with prayer and fasting, committed them to the Lord, in whom they had put their trust. **24** After going through Pisidia, they came into Pamphylia, **25** and when they had preached the word in Perga, they went down to Attalia.

26 From Attalia they sailed back to Antioch, where they had been committed to the grace of God for the work they had now completed. **27** On arriving there, they gathered the church together and reported all th God had done through them an how he had opened the door of fai to the Gentiles. **28** And they staye there a long time with the disciple

The Council at Jerusalem

15 **1** Some men came down fro Judea to Antioch and wer teaching the brothers: "Unless yo are circumcised, according to th custom taught by Moses, you cann be saved." **2** This brought Paul ar Barnabas into sharp dispute ar debate with them. So Paul and Ba nabas were appointed, along wi some other believers, to go up Jerusalem to see the apostles ar elders about this question. **3** T church sent them on their way, ar as they traveled through Phoenic and Samaria, they told how the Ge tiles had been converted. This nev made all the brothers very gla **4** When they came to Jerusalem, the were welcomed by the church ar the apostles and elders, to who they reported everything God ha done through them.

5 Then some of the believers wh belonged to the party of th Pharisees stood up and said, "Th Gentiles must be circumcised and r quired to obey the law of Moses."

6 The apostles and elders met consider this question. **7** After muc discussion, Peter got up and ac dressed them: "Brothers, you kno that some time ago God made choice among you that the Gentile might hear from my lips the messag of the gospel and believe. **8** God, wh knows the heart, showed that he ac cepted them by giving the Holy Spir to them, just as he did to us. **9** H

---

d 23 Or *Barnabas ordained elders;* or *Barnabas had elders elected*

ade no distinction between us and
hem, for he purified their hearts by
aith. **10** Now then, why do you try to
est God by putting on the necks of
he disciples a yoke that neither we
or our fathers have been able to
ear? **11** No! We believe it is through
he grace of our Lord Jesus that we
re saved, just as they are."

12 The whole assembly became
ilent as they listened to Barnabas
nd Paul telling about the miraculous
igns and wonders God had done
mong the Gentiles through them.
3 When they finished, James spoke
p: "Brothers, listen to me. **14** Simon
as described to us how God at first
howed his concern by taking from
he Gentiles a people for himself.
5 The words of the prophets are in
greement with this, as it is written:

16 "'After this I will return
    and rebuild David's fallen tent.
    Its ruins I will rebuild,
    and I will restore it,
17 that the remnant of men may
    seek the Lord,
    and all the Gentiles who bear
    my name,
    says the Lord, who does these
    things^f
18 that have been known for
    ages.^{g}

19 "It is my judgment, therefore,
nat that we should not make it difficult
or the Gentiles who are turning to
iod. **20** Instead we should write to
hem, telling them to abstain from
ood polluted by idols, from sexual
mmorality, from the meat of
trangled animals and from blood.
1 For Moses has been preached in
very city from the earliest times and
is read in the synagogues on every
Sabbath."

The Council's Letter to Gentile Believers

22 Then the apostles and elders,
with the whole church, decided to
choose some of their own men and
send them to Antioch with Paul and
Barnabas. They chose Judas (called
Barsabbas) and Silas, two men who
were leaders among the brothers.
23 With them they sent the following
letter:

The apostles and elders, your
brothers,

To the Gentile believers in Antioch,
Syria and Cilicia:

Greetings.

24 We have heard that some
went out from us without our
authorization and disturbed you,
troubling your minds by what they
said. **25** So we all agreed to choose
some men and send them to you
with our dear friends Barnabas and
Paul — **26** men who have risked
their lives for the name of our Lord
Jesus Christ. **27** Therefore we are
sending Judas and Silas to confirm
by word of mouth what we are
writing. **28** It seemed good to the
Holy Spirit and to us not to burden
you with anything beyond the
following requirements: **29** You are
to abstain from food sacrificed to
idols, from blood, from the meat of
strangled animals and from sexual
immorality. You will do well to
avoid these things.

Farewell.

---

14 Greek *Simeon*, a variant of *Simon*; that is, Peter   *f* **17** Amos 9:11,12   *g* **17,18** Some
anuscripts *things'* — / **18** known to the Lord for ages is his work

30 The men were sent off and went down to Antioch, where they gathered the church together and delivered the letter. **31** The people read it and were glad for its encouraging message. **32** Judas and Silas, who themselves were prophets, said much to encourage and strengthen the brothers. **33** After spending some time there, they were sent off by the brothers with the blessing of peace to return to those who had sent them.*h* **35** But Paul and Barnabas remained in Antioch, where they and many others taught and preached the word of the Lord.

Disagreement Between Paul and Barnabas

36 Some time later Paul said to Barnabas, "Let us go back and visit the brothers in all the towns where we preached the word of the Lord and see how they are doing." **37** Barnabas wanted to take John, also called Mark, with them, **38** but Paul did not think it wise to take him, because he had deserted them in Pamphylia and had not continued with them in the work. **39** They had such a sharp disagreement that they parted company. Barnabas took Mark and sailed for Cyprus, **40** but Paul chose Silas and left, commended by the brothers to the grace of the Lord. **41** He went through Syria and Cilicia, strengthening the churches.

Timothy Joins Paul and Silas

16 **1** He came to Derbe and then to Lystra, where a disciple named Timothy lived, whose mother was a Jewess and a believer, but whose father was a Greek. **2** The brothers at Lystra and Iconium spo[ke] well of him. **3** Paul wanted to ta[ke] him along on the journey, so he c[ir]cumcised him because of the Jew[s] who lived in that area, for they a[ll] knew that his father was a Gree[k.] **4** As they traveled from town [to] town, they delivered the decisio[ns] reached by the apostles and elders [in] Jerusalem for the people to obe[y.] **5** So the churches were strengthene[d] in the faith and grew daily in nur[m]bers.

Paul's Vision of the Man of Macedonia

6 Paul and his companions travele[d] throughout the region of Phrygia a[nd] Galatia, having been kept by the Ho[ly] Spirit from preaching the word in t[he] province of Asia. **7** When they came [to] the border of Mysia, they tried [to] enter Bithynia, but the Spirit of Jes[us] would not allow them to. **8** So the[y] passed by Mysia and went down [to] Troas. **9** During the night Paul had [a] vision of a man of Macedonia stan[d]ing and begging him, "Come over [to] Macedonia and help us." **10** After Pa[ul] had seen the vision, we got ready [at] once to leave for Macedonia, conclu[d]ing that God had called us to preac[h] the gospel to them.

Lydia's Conversion in Philippi

11 From Troas we put out to se[a] and sailed straight for Samothrac[e,] and the next day on to Neapoli[s.] **12** From there we traveled to Phili[p]pi, a Roman colony and the leadi[ng] city of that district of Macedoni[a.] And we stayed there several days. **13** On the Sabbath we went ou[t]side the city gate to the river, whe[re] we expected to find a place of praye[r.]

---

h **33** *Some manuscripts* them, **34** but Silas decided to remain there

We sat down and began to speak to the women who had gathered there. 14 One of those listening was a woman named Lydia, a dealer in purple cloth from the city of Thyatira, who was a worshiper of God. The Lord opened her heart to respond to Paul's message. 15 When she and the members of her household were baptized, she invited us to her home. "If you consider me a believer in the Lord," she said, "come and stay at my house." And she persuaded us.

Paul and Silas in Prison

16 Once when we were going to the place of prayer, we were met by a slave girl who had a spirit by which she predicted the future. She earned a great deal of money for her owners by fortune-telling. 17 This girl followed Paul and the rest of us, shouting, "These men are servants of the Most High God, who are telling you the way to be saved." 18 She kept this up for many days. Finally Paul became so troubled that he turned around and said to the spirit, "In the name of Jesus Christ I command you to come out of her!" At that moment the spirit left her.

19 When the owners of the slave girl realized that their hope of making money was gone, they seized Paul and Silas and dragged them into the marketplace to face the authorities. 20 They brought them before the magistrates and said, "These men are Jews, and are throwing our city into an uproar 21 by advocating customs unlawful for us Romans to accept or practice."

22 The crowd joined in the attack against Paul and Silas, and the magistrates ordered them to be stripped and beaten. 23 After they had been severely flogged, they were thrown into prison, and the jailer was commanded to guard them carefully. 24 Upon receiving such orders, he put them in the inner cell and fastened their feet in the stocks.

25 About midnight Paul and Silas were praying and singing hymns to God, and the other prisoners were listening to them. 26 Suddenly there was such a violent earthquake that the foundations of the prison were shaken. At once all the prison doors flew open, and everybody's chains came loose. 27 The jailer woke up, and when he saw the prison doors open, he drew his sword and was about to kill himself because he thought the prisoners had escaped. 28 But Paul shouted, "Don't harm yourself! We are all here!"

29 The jailer called for lights, rushed in and fell trembling before Paul and Silas. 30 He then brought them out and asked, "Sirs, what must I do to be saved?"

31 They replied, "Believe in the Lord Jesus, and you will be saved—you and your household." 32 Then they spoke the word of the Lord to him and to all the others in his house. 33 At that hour of the night the jailer took them and washed their wounds; then immediately he and all his family were baptized. 34 The jailer brought them into his house and set a meal before them; he was filled with joy because he had come to believe in God—he and his whole family.

35 When it was daylight, the magistrates sent their officers to the jailer with the order: "Release those men." 36 The jailer told Paul, "The magistrates have ordered that you and Silas be released. Now you can leave. Go in peace."

37 But Paul said to the officers: "They beat us publicly without a

trial, even though we are Roman citizens, and threw us into prison. And now do they want to get rid of us quietly? No! Let them come themselves and escort us out."

38 The officers reported this to the magistrates, and when they heard that Paul and Silas were Roman citizens, they were alarmed. **39** They came to appease them and escorted them from the prison, requesting them to leave the city. **40** After Paul and Silas came out of the prison, they went to Lydia's house, where they met with the brothers and encouraged them. Then they left.

In Thessalonica

17 **1** When they had passed through Amphipolis and Apollonia, they came to Thessalonica, where there was a Jewish synagogue. **2** As his custom was, Paul went into the synagogue, and on three Sabbath days he reasoned with them from the Scriptures, **3** explaining and proving that the Christ[i] had to suffer and rise from the dead. "This Jesus I am proclaiming to you is the Christ,[j]" he said. **4** Some of the Jews were persuaded and joined Paul and Silas, as did a large number of God-fearing Greeks and not a few prominent women.

5 But the Jews were jealous; so they rounded up some bad characters from the marketplace, formed a mob and started a riot in the city. They rushed to Jason's house in search of Paul and Silas in order to bring them out to the crowd.[k] **6** But when they did not find them, they dragged Jason and some other brothers before the city officials, shouting: "These men who have

caused trouble all over the worl[d] have now come here, **7** and Jason ha[s] welcomed them into his house. The[y] are all defying Caesar's decree[s,] saying that there is another king, on[e] called Jesus." **8** When they hear[d] this, the crowd and the city officia[ls] were thrown into turmoil. **9** The[n] they made Jason and the others [post] bond and let them go.

In Berea

10 As soon as it was night, th[e] brothers sent Paul and Silas away [to] Berea. On arriving there, they wen[t] to the Jewish synagogue. **11** Now th[e] Bereans were of more noble chara[c-] ter than the Thessalonians, for the[y] received the message with grea[t] eagerness and examined the Scrip[-] tures every day to see if what Pa[ul] said was true. **12** Many of the Jew[s] believed, as did also a number [of] prominent Greek women and man[y] Greek men.

13 When the Jews in Thessalonic[a] learned that Paul was preaching th[e] word of God at Berea, they went the[re] too, agitating the crowds and stirrin[g] them up. **14** The brothers immed[i-] ately sent Paul to the coast, but Sil[as] and Timothy stayed at Berea. **15** Th[e] men who escorted Paul brought hi[m] to Athens and then left with instru[c-] tions for Silas and Timothy to join hi[m] as soon as possible.

In Athens

16 While Paul was waiting for the[m] in Athens, he was greatly distressed [to] see that the city was full of idols. **17** S[o] he reasoned in the synagogue wit[h] the Jews and the God-fearing Greek[s,] as well as in the marketplace day b[y] day with those who happened to b[e]

---

i 3 Or *Messiah*   j 3 Or *Messiah*   k 5 Or *the assembly of the people*

here. **18** A group of Epicurean and Stoic philosophers began to dispute with him. Some of them asked, "What is this babbler trying to say?" Others remarked, "He seems to be advocating foreign gods." They said this because Paul was preaching the good news about Jesus and the resurrection. **19** Then they took him and brought him to a meeting of the Areopagus, where they said to him, "May we know what this new teaching is that you are presenting? **20** You are bringing some strange ideas to our ears, and we want to know what they mean." **21** (All the Athenians and the foreigners who lived there spent their time doing nothing but talking about and listening to the latest ideas.)

22 Paul then stood up in the meeting of the Areopagus and said: "Men of Athens! I see that in every way you are very religious. **23** For as I walked around and looked carefully at your objects of worship, I even found an altar with this inscription: TO AN UNKNOWN GOD. Now what you worship as something unknown I am going to proclaim to you.

24 "The God who made the world and everything in it is the Lord of heaven and earth and does not live in temples built by hands. **25** And he is not served by human hands, as if he needed anything, because he himself gives all men life and breath and everything else. **26** From one man he made every nation of men, that they should inhabit the whole earth; and he determined the times set for them and the exact places where they should live. **27** God did this so that men would seek him and perhaps reach out for him and find him, though he is not far from each one of us. **28** 'For in him we live and move and have our being.' As some of your own poets have said, 'We are his offspring.'

29 "Therefore since we are God's offspring, we should not think that the divine being is like gold or silver or stone—an image made by man's design and skill. **30** In the past God overlooked such ignorance, but now he commands all people everywhere to repent. **31** For he has set a day when he will judge the world with justice by the man he has appointed. He has given proof of this to all men by raising him from the dead."

32 When they heard about the resurrection of the dead, some of them sneered, but others said, "We want to hear you again on this subject." **33** At that, Paul left the Council. **34** A few men became followers of Paul and believed. Among them was Dionysius, a member of the Areopagus, also a woman named Damaris, and a number of others.

In Corinth

18 **1** After this, Paul left Athens and went to Corinth. **2** There he met a Jew named Aquila, a native of Pontus, who had recently come from Italy with his wife Priscilla, because Claudius had ordered all the Jews to leave Rome. Paul went to see them, **3** and because he was a tentmaker as they were, he stayed and worked with them. **4** Every Sabbath he reasoned in the synagogue, trying to persuade Jews and Greeks.

5 When Silas and Timothy came from Macedonia, Paul devoted himself exclusively to preaching, testifying to the Jews that Jesus was the Christ. **6** But when the Jews opposed

5 Or *Messiah*; also in verse 28

Paul and became abusive, he shook out his clothes in protest and said to them, "Your blood be on your own heads! I am clear of my responsibility. From now on I will go to the Gentiles."

7 Then Paul left the synagogue and went next door to the house of Titius Justus, a worshiper of God. **8** Crispus, the synagogue ruler, and his entire household believed in the Lord; and many of the Corinthians who heard him believed and were baptized.

9 One night the Lord spoke to Paul in a vision: "Do not be afraid; keep on speaking, do not be silent. **10** For I am with you, and no one is going to attack and harm you, because I have many people in this city." **11** So Paul stayed for a year and a half, teaching them the word of God.

12 While Gallio was proconsul of Achaia, the Jews made a united attack on Paul and brought him into court. **13** "This man," they charged, "is persuading the people to worship God in ways contrary to the law."

14 Just as Paul was about to speak, Gallio said to the Jews, "If you Jews were making a complaint about some misdemeanor or serious crime, it would be reasonable for me to listen to you. **15** But since it involves questions about words and names and your own law—settle the matter yourselves. I will not be a judge of such things." **16** So he had them ejected from the court. **17** Then they all turned on Sosthenes the synagogue ruler and beat him in front of the court. But Gallio showed no concern whatever.

Priscilla, Aquila and Apollos

18 Paul stayed on in Corinth for some time. Then he left the brothers and sailed for Syria, accompanied b[y] Priscilla and Aquila. Before he saile[d] he had his hair cut off at Cenchre[a] because of a vow he had taken. **19** They arrived at Ephesus, wher[e] Paul left Priscilla and Aquila. He him self went into the synagogue an[d] reasoned with the Jews. **20** Whe[n] they asked him to spend more tim[e] with them, he declined. **21** But as h[e] left, he promised, "I will come bac[k] if it is God's will." Then he set sai[l] from Ephesus. **22** When he landed a[t] Caesarea, he went up and greete[d] the church and then went down t[o] Antioch.

23 After spending some time in An tioch, Paul set out from there an[d] traveled from place to plac[e] throughout the region of Galatia an[d] Phrygia, strengthening all the dis ciples.

24 Meanwhile a Jew named Apol los, a native of Alexandria, came t[o] Ephesus. He was a learned man, wit[h] a thorough knowledge of the Scrip tures. **25** He had been instructed i[n] the way of the Lord, and he spok[e] with great fervor[m] and taught abou[t] Jesus accurately, though he kne[w] only the baptism of John. **26** H[e] began to speak boldly in th[e] synagogue. When Priscilla an[d] Aquila heard him, they invited hi[m] to their home and explained to hi[m] the way of God more adequately.

27 When Apollos wanted to go t[o] Achaia, the brothers encouraged hi[m] and wrote to the disciples there t[o] welcome him. On arriving, he was [a] great help to those who by grace ha[d] believed. **28** For he vigorousl[y] refuted the Jews in public debate[,] proving from the Scriptures tha[t] Jesus was the Christ.

---

m 25 Or *with fervor in the Spirit*

Paul in Ephesus

19 **1** While Apollos was at Corinth, Paul took the road through the interior and arrived at Ephesus. There he found some disciples **2** and asked them, "Did you receive the Holy Spirit when[n] you believed?"

They answered, "No, we have not even heard that there is a Holy Spirit."

3 So Paul asked, "Then what baptism did you receive?"

"John's baptism," they replied.

4 Paul said, "John's baptism was a baptism of repentance. He told the people to believe in the one coming after him, that is, in Jesus." **5** On hearing this, they were baptized into[o] the name of the Lord Jesus. **6** When Paul placed his hands on them, the Holy Spirit came on them, and they spoke in tongues[p] and prophesied. **7** There were about twelve men in all.

8 Paul entered the synagogue and spoke boldly there for three months, arguing persuasively about the kingdom of God. **9** But some of them became obstinate; they refused to believe and publicly maligned the Way. So Paul left them. He took the disciples with him and had discussions daily in the lecture hall of Tyrannus. **10** This went on for two years, so that all the Jews and Greeks who lived in the province of Asia heard the word of the Lord.

11 God did extraordinary miracles through Paul, **12** so that even handkerchiefs and aprons that had touched him were taken to the sick, and their illnesses were cured and the evil spirits left them.

13 Some Jews who went around driving out evil spirits tried to invoke the name of the Lord Jesus over those who were demon-possessed. They would say, "In the name of Jesus, whom Paul preaches, I command you to come out." **14** Seven sons of Sceva, a Jewish chief priest, were doing this. **15** One day the evil spirit answered them, "Jesus I know, and I know about Paul, but who are you?" **16** Then the man who had the evil spirit jumped on them and overpowered them all. He gave them such a beating that they ran out of the house naked and bleeding.

17 When this became known to the Jews and Greeks living in Ephesus, they were all seized with fear, and the name of the Lord Jesus was held in high honor. **18** Many of those who believed now came and openly confessed their evil deeds. **19** A number who had practiced sorcery brought their scrolls together and burned them publicly. When they calculated the value of the scrolls, the total came to fifty thousand drachmas.[q] **20** In this way the word of the Lord spread widely and grew in power.

21 After all this had happened, Paul decided to go to Jerusalem, passing through Macedonia and Achaia. "After I have been there," he said, "I must visit Rome also." **22** He sent two of his helpers, Timothy and Erastus, to Macedonia, while he stayed in the province of Asia a little longer.

The Riot in Ephesus

23 About that time there arose a great disturbance about the Way. **24** A silversmith named Demetrius,

n 2 Or after   o 5 Or in   p 6 Or other languages   q 19 A drachma was a silver coin worth about a day's wages.

who made silver shrines of Artemis, brought in no little business for the craftsmen. 25 He called them together, along with the workmen in related trades, and said: "Men, you know we receive a good income from this business. 26 And you see and hear how this fellow Paul has convinced and led astray large numbers of people here in Ephesus and in practically the whole province of Asia. He says that man-made gods are no gods at all. 27 There is danger not only that our trade will lose its good name, but also that the temple of the great goddess Artemis will be discredited, and the goddess herself, who is worshiped throughout the province of Asia and the world, will be robbed of her divine majesty."

28 When they heard this, they were furious and began shouting: "Great is Artemis of the Ephesians!" 29 Soon the whole city was in an uproar. The people seized Gaius and Aristarchus, Paul's traveling companions from Macedonia, and rushed as one man into the theater. 30 Paul wanted to appear before the crowd, but the disciples would not let him. 31 Even some of the officials of the province, friends of Paul, sent him a message begging him not to venture into the theater.

32 The assembly was in confusion: Some were shouting one thing, some another. Most of the people did not even know why they were there. 33 The Jews pushed Alexander to the front, and some of the crowd shouted instructions to him. He motioned for silence in order to make a defense before the people. 34 But when they realized he was a Jew, they all shouted in unison for about two hours: "Great is Artemis of the Ephesians!"

35 The city clerk quieted the crowd and said: "Men of Ephesus, doesn't all the world know that the city of Ephesus is the guardian of the temple of the great Artemis and of her image, which fell from heaven? 36 Therefore, since these facts are undeniable, you ought to be quiet and not do anything rash. 37 You have brought these men here, though they have neither robbed temples nor blasphemed our goddess. 38 If, then, Demetrius and his fellow craftsmen have a grievance against anybody, the courts are open and there are proconsuls. They can press charges. 39 If there is anything further you want to bring up, it must be settled in a legal assembly. 40 As it is, we are in danger of being charged with rioting because of today's events. In that case we would not be able to account for this commotion, since there is no reason for it." 41 After he had said this, he dismissed the assembly.

Through Macedonia and Greece

20 1 When the uproar had ended, Paul sent for the disciples and, after encouraging them, said good-by and set out for Macedonia. 2 He traveled through that area, speaking many words of encouragement to the people, and finally arrived in Greece, 3 where he stayed three months. Because the Jews made a plot against him just as he was about to sail for Syria, he decided to go back through Macedonia. 4 He was accompanied by Sopater son of Pyrrhus from Berea, Aristarchus and Secundus from Thessalonica, Gaius from Derbe, Timothy also, and Tychicus and Trophimus from the province of Asia. 5 These men went on ahead and waited for us at Troas. 6 But we sailed from Philippi after the Feast of Unleavened Bread, and five days

later joined the others at Troas, where we stayed seven days.

Eutychus Raised From the Dead at Troas

7 On the first day of the week we came together to break bread. Paul spoke to the people and, because he intended to leave the next day, kept on talking until midnight. **8** There were many lamps in the upstairs room where we were meeting. **9** Seated in a window was a young man named Eutychus, who was sinking into a deep sleep as Paul talked on and on. When he was sound asleep, he fell to the ground from the third story and was picked up dead. **10** Paul went down, threw himself on the young man and put his arms around him. "Don't be alarmed," he said. "He's alive!" **11** Then he went upstairs again and broke bread and ate. After talking until daylight, he left. **12** The people took the young man home alive and were greatly comforted.

Paul's Farewell to the Ephesian Elders

13 We went on ahead to the ship and sailed for Assos, where we were going to take Paul aboard. He had made this arrangement because he was going there on foot. **14** When he met us at Assos, we took him aboard and went on to Mitylene. **15** The next day we set sail from there and arrived off Kios. The day after that we crossed over to Samos, and on the following day arrived at Miletus. **16** Paul had decided to sail past Ephesus to avoid spending time in the province of Asia, for he was in a hurry to reach Jerusalem, if possible, by the day of Pentecost.

17 From Miletus, Paul sent to Ephesus for the elders of the church. **18** When they arrived, he said to them: "You know how I lived the whole time I was with you, from the first day I came into the province of Asia. **19** I served the Lord with great humility and with tears, although I was severely tested by the plots of the Jews. **20** You know that I have not hesitated to preach anything that would be helpful to you but have taught you publicly and from house to house. **21** I have declared to both Jews and Greeks that they must turn to God in repentance and have faith in our Lord Jesus.

22 "And now, compelled by the Spirit, I am going to Jerusalem, not knowing what will happen to me there. **23** I only know that in every city the Holy Spirit warns me that prison and hardships are facing me. **24** However, I consider my life worth nothing to me, if only I may finish the race and complete the task the Lord Jesus has given me — the task of testifying to the gospel of God's grace.

25 "Now I know that none of you among whom I have gone about preaching the kingdom will ever see me again. **26** Therefore, I declare to you today that I am innocent of the blood of all men. **27** For I have not hesitated to proclaim to you the whole will of God. **28** Keep watch over yourselves and all the flock of which the Holy Spirit has made you overseers.ʳ Be shepherds of the church of God,ˢ which he bought with his own blood. **29** I know that after I leave, savage wolves will come in among you and will not spare the flock. **30** Even from your own number men will arise and distort the

r 28 Traditionally *bishops*   *s* 28 Many manuscripts *of the Lord* truth in order to draw away disciples after them. **31** So be on your guard! Remember that for three years I never stopped warning each of you night and day with tears.

32 "Now I commit you to God and to the word of his grace, which can build you up and give you an inheritance among all those who are sanctified. **33** I have not coveted anyone's silver or gold or clothing. **34** You yourselves know that these hands of mine have supplied my own needs and the needs of my companions. **35** In everything I did, I showed you that by this kind of hard work we must help the weak, remembering the words the Lord Jesus himself said: 'It is more blessed to give than to receive.'"

36 When he had said this, he knelt down with all of them and prayed. **37** They all wept as they embraced him and kissed him. **38** What grieved them most was his statement that they would never see his face again. Then they accompanied him to the ship.

On to Jerusalem

21 **1** After we had torn ourselves away from them, we put out to sea and sailed straight to Cos. The next day we went to Rhodes and from there to Patara. **2** We found a ship crossing over to Phoenicia, went on board and set sail. **3** After sighting Cyprus and passing to the south of it, we sailed on to Syria. We landed at Tyre, where our ship was to unload its cargo. **4** Finding the disciples there, we stayed with them seven days. Through the Spirit they urged Paul not to go on to Jerusalem. **5** But when our time was up, we left and continued on our way. All the disciples and their wives and children accompanied us out of the city, and

there on the beach we knelt to pray. **6** After saying good-by to each other, we went aboard the ship, and they returned home.

7 We continued our voyage from Tyre and landed at Ptolemais, where we greeted the brothers and stayed with them for a day. **8** Leaving the next day, we reached Caesarea and stayed at the house of Philip the evangelist, one of the Seven. **9** He had four unmarried daughters who prophesied.

10 After we had been there a number of days, a prophet named Agabus came down from Judea. **11** Coming over to us, he took Paul's belt, tied his own hands and feet with it and said, "The Holy Spirit says, 'In this way the Jews of Jerusalem will bind the owner of this belt and will hand him over to the Gentiles.'"

12 When we heard this, we and the people there pleaded with Paul not to go up to Jerusalem. **13** Then Paul answered, "Why are you weeping and breaking my heart? I am ready not only to be bound, but also to die in Jerusalem for the name of the Lord Jesus." **14** When he would not be dissuaded, we gave up and said, "The Lord's will be done."

15 After this, we got ready and went up to Jerusalem. **16** Some of the disciples from Caesarea accompanied us and brought us to the home of Mnason, where we were to stay. He was a man from Cyprus and one of the early disciples.

Paul's Arrival at Jerusalem

17 When we arrived at Jerusalem, the brothers received us warmly. **18** The next day Paul and the rest of us went to see James, and all the elders were present. **19** Paul greeted them and reported in detail what God had done among the Gentiles through his ministry.

20 When they heard this, they praised God. Then they said to Paul: "You see, brother, how many thousands of Jews have believed, and all of them are zealous for the law. 21 They have been informed that you teach all the Jews who live among the Gentiles to turn away from Moses, telling them not to circumcise their children or live according to our customs. 22 What shall we do? They will certainly hear that you have come, 23 so do what we tell you. There are four men with us who have made a vow. 24 Take these men, join in their purification rites and pay their expenses, so that they can have their heads shaved. Then everybody will know there is no truth in these reports about you, but that you yourself are living in obedience to the law. 25 As for the Gentile believers, we have written to them our decision that they should abstain from food sacrificed to idols, from blood, from the meat of strangled animals and from sexual immorality."

26 The next day Paul took the men and purified himself along with them. Then he went to the temple to give notice of the date when the days of purification would end and the offering would be made for each of them.

Paul Arrested

27 When the seven days were nearly over, some Jews from the province of Asia saw Paul at the temple. They stirred up the whole crowd and seized him, 28 shouting, "Men of Israel, help us! This is the man who teaches all men everywhere against our people and our law and this place. And besides, he has brought Greeks into the temple area and defiled this holy place." 29 (They had previously seen Trophimus the Ephesian in the city with Paul and assumed that Paul had brought him into the temple area.)

30 The whole city was aroused, and the people came running from all directions. Seizing Paul, they dragged him from the temple, and immediately the gates were shut. 31 While they were trying to kill him, news reached the commander of the Roman troops that the whole city of Jerusalem was in an uproar. 32 He at once took some officers and soldiers and ran down to the crowd. When the rioters saw the commander and his soldiers, they stopped beating Paul.

33 The commander came up and arrested him and ordered him to be bound with two chains. Then he asked who he was and what he had done. 34 Some in the crowd shouted one thing and some another, and since the commander could not get at the truth because of the uproar, he ordered that Paul be taken into the barracks. 35 When Paul reached the steps, the violence of the mob was so great he had to be carried by the soldiers. 36 The crowd that followed kept shouting, "Away with him!"

Paul Speaks to the Crowd

37 As the soldiers were about to take Paul into the barracks, he asked the commander, "May I say something to you?"

"Do you speak Greek?" he replied. 38 "Aren't you the Egyptian who started a revolt and led four thousand terrorists out into the desert some time ago?"

39 Paul answered, "I am a Jew, from Tarsus in Cilicia, a citizen of no ordinary city. Please let me speak to the people."

40 Having received the commander's permission, Paul stood on

the steps and motioned to the crowd. When they were all silent, he said to them in Aramaic[t]:

22

¹ "Brothers and fathers, listen now to my defense." ² When they heard him speak to them in Aramaic, they became very quiet.

Then Paul said: ³ "I am a Jew, born in Tarsus of Cilicia, but brought up in this city. Under Gamaliel I was thoroughly trained in the law of our fathers and was just as zealous for God as any of you are today. ⁴ I persecuted the followers of this Way to their death, arresting both men and women and throwing them into prison, ⁵ as also the high priest and all the Council can testify. I even obtained letters from them to their brothers in Damascus, and went there to bring these people as prisoners to Jerusalem to be punished.

⁶ "About noon as I came near Damascus, suddenly a bright light from heaven flashed around me. ⁷ I fell to the ground and heard a voice say to me, 'Saul! Saul! Why do you persecute me?'

⁸ "'Who are you, Lord?' I asked.

"'I am Jesus of Nazareth, whom you are persecuting,' he replied. ⁹ My companions saw the light, but they did not understand the voice of him who was speaking to me.

¹⁰ "'What shall I do, Lord?' I asked.

"'Get up,' the Lord said, 'and go into Damascus. There you will be told all that you have been assigned to do.' ¹¹ My companions led me by the hand into Damascus, because the brilliance of the light had blinded me.

¹² "A man named Ananias came to see me. He was a devout observer of the law and highly respected by all the Jews living there. ¹³ He stood beside me and said, 'Brother Saul, receive your sight!' And at that very moment I was able to see him.

¹⁴ "Then he said: 'The God of our fathers has chosen you to know his will and to see the Righteous One and to hear words from his mouth. ¹⁵ You will be his witness to all men of what you have seen and heard. ¹⁶ And now what are you waiting for? Get up, be baptized and wash your sins away, calling on his name.'

¹⁷ "When I returned to Jerusalem and was praying at the temple, I fell into a trance ¹⁸ and saw the Lord speaking. 'Quick!' he said to me. 'Leave Jerusalem immediately, because they will not accept your testimony about me.'

¹⁹ "'Lord,' I replied, 'these men know that I went from one synagogue to another to imprison and beat those who believe in you. ²⁰ And when the blood of your martyr[u] Stephen was shed, I stood there giving my approval and guarding the clothes of those who were killing him.'

²¹ "Then the Lord said to me, 'Go; I will send you far away to the Gentiles.'"

Paul the Roman Citizen

²² The crowd listened to Paul until he said this. Then they raised their voices and shouted, "Rid the earth of him! He's not fit to live!"

²³ As they were shouting and throwing off their cloaks and flinging dust into the air, ²⁴ the commander ordered Paul to be taken into the barracks. He directed that he be flogged and questioned in order to find out why the people were shouting at him like this. ²⁵ As they

t 40 Or possibly Hebrew; also in 22:2   u 20 Or witness

stretched him out to flog him, Paul said to the centurion standing there, "Is it legal for you to flog a Roman citizen who hasn't even been found guilty?"

26 When the centurion heard this, he went to the commander and reported it. "What are you going to do?" he asked. "This man is a Roman citizen."

27 The commander went to Paul and asked, "Tell me, are you a Roman citizen?"

"Yes, I am," he answered.

28 Then the commander said, "I had to pay a big price for my citizenship."

"But I was born a citizen," Paul replied.

29 Those who were about to question him withdrew immediately. The commander himself was alarmed when he realized that he had put Paul, a Roman citizen, in chains.

Before the Sanhedrin

30 The next day, since the commander wanted to find out exactly why Paul was being accused by the Jews, he released him and ordered the chief priests and all the Sanhedrin to assemble. Then he brought Paul and had him stand before them.

23 1 Paul looked straight at the Sanhedrin and said, "My brothers, I have fulfilled my duty to God in all good conscience to this day." 2 At this the high priest Ananias ordered those standing near Paul to strike him on the mouth. 3 Then Paul said to him, "God will strike you, you whitewashed wall! You sit there to judge me according to the law, yet you yourself violate the law by commanding that I be struck!"

4 Those who were standing near Paul said, "You dare to insult God's high priest?"

5 Paul replied, "Brothers, I did not realize that he was the high priest; for it is written: 'Do not speak evil about the ruler of your people.'v"

6 Then Paul, knowing that some of them were Sadducees and the others Pharisees, called out in the Sanhedrin, "My brothers, I am a Pharisee, the son of a Pharisee. I stand on trial because of my hope in the resurrection of the dead." 7 When he said this, a dispute broke out between the Pharisees and the Sadducees, and the assembly was divided. 8 (The Sadducees say that there is no resurrection, and that there are neither angels nor spirits, but the Pharisees acknowledge them all.)

9 There was a great uproar, and some of the teachers of the law who were Pharisees stood up and argued vigorously. "We find nothing wrong with this man," they said. "What if a spirit or an angel has spoken to him?" 10 The dispute became so violent that the commander was afraid Paul would be torn to pieces by them. He ordered the troops to go down and take him away from them by force and bring him into the barracks.

11 The following night the Lord stood near Paul and said, "Take courage! As you have testified about me in Jerusalem, so you must also testify in Rome."

The Plot to Kill Paul

12 The next morning the Jews formed a conspiracy and bound themselves with an oath not to eat or drink until they had killed Paul. 13 More than forty men were in-

v 5 Exodus 22:28

volved in this plot. 14 They went to the chief priests and elders and said, "We have taken a solemn oath not to eat anything until we have killed Paul. 15 Now then, you and the Sanhedrin petition the commander to bring him before you on the pretext of wanting more accurate information about his case. We are ready to kill him before he gets here."

16 But when the son of Paul's sister heard of this plot, he went into the barracks and told Paul.

17 Then Paul called one of the centurions and said, "Take this young man to the commander; he has something to tell him." 18 So he took him to the commander.

The centurion said, "Paul, the prisoner, sent for me and asked me to bring this young man to you because he has something to tell you."

19 The commander took the young man by the hand, drew him aside and asked, "What is it you want to tell me?"

20 He said: "The Jews have agreed to ask you to bring Paul before the Sanhedrin tomorrow on the pretext of wanting more accurate information about him. 21 Don't give in to them, because more than forty of them are waiting in ambush for him. They have taken an oath not to eat or drink until they have killed him. They are ready now, waiting for your consent to their request."

22 The commander dismissed the young man and cautioned him, "Don't tell anyone that you have reported this to me."

Paul Transferred to Caesarea

23 Then he called two of his centurions and ordered them, "Get ready a detachment of two hundred soldiers, seventy horsemen and two hundred spearmen[w] to go to Caesarea at nine tonight. 24 Provide mounts for Paul so that he may be taken safely to Governor Felix."

25 He wrote a letter as follows:

26 Claudius Lysias,

To His Excellency, Governor Felix:

Greetings.

27 This man was seized by the Jews and they were about to kill him, but I came with my troops and rescued him, for I had learned that he is a Roman citizen. 28 I wanted to know why they were accusing him, so I brought him to their Sanhedrin. 29 I found that the accusation had to do with questions about their law, but there was no charge against him that deserved death or imprisonment. 30 When I was informed of a plot to be carried out against the man, I sent him to you at once. I also ordered his accusers to present to you their case against him.

31 So the soldiers, carrying out their orders, took Paul with them during the night and brought him as far as Antipatris. 32 The next day they let the cavalry go on with him, while they returned to the barracks. 33 When the cavalry arrived in Caesarea, they delivered the letter to the governor and handed Paul over to him. 34 The governor read the letter and asked what province he was from. Learning that he was from Cilicia, 35 he said, "I will hear your case when your accusers get here." Then he ordered that Paul be kept under guard in Herod's palace.

w 23 The meaning of the Greek for this word is uncertain.

The Trial Before Felix

24 ¹Five days later the high priest Ananias went down to Caesarea with some of the elders and a lawyer named Tertullus, and they brought their charges against Paul before the governor. ²When Paul was called in, Tertullus presented his case before Felix: "We have enjoyed a long period of peace under you, and your foresight has brought about reforms in this nation. ³Everywhere and in every way, most excellent Felix, we acknowledge this with profound gratitude. ⁴But in order not to weary you further, I would request that you be kind enough to hear us briefly.

⁵"We have found this man to be a troublemaker, stirring up riots among the Jews all over the world. He is a ringleader of the Nazarene sect ⁶and even tried to desecrate the temple; so we seized him. ⁸Byˣ examining him yourself you will be able to learn the truth about all these charges we are bringing against him."

⁹The Jews joined in the accusation, asserting that these things were true.

¹⁰When the governor motioned for him to speak, Paul replied: "I know that for a number of years you have been a judge over this nation; so I gladly make my defense. ¹¹You can easily verify that no more than twelve days ago I went up to Jerusalem to worship. ¹²My accusers did not find me arguing with anyone at the temple, or stirring up a crowd in the synagogues or anywhere else in the city. ¹³And they cannot prove to you the charges they

are now making against me. ¹⁴However, I admit that I worship the God of our fathers as a follower of the Way, which they call a sect. I believe everything that agrees with the Law and that is written in the Prophets, ¹⁵and I have the same hope in God as these men, that there will be a resurrection of both the righteous and the wicked. ¹⁶So I strive always to keep my conscience clear before God and man.

¹⁷"After an absence of several years, I came to Jerusalem to bring my people gifts for the poor and to present offerings. ¹⁸I was ceremonially clean when they found me in the temple courts doing this. There was no crowd with me, nor was I involved in any disturbance. ¹⁹But there are some Jews from the province of Asia, who ought to be here before you and bring charges if they have anything against me. ²⁰Or these who are here should state what crime they found in me when I stood before the Sanhedrin— ²¹unless it was this one thing I shouted as I stood in their presence: 'It is concerning the resurrection of the dead that I am on trial before you today.'"

²²Then Felix, who was well acquainted with the Way, adjourned the proceedings. "When Lysias the commander comes," he said, "I will decide your case." ²³He ordered the centurion to keep Paul under guard but to give him some freedom and permit his friends to take care of his needs.

²⁴Several days later Felix came with his wife Drusilla, who was a Jewess. He sent for Paul and listened to him as he spoke about faith in Christ Jesus. ²⁵As Paul discoursed

---

ˣ 6-8 Some manuscripts *him and wanted to judge him according to our law.* ⁷ *But the commander, Lysias, came and with the use of much force snatched him from our hands* ⁸ *and ordered his accusers to come before you. By*

on righteousness, self-control and the judgment to come, Felix was afraid and said, "That's enough for now! You may leave. When I find it convenient, I will send for you." **26** At the same time he was hoping that Paul would offer him a bribe, so he sent for him frequently and talked with him.

27 When two years had passed, Felix was succeeded by Porcius Festus, but because Felix wanted to grant a favor to the Jews, he left Paul in prison.

The Trial Before Festus

25 **1** Three days after arriving in the province, Festus went up from Caesarea to Jerusalem, **2** where the chief priests and Jewish leaders appeared before him and presented the charges against Paul. **3** They urgently requested Festus, as a favor to them, to have Paul transferred to Jerusalem, for they were preparing an ambush to kill him along the way. **4** Festus answered, "Paul is being held at Caesarea, and I myself am going there soon. **5** Let some of your leaders come with me and press charges against the man there, if he has done anything wrong."

6 After spending eight or ten days with them, he went down to Caesarea, and the next day he convened the court and ordered that Paul be brought before him. **7** When Paul appeared, the Jews who had come down from Jerusalem stood around him, bringing many serious charges against him, which they could not prove.

8 Then Paul made his defense: "I have done nothing wrong against the law of the Jews or against the temple or against Caesar."

9 Festus, wishing to do the Jews a favor, said to Paul, "Are you willing to go up to Jerusalem and stand trial before me there on these charges?"

10 Paul answered: "I am now standing before Caesar's court, where I ought to be tried. I have not done any wrong to the Jews, as you yourself know very well. **11** If, however, I am guilty of doing anything deserving death, I do not refuse to die. But if the charges brought against me by these Jews are not true, no one has the right to hand me over to them. I appeal to Caesar!"

12 After Festus had conferred with his council, he declared: "You have appealed to Caesar. To Caesar you will go!"

Festus Consults King Agrippa

13 A few days later King Agrippa and Bernice arrived at Caesarea to pay their respects to Festus. **14** Since they were spending many days there, Festus discussed Paul's case with the king. He said: "There is a man here whom Felix left as a prisoner. **15** When I went to Jerusalem, the chief priests and elders of the Jews brought charges against him and asked that he be condemned.

16 "I told them that it is not the Roman custom to hand over any man before he has faced his accusers and has had an opportunity to defend himself against their charges. **17** When they came here with me, I did not delay the case, but convened the court the next day and ordered the man to be brought in. **18** When his accusers got up to speak, they did not charge him with any of the crimes I had expected. **19** Instead, they had some points of dispute with him about their own religion and about a dead man named Jesus who Paul claimed was alive. **20** I was at a loss how to investigate such matters; so I asked if he would be willing to go to Jerusalem and stand trial there on these charges. 21 When Paul made his appeal to be held over for the Emperor's decision, I ordered him held until I could send him to Caesar."

22 Then Agrippa said to Festus, "I would like to hear this man myself." He replied, "Tomorrow you will hear him."

Paul Before Agrippa

23 The next day Agrippa and Bernice came with great pomp and entered the audience room with the high ranking officers and the leading men of the city. At the command of Festus, Paul was brought in. 24 Festus said: "King Agrippa, and all who are present with us, you see this man! The whole Jewish community has petitioned me about him in Jerusalem and here in Caesarea, shouting that he ought not to live any longer. 25 I found he had done nothing deserving of death, but because he made his appeal to the Emperor I decided to send him to Rome. 26 But I have nothing definite to write to His Majesty about him. Therefore I have brought him before all of you, and especially before you, King Agrippa, so that as a result of this investigation I may have something to write. 27 For I think it is unreasonable to send on a prisoner without specifying the charges against him."

26 1 Then Agrippa said to Paul, "You have permission to speak for yourself." So Paul motioned with his hand and began his defense: 2 "King Agrippa, I consider myself fortunate to stand before you today as I make my defense against all the accusations of the Jews, 3 and especially so because you are well ac-

quainted with all the Jewish customs and controversies. Therefore, I beg you to listen to me patiently.

4 "The Jews all know the way I have lived ever since I was a child, from the beginning of my life in my own country, and also in Jerusalem. 5 They have known me for a long time and can testify, if they are willing, that according to the strictest sect of our religion, I lived as a Pharisee. 6 And now it is because of my hope in what God has promised our fathers that I am on trial today. 7 This is the promise our twelve tribes are hoping to see fulfilled as they earnestly serve God day and night. O king, it is because of this hope that the Jews are accusing me. 8 Why should any of you consider it incredible that God raises the dead?

9 "I too was convinced that I ought to do all that was possible to oppose the name of Jesus of Nazareth. 10 And that is just what I did in Jerusalem. On the authority of the chief priests I put many of the saints in prison, and when they were put to death, I cast my vote against them. 11 Many a time I went from one synagogue to another to have them punished, and I tried to force them to blaspheme. In my obsession against them, I even went to foreign cities to persecute them.

12 "On one of these journeys I was going to Damascus with the authority and commission of the chief priests. 13 About noon, O king, as I was on the road, I saw a light from heaven, brighter than the sun, blazing around me and my companions. 14 We all fell to the ground, and I heard a voice saying to me in Aramaic,*y* 'Saul, Saul, why do you persecute me? It is hard for you to kick against the goads.'

y 14 Or Hebrew

15 "Then I asked, 'Who are you, Lord?'

" 'I am Jesus, whom you are persecuting,' the Lord replied. **16** 'Now get up and stand on your feet. I have appeared to you to appoint you as a servant and as a witness of what you have seen of me and what I will show you. **17** I will rescue you from your own people and from the Gentiles. I am sending you to them **18** to open their eyes and turn them from darkness to light, and from the power of Satan to God, so that they may receive forgiveness of sins and a place among those who are sanctified by faith in me.'

19 "So then, King Agrippa, I was not disobedient to the vision from heaven. **20** First to those in Damascus, then to those in Jerusalem and in all Judea, and to the Gentiles also, I preached that they should repent and turn to God and prove their repentance by their deeds. **21** That is why the Jews seized me in the temple courts and tried to kill me. **22** But I have had God's help to this very day, and so I stand here and testify to small and great alike. I am saying nothing beyond what the prophets and Moses said would happen— **23** that the Christ[z] would suffer and, as the first to rise from the dead, would proclaim light to his own people and to the Gentiles."

24 At this point Festus interrupted Paul's defense. "You are out of your mind, Paul!" he shouted. "Your great learning is driving you insane."

25 "I am not insane, most excellent Festus," Paul replied. "What I am saying is true and reasonable. **26** The king is familiar with these things, and I can speak freely to him. I am convinced that none of this has escaped his notice, because it was not done in a corner. **27** King Agrippa, do you believe the prophets? I know you do."

28 Then Agrippa said to Paul, "Do you think that in such a short time you can persuade me to be a Christian?"

29 Paul replied, "Short time or long—I pray God that not only you but all who are listening to me today may become what I am, except for these chains."

30 The king rose, and with him the governor and Bernice and those sitting with them. **31** They left the room, and while talking with one another, they said, "This man is not doing anything that deserves death or imprisonment."

32 Agrippa said to Festus, "This man could have been set free if he had not appealed to Caesar."

Paul Sails for Rome

27 **1** When it was decided that we would sail for Italy, Paul and some other prisoners were handed over to a centurion named Julius, who belonged to the Imperial Regiment. **2** We boarded a ship from Adramyttium about to sail for ports along the coast of the province of Asia, and we put out to sea. Aristarchus, a Macedonian from Thessalonica, was with us.

3 The next day we landed at Sidon; and Julius, in kindness to Paul, allowed him to go to his friends so they might provide for his needs. **4** From there we put out to sea again and passed to the lee of Cyprus because the winds were against us. **5** When we had sailed across the open sea off

---

[z] *23* Or *Messiah*

the coast of Cilicia and Pamphylia, we landed at Myra in Lycia. **6** There the centurion found an Alexandrian ship sailing for Italy and put us on board. **7** We made slow headway for many days and had difficulty arriving off Cnidus. When the wind did not allow us to hold our course, we sailed to the lee of Crete, opposite Salmone. **8** We moved along the coast with difficulty and came to a place called Fair Havens, near the town of Lasea.

9 Much time had been lost, and sailing had already become dangerous because by now it was after the Fast.[a] So Paul warned them, **10** "Men, I can see that our voyage is going to be disastrous and bring great loss to ship and cargo, and to our own lives also." **11** But the centurion, instead of listening to what Paul said, followed the advice of the pilot and of the owner of the ship. **12** Since the harbor was unsuitable to winter in, the majority decided that we should sail on, hoping to reach Phoenix and winter there. This was a harbor in Crete, facing both southwest and northwest.

The Storm

13 When a gentle south wind began to blow, they thought they had obtained what they wanted; so they weighed anchor and sailed along the shore of Crete. **14** Before very long, a wind of hurricane force, called the "northeaster," swept down from the island. **15** The ship was caught by the storm and could not head into the wind; so we gave way to it and were driven along. **16** As we passed to the lee of a small island called Cauda, we were hardly able to make the lifeboat secure. **17** When the men had hoisted it aboard, they passed ropes under the ship itself to hold it together. Fearing that they would run aground on the sandbars of Syrtis, they lowered the sea anchor and let the ship be driven along. **18** We took such a violent battering from the storm that the next day they began to throw the cargo overboard. **19** On the third day, they threw the ship's tackle overboard with their own hands. **20** When neither sun nor stars appeared for many days and the storm continued raging, we finally gave up all hope of being saved.

21 After the men had gone a long time without food, Paul stood up before them and said: "Men, you should have taken my advice not to sail from Crete; then you would have spared yourselves this damage and loss. **22** But now I urge you to keep up your courage, because not one of you will be lost; only the ship will be destroyed. **23** Last night an angel of the God whose I am and whom I serve stood beside me **24** and said, 'Do not be afraid, Paul. You must stand trial before Caesar; and God has graciously given you the lives of all who sail with you.' **25** So keep up your courage, men, for I have faith in God that it will happen just as he told me. **26** Nevertheless, we must run aground on some island."

The Shipwreck

27 On the fourteenth night we were still being driven across the Adriatic[b] Sea, when about midnight

---

[a] 9 That is, the Day of Atonement (Yom Kippur)   [b] 27 In ancient times the name referred to an area extending well south of Italy.

the sailors sensed they were approaching land. 28 They took soundings and found that the water was a hundred and twenty feet[c] deep. A short time later they took soundings again and found it was ninety feet[d] deep. 29 Fearing that we would be dashed against the rocks, they dropped four anchors from the stern and prayed for daylight. 30 In an attempt to escape from the ship, the sailors let the lifeboat down into the sea, pretending they were going to lower some anchors from the bow. 31 Then Paul said to the centurion and the soldiers, "Unless these men stay with the ship, you cannot be saved." 32 So the soldiers cut the ropes that held the lifeboat and let it fall away.

33 Just before dawn Paul urged them all to eat. "For the last fourteen days," he said, "you have been in constant suspense and have gone without food—you haven't eaten anything. 34 Now I urge you to take some food. You need it to survive. Not one of you will lose a single hair from his head." 35 After he said this, he took some bread and gave thanks to God in front of them all. Then he broke it and began to eat. 36 They were all encouraged and ate some food themselves. 37 Altogether there were 276 of us on board. 38 When they had eaten as much as they wanted, they lightened the ship by throwing the grain into the sea.

39 When daylight came, they did not recognize the land, but they saw a bay with a sandy beach, where they decided to run the ship aground if they could. 40 Cutting loose the anchors, they left them in the sea and at the same time untied the ropes that held the rudders. Then they hoisted the foresail to the wind and made for the beach. 41 But the ship struck a sandbar and ran aground. The bow stuck fast and would not move, and the stern was broken to pieces by the pounding of the surf.

42 The soldiers planned to kill the prisoners to prevent any of them from swimming away and escaping. 43 But the centurion wanted to spare Paul's life and kept them from carrying out their plan. He ordered those who could swim to jump overboard first and get to land. 44 The rest were to get there on planks or on pieces of the ship. In this way everyone reached land in safety.

Ashore on Malta

28 ¹ Once safely on shore, we found out that the island was called Malta. ² The islanders showed us unusual kindness. They built a fire and welcomed us all because it was raining and cold. ³ Paul gathered a pile of brushwood and, as he put it on the fire, a viper, driven out by the heat, fastened itself on his hand. ⁴ When the islanders saw the snake hanging from his hand, they said to each other, "This man must be a murderer; for though he escaped from the sea, Justice has not allowed him to live." ⁵ But Paul shook the snake off into the fire and suffered no ill effects. ⁶ The people expected him to swell up or suddenly fall dead, but after waiting a long time and seeing nothing unusual happen to him, they changed their minds and said he was a god.

---

c 28 Greek twenty orguias (about 37 meters)   d 28 Greek fifteen orguias (about 27 meters)

7 There was an estate nearby that belonged to Publius, the chief official of the island. He welcomed us to his home and for three days entertained us hospitably. **8** His father was sick in bed, suffering from fever and dysentery. Paul went in to see him and, after prayer, placed his hands on him and healed him. **9** When this had happened, the rest of the sick on the island came and were cured. **10** They honored us in many ways and when we were ready to sail, they furnished us with the supplies we needed.

Arrival at Rome

11 After three months we put out to sea in a ship that had wintered in the island. It was an Alexandrian ship with the figurehead of the twin gods Castor and Pollux. **12** We put in at Syracuse and stayed there three days. **13** From there we set sail and arrived at Rhegium. The next day the south wind came up, and on the following day we reached Puteoli. **14** There we found some brothers who invited us to spend a week with them. And so we came to Rome. **15** The brothers there had heard that we were coming, and they traveled as far as the Forum of Appius and the Three Taverns to meet us. At the sight of these men Paul thanked God and was encouraged. **16** When we got to Rome, Paul was allowed to live by himself, with a soldier to guard him.

Paul Preaches at Rome Under Guard

17 Three days later he called together the leaders of the Jews. When they had assembled, Paul said to them: "My brothers, although I have done nothing against our people or against the customs of our ancestors, I was arrested in Jerusalem and handed over to the Romans. **18** They examined me and wanted to release me, because I was not guilty of any crime deserving death. **19** But when the Jews objected, I was compelled to appeal to Caesar — not that I had any charge to bring against my own people. **20** For this reason I have asked to see you and talk with you. It is because of the hope of Israel that I am bound with this chain." **21** They replied, "We have not received any letters from Judea concerning you, and none of the brothers who have come from there has reported or said anything bad about you. **22** But we want to hear what your views are, for we know that people everywhere are talking against this sect."

23 They arranged to meet Paul on a certain day, and came in even larger numbers to the place where he was staying. From morning till evening he explained and declared to them the kingdom of God and tried to convince them about Jesus from the Law of Moses and from the Prophets. **24** Some were convinced by what he said, but others would not believe. **25** They disagreed among themselves and began to leave after Paul had made this final statement: "The Holy Spirit spoke the truth to your forefathers when he said through Isaiah the prophet:

26 " 'Go to this people and say,
    "You will be ever hearing but
        never understanding;
    you will be ever seeing but
        never perceiving."
27 For this people's heart has
        become calloused;

they hardly hear with their
    ears,
and they have closed their
    eyes.
Otherwise they might see with
    their eyes,
hear with their ears,
understand with their hearts
and turn, and I would heal
    them.'e

28 "Therefore I want you to know that God's salvation has been sent to the Gentiles, and they will listen!"f

30 For two whole years Paul stayed there in his own rented house and welcomed all who came to see him. 31 Boldly and without hindrance he preached the kingdom of God and taught about the Lord Jesus Christ.

---

e 27 Isaiah 6:9,10 f 28 Some manuscripts listen!" 29 After he said this, the Jews left, arguing vigorously among themselves.

Romans

1 **1** Paul, a servant of Christ Jesus, called to be an apostle and set apart for the gospel of God — **2** the gospel he promised beforehand through his prophets in the Holy Scriptures **3** regarding his Son, who as to his human nature was a descendant of David, **4** and who through the Spirit[a] of holiness was declared with power to be the Son of God[b] by his resurrection from the dead: Jesus Christ our Lord. **5** Through him and for his name's sake, we received grace and apostleship to call people from among all the Gentiles to the obedience that comes from faith. **6** And you also are among those who are called to belong to Jesus Christ.

7 To all in Rome who are loved by God and called to be saints:

Grace and peace to you from God our Father and from the Lord Jesus Christ.

Paul's Longing to Visit Rome

8 First, I thank my God through Jesus Christ for all of you, because your faith is being reported all over the world. **9** God, whom I serve with my whole heart in preaching the gospel of his Son, is my witness how constantly I remember you **10** in my prayers at all times; and I pray that now at last by God's will the way may be opened for me to come to you.

11 I long to see you so that I may impart to you some spiritual gift to make you strong — **12** that is, that you and I may be mutually encouraged by each other's faith. **13** I do not want you to be unaware, brothers, that I planned many times to come to you (but have been prevented from doing so until now) in order that I might have a harvest among you, just as I have had among the other Gentiles.

14 I am obligated both to Greeks and non-Greeks, both to the wise and the foolish. **15** That is why I am so eager to preach the gospel also to you who are at Rome.

16 I am not ashamed of the gospel, because it is the power of God for the salvation of everyone who believes: first for the Jew, then for the Gentile. **17** For in the gospel a righteousness from God is revealed, a righteousness that is by faith from first to last,[c] just as it is written: "The righteous will live by faith."[d]

God's Wrath Against Mankind

18 The wrath of God is being revealed from heaven against all the godlessness and wickedness of men who suppress the truth by their wickedness, **19** since what may be known about God is plain to them, because God has made it plain to them. **20** For since the creation of the world God's invisible qualities — his eternal power and divine nature — have been clearly seen, being understood from what has been made, so that men are without excuse.

21 For although they knew God, they neither glorified him as God nor

---

a 4 Or *who as to his spirit* *b 4* Or *was appointed to be the Son of God with power*
c 17 Or *is from faith to faith* *d 17* Hab. 2:4

gave thanks to him, but their thinking became futile and their foolish hearts were darkened. **22** Although they claimed to be wise, they became fools **23** and exchanged the glory of the immortal God for images made to look like mortal man and birds and animals and reptiles.

24 Therefore God gave them over in the sinful desires of their hearts to sexual impurity for the degrading of their bodies with one another. **25** They exchanged the truth of God for a lie, and worshiped and served created things rather than the Creator—who is forever praised. Amen.

26 Because of this, God gave them over to shameful lusts. Even their women exchanged natural relations for unnatural ones. **27** In the same way the men also abandoned natural relations with women and were inflamed with lust for one another. Men committed indecent acts with other men, and received in themselves the due penalty for their perversion.

28 Furthermore, since they did not think it worthwhile to retain the knowledge of God, he gave them over to a depraved mind, to do what ought not to be done. **29** They have become filled with every kind of wickedness, evil, greed and depravity. They are full of envy, murder, strife, deceit and malice. They are gossips, **30** slanderers, God-haters, insolent, arrogant and boastful; they invent ways of doing evil; they disobey their parents; **31** they are senseless, faithless, heartless, ruthless. **32** Although they know God's righteous decree that those who do such things deserve death, they not only continue to do these very things but also approve of those who practice them.

God's Righteous Judgment

2 **1** You, therefore, have no excuse, you who pass judgment on someone else, for at whatever point you judge the other, you are condemning yourself, because you who pass judgment do the same things. **2** Now we know that God's judgment against those who do such things is based on truth. **3** So when you, a mere man, pass judgment on them and yet do the same things, do you think you will escape God's judgment? **4** Or do you show contempt for the riches of his kindness, tolerance and patience, not realizing that God's kindness leads you toward repentance?

5 But because of your stubbornness and your unrepentant heart, you are storing up wrath against yourself for the day of God's wrath, when his righteous judgment will be revealed. **6** God "will give to each person according to what he has done."*e* **7** To those who by persistence in doing good seek glory, honor and immortality, he will give eternal life. **8** But for those who are self-seeking and who reject the truth and follow evil, there will be wrath and anger. **9** There will be trouble and distress for every human being who does evil: first for the Jew, then for the Gentile; **10** but glory, honor and peace for everyone who does good: first for the Jew, then for the Gentile. **11** For God does not show favoritism.

12 All who sin apart from the law will also perish apart from the law, and all who sin under the law will be judged by the law. **13** For it is not those who hear the law who are righteous in God's sight, but it is

e 6 Psalm 62:12; Prov. 24:12

those who obey the law who will be declared righteous. **14** (Indeed, when Gentiles, who do not have the law, do by nature things required by the law, they are a law for themselves, even though they do not have the law, **15** since they show that the requirements of the law are written on their hearts, their consciences also bearing witness, and their thoughts now accusing, now even defending them.) **16** This will take place on the day when God will judge men's secrets through Jesus Christ, as my gospel declares.

The Jews and the Law

17 Now you, if you call yourself a Jew; if you rely on the law and brag about your relationship to God; **18** if you know his will and approve of what is superior because you are instructed by the law; **19** if you are convinced that you are a guide for the blind, a light for those who are in the dark, **20** an instructor of the foolish, a teacher of infants, because you have in the law the embodiment of knowledge and truth— **21** you, then, who teach others, do you not teach yourself? You who preach against stealing, do you steal? **22** You who say that people should not commit adultery, do you commit adultery? You who abhor idols, do you rob temples? **23** You who brag about the law, do you dishonor God by breaking the law? **24** As it is written: "God's name is blasphemed among the Gentiles because of you."*f*

25 Circumcision has value if you observe the law, but if you break the law, you have become as though you had not been circumcised. **26** If those who are not circumcised keep the

law's requirements, will they not be regarded as though they were circumcised? **27** The one who is not circumcised physically and yet obeys the law will condemn you who, even though you have the*g* written code and circumcision, are a lawbreaker.

28 A man is not a Jew if he is only one outwardly, nor is circumcision merely outward and physical. **29** No, a man is a Jew if he is one inwardly; and circumcision is circumcision of the heart, by the Spirit, not by the written code. Such a man's praise is not from men, but from God.

God's Faithfulness

3 **1** What advantage, then, is there in being a Jew, or what value is there in circumcision? **2** Much in every way! First of all, they have been entrusted with the very words of God.

3 What if some did not have faith? Will their lack of faith nullify God's faithfulness? **4** Not at all! Let God be true, and every man a liar. As it is written:

"So that you may be proved right
        when you speak
    and prevail when you judge."*h*

5 But if our unrighteousness brings out God's righteousness more clearly, what shall we say? That God is unjust in bringing his wrath on us? (I am using a human argument.) **6** Certainly not! If that were so, how could God judge the world? **7** Someone might argue, "If my falsehood enhances God's truthfulness and so increases his glory, why am I still condemned as a sinner?" **8** Why not say—as we are being slanderously reported as saying and as some claim

f 24 Isaiah 52:5; Ezek. 36:22   g 27 Or who, by means of a   h 4 Psalm 51:4

that we say—"Let us do evil that good may result"? Their condemnation is deserved.

No One is Righteous

9 What shall we conclude then? Are we any better[i]? Not at all! We have already made the charge that Jews and Gentiles alike are all under sin. **10** As it is written:

"There is no one righteous, not
    even one;
11 there is no one who
    understands,
    no one who seeks God.
12 All have turned away,
    they have together become
    worthless;
there is no one who does good,
    not even one."[j]
13 "Their throats are open graves;
    their tongues practice deceit."[k]
"The poison of vipers is on their
    lips."[l]
14 "Their mouths are full of
    cursing and bitterness."[m]
15 "Their feet are swift to shed
    blood;
16 ruin and misery mark their
    ways,
17 and the way of peace they do
    not know."[n]
18 "There is no fear of God
    before their eyes."[o]

19 Now we know that whatever the law says, it says to those who are under the law, so that every mouth may be silenced and the whole world held accountable to God. **20** Therefore no one will be declared righteous in his sight by observing the law; rather, through the law we become conscious of sin.

Righteousness Through Faith

21 But now a righteousness from God, apart from law, has been made known, to which the Law and the Prophets testify. **22** This righteousness from God comes through faith in Jesus Christ to all who believe. There is no difference, **23** for all have sinned and fall short of the glory of God, **24** and are justified freely by his grace through the redemption that came by Christ Jesus. **25** God presented him as a sacrifice of atonement,[p] through faith in his blood. He did this to demonstrate his justice, because in his forbearance he had left the sins committed beforehand unpunished— **26** he did it to demonstrate his justice at the present time, so as to be just and the one who justifies those who have faith in Jesus.

27 Where, then, is boasting? It is excluded. On what principle? On that of observing the law? No, but on that of faith. **28** For we maintain that a man is justified by faith apart from observing the law. **29** Is God the God of Jews only? Is he not the God of Gentiles too? Yes, of Gentiles too, **30** since there is only one God, who will justify the circumcised by faith and the uncircumcised through that same faith. **31** Do we, then, nullify the law by this faith? Not at all! Rather, we uphold the law.

Abraham Justified by Faith

4 **1** What then shall we say that Abraham, our forefather, discovered in this matter? **2** If, in fact, Abraham was justified by works, he had something to boast about—but not before God. **3** What does the

---

i 9 Or *worse*   *j* 12 Psalms 14:1-3; 53:1-3; Eccles. 7:20   *k* 13 Psalm 5:9
l 13 Psalm 140:3   *m* 14 Psalm 10:7   *n* 17 Isaiah 59:7,8   *o* 18 Psalm 36:1
p 25 Or *as the one who would turn aside his wrath, taking away sin*

Scripture say? "Abraham believed God, and it was credited to him as righteousness."q

4 Now when a man works, his wages are not credited to him as a gift, but as an obligation. 5 However, to the man who does not work but trusts God who justifies the wicked, his faith is credited as righteousness. 6 David says the same thing when he speaks of the blessedness of the man to whom God credits righteousness apart from works:

7 "Blessed are they
    whose transgressions are
        forgiven,
    whose sins are covered.
8 Blessed is the man
    whose sin the Lord will never
        count against him."r

9 Is this blessedness only for the circumcised, or also for the uncircumcised? We have been saying that Abraham's faith was credited to him as righteousness. 10 Under what circumstances was it credited? Was it after he was circumcised, or before? It was not after, but before! 11 And he received the sign of circumcision, a seal of the righteousness that he had by faith while he was still uncircumcised. So then, he is the father of all who believe but have not been circumcised, in order that righteousness might be credited to them. 12 And he is also the father of the circumcised who not only are circumcised but who also walk in the footsteps of the faith that our father Abraham had before he was circumcised.

13 It was not through law that Abraham and his offspring received the promise that he would be heir of the world, but through the righteousness that comes by faith. 14 For if those who live by law are heirs, faith has no value and the promise is worthless, 15 because law brings wrath. And where there is no law there is no transgression.

16 Therefore, the promise comes by faith, so that it may be by grace and may be guaranteed to all Abraham's offspring—not only to those who are of the law but also to those who are of the faith of Abraham. He is the father of us all. 17 As it is written: "I have made you a father of many nations."s He is our father in the sight of God, in whom he believed—the God who gives life to the dead and calls things that are not as though they were.

18 Against all hope, Abraham in hope believed and so became the father of many nations, just as it had been said to him, "So shall your offspring be."t 19 Without weakening in his faith, he faced the fact that his body was as good as dead—since he was about a hundred years old—and that Sarah's womb was also dead. 20 Yet he did not waver through unbelief regarding the promise of God, but was strengthened in his faith and gave glory to God, 21 being fully persuaded that God had power to do what he had promised. 22 This is why "it was credited to him as righteousness." 23 The words "it was credited to him" were written not for him alone, 24 but also for us, to whom God will credit righteousness—for us who believe in him who raised Jesus our Lord from the dead. 25 He was delivered over to death for our sins and was raised to life for our justification.

q 3 Gen. 15:6; also in verse 22   r 8 Psalm 32:1,2   s 17 Gen. 17:5   t 18 Gen. 15:5

Peace and Joy

5 ¹ Therefore, since we have been justified through faith, weᵘ have peace with God through our Lord Jesus Christ, ² through whom we have gained access by faith into this grace in which we now stand. And weᵛ rejoice in the hope of the glory of God. ³ Not only so, but weʷ also rejoice in our sufferings, because we know that suffering produces perseverance; ⁴ perseverance, character; and character, hope. ⁵ And hope does not disappoint us, because God has poured out his love into our hearts by the Holy Spirit, whom he has given us.

⁶ You see, at just the right time, when we were still powerless, Christ died for the ungodly. ⁷ Very rarely will anyone die for a righteous man, though for a good man someone might possibly dare to die. ⁸ But God demonstrates his own love for us in this: While we were still sinners, Christ died for us.

⁹ Since we have now been justified by his blood, how much more shall we be saved from God's wrath through him! ¹⁰ For if, when we were God's enemies, we were reconciled to him through the death of his Son, how much more, having been reconciled, shall we be saved through his life! ¹¹ Not only is this so, but we also rejoice in God through our Lord Jesus Christ, through whom we have now received reconciliation.

Death Through Adam, Life Through Christ

¹² Therefore, just as sin entered the world through one man, and death through sin, and in this way death came to all men, because all sinned— ¹³ for before the law was given, sin was in the world. But sin is not taken into account when there is no law. ¹⁴ Nevertheless, death reigned from the time of Adam to the time of Moses, even over those who did not sin by breaking a command, as did Adam, who was a pattern of the one to come.

¹⁵ But the gift is not like the trespass. For if the many died by the trespass of the one man, how much more did God's grace and the gift that came by the grace of the one man, Jesus Christ, overflow to the many! ¹⁶ Again, the gift of God is not like the result of the one man's sin: The judgment followed one sin and brought condemnation, but the gift followed many trespasses and brought justification. ¹⁷ For if, by the trespass of the one man, death reigned through that one man, how much more will those who receive God's abundant provision of grace and of the gift of righteousness reign in life through the one man, Jesus Christ.

¹⁸ Consequently, just as the result of one trespass was condemnation for all men, so also the result of one act of righteousness was justification that brings life for all men. ¹⁹ For just as through the disobedience of the one man the many were made sinners, so also through the obedience of the one man the many will be made righteous.

²⁰ The law was added so that the trespass might increase. But where sin increased, grace increased all the more, ²¹ so that, just as sin reigned in death, so also grace might reign through righteousness to bring eternal life through Jesus Christ our Lord.

ᵘ *1* Or *let us*   ᵛ *2* Or *let us*   ʷ *3* Or *let us*

Dead to Sin, Alive in Christ

6 1 What shall we say, then? Shall we go on sinning so that grace may increase? 2 By no means! We died to sin; how can we live in it any longer? 3 Or don't you know that all of us who were baptized into Christ Jesus were baptized into his death? 4 We were therefore buried with him through baptism into death in order that, just as Christ was raised from the dead through the glory of the Father, we too may live a new life.

5 If we have been united with him like this in his death, we will certainly also be united with him in his resurrection. 6 For we know that our old self was crucified with him so that the body of sin might be done away with,[x] that we should no longer be slaves to sin — 7 because anyone who has died has been freed from sin.

8 Now if we died with Christ, we believe that we will also live with him. 9 For we know that since Christ was raised from the dead, he cannot die again; death no longer has mastery over him. 10 The death he died, he died to sin once for all; but the life he lives, he lives to God.

11 In the same way, count yourselves dead to sin but alive to God in Christ Jesus. 12 Therefore do not let sin reign in your mortal body so that you obey its evil desires. 13 Do not offer the parts of your body to sin, as instruments of wickedness, but rather offer yourselves to God, as those who have been brought from death to life; and offer the parts of your body to him as instruments of righteousness. 14 For sin shall not be your master, because you are not under law, but under grace.

Slaves to Righteousness

15 What then? Shall we sin because we are not under law but under grace? By no means! 16 Don't you know that when you offer yourselves to someone to obey him as slaves, you are slaves to the one whom you obey — whether you are slaves to sin, which leads to death, or to obedience, which leads to righteousness? 17 But thanks be to God that, though you used to be slaves to sin, you wholeheartedly obeyed the form of teaching to which you were entrusted. 18 You have been set free from sin and have become slaves to righteousness.

19 I put this in human terms because you are weak in your natural selves. Just as you used to offer the parts of your body in slavery to impurity and to ever-increasing wickedness, so now offer them in slavery to righteousness leading to holiness. 20 When you were slaves to sin, you were free from the control of righteousness. 21 What benefit did you reap at that time from the things you are now ashamed of? Those things result in death! 22 But now that you have been set free from sin and have become slaves to God, the benefit you reap leads to holiness, and the result is eternal life. 23 For the wages of sin is death, but the gift of God is eternal life in[y] Christ Jesus our Lord.

An Illustration From Marriage

7 1 Do you not know, brothers — for I am speaking to men who know the law — that the law has authority over a man only as long as he lives? 2 For example, by law a

---

x 6 Or be rendered powerless   *y 23 Or through*

married woman is bound to her husband as long as he is alive, but if her husband dies, she is released from the law of marriage. ³ So then, if she marries another man while her husband is still alive, she is called an adulteress. But if her husband dies, she is released from that law and is not an adulteress, even though she marries another man.

⁴ So, my brothers, you also died to the law through the body of Christ, that you might belong to another, to him who was raised from the dead, in order that we might bear fruit to God. ⁵ For when we were controlled by the sinful nature,^z the sinful passions aroused by the law were at work in our bodies, so that we bore fruit for death. ⁶ But now, by dying to what once bound us, we have been released from the law so that we serve in the new way of the Spirit, and not in the old way of the written code.

Struggling With Sin

⁷ What shall we say, then? Is the law sin? Certainly not! Indeed I would not have known what sin was except through the law. For I would not have known what coveting really was if the law had not said, "Do not covet."^a ⁸ But sin, seizing the opportunity afforded by the commandment, produced in me every kind of covetous desire. For apart from law, sin is dead. ⁹ Once I was alive apart from law; but when the commandment came, sin sprang to life and I died. ¹⁰ I found that the very commandment that was intended to bring life actually brought death. ¹¹ For sin, seizing the opportunity afforded by the commandment,

deceived me, and through the commandment put me to death. ¹² So then, the law is holy, and the commandment is holy, righteous and good. ¹³ Did that which is good, then, become death to me? By no means! But in order that sin might be recognized as sin, it produced death in me through what was good, so that through the commandment sin might become utterly sinful.

¹⁴ We know that the law is spiritual; but I am unspiritual, sold as a slave to sin. ¹⁵ I do not understand what I do. For what I want to do I do not do, but what I hate I do. ¹⁶ And if I do what I do not want to do, I agree that the law is good. ¹⁷ As it is, it is no longer I myself who do it, but it is sin living in me. ¹⁸ I know that nothing good lives in me, that is, in my sinful nature.^b For I have the desire to do what is good, but I cannot carry it out. ¹⁹ For what I do is not the good I want to do; no, the evil I do not want to do—this I keep on doing. ²⁰ Now if I do what I do not want to do, it is no longer I who do it, but it is sin living in me that does it.

²¹ So I find this law at work: When I want to do good, evil is right there with me. ²² For in my inner being I delight in God's law; ²³ but I see another law at work in the members of my body, waging war against the law of my mind and making me a prisoner of the law of sin at work within my members. ²⁴ What a wretched man I am! Who will rescue me from this body of death? ²⁵ Thanks be to God—through Jesus Christ our Lord!

So then, I myself in my mind am a slave to God's law, but in the sinful nature a slave to the law of sin.

---

^z 5 Or *the flesh*; also in verse 25   ^a 7 Exodus 20:17; Deut. 5:21   ^b 18 Or *my flesh*

RW HAMPTON

★ ★ ★

© Cynthia Hunter

THE HEART OF IT ALL...

I've lived the kind of life most men have only dreamed of. I grew up in an urban setting in Texas, but the call of a horseback life in big country lured me out to the Canadian River breaks of the Texas Panhandle and eastern New Mexico.

It was there a green kid from town learned the trade of punchin' cows. During those carefree years I drifted anywhere the wind blew just to see what the country looked like on the other side of the divide. During my wild ramblings I know I was spared many times and survived many a horse wreck due to the fervent prayers of my folks back home.

My life became strangely and miraculously intertwined with music. I went from sitting around the bunkhouse strumming my guitar and singing of an evening, to being asked occasionally to entertain for cattlemen's balls and stock growers' conventions. Before I knew it I was doing a prime time TV special, playing bit parts in Westerns and doing some stunt work alongside the likes of Dick Farnsworth, Ben Johnson, Buck Taylor and Dave Cass, my boyhood heroes.

I helped produce and starred in a play, I've won several industry awards and I've had as much fun singing under the stars by a campfire as I have with a full symphony orchestra. Music has put food on the table, horses in the barn and sent me to such far away places as Australia and Brazil. I was even fortunate enough to play on the Grand Ol' Opry, something I'd always dreamed of.

From cow camps to movie sets to recording studios and then back to the ranch, I've been richly blessed and yet there have been many challenges, disappointments, setbacks and sorrows on the trail. I've experienced the trauma of a horrific car accident where my sister and three others perished because of the selfishness of a drunk driver. Three times now my life has been threatened by deadly Melanoma cancer.

My greatest trial of all came when my family and home of fourteen years were shattered by a divorce I did not want nor understand, and could not stop. Then came the challenges of single parenthood, learning to heal, learning to let go and to love again.

Now, in what some would call the middle of life, I stand at the brink of a new tomorrow. God has sent me a new partner, Lisa, and over the past ten years we have been busy raising our five boys and a daughter on a place of our own. The trail of life has taken me from the mountain top to the dark valley and back again many times. Looking back, I know my Savior Jesus Christ has led me all the way.

★ ★ ★

STRAN SMITH

★★★

I've often said that I don't know how anybody rodeos without being a Christian. Rodeo is such a strain on you mentally, physically, emotionally. There's so much pressure, no sleep, you're away from your family, and it's when you're wore down that things start to attack you.

Being a Christian is everything to me. It's the only reason I've been able to be at the NFR. The things I've been through have only strengthened my faith in God. I'm here to be a witness and an example to kids, to my peers, and maybe even to some folks who are older.

A few years ago I had a stroke. I thought I was really healthy at the time. I was 32 years old and thought I was at the top of my game. But I had a heart condition that we never knew about. The cowboy term for it is that I had a hole in my heart. A blood clot went through it, hit my brain and caused a stroke.

After the stroke it was very hard for me because I didn't feel different, yet people were telling me I had to have heart surgery. I really had to slow down and take a look at that, because they were talking about my odds of not making it off the operating table. It was even more intense and complicated because Jennifer was pregnant with our first son. It was a tough deal for us.

Roping has always been my outlet, but I couldn't rope. I couldn't do anything. I watered grass and talked to the Lord; that was about the extent of how I dealt with it. The scriptures that I had read hundreds of time before jumped off the page with new meaning for me during this time.

You know, they say you really aren't ready to live until you're ready to die. When you look death straight in the face, you look at the things you thought were so important in the world, in the way cowboys live, year to year. But you realize they really aren't that important. The things that are important we often take for granted, like just being able to enjoy life and enjoy family, having the freedom that we have to do the things we love. Those things are what it's all about.

The Lord is so patient with me. He lets me run out ahead, and then I realize I had better wait on the Lord. I fall back on the Lord. He is everything to me. Everything comes from him and we as Christians will be with him forever. In the big picture, what's 75 years, what's 100 years? The important thing is the impact that I will have on this earth. What kind of legacy will I leave? What kind of example am I while I'm here? Those are the things that are really important!

★ ★ ★

KELLY KAMINSKI

If I didn't have faith, I wouldn't be rodeoing. It took a great leap of faith to jump from my safe, secure teaching job to believe God was going to provide for us and take care of us out on the rodeo road. He has! I have been able to make it to the NFR because of my faith in God, prayer and his angels helping me.

The NFR is the most difficult experience any one can go through. I tell people it's like taking ten days of final exams. We pack up like the Clampett's and move to Las Vegas for a month. When we are out there, every night we pray for a safe, secure, solid run. I don't really run around telling everybody about my faith in God, I just hope they see it. I feel my words and actions will be enough; more like modeling, I guess.

God has blessed me with a great horse. I know I'm blessed with lots of people who pray for me every day. It's because of God that I'm here. Going in, if I'm extremely nervous, I thank Jesus for letting me be here to have fun, for a safe run. When it's stressful I remind myself that I'm here to enjoy it. It's a fun game and I've been fortunate enough to make a living out of it.

Gosh, the rodeo community is huge with people of faith. I have wonderful friends in rodeo; and one of the neatest experiences is to visit and hang out. People have the idea that all rodeo cowboys party and carouse and are rowdy, but mainly everyone is just doing their job.

The rodeo is family. We're all in this together and it's fun. It's great for us to be able to ride our horses, which we love to do, see the country, and hang out with people who love to do the same thing.

★ ★ ★

Life Through the Spirit

8 1 Therefore, there is now no condemnation for those who are in
Christ Jesus,*c* 2 because through
Christ Jesus the law of the Spirit of
life set me free from the law of sin
and death. 3 For what the law was
powerless to do in that it was
weakened by the sinful nature,*d* God
did by sending his own Son in the
likeness of sinful man to be a sin
offering.*e* And so he condemned sin
in sinful man,*f* 4 in order that the
righteous requirements of the law
might be fully met in us, who do not
live according to the sinful nature but
according to the Spirit.

5 Those who live according to the
sinful nature have their minds set on
what that nature desires; but those
who live in accordance with the
Spirit have their minds set on what
the Spirit desires. 6 The mind of the
sinful man*g* is death, but the mind controlled by the Spirit is life and peace;
7 the sinful mind*h* is hostile to God.
It does not submit to God's law, nor
can it do so. 8 Those controlled by the
sinful nature cannot please God.

9 You, however, are controlled not
by the sinful nature but by the Spirit,
if the Spirit of God lives in you. And if
anyone does not have the Spirit of
Christ, he does not belong to Christ.
10 But if Christ is in you, your body is
dead because of sin, yet your spirit is
alive because of righteousness.
11 And if the Spirit of him who raised
Jesus from the dead is living in you,
who raised Christ from the dead will
also give life to your mortal bodies
through his Spirit, who lives in you.

12 Therefore, brothers, we have an
obligation—but it is not to the sinful
nature, to live according to it. 13 For
if you live according to the sinful
nature, you will die; but if by the
Spirit you put to death the misdeeds
of the body, you will live, 14 because
those who are led by the Spirit of God
are sons of God. 15 For you did not
receive a spirit that makes you a
slave again to fear, but you received
the Spirit of sonship.*i* And by him we
cry, "Abba,*j* Father." 16 The Spirit
himself testifies with our spirit that
we are God's children. 17 Now if we
are children, then we are heirs—
heirs of God and co-heirs with Christ,
if indeed we share in his sufferings in
order that we may also share in his
glory.

Future Glory

18 I consider that our present sufferings are not worth comparing
with the glory that will be revealed
in us. 19 The creation waits in eager
expectation for the sons of God to be
revealed. 20 For the creation was
subjected to frustration, not by its
own choice, but by the will of the one
who subjected it, in hope 21 that*k* the
creation itself will be liberated from
its bondage to decay and brought
into the glorious freedom of the
children of God.

22 We know that the whole creation has been groaning as in the pains
of childbirth right up to the present
time. 23 Not only so, but we ourselves, who have the firstfruits of the
Spirit, groan inwardly as we wait
eagerly for our adoption as sons, the
redemption of our bodies. 24 For in

c 1 Some later manuscripts *Jesus, who do not live according to the sinful nature but according
to the Spirit,*   *d* 3 Or *the flesh;* also in verses 4, 5, 8, 9, 12 and 13   *e* 3 Or *man, for sin*
f 3 Or *in the flesh*   *g* 6 Or *mind set on the flesh*   *h* 7 Or *The mind set on the flesh*
i 15 Or *adoption*   *j* 15 Aramaic for *Father*   *k* 21 Or *subjected it in hope. 21 For*

this hope we were saved. But hope that is seen is no hope at all. Who hopes for what he already has? **25** But if we hope for what we do not yet have, we wait for it patiently.

26 In the same way, the Spirit helps us in our weakness. We do not know what we ought to pray for, but the Spirit himself intercedes for us with groans that words cannot express. **27** And he who searches our hearts knows the mind of the Spirit, because the Spirit intercedes for the saints in accordance with God's will.

More Than Conquerors

28 And we know that in all things God works for the good of those who love him,*l* who*m* have been called according to his purpose. **29** For those God foreknew he also predestined to be conformed to the likeness of his Son, that he might be the firstborn among many brothers. **30** And those he predestined, he also called; those he called, he also justified; those he justified, he also glorified.

31 What, then, shall we say in response to this? If God is for us, who can be against us? **32** He who did not spare his own Son, but gave him up for us all—how will he not also, along with him, graciously give us all things? **33** Who will bring any charge against those whom God has chosen? It is God who justifies. **34** Who is he that condemns? Christ Jesus, who died—more than that, who was raised to life—is at the right hand of God and is also interceding for us. **35** Who shall separate us from the love of Christ? Shall trouble or

hardship or persecution or famine o nakedness or danger or sword? **36** A it is written:

"For your sake we face death a day long;
we are considered as sheep to be slaughtered."*n*

37 No, in all these things we are mor than conquerors through him who loved us. **38** For I am convinced tha neither death nor life, neither angel nor demons,*o* neither the present no the future, nor any powers **39** neither height nor depth, no anything else in all creation, will be able to separate us from the love o God that is in Christ Jesus our Lord

God's Sovereign Choice

9 **1** I speak the truth in Christ— am not lying, my conscience con firms it in the Holy Spirit— **2** I have great sorrow and unceasing anguis in my heart. **3** For I could wish that myself were cursed and cut off from Christ for the sake of my brothers those of my own race, **4** the people o Israel. Theirs is the adoption as sons theirs the divine glory, the covenants the receiving of the law, the templ worship and the promises. **5** Their are the patriarchs, and from them i traced the human ancestry of Chris who is God over all, forever praised!, Amen.

6 It is not as though God's wor had failed. For not all who are de cended from Israel are Israel. **7** No because they are his descendants ar they all Abraham's children. On th contrary, "It is through Isaac tha your offspring will be reckoned."

---

l 28 Some manuscripts *And we know that all things work together for good to those who love God*   *m 28* Or *works together with those who love him to bring about what is good—with those who* *n 36* Psalm 44:22   *o 38* Or *nor heavenly rulers*   *P 5* Or *Christ, who is over all. God be forever praised! Or Christ. God who is over all be forever praised!*   *q 7* Gen. 21:12

In other words, it is not the natural children who are God's children, but it is the children of the promise who are regarded as Abraham's offspring. 9 For this was how the promise was stated: "At the appointed time I will return, and Sarah will have a son."ʳ

10 Not only that, but Rebekah's children had one and the same father, our father Isaac. 11 Yet, before the twins were born or had done anything good or bad—in order that God's purpose in election might stand: 12 not by works but by him who calls—she was told, "The older will serve the younger."ˢ 13 Just as it is written: "Jacob I loved, but Esau I hated."ᵗ

14 What then shall we say? Is God unjust? Not at all! 15 For he says to Moses,

"I will have mercy on whom I
        have mercy,
    and I will have compassion on
        whom I have
        compassion."ᵘ

16 It does not, therefore, depend on man's desire or effort, but on God's mercy. 17 For the Scripture says to Pharaoh: "I raised you up for this very purpose, that I might display my power in you and that my name might be proclaimed in all the earth."ᵛ 18 Therefore God has mercy on whom he wants to have mercy, and he hardens whom he wants to harden.

19 One of you will say to me: "Then why does God still blame us? For who resists his will?" 20 But who are you, O man, to talk back to God? "Shall what is formed say to him who formed it, 'Why did you make me like this?'"ʷ 21 Does not the potter have the right to make out of the same lump of clay some pottery for noble purposes and some for common use?

22 What if God, choosing to show his wrath and make his power known, bore with great patience the objects of his wrath—prepared for destruction? 23 What if he did this to make the riches of his glory known to the objects of his mercy, whom he prepared in advance for glory—24 even us, whom he also called, not only from the Jews but also from the Gentiles? 25 As he says in Hosea:

"I will call them 'my people' who
        are not my people;
    and I will call her 'my loved one'
        who is not my loved one,"ˣ

26 and,

"It will happen that in the very
        place where it was said to
        them,
    'You are not my people,'
    they will be called 'sons of the
        living God.' "ʸ

27 Isaiah cries out concerning Israel:

"Though the number of the
        Israelites be like the sand by
        the sea,
    only the remnant will be saved.
28 For the Lord will carry out
    his sentence on earth with
        speed and finality."ᶻ

29 It is just as Isaiah said previously:

"Unless the Lord Almighty
    had left us descendants,
we would have become like
        Sodom,
    we would have been like
        Gomorrah."ᵃ

9 Gen. 18:10,14   ˢ 12 Gen. 25:23   ᵗ 13 Mal. 1:2,3   ᵘ 15 Exodus 33:19   ʳ 17 Exodus 9:16   ʷ 20 Isaiah 29:16; 45:9   ˣ 25 Hosea 2:23   ʸ 26 Hosea 1:10   ᶻ 28 Isaiah 10:22,23   ᵃ 29 Isaiah 1:9

Israel's Unbelief

30 What then shall we say? That the Gentiles, who did not pursue righteousness, have obtained it, a righteousness that is by faith; **31** but Israel, who pursued a law of righteousness, has not attained it. **32** Why not? Because they pursued it not by faith but as if it were by works. They stumbled over the "stumbling stone." **33** As it is written:

"See, I lay in Zion a stone that
    causes men to stumble
and a rock that makes them
    fall,
and the one who trusts in him
    will never be put to
    shame."[b]

10 **1** Brothers, my heart's desire and prayer to God for the Israelites is that they may be saved. **2** For I can testify about them that they are zealous for God, but their zeal is not based on knowledge. **3** Since they did not know the righteousness that comes from God and sought to establish their own, they did not submit to God's righteousness. **4** Christ is the end of the law so that there may be righteousness for everyone who believes.

5 Moses describes in this way the righteousness that is by the law: "The man who does these things will live by them."[c] **6** But the righteousness that is by faith says: "Do not say in your heart, 'Who will ascend into heaven?'[d]" (that is, to bring Christ down) **7** "or 'Who will descend into the deep?'[e]" (that is,

to bring Christ up from the dead **8** But what does it say? "The wor is near you; it is in your mouth an in your heart,"[f] that is, the word faith we are proclaiming: **9** That you confess with your mouth "Jesus is Lord," and believe in you heart that God raised him from th dead, you will be saved. **10** For it i with your heart that you believ and are justified, and it is with you mouth that you confess and ar saved. **11** As the Scripture say "Anyone who trusts in him w never be put to shame."[g] **12** Fo there is no difference between Je and Gentile—the same Lord is Lor of all and richly blesses all who ca on him, **13** for, "Everyone who call on the name of the Lord will b saved."[h]

14 How, then, can they call on th one they have not believed in? An how can they believe in the one o whom they have not heard? An how can they hear without some one preaching to them? **15** And ho can they preach unless they are sent? As it is written, "How beaut ful are the feet of those who brin good news!"[i]

16 But not all the Israelites a cepted the good news. For Isaia says, "Lord, who has believed ou message?"[j] **17** Consequently, fait comes from hearing the message and the message is heard throug the word of Christ. **18** But I as Did they not hear? Of course the did:

"Their voice has gone out into a
    the earth,
their words to the ends of the
    world."[k]

---

b 33 Isaiah 8:14; 28:16   *c 5* Lev. 18:5   *d 6* Deut. 30:13   *e 7* Deut. 30:13
f 8 Deut. 30:14   *g 11* Isaiah 28:16   *h 13* Joel 2:32   *i 15* Isaiah 52:7
j 16 Isaiah 53:1   *k 18* Psalm 19:4

19 Again I ask: Did Israel not understand? First, Moses says,

"I will make you envious by those
    who are not a nation;
I will make you angry by a
    nation that has no
    understanding."[l]

20 And Isaiah boldly says,

"I was found by those who did not
    seek me;
I revealed myself to those
    who did not ask for me."[m]

21 But concerning Israel he says,

"All day long I have held out my
    hands
to a disobedient and obstinate
    people."[n]

The Remnant of Israel

11 **1** I ask then: Did God reject his people? By no means! I am an Israelite myself, a descendant of Abraham, from the tribe of Benjamin. **2** God did not reject his people, whom he foreknew. Don't you know what the Scripture says in the passage about Elijah—how he appealed to God against Israel: **3** "Lord, they have killed your prophets and torn down your altars; I am the only one left, and they are trying to kill me"[o]? **4** And what was God's answer to him? "I have reserved for myself seven thousand who have not bowed the knee to Baal."[p] **5** So too, at the present time there is a remnant chosen by grace. **6** And if by grace, then it is no longer by works; if it were, grace would no longer be grace.[q]

7 What then? What Israel sought so earnestly it did not obtain, but the elect did. The others were hardened, **8** as it is written:

"God gave them a spirit of stupor,
    eyes so that they could not see
    and ears so that they could
        not hear,
to this very day."[r]

9 And David says:

"May their table become a snare
    and a trap,
    a stumbling block and a
        retribution for them.
10 May their eyes be darkened so
    they cannot see,
    and their backs be bent
        forever."[s]

Ingrafted Branches

11 Again I ask: Did they stumble so as to fall beyond recovery? Not at all! Rather, because of their transgression, salvation has come to the Gentiles to make Israel envious. **12** But if their transgression means riches for the world, and their loss means riches for the Gentiles, how much greater riches will their fullness bring!

13 I am talking to you Gentiles. Inasmuch as I am the apostle to the Gentiles, I make much of my ministry **14** in the hope that I may somehow arouse my own people to envy and save some of them. **15** For if their rejection is the reconciliation of the world, what will their acceptance be but life from the dead? **16** If the part of the dough offered as firstfruits is holy, then the whole batch is holy; if the root is holy, so are the branches.

17 If some of the branches have been broken off, and you, though a wild olive shoot, have been grafted in

---

[l] 19 Deut. 32:21   [m] 20 Isaiah 65:1   [n] 21 Isaiah 65:2   [o] 3 1 Kings 19:10,14
[p] 4 1 Kings 19:18   [q] 6 Some manuscripts by grace. But if by works, then it is no longer grace; if it were, work would no longer be work.   [r] 8 Deut. 29:4; Isaiah 29:10
[s] 10 Psalm 69:22,23

among the others and now share in the nourishing sap from the olive root, 18 do not boast over those branches. If you do, consider this: You do not support the root, but the root supports you. 19 You will say then, "Branches were broken off so that I could be grafted in." 20 Granted. But they were broken off because of unbelief, and you stand by faith. Do not be arrogant, but be afraid. 21 For if God did not spare the natural branches, he will not spare you either.

22 Consider therefore the kindness and sternness of God: sternness to those who fell, but kindness to you, provided that you continue in his kindness. Otherwise, you also will be cut off. 23 And if they do not persist in unbelief, they will be grafted in, for God is able to graft them in again. 24 After all, if you were cut out of an olive tree that is wild by nature, and contrary to nature were grafted into a cultivated olive tree, how much more readily will these, the natural branches, be grafted into their own olive tree!

All Israel Will Be Saved

25 I do not want you to be ignorant of this mystery, brothers, so that you may not be conceited: Israel has experienced a hardening in part until the full number of the Gentiles has come in. 26 And so all Israel will be saved, as it is written:

> "The deliverer will come from Zion;
> he will turn godlessness away from Jacob.
> 27 And this is^t my covenant with them
> when I take away their sins."^{u}

28 As far as the gospel is concerned, they are enemies on your account; but as far as election is concerned, they are loved on account of the patriarchs, 29 for God's gifts and his call are irrevocable. 30 Just as you who were at one time disobedient to God have now received mercy as a result of their disobedience, 31 so they too have now become disobedient in order that they too may now^v receive mercy as a result of God's mercy to you. 32 For God has bound all men over to disobedience so that he may have mercy on them all.

Doxology

33 Oh, the depth of the riches of the wisdom and^w
knowledge of God!
How unsearchable his judgments,
and his paths beyond tracing out!
34 "Who has known the mind of the Lord?
Or who has been his counselor?"^{x}
35 "Who has ever given to God, that God should repay him?"^{y}
36 For from him and through him and to him are all things.
To him be the glory forever! Amen.

Living Sacrifices

12 1 Therefore, I urge you, brothers, in view of God's mercy, to offer your bodies as living sacrifices, holy and pleasing to God — this is your spiritual^z act of worship. 2 Do not conform any longer to the pattern of this world,

---

^{t} 27 Or will be ^{u} 27 Isaiah 59:20,21; 27:9; Jer. 31:33,34 ^{v} 31 Some manuscripts do not have now. ^{w} 33 Or riches and the wisdom and the ^{x} 34 Isaiah 40:13 ^{y} 35 Job 41:11 ^{z} 1 Or reasonable

but be transformed by the renewing of your mind. Then you will be able to test and approve what God's will is—his good, pleasing and perfect will.

3 For by the grace given me I say to every one of you: Do not think of yourself more highly than you ought, but rather think of yourself with sober judgment, in accordance with the measure of faith God has given you. **4** Just as each of us has one body with many members, and these members do not all have the same function, **5** so in Christ we who are many form one body, and each member belongs to all the others. **6** We have different gifts, according to the grace given us. If a man's gift is prophesying, let him use it in proportion to his*a* faith. **7** If it is serving, let him serve; if it is teaching, let him teach; **8** if it is encouraging, let him encourage; if it is contributing to the needs of others, let him give generously; if it is leadership, let him govern diligently; if it is showing mercy, let him do it cheerfully.

Love

9 Love must be sincere. Hate what is evil; cling to what is good. **10** Be devoted to one another in brotherly love. Honor one another above yourselves. **11** Never be lacking in zeal, but keep your spiritual fervor, serving the Lord. **12** Be joyful in hope, patient in affliction, faithful in prayer. **13** Share with God's people who are in need. Practice hospitality.

14 Bless those who persecute you; bless and do not curse. **15** Rejoice with those who rejoice; mourn with those who mourn. **16** Live in harmony with one another. Do not be proud, but be willing to associate with people of low position.*b* Do not be conceited.

17 Do not repay anyone evil for evil. Be careful to do what is right in the eyes of everybody. **18** If it is possible, as far as it depends on you, live at peace with everyone. **19** Do not take revenge, my friends, but leave room for God's wrath, for it is written: "It is mine to avenge; I will repay,"*c* says the Lord. **20** On the contrary:

> "If your enemy is hungry, feed him;
> if he is thirsty, give him something to drink.
> In doing this, you will heap burning coals on his head."*d*

21 Do not be overcome by evil, but overcome evil with good.

Submission to the Authorities

13 **1** Everyone must submit himself to the governing authorities, for there is no authority except that which God has established. The authorities that exist have been established by God. **2** Consequently, he who rebels against the authority is rebelling against what God has instituted, and those who do so will bring judgment on themselves. **3** For rulers hold no terror for those who do right, but for those who do wrong. Do you want to be free from fear of the one in authority? Then do what is right and he will commend you. **4** For he is God's servant to do you good. But if you do wrong, be afraid, for he does not bear the sword for nothing. He is God's servant, an agent of wrath to bring punishment on the wrongdoer. **5** Therefore, it is necessary to submit to the authorities, not

---

a 6 Or *in agreement with the*   *b* 16 Or *willing to do menial work*   *c* 19 Deut. 32:35
d 20 Prov. 25:21,22

only because of possible punishment but also because of conscience. **6** This is also why you pay taxes, for the authorities are God's servants, who give their full time to governing. **7** Give everyone what you owe him: If you owe taxes, pay taxes; if revenue, then revenue; if respect, then respect; if honor, then honor.

Love, for the Day is Near

8 Let no debt remain outstanding, except the continuing debt to love one another, for he who loves his fellowman has fulfilled the law. **9** The commandments, "Do not commit adultery," "Do not murder," "Do not steal," "Do not covet,"*e* and whatever other commandment there may be, are summed up in this one rule: "Love your neighbor as yourself."*f* **10** Love does no harm to its neighbor. Therefore love is the fulfillment of the law.

11 And do this, understanding the present time. The hour has come for you to wake up from your slumber, because our salvation is nearer now than when we first believed. **12** The night is nearly over; the day is almost here. So let us put aside the deeds of darkness and put on the armor of light. **13** Let us behave decently, as in the daytime, not in orgies and drunkenness, not in sexual immorality and debauchery, not in dissension and jealousy. **14** Rather, clothe yourselves with the Lord Jesus Christ, and do not think about how to gratify the desires of the sinful nature.*g*

The Weak and the Strong

14

1 Accept him whose faith is weak, without passing judgment on disputable matters. **2** One man's faith allows him to eat every-

thing, but another man, whose faith is weak, eats only vegetables. **3** The man who eats everything must not look down on him who does not, and the man who does not eat everything must not condemn the man who does, for God has accepted him. **4** Who are you to judge someone else's servant? To his own master he stands or falls. And he will stand, for the Lord is able to make him stand.

5 One man considers one day more sacred than another; another man considers every day alike. Each one should be fully convinced in his own mind. **6** He who regards one day as special, does so to the Lord. He who eats meat, eats to the Lord, for he gives thanks to God; and he who abstains, does so to the Lord and gives thanks to God. **7** For none of us lives to himself alone and none of us dies to himself alone. **8** If we live, we live to the Lord; and if we die, we die to the Lord. So, whether we live or die, we belong to the Lord.

9 For this very reason, Christ died and returned to life so that he might be the Lord of both the dead and the living. **10** You, then, why do you judge your brother? Or why do you look down on your brother? For we will all stand before God's judgment seat. **11** It is written:

> " 'As surely as I live,' says the
> Lord,
> 'every knee will bow before me;
>   every tongue will confess to
>   God.' "*h*

12 So then, each of us will give an account of himself to God.

13 Therefore let us stop passing judgment on one another. Instead,

---

e 9 Exodus 20:13-15,17; Deut. 5:17-19,21 *f 9* Lev. 19:18 *g 14* Or *the flesh* *h 11* Isaiah 45:23

make up your mind not to put any stumbling block or obstacle in your brother's way. **14** As one who is in the Lord Jesus, I am fully convinced that no food[i] is unclean in itself. But if anyone regards something as unclean, then for him it is unclean. **15** If your brother is distressed because of what you eat, you are no longer acting in love. Do not by your eating destroy your brother for whom Christ died. **16** Do not allow what you consider good to be spoken of as evil. **17** For the kingdom of God is not a matter of eating and drinking, but of righteousness, peace and joy in the Holy Spirit, **18** because anyone who serves Christ in this way is pleasing to God and approved by men.

19 Let us therefore make every effort to do what leads to peace and to mutual edification. **20** Do not destroy the work of God for the sake of food. All food is clean, but it is wrong for a man to eat anything that causes someone else to stumble. **21** It is better not to eat meat or drink wine or to do anything else that will cause your brother to fall.

22 So whatever you believe about these things keep between yourself and God. Blessed is the man who does not condemn himself by what he approves. **23** But the man who has doubts is condemned if he eats, because his eating is not from faith; and everything that does not come from faith is sin.

15 **1** We who are strong ought to bear with the failings of the weak and not to please ourselves. **2** Each of us should please his neighbor for his good, to build him up. **3** For even Christ did not please himself but, as it is written: "The insults

of those who insult you have fallen on me."[j] **4** For everything that was written in the past was written to teach us, so that through endurance and the encouragement of the Scriptures we might have hope.

5 May the God who gives endurance and encouragement give you a spirit of unity among yourselves as you follow Christ Jesus, **6** so that with one heart and mouth you may glorify the God and Father of our Lord Jesus Christ.

7 Accept one another, then, just as Christ accepted you, in order to bring praise to God. **8** For I tell you that Christ has become a servant of the Jews[k] on behalf of God's truth, to confirm the promises made to the patriarchs **9** so that the Gentiles may glorify God for his mercy, as it is written:

> "Therefore I will praise you
>   among the Gentiles;
> I will sing hymns to your name."[l]

10 Again, it says,

> "Rejoice, O Gentiles, with his
>   people."[m]

11 And again,

> "Praise the Lord, all you Gentiles,
> and sing praises to him, all
>   you peoples."[n]

12 And again, Isaiah says,

> "The Root of Jesse will spring up,
> one who will arise to rule
>   over the nations;
> the Gentiles will hope in him."[o]

13 May the God of hope fill you with all joy and peace as you trust in him, so that you may overflow with hope by the power of the Holy Spirit.

---

i 14 Or *that nothing*   *j* 3 Psalm 69:9   *k* 8 Greek *circumcision*   *l* 9 2 Samuel 22:50; Psalm 18:49   *m* 10 Deut. 32:43   *n* 11 Psalm 117:1   *o* 12 Isaiah 11:10

Paul the Minister to the Gentiles

14 I myself am convinced, my brothers, that you yourselves are full of goodness, complete in knowledge and competent to instruct one another. **15** I have written you quite boldly on some points, as if to remind you of them again, because of the grace God gave me **16** to be a minister of Christ Jesus to the Gentiles with the priestly duty of proclaiming the gospel of God, so that the Gentiles might become an offering acceptable to God, sanctified by the Holy Spirit.

17 Therefore I glory in Christ Jesus in my service to God. **18** I will not venture to speak of anything except what Christ has accomplished through me in leading the Gentiles to obey God by what I have said and done— **19** by the power of signs and miracles, through the power of the Spirit. So from Jerusalem all the way around to Illyricum, I have fully proclaimed the gospel of Christ. **20** It has always been my ambition to preach the gospel where Christ was not known, so that I would not be building on someone else's foundation. **21** Rather, as it is written:

> "Those who were not told about
> him will see,
> and those who have not
> heard will understand."*p*

22 This is why I have often been hindered from coming to you.

Paul's Plan to Visit Rome

23 But now that there is no more place for me to work in these regions, and since I have been longing for many years to see you, **24** I plan to do so when I go to Spain. I hope to visit you while passing through and to have you assist me on my journey there, after I have enjoyed your company for a while. **25** Now, however, I am on my way to Jerusalem in the service of the saints there. **26** For Macedonia and Achaia were pleased to make a contribution for the poor among the saints in Jerusalem. **27** They were pleased to do it, and indeed they owe it to them. For if the Gentiles have shared in the Jews' spiritual blessings, they owe it to the Jews to share with them their material blessings. **28** So after I have completed this task and have made sure that they have received this fruit, I will go to Spain and visit you on the way. **29** I know that when I come to you, I will come in the full measure of the blessing of Christ.

30 I urge you, brothers, by our Lord Jesus Christ and by the love of the Spirit, to join me in my struggle by praying to God for me. **31** Pray that I may be rescued from the unbelievers in Judea and that my service in Jerusalem may be acceptable to the saints there, **32** so that by God's will I may come to you with joy and together with you be refreshed. **33** The God of peace be with you all. Amen.

Personal Greetings

16 **1** I commend to you our sister Phoebe, a servant*q* of the church in Cenchrea. **2** I ask you to receive her in the Lord in a way worthy of the saints and to give her any help she may need from you, for she has been a great help to many people, including me.

3 Greet Priscilla*r* and Aquila, my fellow workers in Christ Jesus. **4** They risked their lives for

p 21 Isaiah 52:15   *q 1* Or *deaconess*   *r 3* Greek *Prisca,* a variant of *Priscilla* me. Not only I but all the churches of the Gentiles are grateful to them.

5 Greet also the church that meets at their house.

Greet my dear friend Epenetus, who was the first convert to Christ in the province of Asia.

6 Greet Mary, who worked very hard for you.

7 Greet Andronicus and Junias, my relatives who have been in prison with me. They are outstanding among the apostles, and they were in Christ before I was.

8 Greet Ampliatus, whom I love in the Lord.

9 Greet Urbanus, our fellow worker in Christ, and my dear friend Stachys.

10 Greet Apelles, tested and approved in Christ.

Greet those who belong to the household of Aristobulus.

11 Greet Herodion, my relative.

Greet those in the household of Narcissus who are in the Lord.

12 Greet Tryphena and Tryphosa, those women who work hard in the Lord.

Greet my dear friend Persis, another woman who has worked very hard in the Lord.

13 Greet Rufus, chosen in the Lord, and his mother, who has been a mother to me, too.

14 Greet Asyncritus, Phlegon, Hermes, Patrobas, Hermas and the brothers with them.

15 Greet Philologus, Julia, Nereus and his sister, and Olympas and all the saints with them.

16 Greet one another with a holy kiss.

All the churches of Christ send greetings.

17 I urge you, brothers, to watch out for those who cause divisions and put obstacles in your way that are contrary to the teaching you have learned. Keep away from them. 18 For such people are not serving our Lord Christ, but their own appetites. By smooth talk and flattery they deceive the minds of naive people. 19 Everyone has heard about your obedience, so I am full of joy over you; but I want you to be wise about what is good, and innocent about what is evil.

20 The God of peace will soon crush Satan under your feet.

The grace of our Lord Jesus be with you.

21 Timothy, my fellow worker, sends his greetings to you, as do Lucius, Jason and Sosipater, my relatives.

22 I, Tertius, who wrote down this letter, greet you in the Lord.

23 Gaius, whose hospitality I and the whole church here enjoy, sends you his greetings.

Erastus, who is the city's director of public works, and our brother Quartus send you their greetings.[s]

25 Now to him who is able to establish you by my gospel and the proclamation of Jesus Christ, according to the revelation of the mystery hidden for long ages past, 26 but now revealed and made known through the prophetic writings by the command of the eternal God, so that all nations might believe and obey him— 27 to the only wise God be glory forever through Jesus Christ! Amen.

[s] 23 Some manuscripts their greetings. 24 May the grace of our Lord Jesus Christ be with all of you. Amen.

1 Corinthians

1 ¹Paul, called to be an apostle of Christ Jesus by the will of God, and our brother Sosthenes,

²To the church of God in Corinth, to those sanctified in Christ Jesus and called to be holy, together with all those everywhere who call on the name of our Lord Jesus Christ — their Lord and ours:

³Grace and peace to you from God our Father and the Lord Jesus Christ.

Thanksgiving

⁴I always thank God for you because of his grace given you in Christ Jesus. ⁵For in him you have been enriched in every way — in all your speaking and in all your knowledge — ⁶because our testimony about Christ was confirmed in you. ⁷Therefore you do not lack any spiritual gift as you eagerly wait for our Lord Jesus Christ to be revealed. ⁸He will keep you strong to the end, so that you will be blameless on the day of our Lord Jesus Christ. ⁹God, who has called you into fellowship with his Son Jesus Christ our Lord, is faithful.

Divisions in the Church

¹⁰I appeal to you, brothers, in the name of our Lord Jesus Christ, that all of you agree with one another so that there may be no divisions among you and that you may be perfectly united in mind and thought. ¹¹My brothers, some from Chloe's household have informed me that

there are quarrels among you. ¹²What I mean is this: One of you says, "I follow Paul"; another, "I follow Apollos"; another, "I follow Cephas[a]"; still another, "I follow Christ."

¹³Is Christ divided? Was Paul crucified for you? Were you baptized into[b] the name of Paul? ¹⁴I am thankful that I did not baptize any of you except Crispus and Gaius, ¹⁵so no one can say that you were baptized into my name. ¹⁶(Yes, I also baptized the household of Stephanas; beyond that, I don't remember if I baptized anyone else.) ¹⁷For Christ did not send me to baptize, but to preach the gospel — not with words of human wisdom, lest the cross of Christ be emptied of its power.

Christ the Wisdom and Power of God

¹⁸For the message of the cross is foolishness to those who are perishing, but to us who are being saved it is the power of God. ¹⁹For it is written:

"I will destroy the wisdom of the
  wise;
    the intelligence of the
      intelligent I will frustrate."[c]

²⁰Where is the wise man? Where is the scholar? Where is the philosopher of this age? Has not God made foolish the wisdom of the world? ²¹For since in the wisdom of God the world through its wisdom did not know him, God was pleased through the foolishness of what was

---

a 12 That is, Peter   *b 13* Or *in*; also in verse 15   *c 19* Isaiah 29:14

220

preached to save those who believe. 22 Jews demand miraculous signs and Greeks look for wisdom, 23 but we preach Christ crucified: a stumbling block to Jews and foolishness to Gentiles, 24 but to those whom God has called, both Jews and Greeks, Christ the power of God and the wisdom of God. 25 For the foolishness of God is wiser than man's wisdom, and the weakness of God is stronger than man's strength.

26 Brothers, think of what you were when you were called. Not many of you were wise by human standards; not many were influential; not many were of noble birth. 27 But God chose the foolish things of the world to shame the wise; God chose the weak things of the world to shame the strong. 28 He chose the lowly things of this world and the despised things — and the things that are not — to nullify the things that are, 29 so that no one may boast before him. 30 It is because of him that you are in Christ Jesus, who has become for us wisdom from God — that is, our righteousness, holiness and redemption. 31 Therefore, as it is written: "Let him who boasts boast in the Lord."[d]

2 1 When I came to you, brothers, I did not come with eloquence or superior wisdom as I proclaimed to you the testimony about God.[e] 2 For I resolved to know nothing while I was with you except Jesus Christ and him crucified. 3 I came to you in weakness and fear, and with much trembling. 4 My message and my preaching were not with wise and persuasive words, but with a demonstration of the Spirit's power,

5 so that your faith might not rest on men's wisdom, but on God's power.

Wisdom From the Spirit

6 We do, however, speak a message of wisdom among the mature, but not the wisdom of this age or of the rulers of this age, who are coming to nothing. 7 No, we speak of God's secret wisdom, a wisdom that has been hidden and that God destined for our glory before time began. 8 None of the rulers of this age understood it, for if they had, they would not have crucified the Lord of glory. 9 However, as it is written:

"No eye has seen,
    no ear has heard,
    no mind has conceived
    what God has prepared for
        those who love him"[f]—

10 but God has revealed it to us by his Spirit.

The Spirit searches all things, even the deep things of God. 11 For who among men knows the thoughts of a man except the man's spirit within him? In the same way no one knows the thoughts of God except the Spirit of God. 12 We have not received the spirit of the world but the Spirit who is from God, that we may understand what God has freely given us. 13 This is what we speak, not in words taught us by human wisdom but in words taught by the Spirit, expressing spiritual truths in spiritual words.[g] 14 The man without the Spirit does not accept the things that come from the Spirit of God, for they are foolishness to him, and he cannot understand them, because they are spiritually discerned. 15 The spiritual

---

d 31 Jer. 9:24   e 1 Some manuscripts as I proclaimed to you God's mystery
f 9 Isaiah 64:4   g 13 Or Spirit, interpreting spiritual truths to spiritual men

man makes judgments about all things, but he himself is not subject to any man's judgment:

16 "For who has known the mind
     of the Lord
   that he may instruct him?"[h]

But we have the mind of Christ.

On Divisions in the Church

3 1 Brothers, I could not address you as spiritual but as worldly—mere infants in Christ. 2 I gave you milk, not solid food, for you were not yet ready for it. Indeed, you are still not ready. 3 You are still worldly. For since there is jealousy and quarreling among you, are you not worldly? Are you not acting like mere men? 4 For when one says, "I follow Paul," and another, "I follow Apollos," are you not mere men?

5 What, after all, is Apollos? And what is Paul? Only servants, through whom you came to believe—as the Lord has assigned to each his task. 6 I planted the seed, Apollos watered it, but God made it grow. 7 So neither he who plants nor he who waters is anything, but only God, who makes things grow. 8 The man who plants and the man who waters have one purpose, and each will be rewarded according to his own labor. 9 For we are God's fellow workers; you are God's field, God's building.

10 By the grace God has given me, I laid a foundation as an expert builder, and someone else is building on it. But each one should be careful how he builds. 11 For no one can lay any foundation other than the one already laid, which is Jesus Christ. 12 If any man builds on this foundation using gold, silver, costly stones,

wood, hay or straw, 13 his work will be shown for what it is, because the Day will bring it to light. It will be revealed with fire, and the fire will test the quality of each man's work. 14 If what he has built survives, he will receive his reward. 15 If it is burned up, he will suffer loss; he himself will be saved, but only as one escaping through the flames.

16 Don't you know that you yourselves are God's temple and that God's Spirit lives in you? 17 If anyone destroys God's temple, God will destroy him; for God's temple is sacred, and you are that temple.

18 Do not deceive yourselves. If any one of you thinks he is wise by the standards of this age, he should become a "fool" so that he may become wise. 19 For the wisdom of this world is foolishness in God's sight. As it is written: "He catches the wise in their craftiness"[i]; 20 and again, "The Lord knows that the thoughts of the wise are futile."[j] 21 So then, no more boasting about men! All things are yours, 22 whether Paul or Apollos or Cephas[k] or the world or life or death or the present or the future—all are yours, 23 and you are of Christ, and Christ is of God.

Apostles of Christ

4 1 So then, men ought to regard us as servants of Christ and as those entrusted with the secret things of God. 2 Now it is required that those who have been given a trust must prove faithful. 3 I care very little if I am judged by you or by any human court; indeed, I do not even judge myself. 4 My conscience is clear, but that does not make me innocent. It is the Lord who judges me. 5 Therefore judge

---

h 16 Isaiah 40:13   i 19 Job 5:13   j 20 Psalm 94:11   k 22 That is, Peter

nothing before the appointed time; wait till the Lord comes. He will bring to light what is hidden in darkness and will expose the motives of men's hearts. At that time each will receive his praise from God.

6 Now, brothers, I have applied these things to myself and Apollos for your benefit, so that you may learn from us the meaning of the saying, "Do not go beyond what is written." Then you will not take pride in one man over against another. 7 For who makes you different from anyone else? What do you have that you did not receive? And if you did receive it, why do you boast as though you did not?

8 Already you have all you want! Already you have become rich! You have become kings—and that without us! How I wish that you really had become kings so that we might be kings with you! 9 For it seems to me that God has put us apostles on display at the end of the procession, like men condemned to die in the arena. We have been made a spectacle to the whole universe, to angels as well as to men. 10 We are fools for Christ, but you are so wise in Christ! We are weak, but you are strong! You are honored, we are dishonored! 11 To this very hour we go hungry and thirsty, we are in rags, we are brutally treated, we are homeless. 12 We work hard with our own hands. When we are cursed, we bless; when we are persecuted, we endure it; 13 when we are slandered, we answer kindly. Up to this moment we have become the scum of the earth, the refuse of the world.

14 I am not writing this to shame you, but to warn you, as my dear children. 15 Even though you have ten thousand guardians in Christ, you do not have many fathers, for in Christ Jesus I became your father through the gospel. 16 Therefore I urge you to imitate me. 17 For this reason I am sending to you Timothy, my son whom I love, who is faithful in the Lord. He will remind you of my way of life in Christ Jesus, which agrees with what I teach everywhere in every church.

18 Some of you have become arrogant, as if I were not coming to you. 19 But I will come to you very soon, if the Lord is willing, and then I will find out not only how these arrogant people are talking, but what power they have. 20 For the kingdom of God is not a matter of talk but of power. 21 What do you prefer? Shall I come to you with a whip, or in love and with a gentle spirit?

Expel the Immoral Brother!

5 1 It is actually reported that there is sexual immorality among you, and of a kind that does not occur even among pagans: A man has his father's wife. 2 And you are proud! Shouldn't you rather have been filled with grief and have put out of your fellowship the man who did this? 3 Even though I am not physically present, I am with you in spirit. And I have already passed judgment on the one who did this, just as if I were present. 4 When you are assembled in the name of our Lord Jesus and I am with you in spirit, and the power of our Lord Jesus is present, 5 hand this man over to Satan, so that the sinful nature[l] may be destroyed and his spirit saved on the day of the Lord.

---

l 5 Or *that his body*; or *that the flesh*

6 Your boasting is not good. Don't you know that a little yeast works through the whole batch of dough? 7 Get rid of the old yeast that you may be a new batch without yeast — as you really are. For Christ, our Passover lamb, has been sacrificed. 8 Therefore let us keep the Festival, not with the old yeast, the yeast of malice and wickedness, but with bread without yeast, the bread of sincerity and truth.

9 I have written you in my letter not to associate with sexually immoral people — 10 not at all meaning the people of this world who are immoral, or the greedy and swindlers, or idolaters. In that case you would have to leave this world. 11 But now I am writing you that you must not associate with anyone who calls himself a brother but is sexually immoral or greedy, an idolater or a slanderer, a drunkard or a swindler. With such a man do not even eat.

12 What business is it of mine to judge those outside the church? Are you not to judge those inside? 13 God will judge those outside. "Expel the wicked man from among you."[m]

Lawsuits Among Believers

6 1 If any of you has a dispute with another, dare he take it before the ungodly for judgment instead of before the saints? 2 Do you not know that the saints will judge the world? And if you are to judge the world, are you not competent to judge trivial cases? 3 Do you not know that we will judge angels? How much more the things of this life! 4 Therefore, if you have disputes about such matters, appoint as judges even men of

little account in the church![n] 5 I say this to shame you. Is it possible that there is nobody among you wise enough to judge a dispute between believers? 6 But instead, one brother goes to law against another — and this in front of unbelievers!

7 The very fact that you have lawsuits among you means you have been completely defeated already. Why not rather be wronged? Why not rather be cheated? 8 Instead, you yourselves cheat and do wrong, and you do this to your brothers.

9 Do you not know that the wicked will not inherit the kingdom of God? Do not be deceived: Neither the sexually immoral nor idolaters nor adulterers nor male prostitutes nor homosexual offenders 10 nor thieves nor the greedy nor drunkards nor slanderers nor swindlers will inherit the kingdom of God. 11 And that is what some of you were. But you were washed, you were sanctified, you were justified in the name of the Lord Jesus Christ and by the Spirit of our God.

Sexual Immorality

12 "Everything is permissible for me" — but not everything is beneficial. "Everything is permissible for me" — but I will not be mastered by anything. 13 "Food for the stomach and the stomach for food" — but God will destroy them both. The body is not meant for sexual immorality, but for the Lord, and the Lord for the body. 14 By his power God raised the Lord from the dead, and he will raise us also. 15 Do you not know that your bodies are members of Christ himself? Shall I then take the members

---

m 13 Deut. 17:7; 19:19; 21:21; 22:21,24; 24:7   n 4 Or matters, do you appoint as judges men of little account in the church?

of Christ and unite them with a prostitute? Never! **16** Do you not know that he who unites himself with a prostitute is one with her in body? For it is said, "The two will become one flesh."[o] **17** But he who unites himself with the Lord is one with him in spirit.

18 Flee from sexual immorality. All other sins a man commits are outside his body, but he who sins sexually sins against his own body. **19** Do you not know that your body is a temple of the Holy Spirit, who is in you, whom you have received from God? You are not your own; **20** you were bought at a price. Therefore honor God with your body.

Marriage

7 **1** Now for the matters you wrote about: It is good for a man not to marry.[p] **2** But since there is so much immorality, each man should have his own wife, and each woman her own husband. **3** The husband should fulfill his marital duty to his wife, and likewise the wife to her husband. **4** The wife's body does not belong to her alone but also to her husband. In the same way, the husband's body does not belong to him alone but also to his wife. **5** Do not deprive each other except by mutual consent and for a time, so that you may devote yourselves to prayer. Then come together again so that Satan will not tempt you because of your lack of self-control. **6** I say this as a concession, not as a command. **7** I wish that all men were as I am. But each man has his own gift from God; one has this gift, another has that.

8 Now to the unmarried and the widows I say: It is good for them to stay unmarried, as I am. **9** But if they cannot control themselves, they should marry, for it is better to marry than to burn with passion.

10 To the married I give this command (not I, but the Lord): A wife must not separate from her husband. **11** But if she does, she must remain unmarried or else be reconciled to her husband. And a husband must not divorce his wife.

12 To the rest I say this (I, not the Lord): If any brother has a wife who is not a believer and she is willing to live with him, he must not divorce her. **13** And if a woman has a husband who is not a believer and he is willing to live with her, she must not divorce him. **14** For the unbelieving husband has been sanctified through his wife, and the unbelieving wife has been sanctified through her believing husband. Otherwise your children would be unclean, but as it is, they are holy.

15 But if the unbeliever leaves, let him do so. A believing man or woman is not bound in such circumstances; God has called us to live in peace. **16** How do you know, wife, whether you will save your husband? Or, how do you know, husband, whether you will save your wife?

17 Nevertheless, each one should retain the place in life that the Lord assigned to him and to which God has called him. This is the rule I lay down in all the churches. **18** Was a man already circumcised when he was called? He should not become uncircumcised. Was a man uncircumcised when he was called? He should not be circumcised. **19** Circumcision is nothing and uncircumcision is nothing. Keeping God's com-

---

o 16 Gen. 2:24   *p* 1 Or *"It is good for a man not to have sexual relations with a woman."*

mands is what counts. 20 Each one should remain in the situation which he was in when God called him. 21 Were you a slave when you were called? Don't let it trouble you — although if you can gain your freedom, do so. 22 For he who was a slave when he was called by the Lord is the Lord's freedman; similarly, he who was a free man when he was called is Christ's slave. 23 You were bought at a price; do not become slaves of men. 24 Brothers, each man, as responsible to God, should remain in the situation God called him to.

25 Now about virgins: I have no command from the Lord, but I give a judgment as one who by the Lord's mercy is trustworthy. 26 Because of the present crisis, I think that it is good for you to remain as you are. 27 Are you married? Do not seek a divorce. Are you unmarried? Do not look for a wife. 28 But if you do marry, you have not sinned; and if a virgin marries, she has not sinned. But those who marry will face many troubles in this life, and I want to spare you this.

29 What I mean, brothers, is that the time is short. From now on those who have wives should live as if they had none; 30 those who mourn, as if they did not; those who are happy, as if they were not; those who buy something, as if it were not theirs to keep; 31 those who use the things of the world, as if not engrossed in them. For this world in its present form is passing away.

32 I would like you to be free from concern. An unmarried man is concerned about the Lord's affairs — how he can please the Lord. 33 But a married man is concerned about the affairs of this world — how he can please his wife — 34 and his interests are divided. An unmarried woman or virgin is concerned about the Lord's affairs: Her aim is to be devoted to the Lord in both body and spirit. But a married woman is concerned about the affairs of this world — how she can please her husband. 35 I am saying this for your own good, not to restrict you, but that you may live in a right way in undivided devotion to the Lord.

36 If anyone thinks he is acting improperly toward the virgin he is engaged to, and if she is getting along in years and he feels he ought to marry, he should do as he wants. He is not sinning. They should get married. 37 But the man who has settled the matter in his own mind, who is under no compulsion but has control over his own will, and who has made up his mind not to marry the virgin — this man also does the right thing. 38 So then, he who marries the virgin does right, but he who does not marry her does even better.q

39 A woman is bound to her husband as long as he lives. But if her husband dies, she is free to marry anyone she wishes, but he must belong to the Lord. 40 In my judgment, she is happier if she stays as she is — and I think that I too have the Spirit of God.

q 38 Or 36 If anyone thinks he is not treating his daughter properly, and if she is getting along in years, and he feels she ought to marry, he should do as he wants. He is not sinning. He should let her get married. 37 But the man who has settled the matter in his own mind, who is under no compulsion but has control over his own will, and who has made up his mind to keep the virgin unmarried — this man also does the right thing. 38 So then, he who gives his virgin in marriage does right, but he who does not give her in marriage does even better.

Food Sacrificed to Idols

8 **1** Now about food sacrificed to idols: We know that we all possess knowledge.[r] Knowledge puffs up, but love builds up. **2** The man who thinks he knows something does not yet know as he ought to know. **3** But the man who loves God is known by God.

4 So then, about eating food sacrificed to idols: We know that an idol is nothing at all in the world and that there is no God but one. **5** For even if there are so-called gods, whether in heaven or on earth (as indeed there are many "gods" and many "lords"), **6** yet for us there is but one God, the Father, from whom all things came and for whom we live; and there is but one Lord, Jesus Christ, through whom all things came and through whom we live.

7 But not everyone knows this. Some people are still so accustomed to idols that when they eat such food they think of it as having been sacrificed to an idol, and since their conscience is weak, it is defiled. **8** But food does not bring us near to God; we are no worse if we do not eat, and no better if we do.

9 Be careful, however, that the exercise of your freedom does not become a stumbling block to the weak. **10** For if anyone with a weak conscience sees you who have this knowledge eating in an idol's temple, won't he be emboldened to eat what has been sacrificed to idols? **11** So this weak brother, for whom Christ died, is destroyed by your knowledge. **12** When you sin against your brothers in this way and wound their weak conscience, you sin

against Christ. **13** Therefore, if what I eat causes my brother to fall into sin, I will never eat meat again, so that I will not cause him to fall.

The Rights of an Apostle

9 **1** Am I not free? Am I not an apostle? Have I not seen Jesus our Lord? Are you not the result of my work in the Lord? **2** Even though I may not be an apostle to others, surely I am to you! For you are the seal of my apostleship in the Lord.

3 This is my defense to those who sit in judgment on me. **4** Don't we have the right to food and drink? **5** Don't we have the right to take a believing wife along with us, as do the other apostles and the Lord's brothers and Cephas[s]? **6** Or is it only I and Barnabas who must work for a living?

7 Who serves as a soldier at his own expense? Who plants a vineyard and does not eat of its grapes? Who tends a flock and does not drink of the milk? **8** Do I say this merely from a human point of view? Doesn't the Law say the same thing? **9** For it is written in the Law of Moses: "Do not muzzle an ox while it is treading out the grain."[t] Is it about oxen that God is concerned? **10** Surely he says this for us, doesn't he? Yes, this was written for us, because when the plowman plows and the thresher threshes, they ought to do so in the hope of sharing in the harvest. **11** If we have sown spiritual seed among you, is it too much if we reap a material harvest from you? **12** If others have this right of support from you, shouldn't we have it all the more?

But we did not use this right. On the contrary, we put up with anything rather than hinder the gospel

---

[r] 1 Or *"We all possess knowledge," as you say*   [s] 5 That is, Peter   [t] 9 Deut. 25:4

of Christ. 13 Don't you know that those who work in the temple get their food from the temple, and those who serve at the altar share in what is offered on the altar? 14 In the same way, the Lord has commanded that those who preach the gospel should receive their living from the gospel.

15 But I have not used any of these rights. And I am not writing this in the hope that you will do such things for me. I would rather die than have anyone deprive me of this boast. 16 Yet when I preach the gospel, I cannot boast, for I am compelled to preach. Woe to me if I do not preach the gospel! 17 If I preach voluntarily, I have a reward; if not voluntarily, I am simply discharging the trust committed to me. 18 What then is my reward? Just this: that in preaching the gospel I may offer it free of charge, and so not make use of my rights in preaching it.

19 Though I am free and belong to no man, I make myself a slave to everyone, to win as many as possible. 20 To the Jews I became like a Jew, to win the Jews. To those under the law I became like one under the law (though I myself am not under the law), so as to win those under the law. 21 To those not having the law I became like one not having the law (though I am not free from God's law but am under Christ's law), so as to win those not having the law. 22 To the weak I became weak, to win the weak. I have become all things to all men so that by all possible means I might save some. 23 I do all this for the sake of the gospel, that I may share in its blessings.

24 Do you not know that in a race all the runners run, but only one gets the prize? Run in such a way as to get the prize.

25 Everyone who competes in the games goes into strict training. They do it to get a crown that will not last; but we do it to get a crown that will last forever. 26 Therefore I do not run like a man running aimlessly; I do not fight like a man beating the air. 27 No, I beat my body and make it my slave so that after I have preached to others, I myself will not be disqualified for the prize.

Warnings From Israel's History

10 1 For I do not want you to be ignorant of the fact, brothers, that our forefathers were all under the cloud and that they all passed through the sea. 2 They were all baptized into Moses in the cloud and in the sea. 3 They all ate the same spiritual food 4 and drank the same spiritual drink; for they drank from the spiritual rock that accompanied them, and that rock was Christ. 5 Nevertheless, God was not pleased with most of them; their bodies were scattered over the desert.

6 Now these things occurred as examplesu to keep us from setting our hearts on evil things as they did. 7 Do not be idolaters, as some of them were; as it is written: "The people sat down to eat and drink and got up to indulge in pagan revelry."v 8 We should not commit sexual immorality, as some of them did—and in one day twenty-three thousand of them died. 9 We should not test the Lord, as some of them did—and were killed by snakes. 10 And do not grumble, as some of them did—and were killed by the destroying angel.

u 6 Or types; also in verse 11   v 7 Exodus 32:6

11 These things happened to them as examples and were written down as warnings for us, on whom the fulfillment of the ages has come. 12 So, if you think you are standing firm, be careful that you don't fall! 13 No temptation has seized you except what is common to man. And God is faithful; he will not let you be tempted beyond what you can bear. But when you are tempted, he will also provide a way out so that you can stand up under it.

Idol Feasts and the Lord's Supper

14 Therefore, my dear friends, flee from idolatry. 15 I speak to sensible people; judge for yourselves what I say. 16 Is not the cup of thanksgiving for which we give thanks a participation in the blood of Christ? And is not the bread that we break a participation in the body of Christ? 17 Because there is one loaf, we, who are many, are one body, for we all partake of the one loaf.

18 Consider the people of Israel: Do not those who eat the sacrifices participate in the altar? 19 Do I mean then that a sacrifice offered to an idol is anything, or that an idol is anything? 20 No, but the sacrifices of pagans are offered to demons, not to God, and I do not want you to be participants with demons. 21 You cannot drink the cup of the Lord and the cup of demons too; you cannot have a part in both the Lord's table and the table of demons. 22 Are we trying to arouse the Lord's jealousy? Are we stronger than he?

The Believer's Freedom

23 "Everything is permissible"—but not everything is beneficial. "Every-thing is permissible"—but not every-thing is constructive. 24 Nobody should seek his own good, but the good of others.

25 Eat anything sold in the meat market without raising questions of conscience, 26 for, "The earth is the Lord's, and everything in it."w

27 If some unbeliever invites you to a meal and you want to go, eat whatever is put before you without raising questions of conscience. 28 But if anyone says to you, "This has been offered in sacrifice," then do not eat it, both for the sake of the man who told you and for conscience' sakex— 29 the other man's conscience, I mean, not yours. For why should my freedom be judged by another's conscience? 30 If I take part in the meal with thankfulness, why am I denounced because of something I thank God for?

31 So whether you eat or drink or whatever you do, do it all for the glory of God. 32 Do not cause anyone to stumble, whether Jews, Greeks or the church of God— 33 even as I try to please everybody in every way. For I am not seeking my own good but the good of many, so that they may be saved.

11 1 Follow my example, as I follow the example of Christ.

Propriety in Worship

2 I praise you for remembering me in everything and for holding to the teachings,y just as I passed them on to you.

3 Now I want you to realize that the head of every man is Christ, and the head of the woman is man, and the head of Christ is God. 4 Every

---

w 26 Psalm 24:1   x 28 Some manuscripts conscience' sake, for "the earth is the Lord's and everything in it"   y 2 Or traditions

1 CORINTHIANS 11

230

man who prays or prophesies with his head covered dishonors his head. 5 And every woman who prays or prophesies with her head uncovered dishonors her head—it is just as though her head were shaved. 6 If a woman does not cover her head, she should have her hair cut off; and if it is a disgrace for a woman to have her hair cut or shaved off, she should cover her head. 7 A man ought not to cover his head,z since he is the image and glory of God; but the woman is the glory of man. 8 For man did not come from woman, but woman from man; 9 neither was man created for woman, but woman for man. 10 For this reason, and because of the angels, the woman ought to have a sign of authority on her head.

11 In the Lord, however, woman is not independent of man, nor is man independent of woman. 12 For as woman came from man, so also man is born of woman. But everything comes from God. 13 Judge for yourselves: Is it proper for a woman to pray to God with her head uncovered? 14 Does not the very nature of things teach you that if a man has long hair, it is a disgrace to him, 15 but that if a woman has long hair, it is her glory? For long hair is given to her as a covering. 16 If anyone wants to be contentious about this, we have no other practice—nor do the churches of God.

The Lord's Supper

17 In the following directives I have no praise for you, for your meetings do more harm than good. 18 In the first place, I hear that when you come together as a church, there are divisions among you, and to some extent I believe it. 19 No doubt there have to be differences among you to show which of you have God's approval. 20 When you come together, it is not the Lord's Supper you eat, 21 for as you eat, each of you goes ahead without waiting for anybody else. One remains hungry, another gets drunk. 22 Don't you have homes to eat and drink in? Or do you despise the church of God and humiliate those who have nothing? What shall I say to you? Shall I praise you for this? Certainly not!

23 For I received from the Lord what I also passed on to you: The Lord Jesus, on the night he was betrayed, took bread, 24 and when he had given thanks, he broke it and said, "This is my body, which is for you; do this in remembrance of me." 25 In the same way, after supper he took the cup, saying, "This cup is the new covenant in my blood; do this whenever you drink it, in remembrance of me." 26 For whenever you eat this bread and drink this cup, you proclaim the Lord's death until he comes.

27 Therefore, whoever eats the bread or drinks the cup of the Lord in an unworthy manner will be guilty of sinning against the body and blood of the Lord. 28 A man ought to examine himself before he eats of the bread and drinks of the cup. 29 For anyone who eats and drinks without

z 7 Or 4 Every man who prays or prophesies with long hair dishonors his head. 5 And every woman who prays or prophesies with no covering of hair on her head dishonors her head—she is just like one of the "shorn women." 6 If a woman has no covering, let her be for now with short hair, but since it is a disgrace for a woman to have her hair shorn or shaved, she should grow it again. 7 A man ought not to have long hair

recognizing the body of the Lord eats and drinks judgment on himself. **30** That is why many among you are weak and sick, and a number of you have fallen asleep. **31** But if we judged ourselves, we would not come under judgment. **32** When we are judged by the Lord, we are being disciplined so that we will not be condemned with the world.

33 So then, my brothers, when you come together to eat, wait for each other. **34** If anyone is hungry, he should eat at home, so that when you meet together it may not result in judgment.

And when I come I will give further directions.

Spiritual Gifts

12 **1** Now about spiritual gifts, brothers, I do not want you to be ignorant. **2** You know that when you were pagans, somehow or other you were influenced and led astray to mute idols. **3** Therefore I tell you that no one who is speaking by the Spirit of God says, "Jesus be cursed," and no one can say, "Jesus is Lord," except by the Holy Spirit.

4 There are different kinds of gifts, but the same Spirit. **5** There are different kinds of service, but the same Lord. **6** There are different kinds of working, but the same God works all of them in all men.

7 Now to each one the manifestation of the Spirit is given for the common good. **8** To one there is given through the Spirit the message of wisdom, to another the message of knowledge by means of the same Spirit, **9** to another faith by the same Spirit, to another gifts of healing by

that one Spirit, **10** to another miraculous powers, to another prophecy, to another distinguishing between spirits, to another speaking in different kinds of tongues,*a* and to still another the interpretation of tongues.*b* **11** All these are the work of one and the same Spirit, and he gives them to each one, just as he determines.

12 The body is a unit, though it is made up of many parts; and though all its parts are many, they form one body. So it is with Christ. **13** For we were all baptized by*c* one Spirit into one body—whether Jews or Greeks, slave or free—and we were all given the one Spirit to drink.

14 Now the body is not made up of one part but of many. **15** If the foot should say, "Because I am not a hand, I do not belong to the body," it would not for that reason cease to be part of the body. **16** And if the ear should say, "Because I am not an eye, I do not belong to the body," it would not for that reason cease to be part of the body. **17** If the whole body were an eye, where would the sense of hearing be? If the whole body were an ear, where would the sense of smell be? **18** But in fact God has arranged the parts in the body, every one of them, just as he wanted them to be. **19** If they were all one part, where would the body be? **20** As it is, there are many parts, but one body.

21 The eye cannot say to the hand, "I don't need you!" And the head cannot say to the feet, "I don't need you!" **22** On the contrary, those parts of the body that seem to be weaker are indispensable, **23** and the parts that we think are less honorable we

a 10 Or languages; also in verse 28   *b 10 Or languages; also in verse 28*
c 13 Or with; or in

treat with special honor. And the parts that are unpresentable are treated with special modesty, 24 while our presentable parts need no special treatment. But God has combined the members of the body and has given greater honor to the parts that lacked it, 25 so that there should be no division in the body, but that its parts should have equal concern for each other. 26 If one part suffers, every part suffers with it; if one part is honored, every part rejoices with it.

27 Now you are the body of Christ, and each one of you is a part of it. 28 And in the church God has appointed first of all apostles, second prophets, third teachers, then workers of miracles, also those having gifts of healing, those able to help others, those with gifts of administration, and those speaking in different kinds of tongues. 29 Are all apostles? Are all prophets? Are all teachers? Do all work miracles? 30 Do all have gifts of healing? Do all speak in tongues*d*? Do all interpret? 31 But eagerly desire*e* the greater gifts.

And now I will show you the most excellent way.

Love

13 ¹ If I speak in the tongues*f* of men and of angels, but have not love, I am only a resounding gong or a clanging cymbal. ² If I have the gift of prophecy and can fathom all mysteries and all knowledge, and if I have a faith that can move mountains, but have not love, I am nothing. ³ If I give all I possess to the poor and surrender my body to the flames,*g* but have not love, I gain nothing.

⁴ Love is patient, love is kind. It does not envy, it does not boast, it is not proud. ⁵ It is not rude, it is not self-seeking, it is not easily angered, it keeps no record of wrongs. ⁶ Love does not delight in evil but rejoices with the truth. ⁷ It always protects, always trusts, always hopes, always perseveres.

⁸ Love never fails. But where there are prophecies, they will cease; where there are tongues, they will be stilled; where there is knowledge, it will pass away. ⁹ For we know in part and we prophesy in part, ¹⁰ but when perfection comes, the imperfect disappears. ¹¹ When I was a child, I talked like a child, I thought like a child, I reasoned like a child. When I became a man, I put childish ways behind me. ¹² Now we see but a poor reflection as in a mirror; then we shall see face to face. Now I know in part; then I shall know fully, even as I am fully known.

¹³ And now these three remain: faith, hope and love. But the greatest of these is love.

Gifts of Prophecy and Tongues

14 ¹ Follow the way of love and eagerly desire spiritual gifts, especially the gift of prophecy. ² For anyone who speaks in a tongue*h* does not speak to men but to God. Indeed, no one understands him; he utters mysteries with his spirit.*i* ³ But everyone who prophesies speaks to men for their strengthening, encouragement and comfort. ⁴ He who speaks in a tongue edifies himself, but he who prophesies edifies the

---

d 30 Or *other languages*   *e* 31 Or *But you are eagerly desiring*   *f* 1 Or *languages*
g 3 Some early manuscripts *body that I may boast*   *h* 2 Or *another language; also in verses*
4, 13, 14, 19, 26 and 27   *i* 2 Or *by the Spirit*

church. 5 I would like every one of you to speak in tongues,j but I would rather have you prophesy. He who prophesies is greater than one who speaks in tongues,k unless he interprets, so that the church may be edified.

6 Now, brothers, if I come to you and speak in tongues, what good will I be to you, unless I bring you some revelation or knowledge or prophecy or word of instruction? 7 Even in the case of lifeless things that make sounds, such as the flute or harp, how will anyone know what tune is being played unless there is a distinction in the notes? 8 Again, if the trumpet does not sound a clear call, who will get ready for battle? 9 So it is with you. Unless you speak intelligible words with your tongue, how will anyone know what you are saying? You will just be speaking into the air. 10 Undoubtedly there are all sorts of languages in the world, yet none of them is without meaning. 11 If then I do not grasp the meaning of what someone is saying, I am a foreigner to the speaker, and he is a foreigner to me. 12 So it is with you. Since you are eager to have spiritual gifts, try to excel in gifts that build up the church.

13 For this reason anyone who speaks in a tongue should pray that he may interpret what he says. 14 For if I pray in a tongue, my spirit prays, but my mind is unfruitful. 15 So what shall I do? I will pray with my spirit, but I will also pray with my mind; I will sing with my spirit, but I will also sing with my mind. 16 If you are praising God with your spirit, how can one who finds himself among those who do not understandl say "Amen" to your thanksgiving, since he does not know what you are saying? 17 You may be giving thanks well enough, but the other man is not edified.

18 I thank God that I speak in tongues more than all of you. 19 But in the church I would rather speak five intelligible words to instruct others than ten thousand words in a tongue.

20 Brothers, stop thinking like children. In regard to evil be infants, but in your thinking be adults. 21 In the Law it is written:

> "Through men of strange tongues
>   and through the lips of
>   foreigners
> I will speak to this people,
>   but even then they will not
>   listen to me,"m

says the Lord.

22 Tongues, then, are a sign, not for believers but for unbelievers; prophecy, however, is for believers, not for unbelievers. 23 So if the whole church comes together and everyone speaks in tongues, and some who do not understandn or some unbelievers come in, will they not say that you are out of your mind? 24 But if an unbeliever or someone who does not understando comes in while everybody is prophesying, he will be convinced by all that he is a sinner and will be judged by all, 25 and the secrets of his heart will be laid bare. So he will fall down and worship God, exclaiming, "God is really among you!"

Orderly Worship

26 What then shall we say, brothers? When you come together,

j 5 Or other languages; also in verses 6, 18, 22, 23 and 39   k 5 Or other languages; also in verses 6, 18, 22, 23 and 39   l 16 Or among the inquirers   m 21 Isaiah 28:11,12
n 23 Or some inquirers   o 24 Or or some inquirer

everyone has a hymn, or a word of instruction, a revelation, a tongue or an interpretation. All of these must be done for the strengthening of the church. 27 If anyone speaks in a tongue, two—or at the most three—should speak, one at a time, and someone must interpret. 28 If there is no interpreter, the speaker should keep quiet in the church and speak to himself and God.

29 Two or three prophets should speak, and the others should weigh carefully what is said. 30 And if a revelation comes to someone who is sitting down, the first speaker should stop. 31 For you can all prophesy in turn so that everyone may be instructed and encouraged. 32 The spirits of prophets are subject to the control of prophets. 33 For God is not a God of disorder but of peace.

As in all the congregations of the saints, 34 women should remain silent in the churches. They are not allowed to speak, but must be in submission, as the Law says. 35 If they want to inquire about something, they should ask their own husbands at home; for it is disgraceful for a woman to speak in the church.

36 Did the word of God originate with you? Or are you the only people it has reached? 37 If anybody thinks he is a prophet or spiritually gifted, let him acknowledge that what I am writing to you is the Lord's command. 38 If he ignores this, he himself will be ignored.[p]

39 Therefore, my brothers, be eager to prophesy, and do not forbid speaking in tongues. 40 But everything should be done in a fitting and orderly way.

The Resurrection of Christ

15 1 Now, brothers, I want to remind you of the gospel I preached to you, which you received and on which you have taken your stand. 2 By this gospel you are saved, if you hold firmly to the word I preached to you. Otherwise, you have believed in vain.

3 For what I received I passed on to you as of first importance[q]: that Christ died for our sins according to the Scriptures, 4 that he was buried, that he was raised on the third day according to the Scriptures, 5 and that he appeared to Peter,[r] and then to the Twelve. 6 After that, he appeared to more than five hundred of the brothers at the same time, most of whom are still living, though some have fallen asleep. 7 Then he appeared to James, then to all the apostles, 8 and last of all he appeared to me also, as to one abnormally born.

9 For I am the least of the apostles and do not even deserve to be called an apostle, because I persecuted the church of God. 10 But by the grace of God I am what I am, and his grace to me was not without effect. No, I worked harder than all of them—yet not I, but the grace of God that was with me. 11 Whether, then, it was I or they, this is what we preach, and this is what you believed.

The Resurrection of the Dead

12 But if it is preached that Christ has been raised from the dead, how can some of you say that there is no resurrection of the dead? 13 If there is no resurrection of the dead, then

[p] 38 Some manuscripts *If he is ignorant of this, let him be ignorant* [q] 3 Or *you at the first*
[r] 5 Greek *Cephas*

not even Christ has been raised. 14 And if Christ has not been raised, our preaching is useless and so is your faith. 15 More than that, we are then found to be false witnesses about God, for we have testified about God that he raised Christ from the dead. But he did not raise him if in fact the dead are not raised. 16 For if the dead are not raised, then Christ has not been raised either. 17 And if Christ has not been raised, your faith is futile; you are still in your sins. 18 Then those also who have fallen asleep in Christ are lost. 19 If only for this life we have hope in Christ, we are to be pitied more than all men.

20 But Christ has indeed been raised from the dead, the firstfruits of those who have fallen asleep. 21 For since death came through a man, the resurrection of the dead comes also through a man. 22 For as in Adam all die, so in Christ all will be made alive. 23 But each in his own turn: Christ, the firstfruits; then, when he comes, those who belong to him. 24 Then the end will come, when he hands over the kingdom to God the Father after he has destroyed all dominion, authority and power. 25 For he must reign until he has put all his enemies under his feet. 26 The last enemy to be destroyed is death. 27 For he "has put everything under his feet."s Now when it says that "everything" has been put under him, it is clear that this does not include God himself, who put everything under Christ. 28 When he has done this, then the Son himself will be made subject to him who put everything under him, so that God may be all in all.

29 Now if there is no resurrection, what will those do who are baptized for the dead? If the dead are not raised at all, why are people baptized for them? 30 And as for us, why do we endanger ourselves every hour? 31 I die every day—I mean that, brothers—just as surely as I glory over you in Christ Jesus our Lord. 32 If I fought wild beasts in Ephesus for merely human reasons, what have I gained? If the dead are not raised,

"Let us eat and drink,
    for tomorrow we die."t

33 Do not be misled: "Bad company corrupts good character." 34 Come back to your senses as you ought, and stop sinning; for there are some who are ignorant of God—I say this to your shame.

The Resurrection Body

35 But someone may ask, "How are the dead raised? With what kind of body will they come?" 36 How foolish! What you sow does not come to life unless it dies. 37 When you sow, you do not plant the body that will be, but just a seed, perhaps of wheat or of something else. 38 But God gives it a body as he has determined, and to each kind of seed he gives its own body. 39 All flesh is not the same: Men have one kind of flesh, animals have another, birds another and fish another. 40 There are also heavenly bodies and there are earthly bodies; but the splendor of the heavenly bodies is one kind, and the splendor of the earthly bodies is another. 41 The sun has one kind of splendor, the moon another and the stars another; and star differs from star in splendor.

42 So will it be with the resurrection of the dead. The body that is

---

s 27 Psalm 8:6   *t* 32 Isaiah 22:13

sown is perishable, it is raised imperishable; 43 it is sown in dishonor, it is raised in glory; it is sown in weakness, it is raised in power; 44 it is sown a natural body, it is raised a spiritual body.

If there is a natural body, there is also a spiritual body. 45 So it is written: "The first man Adam became a living being"[u]; the last Adam, a lifegiving spirit. 46 The spiritual did not come first, but the natural, and after that the spiritual. 47 The first man was of the dust of the earth, the second man from heaven. 48 As was the earthly man, so are those who are of the earth; and as is the man from heaven, so also are those who are of heaven. 49 And just as we have borne the likeness of the earthly man, so shall we[v] bear the likeness of the man from heaven.

50 I declare to you, brothers, that flesh and blood cannot inherit the kingdom of God, nor does the perishable inherit the imperishable. 51 Listen, I tell you a mystery: We will not all sleep, but we will all be changed— 52 in a flash, in the twinkling of an eye, at the last trumpet. For the trumpet will sound, the dead will be raised imperishable, and we will be changed. 53 For the perishable must clothe itself with the imperishable, and the mortal with immortality. 54 When the perishable has been clothed with the imperishable, and the mortal with immortality, then the saying that is written will come true: "Death has been swallowed up in victory."[w]

55 "Where, O death, is your victory?
    Where, O death, is your sting?"[x]

56 The sting of death is sin, and the power of sin is the law. 57 But thanks be to God! He gives us the victory through our Lord Jesus Christ.

58 Therefore, my dear brothers, stand firm. Let nothing move you. Always give yourselves fully to the work of the Lord, because you know that your labor in the Lord is not in vain.

The Collection for God's People

16 1 Now about the collection for God's people: Do what I told the Galatian churches to do. 2 On the first day of every week, each one of you should set aside a sum of money in keeping with his income, saving it up, so that when I come no collections will have to be made. 3 Then, when I arrive, I will give letters of introduction to the men you approve and send them with your gift to Jerusalem. 4 If it seems advisable for me to go also, they will accompany me.

Personal Requests

5 After I go through Macedonia, I will come to you—for I will be going through Macedonia. 6 Perhaps I will stay with you awhile, or even spend the winter, so that you can help me on my journey, wherever I go. 7 I do not want to see you now and make only a passing visit; I hope to spend some time with you, if the Lord permits. 8 But I will stay on at Ephesus until Pentecost, 9 because a great door for effective work has opened to me, and there are many who oppose me.

10 If Timothy comes, see to it that he has nothing to fear while he is

u 45 Gen. 2:7   v 49 Some early manuscripts *so let us*   w 54 Isaiah 25:8
x 55 Hosea 13:14

with you, for he is carrying on the work of the Lord, just as I am. **11** No one, then, should refuse to accept him. Send him on his way in peace so that he may return to me. I am expecting him along with the brothers.

12 Now about our brother Apollos: I strongly urged him to go to you with the brothers. He was quite unwilling to go now, but he will go when he has the opportunity.

13 Be on your guard; stand firm in the faith; be men of courage; be strong. **14** Do everything in love.

15 You know that the household of Stephanas were the first converts in Achaia, and they have devoted themselves to the service of the saints. I urge you, brothers, **16** to submit to such as these and to everyone who joins in the work, and labors at it. **17** I was glad when Stephanas, For-

tunatus and Achaicus arrived, because they have supplied what was lacking from you. **18** For they refreshed my spirit and yours also. Such men deserve recognition.

Final Greetings

19 The churches in the province of Asia send you greetings. Aquila and Priscilla*y* greet you warmly in the Lord, and so does the church that meets at their house. **20** All the brothers here send you greetings. Greet one another with a holy kiss.

21 I, Paul, write this greeting in my own hand.

22 If anyone does not love the Lord—a curse be on him. Come, O Lord*z*!

23 The grace of the Lord Jesus be with you.

24 My love to all of you in Christ Jesus. Amen.*a*

---

y 19 Greek *Prisca*, a variant of *Priscilla* *z* 22 In Aramaic the expression *Come, O Lord* is *Marana tha*. *a* 24 Some manuscripts do not have *Amen*.

2 Corinthians

1 ¹ Paul, an apostle of Christ Jesus by the will of God, and Timothy our brother,

To the church of God in Corinth, together with all the saints throughout Achaia:

² Grace and peace to you from God our Father and the Lord Jesus Christ.

The God of All Comfort

³ Praise be to the God and Father of our Lord Jesus Christ, the Father of compassion and the God of all comfort, ⁴ who comforts us in all our troubles, so that we can comfort those in any trouble with the comfort we ourselves have received from God. ⁵ For just as the sufferings of Christ flow over into our lives, so also through Christ our comfort overflows. ⁶ If we are distressed, it is for your comfort and salvation; if we are comforted, it is for your comfort, which produces in you patient endurance of the same sufferings we suffer. ⁷ And our hope for you is firm, because we know that just as you share in our sufferings, so also you share in our comfort.

⁸ We do not want you to be uninformed, brothers, about the hardships we suffered in the province of Asia. We were under great pressure, far beyond our ability to endure, so that we despaired even of life. ⁹ Indeed, in our hearts we felt the sentence of death. But this happened that we might not rely on ourselves but on God, who raises the dead. ¹⁰ He has delivered us from such a deadly peril, and he will deliver us. On him we have set our hope that he will continue to deliver us, ¹¹ as you help us by your prayers. Then many will give thanks on our[a] behalf for the gracious favor granted us in answer to the prayers of many.

Paul's Change of Plans

¹² Now this is our boast: Our conscience testifies that we have conducted ourselves in the world, and especially in our relations with you, in the holiness and sincerity that are from God. We have done so not according to worldly wisdom but according to God's grace. ¹³ For we do not write you anything you cannot read or understand. And I hope that, ¹⁴ as you have understood us in part, you will come to understand fully that you can boast of us just as we will boast of you in the day of the Lord Jesus.

¹⁵ Because I was confident of this, I planned to visit you first so that you might benefit twice. ¹⁶ I planned to visit you on my way to Macedonia and to come back to you from Macedonia, and then to have you send me on my way to Judea. ¹⁷ When I planned this, did I do it lightly? Or do I make my plans in a worldly manner so that in the same breath I say, "Yes, yes" and "No, no"?

¹⁸ But as surely as God is faithful, our message to you is not "Yes" and "No." ¹⁹ For the Son of God, Jesus Christ, who was preached among you

---

a 11 Many manuscripts *your*

238

by me and Silas[b] and Timothy, was not "Yes" and "No," but in him it has always been "Yes." **20** For no matter how many promises God has made, they are "Yes" in Christ. And so through him the "Amen" is spoken by us to the glory of God. **21** Now it is God who makes both us and you stand firm in Christ. He anointed us, **22** set his seal of ownership on us, and put his Spirit in our hearts as a deposit, guaranteeing what is to come.

23 I call God as my witness that it was in order to spare you that I did not return to Corinth. **24** Not that we lord it over your faith, but we work with you for your joy, because it is by faith you stand firm.

2 **1** So I made up my mind that I would not make another painful visit to you. **2** For if I grieve you, who is left to make me glad but you whom I have grieved? **3** I wrote as I did so that when I came I should not be distressed by those who ought to make me rejoice. I had confidence in all of you, that you would all share my joy. **4** For I wrote you out of great distress and anguish of heart and with many tears, not to grieve you but to let you know the depth of my love for you.

Forgiveness for the Sinner

5 If anyone has caused grief, he has not so much grieved me as he has grieved all of you, to some extent— not to put it too severely. **6** The punishment inflicted on him by the majority is sufficient for him. **7** Now instead, you ought to forgive and comfort him, so that he will not be overwhelmed by excessive sorrow. **8** I urge you, therefore, to reaffirm your love for him. **9** The reason I wrote

you was to see if you would stand the test and be obedient in everything. **10** If you forgive anyone, I also forgive him. And what I have forgiven— if there was anything to forgive—I have forgiven in the sight of Christ for your sake, **11** in order that Satan might not outwit us. For we are not unaware of his schemes.

Ministers of the New Covenant

12 Now when I went to Troas to preach the gospel of Christ and found that the Lord had opened a door for me, **13** I still had no peace of mind, because I did not find my brother Titus there. So I said good-by to them and went on to Macedonia.

14 But thanks be to God, who always leads us in triumphal procession in Christ and through us spreads everywhere the fragrance of the knowledge of him. **15** For we are to God the aroma of Christ among those who are being saved and those who are perishing. **16** To the one we are the smell of death; to the other, the fragrance of life. And who is equal to such a task? **17** Unlike so many, we do not peddle the word of God for profit. On the contrary, in Christ we speak before God with sincerity, like men sent from God.

3 **1** Are we beginning to commend ourselves again? Or do we need, like some people, letters of recommendation to you or from you? **2** You yourselves are our letter, written on our hearts, known and read by everybody. **3** You show that you are a letter from Christ, the result of our ministry, written not with ink but with the Spirit of the living God, not on tablets of stone but on tablets of human hearts.

---

b **19** Greek *Silvanus,* a variant of *Silas*

4 Such confidence as this is ours through Christ before God. **5** Not that we are competent in ourselves to claim anything for ourselves, but our competence comes from God. **6** He has made us competent as ministers of a new covenant—not of the letter but of the Spirit; for the letter kills, but the Spirit gives life.

The Glory of the New Covenant

7 Now if the ministry that brought death, which was engraved in letters on stone, came with glory, so that the Israelites could not look steadily at the face of Moses because of its glory, fading though it was, **8** will not the ministry of the Spirit be even more glorious? **9** If the ministry that condemns men is glorious, how much more glorious is the ministry that brings righteousness! **10** For what was glorious has no glory now in comparison with the surpassing glory. **11** And if what was fading away came with glory, how much greater is the glory of that which lasts!

12 Therefore, since we have such a hope, we are very bold. **13** We are not like Moses, who would put a veil over his face to keep the Israelites from gazing at it while the radiance was fading away. **14** But their minds were made dull, for to this day the same veil remains when the old covenant is read. It has not been removed, because only in Christ is it taken away. **15** Even to this day when Moses is read, a veil covers their hearts. **16** But whenever anyone turns to the Lord, the veil is taken away. **17** Now the Lord is the Spirit, and where the Spirit of the Lord is, there is freedom. **18** And we, who with unveiled faces all reflect[c] the

Lord's glory, are being transformed into his likeness with ever-increasing glory, which comes from the Lord, who is the Spirit.

Treasures in Jars of Clay

4 **1** Therefore, since through God's mercy we have this ministry, we do not lose heart. **2** Rather, we have renounced secret and shameful ways; we do not use deception, nor do we distort the word of God. On the contrary, by setting forth the truth plainly we commend ourselves to every man's conscience in the sight of God. **3** And even if our gospel is veiled, it is veiled to those who are perishing. **4** The god of this age has blinded the minds of unbelievers, so that they cannot see the light of the gospel of the glory of Christ, who is the image of God. **5** For we do not preach ourselves, but Jesus Christ as Lord, and ourselves as your servants for Jesus' sake. **6** For God, who said, "Let light shine out of darkness,"[d] made his light shine in our hearts to give us the light of the knowledge of the glory of God in the face of Christ.

7 But we have this treasure in jars of clay to show that this all-surpassing power is from God and not from us. **8** We are hard pressed on every side, but not crushed; perplexed, but not in despair; **9** persecuted, but not abandoned; struck down, but not destroyed. **10** We always carry around in our body the death of Jesus, so that the life of Jesus may also be revealed in our body. **11** For we who are alive are always being given over to death for Jesus' sake, so that his life may be revealed in our mortal body. **12** So then, death is at work in us, but life is at work in you.

c 18 Or *contemplate*   *d 6* Gen. 1:3

13 It is written: "I believed; therefore I have spoken."* With that same spirit of faith we also believe and therefore speak, 14 because we know that the one who raised the Lord Jesus from the dead will also raise us with Jesus and present us with you in his presence. 15 All this is for your benefit, so that the grace that is reaching more and more people may cause thanksgiving to overflow to the glory of God.

16 Therefore we do not lose heart. Though outwardly we are wasting away, yet inwardly we are being renewed day by day. 17 For our light and momentary troubles are achieving for us an eternal glory that far outweighs them all. 18 So we fix our eyes not on what is seen, but on what is unseen. For what is seen is temporary, but what is unseen is eternal.

Our Heavenly Dwelling

5 1 Now we know that if the earthly tent we live in is destroyed, we have a building from God, an eternal house in heaven, not built by human hands. 2 Meanwhile we groan, longing to be clothed with our heavenly dwelling, 3 because when we are clothed, we will not be found naked. 4 For while we are in this tent, we groan and are burdened, because we do not wish to be unclothed but to be clothed with our heavenly dwelling, so that what is mortal may be swallowed up by life. 5 Now it is God who has made us for this very purpose and has given us the Spirit as a deposit, guaranteeing what is to come.

6 Therefore we are always confident and know that as long as we are at home in the body we are away from the Lord. 7 We live by faith, not by sight. 8 We are confident, I say, and would prefer to be away from the body and at home with the Lord. 9 So we make it our goal to please him, whether we are at home in the body or away from it. 10 For we must all appear before the judgment seat of Christ, that each one may receive what is due him for the things done while in the body, whether good or bad.

The Ministry of Reconciliation

11 Since, then, we know what it is to fear the Lord, we try to persuade men. What we are is plain to God, and I hope it is also plain to your conscience. 12 We are not trying to commend ourselves to you again, but are giving you an opportunity to take pride in us, so that you can answer those who take pride in what is seen rather than in what is in the heart. 13 If we are out of our mind, it is for the sake of God; if we are in our right mind, it is for you. 14 For Christ's love compels us, because we are convinced that one died for all, and therefore all died. 15 And he died for all, that those who live should no longer live for themselves but for him who died for them and was raised again.

16 So from now on we regard no one from a worldly point of view. Though we once regarded Christ in this way, we do so no longer. 17 Therefore, if anyone is in Christ, he is a new creation; the old has gone, the new has come! 18 All this is from God, who reconciled us to himself through Christ and gave us the ministry of reconciliation: 19 that God was reconciling the world to

13 Psalm 116:10

himself in Christ, not counting men's sins against them. And he has committed to us the message of reconciliation. 20 We are therefore Christ's ambassadors, as though God were making his appeal through us. We implore you on Christ's behalf: Be reconciled to God. 21 God made him who had no sin to be sin*f* for us, so that in him we might become the righteousness of God.

6 1 As God's fellow workers we urge you not to receive God's grace in vain. 2 For he says,

"In the time of my favor I heard you,
    and in the day of salvation I helped you."*g*

I tell you, now is the time of God's favor, now is the day of salvation.

Paul's Hardships

3 We put no stumbling block in anyone's path, so that our ministry will not be discredited. 4 Rather, as servants of God we commend ourselves in every way: in great endurance; in troubles, hardships and distresses; 5 in beatings, imprisonments and riots; in hard work, sleepless nights and hunger; 6 in purity, understanding, patience and kindness; in the Holy Spirit and in sincere love; 7 in truthful speech and in the power of God; with weapons of righteousness in the right hand and in the left; 8 through glory and dishonor, bad report and good report; genuine, yet regarded as impostors; 9 known, yet regarded as unknown; dying, and yet we live on; beaten, and yet not killed; 10 sorrowful, yet always rejoicing; poor, yet making many rich; having

nothing, and yet possessing every thing.

11 We have spoken freely to yo Corinthians, and opened wide o hearts to you. 12 We are not withhold ing our affection from you, but you ar withholding yours from us. 13 As a fa exchange—I speak as to m children—open wide your hearts als

Do Not Be Yoked With Unbelievers

14 Do not be yoked together wi unbelievers. For what do righteou ness and wickedness have in com mon? Or what fellowship can lig have with darkness? 15 What ha mony is there between Christ an Belial*h*? What does a believer have common with an unbeliever? 16 Wha agreement is there between th temple of God and idols? For we ar the temple of the living God. As Go has said: "I will live with them an walk among them, and I will be the God, and they will be my people."*i*

17 "Therefore come out from then and be separate,
                    says the Lor
    Touch no unclean thing,
        and I will receive you."*j*
18 "I will be a Father to you,
    and you will be my sons and daughters,
        says the Lord Almighty.

7 1 Since we have these promise dear friends, let us purify ourse ves from everything that con taminates body and spirit, perfectir holiness out of reverence for God.

Paul's Joy

2 Make room for us in your heart We have wronged no one, we hav

---

f 21 Or *be a sin offering*   *g* 2 Isaiah 49:8   *h* 15 Greek *Beliar,* a variant of *Belial*
i 16 Lev. 26:12; Jer. 32:38; Ezek. 37:27   *j* 17 Isaiah 52:11; Ezek. 20:34,41
k 18 2 Samuel 7:14; 7:8

orrupted no one, we have exploited o one. 3 I do not say this to condemn ou; I have said before that you have uch a place in our hearts that we would live or die with you. 4 I have reat confidence in you; I take great ride in you. I am greatly encouraged; in all our troubles my joy nows no bounds.

5 For when we came into Macedonia, this body of ours had no est, but we were harassed at every urn — conflicts on the outside, fears vithin. 6 But God, who comforts the lowncast, comforted us by the coming of Titus, 7 and not only by his oming but also by the comfort you ad given him. He told us about your onging for me, your deep sorrow, our ardent concern for me, so that ny joy was greater than ever.

8 Even if I caused you sorrow by ny letter, I do not regret it. Though I did regret it — I see that my letter urt you, but only for a little while — 9 yet now I am happy, not because ou were made sorry, but because our sorrow led you to repentance. For you became sorrowful as God intended and so were not harmed in iny way by us. 10 Godly sorrow brings repentance that leads to salvation and leaves no regret, but worldly sorrow brings death. 11 See what this godly sorrow has produced n you: what earnestness, what eagerness to clear yourselves, what ndignation, what alarm, what longing, what concern, what readiness to see justice done. At every point you nave proved yourselves to be innocent in this matter. 12 So even hough I wrote to you, it was not on iccount of the one who did the vrong or of the injured party, but

rather that before God you could see for yourselves how devoted to us you are. 13 By all this we are encouraged.

In addition to our own encouragement, we were especially delighted to see how happy Titus was, because his spirit has been refreshed by all of you. 14 I had boasted to him about you, and you have not embarrassed me. But just as everything we said to you was true, so our boasting about you to Titus has proved to be true as well. 15 And his affection for you is all the greater when he remembers that you were all obedient, receiving him with fear and trembling. 16 I am glad I can have complete confidence in you.

Generosity Encouraged

8 1 And now, brothers, we want you to know about the grace that God has given the Macedonian churches. 2 Out of the most severe trial, their overflowing joy and their extreme poverty welled up in rich generosity. 3 For I testify that they gave as much as they were able, and even beyond their ability. Entirely on their own, 4 they urgently pleaded with us for the privilege of sharing in this service to the saints. 5 And they did not do as we expected, but they gave themselves first to the Lord and then to us in keeping with God's will. 6 So we urged Titus, since he had earlier made a beginning, to bring also to completion this act of grace on your part. 7 But just as you excel in everything — in faith, in speech, in knowledge, in complete earnestness and in your love for us[f] — see that you also excel in this grace of giving.

8 I am not commanding you, but I want to test the sincerity of your love

---

7 Some manuscripts in our love for you

by comparing it with the earnestness of others. **9** For you know the grace of our Lord Jesus Christ, that though he was rich, yet for your sakes he became poor, so that you through his poverty might become rich.

10 And here is my advice about what is best for you in this matter: Last year you were the first not only to give but also to have the desire to do so. **11** Now finish the work, so that your eager willingness to do it may be matched by your completion of it, according to your means. **12** For if the willingness is there, the gift is acceptable according to what one has, not according to what he does not have.

13 Our desire is not that others might be relieved while you are hard pressed, but that there might be equality. **14** At the present time your plenty will supply what they need, so that in turn their plenty will supply what you need. Then there will be equality, **15** as it is written: "He who gathered much did not have too much, and he who gathered little did not have too little."*m*

Titus Sent to Corinth

16 I thank God, who put into the heart of Titus the same concern I have for you. **17** For Titus not only welcomed our appeal, but he is coming to you with much enthusiasm and on his own initiative. **18** And we are sending along with him the brother who is praised by all the churches for his service to the gospel. **19** What is more, he was chosen by the churches to accompany us as we carry the offering, which we administer in order to honor the Lord himself and to show our eagerness to help. **20** We want to avoid any

criticism of the way we administe this liberal gift. **21** For we are takin pains to do what is right, not only i the eyes of the Lord but also in th eyes of men.

22 In addition, we are sendin with them our brother who has ofte proved to us in many ways that he i zealous, and now even more so be cause of his great confidence in you **23** As for Titus, he is my partner an fellow worker among you; as for ou brothers, they are representatives c the churches and an honor to Chris **24** Therefore show these men th proof of your love and the reason fc our pride in you, so that the churche can see it.

9 **1** There is no need for me to wri to you about this service to th saints. **2** For I know your eagerness t help, and I have been boasting abou it to the Macedonians, telling ther that since last year you in Achaia wer ready to give; and your enthusiasr has stirred most of them to actior **3** But I am sending the brothers i order that our boasting about you i this matter should not prove hollov but that you may be ready, as I sai you would be. **4** For if an Macedonians come with me and fin you unprepared, we — not to say any thing about you — would be ashame of having been so confident. **5** So thought it necessary to urge th brothers to visit you in advance an finish the arrangements for th generous gift you had promised. The it will be ready as a generous gift, no as one grudgingly given.

Sowing Generously

6 Remember this: Whoever sow sparingly will also reap sparingly

---

m 15 Exodus 16:18

and whoever sows generously will also reap generously. 7 Each man should give what he has decided in his heart to give, not reluctantly or under compulsion, for God loves a cheerful giver. 8 And God is able to make all grace abound to you, so that in all things at all times, having all that you need, you will abound in every good work. 9 As it is written:

> "He has scattered abroad his gifts
>   to the poor;
> his righteousness endures
>   forever."[n]

10 Now he who supplies seed to the sower and bread for food will also supply and increase your store of seed and will enlarge the harvest of your righteousness. 11 You will be made rich in every way so that you can be generous on every occasion, and through us your generosity will result in thanksgiving to God.

12 This service that you perform is not only supplying the needs of God's people but is also overflowing in many expressions of thanks to God. 13 Because of the service by which you have proved yourselves, men will praise God for the obedience that accompanies your confession of the gospel of Christ, and for your generosity in sharing with them and with everyone else. 14 And in their prayers for you their hearts will go out to you, because of the surpassing grace God has given you. 15 Thanks be to God for his indescribable gift!

Paul's Defense of His Ministry

10 1 By the meekness and gentleness of Christ, I appeal to you—I, Paul, who am "timid" when face to face with you, but "bold"

when away! 2 I beg you that when I come I may not have to be as bold as I expect to be toward some people who think that we live by the standards of this world. 3 For though we live in the world, we do not wage war as the world does. 4 The weapons we fight with are not the weapons of the world. On the contrary, they have divine power to demolish strongholds. 5 We demolish arguments and every pretension that sets itself up against the knowledge of God, and we take captive every thought to make it obedient to Christ. 6 And we will be ready to punish every act of disobedience, once your obedience is complete.

7 You are looking only on the surface of things.[o] If anyone is confident that he belongs to Christ, he should consider again that we belong to Christ just as much as he. 8 For even if I boast somewhat freely about the authority the Lord gave us for building you up rather than pulling you down, I will not be ashamed of it. 9 I do not want to seem to be trying to frighten you with my letters. 10 For some say, "His letters are weighty and forceful, but in person he is unimpressive and his speaking amounts to nothing." 11 Such people should realize that what we are in our letters when we are absent, we will be in our actions when we are present.

12 We do not dare to classify or compare ourselves with some who commend themselves. When they measure themselves by themselves and compare themselves with themselves, they are not wise. 13 We, however, will not boast beyond proper limits, but will confine our boasting

---

n 9 Psalm 112:9   o 7 Or *Look at the obvious facts*

to the field God has assigned to us, a field that reaches even to you. **14** We are not going too far in our boasting, as would be the case if we had not come to you, for we did get as far as you with the gospel of Christ. **15** Neither do we go beyond our limits by boasting of work done by others.*p* Our hope is that, as your faith continues to grow, our area of activity among you will greatly expand, **16** so that we can preach the gospel in the regions beyond you. For we do not want to boast about work already done in another man's territory. **17** But, "Let him who boasts boast in the Lord."*q* **18** For it is not the one who commends himself who is approved, but the one whom the Lord commends.

Paul and the False Apostles

11 **1** I hope you will put up with a little of my foolishness; but you are already doing that. **2** I am jealous for you with a godly jealousy. I promised you to one husband, to Christ, so that I might present you as a pure virgin to him. **3** But I am afraid that just as Eve was deceived by the serpent's cunning, your minds may somehow be led astray from your sincere and pure devotion to Christ. **4** For if someone comes to you and preaches a Jesus other than the Jesus we preached, or if you receive a different spirit from the one you received, or a different gospel from the one you accepted, you put up with it easily enough. **5** But I do not think I am in the least inferior to those "super-apostles." **6** I may not be a trained speaker, but I do have

knowledge. We have made this perfectly clear to you in every way.

7 Was it a sin for me to lower myself in order to elevate you by preaching the gospel of God to you free of charge? **8** I robbed other churches by receiving support from them so as to serve you. **9** And when I was with you and needed something, I was not a burden to anyone, for the brothers who came from Macedonia supplied what I needed. I have kept myself from being a burden to you in any way, and will continue to do so. **10** As surely as the truth of Christ is in me, nobody in the regions of Achaia will stop this boasting of mine. **11** Why? Because I do not love you? God knows I do! **12** And I will keep on doing what I am doing in order to cut the ground from under those who want an opportunity to be considered equal with us in the things they boast about. **13** For such men are false apostles, deceitful workmen, masquerading as apostles of Christ. **14** And no wonder, for Satan himself masquerades as an angel of light. **15** It is not surprising, then, if his servants masquerade as servants of righteousness. Their end will be what their actions deserve.

Paul Boasts About His Sufferings

16 I repeat: Let no one take me for a fool. But if you do, then receive me just as you would a fool, so that I may do a little boasting. **17** In this self-confident boasting I am not talking as the Lord would, but as a fool. **18** Since many are boasting in the

p 13-15 Or *13 We, however, will not boast about things that cannot be measured, but we will boast according to the standard of measurement that the God of measure has assigned us — a measurement that relates even to you. 14 ... 15 Neither do we boast about things that cannot be measured in regard to the work done by others.*   *q 17* Jer. 9:24

way the world does, I too will boast. 19 You gladly put up with fools since you are so wise! 20 In fact, you even put up with anyone who enslaves you or exploits you or takes advantage of you or pushes himself forward or slaps you in the face. 21 To my shame I admit that we were too weak for that!

What anyone else dares to boast about—I am speaking as a fool—I also dare to boast about. 22 Are they Hebrews? So am I. Are they Israelites? So am I. Are they Abraham's descendants? So am I. 23 Are they servants of Christ? (I am out of my mind to talk like this.) I am more. I have worked much harder, been in prison more frequently, been flogged more severely, and been exposed to death again and again. 24 Five times I received from the Jews the forty lashes minus one. 25 Three times I was beaten with rods, once I was stoned, three times I was shipwrecked, I spent a night and a day in the open sea, 26 I have been constantly on the move. I have been in danger from rivers, in danger from bandits, in danger from my own countrymen, in danger from Gentiles; in danger in the city, in danger in the country, in danger at sea; and in danger from false brothers. 27 I have labored and toiled and have often gone without sleep; I have known hunger and thirst and have often gone without food; I have been cold and naked. 28 Besides everything else, I face daily the pressure of my concern for all the churches. 29 Who is weak, and I do not feel weak? Who is led into sin, and I do not inwardly burn?

30 If I must boast, I will boast of the things that show my weakness.

31 The God and Father of the Lord Jesus, who is to be praised forever, knows that I am not lying. 32 In Damascus the governor under King Aretas had the city of the Damascenes guarded in order to arrest me. 33 But I was lowered in a basket from a window in the wall and slipped through his hands.

Paul's Vision and His Thorn

12 1 I must go on boasting. Although there is nothing to be gained, I will go on to visions and revelations from the Lord. 2 I know a man in Christ who fourteen years ago was caught up to the third heaven. Whether it was in the body or out of the body I do not know—God knows. 3 And I know that this man—whether in the body or apart from the body I do not know, but God knows— 4 was caught up to paradise. He heard inexpressible things, things that man is not permitted to tell. 5 I will boast about a man like that, but I will not boast about myself, except about my weaknesses. 6 Even if I should choose to boast, I would not be a fool, because I would be speaking the truth. But I refrain, so no one will think more of me than is warranted by what I do or say.

7 To keep me from becoming conceited because of these surpassingly great revelations, there was given me a thorn in my flesh, a messenger of Satan, to torment me. 8 Three times I pleaded with the Lord to take it away from me. 9 But he said to me, "My grace is sufficient for you, for my power is made perfect in weakness." Therefore I will boast all the more gladly about my weaknesses, so that Christ's power may rest on me. 10 That is why, for Christ's sake, I delight in weaknesses, in insults, in

hardships, in persecutions, in difficulties. For when I am weak, then I am strong.

Paul's Concern for the Corinthians

11 I have made a fool of myself, but you drove me to it. I ought to have been commended by you, for I am not in the least inferior to the "super-apostles," even though I am nothing. 12 The things that mark an apostle — signs, wonders and miracles — were done among you with great perseverance. 13 How were you inferior to the other churches, except that I was never a burden to you? Forgive me this wrong!

14 Now I am ready to visit you for the third time, and I will not be a burden to you, because what I want is not your possessions but you. After all, children should not have to save up for their parents, but parents for their children. 15 So I will very gladly spend for you everything I have and expend myself as well. If I love you more, will you love me less? 16 Be that as it may, I have not been a burden to you. Yet, crafty fellow that I am, I caught you by trickery! 17 Did I exploit you through any of the men I sent you? 18 I urged Titus to go to you and I sent our brother with him. Titus did not exploit you, did he? Did we not act in the same spirit and follow the same course?

19 Have you been thinking all along that we have been defending ourselves to you? We have been speaking in the sight of God as those in Christ; and everything we do, dear friends, is for your strengthening. 20 For I am afraid that when I come I may not find you as I want you to be, and you may not find me as you want me to be. I fear that there may be quarreling, jealousy, outbursts of anger, factions, slander, gossip, arrogance and disorder. 21 I am afraid that when I come again my God will humble me before you, and I will be grieved over many who have sinned earlier and have not repented of the impurity, sexual sin and debauchery in which they have indulged.

Final Warnings

13 1 This will be my third visit to you. "Every matter must be established by the testimony of two or three witnesses."r 2 I already gave you a warning when I was with you the second time. I now repeat it while absent: On my return I will not spare those who sinned earlier or any of the others, 3 since you are demanding proof that Christ is speaking through me. He is not weak in dealing with you, but is powerful among you. 4 For to be sure, he was crucified in weakness, yet he lives by God's power. Likewise, we are weak in him, yet by God's power we will live with him to serve you.

5 Examine yourselves to see whether you are in the faith; test yourselves. Do you not realize that Christ Jesus is in you — unless, of course, you fail the test? 6 And I trust that you will discover that we have not failed the test. 7 Now we pray to God that you will do not anything wrong. Not that people will see that we have stood the test but that you will do what is right even though we may seem to have failed. 8 For we cannot do anything against the truth, but only for the truth. 9 We are glad whenever we are weak but you are strong; and our prayer is for your

r 1 Deut. 19:15

perfection. **10** This is why I write these things when I am absent, that when I come I may not have to be harsh in my use of authority—the authority the Lord gave me for building you up, not for tearing you down.

Final Greetings

11 Finally, brothers, good-by. Aim for perfection, listen to my appeal, be of one mind, live in peace. And the God of love and peace will be with you.

12 Greet one another with a holy kiss. **13** All the saints send their greetings.

14 May the grace of the Lord Jesus Christ, and the love of God, and the fellowship of the Holy Spirit be with you all.

Galatians

1

1 Paul, an apostle—sent not from men nor by man, but by Jesus Christ and God the Father, who raised him from the dead— **2** and all the brothers with me,

To the churches in Galatia:

3 Grace and peace to you from God our Father and the Lord Jesus Christ, **4** who gave himself for our sins to rescue us from the present evil age, according to the will of our God and Father, **5** to whom be glory for ever and ever. Amen.

No Other Gospel

6 I am astonished that you are so quickly deserting the one who called you by the grace of Christ and are turning to a different gospel— **7** which is really no gospel at all. Evidently some people are throwing you into confusion and are trying to pervert the gospel of Christ. **8** But even if we or an angel from heaven should preach a gospel other than the one we preached to you, let him be eternally condemned! **9** As we have already said, so now I say again: If anybody is preaching to you a gospel other than what you accepted, let him be eternally condemned!

10 Am I now trying to win the approval of men, or of God? Or am I trying to please men? If I were still trying to please men, I would not be a servant of Christ.

Paul Called by God

11 I want you to know, brothers, that the gospel I preached is not something that man made up. **12** I did not receive it from any man, nor was I taught it; rather, I received it by revelation from Jesus Christ.

13 For you have heard of my previous way of life in Judaism, how intensely I persecuted the church of God and tried to destroy it. **14** I was advancing in Judaism beyond many Jews of my own age and was extremely zealous for the traditions of my fathers. **15** But when God, who set me apart from birth[a] and called me by his grace, was pleased **16** to reveal his Son in me so that I might preach him among the Gentiles, I did not consult any man, **17** nor did I go up to Jerusalem to see those who were apostles before I was, but I went immediately into Arabia and later returned to Damascus.

18 Then after three years, I went up to Jerusalem to get acquainted with Peter[b] and stayed with him fifteen days. **19** I saw none of the other apostles—only James, the Lord's brother. **20** I assure you before God that what I am writing you is no lie. **21** Later I went to Syria and Cilicia. **22** I was personally unknown to the churches of Judea that are in Christ. **23** They only heard the report: "The man who formerly persecuted us is now preaching the faith he once tried to destroy." **24** And they praised God because of me.

---

a 15 Or *from my mother's womb*   *b* 18 Greek *Cephas*

Paul Accepted by the Apostles

2 ¹ Fourteen years later I went up again to Jerusalem, this time with Barnabas. I took Titus along also. ² I went in response to a revelation and set before them the gospel that I preach among the Gentiles. But I did this privately to those who seemed to be leaders, for fear that I was running or had run my race in vain. ³ Yet not even Titus, who was with me, was compelled to be circumcised, even though he was a Greek. ⁴ This matter arose because some false brothers had infiltrated our ranks to spy on the freedom we have in Christ Jesus and to make us slaves. ⁵ We did not give in to them for a moment, so that the truth of the gospel might remain with you.

⁶ As for those who seemed to be important—whatever they were makes no difference to me; God does not judge by external appearance—those men added nothing to my message. ⁷ On the contrary, they saw that I had been entrusted with the task of preaching the gospel to the Gentiles,^c just as Peter had been to the Jews.^d ⁸ For God, who was at work in the ministry of Peter as an apostle to the Jews, was also at work in my ministry as an apostle to the Gentiles. ⁹ James, Peter^e and John, those reputed to be pillars, gave me and Barnabas the right hand of fellowship when they recognized the grace given to me. They agreed that we should go to the Gentiles, and they to the Jews. ¹⁰ All they asked was that we should continue to remember the poor, the very thing I was eager to do.

Paul Opposes Peter

¹¹ When Peter came to Antioch, I opposed him to his face, because he was clearly in the wrong. ¹² Before certain men came from James, he used to eat with the Gentiles. But when they arrived, he began to draw back and separate himself from the Gentiles because he was afraid of those who belonged to the circumcision group. ¹³ The other Jews joined him in his hypocrisy, so that by their hypocrisy even Barnabas was led astray.

¹⁴ When I saw that they were not acting in line with the truth of the gospel, I said to Peter in front of them all, "You are a Jew, yet you live like a Gentile and not like a Jew. How is it, then, that you force Gentiles to follow Jewish customs?

¹⁵ "We who are Jews by birth and not 'Gentile sinners' ¹⁶ know that a man is not justified by observing the law, but by faith in Jesus Christ. So we, too, have put our faith in Christ Jesus that we may be justified by faith in Christ and not by observing the law, because by observing the law no one will be justified.

¹⁷ "If, while we seek to be justified in Christ, it becomes evident that we ourselves are sinners, does that mean that Christ promotes sin? Absolutely not! ¹⁸ If I rebuild what I destroyed, I prove that I am a lawbreaker. ¹⁹ For through the law I died to the law so that I might live for God. ²⁰ I have been crucified with Christ and I no longer live, but Christ lives in me. The life I live in the body, I live by faith in the Son of God, who loved me and gave himself for me. ²¹ I do

---

^c 7 Greek *uncircumcised*   ^d 7 Greek *circumcised*; also in verses 8 and 9   ^e 9 Greek *Cephas*; also in verses 11 and 14

not set aside the grace of God, for if righteousness could be gained through the law, Christ died for nothing!"*f*

Faith or Observance of the Law

3 ¹ You foolish Galatians! Who has bewitched you? Before your very eyes Jesus Christ was clearly portrayed as crucified. ² I would like to learn just one thing from you: Did you receive the Spirit by observing the law, or by believing what you heard? ³ Are you so foolish? After beginning with the Spirit, are you now trying to attain your goal by human effort? ⁴ Have you suffered so much for nothing—if it really was for nothing? ⁵ Does God give you his Spirit and work miracles among you because you observe the law, or because you believe what you heard?

⁶ Consider Abraham: "He believed God, and it was credited to him as righteousness."*g* ⁷ Understand, then, that those who believe are children of Abraham. ⁸ The Scripture foresaw that God would justify the Gentiles by faith, and announced the gospel in advance to Abraham: "All nations will be blessed through you."*h* ⁹ So those who have faith are blessed along with Abraham, the man of faith.

¹⁰ All who rely on observing the law are under a curse, for it is written: "Cursed is everyone who does not continue to do everything written in the Book of the Law."*i* ¹¹ Clearly no one is justified before God by the law, because, "The righteous will live by faith."*j* ¹² The law is not based on faith; on the contrary, "The man who does these things will live by them."*k* ¹³ Christ redeemed us from the curse of the law by becoming a curse for us, for it is written: "Cursed is everyone who is hung on a tree."*l* ¹⁴ He redeemed us in order that the blessing given to Abraham might come to the Gentiles through Christ Jesus, so that by faith we might receive the promise of the Spirit.

The Law and the Promise

¹⁵ Brothers, let me take an example from everyday life. Just as no one can set aside or add to a human covenant that has been duly established, so it is in this case. ¹⁶ The promises were spoken to Abraham and to his seed. The Scripture does not say "and to seeds," meaning many people, but "and to your seed,"*m* meaning one person, who is Christ. ¹⁷ What I mean is this: The law, introduced 430 years later, does not set aside the covenant previously established by God and thus do away with the promise. ¹⁸ For if the inheritance depends on the law, then it no longer depends on a promise; but God in his grace gave it to Abraham through a promise.

¹⁹ What, then, was the purpose of the law? It was added because of transgressions until the Seed to whom the promise referred had come. The law was put into effect through angels by a mediator. ²⁰ A mediator, however, does not represent just one party; but God is one.

²¹ Is the law, therefore, opposed to the promises of God? Absolutely not! For if a law had been given that could impart life, then righteousness would certainly have come by the law. ²² But the Scripture declares that the whole world is a prisoner of sin, so that what was promised, being

---

f 21 Some interpreters end the quotation after verse 14.   *g* 6 Gen. 15:6   *h* 8 Gen. 12:3; 18:18; 22:18   *i* 10 Deut. 27:26   *j* 11 Hab. 2:4   *k* 12 Lev. 18:5   *l* 13 Deut. 21:23   *m* 16 Gen. 12:7; 13:15; 24:7

given through faith in Jesus Christ, might be given to those who believe.

23 Before this faith came, we were held prisoners by the law, locked up until faith should be revealed. **24** So the law was put in charge to lead us to Christ[n] that we might be justified by faith. **25** Now that faith has come, we are no longer under the supervision of the law.

Sons of God

26 You are all sons of God through faith in Christ Jesus, **27** for all of you who were baptized into Christ have clothed yourselves with Christ. **28** There is neither Jew nor Greek, slave nor free, male nor female, for you are all one in Christ Jesus. **29** If you belong to Christ, then you are Abraham's seed, and heirs according to the promise.

4 **1** What I am saying is that as long as the heir is a child, he is no different from a slave, although he owns the whole estate. **2** He is subject to guardians and trustees until the time set by his father. **3** So also, when we were children, we were in slavery under the basic principles of the world. **4** But when the time had fully come, God sent his Son, born of a woman, born under law, **5** to redeem those under law, that we might receive the full rights of sons. **6** Because you are sons, God sent the Spirit of his Son into our hearts, the Spirit who calls out, "Abba,[o] Father." **7** So you are no longer a slave, but a son; and since you are a son, God has made you also an heir.

Paul's Concern for the Galatians

8 Formerly, when you did not know God, you were slaves to those who by nature are not gods. **9** But now that you know God — or rather are known by God — how is it that you are turning back to those weak and miserable principles? Do you wish to be enslaved by them all over again? **10** You are observing special days and months and seasons and years! **11** I fear for you, that somehow I have wasted my efforts on you.

12 I plead with you, brothers, become like me, for I became like you. You have done me no wrong. **13** As you know, it was because of an illness that I first preached the gospel to you. **14** Even though my illness was a trial to you, you did not treat me with contempt or scorn. Instead, you welcomed me as if I were an angel of God, as if I were Christ Jesus himself. **15** What has happened to all your joy? I can testify that, if you could have done so, you would have torn out your eyes and given them to me. **16** Have I now become your enemy by telling you the truth?

17 Those people are zealous to win you over, but for no good. What they want is to alienate you from us, so that you may be zealous for them. **18** It is fine to be zealous, provided the purpose is good, and to be so always and not just when I am with you. **19** My dear children, for whom I am again in the pains of childbirth until Christ is formed in you, **20** how I wish I could be with you now and change my tone, because I am perplexed about you!

Hagar and Sarah

21 Tell me, you who want to be under the law, are you not aware of what the law says? **22** For it is written that Abraham had two sons, one by

---

n 24 Or *charge until Christ came*   o 6 Aramaic for *Father* the slave woman and the other by the free woman. **23** His son by the slave woman was born in the ordinary way; but his son by the free woman was born as the result of a promise.

24 These things may be taken figuratively, for the women represent two covenants. One covenant is from Mount Sinai and bears children who are to be slaves: This is Hagar. **25** Now Hagar stands for Mount Sinai in Arabia and corresponds to the present city of Jerusalem, because she is in slavery with her children. **26** But the Jerusalem that is above is free, and she is our mother. **27** For it is written:

> "Be glad, O barren woman,
>   who bears no children;
> break forth and cry aloud,
>   you who have no labor pains;
> because more are the children
>   of the desolate woman
> than of her who has a
>   husband."[p]

28 Now you, brothers, like Isaac, are children of promise. **29** At that time the son born in the ordinary way persecuted the son born by the power of the Spirit. It is the same now. **30** But what does the Scripture say? "Get rid of the slave woman and her son, for the slave woman's son will never share in the inheritance with the free woman's son."[q] **31** Therefore, brothers, we are not children of the slave woman, but of the free woman.

Freedom in Christ

5 **1** It is for freedom that Christ has set us free. Stand firm, then, and do not let yourselves be burdened again by a yoke of slavery.

2 Mark my words! I, Paul, tell you that if you let yourselves be circumcised, Christ will be of no value to you at all. **3** Again I declare to every man who lets himself be circumcised that he is obligated to obey the whole law. **4** You who are trying to be justified by law have been alienated from Christ; you have fallen away from grace. **5** But by faith we eagerly await through the Spirit the righteousness for which we hope. **6** For in Christ Jesus neither circumcision nor uncircumcision has any value. The only thing that counts is faith expressing itself through love.

7 You were running a good race. Who cut in on you and kept you from obeying the truth? **8** That kind of persuasion does not come from the one who calls you. **9** "A little yeast works through the whole batch of dough." **10** I am confident in the Lord that you will take no other view. The one who is throwing you into confusion will pay the penalty, whoever he may be. **11** Brothers, if I am still preaching circumcision, why am I still being persecuted? In that case the offense of the cross has been abolished. **12** As for those agitators, I wish they would go the whole way and emasculate themselves!

13 You, my brothers, were called to be free. But do not use your freedom to indulge the sinful nature[r]; rather, serve one another in love. **14** The entire law is summed up in a single command: "Love your neighbor as yourself."[s] **15** If you keep on biting and devouring each other, watch out or you will be destroyed by each other.

---

p 27 Isaiah 54:1   *q* 30 Gen. 21:10   *r* 13 Or *the flesh*; also in verses 16, 17, 19 and 24   *s* 14 Lev. 19:18

Life by the Spirit

16 So I say, live by the Spirit, and you will not gratify the desires of the sinful nature. 17 For the sinful nature desires what is contrary to the Spirit, and the Spirit what is contrary to the sinful nature. They are in conflict with each other, so that you do not do what you want. 18 But if you are led by the Spirit, you are not under law.

19 The acts of the sinful nature are obvious: sexual immorality, impurity and debauchery; 20 idolatry and witchcraft; hatred, discord, jealousy, fits of rage, selfish ambition, dissensions, factions 21 and envy; drunkenness, orgies, and the like. I warn you, as I did before, that those who live like this will not inherit the kingdom of God.

22 But the fruit of the Spirit is love, joy, peace, patience, kindness, goodness, faithfulness, 23 gentleness and self-control. Against such things there is no law. 24 Those who belong to Christ Jesus have crucified the sinful nature with its passions and desires. 25 Since we live by the Spirit, let us keep in step with the Spirit. 26 Let us not become conceited, provoking and envying each other.

Doing Good to All

6 1 Brothers, if someone is caught in a sin, you who are spiritual should restore him gently. But watch yourself, or you also may be tempted. 2 Carry each other's burdens, and in this way you will fulfill the law of Christ. 3 If anyone thinks he is something when he is nothing, he deceives himself. 4 Each one should test his own actions. Then he can take pride in himself, without comparing himself to somebody else, 5 for each one should carry his own load.

6 Anyone who receives instruction in the word must share all good things with his instructor.

7 Do not be deceived: God cannot be mocked. A man reaps what he sows. 8 The one who sows to please his sinful nature, from that nature[t] will reap destruction; the one who sows to please the Spirit, from the Spirit will reap eternal life. 9 Let us not become weary in doing good, for at the proper time we will reap a harvest if we do not give up. 10 Therefore, as we have opportunity, let us do good to all people, especially to those who belong to the family of believers.

Not Circumcision but a New Creation

11 See what large letters I use as I write to you with my own hand! 12 Those who want to make a good impression outwardly are trying to compel you to be circumcised. The only reason they do this is to avoid being persecuted for the cross of Christ. 13 Not even those who are circumcised obey the law, yet they want you to be circumcised that they may boast about your flesh. 14 May I never boast except in the cross of our Lord Jesus Christ, through which[u] the world has been crucified to me, and I to the world. 15 Neither circumcision nor uncircumcision means anything; what counts is a new creation. 16 Peace and mercy to all who follow this rule, even to the Israel of God.

17 Finally, let no one cause me trouble, for I bear on my body the marks of Jesus.

18 The grace of our Lord Jesus Christ be with your spirit, brothers. Amen.

t 8 Or *his flesh, from the flesh*   u 14 Or *whom*

Ephesians

1

1 Paul, an apostle of Christ Jesus by the will of God,

To the saints in Ephesus,[a] the faithful[b] in Christ Jesus:

2 Grace and peace to you from God our Father and the Lord Jesus Christ.

Spiritual Blessings in Christ

3 Praise be to the God and Father of our Lord Jesus Christ, who has blessed us in the heavenly realms with every spiritual blessing in Christ. **4** For he chose us in him before the creation of the world to be holy and blameless in his sight. In love **5** he[c] predestined us to be adopted as his sons through Jesus Christ, in accordance with his pleasure and will — **6** to the praise of his glorious grace, which he has freely given us in the One he loves. **7** In him we have redemption through his blood, the forgiveness of sins, in accordance with the riches of God's grace **8** that he lavished on us with all wisdom and understanding. **9** And he[d] made known to us the mystery of his will according to his good pleasure, which he purposed in Christ, **10** to be put into effect when the times will have reached their fulfillment — to bring all things in heaven and on earth together under one head, even Christ.

11 In him we were also chosen,[e] having been predestined according to the plan of him who works out everything in conformity with the purpose of his will, **12** in order that we, who were the first to hope in Christ, might be for the praise of his glory. **13** And you also were included in Christ when you heard the word of truth, the gospel of your salvation. Having believed, you were marked in him with a seal, the promised Holy Spirit, **14** who is a deposit guaranteeing our inheritance until the redemption of those who are God's possession — to the praise of his glory.

Thanksgiving and Prayer

15 For this reason, ever since I heard about your faith in the Lord Jesus and your love for all the saints, **16** I have not stopped giving thanks for you, remembering you in my prayers. **17** I keep asking that the God of our Lord Jesus Christ, the glorious Father, may give you the Spirit[f] of wisdom and revelation, so that you may know him better. **18** I pray also that the eyes of your heart may be enlightened in order that you may know the hope to which he has called you, the riches of his glorious inheritance in the saints, **19** and his incomparably great power for us who believe. That power is like the working of his mighty strength, **20** which he exerted in Christ when he raised him from the dead and seated him at his right hand in the heavenly realms, **21** far above all rule and authority, power and dominion, and every title that can be given, not only in the present age but also in the

---

a 1 Some early manuscripts do not have in Ephesus.   *b 1 Or believers who are*
c 5 Or sight in love. 5 He   *d 9 Or us. With all wisdom and understanding,* 9 he
e 11 Or were made heirs   *f 17 Or a spirit*

one to come. **22** And God placed all things under his feet and appointed him to be head over everything for the church, **23** which is his body, the fullness of him who fills everything in every way.

Made Alive in Christ

2 **1** As for you, you were dead in your transgressions and sins, **2** in which you used to live when you followed the ways of this world and of the ruler of the kingdom of the air, the spirit who is now at work in those who are disobedient. **3** All of us also lived among them at one time, gratifying the cravings of our sinful nature*a* and following its desires and thoughts. Like the rest, we were by nature objects of wrath. **4** But because of his great love for us, God, who is rich in mercy, **5** made us alive with Christ even when we were dead in transgressions—it is by grace you have been saved. **6** And God raised us up with Christ and seated us with him in the heavenly realms in Christ Jesus, **7** in order that in the coming ages he might show the incomparable riches of his grace, expressed in his kindness to us in Christ Jesus. **8** For it is by grace you have been saved, through faith—and this not from yourselves, it is the gift of God— **9** not by works, so that no one can boast. **10** For we are God's workmanship, created in Christ Jesus to do good works, which God prepared in advance for us to do.

One in Christ

11 Therefore, remember that formerly you who are Gentiles by birth and called "uncircumcised" by those who call themselves "the cir-

cumcision" (that done in the body by the hands of men)— **12** remember that at that time you were separate from Christ, excluded from citizenship in Israel and foreigners to the covenants of the promise, without hope and without God in the world. **13** But now in Christ Jesus you who once were far away have been brought near through the blood of Christ.

14 For he himself is our peace, who has made the two one and has destroyed the barrier, the dividing wall of hostility, **15** by abolishing in his flesh the law with its commandments and regulations. His purpose was to create in himself one new man out of the two, thus making peace, **16** and in this one body to reconcile both of them to God through the cross, by which he put to death their hostility. **17** He came and preached peace to you who were far away and peace to those who were near. **18** For through him we both have access to the Father by one Spirit.

19 Consequently, you are no longer foreigners and aliens, but fellow citizens with God's people and members of God's household, **20** built on the foundation of the apostles and prophets, with Christ Jesus himself as the chief cornerstone. **21** In him the whole building is joined together and rises to become a holy temple in the Lord. **22** And in him you too are being built together to become a dwelling in which God lives by his Spirit.

Paul the Preacher to the Gentiles

3 **1** For this reason I, Paul, the prisoner of Christ Jesus for the sake of you Gentiles—

---

a **3** Or *our flesh*

2 Surely you have heard about the administration of God's grace that was given to me for you, 3 that is, the mystery made known to me by revelation, as I have already written briefly. 4 In reading this, then, you will be able to understand my insight into the mystery of Christ, 5 which was not made known to men in other generations as it has now been revealed by the Spirit to God's holy apostles and prophets. 6 This mystery is that through the gospel the Gentiles are heirs together with Israel, members together of one body, and sharers together in the promise in Christ Jesus.

7 I became a servant of this gospel by the gift of God's grace given me through the working of his power. 8 Although I am less than the least of all God's people, this grace was given me: to preach to the Gentiles the unsearchable riches of Christ, 9 and to make plain to everyone the administration of this mystery, which for ages past was kept hidden in God, who created all things. 10 His intent was that now, through the church, the manifold wisdom of God should be made known to the rulers and authorities in the heavenly realms, 11 according to his eternal purpose which he accomplished in Christ Jesus our Lord. 12 In him and through faith in him we may approach God with freedom and confidence. 13 I ask you, therefore, not to be discouraged because of my sufferings for you, which are your glory.

A Prayer for the Ephesians

14 For this reason I kneel before the Father, 15 from whom his whole family[h] in heaven and on earth

derives its name. 16 I pray that out of his glorious riches he may strengthen you with power through his Spirit in your inner being, 17 so that Christ may dwell in your hearts through faith. And I pray that you, being rooted and established in love, 18 may have power, together with all the saints, to grasp how wide and long and high and deep is the love of Christ, 19 and to know this love that surpasses knowledge—that you may be filled to the measure of all the fullness of God.

20 Now to him who is able to do immeasurably more than all we ask or imagine, according to his power that is at work within us, 21 to him be glory in the church and in Christ Jesus throughout all generations, for ever and ever! Amen.

Unity in the Body of Christ

4 1 As a prisoner for the Lord, then, I urge you to live a life worthy of the calling you have received. 2 Be completely humble and gentle; be patient, bearing with one another in love. 3 Make every effort to keep the unity of the Spirit through the bond of peace. 4 There is one body and one Spirit—just as you were called to one hope when you were called— 5 one Lord, one faith, one baptism; 6 one God and Father of all, who is over all and through all and in all.

7 But to each one of us grace has been given as Christ apportioned it. 8 This is why it[i] says:

"When he ascended on high,
he led captives in his train
and gave gifts to men."[j]

9 (What does "he ascended" mean except that he also descended to the

h 15 Or whom all fatherhood   i 8 Or God   j 8 Psalm 68:18

lower, earthly regions[k]? 10 He who descended is the very one who ascended higher than all the heavens, in order to fill the whole universe.) 11 It was he who gave some to be apostles, some to be prophets, some to be evangelists, and some to be pastors and teachers, 12 to prepare God's people for works of service, so that the body of Christ may be built up 13 until we all reach unity in the faith and in the knowledge of the Son of God and become mature, attaining to the whole measure of the fullness of Christ.

14 Then we will no longer be infants, tossed back and forth by the waves, and blown here and there by every wind of teaching and by the cunning and craftiness of men in their deceitful scheming. 15 Instead, speaking the truth in love, we will in all things grow up into him who is the Head, that is, Christ. 16 From him the whole body, joined and held together by every supporting ligament, grows and builds itself up in love, as each part does its work.

Living as Children of Light

17 So I tell you this, and insist on it in the Lord, that you must no longer live as the Gentiles do, in the futility of their thinking. 18 They are darkened in their understanding and separated from the life of God because of the ignorance that is in them due to the hardening of their hearts. 19 Having lost all sensitivity, they have given themselves over to sensuality so as to indulge in every kind of impurity, with a continual lust for more.

20 You, however, did not come to know Christ that way. 21 Surely you heard of him and were taught in him in accordance with the truth that is in Jesus. 22 You were taught, with regard to your former way of life, to put off your old self, which is being corrupted by its deceitful desires; 23 to be made new in the attitude of your minds; 24 and to put on the new self, created to be like God in true righteousness and holiness.

25 Therefore each of you must put off falsehood and speak truthfully to his neighbor, for we are all members of one body. 26 "In your anger do not sin"[l]: Do not let the sun go down while you are still angry, 27 and do not give the devil a foothold. 28 He who has been stealing must steal no longer, but must work, doing something useful with his own hands, that he may have something to share with those in need.

29 Do not let any unwholesome talk come out of your mouths, but only what is helpful for building others up according to their needs, that it may benefit those who listen. 30 And do not grieve the Holy Spirit of God, with whom you were sealed for the day of redemption. 31 Get rid of all bitterness, rage and anger, brawling and slander, along with every form of malice. 32 Be kind and compassionate to one another, forgiving each other, just as in Christ God forgave you.

5 1 Be imitators of God, therefore, as dearly loved children 2 and live a life of love, just as Christ loved us and gave himself up for us as a fragrant offering and sacrifice to God.

3 But among you there must not be even a hint of sexual immorality, or of any kind of impurity, or of greed,

---

k 9 Or the depths of the earth   l 26 Psalm 4:4

because these are improper for God's holy people. 4 Nor should there be obscenity, foolish talk or coarse joking, which are out of place, but rather thanksgiving. 5 For of this you can be sure: No immoral, impure or greedy person—such a man is an idolater—has any inheritance in the kingdom of Christ and of God.*m* 6 Let no one deceive you with empty words, for because of such things God's wrath comes on those who are disobedient. 7 Therefore do not be partners with them.

8 For you were once darkness, but now you are light in the Lord. Live as children of light 9 (for the fruit of the light consists in all goodness, righteousness and truth) 10 and find out what pleases the Lord. 11 Have nothing to do with the fruitless deeds of darkness, but rather expose them. 12 For it is shameful even to mention what the disobedient do in secret. 13 But everything exposed by the light becomes visible, 14 for it is light that makes everything visible. This is why it is said:

"Wake up, O sleeper,
    rise from the dead,
and Christ will shine on you."

15 Be very careful, then, how you live—not as unwise but as wise, 16 making the most of every opportunity, because the days are evil. 17 Therefore do not be foolish, but understand what the Lord's will is. 18 Do not get drunk on wine, which leads to debauchery. Instead, be filled with the Spirit. 19 Speak to one another with psalms, hymns and spiritual songs. Sing and make music in your heart to the Lord, 20 always giving thanks to God the Father for everything, in the name of our Lord Jesus Christ.

21 Submit to one another out of reverence for Christ.

Wives and Husbands

22 Wives, submit to your husbands as to the Lord. 23 For the husband is the head of the wife as Christ is the head of the church, his body, of which he is the Savior. 24 Now as the church submits to Christ, so also wives should submit to their husbands in everything.

25 Husbands, love your wives, just as Christ loved the church and gave himself up for her 26 to make her holy, cleansing*n* her by the washing with water through the word, 27 and to present her to himself as a radiant church, without stain or wrinkle or any other blemish, but holy and blameless. 28 In this same way, husbands ought to love their wives as their own bodies. He who loves his wife loves himself. 29 After all, no one ever hated his own body, but he feeds and cares for it, just as Christ does the church— 30 for we are members of his body. 31 "For this reason a man will leave his father and mother and be united to his wife, and the two will become one flesh."*o* 32 This is a profound mystery—but I am talking about Christ and the church. 33 However, each one of you also must love his wife as he loves himself, and the wife must respect her husband.

Children and Parents

6 1 Children, obey your parents in the Lord, for this is right. 2 "Honor your father and mother"— which is the first commandment with

---

m 5 Or kingdom of the Christ and God   n 26 Or having cleansed   o 31 Gen. 2:24 a promise— 3 "that it may go well with you and that you may enjoy long life on the earth."*p* 4 Fathers, do not exasperate your children; instead, bring them up in the training and instruction of the Lord.

Slaves and Masters

5 Slaves, obey your earthly masters with respect and fear, and with sincerity of heart, just as you would obey Christ. 6 Obey them not only to win their favor when their eye is on you, but like slaves of Christ, doing the will of God from your heart. 7 Serve wholeheartedly, as if you were serving the Lord, not men, 8 because you know that the Lord will reward everyone for whatever good he does, whether he is slave or free.

9 And masters, treat your slaves in the same way. Do not threaten them, since you know that he who is both their Master and yours is in heaven, and there is no favoritism with him.

The Armor of God

10 Finally, be strong in the Lord and in his mighty power. 11 Put on the full armor of God so that you can take your stand against the devil's schemes. 12 For our struggle is not against flesh and blood, but against the rulers, against the authorities, against the powers of this dark world and against the spiritual forces of evil in the heavenly realms. 13 Therefore put on the full armor of God, so that when the day of evil comes, you may be able to stand your ground, and

after you have done everything, to stand. 14 Stand firm then, with the belt of truth buckled around your waist, with the breastplate of righteousness in place, 15 and with your feet fitted with the readiness that comes from the gospel of peace. 16 In addition to all this, take up the shield of faith, with which you can extinguish all the flaming arrows of the evil one. 17 Take the helmet of salvation and the sword of the Spirit, which is the word of God. 18 And pray in the Spirit on all occasions with all kinds of prayers and requests. With this in mind, be alert and always keep on praying for all the saints.

19 Pray also for me, that whenever I open my mouth, words may be given me so that I will fearlessly make known the mystery of the gospel, 20 for which I am an ambassador in chains. Pray that I may declare it fearlessly, as I should.

Final Greetings

21 Tychicus, the dear brother and faithful servant in the Lord, will tell you everything, so that you also may know how I am and what I am doing. 22 I am sending him to you for this very purpose, that you may know how we are, and that he may encourage you.

23 Peace to the brothers, and love with faith from God the Father and the Lord Jesus Christ. 24 Grace to all who love our Lord Jesus Christ with an undying love.

p 3 Deut. 5:16

Philippians

1

1 Paul and Timothy, servants of Christ Jesus,

To all the saints in Christ Jesus at Philippi, together with the overseers[a] and deacons:

2 Grace and peace to you from God our Father and the Lord Jesus Christ.

Thanksgiving and Prayer

3 I thank my God every time I remember you. **4** In all my prayers for all of you, I always pray with joy **5** because of your partnership in the gospel from the first day until now, **6** being confident of this, that he who began a good work in you will carry it on to completion until the day of Christ Jesus.

7 It is right for me to feel this way about all of you, since I have you in my heart; for whether I am in chains or defending and confirming the gospel, all of you share in God's grace with me. **8** God can testify how I long for all of you with the affection of Christ Jesus.

9 And this is my prayer: that your love may abound more and more in knowledge and depth of insight, **10** so that you may be able to discern what is best and may be pure and blameless until the day of Christ, **11** filled with the fruit of righteousness that comes through Jesus Christ — to the glory and praise of God.

Paul's Chains Advance the Gospel

12 Now I want you to know, brothers, that what has happened to me has really served to advance the gospel. **13** As a result, it has become clear throughout the whole palace guard[b] and to everyone else that I am in chains for Christ. **14** Because of my chains, most of the brothers in the Lord have been encouraged to speak the word of God more courageously and fearlessly.

15 It is true that some preach Christ out of envy and rivalry, but others out of goodwill. **16** The latter do so in love, knowing that I am put here for the defense of the gospel. **17** The former preach Christ out of selfish ambition, not sincerely, supposing that they can stir up trouble for me while I am in chains.[c] **18** But what does it matter? The important thing is that in every way, whether from false motives or true, Christ is preached. And because of this I rejoice.

Yes, and I will continue to rejoice, **19** for I know that through your prayers and the help given by the Spirit of Jesus Christ, what has happened to me will turn out for my deliverance.[d] **20** I eagerly expect and hope that I will in no way be ashamed, but will have sufficient courage so that now as always Christ will be exalted in my body, whether by life or by death. **21** For to me, to live is Christ and to die is gain. **22** If

---

[a] 1 Traditionally *bishops*   [b] 13 Or *whole palace*   [c] 17 Some late manuscripts have verses 16 and 17 in reverse order.   [d] 19 Or *salvation*

I am to go on living in the body, this will mean fruitful labor for me. Yet what shall I choose? I do not know! 23 I am torn between the two: I desire to depart and be with Christ, which is better by far; 24 but it is more necessary for you that I remain in the body. 25 Convinced of this, I know that I will remain, and I will continue with all of you for your progress and joy in the faith, 26 so that through my being with you again your joy in Christ Jesus will overflow on account of me.

27 Whatever happens, conduct yourselves in a manner worthy of the gospel of Christ. Then, whether I come and see you or only hear about you in my absence, I will know that you stand firm in one spirit, contending as one man for the faith of the gospel 28 without being frightened in any way by those who oppose you. This is a sign to them that they will be destroyed, but that you will be saved — and that by God. 29 For it has been granted to you on behalf of Christ not only to believe on him, but also to suffer for him, 30 since you are going through the same struggle you saw I had, and now hear that I still have.

Imitating Christ's Humility

2 1 If you have any encouragement from being united with Christ, if any comfort from his love, if any fellowship with the Spirit, if any tenderness and compassion, 2 then make my joy complete by being like-minded, having the same love, being one in spirit and purpose. 3 Do nothing out of selfish ambition or vain conceit, but in humility consider others better than yourselves.

4 Each of you should look not only to your own interests, but also to the interests of others.

5 Your attitude should be the same as that of Christ Jesus:

6 Who, being in very nature[e] God,
   did not consider equality with
      God something to be
         grasped,
7 but made himself nothing,
   taking the very nature[f] of a
      servant,
   being made in human
      likeness.
8 And being found in appearance
      as a man,
   he humbled himself
   and became obedient to
      death — even death on a
         cross!
9 Therefore God exalted him to
      the highest place
   and gave him the name that
      is above every name,
10 that at the name of Jesus every
      knee should bow,
   in heaven and on earth and
      under the earth,
11 and every tongue confess that
      Jesus Christ is Lord,
   to the glory of God the Father.

Shining as Stars

12 Therefore, my dear friends, as you have always obeyed — not only in my presence, but now much more in my absence — continue to work out your salvation with fear and trembling, 13 for it is God who works in you to will and to act according to his good purpose.

14 Do everything without complaining or arguing, 15 so that you may become blameless and pure, children of God without fault in a

---

e 6 Or in the form of   f 7 Or the form

crooked and depraved generation, in which you shine like stars in the universe 16 as you hold out[g] the word of life—in order that I may boast on the day of Christ that I did not run or labor for nothing. 17 But even if I am being poured out like a drink offering on the sacrifice and service coming from your faith, I am glad and rejoice with all of you. 18 So you too should be glad and rejoice with me.

Timothy and Epaphroditus

19 I hope in the Lord Jesus to send Timothy to you soon, that I also may be cheered when I receive news about you. 20 I have no one else like him, who takes a genuine interest in your welfare. 21 For everyone looks out for his own interests, not those of Jesus Christ. 22 But you know that Timothy has proved himself, because as a son with his father he has served with me in the work of the gospel. 23 I hope, therefore, to send him as soon as I see how things go with me. 24 And I am confident in the Lord that I myself will come soon.

25 But I think it is necessary to send back to you Epaphroditus, my brother, fellow worker and fellow soldier, who is also your messenger, whom you sent to take care of my needs. 26 For he longs for all of you and is distressed because you heard he was ill. 27 Indeed he was ill, and almost died. But God had mercy on him, and not on him only but also on me, to spare me sorrow upon sorrow. 28 Therefore I am all the more eager to send him, so that when you see him again you may be glad and I may have less anxiety. 29 Welcome him in the Lord with great joy, and honor men like him, 30 because he almost

died for the work of Christ, risking his life to make up for the help you could not give me.

No Confidence in the Flesh

3 1 Finally, my brothers, rejoice in the Lord! It is no trouble for me to write the same things to you again, and it is a safeguard for you.

2 Watch out for those dogs, those men who do evil, those mutilators of the flesh. 3 For it is we who are the circumcision, we who worship by the Spirit of God, who glory in Christ Jesus, and who put no confidence in the flesh— 4 though I myself have reasons for such confidence.

If anyone else thinks he has reason to put confidence in the flesh, I have more: 5 circumcised on the eighth day, of the people of Israel, of the tribe of Benjamin, a Hebrew of Hebrews; in regard to the law, a Pharisee; 6 as for zeal, persecuting the church; as for legalistic righteousness, faultless.

7 But whatever was to my profit I now consider loss for the sake of Christ. 8 What is more, I consider everything a loss compared to the surpassing greatness of knowing Christ Jesus my Lord, for whose sake I have lost all things. I consider them rubbish, that I may gain Christ 9 and be found in him, not having a righteousness of my own that comes from the law, but that which is through faith in Christ—the righteousness that comes from God and is by faith. 10 I want to know Christ and the power of his resurrection and the fellowship of sharing in his sufferings, becoming like him in his death, 11 and so, somehow, to attain to the resurrection from the dead.

g 16 Or hold on to

Pressing on Toward the Goal

12 Not that I have already obtained all this, or have already been made perfect, but I press on to take hold of that for which Christ Jesus took hold of me. **13** Brothers, I do not consider myself yet to have taken hold of it. But one thing I do: Forgetting what is behind and straining toward what is ahead, **14** I press on toward the goal to win the prize for which God has called me heavenward in Christ Jesus.

15 All of us who are mature should take such a view of things. And if on some point you think differently, that too God will make clear to you. **16** Only let us live up to what we have already attained.

17 Join with others in following my example, brothers, and take note of those who live according to the pattern we gave you. **18** For, as I have often told you before and now say again even with tears, many live as enemies of the cross of Christ. **19** Their destiny is destruction, their god is their stomach, and their glory is in their shame. Their mind is on earthly things. **20** But our citizenship is in heaven. And we eagerly await a Savior from there, the Lord Jesus Christ, **21** who, by the power that enables him to bring everything under his control, will transform our lowly bodies so that they will be like his glorious body.

4 **1** Therefore, my brothers, you whom I love and long for, my joy and crown, that is how you should stand firm in the Lord, dear friends!

Exhortations

2 I plead with Euodia and I plead with Syntyche to agree with each other in the Lord. **3** Yes, and I ask you, loyal yokefellow,[h] help these women who have contended at my side in the cause of the gospel, along with Clement and the rest of my fellow workers, whose names are in the book of life.

4 Rejoice in the Lord always. I will say it again: Rejoice! **5** Let your gentleness be evident to all. The Lord is near. **6** Do not be anxious about anything, but in everything, by prayer and petition, with thanksgiving, present your requests to God. **7** And the peace of God, which transcends all understanding, will guard your hearts and your minds in Christ Jesus.

8 Finally, brothers, whatever is true, whatever is noble, whatever is right, whatever is pure, whatever is lovely, whatever is admirable—if anything is excellent or praiseworthy—think about such things. **9** Whatever you have learned or received or heard from me, or seen in me—put it into practice. And the God of peace will be with you.

Thanks for Their Gifts

10 I rejoice greatly in the Lord that at last you have renewed your concern for me. Indeed, you have been concerned, but you had no opportunity to show it. **11** I am not saying this because I am in need, for I have learned to be content whatever the circumstances. **12** I know what it is to be in need, and I know what it is to have plenty. I have learned the secret of being content in any and every situation, whether well fed or hungry, whether living in plenty or in want. **13** I can do everything through him who gives me strength.

---

h 3 Or loyal Syzygus

14 Yet it was good of you to share in my troubles. **15** Moreover, as you Philippians know, in the early days of your acquaintance with the gospel, when I set out from Macedonia, not one church shared with me in the matter of giving and receiving, except you only; **16** for even when I was in Thessalonica, you sent me aid again and again when I was in need. **17** Not that I am looking for a gift, but I am looking for what may be credited to your account. **18** I have received full payment and even more; I am amply supplied, now that I have received from Epaphroditus the gifts you sent. They are a fragrant offering, an acceptable sacrifice, pleasing to God. **19** And my God will meet all your needs according to his glorious riches in Christ Jesus.

20 To our God and Father be glory for ever and ever. Amen.

Final Greetings

21 Greet all the saints in Christ Jesus. The brothers who are with me send greetings. **22** All the saints send you greetings, especially those who belong to Caesar's household.

23 The grace of the Lord Jesus Christ be with your spirit. Amen.[i]

---

i **23** Some manuscripts do not have *Amen*.

Colossians

1 ¹Paul, an apostle of Christ Jesus by the will of God, and Timothy our brother,

²To the holy and faithful[a] brothers in Christ at Colosse:

Grace and peace to you from God our Father.[b]

Thanksgiving and Prayer

³We always thank God, the Father of our Lord Jesus Christ, when we pray for you, ⁴because we have heard of your faith in Christ Jesus and of the love you have for all the saints — ⁵the faith and love that spring from the hope that is stored up for you in heaven and that you have already heard about in the word of truth, the gospel ⁶that has come to you. All over the world this gospel is bearing fruit and growing, just as it has been doing among you since the day you heard it and understood God's grace in all its truth. ⁷You learned it from Epaphras, our dear fellow servant, who is a faithful minister of Christ on our[c] behalf, ⁸and who also told us of your love in the Spirit.

⁹For this reason, since the day we heard about you, we have not stopped praying for you and asking God to fill you with the knowledge of his will through all spiritual wisdom and understanding. ¹⁰And we pray this in order that you may live a life worthy of the Lord and may please him in every way: bearing fruit in every good work, growing in the knowledge of God, ¹¹being strengthened with all power according to his glorious might so that you may have great endurance and patience, and joyfully ¹²giving thanks to the Father, who has qualified you[d] to share in the inheritance of the saints in the kingdom of light. ¹³For he has rescued us from the dominion of darkness and brought us into the kingdom of the Son he loves, ¹⁴in whom we have redemption,[e] the forgiveness of sins.

The Supremacy of Christ

¹⁵He is the image of the invisible God, the firstborn over all creation. ¹⁶For by him all things were created: things in heaven and on earth, visible and invisible, whether thrones or powers or rulers or authorities; all things were created by him and for him. ¹⁷He is before all things, and in him all things hold together. ¹⁸And he is the head of the body, the church; he is the beginning and the firstborn from among the dead, so that in everything he might have the supremacy. ¹⁹For God was pleased to have all his fullness dwell in him, ²⁰and through him to reconcile to himself all things, whether things on earth or things in heaven, by making peace through his blood, shed on the cross.

²¹Once you were alienated from God and were enemies in your minds because of[f] your evil behavior. ²²But now he has reconciled you by Christ's physical body through death to present you holy in his sight, without

---

a 2 Or *believing*   *b 2* Some manuscripts *Father and the Lord Jesus Christ*   *c 7* Some manuscripts *your*   *d 12* Some manuscripts *us*   *e 14* A few late manuscripts *redemption through his blood*   *f 21* Or *minds, as shown by*

blemish and free from accusation—
23 if you continue in your faith, established and firm, not moved from the hope held out in the gospel. This is the gospel that you heard and that has been proclaimed to every creature under heaven, and of which I, Paul, have become a servant.

Paul's Labor for the Church

24 Now I rejoice in what was suffered for you, and I fill up in my flesh what is still lacking in regard to Christ's afflictions, for the sake of his body, which is the church. 25 I have become its servant by the commission God gave me to present to you the word of God in its fullness— 26 the mystery that has been kept hidden for ages and generations, but is now disclosed to the saints. 27 To them God has chosen to make known among the Gentiles the glorious riches of this mystery, which is Christ in you, the hope of glory.

28 We proclaim him, admonishing and teaching everyone with all wisdom, so that we may present everyone perfect in Christ. 29 To this end I labor, struggling with all his energy, which so powerfully works in me.

2 1 I want you to know how much I am struggling for you and for those at Laodicea, and for all who have not met me personally. 2 My purpose is that they may be encouraged in heart and united in love, so that they may have the full riches of complete understanding, in order that they may know the mystery of God, namely, Christ, 3 in whom are hidden all the treasures of wisdom and knowledge. 4 I tell you this so that no one may deceive you by fine-sounding arguments. 5 For though I

am absent from you in body, I am present with you in spirit and delight to see how orderly you are and how firm your faith in Christ is.

Freedom From Human Regulations Through Life With Christ

6 So then, just as you received Christ Jesus as Lord, continue to live in him, 7 rooted and built up in him, strengthened in the faith as you were taught, and overflowing with thankfulness.

8 See to it that no one takes you captive through hollow and deceptive philosophy, which depends on human tradition and the basic principles of this world rather than on Christ.

9 For in Christ all the fullness of the Deity lives in bodily form, 10 and you have been given fullness in Christ, who is the head over every power and authority. 11 In him you were also circumcised, in the putting off of the sinful nature,*g* not with a circumcision done by the hands of men but with the circumcision done by Christ, 12 having been buried with him in baptism and raised with him through your faith in the power of God, who raised him from the dead.

13 When you were dead in your sins and in the uncircumcision of your sinful nature,*h* God made you alive with Christ. He forgave us all*i* our sins, 14 having canceled the written code, with its regulations, that was against us and that stood opposed to us; he took it away, nailing it to the cross. 15 And having disarmed the powers and authorities, he made a public spectacle of them, triumphing over them by the cross.*j*

16 Therefore do not let anyone judge you by what you eat or drink

---

g 11 Or *the flesh*   *h* 13 Or *your flesh*   *i* 13 Some manuscripts *us*   *j* 15 Or *them in him*

r with regard to a religious festival, a New Moon celebration or a Sabbath day. **17** These are a shadow of the things that were to come; the reality, however, is found in Christ. **18** Do not let anyone who delights in false humility and the worship of angels disqualify you for the prize. Such a person goes into great detail about what he has seen, and his unspiritual mind puffs him up with idle notions. **19** He has lost connection with the Head, from whom the whole body, supported and held together by its ligaments and sinews, grows as God causes it to grow.

20 Since you died with Christ to the basic principles of this world, why, as though you still belonged to it, do you submit to its rules: **21** "Do not handle! Do not taste! Do not touch!"? **22** These are all destined to perish with use, because they are based on human commands and teachings. **23** Such regulations indeed have an appearance of wisdom, with their self-imposed worship, their false humility and their harsh treatment of the body, but they lack any value in restraining sensual indulgence.

Rules for Holy Living

3 **1** Since, then, you have been raised with Christ, set your hearts on things above, where Christ is seated at the right hand of God. **2** Set your minds on things above, not on earthly things. **3** For you died, and your life is now hidden with Christ in God. **4** When Christ, who is your* life, appears, then you also will appear with him in glory.

5 Put to death, therefore, whatever belongs to your earthly nature:

sexual immorality, impurity, lust, evil desires and greed, which is idolatry. **6** Because of these, the wrath of God is coming.¹ **7** You used to walk in these ways, in the life you once lived. **8** But now you must rid yourselves of all such things as these: anger, rage, malice, slander, and filthy language from your lips. **9** Do not lie to each other, since you have taken off your old self with its practices **10** and have put on the new self, which is being renewed in knowledge in the image of its Creator. **11** Here there is no Greek or Jew, circumcised or uncircumcised, barbarian, Scythian, slave or free, but Christ is all, and is in all.

12 Therefore, as God's chosen people, holy and dearly loved, clothe yourselves with compassion, kindness, humility, gentleness and patience. **13** Bear with each other and forgive whatever grievances you may have against one another. Forgive as the Lord forgave you. **14** And over all these virtues put on love, which binds them all together in perfect unity.

15 Let the peace of Christ rule in your hearts, since as members of one body you were called to peace. And be thankful. **16** Let the word of Christ dwell in you richly as you teach and admonish one another with all wisdom, and as you sing psalms, hymns and spiritual songs with gratitude in your hearts to God. **17** And whatever you do, whether in word or deed, do it all in the name of the Lord Jesus, giving thanks to God the Father through him.

Rules for Christian Households

18 Wives, submit to your husbands, as is fitting in the Lord.

---

k 4 Some manuscripts *our* l 6 Some early manuscripts *coming on those who are disobedient*

19 Husbands, love your wives and do not be harsh with them.

20 Children, obey your parents in everything, for this pleases the Lord.

21 Fathers, do not embitter your children, or they will become discouraged.

22 Slaves, obey your earthly masters in everything; and do it, not only when their eye is on you and to win their favor, but with sincerity of heart and reverence for the Lord. **23** Whatever you do, work at it with all your heart, as working for the Lord, not for men, **24** since you know that you will receive an inheritance from the Lord as a reward. It is the Lord Christ you are serving. **25** Anyone who does wrong will be repaid for his wrong, and there is no favoritism.

4 **1** Masters, provide your slaves with what is right and fair, because you know that you also have a Master in heaven.

Further Instructions

2 Devote yourselves to prayer, being watchful and thankful. **3** And pray for us, too, that God may open a door for our message, so that we may proclaim the mystery of Christ, for which I am in chains. **4** Pray that I may proclaim it clearly, as I should. **5** Be wise in the way you act toward outsiders; make the most of every opportunity. **6** Let your conversation be always full of grace, seasoned with salt, so that you may know how to answer everyone.

Final Greetings

7 Tychicus will tell you all the news about me. He is a dear brother, a faithful minister and fellow servant in the Lord. **8** I am sending him to you for the express purpose that you may know about our*m* circumstances and that he may encourage your hearts. **9** He is coming with Onesimus, our faithful and dear brother, who is one of you. They will tell you everything that is happening here.

10 My fellow prisoner Aristarchus sends you his greetings, as does Mark, the cousin of Barnabas. (You have received instructions about him; if he comes to you, welcome him.) **11** Jesus, who is called Justus, also sends greetings. These are the only Jews among my fellow workers for the kingdom of God, and they have proved a comfort to me. **12** Epaphras, who is one of you and a servant of Christ Jesus, sends greetings. He is always wrestling in prayer for you, that you may stand firm in all the will of God, mature and fully assured. **13** I vouch for him that he is working hard for you and for those at Laodicea and Hierapolis. **14** Our dear friend Luke, the doctor, and Demas send greetings. **15** Give my greetings to the brothers at Laodicea, and to Nympha and the church in her house.

16 After this letter has been read to you, see that it is also read in the church of the Laodiceans and that you in turn read the letter from Laodicea.

17 Tell Archippus: "See to it that you complete the work you have received in the Lord."

18 I, Paul, write this greeting in my own hand. Remember my chains. Grace be with you.

---

m 8 Some manuscripts *that he may know about your*

1 Thessalonians

1 Paul, Silas[a] and Timothy,

To the church of the Thessalonians in God the Father and the Lord Jesus Christ:

Grace and peace to you.[b]

Thanksgiving for the Thessalonians' Faith

2 We always thank God for all of you, mentioning you in our prayers. **3** We continually remember before our God and Father your work produced by faith, your labor prompted by love, and your endurance inspired by hope in our Lord Jesus Christ.

4 For we know, brothers loved by God, that he has chosen you, **5** because our gospel came to you not simply with words, but also with power, with the Holy Spirit and with deep conviction. You know how we lived among you for your sake. **6** You became imitators of us and of the Lord; in spite of severe suffering, you welcomed the message with the joy given by the Holy Spirit. **7** And so you became a model to all the believers in Macedonia and Achaia. **8** The Lord's message rang out from you not only in Macedonia and Achaia—your faith in God has become known everywhere. Therefore we do not need to say anything about it, **9** for they themselves report what kind of reception you gave us. They tell how you turned to God from idols to serve the living and true God, **10** and to wait for his Son from heaven, whom he raised from the dead—Jesus, who rescues us from the coming wrath.

Paul's Ministry in Thessalonica

2 You know, brothers, that our visit to you was not a failure. **2** We had previously suffered and been insulted in Philippi, as you know, but with the help of our God we dared to tell you his gospel in spite of strong opposition. **3** For the appeal we make does not spring from error or impure motives, nor are we trying to trick you. **4** On the contrary, we speak as men approved by God to be entrusted with the gospel. We are not trying to please men but God, who tests our hearts. **5** You know we never used flattery, nor did we put on a mask to cover up greed—God is our witness. **6** We were not looking for praise from men, not from you or anyone else.

As apostles of Christ we could have been a burden to you, **7** but we were gentle among you, like a mother caring for her little children. **8** We loved you so much that we were delighted to share with you not only the gospel of God but our lives as well, because you had become so dear to us. **9** Surely you remember, brothers, our toil and hardship; we worked night and day in order not to be a burden to anyone while we preached the gospel of God to you.

10 You are witnesses, and so is God, of how holy, righteous and

---

a 1 Greek *Silvanus*, a variant of *Silas*   *b 1* Some early manuscripts *you from God our Father and the Lord Jesus Christ*

blameless we were among you who believed. **11** For you know that we dealt with each of you as a father deals with his own children, **12** encouraging, comforting and urging you to live lives worthy of God, who calls you into his kingdom and glory.

13 And we also thank God continually because, when you received the word of God, which you heard from us, you accepted it not as the word of men, but as it actually is, the word of God, which is at work in you who believe. **14** For you, brothers, became imitators of God's churches in Judea, which are in Christ Jesus: You suffered from your own countrymen the same things those churches suffered from the Jews, **15** who killed the Lord Jesus and the prophets and also drove us out. They displease God and are hostile to all men **16** in their effort to keep us from speaking to the Gentiles so that they may be saved. In this way they always heap up their sins to the limit. The wrath of God has come upon them at last.[c]

Paul's Longing to See the Thessalonians

17 But, brothers, when we were torn away from you for a short time (in person, not in thought), out of our intense longing we made every effort to see you. **18** For we wanted to come to you — certainly I, Paul, did, again and again — but Satan stopped us. **19** For what is our hope, our joy, or the crown in which we will glory in the presence of our Lord Jesus when he comes? Is it not you? **20** Indeed, you are our glory and joy.

3 **1** So when we could stand it no longer, we thought it best to be left by ourselves in Athens. **2** We sent Timothy, who is our brother and God's fellow worker[d] in spreading the gospel of Christ, to strengthen and encourage you in your faith, **3** so that no one would be unsettled by these trials. You know quite well that we were destined for them. **4** In fact, when we were with you, we kept telling you that we would be persecuted. And it turned out that way, as you well know. **5** For this reason, when I could stand it no longer, I sent to find out about your faith. I was afraid that in some way the tempter might have tempted you and our efforts might have been useless.

Timothy's Encouraging Report

6 But Timothy has just now come to us from you and has brought good news about your faith and love. He has told us that you always have pleasant memories of us and that you long to see us, just as we also long to see you. **7** Therefore, brothers, in all our distress and persecution we were encouraged about you because of your faith. **8** For now we really live, since you are standing firm in the Lord. **9** How can we thank God enough for you in return for all the joy we have in the presence of our God because of you? **10** Night and day we pray most earnestly that we may see you again and supply what is lacking in your faith.

11 Now may our God and Father himself and our Lord Jesus clear the way for us to come to you. **12** May the Lord make your love increase and overflow for each other and for

---

[c] 16 Or *them fully*   [d] 2 Some manuscripts *brother and fellow worker;* other manuscripts *brother and God's servant*

everyone else, just as ours does for you. **13** May he strengthen your hearts so that you will be blameless and holy in the presence of our God and Father when our Lord Jesus comes with all his holy ones.

Living to Please God

4 **1** Finally, brothers, we instructed you how to live in order to please God, as in fact you are living. Now we ask you and urge you in the Lord Jesus to do this more and more. **2** For you know what instructions we gave you by the authority of the Lord Jesus.

3 It is God's will that you should be sanctified: that you should avoid sexual immorality; **4** that each of you should learn to control his own body*e* in a way that is holy and honorable, **5** not in passionate lust like the heathen, who do not know God; **6** and that in this matter no one should wrong his brother or take advantage of him. The Lord will punish men for all such sins, as we have already told you and warned you. **7** For God did not call us to be impure, but to live a holy life. **8** Therefore, he who rejects this instruction does not reject man but God, who gives you his Holy Spirit.

9 Now about brotherly love we do not need to write to you, for you yourselves have been taught by God to love each other. **10** And in fact, you do love all the brothers throughout Macedonia. Yet we urge you, brothers, to do so more and more. **11** Make it your ambition to lead a quiet life, to mind your own business and to work with your hands, just as we told you, **12** so that your daily life may win the respect of outsiders and so that you will not be dependent on anybody.

The Coming of the Lord

13 Brothers, we do not want you to be ignorant about those who fall asleep, or to grieve like the rest of men, who have no hope. **14** We believe that Jesus died and rose again and so we believe that God will bring with Jesus those who have fallen asleep in him. **15** According to the Lord's own word, we tell you that we who are still alive, who are left till the coming of the Lord, will certainly not precede those who have fallen asleep. **16** For the Lord himself will come down from heaven, with a loud command, with the voice of the archangel and with the trumpet call of God, and the dead in Christ will rise first. **17** After that, we who are still alive and are left will be caught up together with them in the clouds to meet the Lord in the air. And so we will be with the Lord forever. **18** Therefore encourage each other with these words.

5 **1** Now, brothers, about times and dates we do not need to write to you, **2** for you know very well that the day of the Lord will come like a thief in the night. **3** While people are saying, "Peace and safety," destruction will come on them suddenly, as labor pains on a pregnant woman, and they will not escape.

4 But you, brothers, are not in darkness so that this day should surprise you like a thief. **5** You are all sons of the light and sons of the day. We do not belong to the night or to the darkness. **6** So then, let us not be like others, who are asleep, but let us be alert and self-controlled. **7** For those who sleep, sleep at night, and

---

e 4 Or *learn to live with his own wife;* or *learn to acquire a wife*

those who get drunk, get drunk at night. **8** But since we belong to the day, let us be self-controlled, putting on faith and love as a breastplate, and the hope of salvation as a helmet. **9** For God did not appoint us to suffer wrath but to receive salvation through our Lord Jesus Christ. **10** He died for us so that, whether we are awake or asleep, we may live together with him. **11** Therefore encourage one another and build each other up, just as in fact you are doing.

Final Instructions

12 Now we ask you, brothers, to respect those who work hard among you, who are over you in the Lord and who admonish you. **13** Hold them in the highest regard in love because of their work. Live in peace with each other. **14** And we urge you, brothers, warn those who are idle, encourage the timid, help the weak, be patient with everyone.

15 Make sure that nobody pays back wrong for wrong, but always try to be kind to each other and to everyone else.

16 Be joyful always; **17** pray continually; **18** give thanks in all circumstances, for this is God's will for you in Christ Jesus.

19 Do not put out the Spirit's fire; **20** do not treat prophecies with contempt. **21** Test everything. Hold on to the good. **22** Avoid every kind of evil.

23 May God himself, the God of peace, sanctify you through and through. May your whole spirit, soul and body be kept blameless at the coming of our Lord Jesus Christ. **24** The one who calls you is faithful and he will do it.

25 Brothers, pray for us. **26** Greet all the brothers with a holy kiss. **27** I charge you before the Lord to have this letter read to all the brothers.

28 The grace of our Lord Jesus Christ be with you.

2 Thessalonians

1 ¹ Paul, Silas[a] and Timothy,

To the church of the Thessalonians in God our Father and the Lord Jesus Christ:

² Grace and peace to you from God the Father and the Lord Jesus Christ.

Thanksgiving and Prayer

³ We ought always to thank God for you, brothers, and rightly so, because your faith is growing more and more, and the love every one of you has for each other is increasing. ⁴ Therefore, among God's churches we boast about your perseverance and faith in all the persecutions and trials you are enduring.

⁵ All this is evidence that God's judgment is right, and as a result you will be counted worthy of the kingdom of God, for which you are suffering. ⁶ God is just: He will pay back trouble to those who trouble you ⁷ and give relief to you who are troubled, and to us as well. This will happen when the Lord Jesus is revealed from heaven in blazing fire with his powerful angels. ⁸ He will punish those who do not know God and do not obey the gospel of our Lord Jesus. ⁹ They will be punished with everlasting destruction and shut out from the presence of the Lord and from the majesty of his power ¹⁰ on the day he comes to be glorified in his holy people and to be marveled at among all those who

have believed. This includes you, because you believed our testimony to you.

¹¹ With this in mind, we constantly pray for you, that our God may count you worthy of his calling, and that by his power he may fulfill every good purpose of yours and every act prompted by your faith. ¹² We pray this so that the name of our Lord Jesus may be glorified in you, and you in him, according to the grace of our God and the Lord Jesus Christ.[b]

The Man of Lawlessness

2 ¹ Concerning the coming of our Lord Jesus Christ and our being gathered to him, we ask you, brothers, ² not to become easily unsettled or alarmed by some prophecy, report or letter supposed to have come from us, saying that the day of the Lord has already come. ³ Don't let anyone deceive you in any way, for that day will not come until the rebellion occurs and the man of lawlessness[c] is revealed, the man doomed to destruction. ⁴ He will oppose and will exalt himself over everything that is called God or is worshiped, so that he sets himself up in God's temple, proclaiming himself to be God.

⁵ Don't you remember that when I was with you I used to tell you these things? ⁶ And now you know what is holding him back, so that he may be revealed at the proper time. ⁷ For the

---

a 1 Greek *Silvanus*, a variant of *Silas*   *b* 12 Or *God and Lord, Jesus Christ*   *c* 3 Some manuscripts *sin*

secret power of lawlessness is already at work; but the one who now holds it back will continue to do so till he is taken out of the way. 8 And then the lawless one will be revealed, whom the Lord Jesus will overthrow with the breath of his mouth and destroy by the splendor of his coming. 9 The coming of the lawless one will be in accordance with the work of Satan displayed in all kinds of counterfeit miracles, signs and wonders, 10 and in every sort of evil that deceives those who are perishing. They perish because they refused to love the truth and so be saved. 11 For this reason God sends them a powerful delusion so that they will believe the lie 12 and so that all will be condemned who have not believed the truth but have delighted in wickedness.

Stand Firm

13 But we ought always to thank God for you, brothers loved by the Lord, because from the beginning God chose you^d to be saved through the sanctifying work of the Spirit and through belief in the truth. 14 He called you to this through our gospel, that you might share in the glory of our Lord Jesus Christ. 15 So then, brothers, stand firm and hold to the teachings^e we passed on to you, whether by word of mouth or by letter.

16 May our Lord Jesus Christ himself and God our Father, who loved us and by his grace gave us eternal encouragement and good hope, 17 encourage your hearts and strengthen you in every good deed and word.

Request for Prayer

3 1 Finally, brothers, pray for us that the message of the Lord may spread rapidly and be honored, just as it was with you. 2 And pray that we may be delivered from wicked and evil men, for not everyone has faith. 3 But the Lord is faithful, and he will strengthen and protect you from the evil one. 4 We have confidence in the Lord that you are doing and will continue to do the things we command. 5 May the Lord direct your hearts into God's love and Christ's perseverance.

Warning Against Idleness

6 In the name of the Lord Jesus Christ, we command you, brothers, to keep away from every brother who is idle and does not live according to the teaching^f you received from us. 7 For you yourselves know how you ought to follow our example. We were not idle when we were with you, 8 nor did we eat anyone's food without paying for it. On the contrary, we worked night and day, laboring and toiling so that we would not be a burden to any of you. 9 We did this, not because we do not have the right to such help, but in order to make ourselves a model for you to follow. 10 For even when we were with you, we gave you this rule: "If a man will not work, he shall not eat."

11 We hear that some among you are idle. They are not busy; they are busybodies. 12 Such people we command and urge in the Lord Jesus Christ to settle down and earn the bread they eat. 13 And as for you, brothers, never tire of doing what is right.

---

^d 13 Some manuscripts *because God chose you as his firstfruits*   ^e 15 Or *traditions*   ^f 6 Or *tradition*

14 If anyone does not obey our instruction in this letter, take special note of him. Do not associate with him, in order that he may feel ashamed. **15** Ye* do not regard him as an enemy, but warn him as a brother.

Special Greetings

16 Now may the Lord of peace himself give you peace at all times and in every way. The Lord be with all of you.

17 I, Paul, write this greeting in my own hand, which is the distinguishing mark in all my letters. This is how I write.

18 The grace of our Lord Jesus Christ be with you all.

1 Timothy

1 ¹ Paul, an apostle of Christ Jesus by the command of God our Savior and of Christ Jesus our hope,

² To Timothy my true son in the faith:

Grace, mercy and peace from God the Father and Christ Jesus our Lord.

Warning Against False Teachers of the Law

³ As I urged you when I went into Macedonia, stay there in Ephesus so that you may command certain men not to teach false doctrines any longer ⁴ nor to devote themselves to myths and endless genealogies. These promote controversies rather than God's work—which is by faith. ⁵ The goal of this command is love, which comes from a pure heart and a good conscience and a sincere faith. ⁶ Some have wandered away from these and turned to meaningless talk. ⁷ They want to be teachers of the law, but they do not know what they are talking about or what they so confidently affirm.

⁸ We know that the law is good if one uses it properly. ⁹ We also know that law*ᵃ* is made not for the righteous but for lawbreakers and rebels, the ungodly and sinful, the unholy and irreligious; for those who kill their fathers or mothers, for murderers, ¹⁰ for adulterers and perverts, for slave traders and liars and perjurers—and for whatever else is contrary to the sound doctrine ¹¹ that conforms to the glorious gospel of the blessed God, which he entrusted to me.

The Lord's Grace to Paul

¹² I thank Christ Jesus our Lord, who has given me strength, that he considered me faithful, appointing me to his service. ¹³ Even though I was once a blasphemer and a persecutor and a violent man, I was shown mercy because I acted in ignorance and unbelief. ¹⁴ The grace of our Lord was poured out on me abundantly, along with the faith and love that are in Christ Jesus.

¹⁵ Here is a trustworthy saying that deserves full acceptance: Christ Jesus came into the world to save sinners—of whom I am the worst. ¹⁶ But for that very reason I was shown mercy so that in me, the worst of sinners, Christ Jesus might display his unlimited patience as an example for those who would believe on him and receive eternal life. ¹⁷ Now to the King eternal, immortal, invisible, the only God, be honor and glory for ever and ever. Amen.

¹⁸ Timothy, my son, I give you this instruction in keeping with the prophecies once made about you, so that by following them you may fight the good fight, ¹⁹ holding on to faith and a good conscience. Some have rejected these and so have shipwrecked their faith. ²⁰ Among them are Hymenaeus and Alexander, whom I have handed over to Satan to be taught not to blaspheme.

ᵃ 9 Or that the law

278

Instructions on Worship

2 1 I urge, then, first of all, that requests, prayers, intercession and thanksgiving be made for everyone— 2 for kings and all those in authority, that we may live peaceful and quiet lives in all godliness and holiness. 3 This is good, and pleases God our Savior, 4 who wants all men to be saved and to come to a knowledge of the truth. 5 For there is one God and one mediator between God and men, the man Christ Jesus, 6 who gave himself as a ransom for all men— the testimony given in its proper time. 7 And for this purpose I was appointed a herald and an apostle—I am telling the truth, I am not lying—and a teacher of the true faith to the Gentiles.

8 I want men everywhere to lift up holy hands in prayer, without anger or disputing.

9 I also want women to dress modestly, with decency and propriety, not with braided hair or gold or pearls or expensive clothes, 10 but with good deeds, appropriate for women who profess to worship God.

11 A woman should learn in quietness and full submission. 12 I do not permit a woman to teach or to have authority over a man; she must be silent. 13 For Adam was formed first, then Eve. 14 And Adam was not the one deceived; it was the woman who was deceived and became a sinner. 15 But women[b] will be saved[c] through childbearing—if they continue in faith, love and holiness with propriety.

Overseers and Deacons

3 1 Here is a trustworthy saying: If anyone sets his heart on being an overseer,[d] he desires a noble task. 2 Now the overseer must be above reproach, the husband of but one wife, temperate, self-controlled, respectable, hospitable, able to teach, 3 not given to drunkenness, not violent but gentle, not quarrelsome, not a lover of money. 4 He must manage his own family well and see that his children obey him with proper respect. 5 (If anyone does not know how to manage his own family, how can he take care of God's church?) 6 He must not be a recent convert, or he may become conceited and fall under the same judgment as the devil. 7 He must also have a good reputation with outsiders, so that he will not fall into disgrace and into the devil's trap.

8 Deacons, likewise, are to be men worthy of respect, sincere, not indulging in much wine, and not pursuing dishonest gain. 9 They must keep hold of the deep truths of the faith with a clear conscience. 10 They must first be tested; and then if there is nothing against them, let them serve as deacons.

11 In the same way, their wives[e] are to be women worthy of respect, not malicious talkers but temperate and trustworthy in everything.

12 A deacon must be the husband of but one wife and must manage his children and his household well. 13 Those who have served well gain an excellent standing and great assurance in their faith in Christ Jesus.

---

b 15 Greek she   c 15 Or restored   d 1 Traditionally bishop; also in verse 2
e 11 Or way, deaconesses

14 Although I hope to come to you soon, I am writing you these instructions so that, 15 if I am delayed, you will know how people ought to conduct themselves in God's household, which is the church of the living God, the pillar and foundation of the truth. 16 Beyond all question, the mystery of godliness is great:

He*f* appeared in a body,*g*
was vindicated by the Spirit,
was seen by angels,
was preached among the
nations,
was believed on in the world,
was taken up in glory.

Instructions to Timothy

4 ¹ The Spirit clearly says that in later times some will abandon the faith and follow deceiving spirits and things taught by demons. 2 Such teachings come through hypocritical liars, whose consciences have been seared as with a hot iron. 3 They forbid people to marry and order them to abstain from certain foods, which God created to be received with thanksgiving by those who believe and who know the truth. 4 For everything God created is good, and nothing is to be rejected if it is received with thanksgiving, 5 because it is consecrated by the word of God and prayer.

6 If you point these things out to the brothers, you will be a good minister of Christ Jesus, brought up in the truths of the faith and of the good teaching that you have followed. 7 Have nothing to do with godless myths and old wives' tales; rather, train yourself to be godly. 8 For physical training is of some value, but

godliness has value for all things, holding promise for both the present life and the life to come.

9 This is a trustworthy saying that deserves full acceptance 10 (and for this we labor and strive), that we have put our hope in the living God, who is the Savior of all men, and especially of those who believe.

11 Command and teach these things. 12 Don't let anyone look down on you because you are young, but set an example for the believers in speech, in life, in love, in faith and in purity. 13 Until I come, devote yourself to the public reading of Scripture, to preaching and to teaching. 14 Do not neglect your gift, which was given you through a prophetic message when the body of elders laid their hands on you.

15 Be diligent in these matters; give yourself wholly to them, so that everyone may see your progress. 16 Watch your life and doctrine closely. Persevere in them, because if you do, you will save both yourself and your hearers.

Advice About Widows, Elders and Slaves

5 ¹ Do not rebuke an older man harshly, but exhort him as if he were your father. Treat younger men as brothers, 2 older women as mothers, and younger women as sisters, with absolute purity.

3 Give proper recognition to those widows who are really in need. 4 But if a widow has children or grandchildren, these should learn first of all to put their religion into practice by caring for their own family and so repaying their parents and grandparents, for this is pleasing to

f 16 Some manuscripts God   g 16 Or in the flesh

God. **5** The widow who is really in need and left all alone puts her hope in God and continues night and day to pray and to ask God for help. **6** But the widow who lives for pleasure is dead even while she lives. **7** Give the people these instructions, too, so that no one may be open to blame. **8** If anyone does not provide for his relatives, and especially for his immediate family, he has denied the faith and is worse than an unbeliever.

9 No widow may be put on the list of widows unless she is over sixty, has been faithful to her husband,[h] **10** and is well known for her good deeds, such as bringing up children, showing hospitality, washing the feet of the saints, helping those in trouble and devoting herself to all kinds of good deeds.

11 As for younger widows, do not put them on such a list. For when their sensual desires overcome their dedication to Christ, they want to marry. **12** Thus they bring judgment on themselves, because they have broken their first pledge. **13** Besides, they get into the habit of being idle and going about from house to house. And not only do they become idlers, but also gossips and busybodies, saying things they ought not to. **14** So I counsel younger widows to marry, to have children, to manage their homes and to give the enemy no opportunity for slander. **15** Some have in fact already turned away to follow Satan.

16 If any woman who is a believer has widows in her family, she should help them and not let the church be burdened with them, so that the church can help those widows who are really in need.

17 The elders who direct the affairs of the church well are worthy of double honor, especially those whose work is preaching and teaching. **18** For the Scripture says, "Do not muzzle the ox while it is treading out the grain,"[i] and "The worker deserves his wages."[j] **19** Do not entertain an accusation against an elder unless it is brought by two or three witnesses. **20** Those who sin are to be rebuked publicly, so that the others may take warning.

21 I charge you, in the sight of God and Christ Jesus and the elect angels, to keep these instructions without partiality, and to do nothing out of favoritism.

22 Do not be hasty in the laying on of hands, and do not share in the sins of others. Keep yourself pure.

23 Stop drinking only water, and use a little wine because of your stomach and your frequent illnesses.

24 The sins of some men are obvious, reaching the place of judgment ahead of them; the sins of others trail behind them. **25** In the same way, good deeds are obvious, and even those that are not cannot be hidden.

6 **1** All who are under the yoke of slavery should consider their masters worthy of full respect, so that God's name and our teaching may not be slandered. **2** Those who have believing masters are not to show less respect for them because they are brothers. Instead, they are to serve them even better, because those who benefit from their service are believers, and dear to them. These are the things you are to teach and urge on them.

---

h 9 Or has had but one husband   i 18 Deut. 25:4   j 18 Luke 10:7

Love of Money

3 If anyone teaches false doctrines and does not agree to the sound instruction of our Lord Jesus Christ and to godly teaching, 4 he is conceited and understands nothing. He has an unhealthy interest in controversies and quarrels about words that result in envy, strife, malicious talk, evil suspicions 5 and constant friction between men of corrupt mind, who have been robbed of the truth and who think that godliness is a means to financial gain.

6 But godliness with contentment is great gain. 7 For we brought nothing into the world, and we can take nothing out of it. 8 But if we have food and clothing, we will be content with that. 9 People who want to get rich fall into temptation and a trap and into many foolish and harmful desires that plunge men into ruin and destruction. 10 For the love of money is a root of all kinds of evil. Some people, eager for money, have wandered from the faith and pierced themselves with many griefs.

Paul's Charge to Timothy

11 But you, man of God, flee from all this, and pursue righteousness, godliness, faith, love, endurance and gentleness. 12 Fight the good fight of the faith. Take hold of the eternal life to which you were called when you made your good confession in the presence of many witnesses. 13 In the sight of God, who gives life to everything, and of Christ Jesus, who while testifying before Pontius Pilate made the good confession, I charge you 14 to keep this command without spot or blame until the appearing of our Lord Jesus Christ, 15 which God will bring about in his own time — God, the blessed and only Ruler, the King of kings and Lord of lords, 16 who alone is immortal and who lives in unapproachable light, whom no one has seen or can see. To him be honor and might forever. Amen.

17 Command those who are rich in this present world not to be arrogant nor to put their hope in wealth, which is so uncertain, but to put their hope in God, who richly provides us with everything for our enjoyment. 18 Command them to do good, to be rich in good deeds, and to be generous and willing to share. 19 In this way they will lay up treasure for themselves as a firm foundation for the coming age, so that they may take hold of the life that is truly life.

20 Timothy, guard what has been entrusted to your care. Turn away from godless chatter and the opposing ideas of what is falsely called knowledge, 21 which some have professed and in so doing have wandered from the faith.

Grace be with you.

2 Timothy

1 1 Paul, an apostle of Christ Jesus by the will of God, according to the promise of life that is in Christ Jesus,

2 To Timothy, my dear son:

Grace, mercy and peace from God the Father and Christ Jesus our Lord.

Encouragement to Be Faithful

3 I thank God, whom I serve, as my forefathers did, with a clear conscience, as night and day I constantly remember you in my prayers. 4 Recalling your tears, I long to see you, so that I may be filled with joy. 5 I have been reminded of your sincere faith, which first lived in your grandmother Lois and in your mother Eunice and, I am persuaded, now lives in you also. 6 For this reason I remind you to fan into flame the gift of God, which is in you through the laying on of my hands. 7 For God did not give us a spirit of timidity, but a spirit of power, of love and of self-discipline.

8 So do not be ashamed to testify about our Lord, or ashamed of me his prisoner. But join with me in suffering for the gospel, by the power of God, 9 who has saved us and called us to a holy life — not because of anything we have done but because of his own purpose and grace. This grace was given us in Christ Jesus before the beginning of time, 10 but it has now been revealed through the appearing of our Savior, Christ Jesus, who has destroyed death and has brought life and immortality to light through the gospel. 11 And of this gospel I was appointed a herald and an apostle and a teacher. 12 That is why I am suffering as I am. Yet I am not ashamed, because I know whom I have believed, and am convinced that he is able to guard what I have entrusted to him for that day.

13 What you heard from me, keep as the pattern of sound teaching, with faith and love in Christ Jesus. 14 Guard the good deposit that was entrusted to you — guard it with the help of the Holy Spirit who lives in us.

15 You know that everyone in the province of Asia has deserted me, including Phygelus and Hermogenes.

16 May the Lord show mercy to the household of Onesiphorus, because he often refreshed me and was not ashamed of my chains. 17 On the contrary, when he was in Rome, he searched hard for me until he found me. 18 May the Lord grant that he will find mercy from the Lord on that day! You know very well in how many ways he helped me in Ephesus.

2 1 You then, my son, be strong in the grace that is in Christ Jesus. 2 And the things you have heard me say in the presence of many witnesses entrust to reliable men who will also be qualified to teach others. 3 Endure hardship with us like a good soldier of Christ Jesus. 4 No one serving as a soldier gets involved in civilian affairs — he wants to please his commanding officer. 5 Similarly, if anyone competes as an athlete, he does not receive the victor's crown unless he competes according to the rules. 6 The hardworking farmer should be the first to receive a share of the crops. 7 Reflect on what I am saying, for the Lord will give you insight into all this.

8 Remember Jesus Christ, raised from the dead, descended from David. This is my gospel, 9 for which I am suffering even to the point of being chained like a criminal. But God's word is not chained. 10 Therefore I endure everything for the sake of the elect, that they too may obtain the salvation that is in Christ Jesus, with eternal glory.

11 Here is a trustworthy saying:

If we died with him,
    we will also live with him;
12 if we endure,
    we will also reign with him.
If we disown him,
    he will also disown us;
13 if we are faithless,
    he will remain faithful,
    for he cannot disown himself.

A Workman Approved by God

14 Keep reminding them of these things. Warn them before God against quarreling about words; it is of no value, and only ruins those who listen. 15 Do your best to present yourself to God as one approved, a workman who does not need to be ashamed and who correctly handles the word of truth. 16 Avoid godless chatter, because those who indulge in it will become more and more ungodly. 17 Their teaching will spread like gangrene. Among them are Hymenaeus and Philetus, 18 who have wandered away from the truth. They say that the resurrection has already taken place, and they destroy the faith of some. 19 Nevertheless, God's solid foundation stands firm,

sealed with this inscription: "The Lord knows those who are his,"[a] and, "Everyone who confesses the name of the Lord must turn away from wickedness."

20 In a large house there are articles not only of gold and silver, but also of wood and clay; some are for noble purposes and some for ignoble. 21 If a man cleanses himself from the latter, he will be an instrument for noble purposes, made holy, useful to the Master and prepared to do any good work.

22 Flee the evil desires of youth, and pursue righteousness, faith, love and peace, along with those who call on the Lord out of a pure heart. 23 Don't have anything to do with foolish and stupid arguments, because you know they produce quarrels. 24 And the Lord's servant must not quarrel; instead, he must be kind to everyone, able to teach, not resentful. 25 Those who oppose him he must gently instruct, in the hope that God will grant them repentance leading them to a knowledge of the truth, 26 and that they will come to their senses and escape from the trap of the devil, who has taken them captive to do his will.

Godlessness in the Last Days

3 1 But mark this: There will be terrible times in the last days. 2 People will be lovers of themselves, lovers of money, boastful, proud, abusive, disobedient to their parents, ungrateful, unholy, 3 without love, unforgiving, slanderous, without self-control, brutal, not lovers of the good, 4 treacherous, rash, conceited, lovers of pleasure rather than lovers of God — 5 having a form of godliness

a 19 Num. 16:5 (see Septuagint)

ut denying its power. Have nothing o do with them.

6 They are the kind who worm heir way into homes and gain control over weak-willed women, who re loaded down with sins and are wayed by all kinds of evil desires, always learning but never able to cknowledge the truth. 8 Just as Janes and Jambres opposed Moses, so also these men oppose the truth—men of depraved minds, who, as far as the faith is concerned, are ejected. 9 But they will not get very ar because, as in the case of those nen, their folly will be clear to veryone.

Paul's Charge to Timothy

10 You, however, know all about ny teaching, my way of life, my purose, faith, patience, love, endurance, 11 persecutions, sufferings—what kinds of things happened o me in Antioch, Iconium and Lystra, the persecutions I endured. Yet the Lord rescued me from all of hem. 12 In fact, everyone who wants o live a godly life in Christ Jesus will be persecuted, 13 while evil men and mpostors will go from bad to worse, deceiving and being deceived. 14 But as for you, continue in what you have earned and have become convinced of, because you know those from whom you learned it, 15 and how from infancy you have known the holy Scriptures, which are able to make you wise for salvation through faith in Christ Jesus. 16 All Scripture is God-breathed and is useful for teaching, rebuking, correcting and training in righteousness, 17 so that the man of God may be thoroughly equipped for every good work.

4 1 In the presence of God and of Christ Jesus, who will judge the living and the dead, and in view of his appearing and his kingdom, I give you this charge: 2 Preach the Word; be prepared in season and out of season; correct, rebuke and encourage—with great patience and careful instruction. 3 For the time will come when men will not put up with sound doctrine. Instead, to suit their own desires, they will gather around them a great number of teachers to say what their itching ears want to hear. 4 They will turn their ears away from the truth and turn aside to myths. 5 But you, keep your head in all situations, endure hardship, do the work of an evangelist, discharge all the duties of your ministry.

6 For I am already being poured out like a drink offering, and the time has come for my departure. 7 I have fought the good fight, I have finished the race, I have kept the faith. 8 Now there is in store for me the crown of righteousness, which the Lord, the righteous Judge, will award to me on that day—and not only to me, but also to all who have longed for his appearing.

Personal Remarks

9 Do your best to come to me quickly, 10 for Demas, because he loved this world, has deserted me and has gone to Thessalonica. Crescens has gone to Galatia, and Titus to Dalmatia. 11 Only Luke is with me. Get Mark and bring him with you, because he is helpful to me in my ministry. 12 I sent Tychicus to Ephesus. 13 When you come, bring the cloak that I left with Carpus at Troas, and my scrolls, especially the parchments.

14 Alexander the metalworker did me a great deal of harm. The Lord will repay him for what he has done. 15 You too should be on your guard

against him, because he strongly opposed our message.

16 At my first defense, no one came to my support, but everyone deserted me. May it not be held against them. 17 But the Lord stood at my side and gave me strength, so that through me the message might be fully proclaimed and all the Gentiles might hear it. And I was delivered from the lion's mouth. 18 The Lord will rescue me from every evil attack and will bring me

safely to his heavenly kingdom. To him be glory for ever and ever. Amen.

Final Greetings

19 Greet Priscillab and Aquila and the household of Onesiphorus. 20 Erastus stayed in Corinth, and I left Trophimus sick in Miletus. 21 Do your best to get here before winter. Eubulus greets you, and so do Pudens, Linus, Claudia and all the brothers.

22 The Lord be with your spirit. Grace be with you.

Titus

1 ¹ Paul, a servant of God and an apostle of Jesus Christ for the faith of God's elect and the knowledge of the truth that leads to godliness— ² a faith and knowledge resting on the hope of eternal life, which God, who does not lie, promised before the beginning of time, ³ and at his appointed season he brought his word to light through the preaching entrusted to me by the command of God our Savior,

⁴ To Titus, my true son in our common faith:

Grace and peace from God the Father and Christ Jesus our Savior.

Titus' Task on Crete

⁵ The reason I left you in Crete was that you might straighten out what was left unfinished and appoint[a] elders in every town, as I directed you. ⁶ An elder must be blameless, the husband of but one wife, a man whose children believe and are not open to the charge of being wild and disobedient. ⁷ Since an overseer[b] is entrusted with God's work, he must be blameless—not overbearing, not quick-tempered, not given to drunkenness, not violent, not pursuing dishonest gain. ⁸ Rather he must be hospitable, one who loves what is good, who is self-controlled, upright, holy and disciplined. ⁹ He must hold firmly to the trustworthy message as it has been taught, so that he can encourage others by sound doctrine and refute those who oppose it.

¹⁰ For there are many rebellious people, mere talkers and deceivers, especially those of the circumcision group. ¹¹ They must be silenced, because they are ruining whole households by teaching things they ought not to teach—and that for the sake of dishonest gain. ¹² Even one of their own prophets has said, "Cretans are always liars, evil brutes, lazy gluttons." ¹³ This testimony is true. Therefore, rebuke them sharply, so that they will be sound in the faith ¹⁴ and will pay no attention to Jewish myths or to the commands of those who reject the truth. ¹⁵ To the pure, all things are pure, but to those who are corrupted and do not believe, nothing is pure. In fact, both their minds and consciences are corrupted. ¹⁶ They claim to know God, but by their actions they deny him. They are detestable, disobedient and unfit for doing anything good.

What Must Be Taught to Various Groups

2 ¹ You must teach what is in accord with sound doctrine. ² Teach the older men to be temperate, worthy of respect, self-controlled, and sound in faith, in love and in endurance.

³ Likewise, teach the older women to be reverent in the way they live, not to be slanderers or addicted to much wine, but to teach what is good. ⁴ Then they can train the younger women to love their husbands and children, ⁵ to be self-con-

---

a 5 Or *ordain*   *b 7* Traditionally *bishop*

trolled and pure, to be busy at home, to be kind, and to be subject to their husbands, so that no one will malign the word of God.

6 Similarly, encourage the young men to be self-controlled. 7 In everything set them an example by doing what is good. In your teaching show integrity, seriousness 8 and soundness of speech that cannot be condemned, so that those who oppose you may be ashamed because they have nothing bad to say about us.

9 Teach slaves to be subject to their masters in everything, to try to please them, not to talk back to them, 10 and not to steal from them, but to show that they can be fully trusted, so that in every way they will make the teaching about God our Savior attractive.

11 For the grace of God that brings salvation has appeared to all men. 12 It teaches us to say "No" to ungodliness and worldly passions, and to live self-controlled, upright and godly lives in this present age, 13 while we wait for the blessed hope — the glorious appearing of our great God and Savior, Jesus Christ, 14 who gave himself for us to redeem us from all wickedness and to purify for himself a people that are his very own, eager to do what is good.

15 These, then, are the things you should teach. Encourage and rebuke with all authority. Do not let anyone despise you.

Doing What is Good

3 1 Remind the people to be subject to rulers and authorities, to be obedient, to be ready to do whatever is good, 2 to slander no one, to be peaceable and considerate, and to show true humility toward all men.

3 At one time we too were foolish, disobedient, deceived and enslaved by all kinds of passions and pleasures. We lived in malice and envy, being hated and hating one another. 4 But when the kindness and love of God our Savior appeared 5 he saved us, not because of righteous things we had done, but because of his mercy. He saved us through the washing of rebirth and renewal by the Holy Spirit, 6 whom he poured out on us generously through Jesus Christ our Savior, 7 so that, having been justified by his grace, we might become heirs having the hope of eternal life. 8 This is a trustworthy saying. And I want you to stress these things, so that those who have trusted in God may be careful to devote themselves to doing what is good. These things are excellent and profitable for everyone.

9 But avoid foolish controversies and genealogies and arguments and quarrels about the law, because these are unprofitable and useless. 10 Warn a divisive person once, and then warn him a second time. After that, have nothing to do with him. 11 You may be sure that such a man is warped and sinful; he is self-condemned.

Final Remarks

12 As soon as I send Artemas or Tychicus to you, do your best to come to me at Nicopolis, because I have decided to winter there. 13 Do everything you can to help Zenas the lawyer and Apollos on their way and see that they have everything they need. 14 Our people must learn to devote themselves to doing what is good, in order that they may provide for daily necessities and not live unproductive lives.

15 Everyone with me sends you greetings. Greet those who love us in the faith.

Grace be with you all.

CORBIN CARPENTER

★ ★ ★

I was riding at the 2008 National Finals High School Rodeo in Farmington, New Mexico. I had already ridden my second bull and knew one more score would put me in the short round, sittin' in a pretty good position to win. I had seen the bull a few days earlier in the back pens and knew by the way he was acting he was pretty "hooky" and whoever drew him would have to hit the ground moving.

I had no idea at the time that it would be me who drew him. I've always ridden jump for jump and my game plan was the same with him. The first jump out of the chute, I lost my rope and was ridin' with only two fingers. I knew I had to make the whistle and was doing whatever it took.

About six seconds into the ride, I was ridin' with only the tail of my rope and had slid too far back. I fell off into the well. Before I could move, the bull came around and was hooking me. I couldn't get out of the way when he spun around and his leg caught the back of my head and pushed it down. Something had to give and it was my neck. The bull kicked me and I landed on my left side. In my mind, I was scrambling out of the way, but I soon realized I wasn't moving at all. So I tried again. I couldn't move; I was scared.

As I laid in the dirt on the arena floor, God told me not to be afraid, that everything would be alright. I felt pretty good after that and trusted him.

I had two surgeries at San Juan Regional Medical Center in Farmington to repair the C6 and C7 vertebrae that were broken.

Even with the surgeries, the doctors didn't believe I would ever walk again. I was totally paralyzed from the chest down. But on the fifth day, my parents saw the muscle in the top of my left leg move.

More and more feeling and movement began to come back over the next couple of months. I stayed in the hospital in Farmington for 11 days, before being moved to Baylor Institute of Rehabilitation in Dallas, Texas.

Our insurance didn't cover much, so for Baylor to admit me, they had to have $26,700 in a cashiers check. My buddies worked to raise money for my medical expenses during the short go round at the finals the week before. An account had been opened for me at a bank in Farmington but we didn't have any idea how much was there.

My mom flew to Dallas with me while my dad stayed behind to go to the bank with Tilt James from The Fellowship of Christian Cowboys. By the time all the totals were added up, there was $26,800. A cashier's check was cut and a copy was faxed to Baylor. When my mom and I got off the elevator at Baylor, they took me right in. God just keeps working miracles!

My physical therapist asked me what my goal was when I left Baylor. I told him I was going to walk out and that my long term goal was to be 100% and ride bulls again. God had already told me that I was going to be alright and I never gave a second thought to anything different.

I know without a doubt that being a Christian is how I dealt with the physical and mental challenges that I faced. I stayed in rehab at Baylor for 6-1/2 weeks and the day I left, with my dad's help, I walked out.

One day short of seven months since my accident, I started back practicing team roping. One day short of nine months since the accident, I was back roping in competition. I thank God everyday that he is letting me tell my story and do what I love to do—rodeo.

★ ★ ★

JEFF GORE

At an early age, I longed to grow up and be a cowboy. Everything about the cowboy life and image interested me. To the astonishment of my parents, these interests didn't remain that of a small boy. They grew as I grew.

With the help of family friends who owned a small farm and ranch outside Sherman, Texas, I began ranch work and a learning process that would teach me not only about horses and cattle, but about life itself. Working afternoons and on weekends, I soon earned enough money to begin buying my own cattle for Future Farmers of America (FFA) projects at school.

From the time I was three years old, I have been performing gospel and pop music with family and friends for church and civic organizations and banquets. When I was seven, I began asking my dad what it meant to be a Christian. As a young boy sitting on my father's lap in the church parsonage late one night, I prayed to receive Christ as my Lord and Savior. I didn't understand everything that it meant at the time, but I believed as God's Word tells us in Romans, *"Everyone who calls on the name of the Lord will be saved"* (page 212). That day God began molding me to be what he wanted me to be.

I felt God call me to serve him full-time in a ministry at age twelve. I knew this calling was true, but I still longed for the cowboy life. I pursued a career in ministry, but I also took every opportunity to cowboy. I went to school at Howard Payne University and then to Southwestern Baptist Theological Seminary. I just figured I would work with teenagers the rest of my life. However, I also wanted to be a cowboy.

After twelve years of working in a local church along with singing cowboy and gospel music across the Southwest, I began a singing and preaching ministry geared toward cowboys, rural churches and ranching families.

As I grow older in age and in the Lord, I see that God has worked out all things. It was no coincidence that I loved the cowboy life and grew up working for friends on their ranch. It was no coincidence that I grew up in a preacher's home. It was all part of God's purpose for my life. I'm honored and privileged to serve God as a minister, striving to be a godly husband and father. I've seen all of my children pray to receive Christ into their hearts, just as my dad helped me more than thirty years ago.

Today, after neary twenty years of working with cowboys, their families and churches in rural areas, we have truly seen Christ's words come true when he said, *"But I, when I am lifted up from the earth, will draw all men to myself"* (John 12:32, page 142).

The letter of Second Corinthians says, *"Therefore, if anyone is in Christ, he is a new creation; the old has gone, the new has come!"* (page 241). We have seen Christ change people's lives and he continues to change ours through his word. We will always praise him for what he has done for us and continue to have copies of his word available for anyone who will take one.

★ ★ ★

© Jeff Gore

Philemon

1 Paul, a prisoner of Christ Jesus, and Timothy our brother,

To Philemon our dear friend and fellow worker, 2 to Apphia our sister, to Archippus our fellow soldier and to the church that meets in your home:

3 Grace to you and peace from God our Father and the Lord Jesus Christ.

Thanksgiving and Prayer

4 I always thank my God as I remember you in my prayers, 5 because I hear about your faith in the Lord Jesus and your love for all the saints. 6 I pray that you may be active in sharing your faith, so that you will have a full understanding of every good thing we have in Christ. 7 Your love has given me great joy and encouragement, because you, brother, have refreshed the hearts of the saints.

Paul's Plea for Onesimus

8 Therefore, although in Christ I could be bold and order you to do what you ought to do, 9 yet I appeal to you on the basis of love. I then, as Paul—an old man and now also a prisoner of Christ Jesus— 10 I appeal to you for my son Onesimus,[a] who became my son while I was in chains. 11 Formerly he was useless to you, but now he has become useful both to you and to me.

12 I am sending him—who is my very heart—back to you. 13 I would have liked to keep him with me so that he could take your place in helping me while I am in chains for the gospel. 14 But I did not want to do anything without your consent, so that any favor you do will be spontaneous and not forced. 15 Perhaps the reason he was separated from you for a little while was that you might have him back for good— 16 no longer as a slave, but better than a slave, as a dear brother. He is very dear to me but even dearer to you, both as a man and as a brother in the Lord.

17 So if you consider me a partner, welcome him as you would welcome me. 18 If he has done you any wrong or owes you anything, charge it to me. 19 I, Paul, am writing this with my own hand. I will pay it back—not to mention that you owe me your very self. 20 I do wish, brother, that I may have some benefit from you in the Lord; refresh my heart in Christ. 21 Confident of your obedience, I write to you, knowing that you will do even more than I ask.

22 And one thing more: Prepare a guest room for me, because I hope to be restored to you in answer to your prayers.

23 Epaphras, my fellow prisoner in Christ Jesus, sends you greetings. 24 And so do Mark, Aristarchus, Demas and Luke, my fellow workers.

25 The grace of the Lord Jesus Christ be with your spirit.

---

a 10 Onesimus means useful.

Hebrews

The Son Superior to Angels

1 ¹ In the past God spoke to our forefathers through the prophets at many times and in various ways, ² but in these last days he has spoken to us by his Son, whom he appointed heir of all things, and through whom he made the universe. ³ The Son is the radiance of God's glory and the exact representation of his being, sustaining all things by his powerful word. After he had provided purification for sins, he sat down at the right hand of the Majesty in heaven. ⁴ So he became as much superior to the angels as the name he has inherited is superior to theirs.

⁵ For to which of the angels did God ever say,

> "You are my Son;
> today I have become your Father^a"^{b}?

Or again,

> "I will be his Father,
> and he will be my Son"^{c}?

⁶ And again, when God brings his firstborn into the world, he says,

> "Let all God's angels worship him."^{d}

⁷ In speaking of the angels he says,

> "He makes his angels winds,
> his servants flames of fire."^{e}

⁸ But about the Son he says,

> "Your throne, O God, will last for ever and ever,
> and righteousness will be the scepter of your kingdom.
> ⁹ You have loved righteousness and hated wickedness;
> therefore God, your God, has set you above your companions
> by anointing you with the oil of joy."^{f}

¹⁰ He also says,

> "In the beginning, O Lord, you laid the foundations of the earth,
> and the heavens are the work of your hands.
> ¹¹ They will perish, but you remain;
> they will all wear out like a garment.
> ¹² You will roll them up like a robe;
> like a garment they will be changed.
> But you remain the same,
> and your years will never end."^{g}

¹³ To which of the angels did God ever say,

> "Sit at my right hand
> until I make your enemies a footstool for your feet"^{h}?

¹⁴ Are not all angels ministering spirits sent to serve those who will inherit salvation?

---

^{a} 5 Or *have begotten you* ^{b} 5 Psalm 2:7 ^{c} 5 2 Samuel 7:14; 1 Chron. 17:13
^{d} 6 Deut. 32:43 (see Dead Sea Scrolls and Septuagint) ^{e} 7 Psalm 104:4
^{f} 9 Psalm 45:6,7 ^{g} 12 Psalm 102:25-27 ^{h} 13 Psalm 110:1

Warning to Pay Attention

2 **1** We must pay more careful attention, therefore, to what we have heard, so that we do not drift away. **2** For if the message spoken by angels was binding, and every violation and disobedience received its just punishment, **3** how shall we escape if we ignore such a great salvation? This salvation, which was first announced by the Lord, was confirmed to us by those who heard him. **4** God also testified to it by signs, wonders and various miracles, and gifts of the Holy Spirit distributed according to his will.

Jesus Made Like His Brothers

5 It is not to angels that he has subjected the world to come, about which we are speaking. **6** But there is a place where someone has testified:

> "What is man that you are mindful of him,
> the son of man that you care for him?
> **7** You made him a little[i] lower than the angels;
> you crowned him with glory and honor
> **8** and put everything under his feet."[j]

In putting everything under him, God left nothing that is not subject to him. Yet at present we do not see everything subject to him. **9** But we see Jesus, who was made a little lower than the angels, now crowned with glory and honor because he suffered death, so that by the grace of God he might taste death for everyone.

10 In bringing many sons to glory, it was fitting that God, for whom and through whom everything exists, should make the author of their salvation perfect through suffering. **11** Both the one who makes men holy and those who are made holy are of the same family. So Jesus is not ashamed to call them brothers. **12** He says,

> "I will declare your name to my brothers;
> in the presence of the congregation I will sing your praises."[k]

13 And again,

> "I will put my trust in him."[l]

And again he says,

> "Here am I, and the children God has given me."[m]

14 Since the children have flesh and blood, he too shared in their humanity so that by his death he might destroy him who holds the power of death—that is, the devil— **15** and free those who all their lives were held in slavery by their fear of death. **16** For surely it is not angels he helps, but Abraham's descendants. **17** For this reason he had to be made like his brothers in every way, in order that he might become a merciful and faithful high priest in service to God, and that he might make atonement for[n] the sins of the people. **18** Because he himself suffered when he was tempted, he is able to help those who are being tempted.

---

i 7 Or him for a little while; also in verse 9   j 8 Psalm 8:4-6   k 12 Psalm 22:22   l 13 Isaiah 8:17   m 13 Isaiah 8:18   n 17 Or and that he might turn aside God's wrath, taking away

Jesus Greater Than Moses

3 1 Therefore, holy brothers, who share in the heavenly calling, fix your thoughts on Jesus, the apostle and high priest whom we confess. 2 He was faithful to the one who appointed him, just as Moses was faithful in all God's house. 3 Jesus has been found worthy of greater honor than Moses, just as the builder of a house has greater honor than the house itself. 4 For every house is built by someone, but God is the builder of everything. 5 Moses was faithful as a servant in all God's house, testifying to what would be said in the future. 6 But Christ is faithful as a son over God's house. And we are his house, if we hold on to our courage and the hope of which we boast.

Warning Against Unbelief

7 So, as the Holy Spirit says:

"Today, if you hear his voice,
8   do not harden your hearts
    as you did in the rebellion,
       during the time of testing in
          the desert,
9   where your fathers tested and
       tried me
    and for forty years saw what I
       did.
10 That is why I was angry with
       that generation,
    and I said, 'Their hearts are
       always going astray,
    and they have not known my
       ways.'
11 So I declared on oath in my
       anger,
    'They shall never enter my
       rest.' "*o*

12 See to it, brothers, that none of you has a sinful, unbelieving heart that turns away from the living God. 13 But encourage one another daily, as long as it is called Today, so that none of you may be hardened by sin's deceitfulness. 14 We have come to share in Christ if we hold firmly till the end the confidence we had at first. 15 As has just been said:

"Today, if you hear his voice,
   do not harden your hearts
   as you did in the rebellion."*p*

16 Who were they who heard and rebelled? Were they not all those Moses led out of Egypt? 17 And with whom was he angry for forty years? Was it not with those who sinned, whose bodies fell in the desert? 18 And to whom did God swear that they would never enter his rest if not to those who disobeyed*q*? 19 So we see that they were not able to enter, because of their unbelief.

A Sabbath-Rest for the People of God

4 1 Therefore, since the promise of entering his rest still stands, let us be careful that none of you be found to have fallen short of it. 2 For we also have had the gospel preached to us, just as they did; but the message they heard was of no value to them, because those who heard did not combine it with faith.*r* 3 Now we who have believed enter that rest, just as God has said,

"So I declared on oath in my
   anger,
'They shall never enter my
   rest.' "*s*

---

o 11 Psalm 95:7-11   *p* 15 Psalm 95:7,8   *q* 18 Or *disbelieved*   *r* 2 Many manuscripts *because they did not share in the faith of those who obeyed*   *s* 3 Psalm 95:11; also in verse 5

And yet his work has been finished since the creation of the world. 4 For somewhere he has spoken about the seventh day in these words: "And on the seventh day God rested from all his work."[t] 5 And again in the passage above he says, "They shall never enter my rest."

6 It still remains that some will enter that rest, and those who formerly had the gospel preached to them did not go in, because of their disobedience. 7 Therefore God again set a certain day, calling it Today, when a long time later he spoke through David, as was said before:

"Today, if you hear his voice,
    do not harden your hearts."[u]

8 For if Joshua had given them rest, God would not have spoken later about another day. 9 There remains, then, a Sabbath-rest for the people of God; 10 for anyone who enters God's rest also rests from his own work, just as God did from his. 11 Let us, therefore, make every effort to enter that rest, so that no one will fall by following their example of disobedience.

12 For the word of God is living and active. Sharper than any double-edged sword, it penetrates even to dividing soul and spirit, joints and marrow; it judges the thoughts and attitudes of the heart. 13 Nothing in all creation is hidden from God's sight. Everything is uncovered and laid bare before the eyes of him to whom we must give account.

Jesus the Great High Priest

14 Therefore, since we have a great high priest who has gone through the heavens,[v] Jesus the Son of God, let us hold firmly to the faith we profess. 15 For we do not have a high priest who is unable to sympathize with our weaknesses, but we have one who has been tempted in every way, just as we are—yet was without sin. 16 Let us then approach the throne of grace with confidence, so that we may receive mercy and find grace to help us in our time of need.

5 1 Every high priest is selected from among men and is appointed to represent them in matters related to God, to offer gifts and sacrifices for sins. 2 He is able to deal gently with those who are ignorant and are going astray, since he himself is subject to weakness. 3 This is why he has to offer sacrifices for his own sins, as well as for the sins of the people.

4 No one takes this honor upon himself; he must be called by God, just as Aaron was. 5 So Christ also did not take upon himself the glory of becoming a high priest. But God said to him,

"You are my Son;
    today I have become your
        Father."[w][x]

6 And he says in another place,

"You are a priest forever,
    in the order of Melchizedek."[y]

7 During the days of Jesus' life on earth, he offered up prayers and petitions with loud cries and tears to the one who could save him from death, and he was heard because of his reverent submission. 8 Although he was a son, he learned obedience

t 4 Gen. 2:2   u 7 Psalm 95:7,8   v 14 Or gone into heaven   w 5 Or have begotten you
x 5 Psalm 2:7   y 6 Psalm 110:4

from what he suffered 9 and, once made perfect, he became the source of eternal salvation for all who obey him 10 and was designated by God to be high priest in the order of Melchizedek.

Warning Against Falling Away

11 We have much to say about this, but it is hard to explain because you are slow to learn. 12 In fact, though by this time you ought to be teachers, you need someone to teach you the elementary truths of God's word all over again. You need milk, not solid food! 13 Anyone who lives on milk, being still an infant, is not acquainted with the teaching about righteousness. 14 But solid food is for the mature, who by constant use have trained themselves to distinguish good from evil.

6 1 Therefore let us leave the elementary teachings about Christ and go on to maturity, not laying again the foundation of repentance from acts that lead to death,^{z} and of faith in God, 2 instruction about baptisms, the laying on of hands, the resurrection of the dead, and eternal judgment. 3 And God permitting, we will do so.

4 It is impossible for those who have once been enlightened, who have tasted the heavenly gift, who have shared in the Holy Spirit, 5 who have tasted the goodness of the word of God and the powers of the coming age, 6 if they fall away, to be brought back to repentance, because^a to their loss they are crucifying the Son of God all over again and subjecting him to public disgrace.

7 Land that drinks in the rain often falling on it and that produces a crop useful to those for whom it is farmed receives the blessing of God. 8 But land that produces thorns and thistles is worthless and is in danger of being cursed. In the end it will be burned.

9 Even though we speak like this, dear friends, we are confident of better things in your case—things that accompany salvation. 10 God is not unjust; he will not forget your work and the love you have shown him as you have helped his people and continue to help them. 11 We want each of you to show this same diligence to the very end, in order to make your hope sure. 12 We do not want you to become lazy, but to imitate those who through faith and patience inherit what has been promised.

The Certainty of God's Promise

13 When God made his promise to Abraham, since there was no one greater for him to swear by, he swore by himself, 14 saying, "I will surely bless you and give you many descendants."^{b} 15 And so after waiting patiently, Abraham received what was promised.

16 Men swear by someone greater than themselves, and the oath confirms what is said and puts an end to all argument. 17 Because God wanted to make the unchanging nature of his purpose very clear to the heirs of what was promised, he confirmed it with an oath. 18 God did this so that, by two unchangeable things in which it is impossible for God to lie, we who have fled to take hold of the hope offered to us may be greatly encouraged. 19 We have this hope as an anchor for the soul, firm and secure. It enters the inner

---

^{z} 1 Or *from useless rituals* ^{a} 6 Or *repentance while* ^{b} 14 Gen. 22:17

sanctuary behind the curtain, **20** where Jesus, who went before us, has entered on our behalf. He has become a high priest forever, in the order of Melchizedek.

Melchizedek the Priest

7 ¹ This Melchizedek was king of Salem and priest of God Most High. He met Abraham returning from the defeat of the kings and blessed him, **2** and Abraham gave him a tenth of everything. First, his name means "king of righteousness"; then also, "king of Salem" means "king of peace." **3** Without father or mother, without genealogy, without beginning of days or end of life, like the Son of God he remains a priest forever.

4 Just think how great he was: Even the patriarch Abraham gave him a tenth of the plunder! **5** Now the law requires the descendants of Levi who become priests to collect a tenth from the people — that is, their brothers — even though their brothers are descended from Abraham. **6** This man, however, did not trace his descent from Levi, yet he collected a tenth from Abraham and blessed him who had the promises. **7** And without doubt the lesser person is blessed by the greater. **8** In the one case, the tenth is collected by men who die; but in the other case, by him who is declared to be living. **9** One might even say that Levi, who collects the tenth, paid the tenth through Abraham, **10** because when Melchizedek met Abraham, Levi was still in the body of his ancestor.

Jesus Like Melchizedek

11 If perfection could have been attained through the Levitical priest-

hood (for on the basis of it the law was given to the people), why was there still need for another priest to come — one in the order of Melchizedek, not in the order of Aaron? **12** For when there is a change of the priesthood, there must also be a change of the law. **13** He of whom these things are said belonged to a different tribe, and no one from that tribe has ever served at the altar. **14** For it is clear that our Lord descended from Judah, and in regard to that tribe Moses said nothing about priests. **15** And what we have said is even more clear if another priest like Melchizedek appears, **16** one who has become a priest not on the basis of a regulation as to his ancestry but on the basis of the power of an indestructible life. **17** For it is declared:

> "You are a priest forever,
>   in the order of Melchizedek."ᶜ

18 The former regulation is set aside because it was weak and useless **19** (for the law made nothing perfect), and a better hope is introduced, by which we draw near to God.

20 And it was not without an oath! Others became priests without any oath, **21** but he became a priest with an oath when God said to him:

> "The Lord has sworn
>   and will not change his mind:
>   'You are a priest forever.'"ᵈ

22 Because of this oath, Jesus has become the guarantee of a better covenant.

23 Now there have been many of those priests, since death prevented them from continuing in office; **24** but because Jesus lives forever, he

---

ᶜ *17* Psalm 110:4   ᵈ *21* Psalm 110:4

has a permanent priesthood.
25 Therefore he is able to save completely[e] those who come to God through him, because he always lives to intercede for them.

26 Such a high priest meets our need—one who is holy, blameless, pure, set apart from sinners, exalted above the heavens. **27** Unlike the other high priests, he does not need to offer sacrifices day after day, first for his own sins, and then for the sins of the people. He sacrificed for their sins once for all when he offered himself. **28** For the law appoints as high priests men who are weak; but the oath, which came after the law, appointed the Son, who has been made perfect forever.

The High Priest of a New Covenant

8 **1** The point of what we are saying is this: We do have such a high priest, who sat down at the right hand of the throne of the Majesty in heaven, **2** and who serves in the sanctuary, the true tabernacle set up by the Lord, not by man.

3 Every high priest is appointed to offer both gifts and sacrifices, and so it was necessary for this one also to have something to offer. **4** If he were on earth, he would not be a priest, for there are already men who offer the gifts prescribed by the law. **5** They serve at a sanctuary that is a copy and shadow of what is in heaven. This is why Moses was warned when he was about to build the tabernacle: "See to it that you make everything according to the pattern shown you on the mountain."[f] **6** But the ministry Jesus has received is as superior to theirs as the covenant of which he is mediator

is superior to the old one, and it is founded on better promises.

7 For if there had been nothing wrong with that first covenant, no place would have been sought for another. **8** But God found fault with the people and said:[g]

"The time is coming, declares the Lord,
  when I will make a new covenant
with the house of Israel
  and with the house of Judah.
9 It will not be like the covenant
  I made with their forefathers
when I took them by the hand
  to lead them out of Egypt,
because they did not remain
  faithful to my covenant,
  and I turned away from them,
    declares the Lord.
10 This is the covenant I will make
  with the house of Israel
after that time, declares the Lord.
I will put my laws in their minds
  and write them on their hearts.
I will be their God,
  and they will be my people.
11 No longer will a man teach his neighbor,
  or a man his brother, saying,
  'Know the Lord,'
because they will all know me,
  from the least of them to the greatest.
12 For I will forgive their wickedness
  and will remember their sins no more."[h]

13 By calling this covenant "new," he has made the first one obsolete; and what is obsolete and aging will soon disappear.

---

e 25 Or *forever*   *f* 5 Exodus 25:40   *g* 8 Some manuscripts may be translated *fault and said to the people.*   *h* 12 Jer. 31:31-34

Worship in the Earthly Tabernacle

9 1 Now the first covenant had regulations for worship and also an earthly sanctuary. 2 A tabernacle was set up. In its first room were the lampstand, the table and the consecrated bread; this was called the Holy Place. 3 Behind the second curtain was a room called the Most Holy Place, 4 which had the golden altar of incense and the gold-covered ark of the covenant. This ark contained the gold jar of manna, Aaron's staff that had budded, and the stone tablets of the covenant. 5 Above the ark were the cherubim of the Glory, overshadowing the atonement cover.[i] But we cannot discuss these things in detail now.

6 When everything had been arranged like this, the priests entered regularly into the outer room to carry on their ministry. 7 But only the high priest entered the inner room, and that only once a year, and never without blood, which he offered for himself and for the sins the people had committed in ignorance. 8 The Holy Spirit was showing by this that the way into the Most Holy Place had not yet been disclosed as long as the first tabernacle was still standing. 9 This is an illustration for the present time, indicating that the gifts and sacrifices being offered were not able to clear the conscience of the worshiper. 10 They are only a matter of food and drink and various ceremonial washings—external regulations applying until the time of the new order.

The Blood of Christ

11 When Christ came as high priest of the good things that are already here,[j] he went through the greater and more perfect tabernacle that is not man-made, that is to say, not a part of this creation. 12 He did not enter by means of the blood of goats and calves; but he entered the Most Holy Place once for all by his own blood, having obtained eternal redemption. 13 The blood of goats and bulls and the ashes of a heifer sprinkled on those who are ceremonially unclean sanctify them so that they are outwardly clean. 14 How much more, then, will the blood of Christ, who through the eternal Spirit offered himself unblemished to God, cleanse our consciences from acts that lead to death,[k] so that we may serve the living God!

15 For this reason Christ is the mediator of a new covenant, that those who are called may receive the promised eternal inheritance—now that he has died as a ransom to set them free from the sins committed under the first covenant.

16 In the case of a will,[l] it is necessary to prove the death of the one who made it, 17 because a will is in force only when somebody has died; it never takes effect while the one who made it is living. 18 This is why even the first covenant was not put into effect without blood. 19 When Moses had proclaimed every commandment of the law to all the people, he took the blood of calves, together with water, scarlet wool and branches of hyssop, and sprinkled

---

i 5 Traditionally *the mercy seat* j 11 Some early manuscripts *are to come* k 14 Or *from useless rituals* l 16 Same Greek word as *covenant*; also in verse 17

the scroll and all the people. **20** He said, "This is the blood of the covenant, which God has commanded you to keep."[m] **21** In the same way, he sprinkled with the blood both the tabernacle and everything used in its ceremonies. **22** In fact, the law requires that nearly everything be cleansed with blood, and without the shedding of blood there is no forgiveness.

23 It was necessary, then, for the copies of the heavenly things to be purified with these sacrifices, but the heavenly things themselves with better sacrifices than these. **24** For Christ did not enter a man-made sanctuary that was only a copy of the true one; he entered heaven itself, now to appear for us in God's presence. **25** Nor did he enter heaven to offer himself again and again, the way the high priest enters the Most Holy Place every year with blood that is not his own. **26** Then Christ would have had to suffer many times since the creation of the world. But now he has appeared once for all at the end of the ages to do away with sin by the sacrifice of himself. **27** Just as man is destined to die once, and after that to face judgment, **28** so Christ was sacrificed once to take away the sins of many people; and he will appear a second time, not to bear sin, but to bring salvation to those who are waiting for him.

Christ's Sacrifice Once for All

10 **1** The law is only a shadow of the good things that are coming—not the realities themselves. For this reason it can never, by the same sacrifices repeated endlessly year after year, make perfect those who draw near to worship. **2** If it could, would they not have stopped being offered? For the worshipers would have been cleansed once for all, and would no longer have felt guilty for their sins. **3** But those sacrifices are an annual reminder of sins, **4** because it is impossible for the blood of bulls and goats to take away sins.

5 Therefore, when Christ came into the world, he said:

> "Sacrifice and offering you did
> not desire,
>   but a body you prepared for me;
> **6** with burnt offerings and sin
> offerings
>   you were not pleased.
> **7** Then I said, 'Here I am—it is
>   written about me in the
>   scroll—
>   I have come to do your will,
>   O God.'"[n]

8 First he said, "Sacrifices and offerings, burnt offerings and sin offerings you did not desire, nor were you pleased with them" (although the law required them to be made). **9** Then he said, "Here I am, I have come to do your will." He sets aside the first to establish the second. **10** And by that will, we have been made holy through the sacrifice of the body of Jesus Christ once for all.

11 Day after day every priest stands and performs his religious duties; again and again he offers the same sacrifices, which can never take away sins. **12** But when this priest had offered for all time one sacrifice for sins, he sat down at the right hand of God. **13** Since that time he waits for his enemies to be made his footstool, **14** because by one

---

m 20 Exodus 24:8   *n 7* Psalm 40:6-8 (see Septuagint)

sacrifice he has made perfect forever those who are being made holy.

15 The Holy Spirit also testifies to us about this. First he says:

16 "This is the covenant I will
make with them
after that time, says the Lord.
I will put my laws in their hearts,
and I will write them on their
minds."[o]

17 Then he adds:

"Their sins and lawless acts
I will remember no more."[p]

18 And where these have been forgiven, there is no longer any sacrifice for sin. **19** Therefore, brothers, since we have confidence to enter the Most Holy Place by the blood of Jesus, **20** by a new and living way opened for us through the curtain, that is, his body, **21** and since we have a great priest over the house of God, **22** let us draw near to God with a sincere heart in full assurance of faith, having our hearts sprinkled to cleanse us from a guilty conscience and having our bodies washed with pure water. **23** Let us hold unswervingly to the hope we profess, for he who promised is faithful. **24** And let us consider how we may spur one another on toward love and good deeds. **25** Let us not give up meeting together, as some are in the habit of doing, but let us encourage one another—and all the more as you see the Day approaching.

26 If we deliberately keep on sinning after we have received the knowledge of the truth, no sacrifice for sins is left, **27** but only a fearful expectation of judgment and of raging fire that will consume the enemies of God. **28** Anyone who rejected the law of Moses died without mercy on the testimony of two or three witnesses. **29** How much more severely do you think a man deserves to be punished who has trampled the Son of God under foot, who has treated as an unholy thing the blood of the covenant that sanctified him, and who has insulted the Spirit of grace? **30** For we know him who said, "It is mine to avenge; I will repay,"[q] and again, "The Lord will judge his people."[r] **31** It is a dreadful thing to fall into the hands of the living God.

32 Remember those earlier days after you had received the light, when you stood your ground in a great contest in the face of suffering. **33** Sometimes you were publicly exposed to insult and persecution; at other times you stood side by side with those who were so treated. **34** You sympathized with those in prison and joyfully accepted the confiscation of your property, because you knew that you yourselves had better and lasting possessions.

35 So do not throw away your confidence; it will be richly rewarded. **36** You need to persevere so that when you have done the will of God, you will receive what he has promised. **37** For in just a very little while,

"He who is coming will come and
will not delay.
38 But my righteous one[s] will
live by faith.
And if he shrinks back,
I will not be pleased with him."[t]

o 16 Jer. 31:33   p 17 Jer. 31:34   q 30 Deut. 32:35   r 30 Deut. 32:36; Psalm 135:14   s 38 One early manuscript But the righteous   t 38 Hab. 2:3,4

39 But we are not of those who shrink back and are destroyed, but of those who believe and are saved.

By Faith

11 **1** Now faith is being sure of what we hope for and certain of what we do not see. **2** This is what the ancients were commended for.

3 By faith we understand that the universe was formed at God's command, so that what is seen was not made out of what was visible. **4** By faith Abel offered God a better sacrifice than Cain did. By faith he was commended as a righteous man, when God spoke well of his offerings. And by faith he still speaks, even though he is dead.

5 By faith Enoch was taken from this life, so that he did not experience death; he could not be found, because God had taken him away. For before he was taken, he was commended as one who pleased God. **6** And without faith it is impossible to please God, because anyone who comes to him must believe that he exists and that he rewards those who earnestly seek him.

7 By faith Noah, when warned about things not yet seen, in holy fear built an ark to save his family. By his faith he condemned the world and became heir of the righteousness that comes by faith.

8 By faith Abraham, when called to go to a place he would later receive as his inheritance, obeyed and went, even though he did not know where he was going. **9** By faith he made his home in the promised land like a stranger in a foreign country; he lived in tents, as did Isaac and Jacob, who were heirs with him of the same promise. **10** For he was looking forward to the city with foundations, whose architect and builder is God.

11 By faith Abraham, even though he was past age — and Sarah herself was barren — was enabled to become a father because heu considered him faithful who had made the promise. **12** And so from this one man, and he as good as dead, came descendants as numerous as the stars in the sky and as countless as the sand on the seashore.

13 All these people were still living by faith when they died. They did not receive the things promised; they only saw them and welcomed them from a distance. And they admitted that they were aliens and strangers on earth. **14** People who say such things show that they are looking for a country of their own. **15** If they had been thinking of the country they had left, they would have had opportunity to return. **16** Instead, they were longing for a better country — a heavenly one. Therefore God is not ashamed to be called their God, for he has prepared a city for them.

17 By faith Abraham, when God tested him, offered Isaac as a sacrifice. He who had received the promises was about to sacrifice his one and only son, **18** even though God had said to him, "It is through Isaac that your offspringv will be reckoned."w **19** Abraham reasoned that God could raise the dead, and figuratively speaking, he did receive Isaac back from death.

20 By faith Isaac blessed Jacob and Esau in regard to their future.

---

u 11 Or *By faith even Sarah, who was past age, was enabled to bear children because she*
v 18 Greek *seed*   w 18 Gen. 21:12

21 By faith Jacob, when he was dying, blessed each of Joseph's sons, and worshiped as he leaned on the top of his staff.

22 By faith Joseph, when his end was near, spoke about the exodus of the Israelites from Egypt and gave instructions about his bones.

23 By faith Moses' parents hid him for three months after he was born, because they saw he was no ordinary child, and they were not afraid of the king's edict.

24 By faith Moses, when he had grown up, refused to be known as the son of Pharaoh's daughter. **25** He chose to be mistreated along with the people of God rather than to enjoy the pleasures of sin for a short time. **26** He regarded disgrace for the sake of Christ as of greater value than the treasures of Egypt, because he was looking ahead to his reward. **27** By faith he left Egypt, not fearing the king's anger; he persevered because he saw him who is invisible. **28** By faith he kept the Passover and the sprinkling of blood, so that the destroyer of the firstborn would not touch the firstborn of Israel.

29 By faith the people passed through the Red Sea[x] as on dry land; but when the Egyptians tried to do so, they were drowned.

30 By faith the walls of Jericho fell, after the people had marched around them for seven days.

31 By faith the prostitute Rahab, because she welcomed the spies, was not killed with those who were disobedient.[y]

32 And what more shall I say? I do not have time to tell about Gideon, Barak, Samson, Jephthah, David, Samuel and the prophets, **33** who through faith conquered kingdoms, administered justice, and gained what was promised; who shut the mouths of lions, **34** quenched the fury of the flames, and escaped the edge of the sword; whose weakness was turned to strength; and who became powerful in battle and routed foreign armies. **35** Women received back their dead, raised to life again. Others were tortured and refused to be released, so that they might gain a better resurrection. **36** Some faced jeers and flogging, while still others were chained and put in prison. **37** They were stoned[z]; they were sawed in two; they were put to death by the sword. They went about in sheepskins and goatskins, destitute, persecuted and mistreated— **38** the world was not worthy of them. They wandered in deserts and mountains, and in caves and holes in the ground.

39 These were all commended for their faith, yet none of them received what had been promised. **40** God had planned something better for us so that only together with us would they be made perfect.

God Disciplines His Sons

12 **1** Therefore, since we are surrounded by such a great cloud of witnesses, let us throw off everything that hinders and the sin that so easily entangles, and let us run with perseverance the race marked out for us. **2** Let us fix our eyes on Jesus, the author and perfecter of our faith, who for the joy set before him en-

---

x 29 That is, Sea of Reeds   *y 31* Or *unbelieving*   *z 37* Some early manuscripts *stoned; they were put to the test;*

dured the cross, scorning its shame, and sat down at the right hand of the throne of God. **3** Consider him who endured such opposition from sinful men, so that you will not grow weary and lose heart.

4 In your struggle against sin, you have not yet resisted to the point of shedding your blood. **5** And you have forgotten that word of encouragement that addresses you as sons:

> "My son, do not make light of the
>   Lord's discipline,
>   and do not lose heart when
>   he rebukes you,
> **6** because the Lord disciplines
>   those he loves,
>   and he punishes everyone he
>   accepts as a son."[a]

7 Endure hardship as discipline; God is treating you as sons. For what son is not disciplined by his father? **8** If you are not disciplined (and everyone undergoes discipline), then you are illegitimate children and not true sons. **9** Moreover, we have all had human fathers who disciplined us and we respected them for it. How much more should we submit to the Father of our spirits and live! **10** Our fathers disciplined us for a little while as they thought best; but God disciplines us for our good, that we may share in his holiness. **11** No discipline seems pleasant at the time, but painful. Later on, however, it produces a harvest of righteousness and peace for those who have been trained by it.

12 Therefore, strengthen your feeble arms and weak knees. **13** "Make level paths for your feet,"[b]

so that the lame may not be disabled, but rather healed.

Warning Against Refusing God

14 Make every effort to live in peace with all men and to be holy; without holiness no one will see the Lord. **15** See to it that no one misses the grace of God and that no bitter root grows up to cause trouble and defile many. **16** See that no one is sexually immoral, or is godless like Esau, who for a single meal sold his inheritance rights as the oldest son. **17** Afterward, as you know, when he wanted to inherit this blessing, he was rejected. He could bring about no change of mind, though he sought the blessing with tears.

18 You have not come to a mountain that can be touched and that is burning with fire; to darkness, gloom and storm; **19** to a trumpet blast or to such a voice speaking words that those who heard it begged that no further word be spoken to them, **20** because they could not bear what was commanded: "If even an animal touches the mountain, it must be stoned."[c] **21** The sight was so terrifying that Moses said, "I am trembling with fear."[d]

22 But you have come to Mount Zion, to the heavenly Jerusalem, the city of the living God. You have come to thousands upon thousands of angels in joyful assembly, **23** to the church of the firstborn, whose names are written in heaven. You have come to God, the judge of all men, to the spirits of righteous men made perfect, **24** to Jesus the mediator of a new covenant, and to the sprinkled blood that speaks a better word than the blood of Abel.

---

a 6 Prov. 3:11,12   *b* 13 Prov. 4:26   *c* 20 Exodus 19:12,13   *d* 21 Deut. 9:19

25 See to it that you do not refuse him who speaks. If they did not escape when they refused him who warned them on earth, how much less will we, if we turn away from him who warns us from heaven? 26 At that time his voice shook the earth, but now he has promised, "Once more I will shake not only the earth but also the heavens."*e* 27 The words "once more" indicate the removing of what can be shaken—that is, created things—so that what cannot be shaken may remain.

28 Therefore, since we are receiving a kingdom that cannot be shaken, let us be thankful, and so worship God acceptably with reverence and awe, 29 for our "God is a consuming fire."*f*

Concluding Exhortations

13 1 Keep on loving each other as brothers. 2 Do not forget to entertain strangers, for by so doing some people have entertained angels without knowing it. 3 Remember those in prison as if you were their fellow prisoners, and those who are mistreated as if you yourselves were suffering.

4 Marriage should be honored by all, and the marriage bed kept pure, for God will judge the adulterer and all the sexually immoral. 5 Keep your lives free from the love of money and be content with what you have, because God has said,

"Never will I leave you;
    never will I forsake you."*g*

6 So we say with confidence,

"The Lord is my helper; I will not
    be afraid.
What can man do to me?"*h*

7 Remember your leaders, who spoke the word of God to you. Consider the outcome of their way of life and imitate their faith. 8 Jesus Christ is the same yesterday and today and forever.

9 Do not be carried away by all kinds of strange teachings. It is good for our hearts to be strengthened by grace, not by ceremonial foods, which are of no value to those who eat them. 10 We have an altar from which those who minister at the tabernacle have no right to eat.

11 The high priest carries the blood of animals into the Most Holy Place as a sin offering, but the bodies are burned outside the camp. 12 And so Jesus also suffered outside the city gate to make the people holy through his own blood. 13 Let us, then, go to him outside the camp, bearing the disgrace he bore. 14 For here we do not have an enduring city, but we are looking for the city that is to come.

15 Through Jesus, therefore, let us continually offer to God a sacrifice of praise—the fruit of lips that confess his name. 16 And do not forget to do good and to share with others, for with such sacrifices God is pleased. 17 Obey your leaders and submit to their authority. They keep watch over you as men who must give an account. Obey them so that their work will be a joy, not a burden, for that would be of no advantage to you.

18 Pray for us. We are sure that we have a clear conscience and desire to

---

e 26 Haggai 2:6   *f* 29 Deut. 4:24   *g* 5 Deut. 31:6   *h* 6 Psalm 118:6,7 live honorably in every way. **19** I particularly urge you to pray so that I may be restored to you soon.

20 May the God of peace, who through the blood of the eternal covenant brought back from the dead our Lord Jesus, that great Shepherd of the sheep, **21** equip you with everything good for doing his will, and may he work in us what is pleasing to him, through Jesus Christ, to whom be glory for ever and ever. Amen.

22 Brothers, I urge you to bear with my word of exhortation, for I have written you only a short letter.

23 I want you to know that our brother Timothy has been released. If he arrives soon, I will come with him to see you.

24 Greet all your leaders and all God's people. Those from Italy send you their greetings.

25 Grace be with you all.

James

1 ¹ James, a servant of God and of the Lord Jesus Christ,

To the twelve tribes scattered among the nations:

Greetings.

Trials and Temptations

² Consider it pure joy, my brothers, whenever you face trials of many kinds, ³ because you know that the testing of your faith develops perseverance. ⁴ Perseverance must finish its work so that you may be mature and complete, not lacking anything. ⁵ If any of you lacks wisdom, he should ask God, who gives generously to all without finding fault, and it will be given to him. ⁶ But when he asks, he must believe and not doubt, because he who doubts is like a wave of the sea, blown and tossed by the wind. ⁷ That man should not think he will receive anything from the Lord; ⁸ he is a double-minded man, unstable in all he does.

⁹ The brother in humble circumstances ought to take pride in his high position. ¹⁰ But the one who is rich should take pride in his low position, because he will pass away like a wild flower. ¹¹ For the sun rises with scorching heat and withers the plant; its blossom falls and its beauty is destroyed. In the same way, the rich man will fade away even while he goes about his business.

¹² Blessed is the man who perseveres under trial, because when he has stood the test, he will receive the crown of life that God has promised to those who love him.

¹³ When tempted, no one should say, "God is tempting me." For God cannot be tempted by evil, nor does he tempt anyone; ¹⁴ but each one is tempted when, by his own evil desire, he is dragged away and enticed. ¹⁵ Then, after desire has conceived, it gives birth to sin; and sin, when it is full-grown, gives birth to death.

¹⁶ Don't be deceived, my dear brothers. ¹⁷ Every good and perfect gift is from above, coming down from the Father of the heavenly lights, who does not change like shifting shadows. ¹⁸ He chose to give us birth through the word of truth, that we might be a kind of firstfruits of all he created.

Listening and Doing

¹⁹ My dear brothers, take note of this: Everyone should be quick to listen, slow to speak and slow to become angry, ²⁰ for man's anger does not bring about the righteous life that God desires. ²¹ Therefore, get rid of all moral filth and the evil that is so prevalent and humbly accept the word planted in you, which can save you.

²² Do not merely listen to the word, and so deceive yourselves. Do what it says. ²³ Anyone who listens to the word but does not do what it says is like a man who looks at his face in a mirror ²⁴ and, after looking at himself, goes away and immediately forgets what he looks like. ²⁵ But the man who looks intently into the perfect law that gives freedom, and continues to do this,

not forgetting what he has heard, but doing it—he will be blessed in what he does.

26 If anyone considers himself religious and yet does not keep a tight rein on his tongue, he deceives himself and his religion is worthless. 27 Religion that God our Father accepts as pure and faultless is this: to look after orphans and widows in their distress and to keep oneself from being polluted by the world.

Favoritism Forbidden

2 1 My brothers, as believers in our glorious Lord Jesus Christ, don't show favoritism. 2 Suppose a man comes into your meeting wearing a gold ring and fine clothes, and a poor man in shabby clothes also comes in. 3 If you show special attention to the man wearing fine clothes and say, "Here's a good seat for you," but say to the poor man, "You stand there" or "Sit on the floor by my feet," 4 have you not discriminated among yourselves and become judges with evil thoughts?

5 Listen, my dear brothers: Has not God chosen those who are poor in the eyes of the world to be rich in faith and to inherit the kingdom he promised those who love him? 6 But you have insulted the poor. Is it not the rich who are exploiting you? Are they not the ones who are dragging you into court? 7 Are they not the ones who are slandering the noble name of him to whom you belong?

8 If you really keep the royal law found in Scripture, "Love your neighbor as yourself,"[a] you are doing right. 9 But if you show favoritism, you sin and are convicted by the law as lawbreakers. 10 For whoever keeps the whole law and yet stumbles at just one point is guilty of breaking all of it. 11 For he who said, "Do not commit adultery,"[b] also said, "Do not murder."[c] If you do not commit adultery but do commit murder, you have become a lawbreaker.

12 Speak and act as those who are going to be judged by the law that gives freedom, 13 because judgment without mercy will be shown to anyone who has not been merciful. Mercy triumphs over judgment!

Faith and Deeds

14 What good is it, my brothers, if a man claims to have faith but has no deeds? Can such faith save him? 15 Suppose a brother or sister is without clothes and daily food. 16 If one of you says to him, "Go, I wish you well; keep warm and well fed," but does nothing about his physical needs, what good is it? 17 In the same way, faith by itself, if it is not accompanied by action, is dead.

18 But someone will say, "You have faith; I have deeds."

Show me your faith without deeds, and I will show you my faith by what I do. 19 You believe that there is one God. Good! Even the demons believe that—and shudder.

20 You foolish man, do you want evidence that faith without deeds is useless[d]? 21 Was not our ancestor Abraham considered righteous for what he did when he offered his son Isaac on the altar? 22 You see that his faith and his actions were working together, and his faith was made complete by what he did. 23 And the scripture was fulfilled that says,

---

[a] 8 Lev. 19:18   [b] 11 Exodus 20:14; Deut. 5:18   [c] 11 Exodus 20:13; Deut. 5:17
[d] 20 Some early manuscripts dead

"Abraham believed God, and it was credited to him as righteousness,"ᵉ and he was called God's friend. **24** You see that a person is justified by what he does and not by faith alone.

25 In the same way, was not even Rahab the prostitute considered righteous for what she did when she gave lodging to the spies and sent them off in a different direction? **26** As the body without the spirit is dead, so faith without deeds is dead.

Taming the Tongue

3 **1** Not many of you should presume to be teachers, my brothers, because you know that we who teach will be judged more strictly. **2** We all stumble in many ways. If anyone is never at fault in what he says, he is a perfect man, able to keep his whole body in check.

3 When we put bits into the mouths of horses to make them obey us, we can turn the whole animal. **4** Or take ships as an example. Although they are so large and are driven by strong winds, they are steered by a very small rudder wherever the pilot wants to go. **5** Likewise the tongue is a small part of the body, but it makes great boasts. Consider what a great forest is set on fire by a small spark. **6** The tongue also is a fire, a world of evil among the parts of the body. It corrupts the whole person, sets the whole course of his life on fire, and is itself set on fire by hell.

7 All kinds of animals, birds, reptiles and creatures of the sea are being tamed and have been tamed by man, **8** but no man can tame the tongue. It is a restless evil, full of deadly poison.

9 With the tongue we praise our Lord and Father, and with it we curse men, who have been made in God's likeness. **10** Out of the same mouth come praise and cursing. My brothers, this should not be. **11** Can both fresh water and saltᶠ water flow from the same spring? **12** My brothers, can a fig tree bear olives, or a grapevine bear figs? Neither can a salt spring produce fresh water.

Two Kinds of Wisdom

13 Who is wise and understanding among you? Let him show it by his good life, by deeds done in the humility that comes from wisdom. **14** But if you harbor bitter envy and selfish ambition in your hearts, do not boast about it or deny the truth. **15** Such "wisdom" does not come down from heaven but is earthly, unspiritual, of the devil. **16** For where you have envy and selfish ambition, there you find disorder and every evil practice.

17 But the wisdom that comes from heaven is first of all pure; then peace-loving, considerate, submissive, full of mercy and good fruit, impartial and sincere. **18** Peacemakers who sow in peace raise a harvest of righteousness.

Submit Yourselves to God

4 **1** What causes fights and quarrels among you? Don't they come from your desires that battle within you? **2** You want something but don't get it. You kill and covet, but you cannot have what you want. You quarrel and fight. You do not have, because you do not ask God. **3** When you ask, you do not receive, because you ask with wrong motives, that you

ᵉ *23* Gen. 15:6 ᶠ *11* Greek *bitter* (see also verse 14)

may spend what you get on your pleasures.

4 You adulterous people, don't you know that friendship with the world is hatred toward God? Anyone who chooses to be a friend of the world becomes an enemy of God. **5** Or do you think Scripture says without reason that the spirit he caused to live in us envies intensely?[g] **6** But he gives us more grace. That is why Scripture says:

> "God opposes the proud
> but gives grace to the
> humble."[h]

7 Submit yourselves, then, to God. Resist the devil, and he will flee from you. **8** Come near to God and he will come near to you. Wash your hands, you sinners, and purify your hearts, you double-minded. **9** Grieve, mourn and wail. Change your laughter to mourning and your joy to gloom. **10** Humble yourselves before the Lord, and he will lift you up.

11 Brothers, do not slander one another. Anyone who speaks against his brother or judges him speaks against the law and judges it. When you judge the law, you are not keeping it, but sitting in judgment on it. **12** There is only one Lawgiver and Judge, the one who is able to save and destroy. But you—who are you to judge your neighbor?

Boasting About Tomorrow

13 Now listen, you who say, "Today or tomorrow we will go to this or that city, spend a year there, carry on business and make money." **14** Why, you do not even know what will happen tomorrow. What is your life? You are a mist that appears for a little while and then vanishes. **15** Instead, you ought to say, "If it is the Lord's will, we will live and do this or that." **16** As it is, you boast and brag. All such boasting is evil. **17** Anyone, then, who knows the good he ought to do and doesn't do it, sins.

Warning to Rich Oppressors

5 **1** Now listen, you rich people, weep and wail because of the misery that is coming upon you. **2** Your wealth has rotted, and moths have eaten your clothes. **3** Your gold and silver are corroded. Their corrosion will testify against you and eat your flesh like fire. You have hoarded wealth in the last days. **4** Look! The wages you failed to pay the workmen who mowed your fields are crying out against you. The cries of the harvesters have reached the ears of the Lord Almighty. **5** You have lived on earth in luxury and self-indulgence. You have fattened yourselves in the day of slaughter.[i] **6** You have condemned and murdered innocent men, who were not opposing you.

Patience in Suffering

7 Be patient, then, brothers, until the Lord's coming. See how the farmer waits for the land to yield its valuable crop and how patient he is for the autumn and spring rains. **8** You too, be patient and stand firm, because the Lord's coming is near. **9** Don't grumble against each other, brothers, or you will be judged. The Judge is standing at the door!

10 Brothers, as an example of patience in the face of suffering, take the prophets who spoke in the name

---

g 5 Or that God jealously longs for the spirit that he made to live in us; or that the Spirit he caused to live in us longs jealously   h 6 Prov. 3:34   i 5 Or yourselves as in a day of feasting

of the Lord. **11** As you know, we consider blessed those who have persevered. You have heard of Job's perseverance and have seen what the Lord finally brought about. The Lord is full of compassion and mercy.

12 Above all, my brothers, do not swear—not by heaven or by earth or by anything else. Let your "Yes" be yes, and your "No," no, or you will be condemned.

The Prayer of Faith

13 Is any one of you in trouble? He should pray. Is anyone happy? Let him sing songs of praise. **14** Is any one of you sick? He should call the elders of the church to pray over him and anoint him with oil in the name of the Lord. **15** And the prayer offered in faith will make the sick person well; the Lord will raise him up. If he has sinned, he will be forgiven. **16** Therefore confess your sins to each other and pray for each other so that you may be healed. The prayer of a righteous man is powerful and effective.

17 Elijah was a man just like us. He prayed earnestly that it would not rain, and it did not rain on the land for three and a half years. **18** Again he prayed, and the heavens gave rain, and the earth produced its crops. **19** My brothers, if one of you should wander from the truth and someone should bring him back, **20** remember this: Whoever turns a sinner from the error of his way will save him from death and cover over a multitude of sins.

1 Peter

1 **1** Peter, an apostle of Jesus Christ,

To God's elect, strangers in the world, scattered throughout Pontus, Galatia, Cappadocia, Asia and Bithynia, **2** who have been chosen according to the foreknowledge of God the Father, through the sanctifying work of the Spirit, for obedience to Jesus Christ and sprinkling by his blood:

Grace and peace be yours in abundance.

Praise to God for a Living Hope

3 Praise be to the God and Father of our Lord Jesus Christ! In his great mercy he has given us new birth into a living hope through the resurrection of Jesus Christ from the dead, **4** and into an inheritance that can never perish, spoil or fade — kept in heaven for you, **5** who through faith are shielded by God's power until the coming of the salvation that is ready to be revealed in the last time. **6** In this you greatly rejoice, though now for a little while you may have had to suffer grief in all kinds of trials. **7** These have come so that your faith — of greater worth than gold, which perishes even though refined by fire — may be proved genuine and may result in praise, glory and honor when Jesus Christ is revealed. **8** Though you have not seen him, you love him; and even though you do not see him now, you believe in him and are filled with an inexpressible

and glorious joy, **9** for you are receiving the goal of your faith, the salvation of your souls.

10 Concerning this salvation, the prophets, who spoke of the grace that was to come to you, searched intently and with the greatest care, **11** trying to find out the time and circumstances to which the Spirit of Christ in them was pointing when he predicted the sufferings of Christ and the glories that would follow. **12** It was revealed to them that they were not serving themselves but you, when they spoke of the things that have now been told you by those who have preached the gospel to you by the Holy Spirit sent from heaven. Even angels long to look into these things.

Be Holy

13 Therefore, prepare your minds for action; be self-controlled; set your hope fully on the grace to be given you when Jesus Christ is revealed. **14** As obedient children, do not conform to the evil desires you had when you lived in ignorance. **15** But just as he who called you is holy, so be holy in all you do; **16** for it is written: "Be holy, because I am holy."[a]

17 Since you call on a Father who judges each man's work impartially, live your lives as strangers here in reverent fear. **18** For you know that it was not with perishable things such as silver or gold that you were redeemed from the empty way of

---

a 16 Lev. 11:44,45; 19:2; 20:7

life handed down to you from your forefathers, **19** but with the precious blood of Christ, a lamb without blemish or defect. **20** He was chosen before the creation of the world, but was revealed in these last times for your sake. **21** Through him you believe in God, who raised him from the dead and glorified him, and so your faith and hope are in God.

22 Now that you have purified yourselves by obeying the truth so that you have sincere love for your brothers, love one another deeply, from the heart.[b] **23** For you have been born again, not of perishable seed, but of imperishable, through the living and enduring word of God. **24** For,

> "All men are like grass,
>   and all their glory is like the
>   flowers of the field;
> the grass withers and the
>   flowers fall,
> **25**   but the word of the Lord
>   stands forever."[c]

And this is the word that was preached to you.

2 **1** Therefore, rid yourselves of all malice and all deceit, hypocrisy, envy, and slander of every kind. **2** Like newborn babies, crave pure spiritual milk, so that by it you may grow up in your salvation, **3** now that you have tasted that the Lord is good.

The Living Stone and a Chosen People

4 As you come to him, the living Stone—rejected by men but chosen by God and precious to him— **5** you

also, like living stones, are being built into a spiritual house to be a holy priesthood, offering spiritual sacrifices acceptable to God through Jesus Christ. **6** For in Scripture it says:

> "See, I lay a stone in Zion,
>   a chosen and precious
>   cornerstone,
> and the one who trusts in him
>   will never be put to shame."[d]

7 Now to you who believe, this stone is precious. But to those who do not believe,

> "The stone the builders rejected
>   has become the capstone,[e]"[f]

8 and,

> "A stone that causes men to
>   stumble
>   and a rock that makes them
>   fall."[g]

They stumble because they disobey the message—which is also what they were destined for.

9 But you are a chosen people, a royal priesthood, a holy nation, a people belonging to God, that you may declare the praises of him who called you out of darkness into his wonderful light. **10** Once you were not a people, but now you are the people of God; once you had not received mercy, but now you have received mercy.

11 Dear friends, I urge you, as aliens and strangers in the world, to abstain from sinful desires, which war against your soul. **12** Live such good lives among the pagans that, though they accuse you of doing wrong, they may see your good

---

b 22 Some early manuscripts *from a pure heart*   *c 25* Isaiah 40:6-8   *d 6* Isaiah 28:16
e 7 Or *cornerstone*   *f 7* Psalm 118:22   *g 8* Isaiah 8:14

deeds and glorify God on the day he visits us.

Submission to Rulers and Masters

13 Submit yourselves for the Lord's sake to every authority instituted among men: whether to the king, as the supreme authority, 14 or to governors, who are sent by him to punish those who do wrong and to commend those who do right. 15 For it is God's will that by doing good you should silence the ignorant talk of foolish men. 16 Live as free men, but do not use your freedom as a cover-up for evil; live as servants of God. 17 Show proper respect to everyone: Love the brotherhood of believers, fear God, honor the king.

18 Slaves, submit yourselves to your masters with all respect, not only to those who are good and considerate, but also to those who are harsh. 19 For it is commendable if a man bears up under the pain of unjust suffering because he is conscious of God. 20 But how is it to your credit if you receive a beating for doing wrong and endure it? But if you suffer for doing good and you endure it, this is commendable before God. 21 To this you were called, because Christ suffered for you, leaving you an example, that you should follow in his steps.

22 "He committed no sin,
    and no deceit was found in
        his mouth."[h]

23 When they hurled their insults at him, he did not retaliate; when he suffered, he made no threats. Instead, he entrusted himself to him who judges justly. 24 He himself bore our sins in his body on the tree, so that we might die to sins and live for righteousness; by his wounds you have been healed. 25 For you were like sheep going astray, but now you have returned to the Shepherd and Overseer of your souls.

Wives and Husbands

3 1 Wives, in the same way be submissive to your husbands so that, if any of them do not believe the word, they may be won over without words by the behavior of their wives, 2 when they see the purity and reverence of your lives. 3 Your beauty should not come from outward adornment, such as braided hair and the wearing of gold jewelry and fine clothes. 4 Instead, it should be that of your inner self, the unfading beauty of a gentle and quiet spirit, which is of great worth in God's sight. 5 For this is the way the holy women of the past who put their hope in God used to make themselves beautiful. They were submissive to their own husbands, 6 like Sarah, who obeyed Abraham and called him her master. You are her daughters if you do what is right and do not give way to fear.

7 Husbands, in the same way be considerate as you live with your wives, and treat them with respect as the weaker partner and as heirs with you of the gracious gift of life, so that nothing will hinder your prayers.

Suffering for Doing Good

8 Finally, all of you, live in harmony with one another; be sympathetic, love as brothers, be compassionate and humble. 9 Do not repay evil with evil or insult with insult, but with blessing, because to

h 22 Isaiah 53:9

this you were called so that you may inherit a blessing. 10 For,

> "Whoever would love life
>   and see good days
> must keep his tongue from evil
>   and his lips from deceitful
>   speech.
> 11 He must turn from evil and do
>   good;
>   he must seek peace and
>   pursue it.
> 12 For the eyes of the Lord are on
>   the righteous
>   and his ears are attentive to
>   their prayer,
> but the face of the Lord is
>   against those who do evil."[i]

13 Who is going to harm you if you are eager to do good? 14 But even if you should suffer for what is right, you are blessed. "Do not fear what they fear[j]; do not be frightened."[k] 15 But in your hearts set apart Christ as Lord. Always be prepared to give an answer to everyone who asks you to give the reason for the hope that you have. But do this with gentleness and respect, 16 keeping a clear conscience, so that those who speak maliciously against your good behavior in Christ may be ashamed of their slander. 17 It is better, if it is God's will, to suffer for doing good than for doing evil. 18 For Christ died for sins once for all, the righteous for the unrighteous, to bring you to God. He was put to death in the body but made alive by the Spirit, 19 through whom[l] also he went and preached to the spirits in prison 20 who disobeyed long ago when God waited patiently in the days of Noah while the ark was being built. In it only a few people, eight in all, were saved through water, 21 and this water symbolizes baptism that now saves you also—not the removal of dirt from the body but the pledge[m] of a good conscience toward God. It saves you by the resurrection of Jesus Christ, 22 who has gone into heaven and is at God's right hand—with angels, authorities and powers in submission to him.

Living for God

4 1 Therefore, since Christ suffered in his body, arm yourselves also with the same attitude, because he who has suffered in his body is done with sin. 2 As a result, he does not live the rest of his earthly life for evil human desires, but rather for the will of God. 3 For you have spent enough time in the past doing what pagans choose to do—living in debauchery, lust, drunkenness, orgies, carousing and detestable idolatry. 4 They think it strange that you do not plunge with them into the same flood of dissipation, and they heap abuse on you. 5 But they will have to give account to him who is ready to judge the living and the dead. 6 For this is the reason the gospel was preached even to those who are now dead, so that they might be judged according to men in regard to the body, but live according to God in regard to the spirit.

7 The end of all things is near. Therefore be clear minded and self-controlled so that you can pray. 8 Above all, love each other deeply, because love covers over a multitude of sins. 9 Offer hospitality to one another without grumbling. 10 Each

---

i 12 Psalm 34:12-16   *j 14* Or *not fear their threats*   *k 14* Isaiah 8:12   *l 19* Or *alive in the spirit, 19 through which*   *m 21* Or *response*

one should use whatever gift he has received to serve others, faithfully administering God's grace in its various forms. 11 If anyone speaks, he should do it as one speaking the very words of God. If anyone serves, he should do it with the strength God provides, so that in all things God may be praised through Jesus Christ. To him be the glory and the power for ever and ever. Amen.

Suffering for Being a Christian

12 Dear friends, do not be surprised at the painful trial you are suffering, as though something strange were happening to you. 13 But rejoice that you participate in the sufferings of Christ, so that you may be overjoyed when his glory is revealed. 14 If you are insulted because of the name of Christ, you are blessed, for the Spirit of glory and of God rests on you. 15 If you suffer, it should not be as a murderer or thief or any other kind of criminal, or even as a meddler. 16 However, if you suffer as a Christian, do not be ashamed, but praise God that you bear that name. 17 For it is time for judgment to begin with the family of God; and if it begins with us, what will the outcome be for those who do not obey the gospel of God? 18 And,

> "If it is hard for the righteous to
> be saved,
>   what will become of the
>   ungodly and the sinner?"[n]

19 So then, those who suffer according to God's will should commit themselves to their faithful Creator and continue to do good.

To Elders and Young Men

5 1 To the elders among you, I appeal as a fellow elder, a witness of Christ's sufferings and one who also will share in the glory to be revealed: 2 Be shepherds of God's flock that is under your care, serving as overseers — not because you must, but because you are willing, as God wants you to be; not greedy for money, but eager to serve; 3 not lording it over those entrusted to you, but being examples to the flock. 4 And when the Chief Shepherd appears, you will receive the crown of glory that will never fade away.

5 Young men, in the same way be submissive to those who are older. All of you, clothe yourselves with humility toward one another, because,

> "God opposes the proud
>   but gives grace to the
>   humble."[o]

6 Humble yourselves, therefore, under God's mighty hand, that he may lift you up in due time. 7 Cast all your anxiety on him because he cares for you.

8 Be self-controlled and alert. Your enemy the devil prowls around like a roaring lion looking for someone to devour. 9 Resist him, standing firm in the faith, because you know that your brothers throughout the world are undergoing the same kind of sufferings.

10 And the God of all grace, who called you to his eternal glory in Christ, after you have suffered a little while, will himself restore you and make you strong, firm and steadfast.

---

n 18 Prov. 11:31   o 5 Prov. 3:34

1 To him be the power for ever and ever. Amen.

Final Greetings

12 With the help of Silas,p whom I regard as a faithful brother, I have written to you briefly, encouraging you and testifying that this is the true grace of God. Stand fast in it. 13 She who is in Babylon, chosen together with you, sends you her greetings, and so does my son Mark. 14 Greet one another with a kiss of love. Peace to all of you who are in Christ.

p 12 Greek *Silvanus*, a variant of *Silas*

2 Peter

1

1 Simon Peter, a servant and apostle of Jesus Christ,

To those who through the righteousness of our God and Savior Jesus Christ have received a faith as precious as ours:

2 Grace and peace be yours in abundance through the knowledge of God and of Jesus our Lord.

Making One's Calling and Election Sure

3 His divine power has given us everything we need for life and godliness through our knowledge of him who called us by his own glory and goodness. **4** Through these he has given us his very great and precious promises, so that through them you may participate in the divine nature and escape the corruption in the world caused by evil desires.

5 For this very reason, make every effort to add to your faith goodness; and to goodness, knowledge; **6** and to knowledge, self-control; and to self-control, perseverance; and to perseverance, godliness; **7** and to godliness, brotherly kindness; and to brotherly kindness, love. **8** For if you possess these qualities in increasing measure, they will keep you from being ineffective and unproductive in your knowledge of our Lord Jesus Christ. **9** But if anyone does not have them, he is nearsighted and blind, and has forgotten that he has been cleansed from his past sins.

10 Therefore, my brothers, be all the more eager to make your calling and election sure. For if you do these things, you will never fall, **11** and you will receive a rich welcome into the eternal kingdom of our Lord and Savior Jesus Christ.

Prophecy of Scripture

12 So I will always remind you of these things, even though you know them and are firmly established in the truth you now have. **13** I think it is right to refresh your memory as long as I live in the tent of this body, **14** because I know that I will soon put it aside, as our Lord Jesus Christ has made clear to me. **15** And I will make every effort to see that after my departure you will always be able to remember these things.

16 We did not follow cleverly invented stories when we told you about the power and coming of our Lord Jesus Christ, but we were eyewitnesses of his majesty. **17** For he received honor and glory from God the Father when the voice came to him from the Majestic Glory, saying, "This is my Son, whom I love; with him I am well pleased."*a* **18** We ourselves heard this voice that came from heaven when we were with him on the sacred mountain.

19 And we have the word of the prophets made more certain, and you will do well to pay attention to it, as to a light shining in a dark place, until the day dawns and the morning star rises in your hearts. **20** Above all,

---

a 17 Matt. 17:5; Mark 9:7; Luke 9:35

ou must understand that no prophecy of Scripture came about by the prophet's own interpretation. 21 For prophecy never had its origin in the will of man, but men spoke from God as they were carried along by the Holy Spirit.

False Teachers and Their Destruction

2 1 But there were also false prophets among the people, just as there will be false teachers among you. They will secretly introduce destructive heresies, even denying the sovereign Lord who bought them—bringing swift destruction on themselves. 2 Many will follow their shameful ways and will bring the way of truth into disrepute. 3 In their greed these teachers will exploit you with stories they have made up. Their condemnation has long been hanging over them, and their destruction has not been sleeping.

4 For if God did not spare angels when they sinned, but sent them to hell,b putting them into gloomy dungeonsc to be held for judgment; 5 if he did not spare the ancient world when he brought the flood on its ungodly people, but protected Noah, a preacher of righteousness, and seven others; 6 if he condemned the cities of Sodom and Gomorrah by burning them to ashes, and made them an example of what is going to happen to the ungodly; 7 and if he rescued Lot, a righteous man, who was distressed by the filthy lives of lawless men 8 (for that righteous man, living among them day after day, was tormented in his righteous soul by the lawless deeds he saw and heard)— 9 if this is so, then the Lord

knows how to rescue godly men from trials and to hold the unrighteous for the day of judgment, while continuing their punishment.d 10 This is especially true of those who follow the corrupt desire of the sinful naturee and despise authority.

Bold and arrogant, these men are not afraid to slander celestial beings; 11 yet even angels, although they are stronger and more powerful, do not bring slanderous accusations against such beings in the presence of the Lord. 12 But these men blaspheme in matters they do not understand. They are like brute beasts, creatures of instinct, born only to be caught and destroyed, and like beasts they too will perish.

13 They will be paid back with harm for the harm they have done. Their idea of pleasure is to carouse in broad daylight. They are blots and blemishes, reveling in their pleasures while they feast with you.f 14 With eyes full of adultery, they never stop sinning; they seduce the unstable; they are experts in greed—an accursed brood! 15 They have left the straight way and wandered off to follow the way of Balaam son of Beor, who loved the wages of wickedness. 16 But he was rebuked for his wrongdoing by a donkey—a beast without speech—who spoke with a man's voice and restrained the prophet's madness.

17 These men are springs without water and mists driven by a storm. Blackest darkness is reserved for them. 18 For they mouth empty, boastful words and, by appealing to the lustful desires of sinful human nature, they entice people who are

just escaping from those who live in error. **19** They promise them freedom, while they themselves are slaves of depravity—for a man is a slave to whatever has mastered him. **20** If they have escaped the corruption of the world by knowing our Lord and Savior Jesus Christ and are again entangled in it and overcome, they are worse off at the end than they were at the beginning. **21** It would have been better for them not to have known the way of righteousness, than to have known it and then to turn their backs on the sacred command that was passed on to them. **22** Of them the proverbs are true: "A dog returns to its vomit,"*g* and, "A sow that is washed goes back to her wallowing in the mud."

The Day of the Lord

3 **1** Dear friends, this is now my second letter to you. I have written both of them as reminders to stimulate you to wholesome thinking. **2** I want you to recall the words spoken in the past by the holy prophets and the command given by our Lord and Savior through your apostles. **3** First of all, you must understand that in the last days scoffers will come, scoffing and following their own evil desires. **4** They will say, "Where is this 'coming' he promised? Ever since our fathers died, everything goes on as it has since the beginning of creation." **5** But they deliberately forget that long ago by God's word the heavens existed and the earth was formed out of water and by water. **6** By these waters also the world of that time was deluged

and destroyed. **7** By the same word the present heavens and earth are reserved for fire, being kept for the day of judgment and destruction of ungodly men.

8 But do not forget this one thing, dear friends: With the Lord a day is like a thousand years, and a thousand years are like a day. **9** The Lord is not slow in keeping his promise, as some understand slowness. He is patient with you, not wanting anyone to perish, but everyone to come to repentance.

10 But the day of the Lord will come like a thief. The heavens will disappear with a roar; the elements will be destroyed by fire, and the earth and everything in it will be laid bare.*h*

11 Since everything will be destroyed in this way, what kind of people ought you to be? You ought to live holy and godly lives **12** as you look forward to the day of God and speed its coming.*i* That day will bring about the destruction of the heavens by fire, and the elements will melt in the heat. **13** But in keeping with his promise we are looking forward to a new heaven and a new earth, the home of righteousness.

14 So then, dear friends, since you are looking forward to this, make every effort to be found spotless, blameless and at peace with him. **15** Bear in mind that our Lord's patience means salvation, just as our dear brother Paul also wrote you with the wisdom that God gave him. **16** He writes the same way in all his letters, speaking in them of these matters. His letters contain some things that are hard to understand,

g 22 Prov. 26:11   *h* 10 Some manuscripts *be burned up*   *i* 12 Or *as you wait eagerly for the day of God to come*

which ignorant and unstable people distort, as they do the other Scriptures, to their own destruction.

17 Therefore, dear friends, since you already know this, be on your guard so that you may not be carried away by the error of lawless men and fall from your secure position. **18** But grow in the grace and knowledge of our Lord and Savior Jesus Christ. To him be glory both now and forever! Amen.

1 John

The Word of Life

1 ¹That which was from the beginning, which we have heard, which we have seen with our eyes, which we have looked at and our hands have touched—this we proclaim concerning the Word of life. ²The life appeared; we have seen it and testify to it, and we proclaim to you the eternal life, which was with the Father and has appeared to us. ³We proclaim to you what we have seen and heard, so that you also may have fellowship with us. And our fellowship is with the Father and with his Son, Jesus Christ. ⁴We write this to make our[a] joy complete.

Walking in the light

⁵This is the message we have heard from him and declare to you: God is light; in him there is no darkness at all. ⁶If we claim to have fellowship with him yet walk in the darkness, we lie and do not live by the truth. ⁷But if we walk in the light, as he is in the light, we have fellowship with one another, and the blood of Jesus, his Son, purifies us from all[b] sin.

⁸If we claim to be without sin, we deceive ourselves and the truth is not in us. ⁹If we confess our sins, he is faithful and just and will forgive us our sins and purify us from all unrighteousness. ¹⁰If we claim we have not sinned, we make him out to be a liar and his word has no place in our lives.

2 ¹My dear children, I write this to you so that you will not sin. But if anybody does sin, we have one who speaks to the Father in our defense—Jesus Christ, the Righteous One. ²He is the atoning sacrifice for our sins, and not only for ours but also for[c] the sins of the whole world.

³We know that we have come to know him if we obey his commands. ⁴The man who says, "I know him," but does not do what he commands is a liar, and the truth is not in him. ⁵But if anyone obeys his word, God's love[d] is truly made complete in him. This is how we know we are in him: ⁶Whoever claims to live in him must walk as Jesus did.

⁷Dear friends, I am not writing you a new command but an old one, which you have had since the beginning. This old command is the message you have heard. ⁸Yet I am writing you a new command; its truth is seen in him and you, because the darkness is passing and the true light is already shining.

⁹Anyone who claims to be in the light but hates his brother is still in the darkness. ¹⁰Whoever loves his brother lives in the light, and there is nothing in him[e] to make him stumble. ¹¹But whoever hates his brother is in the darkness and walks around in the darkness; he does not know where he is going, because the darkness has blinded him.

---

a 4 Some manuscripts *your*   *b* 7 Or *every*   *c* 2 Or *He is the one who turns aside God's wrath, taking away our sins, and not only ours but also*   *d* 5 Or *word, love for God*
e 10 Or *it*

12 I write to you, dear children,
    because your sins have been
        forgiven on account of his
            name.
13 I write to you, fathers,
    because you have known him
        who is from the beginning.
I write to you, young men,
    because you have overcome
        the evil one.
I write to you, dear children,
    because you have known the
        Father.
14 I write to you, fathers,
    because you have known him
        who is from the beginning.
I write to you, young men,
    because you are strong,
        and the word of God lives in
            you,
    and you have overcome the
        evil one.

Do Not Love the World

15 Do not love the world or anything in the world. If anyone loves
the world, the love of the Father is
not in him. 16 For everything in the
world—the cravings of sinful man,
the lust of his eyes and the boasting
of what he has and does—comes not
from the Father but from the world.
17 The world and its desires pass
away, but the man who does the will
of God lives forever.

Warning Against Antichrists

18 Dear children, this is the last
hour; and as you have heard that the
antichrist is coming, even now many
antichrists have come. This is how we
know it is the last hour. 19 They went
out from us, but they did not really
belong to us. For if they had belonged
to us, they would have remained with

us; but their going showed that none
of them belonged to us.

20 But you have an anointing from
the Holy One, and all of you know
the truth ƒ 21 I do not write to you
because you do not know the truth,
but because you do know it and because no lie comes from the truth.
22 Who is the liar? It is the man who
denies that Jesus is the Christ. Such
a man is the antichrist—he denies
the Father and the Son. 23 No one
who denies the Son has the Father;
whoever acknowledges the Son has
the Father also.

24 See that what you have heard
from the beginning remains in you.
If it does, you also will remain in the
Son and in the Father. 25 And this is
what he promised us—even eternal
life.

26 I am writing these things to you
about those who are trying to lead
you astray. 27 As for you, the anointing you received from him remains in
you, and you do not need anyone to
teach you. But as his anointing
teaches you about all things and as
that anointing is real, not counterfeit—just as it has taught you,
remain in him.

Children of God

28 And now, dear children, continue in him, so that when he appears
we may be confident and unashamed
before him at his coming.

29 If you know that he is righteous,
you know that everyone who does
what is right has been born of him.

3 1 How great is the love the
    Father has lavished on us, that
we should be called children of God!
And that is what we are! The reason
the world does not know us is that it

ƒ 20 Some manuscripts and you know all things

did not know him. **2** Dear friends, now we are children of God, and what we will be has not yet been made known. But we know that when he appears,*g* we shall be like him, for we shall see him as he is. **3** Everyone who has this hope in him purifies himself, just as he is pure.

4 Everyone who sins breaks the law; in fact, sin is lawlessness. **5** But you know that he appeared so that he might take away our sins. And in him is no sin. **6** No one who lives in him keeps on sinning. No one who continues to sin has either seen him or known him.

7 Dear children, do not let anyone lead you astray. He who does what is right is righteous, just as he is righteous. **8** He who does what is sinful is of the devil, because the devil has been sinning from the beginning. The reason the Son of God appeared was to destroy the devil's work. **9** No one who is born of God will continue to sin, because God's seed remains in him; he cannot go on sinning, because he has been born of God. **10** This is how we know who the children of God are and who the children of the devil are: Anyone who does not do what is right is not a child of God; nor is anyone who does not love his brother.

Love one another

11 This is the message you heard from the beginning: We should love one another. **12** Do not be like Cain, who belonged to the evil one and murdered his brother. And why did he murder him? Because his own actions were evil and his brother's were righteous. **13** Do not be surprised, my brothers, if the world

hates you. **14** We know that we have passed from death to life, because we love our brothers. Anyone who does not love remains in death. **15** Anyone who hates his brother is a murderer, and you know that no murderer has eternal life in him.

16 This is how we know what love is: Jesus Christ laid down his life for us. And we ought to lay down our lives for our brothers. **17** If anyone has material possessions and sees his brother in need but has no pity on him, how can the love of God be in him? **18** Dear children, let us not love with words or tongue but with actions and in truth. **19** This then is how we know that we belong to the truth, and how we set our hearts at rest in his presence **20** whenever our hearts condemn us. For God is greater than our hearts, and he knows everything.

21 Dear friends, if our hearts do not condemn us, we have confidence before God **22** and receive from him anything we ask, because we obey his commands and do what pleases him. **23** And this is his command: to believe in the name of his Son, Jesus Christ, and to love one another as he commanded us. **24** Those who obey his commands live in him, and he in them. And this is how we know that he lives in us: We know it by the Spirit he gave us.

Test the Spirits

4 **1** Dear friends, do not believe every spirit, but test the spirits to see whether they are from God, because many false prophets have gone out into the world. **2** This is how you can recognize the Spirit of God: Every spirit that acknowledges that Jesus Christ has come in the flesh is

8 2 Or when it is made known

from God, **3** but every spirit that does not acknowledge Jesus is not from God. This is the spirit of the antichrist, which you have heard is coming and even now is already in the world.

4 You, dear children, are from God and have overcome them, because the one who is in you is greater than the one who is in the world. **5** They are from the world and therefore speak from the viewpoint of the world, and the world listens to them. **6** We are from God, and whoever knows God listens to us; but whoever is not from God does not listen to us. This is how we recognize the Spirit[h] of truth and the spirit of falsehood.

God's Love and Ours

7 Dear friends, let us love one another, for love comes from God. Everyone who loves has been born of God and knows God. **8** Whoever does not love does not know God, because God is love. **9** This is how God showed his love among us: He sent his one and only Son[i] into the world that we might live through him. **10** This is love: not that we loved God, but that he loved us and sent his Son as an atoning sacrifice for[j] our sins. **11** Dear friends, since God so loved us, we also ought to love one another. **12** No one has ever seen God; but if we love one another, God lives in us and his love is made complete in us.

13 We know that we live in him and he in us, because he has given us of his Spirit. **14** And we have seen and testify that the Father has sent his Son to be the Savior of the world. **15** If anyone acknowledges that Jesus is the Son of God, God lives in him and he in God. **16** And so we know and rely on the love God has for us.

God is love. Whoever lives in love lives in God, and God in him. **17** In this way, love is made complete among us so that we will have confidence on the day of judgment, because in this world we are like him. **18** There is no fear in love. But perfect love drives out fear, because fear has to do with punishment. The one who fears is not made perfect in love.

19 We love because he first loved us. **20** If anyone says, "I love God," yet hates his brother, he is a liar. For anyone who does not love his brother, whom he has seen, cannot love God, whom he has not seen. **21** And he has given us this command: Whoever loves God must also love his brother.

Faith in the Son of God

5 **1** Everyone who believes that Jesus is the Christ is born of God, and everyone who loves the father loves his child as well. **2** This is how we know that we love the children of God: by loving God and carrying out his commands. **3** This is love for God: to obey his commands. And his commands are not burdensome, **4** for everyone born of God overcomes the world. This is the victory that has overcome the world, even our faith. **5** Who is it that overcomes the world? Only he who believes that Jesus is the Son of God.

6 This is the one who came by water and blood—Jesus Christ. He did not come by water only, but by water and blood. And it is the Spirit

---

h 6 Or *spirit*   *i* 9 Or *his only begotten Son*   *j* 10 Or *as the one who would turn aside his wrath, taking away*

who testifies, because the Spirit is the truth. 7 For there are three that testify: 8 the*k* Spirit, the water and the blood; and the three are in agreement. 9 We accept man's testimony, but God's testimony is greater because it is the testimony of God, which he has given about his Son. 10 Anyone who believes in the Son of God has this testimony in his heart. Anyone who does not believe God has made him out to be a liar, because he has not believed the testimony God has given about his Son. 11 And this is the testimony: God has given us eternal life, and this life is in his Son. 12 He who has the Son has life; he who does not have the Son of God does not have life.

Concluding Remarks

13 I write these things to you who believe in the name of the Son of God so that you may know that you have eternal life. 14 This is the confidence we have in approaching God: that if we ask anything according to his will, he hears us. 15 And if we know that

he hears us—whatever we ask—we know that we have what we asked of him.

16 If anyone sees his brother commit a sin that does not lead to death, he should pray and God will give him life. I refer to those whose sin does not lead to death. There is a sin that leads to death. I am not saying that he should pray about that. 17 All wrongdoing is sin, and there is sin that does not lead to death.

18 We know that anyone born of God does not continue to sin; the one who was born of God keeps him safe, and the evil one cannot harm him. 19 We know that we are children of God, and that the whole world is under the control of the evil one. 20 We know also that the Son of God has come and has given us understanding, so that we may know him who is true. And we are in him who is true—even in his Son Jesus Christ. He is the true God and eternal life.

21 Dear children, keep yourselves from idols.

---

k 8 Late manuscripts of the Vulgate *testify in heaven: the Father, the Word and the Holy Spirit, and these three are one.* 8 *And there are three that testify on earth: the* (not found in any Greek manuscript before the sixteenth century)

2 John

1 The elder,

To the chosen lady and her children, whom I love in the truth—and not I only, but also all who know the truth— **2** because of the truth, which lives in us and will be with us forever:

3 Grace, mercy and peace from God the Father and from Jesus Christ, the Father's Son, will be with us in truth and love.

4 It has given me great joy to find some of your children walking in the truth, just as the Father commanded us. **5** And now, dear lady, I am not writing you a new command but one we have had from the beginning. I ask that we love one another. **6** And this is love: that we walk in obedience to his commands. As you have heard from the beginning, his command is that you walk in love.

7 Many deceivers, who do not acknowledge Jesus Christ as coming in the flesh, have gone out into the world. Any such person is the deceiver and the antichrist. **8** Watch out that you do not lose what you have worked for, but that you may be rewarded fully. **9** Anyone who runs ahead and does not continue in the teaching of Christ does not have God; whoever continues in the teaching has both the Father and the Son. **10** If anyone comes to you and does not bring this teaching, do not take him into your house or welcome him. **11** Anyone who welcomes him shares in his wicked work.

12 I have much to write to you, but I do not want to use paper and ink. Instead, I hope to visit you and talk with you face to face, so that our joy may be complete.

13 The children of your chosen sister send their greetings.

3 John

¹ The elder,

To my dear friend Gaius, whom I love in the truth.

² Dear friend, I pray that you may enjoy good health and that all may go well with you, even as your soul is getting along well. ³ It gave me great joy to have some brothers come and tell about your faithfulness to the truth and how you continue to walk in the truth. ⁴ I have no greater joy than to hear that my children are walking in the truth.

⁵ Dear friend, you are faithful in what you are doing for the brothers, even though they are strangers to you. ⁶ They have told the church about your love. You will do well to send them on their way in a manner worthy of God. ⁷ It was for the sake of the Name that they went out, receiving no help from the pagans. ⁸ We ought therefore to show hospitality to such men so that we may work together for the truth.

⁹ I wrote to the church, but Diotrephes, who loves to be first, will have nothing to do with us. ¹⁰ So if I come, I will call attention to what he is doing, gossiping maliciously about us. Not satisfied with that, he refuses to welcome the brothers. He also stops those who want to do so and puts them out of the church.

¹¹ Dear friend, do not imitate what is evil but what is good. Anyone who does what is good is from God. Anyone who does what is evil has not seen God. ¹² Demetrius is well spoken of by everyone — and even by the truth itself. We also speak well of him, and you know that our testimony is true.

¹³ I have much to write you, but I do not want to do so with pen and ink. ¹⁴ I hope to see you soon, and we will talk face to face.

Peace to you. The friends here send their greetings. Greet the friends there by name.

Jude

1 Jude, a servant of Jesus Christ and a brother of James,

To those who have been called, who are loved by God the Father and kept by[a] Jesus Christ:

2 Mercy, peace and love be yours in abundance.

The sin and doom of Godless men

3 Dear friends, although I was very eager to write to you about the salvation we share, I felt I had to write and urge you to contend for the faith that was once for all entrusted to the saints. 4 For certain men whose condemnation was written about[b] long ago have secretly slipped in among you. They are godless men, who change the grace of our God into a license for immorality and deny Jesus Christ our only Sovereign and Lord.

5 Though you already know all this, I want to remind you that the Lord[c] delivered his people out of Egypt, but later destroyed those who did not believe. 6 And the angels who did not keep their positions of authority but abandoned their own home—these he has kept in darkness, bound with everlasting chains for judgment on the great Day. 7 In a similar way, Sodom and Gomorrah and the surrounding towns gave themselves up to sexual immorality and perversion. They serve as an example of those who suffer the punishment of eternal fire.

8 In the very same way, these dreamers pollute their own bodies, reject authority and slander celestial beings. 9 But even the archangel Michael, when he was disputing with the devil about the body of Moses, did not dare to bring a slanderous accusation against him, but said, "The Lord rebuke you!" 10 Yet these men speak abusively against whatever they do not understand; and what things they do understand by instinct, like unreasoning animals—these are the very things that destroy them.

11 Woe to them! They have taken the way of Cain; they have rushed for profit into Balaam's error; they have been destroyed in Korah's rebellion.

12 These men are blemishes at your love feasts, eating with you without the slightest qualm— shepherds who feed only themselves. They are clouds without rain, blown along by the wind; autumn trees, without fruit and uprooted—twice dead. 13 They are wild waves of the sea, foaming up their shame; wandering stars, for whom blackest darkness has been reserved forever.

14 Enoch, the seventh from Adam, prophesied about these men: "See, the Lord is coming with thousands upon thousands of his holy ones 15 to judge everyone, and to convict all the ungodly of all the ungodly acts they have done in the ungodly way, and of all the harsh words ungodly sinners have spoken against him." 16 These

---

a 1 Or for; or in b 4 Or men who were marked out for condemnation c 5 Some early manuscripts Jesus

men are grumblers and faultfinders; they follow their own evil desires; they boast about themselves and flatter others for their own advantage.

A call to persevere

17 But, dear friends, remember what the apostles of our Lord Jesus Christ foretold. **18** They said to you, "In the last times there will be scoffers who will follow their own ungodly desires." **19** These are the men who divide you, who follow mere natural instincts and do not have the Spirit.

20 But you, dear friends, build yourselves up in your most holy faith and pray in the Holy Spirit. **21** Keep yourselves in God's love as you wait for the mercy of our Lord Jesus Christ to bring you to eternal life.

22 Be merciful to those who doubt; **23** snatch others from the fire and save them; to others show mercy, mixed with fear — hating even the clothing stained by corrupted flesh.

Doxology

24 To him who is able to keep you from falling and to present you before his glorious presence without fault and with great joy — **25** to the only God our Savior be glory, majesty, power and authority, through Jesus Christ our Lord, before all ages, now and forevermore! Amen.

Revelation

Prologue

1 **1** The revelation of Jesus Christ, which God gave him to show his servants what must soon take place. He made it known by sending his angel to his servant John, **2** who testifies to everything he saw—that is, the word of God and the testimony of Jesus Christ. **3** Blessed is the one who reads the words of this prophecy, and blessed are those who hear it and take to heart what is written in it, because the time is near.

Greetings and doxology

4 John,

To the seven churches in the province of Asia:

Grace and peace to you from him who is, and who was, and who is to come, and from the seven spirits*a* before his throne, **5** and from Jesus Christ, who is the faithful witness, the firstborn from the dead, and the ruler of the kings of the earth.

To him who loves us and has freed us from our sins by his blood, **6** and has made us to be a kingdom and priests to serve his God and Father—to him be glory and power for ever and ever! Amen.

7 Look, he is coming with the clouds,
and every eye will see him,

even those who pierced him;
and all the peoples of the
earth will mourn because
of him.

So shall it be! Amen.

8 "I am the Alpha and the Omega," says the Lord God, "who is, and who was, and who is to come, the Almighty."

One like a Son of Man

9 I, John, your brother and companion in the suffering and kingdom and patient endurance that are ours in Jesus, was on the island of Patmos because of the word of God and the testimony of Jesus. **10** On the Lord's Day I was in the Spirit, and I heard behind me a loud voice like a trumpet, **11** which said: "Write on a scroll what you see and send it to the seven churches: to Ephesus, Smyrna, Pergamum, Thyatira, Sardis, Philadelphia and Laodicea."

12 I turned around to see the voice that was speaking to me. And when I turned I saw seven golden lampstands, **13** and among the lampstands was someone "like a son of man,"*b* dressed in a robe reaching down to his feet and with a golden sash around his chest. **14** His head and hair were white like wool, as white as snow, and his eyes were like blazing fire. **15** His feet were like bronze glowing in a furnace, and his voice was like the sound of rushing waters. **16** In his right hand he held seven stars, and out of his mouth

---

a 4 Or *the sevenfold Spirit*   *b 13* Daniel 7:13

came a sharp double-edged sword. His face was like the sun shining in all its brilliance.

17 When I saw him, I fell at his feet as though dead. Then he placed his right hand on me and said: "Do not be afraid. I am the First and the Last. 18 I am the Living One; I was dead, and behold I am alive for ever and ever! And I hold the keys of death and Hades.

19 "Write, therefore, what you have seen, what is now and what will take place later. 20 The mystery of the seven stars that you saw in my right hand and of the seven golden lampstands is this: The seven stars are the angels[c] of the seven churches, and the seven lampstands are the seven churches.

To the church in Ephesus

2 1 "To the angel[d] of the church in Ephesus write:

These are the words of him who holds the seven stars in his right hand and walks among the seven golden lampstands: 2 I know your deeds, your hard work and your perseverance. I know that you cannot tolerate wicked men, that you have tested those who claim to be apostles but are not, and have found them false. 3 You have persevered and have endured hardships for my name, and have not grown weary.

4 Yet I hold this against you: You have forsaken your first love. 5 Remember the height from which you have fallen! Repent and do the things you did at first. If you do not repent, I will come to you and remove your lampstand from

its place. 6 But you have this in your favor: You hate the practices of the Nicolaitans, which I also hate.

7 He who has an ear, let him hear what the Spirit says to the churches. To him who overcomes, I will give the right to eat from the tree of life, which is in the paradise of God.

To the Church in Smyrna

8 "To the angel of the church in Smyrna write:

These are the words of him who is the First and the Last, who died and came to life again. 9 I know your afflictions and your poverty—yet you are rich! I know the slander of those who say they are Jews and are not, but are a synagogue of Satan. 10 Do not be afraid of what you are about to suffer. I tell you, the devil will put some of you in prison to test you, and you will suffer persecution for ten days. Be faithful, even to the point of death, and I will give you the crown of life.

11 He who has an ear, let him hear what the Spirit says to the churches. He who overcomes will not be hurt at all by the second death.

To the Church in Pergamum

12 "To the angel of the church in Pergamum write:

These are the words of him who has the sharp, double-edged sword. 13 I know where you live—where Satan has his throne. Yet you remain true to my name. You did not renounce your faith in me, even in the days of Antipas, my faithful witness, who was put to death in your city—where Satan lives.

14 Nevertheless, I have a few things against you: You have people there who hold to the teaching of Balaam, who taught Balak to entice the Israelites to sin by eating food sacrificed to idols and by committing sexual immorality. **15** Likewise you also have those who hold to the teaching of the Nicolaitans. **16** Repent therefore! Otherwise, I will soon come to you and will fight against them with the sword of my mouth.

17 He who has an ear, let him hear what the Spirit says to the churches. To him who overcomes, I will give some of the hidden manna. I will also give him a white stone with a new name written on it, known only to him who receives it.

To the Church in Thyatira

18 "To the angel of the church in Thyatira write:

These are the words of the Son of God, whose eyes are like blazing fire and whose feet are like burnished bronze. **19** I know your deeds, your love and faith, your service and perseverance, and that you are now doing more than you did at first.

20 Nevertheless, I have this against you: You tolerate that woman Jezebel, who calls herself a prophetess. By her teaching she misleads my servants into sexual immorality and the eating of food sacrificed to idols. **21** I have given her time to repent of her

immorality, but she is unwilling. **22** So I will cast her on a bed of suffering, and I will make those who commit adultery with her suffer intensely, unless they repent of her ways. **23** I will strike her children dead. Then all the churches will know that I am he who searches hearts and minds, and I will repay each of you according to your deeds. **24** Now I say to the rest of you in Thyatira, to you who do not hold to her teaching and have not learned Satan's so-called deep secrets (I will not impose any other burden on you): **25** Only hold on to what you have until I come.

26 To him who overcomes and does my will to the end, I will give authority over the nations—

27 'He will rule them with an iron scepter;
he will dash them to pieces like pottery'*e*—

just as I have received authority from my Father. **28** I will also give him the morning star. **29** He who has an ear, let him hear what the Spirit says to the churches.

To the Church in Sardis

3 **1** "To the angel*f* of the church in Sardis write:

These are the words of him who holds the seven spirits*g* of God and the seven stars. I know your deeds; you have a reputation of being alive, but you are dead. **2** Wake up! Strengthen what remains and is about to die, for I have not found your deeds complete in the sight of my God. **3** Remember, therefore, what you have received and heard;

obey it, and repent. But if you do not wake up, I will come like a thief, and you will not know at what time I will come to you.

4 Yet you have a few people in Sardis who have not soiled their clothes. They will walk with me, dressed in white, for they are worthy. **5** He who overcomes will, like them, be dressed in white. I will never blot out his name from the book of life, but will acknowledge his name before my Father and his angels. **6** He who has an ear, let him hear what the Spirit says to the churches.

To the Church in Philadelphia

7 "To the angel of the church in Philadelphia write:

These are the words of him who is holy and true, who holds the key of David. What he opens no one can shut, and what he shuts no one can open. **8** I know your deeds. See, I have placed before you an open door that no one can shut. I know that you have little strength, yet you have kept my word and have not denied my name. **9** I will make those who are of the synagogue of Satan, who claim to be Jews though they are not, but are liars—I will make them come and fall down at your feet and acknowledge that I have loved you. **10** Since you have kept my command to endure patiently, I will also keep you from the hour of trial that is going to come upon the whole world to test those who live on the earth.

11 I am coming soon. Hold on to what you have, so that no one will take your crown. **12** Him who overcomes I will make a pillar in the temple of my God. Never again

will he leave it. I will write on him the name of my God and the name of the city of my God, the new Jerusalem, which is coming down out of heaven from my God; and I will also write on him my new name. **13** He who has an ear, let him hear what the Spirit says to the churches.

To the Church in Laodicea

14 "To the angel of the church in Laodicea write:

These are the words of the Amen, the faithful and true witness, the ruler of God's creation. **15** I know your deeds, that you are neither cold nor hot. I wish you were either one or the other! **16** So, because you are lukewarm—neither hot nor cold—I am about to spit you out of my mouth. **17** You say, 'I am rich; I have acquired wealth and do not need a thing.' But you do not realize that you are wretched, pitiful, poor, blind and naked. **18** I counsel you to buy from me gold refined in the fire, so you can become rich; and white clothes to wear, so you can cover your shameful nakedness; and salve to put on your eyes, so you can see.

19 Those whom I love I rebuke and discipline. So be earnest, and repent. **20** Here I am! I stand at the door and knock. If anyone hears my voice and opens the door, I will come in and eat with him, and he with me.

21 To him who overcomes, I will give the right to sit with me on my throne, just as I overcame and sat down with my Father on his throne. **22** He who has an ear, let him hear what the Spirit says to the churches."

The Throne in Heaven

4 ¹ After this I looked, and there before me was a door standing open in heaven. And the voice I had first heard speaking to me like a trumpet said, "Come up here, and I will show you what must take place after this." ² At once I was in the Spirit, and there before me was a throne in heaven with someone sitting on it. ³ And the one who sat there had the appearance of jasper and carnelian. A rainbow, resembling an emerald, encircled the throne. ⁴ Surrounding the throne were twenty-four other thrones, and seated on them were twenty-four elders. They were dressed in white and had crowns of gold on their heads. ⁵ From the throne came flashes of lightning, rumblings and peals of thunder. Before the throne, seven lamps were blazing. These are the seven spirits[h] of God. ⁶ Also before the throne there was what looked like a sea of glass, clear as crystal.

In the center, around the throne, were four living creatures, and they were covered with eyes, in front and in back. ⁷ The first living creature was like a lion, the second was like an ox, the third had a face like a man, the fourth was like a flying eagle. ⁸ Each of the four living creatures had six wings and was covered with eyes all around, even under his wings. Day and night they never stop saying:

"Holy, holy, holy
    is the Lord God Almighty,
who was, and is, and is to come."

⁹ Whenever the living creatures give glory, honor and thanks to him who sits on the throne and who lives for ever and ever, ¹⁰ the twenty-four elders fall down before him who sits on the throne, and worship him who lives for ever and ever. They lay their crowns before the throne and say:

¹¹ "You are worthy, our Lord and God,
    to receive glory and honor and power,
for you created all things,
    and by your will they were created
    and have their being."

The Scroll and the Lamb

5 ¹ Then I saw in the right hand of him who sat on the throne a scroll with writing on both sides and sealed with seven seals. ² And I saw a mighty angel proclaiming in a loud voice, "Who is worthy to break the seals and open the scroll?" ³ But no one in heaven or on earth or under the earth could open the scroll or even look inside it. ⁴ I wept and wept because no one was found who was worthy to open the scroll or look inside. ⁵ Then one of the elders said to me, "Do not weep! See, the Lion of the tribe of Judah, the Root of David, has triumphed. He is able to open the scroll and its seven seals."

⁶ Then I saw a Lamb, looking as if it had been slain, standing in the center of the throne, encircled by the four living creatures and the elders. He had seven horns and seven eyes, which are the seven spirits[i] of God sent out into all the earth. ⁷ He came and took the scroll from the right hand of him who sat on the throne. ⁸ And when he had taken it, the four living creatures and the twenty-four

h 5 Or *the sevenfold Spirit*   i 6 Or *the sevenfold Spirit*

elders fell down before the Lamb. Each one had a harp and they were holding golden bowls full of incense, which are the prayers of the saints. 9 And they sang a new song:

"You are worthy to take the scroll
   and to open its seals,
because you were slain,
   and with your blood you
      purchased men for God
from every tribe and language
   and people and nation.
10 You have made them to be a
   kingdom and priests to
     serve our God,
and they will reign on the
   earth."

11 Then I looked and heard the voice of many angels, numbering thousands upon thousands, and ten thousand times ten thousand. They encircled the throne and the living creatures and the elders. 12 In a loud voice they sang:

"Worthy is the Lamb, who was
   slain,
to receive power and wealth
   and wisdom and strength
and honor and glory and
   praise!"

13 Then I heard every creature in heaven and on earth and under the earth and on the sea, and all that is in them, singing:

"To him who sits on the throne
   and to the Lamb
be praise and honor and glory
   and power,
for ever and ever!"

14 The four living creatures said, "Amen," and the elders fell down and worshiped.

The Seals

6 1 I watched as the Lamb opened the first of the seven seals. Then I heard one of the four living creatures say in a voice like thunder, "Come!" 2 I looked, and there before me was a white horse! Its rider held a bow, and he was given a crown, and he rode out as a conqueror bent on conquest.

3 When the Lamb opened the second seal, I heard the second living creature say, "Come!" 4 Then another horse came out, a fiery red one. Its rider was given power to take peace from the earth and to make men slay each other. To him was given a large sword.

5 When the Lamb opened the third seal, I heard the third living creature say, "Come!" I looked, and there before me was a black horse! Its rider was holding a pair of scales in his hand. 6 Then I heard what sounded like a voice among the four living creatures, saying, "A quart*j* of wheat for a day's wages,*k* and three quarts of barley for a day's wages,*l* and do not damage the oil and the wine!"

7 When the Lamb opened the fourth seal, I heard the voice of the fourth living creature say, "Come!" 8 I looked, and there before me was a pale horse! Its rider was named Death, and Hades was following close behind him. They were given power over a fourth of the earth to kill by sword, famine and plague, and by the wild beasts of the earth.

9 When he opened the fifth seal, I saw under the altar the souls of those who had been slain because of the word of God and the testimony they had maintained. 10 They called out

---

j 6 Greek *a choinix* (probably about a liter)   *k* 6 Greek *a denarius*   *l* 6 Greek *a denarius*

in a loud voice, "How long, Sovereign Lord, holy and true, until you judge the inhabitants of the earth and avenge our blood?" **11** Then each of them was given a white robe, and they were told to wait a little longer, until the number of their fellow servants and brothers who were to be killed as they had been was completed.

12 I watched as he opened the sixth seal. There was a great earthquake. The sun turned black like sackcloth made of goat hair, the whole moon turned blood red, **13** and the stars in the sky fell to earth, as late figs drop from a fig tree when shaken by a strong wind. **14** The sky receded like a scroll, rolling up, and every mountain and island was removed from its place.

15 Then the kings of the earth, the princes, the generals, the rich, the mighty, and every slave and every free man hid in caves and among the rocks of the mountains. **16** They called to the mountains and the rocks, "Fall on us and hide us from the face of him who sits on the throne and from the wrath of the Lamb! **17** For the great day of their wrath has come, and who can stand?"

144,000 Sealed

7 **1** After this I saw four angels standing at the four corners of the earth, holding back the four winds of the earth to prevent any wind from blowing on the land or on the sea or on any tree. **2** Then I saw another angel coming up from the east, having the seal of the living God. He called out in a loud voice to the four angels who had been given power to harm the land and the sea: **3** "Do not harm the land or the sea or the trees until we put a seal on the

foreheads of the servants of our God." **4** Then I heard the number of those who were sealed: 144,000 from all the tribes of Israel.

5 From the tribe of Judah 12,000 were sealed,
  from the tribe of Reuben 12,000,
  from the tribe of Gad 12,000,
6 from the tribe of Asher 12,000,
  from the tribe of Naphtali 12,000,
  from the tribe of Manasseh 12,000,
7 from the tribe of Simeon 12,000,
  from the tribe of Levi 12,000,
  from the tribe of Issachar 12,000,
8 from the tribe of Zebulun 12,000,
  from the tribe of Joseph 12,000,
  from the tribe of Benjamin 12,000.

The Great Multitude in White Robes

9 After this I looked and there before me was a great multitude that no one could count, from every nation, tribe, people and language, standing before the throne and in front of the Lamb. They were wearing white robes and were holding palm branches in their hands. **10** And they cried out in a loud voice:

  "Salvation belongs to our God,
  who sits on the throne,
  and to the Lamb."

11 All the angels were standing around the throne and around the elders and the four living creatures. They fell down on their faces before the throne and worshiped God, **12** saying:

  "Amen!
  Praise and glory
  and wisdom and thanks and honor
  and power and strength
  be to our God for ever and ever. Amen!"

13 Then one of the elders asked me, "These in white robes – who are they, and where did they come from?"

14 I answered, "Sir, you know."

And he said, "These are they who have come out of the great tribulation; they have washed their robes and made them white in the blood of the Lamb. 15 Therefore,

"they are before the throne of
        God
    and serve him day and night
        in his temple;
    and he who sits on the throne will
        spread his tent over them.
16 Never again will they hunger;
    never again will they thirst.
    The sun will not beat upon them,
        nor any scorching heat.
17 For the Lamb at the center of
        the throne will be their
        shepherd;
    he will lead them to springs
        of living water.
    And God will wipe away every
        tear from their eyes."

The Seventh Seal and the Golden Censer

8 1 When he opened the seventh seal, there was silence in heaven for about half an hour.

2 And I saw the seven angels who stand before God, and to them were given seven trumpets.

3 Another angel, who had a golden censer, came and stood at the altar. He was given much incense to offer, with the prayers of all the saints, on the golden altar before the throne. 4 The smoke of the incense, together with the prayers of the saints, went up before God from the angel's hand. 5 Then the angel took the censer, filled it with fire from the altar, and hurled it on the earth; and there came peals of thunder, rumblings, flashes of lightning and an earthquake.

The Trumpets

6 Then the seven angels who had the seven trumpets prepared to sound them.

7 The first angel sounded his trumpet, and there came hail and fire mixed with blood, and it was hurled down upon the earth. A third of the earth was burned up, a third of the trees were burned up, and all the green grass was burned up.

8 The second angel sounded his trumpet, and something like a huge mountain, all ablaze, was thrown into the sea. A third of the sea turned into blood, 9 a third of the living creatures in the sea died, and a third of the ships were destroyed.

10 The third angel sounded his trumpet, and a great star, blazing like a torch, fell from the sky on a third of the rivers and on the springs of water— 11 the name of the star is Wormwood.m A third of the waters turned bitter, and many people died from the waters that had become bitter.

12 The fourth angel sounded his trumpet, and a third of the sun was struck, a third of the moon, and a third of the stars, so that a third of them turned dark. A third of the day was without light, and also a third of the night.

13 As I watched, I heard an eagle that was flying in midair call out in a loud voice: "Woe! Woe! Woe to the inhabitants of the earth, because of the trumpet blasts about to be sounded by the other three angels!"

m 11 That is, Bitterness

9 1 The fifth angel sounded his trumpet, and I saw a star that had fallen from the sky to the earth. The star was given the key to the shaft of the Abyss. 2 When he opened the Abyss, smoke rose from it like the smoke from a gigantic furnace. The sun and sky were darkened by the smoke from the Abyss. 3 And out of the smoke locusts came down upon the earth and were given power like that of scorpions of the earth. 4 They were told not to harm the grass of the earth or any plant or tree, but only those people who did not have the seal of God on their foreheads. 5 They were not given power to kill them, but only to torture them for five months. And the agony they suffered was like that of the sting of a scorpion when it strikes a man. 6 During those days men will seek death, but will not find it; they will long to die, but death will elude them.

7 The locusts looked like horses prepared for battle. On their heads they wore something like crowns of gold, and their faces resembled human faces. 8 Their hair was like women's hair, and their teeth were like lions' teeth. 9 They had breastplates like breastplates of iron, and the sound of their wings was like the thundering of many horses and chariots rushing into battle. 10 They had tails and stings like scorpions, and in their tails they had power to torment people for five months. 11 They had as king over them the angel of the Abyss, whose name in Hebrew is Abaddon, and in Greek, Apollyon.[n]

12 The first woe is past; two other woes are yet to come.

13 The sixth angel sounded his trumpet, and I heard a voice coming from the horns[o] of the golden altar that is before God. 14 It said to the sixth angel who had the trumpet, "Release the four angels who are bound at the great river Euphrates." 15 And the four angels who had been kept ready for this very hour and day and month and year were released to kill a third of mankind. 16 The number of the mounted troops was two hundred million. I heard their number.

17 The horses and riders I saw in my vision looked like this: Their breastplates were fiery red, dark blue, and yellow as sulfur. The heads of the horses resembled the heads of lions, and out of their mouths came fire, smoke and sulfur. 18 A third of mankind was killed by the three plagues of fire, smoke and sulfur that came out of their mouths. 19 The power of the horses was in their mouths and in their tails; for their tails were like snakes, having heads with which they inflict injury.

20 The rest of mankind that were not killed by these plagues still did not repent of the work of their hands; they did not stop worshiping demons, and idols of gold, silver, bronze, stone and wood—idols that cannot see or hear or walk. 21 Nor did they repent of their murders, their magic arts, their sexual immorality or their thefts.

The Angel and the Little Scroll

10 1 Then I saw another mighty angel coming down from heaven. He was robed in a cloud, with a rainbow above his head; his face was like the sun, and his legs

---

[n] 11 Abaddon and Apollyon mean Destroyer.   [o] 13 That is, projections

were like fiery pillars. **2** He was holding a little scroll, which lay open in his hand. He planted his right foot on the sea and his left foot on the land, **3** and he gave a loud shout like the roar of a lion. When he shouted, the voices of the seven thunders spoke. **4** And when the seven thunders spoke, I was about to write; but I heard a voice from heaven say, "Seal up what the seven thunders have said and do not write it down."

5 Then the angel I had seen standing on the sea and on the land raised his right hand to heaven. **6** And he swore by him who lives for ever and ever, who created the heavens and all that is in them, the earth and all that is in it, and the sea and all that is in it, and said, "There will be no more delay! **7** But in the days when the seventh angel is about to sound his trumpet, the mystery of God will be accomplished, just as he announced to his servants the prophets."

8 Then the voice that I had heard from heaven spoke to me once more: "Go, take the scroll that lies open in the hand of the angel who is standing on the sea and on the land."

9 So I went to the angel and asked him to give me the little scroll. He said to me, "Take it and eat it. It will turn your stomach sour, but in your mouth it will be as sweet as honey." **10** I took the little scroll from the angel's hand and ate it. It tasted as sweet as honey in my mouth, but when I had eaten it, my stomach turned sour. **11** Then I was told, "You must prophesy again about many peoples, nations, languages and kings."

The Two Witnesses

11 **1** I was given a reed like a measuring rod and was told, "Go and measure the temple of God and the altar, and count the wor-shipers there. **2** But exclude the outer court; do not measure it, because it has been given to the Gentiles. They will trample on the holy city for 42 months. **3** And I will give power to my two witnesses, and they will prophesy for 1,260 days, clothed in sackcloth." **4** These are the two olive trees and the two lampstands that stand before the Lord of the earth. **5** If anyone tries to harm them, fire comes from their mouths and devours their enemies. This is how anyone who wants to harm them must die. **6** These men have power to shut up the sky so that it will not rain during the time they are prophesying; and they have power to turn the waters into blood and to strike the earth with every kind of plague as often as they want.

7 Now when they have finished their testimony, the beast that comes up from the Abyss will attack them, and overpower and kill them. **8** Their bodies will lie in the street of the great city, which is figuratively called Sodom and Egypt, where also their Lord was crucified. **9** For three and a half days men from every people, tribe, language and nation will gaze on their bodies and refuse them burial. **10** The inhabitants of the earth will gloat over them and will celebrate by sending each other gifts, because these two prophets had tormented those who live on the earth.

11 But after the three and a half days a breath of life from God entered them, and they stood on their feet, and terror struck those who saw them. **12** Then they heard a loud voice from heaven saying to them, "Come up here." And they went up to heaven in a cloud, while their enemies looked on.

13 At that very hour there was a severe earthquake and a tenth of the city collapsed. Seven thousand people were killed in the earthquake, and the survivors were terrified and gave glory to the God of heaven.

14 The second woe has passed; the third woe is coming soon.

The Seventh Trumpet

15 The seventh angel sounded his trumpet, and there were loud voices in heaven, which said:

> "The kingdom of the world has
>   become the kingdom of our
>   Lord and of his Christ,
> and he will reign for ever and
>   ever."

16 And the twenty-four elders, who were seated on their thrones before God, fell on their faces and worshiped God, **17** saying:

> "We give thanks to you, Lord God
>   Almighty,
>   the One who is and who was,
> because you have taken your
>   great power
>   and have begun to reign.
> **18** The nations were angry; and
>   your wrath has come.
> The time has come for judging
>   the dead,
>   and for rewarding your
>   servants the prophets
> and your saints and those who
>   reverence your name,
>   both small and great—
> and for destroying those who
>   destroy the earth."

19 Then God's temple in heaven was opened, and within his temple was seen the ark of his covenant. And there came flashes of lightning, rumblings, peals of thunder, an earthquake and a great hailstorm.

The Woman and the Dragon

12 **1** A great and wondrous sign appeared in heaven: a woman clothed with the sun, with the moon under her feet and a crown of twelve stars on her head. **2** She was pregnant and cried out in pain as she was about to give birth. **3** Then another sign appeared in heaven: an enormous red dragon with seven heads and ten horns and seven crowns on his heads. **4** His tail swept a third of the stars out of the sky and flung them to the earth. The dragon stood in front of the woman who was about to give birth, so that he might devour her child the moment it was born. **5** She gave birth to a son, a male child, who will rule all the nations with an iron scepter. And her child was snatched up to God and to his throne. **6** The woman fled into the desert to a place prepared for her by God, where she might be taken care of for 1,260 days.

7 And there was war in heaven. Michael and his angels fought against the dragon, and the dragon and his angels fought back. **8** But he was not strong enough, and they lost their place in heaven. **9** The great dragon was hurled down—that ancient serpent called the devil, or Satan, who leads the whole world astray. He was hurled to the earth, and his angels with him.

10 Then I heard a loud voice in heaven say:

> "Now have come the salvation
>   and the power and the
>   kingdom of our God,
>   and the authority of his Christ.
> For the accuser of our brothers,
>   who accuses them before our
>   God day and night,
>   has been hurled down.

11 They overcame him
by the blood of the Lamb
and by the word of their
testimony;
they did not love their lives so
much
as to shrink from death.
12 Therefore rejoice, you heavens
and you who dwell in them!
But woe to the earth and the sea,
because the devil has gone
down to you!
He is filled with fury,
because he knows that his
time is short."

13 When the dragon saw that he had been hurled to the earth, he pursued the woman who had given birth to the male child. 14 The woman was given the two wings of a great eagle, so that she might fly to the place prepared for her in the desert, where she would be taken care of for a time, times and half a time, out of the serpent's reach. 15 Then from his mouth the serpent spewed water like a river, to overtake the woman and sweep her away with the torrent. 16 But the earth helped the woman by opening its mouth and swallowing the river that the dragon had spewed out of his mouth. 17 Then the dragon was enraged at the woman and went off to make war against the rest of her offspring— those who obey God's commandments and hold to the testimony of Jesus.

13 ¹ And the dragon[p] stood on the shore of the sea.

The Beast out of the Sea

And I saw a beast coming out of the sea. He had ten horns and seven heads, with ten crowns on his horns, and on each head a blasphemous name. ² The beast I saw resembled a leopard, but had feet like those of a bear and a mouth like that of a lion. The dragon gave the beast his power and his throne and great authority. ³ One of the heads of the beast seemed to have had a fatal wound, but the fatal wound had been healed. The whole world was astonished and followed the beast. ⁴ Men worshiped the dragon because he had given authority to the beast, and they also worshiped the beast and asked, "Who is like the beast? Who can make war against him?"

⁵ The beast was given a mouth to utter proud words and blasphemies and to exercise his authority for forty-two months. ⁶ He opened his mouth to blaspheme God, and to slander his name and his dwelling place and those who live in heaven. ⁷ He was given power to make war against the saints and to conquer them. And he was given authority over every tribe, people, language and nation. ⁸ All inhabitants of the earth will worship the beast—all whose names have not been written in the book of life belonging to the Lamb that was slain from the creation of the world.[q]

⁹ He who has an ear, let him hear.

10 If anyone is to go into captivity,
into captivity he will go.
If anyone is to be killed[r] with
the sword,
with the sword he will be
killed.

This calls for patient endurance and faithfulness on the part of the saints.

---

p 1 Some late manuscripts *And I*   q 8 Or *written from the creation of the world in the book of life belonging to the Lamb that was slain*   r 10 Some manuscripts *anyone kills*

The Beast out of the Earth

11 Then I saw another beast, coming out of the earth. He had two horns like a lamb, but he spoke like a dragon. 12 He exercised all the authority of the first beast on his behalf, and made the earth and its inhabitants worship the first beast, whose fatal wound had been healed. 13 And he performed great and miraculous signs, even causing fire to come down from heaven to earth in full view of men. 14 Because of the signs he was given power to do on behalf of the first beast, he deceived the inhabitants of the earth. He ordered them to set up an image in honor of the beast who was wounded by the sword and yet lived. 15 He was given power to give breath to the image of the first beast, so that it could speak and cause all who refused to worship the image to be killed. 16 He also forced everyone, small and great, rich and poor, free and slave, to receive a mark on his right hand or on his forehead, 17 so that no one could buy or sell unless he had the mark, which is the name of the beast or the number of his name.

18 This calls for wisdom. If anyone has insight, let him calculate the number of the beast, for it is man's number. His number is 666.

The Lamb and the 144,000

14 1 Then I looked, and there before me was the Lamb, standing on Mount Zion, and with him 144,000 who had his name and his Father's name written on their foreheads. 2 And I heard a sound from heaven like the roar of rushing waters and like a loud peal of thunder. The sound I heard was like that of harpists playing their harps.

3 And they sang a new song before the throne and before the four living creatures and the elders. No one could learn the song except the 144,000 who had been redeemed from the earth. 4 These are those who did not defile themselves with women, for they kept themselves pure. They follow the Lamb wherever he goes. They were purchased from among men and offered as firstfruits to God and the Lamb. 5 No lie was found in their mouths; they are blameless.

The Three Angels

6 Then I saw another angel flying in midair, and he had the eternal gospel to proclaim to those who live on the earth — to every nation, tribe, language and people. 7 He said in a loud voice, "Fear God and give him glory, because the hour of his judgment has come. Worship him who made the heavens, the earth, the sea and the springs of water."

8 A second angel followed and said, "Fallen! Fallen is Babylon the Great, which made all the nations drink the maddening wine of her adulteries."

9 A third angel followed them and said in a loud voice: "If anyone worships the beast and his image and receives his mark on the forehead or on the hand, 10 he, too, will drink of the wine of God's fury, which has been poured in full strength into the cup of his wrath. He will be tormented with burning sulfur in the presence of the holy angels and of the Lamb. 11 And the smoke of their torment rises for ever and ever. There is no rest day or night for those who worship the beast and his image, or for anyone who receives the mark of his name."

¹²This calls for patient endurance on the part of the saints who obey God's commandments and remain faithful to Jesus.

¹³Then I heard a voice from heaven say, "Write: Blessed are the dead who die in the Lord from now on."

"Yes," says the Spirit, "they will rest from their labor, for their deeds will follow them."

The Harvest of the Earth

¹⁴I looked, and there before me was a white cloud, and seated on the cloud was one "like a son of man"ˢ with a crown of gold on his head and a sharp sickle in his hand. ¹⁵Then another angel came out of the temple and called in a loud voice to him who was sitting on the cloud, "Take your sickle and reap, because the time to reap has come, for the harvest of the earth is ripe." ¹⁶So he who was seated on the cloud swung his sickle over the earth, and the earth was harvested.

¹⁷Another angel came out of the temple in heaven, and he too had a sharp sickle. ¹⁸Still another angel, who had charge of the fire, came from the altar and called in a loud voice to him who had the sharp sickle, "Take your sharp sickle and gather the clusters of grapes from the earth's vine, because its grapes are ripe." ¹⁹The angel swung his sickle on the earth, gathered its grapes and threw them into the great winepress of God's wrath. ²⁰They were trampled in the winepress outside the city, and blood flowed out of the press, rising as high as the horses' bridles for a distance of 1,600 stadia.ᵗ

Seven Angels with Seven Plagues

15 ¹I saw in heaven another great and marvelous sign: seven angels with the seven last plagues—last, because with them God's wrath is completed. ²And I saw what looked like a sea of glass mixed with fire and, standing beside the sea, those who had been victorious over the beast and his image and over the number of his name. They held harps given them by God ³and sang the song of Moses the servant of God and the song of the Lamb:

> "Great and marvelous are your deeds,
>   Lord God Almighty.
> Just and true are your ways,
>   King of the ages.
> ⁴Who will not fear you, O Lord,
>   and bring glory to your name?
> For you alone are holy.
> All nations will come
>   and worship before you,
> for your righteous acts have
>   been revealed."

⁵After this I looked and in heaven the temple, that is, the tabernacle of the Testimony, was opened. ⁶Out of the temple came the seven angels with the seven plagues. They were dressed in clean, shining linen and wore golden sashes around their chests. ⁷Then one of the four living creatures gave to the seven angels seven golden bowls filled with the wrath of God, who lives for ever and ever. ⁸And the temple was filled with smoke from the glory of God and from his power, and no one could enter the temple until the seven plagues of the seven angels were completed.

ˢ *14* Daniel 7:13   ᵗ *20* That is, about 180 miles (about 300 kilometers)

The Seven Bowls of God's Wrath

16 **1** Then I heard a loud voice from the temple saying to the seven angels, "Go, pour out the seven bowls of God's wrath on the earth." **2** The first angel went and poured out his bowl on the land, and ugly and painful sores broke out on the people who had the mark of the beast and worshiped his image.

3 The second angel poured out his bowl on the sea, and it turned into blood like that of a dead man, and every living thing in the sea died.

4 The third angel poured out his bowl on the rivers and springs of water, and they became blood. **5** Then I heard the angel in charge of the waters say:

"You are just in these judgments,
  you who are and who were,
    the Holy One,
  because you have so judged;
6 for they have shed the blood of
    your saints and prophets,
  and you have given them
    blood to drink as they
      deserve."

7 And I heard the altar respond:

"Yes, Lord God Almighty,
  true and just are your
    judgments."

8 The fourth angel poured out his bowl on the sun, and the sun was given power to scorch people with fire. **9** They were seared by the intense heat and they cursed the name of God, who had control over these plagues, but they refused to repent and glorify him.

10 The fifth angel poured out his bowl on the throne of the beast, and his kingdom was plunged into darkness. Men gnawed their tongues in agony **11** and cursed the God of heaven because of their pains and their sores, but they refused to repent of what they had done.

12 The sixth angel poured out his bowl on the great river Euphrates, and its water was dried up to prepare the way for the kings from the East. **13** Then I saw three evil[u] spirits that looked like frogs; they came out of the mouth of the dragon, out of the mouth of the beast and out of the mouth of the false prophet. **14** They are spirits of demons performing miraculous signs, and they go out to the kings of the whole world, to gather them for the battle on the great day of God Almighty.

15 "Behold, I come like a thief! Blessed is he who stays awake and keeps his clothes with him, so that he may not go naked and be shamefully exposed."

16 Then they gathered the kings together to the place that in Hebrew is called Armageddon.

17 The seventh angel poured out his bowl into the air, and out of the temple came a loud voice from the throne, saying, "It is done!" **18** Then there came flashes of lightning, rumblings, peals of thunder and a severe earthquake. No earthquake like it has ever occurred since man has been on earth, so tremendous was the quake. **19** The great city split into three parts, and the cities of the nations collapsed. God remembered Babylon the Great and gave her the cup filled with the wine of the fury of his wrath. **20** Every island fled away and the mountains could not be found. **21** From the sky huge

---

u 13 Greek *unclean*

hailstones of about a hundred pounds each fell upon men. And they cursed God on account of the plague of hail, because the plague was so terrible.

The Woman and the Beast

17 1 One of the seven angels who had the seven bowls came and said to me, "Come, I will show you the punishment of the great prostitute, who sits on many waters. 2 With her the kings of the earth committed adultery and the inhabitants of the earth were intoxicated with the wine of her adulteries."

3 Then the angel carried me away in the Spirit into a desert. There I saw a woman sitting on a scarlet beast that was covered with blasphemous names and had seven heads and ten horns. 4 The woman was dressed in purple and scarlet, and was glittering with gold, precious stones and pearls. She held a golden cup in her hand, filled with abominable things and the filth of her adulteries. 5 This title was written on her forehead:

MYSTERY
BABYLON THE GREAT
THE MOTHER OF PROSTITUTES
AND OF THE ABOMINATIONS OF THE EARTH.

6 I saw that the woman was drunk with the blood of the saints, the blood of those who bore testimony to Jesus.

When I saw her, I was greatly astonished. 7 Then the angel said to me: "Why are you astonished? I will explain to you the mystery of the woman and of the beast she rides, which has the seven heads and ten horns. 8 The beast, which you saw, once was, now is not, and will come up out of the Abyss and go to his destruction. The inhabitants of the earth whose names have not been written in the book of life from the creation of the world will be astonished when they see the beast, because he once was, now is not, and yet will come.

9 "This calls for a mind with wisdom. The seven heads are seven hills on which the woman sits. 10 They are also seven kings. Five have fallen, one is, the other has not yet come; but when he does come, he must remain for a little while. 11 The beast who once was, and now is not, is an eighth king. He belongs to the seven and is going to his destruction.

12 "The ten horns you saw are ten kings who have not yet received a kingdom, but who for one hour will receive authority as kings along with the beast. 13 They have one purpose and will give their power and authority to the beast. 14 They will make war against the Lamb, but the Lamb will overcome them because he is Lord of lords and King of kings— and with him will be his called, chosen and faithful followers."

15 Then the angel said to me, "The waters you saw, where the prostitute sits, are peoples, multitudes, nations and languages. 16 The beast and the ten horns you saw will hate the prostitute. They will bring her to ruin and leave her naked; they will eat her flesh and burn her with fire. 17 For God has put it into their hearts to accomplish his purpose by agreeing to give the beast their power to rule, until God's words are fulfilled. 18 The woman you saw is the great city that rules over the kings of the earth."

18 1 After this I saw another angel coming down from heaven. He had great authority, and the earth was illuminated by his splendor. 2 With a mighty voice he shouted:

"Fallen! Fallen is Babylon the
Great!
She has become a home for
demons
and a haunt for every evil[v]
spirit,
a haunt for every unclean and
detestable bird.
3 For all the nations have drunk
the maddening wine of her
adulteries.
The kings of the earth committed
adultery with her,
and the merchants of the
earth grew rich from her
excessive luxuries."

4 Then I heard another voice from
heaven say:

"Come out of her, my people,
so that you will not share in
her sins,
so that you will not receive
any of her plagues;
5 for her sins are piled up to
heaven,
and God has remembered her
crimes.
6 Give back to her as she has
given;
pay her back double for what
she has done.
Mix her a double portion
from her own cup.
7 Give her as much torture and
grief
as the glory and luxury she
gave herself.
In her heart she boasts,
'I sit as queen; I am not a
widow,
and I will never mourn.'
8 Therefore in one day her
plagues will overtake her:
death, mourning and famine.

She will be consumed by fire,
for mighty is the Lord God
who judges her.

9 "When the kings of the earth who
committed adultery with her and
shared her luxury see the smoke of
her burning, they will weep and
mourn over her. 10 Terrified at her
torment, they will stand far off and
cry:

"'Woe! Woe, O great city,
O Babylon, city of power!
In one hour your doom has come!'

11 "The merchants of the earth will
weep and mourn over her because no
one buys their cargoes any more—
12 cargoes of gold, silver, precious
stones and pearls; fine linen, purple,
silk and scarlet cloth; every sort of
citron wood, and articles of every
kind made of ivory, costly wood,
bronze, iron and marble; 13 cargoes
of cinnamon and spice, of incense,
myrrh and frankincense, of wine and
olive oil, of fine flour and wheat;
cattle and sheep; horses and car-
riages; and bodies and souls of men.

14 "They will say, 'The fruit you
longed for is gone from you. All your
riches and splendor have vanished,
never to be recovered.' 15 The merchants who sold these things and
gained their wealth from her will
stand far off, terrified at her torment.
They will weep and mourn 16 and cry
out:

"'Woe! Woe, O great city,
dressed in fine linen, purple
and scarlet,
and glittering with gold,
precious stones and pearls!
17 In one hour such great wealth
has been brought to ruin!'

v 2 Greek *unclean*

"Every sea captain, and all who travel by ship, the sailors, and all who earn their living from the sea, will stand far off. **18** When they see the smoke of her burning, they will exclaim, 'Was there ever a city like this great city?' **19** They will throw dust on their heads, and with weeping and mourning cry out:

"'Woe! Woe, O great city,
where all who had ships on
the sea
became rich through her
wealth!
In one hour she has been
brought to ruin!
20 Rejoice over her, O heaven!
Rejoice, saints and apostles
and prophets!
God has judged her for the way
she treated you.'"

21 Then a mighty angel picked up a boulder the size of a large millstone and threw it into the sea, and said:

"With such violence
the great city of Babylon will
be thrown down,
never to be found again.
22 The music of harpists and
musicians, flute players
and trumpeters,
will never be heard in you
again.
No workman of any trade
will ever be found in you
again.
The sound of a millstone
will never be heard in you
again.
23 The light of a lamp will never
shine in you again.
The voice of bridegroom and
bride
will never be heard in you
again.

Your merchants were the
world's great men.
By your magic spell all the
nations were led astray.
24 In her was found the blood of
prophets and of the saints,
and of all who have been
killed on the earth."

Hallelujah!

19 **1** After this I heard what sounded like the roar of a great multitude in heaven shouting:

"Hallelujah!
Salvation and glory and power
belong to our God,
2 for true and just are his
judgments.
He has condemned the great
prostitute
who corrupted the earth by
her adulteries.
He has avenged on her the
blood of his servants."

3 And again they shouted:

"Hallelujah!
The smoke from her goes up
for ever and ever."

4 The twenty-four elders and the four living creatures fell down and worshiped God, who was seated on the throne. And they cried:

"Amen, Hallelujah!"

5 Then a voice came from the throne, saying:

"Praise our God,
all you his servants,
you who fear him,
both small and great!"

6 Then I heard what sounded like a great multitude, like the roar of rushing waters and like loud peals of thunder, shouting:

"Hallelujah!
For our Lord God Almighty
reigns.
7 Let us rejoice and be glad
and give him glory!
For the wedding of the Lamb
has come,
and his bride has made
herself ready.
8 Fine linen, bright and clean,
was given her to wear."
(Fine linen stands for the righteous
acts of the saints.)

9 Then the angel said to me,
'Write: 'Blessed are those who are
invited to the wedding supper of the
Lamb!'" And he added, "These are
the true words of God."

10 At this I fell at his feet to worship him. But he said to me, "Do not
do it! I am a fellow servant with you
and with your brothers who hold to
the testimony of Jesus. Worship God!
For the testimony of Jesus is the spirit
of prophecy."

The Rider on the White Horse

11 I saw heaven standing open and
there before me was a white horse,
whose rider is called Faithful and
True. With justice he judges and
makes war. 12 His eyes are like blazing fire, and on his head are many
crowns. He has a name written on
him that no one knows but he himself.
13 He is dressed in a robe dipped in
blood, and his name is the Word of
God. 14 The armies of heaven were
following him, riding on white horses
and dressed in fine linen, white and
clean. 15 Out of his mouth comes a
sharp sword with which to strike
down the nations. "He will rule them
with an iron scepter."w He treads the
winepress of the fury of the wrath of
God Almighty. 16 On his robe and on
his thigh he has this name written:

KING OF KINGS AND LORD OF LORDS.

17 And I saw an angel standing in
the sun, who cried in a loud voice to
all the birds flying in midair, "Come,
gather together for the great supper
of God, 18 so that you may eat the
flesh of kings, generals, and mighty
men, of horses and their riders, and
the flesh of all people, free and slave,
small and great."

19 Then I saw the beast and the
kings of the earth and their armies
gathered together to make war
against the rider on the horse and his
army. 20 But the beast was captured,
and with him the false prophet who
had performed the miraculous signs
on his behalf. With these signs he had
deluded those who had received the
mark of the beast and worshiped his
image. The two of them were thrown
alive into the fiery lake of burning
sulfur. 21 The rest of them were
killed with the sword that came out
of the mouth of the rider on the
horse, and all the birds gorged themselves on their flesh.

The Thousand Years

20 1 And I saw an angel coming
down out of heaven, having
the key to the Abyss and holding in
his hand a great chain. 2 He seized
the dragon, that ancient serpent,
who is the devil, or Satan, and bound
him for a thousand years. 3 He threw
him into the Abyss, and locked and
sealed it over him, to keep him from
deceiving the nations anymore until
the thousand years were ended.
After that, he must be set free for a
short time.

w 15 Psalm 2:9

4 I saw thrones on which were seated those who had been given authority to judge. And I saw the souls of those who had been beheaded because of their testimony for Jesus and because of the word of God. They had not worshiped the beast or his image and had not received his mark on their foreheads or their hands. They came to life and reigned with Christ a thousand years. **5** (The rest of the dead did not come to life until the thousand years were ended.) This is the first resurrection. **6** Blessed and holy are those who have part in the first resurrection. The second death has no power over them, but they will be priests of God and of Christ and will reign with him for a thousand years.

Satan's Doom

7 When the thousand years are over, Satan will be released from his prison **8** and will go out to deceive the nations in the four corners of the earth — Gog and Magog — to gather them for battle. In number they are like the sand on the seashore. **9** They marched across the breadth of the earth and surrounded the camp of God's people, the city he loves. But fire came down from heaven and devoured them. **10** And the devil, who deceived them, was thrown into the lake of burning sulfur, where the beast and the false prophet had been thrown. They will be tormented day and night for ever and ever.

The Dead Are Judged

11 Then I saw a great white throne and him who was seated on it. Earth and sky fled from his presence, and there was no place for them. **12** And I saw the dead, great and small, standing before the throne, and books were opened. Another book was opened, which is the book of life. The dead were judged according to what they had done as recorded in the books. **13** The sea gave up the dead that were in it, and death and Hades gave up the dead that were in them, and each person was judged according to what he had done. **14** Then death and Hades were thrown into the lake of fire. The lake of fire is the second death. **15** If anyone's name was not found written in the book of life, he was thrown into the lake of fire.

The New Jerusalem

21 **1** Then I saw a new heaven and a new earth, for the first heaven and the first earth had passed away, and there was no longer any sea. **2** I saw the Holy City, the new Jerusalem, coming down out of heaven from God, prepared as a bride beautifully dressed for her husband. **3** And I heard a loud voice from the throne saying, "Now the dwelling of God is with men, and he will live with them. They will be his people and God himself will be with them and be their God. **4** He will wipe every tear from their eyes. There will be no more death or mourning or crying or pain, for the old order of things has passed away."

5 He who was seated on the throne said, "I am making everything new!" Then he said, "Write this down, for these words are trustworthy and true."

6 He said to me: "It is done. I am the Alpha and the Omega, the Beginning and the End. To him who is thirsty I will give to drink without cost from the spring of the water of life. **7** He who overcomes will inherit all this, and I will be his God and he will be my son. **8** But the cowardly, the unbelieving, the vile, the mur-

...erers, the sexually immoral, those who practice magic arts, the idolaters and all liars—their place will be in the fiery lake of burning sulfur. This is the second death."

9 One of the seven angels who had the seven bowls full of the seven last plagues came and said to me, "Come, I will show you the bride, the wife of the Lamb." **10** And he carried me away in the Spirit to a mountain great and high, and showed me the Holy City, Jerusalem, coming down out of heaven from God. **11** It shone with the glory of God, and its brilliance was like that of a very precious jewel, like a jasper, clear as crystal. **12** It had a great, high wall with twelve gates, and with twelve angels at the gates. On the gates were written the names of the twelve tribes of Israel. **13** There were three gates on the east, three on the north, three on the south and three on the west. **14** The wall of the city had twelve foundations, and on them were the names of the twelve apostles of the Lamb.

15 The angel who talked with me had a measuring rod of gold to measure the city, its gates and its walls. **16** The city was laid out like a square, as long as it was wide. He measured the city with the rod and found it to be 12,000 stadia[x] in length, and as wide and high as it is long. **17** He measured its wall and it was 144 cubits[y] thick,[z] by man's measurement, which the angel was using. **18** The wall was made of jasper, and the city of pure gold, as pure as glass. **19** The foundations of the city walls were decorated with every kind of precious stone. The first foundation was jasper, the second sapphire, the third chalcedony, the fourth emerald, **20** the fifth sardonyx, the sixth carnelian, the seventh chrysolite, the eighth beryl, the ninth topaz, the tenth chrysoprase, the eleventh jacinth, and the twelfth amethyst.[a] **21** The twelve gates were twelve pearls, each gate made of a single pearl. The great street of the city was of pure gold, like transparent glass.

22 I did not see a temple in the city, because the Lord God Almighty and the Lamb are its temple. **23** The city does not need the sun or the moon to shine on it, for the glory of God gives it light, and the Lamb is its lamp. **24** The nations will walk by its light, and the kings of the earth will bring their splendor into it. **25** On no day will its gates ever be shut, for there will be no night there. **26** The glory and honor of the nations will be brought into it. **27** Nothing impure will ever enter it, nor will anyone who does what is shameful or deceitful, but only those whose names are written in the Lamb's book of life.

The River of Life

22 **1** Then the angel showed me the river of the water of life, as clear as crystal, flowing from the throne of God and of the Lamb **2** down the middle of the great street of the city. On each side of the river stood the tree of life, bearing twelve crops of fruit, yielding its fruit every month. And the leaves of the tree are for the healing of the nations. **3** No longer will there be any curse. The throne of God and of the Lamb will be in the city, and his servants will

---

[x] *16* That is, about 1,400 miles (about 2,200 kilometers)   [y] *17* That is, about 200 feet (about 65 meters)   [z] *17* Or *high*   [a] *20* The precise identification of some of these precious stones is uncertain.

serve him. 4 They will see his face, and his name will be on their foreheads. 5 There will be no more night. They will not need the light of a lamp or the light of the sun, for the Lord God will give them light. And they will reign for ever and ever. 6 The angel said to me, "These words are trustworthy and true. The Lord, the God of the spirits of the prophets, sent his angel to show his servants the things that must soon take place."

Jesus Is Coming

7 "Behold, I am coming soon! Blessed is he who keeps the words of the prophecy in this book."

8 I, John, am the one who heard and saw these things. And when I had heard and seen them, I fell down to worship at the feet of the angel who had been showing them to me. 9 But he said to me, "Do not do it! I am a fellow servant with you and with your brothers the prophets and of all who keep the words of this book. Worship God!"

10 Then he told me, "Do not seal up the words of the prophecy of this book, because the time is near. 11 Let him who does wrong continue to do wrong; let him who is vile continue to be vile; let him who does right continue to do right; and let him who is holy continue to be holy."

12 "Behold, I am coming soon! My reward is with me, and I will give to everyone according to what he has done. 13 I am the Alpha and the Omega, the First and the Last, the Beginning and the End.

14 "Blessed are those who wash their robes, that they may have the right to the tree of life and may go through the gates into the city. 15 Outside are the dogs, those who practice magic arts, the sexually immoral, the murderers, the idolaters and everyone who loves and practices falsehood.

16 "I, Jesus, have sent my angel to give you[b] this testimony for the churches. I am the Root and the Offspring of David, and the bright Morning Star."

17 The Spirit and the bride say, "Come!" And let him who hears say, "Come!" Whoever is thirsty, let him come; and whoever wishes, let him take the free gift of the water of life.

18 I warn everyone who hears the words of the prophecy of this book: If anyone adds anything to them, God will add to him the plagues described in this book. 19 And if anyone takes words away from this book of prophecy, God will take away from him his share in the tree of life and in the holy city, which are described in this book.

20 He who testifies to these things says, "Yes, I am coming soon."

Amen. Come, Lord Jesus.

21 The grace of the Lord Jesus be with God's people. Amen.

b 16 The Greek is plural.

Psalms

BOOK I

Psalms 1-41

Psalm 1

1 Blessed is the man
    who does not walk in the
        counsel of the wicked
or stand in the way of sinners
    or sit in the seat of mockers.
2 But his delight is in the law of
        the LORD,
    and on his law he meditates
        day and night.
3 He is like a tree planted by
        streams of water,
    which yields its fruit in season
    and whose leaf does not wither.
    Whatever he does prospers.

4 Not so the wicked!
    They are like chaff
    that the wind blows away.
5 Therefore the wicked will not
        stand in the judgment,
    nor sinners in the assembly of
        the righteous.

6 For the LORD watches over the
        way of the righteous,
    but the way of the wicked
        will perish.

Psalm 2

1 Why do the nations conspire*a*
    and the peoples plot in vain?
2 The kings of the earth take
        their stand
    and the rulers gather together
against the LORD

and against his Anointed One.*b*
3 "Let us break their chains,"
    they say,
    "and throw off their fetters."

4 The One enthroned in heaven
        laughs;
    the Lord scoffs at them.
5 Then he rebukes them in his
        anger
    and terrifies them in his
        wrath, saying,
6 "I have installed my King*c*
    on Zion, my holy hill."

7 I will proclaim the decree of the
LORD:

He said to me, "You are my Son*d*;
    today I have become your
        Father.*e*
8 Ask of me,
    and I will make the nations
        your inheritance,
    the ends of the earth your
        possession.
9 You will rule them with an iron
        scepter*f*;
    you will dash them to pieces
        like pottery."

10 Therefore, you kings, be wise;
    be warned, you rulers of the
        earth.
11 Serve the LORD with fear
    and rejoice with trembling.
12 Kiss the Son, lest he be angry
    and you be destroyed in your
        way,
    for his wrath can flare up in a
        moment.

---

*1 Hebrew; Septuagint rage   b 2 Or anointed one   c 6 Or king   d 7 Or son; also in
verse 12   e 7 Or have begotten you   f 9 Or will break them with a rod of iron*

Blessed are all who take
refuge in him.

Psalm 3

*A psalm of David. When he fled
from his son Absalom.*

1 O LORD, how many are my foes!
 How many rise up against me!
2 Many are saying of me,
 "God will not deliver him."
 Selah[g]

3 But you are a shield around
 me, O LORD;
 you bestow glory on me and
 lift[h] up my head.
4 To the LORD I cry aloud,
 and he answers me from his
 holy hill.   *Selah*

5 I lie down and sleep;
 I wake again, because the
 LORD sustains me.
6 I will not fear the tens of
 thousands
 drawn up against me on
 every side.

7 Arise, O LORD!
 Deliver me, O my God!
 Strike all my enemies on the jaw;
 break the teeth of the wicked.

8 From the LORD comes
 deliverance.
 May your blessing be on your
 people.   *Selah*

Psalm 4

*For the director of music. With stringed
instruments. A psalm of David.*

1 Answer me when I call to you,
 O my righteous God.
 Give me relief from my distress;
 be merciful to me and hear
 my prayer.

2 How long, O men, will you
 turn my glory into shame[i]?
 How long will you love
 delusions and seek false
 gods[j]?   *Selah*

3 Know that the LORD has set
 apart the godly for himself;
 the LORD will hear when I
 call to him.

4 In your anger do not sin;
 when you are on your beds,
 search your hearts and be
 silent.   *Selah*

5 Offer right sacrifices
 and trust in the LORD.

6 Many are asking, "Who can
 show us any good?"
 Let the light of your face
 shine upon us, O LORD.
7 You have filled my heart with
 greater joy
 than when their grain and
 new wine abound.
8 I will lie down and sleep in
 peace,
 for you alone, O LORD,
 make me dwell in safety.

Psalm 5

*For the director of music. For flutes.
A psalm of David.*

1 Give ear to my words, O LORD,
 consider my sighing.
2 Listen to my cry for help,
 my King and my God,
 for to you I pray.
3 In the morning, O LORD, you
 hear my voice;
 in the morning I lay my
 requests before you
 and wait in expectation.

4 You are not a God who takes
 pleasure in evil;

---

g 2 A word of uncertain meaning, occurring frequently in the Psalms; possibly a musical ter
*h 3 Or LORD, / my Glorious One, who lifts   i 2 Or you dishonor my Glorious One   j 2 Or
seek lies*

with you the wicked cannot
dwell.
5 The arrogant cannot stand in
your presence;
you hate all who do wrong.
6 You destroy those who tell lies;
bloodthirsty and deceitful men
the LORD abhors.

7 But I, by your great mercy,
will come into your house;
in reverence will I bow down
toward your holy temple.
8 Lead me, O LORD, in your
righteousness
because of my enemies—
make straight your way
before me.

9 Not a word from their mouth
can be trusted;
their heart is filled with
destruction.
Their throat is an open grave;
with their tongue they speak
deceit.
10 Declare them guilty, O God!
Let their intrigues be their
downfall.
Banish them for their many
sins,
for they have rebelled against
you.

11 But let all who take refuge in
you be glad;
let them ever sing for joy.
Spread your protection over
them,
that those who love your
name may rejoice in you.
12 For surely, O LORD, you bless
the righteous;
you surround them with your
favor as with a shield.

Psalm 6

For the director of music. With stringed
instruments. According to *sheminith*.[k]
A psalm of David.

1 O LORD, do not rebuke me in
your anger
or discipline me in your
wrath.
2 Be merciful to me, LORD, for I
am faint;
O LORD, heal me, for my
bones are in agony.
3 My soul is in anguish.
How long, O LORD, how long?

4 Turn, O LORD, and deliver me;
save me because of your
unfailing love.
5 No one remembers you when
he is dead.
Who praises you from the
grave[l]?

6 I am worn out from groaning;
all night long I flood my bed
with weeping
and drench my couch with
tears.
7 My eyes grow weak with
sorrow;
they fail because of all my
foes.

8 Away from me, all you who do
evil,
for the LORD has heard my
weeping.
9 The LORD has heard my cry
for mercy;
the LORD accepts my
prayer.
10 All my enemies will be
ashamed and dismayed;
they will turn back in
sudden disgrace.

---

k Title: Probably a musical term   *l 5* Hebrew *Sheol*

Psalm 7

A *shiggaion*[m] of David, which he sang to the LORD concerning Cush, a Benjamite.

1 O LORD my God, I take refuge
    in you;
    save and deliver me from all
    who pursue me,

2 or they will tear me like a lion
    and rip me to pieces with no
    one to rescue me.

3 O LORD my God, if I have done
    this
    and there is guilt on my
    hands—

4 if I have done evil to him who
    is at peace with me
    or without cause have robbed
    my foe—

5 then let my enemy pursue and
    overtake me;
    let him trample my life to the
    ground
    and make me sleep in the
    dust.   *Selah*

6 Arise, O LORD, in your anger;
    rise up against the rage of my
    enemies.
    Awake, my God; decree justice.

7 Let the assembled peoples
    gather around you.
    Rule over them from on high;

8 let the LORD judge the
    peoples.
    Judge me, O LORD, according
    to my righteousness,
    according to my integrity, O
    Most High.

9 O righteous God,
    who searches minds and hearts,
    bring to an end the violence of
    the wicked
    and make the righteous secure.

10 My shield[n] is God Most High,
    who saves the upright in
    heart.

11 God is a righteous judge,
    a God who expresses his
    wrath every day.

12 If he does not relent,
    he[o] will sharpen his sword;
    he will bend and string his
    bow.

13 He has prepared his deadly
    weapons;
    he makes ready his flaming
    arrows.

14 He who is pregnant with evil
    and conceives trouble gives
    birth to disillusionment.

15 He who digs a hole and scoops
    it out
    falls into the pit he has made.

16 The trouble he causes recoils
    on himself;
    his violence comes down on
    his own head.

17 I will give thanks to the LORD
    because of his righteousness
    and will sing praise to the
    name of the LORD Most High.

Psalm 8

For the director of music. According to *gittith*.[p] A psalm of David.

1 O LORD, our Lord,
    how majestic is your name in
    all the earth!

You have set your glory
    above the heavens.

2 From the lips of children and
    infants
    you have ordained praise[q]
    because of your enemies,
    to silence the foe and the
    avenger.

---

m Title: Probably a literary or musical term   *n* 10 Or *sovereign*   *o* 12 Or *If a man does not repent, / God*   *p* Title: Probably a musical term   *q* 2 Or *strength*

3 When I consider your heavens,
  the work of your fingers,
the moon and the stars,
  which you have set in place,
4 what is man that you are
    mindful of him,
  the son of man that you care
    for him?
5 You made him a little lower
    than the heavenly beings⁵
  and crowned him with glory
    and honor.

6 You made him ruler over the
    works of your hands;
  you put everything under his
    feet:
7 all flocks and herds,
  and the beasts of the field,
8 the birds of the air,
  and the fish of the sea,
  all that swim the paths of the
    seas.

9 O LORD, our Lord,
  how majestic is your name in
    all the earth!

Psalm 9 ˢ

For the director of music. To [the tune
of] "The Death of the Son."
  A psalm of David.

1 I will praise you, O LORD, with
    all my heart;
  I will tell of all your wonders.
2 I will be glad and rejoice in
    you;
  I will sing praise to your
    name, O Most High.

3 My enemies turn back;
  they stumble and perish
    before you.
4 For you have upheld my right
    and my cause;

you have sat on your throne,
  judging righteously.
5 You have rebuked the nations
    and destroyed the wicked;
  you have blotted out their
    name for ever and ever.
6 Endless ruin has overtaken the
    enemy,
  you have uprooted their cities;
  even the memory of them has
    perished.

7 The LORD reigns forever;
  he has established his throne
    for judgment.
8 He will judge the world in
    righteousness;
  he will govern the peoples
    with justice.
9 The LORD is a refuge for the
    oppressed,
  a stronghold in times of trouble.
10 Those who know your name
    will trust in you,
  for you, LORD, have never for-
    saken those who seek you.

11 Sing praises to the LORD,
    enthroned in Zion;
  proclaim among the nations
    what he has done.
12 For he who avenges blood
    remembers;
  he does not ignore the cry of
    the afflicted.

13 O LORD, see how my enemies
    persecute me!
  Have mercy and lift me up
    from the gates of death,
14 that I may declare your praises
    in the gates of the Daughter
    of Zion
  and there rejoice in your
    salvation.

---

⁵ Or *than God*   ˢ Psalms 9 and 10 may have been originally a single acrostic poem, the
stanzas of which begin with the successive letters of the Hebrew alphabet. In the Septuagint
they constitute one psalm.

15 The nations have fallen into
      the pit they have dug;
   their feet are caught in the
      net they have hidden.
16 The LORD is known by his justice;
   the wicked are ensnared by
      the work of their hands.
                         Higgaion.^t *Selah*
17 The wicked return to the
      grave,^u
   all the nations that forget God.
18 But the needy will not always
      be forgotten,
   nor the hope of the afflicted
      ever perish.

19 Arise, O LORD, let not man
      triumph;
   let the nations be judged in
      your presence.
20 Strike them with terror, O LORD;
   let the nations know they are
      but men.   *Selah*

Psalm 10^v

1 Why, O LORD, do you stand far
      off?
   Why do you hide yourself in
      times of trouble?

2 In his arrogance the wicked
      man hunts down the weak,
   who are caught in the
      schemes he devises.
3 He boasts of the cravings of his
      heart;
   he blesses the greedy and
      reviles the LORD.
4 In his pride the wicked does
      not seek him;
   in all his thoughts there is no
      room for God.
5 His ways are always prosperous;
   he is haughty and your laws
      are far from him;

he sneers at all his enemies.
6 He says to himself, "Nothing
      will shake me;
   I'll always be happy and
      never have trouble."
7 His mouth is full of curses and
      lies and threats;
   trouble and evil are under his
      tongue.
8 He lies in wait near the villages
   from ambush he murders the
      innocent,
   watching in secret for his
      victims.
9 He lies in wait like a lion in
      cover;
   he lies in wait to catch the
      helpless;
   he catches the helpless and
      drags them off in his net.
10 His victims are crushed, they
      collapse;
   they fall under his strength.
11 He says to himself, "God has
      forgotten;
   he covers his face and never
      sees."

12 Arise, LORD! Lift up your hand,
      O God.
   Do not forget the helpless.
13 Why does the wicked man
      revile God?
   Why does he say to himself,
   "He won't call me to account"?
14 But you, O God, do see trouble
      and grief;
   you consider it to take it in
      hand.
   The victim commits himself to
      you;
   you are the helper of the
      fatherless.
15 Break the arm of the wicked
      and evil man;

^t *16* Or *Meditation*; possibly a musical notation   ^u *17* Hebrew *Sheol*   ^v Psalms 9 and 10
may have been originally a single acrostic poem, the stanzas of which begin with the
successive letters of the Hebrew alphabet. In the Septuagint they constitute one psalm.

call him to account for his
wickedness
that would not be found out.

16 The LORD is King for ever and
ever;
the nations will perish from
his land.
17 You hear, O LORD, the desire of
the afflicted;
you encourage them, and you
listen to their cry,
18 defending the fatherless and
the oppressed,
in order that man, who is of the
earth, may terrify no more.

Psalm 11

For the director of music. Of David.

1 In the LORD I take refuge.
How then can you say to me:
"Flee like a bird to your
mountain.
2 For look, the wicked bend their
bows;
they set their arrows against
the strings
to shoot from the shadows
at the upright in heart.
3 When the foundations are
being destroyed,
what can the righteous
do^w?"

4 The LORD is in his holy temple;
the LORD is on his heavenly
throne.
He observes the sons of men;
his eyes examine them.
5 The LORD examines the
righteous,
but the wicked^x and those
who love violence
his soul hates.

6 On the wicked he will rain
fiery coals and burning sulfur;
a scorching wind will be their
lot.
7 For the LORD is righteous,
he loves justice;
upright men will see his face.

Psalm 12

For the director of music. According to
sheminith.^y A psalm of David.

1 Help, LORD, for the godly are
no more;
the faithful have vanished
from among men.
2 Everyone lies to his neighbor;
their flattering lips speak
with deception.

3 May the LORD cut off all
flattering lips
and every boastful tongue
4 that says, "We will triumph
with our tongues;
we own our lips^z — who is
our master?"

5 "Because of the oppression of
the weak
and the groaning of the needy,
I will now arise," says the LORD.
"I will protect them from
those who malign them."
6 And the words of the LORD are
flawless,
like silver refined in a furnace
of clay,
purified seven times.

7 O LORD, you will keep us safe
and protect us from such
people forever.
8 The wicked freely strut about
when what is vile is honored
among men.

---

^w 3 Or what is the Righteous One doing   ^x 5 Or The LORD, the Righteous One, examines the
wicked, /   ^y Title: Probably a musical term   ^z 4 Or / our lips are our plowshares

Psalm 13
For the director of music.
A psalm of David.

1 How long, O LORD? Will you forget me forever?
How long will you hide your face from me?
2 How long must I wrestle with my thoughts
and every day have sorrow in my heart?
How long will my enemy triumph over me?

3 Look on me and answer, O LORD my God.
Give light to my eyes, or I will sleep in death;
4 my enemy will say, "I have overcome him,"
and my foes will rejoice when I fall.

5 But I trust in your unfailing love;
my heart rejoices in your salvation.
6 I will sing to the LORD,
for he has been good to me.

Psalm 14
For the director of music. Of David.

1 The fool[a] says in his heart,
"There is no God."
They are corrupt, their deeds are vile;
there is no one who does good.

2 The LORD looks down from heaven
on the sons of men
to see if there are any who understand,
any who seek God.
3 All have turned aside,
they have together become corrupt;
there is no one who does good,
not even one.

4 Will evildoers never learn —
those who devour my people
as men eat bread
and who do not call on the LORD?
5 There they are, overwhelmed with dread,
for God is present in the company of the righteous.
6 You evildoers frustrate the plans of the poor,
but the LORD is their refuge.

7 Oh, that salvation for Israel would come out of Zion!
When the LORD restores the fortunes of his people,
let Jacob rejoice and Israel be glad!

Psalm 15
A psalm of David.

1 LORD, who may dwell in your sanctuary?
Who may live on your holy hill?

2 He whose walk is blameless
and who does what is righteous,
who speaks the truth from his heart
3 and has no slander on his tongue,
who does his neighbor no wrong
and casts no slur on his fellowman,
4 who despises a vile man
but honors those who fear the LORD,
who keeps his oath
even when it hurts,
5 who lends his money without usury

---

a 1 The Hebrew words rendered *fool* in Psalms denote one who is morally deficient.

and does not accept a bribe
against the innocent.

He who does these things
will never be shaken.

Psalm 16

A *miktam*[b] of David.

1 Keep me safe, O God,
for in you I take refuge.

2 I said to the LORD, "You are my
Lord;
apart from you I have no
good thing."

3 As for the saints who are in the
land,
they are the glorious ones in
whom is all my delight.[c]

4 The sorrows of those will
increase
who run after other gods.
I will not pour out their liba-
tions of blood
or take up their names on my
lips.

5 LORD, you have assigned me
my portion and my cup;
you have made my lot secure.

6 The boundary lines have fallen
for me in pleasant places;
surely I have a delightful
inheritance.

7 I will praise the LORD, who
counsels me;
even at night my heart
instructs me.

8 I have set the LORD always
before me.
Because he is at my right
hand,
I will not be shaken.

9 Therefore my heart is glad and
my tongue rejoices;
my body also will rest secure,

10 because you will not abandon
me to the grave,[d]
nor will you let your Holy
One[e] see decay.

11 You have made[f] known to me
the path of life;
you will fill me with joy in
your presence,
with eternal pleasures at your
right hand.

Psalm 17

A prayer of David.

1 Hear, O LORD, my righteous
plea;
listen to my cry.
Give ear to my prayer—
it does not rise from deceitful
lips.

2 May my vindication come from
you;
may your eyes see what is
right.

3 Though you probe my heart
and examine me at night,
though you test me, you will
find nothing;
I have resolved that my
mouth will not sin.

4 As for the deeds of men—
by the word of your lips
I have kept myself
from the ways of the violent.

5 My steps have held to your
paths;
my feet have not slipped.

6 I call on you, O God, for you
will answer me;

---

b Title: Probably a literary or musical term   *c* 3 Or *As for the pagan priests who are in the*
and / and the nobles in whom all delight, I said: *d* 10 Hebrew *Sheol*   *e* 10 Or *Your*
faithful one   *f* 11 Or *You will make*

give ear to me and hear my
prayer.

7 Show the wonder of your great
love,
you who save by your right
hand
those who take refuge in you
from their foes.

8 Keep me as the apple of your
eye;
hide me in the shadow of
your wings

9 from the wicked who assail
me,
from my mortal enemies who
surround me.

10 They close up their callous
hearts,
and their mouths speak with
arrogance.

11 They have tracked me down,
they now surround me,
with eyes alert, to throw me
to the ground.

12 They are like a lion hungry for
prey,
like a great lion crouching in
cover.

13 Rise up, O LORD, confront
them, bring them down;
rescue me from the wicked
by your sword.

14 O LORD, by your hand save me
from such men,
from men of this world
whose reward is in this
life.

You still the hunger of those you
cherish;
their sons have plenty,
and they store up wealth for
their children.

15 And I—in righteousness I will
see your face;
when I awake, I will be
satisfied with seeing your
likeness.

Psalm 18

For the director of music. Of David the
servant of the LORD. He sang to the
LORD the words of this song when the
LORD delivered him from the hand of all
his enemies and from the hand of Saul.

He said:

1 I love you, O LORD, my strength.

2 The LORD is my rock, my
fortress and my deliverer;
my God is my rock, in whom
I take refuge.
He is my shield and the horn[g]
of my salvation, my
stronghold.

3 I call to the LORD, who is
worthy of praise,
and I am saved from my
enemies.

4 The cords of death entangled me;
the torrents of destruction
overwhelmed me.

5 The cords of the grave[h] coiled
around me;
the snares of death
confronted me.

6 In my distress I called to the
LORD;
I cried to my God for help.
From his temple he heard my
voice;
my cry came before him, into
his ears.

7 The earth trembled and quaked,
and the foundations of the
mountains shook;

___

g 2 Horn here symbolizes strength.   h 5 Hebrew Sheol

they trembled because he
was angry.

8 Smoke rose from his nostrils;
consuming fire came from his
mouth,
burning coals blazed out of it.

9 He parted the heavens and
came down;
dark clouds were under his
feet.

10 He mounted the cherubim and
flew;
he soared on the wings of the
wind.

11 He made darkness his
covering, his canopy around
him—
the dark rain clouds of the sky.

12 Out of the brightness of his
presence clouds advanced,
with hailstones and bolts of
lightning.

13 The LORD thundered from
heaven;
the voice of the Most High
resounded.[i]

14 He shot his arrows and
scattered [the enemies],
great bolts of lightning and
routed them.

15 The valleys of the sea were
exposed
and the foundations of the
earth laid bare
at your rebuke, O LORD,
at the blast of breath from
your nostrils.

16 He reached down from on high
and took hold of me;
he drew me out of deep waters.

17 He rescued me from my
powerful enemy,
from my foes, who were too
strong for me.

18 They confronted me in the day
of my disaster,
but the LORD was my support.

19 He brought me out into a
spacious place;
he rescued me because he
delighted in me.

20 The LORD has dealt with me
according to my
righteousness;
according to the cleanness of
my hands he has rewarded
me.

21 For I have kept the ways of the
LORD;
I have not done evil by
turning from my God.

22 All his laws are before me;
I have not turned away from
his decrees.

23 I have been blameless before
him
and have kept myself from sin.

24 The LORD has rewarded me
according to my
righteousness,
according to the cleanness of
my hands in his sight.

25 To the faithful you show
yourself faithful,
to the blameless you show
yourself blameless,

26 to the pure you show yourself
pure,
but to the crooked you show
yourself shrewd.

27 You save the humble
but bring low those whose
eyes are haughty.

28 You, O LORD, keep my lamp
burning;
my God turns my darkness
into light.

---

i 13 Some Hebrew manuscripts and Septuagint (see also 2 Samuel 22:14); most Hebrew
manuscripts resounded, / amid hailstones and bolts of lightning

29 With your help I can advance
    against a troop*j*;
  with my God I can scale a
    wall.

30 As for God, his way is perfect;
    the word of the LORD is
      flawless.
  He is a shield
    for all who take refuge in him.

31 For who is God besides the
    LORD?
  And who is the Rock except
    our God?

32 It is God who arms me with
    strength
  and makes my way perfect.

33 He makes my feet like the feet
    of a deer;
  he enables me to stand on
    the heights.

34 He trains my hands for battle;
  my arms can bend a bow of
    bronze.

35 You give me your shield of
    victory,
  and your right hand sustains
    me;
  you stoop down to make me
    great.

36 You broaden the path beneath
    me,
  so that my ankles do not turn.

37 I pursued my enemies and
    overtook them;
  I did not turn back till they
    were destroyed.

38 I crushed them so that they
    could not rise;
  they fell beneath my feet.

39 You armed me with strength
    for battle;
  you made my adversaries
    bow at my feet.

40 You made my enemies turn
    their backs in flight,
  and I destroyed my foes.

41 They cried for help, but there
    was no one to save them—
  to the LORD, but he did not
    answer.

42 I beat them as fine as dust
    borne on the wind;
  I poured them out like mud
    in the streets.

43 You have delivered me from
    the attacks of the people;
  you have made me the head
    of nations;
  people I did not know are
    subject to me.

44 As soon as they hear me, they
    obey me;
  foreigners cringe before me.

45 They all lose heart;
  they come trembling from
    their strongholds.

46 The LORD lives! Praise be to my
    Rock!
  Exalted be God my Savior!

47 He is the God who avenges me,
  who subdues nations under
    me,

48   who saves me from my
      enemies.
  You exalted me above my foes;
  from violent men you rescued
    me.

49 Therefore I will praise you
    among the nations, O LORD;
  I will sing praises to your
    name.

50 He gives his king great
    victories;
  he shows unfailing kindness
    to his anointed,
  to David and his descendants
    forever.

j 29 Or can run through a barricade

Psalm 19

For the director of music.
A psalm of David.

1 The heavens declare the glory
    of God;
  the skies proclaim the work
    of his hands.
2 Day after day they pour forth
    speech;
  night after night they display
    knowledge.
3 There is no speech or language
  where their voice is not heard.[k]
4 Their voice[l] goes out into all
    the earth,
  their words to the ends of the
    world.

  In the heavens he has pitched a
    tent for the sun,
5 which is like a bridegroom
    coming forth from his
    pavilion,
  like a champion rejoicing to
    run his course.
6 It rises at one end of the heavens
  and makes its circuit to the
    other;
  nothing is hidden from its
    heat.

7 The law of the LORD is perfect,
    reviving the soul.
  The statutes of the LORD are
    trustworthy,
  making wise the simple.
8 The precepts of the LORD are
    right,
  giving joy to the heart.
  The commands of the LORD are
    radiant,
  giving light to the eyes.
9 The fear of the LORD is pure,
    enduring forever.

The ordinances of the LORD are
    sure
  and altogether righteous.
10 They are more precious than
    gold,
  than much pure gold;
  they are sweeter than honey,
    than honey from the comb.
11 By them is your servant
    warned;
  in keeping them there is
    great reward.

12 Who can discern his errors?
  Forgive my hidden faults.
13 Keep your servant also from
    willful sins;
  may they not rule over me.
  Then will I be blameless,
    innocent of great
    transgression.

14 May the words of my mouth
  and the meditation of my
    heart
  be pleasing in your sight,
  O LORD, my Rock and my
    Redeemer.

Psalm 20

For the director of music.
A psalm of David.

1 May the LORD answer you when
    you are in distress;
  may the name of the God of
    Jacob protect you.
2 May he send you help from the
    sanctuary
  and grant you support from
    Zion.
3 May he remember all your
    sacrifices
  and accept your burnt
    offerings.   Selah

---

k 3 Or They have no speech, there are no words; / no sound is heard from them
l 4 Septuagint, Jerome and Syriac; Hebrew line

4 May he give you the desire of
   your heart
      and make all your plans
      succeed.
5 We will shout for joy when you
   are victorious
      and will lift up our banners in
      the name of our God.
   May the LORD grant all your
   requests.

6 Now I know that the LORD
   saves his anointed;
      he answers him from his holy
      heaven
      with the saving power of his
      right hand.
7 Some trust in chariots and
   some in horses,
      but we trust in the name of
      the LORD our God.
8 They are brought to their knees
   and fall,
      but we rise up and stand firm.

9 O LORD, save the king!
      Answer[m] us when we call!

Psalm 21

For the director of music.
A psalm of David.

1 O LORD, the king rejoices in
   your strength.
      How great is his joy in the
      victories you give!
2 You have granted him the
   desire of his heart
      and have not withheld the
      request of his lips.   *Selah*
3 You welcomed him with rich
   blessings
      and placed a crown of pure
      gold on his head.
4 He asked you for life, and you
   gave it to him—

length of days, for ever and
   ever.
5 Through the victories you
   gave, his glory is great;
      you have bestowed on him
      splendor and majesty.
6 Surely you have granted him
   eternal blessings
      and made him glad with the
      joy of your presence.
7 For the king trusts in the
   LORD;
      through the unfailing love
      of the Most High
      he will not be shaken.

8 Your hand will lay hold on all
   your enemies;
      your right hand will seize
      your foes.
9 At the time of your appearing
   you will make them like a
   fiery furnace.
      In his wrath the LORD will
      swallow them up,
      and his fire will consume
      them.
10 You will destroy their
   descendants from the
   earth,
      their posterity from
      mankind.
11 Though they plot evil against
   you
      and devise wicked schemes,
      they cannot succeed;
12 for you will make them turn
   their backs
      when you aim at them with
      drawn bow.

13 Be exalted, O LORD, in your
   strength;
      we will sing and praise your
      might.

---

m 9 Or *save / O King, answer*

Psalm 22

For the director of music. To [the tune of] "The Doe of the Morning." A psalm of David.

1 My God, my God, why have
     you forsaken me?
   Why are you so far from
     saving me,
   so far from the words of my
     groaning?
2 O my God, I cry out by day, but
     you do not answer,
   by night, and am not silent.

3 Yet you are enthroned as the
     Holy One;
   you are the praise of Israel.[n]
4 In you our fathers put their
     trust;
   they trusted and you
     delivered them.
5 They cried to you and were
     saved;
   in you they trusted and were
     not disappointed.

6 But I am a worm and not a
     man,
   scorned by men and despised
     by the people.
7 All who see me mock me;
   they hurl insults, shaking
     their heads:
8 "He trusts in the LORD;
   let the LORD rescue him.
   Let him deliver him,
     since he delights in him."

9 Yet you brought me out of the
     womb;
   you made me trust in you
     even at my mother's breast.
10 From birth I was cast upon you;
    from my mother's womb you
      have been my God.

11 Do not be far from me,
     for trouble is near
     and there is no one to help.

12 Many bulls surround me;
     strong bulls of Bashan
       encircle me.
13 Roaring lions tearing their prey
     open their mouths wide
       against me.
14 I am poured out like water,
     and all my bones are out of
       joint.
   My heart has turned to wax;
     it has melted away within me.
15 My strength is dried up like a
     potsherd,
   and my tongue sticks to the
     roof of my mouth;
   you lay me[o] in the dust of
     death.
16 Dogs have surrounded me;
     a band of evil men has
       encircled me,
   they have pierced[p] my hands
     and my feet.
17 I can count all my bones;
     people stare and gloat over
       me.
18 They divide my garments
     among them
     and cast lots for my clothing.

19 But you, O LORD, be not far off;
     O my Strength, come quickly
       to help me.
20 Deliver my life from the sword,
     my precious life from the
       power of the dogs.
21 Rescue me from the mouth of
     the lions;
   save[q] me from the horns of
     the wild oxen.

22 I will declare your name to my
     brothers;

---

n 3 Or Yet you are holy, / enthroned on the praises of Israel   o 15 Or / I am laid
p 16 Some Hebrew manuscripts, Septuagint and Syriac; most Hebrew manuscripts / like the
lion,   q 21 Or / you have heard

in the congregation I will
praise you.

23 You who fear the LORD, praise
him!
All you descendants of Jacob,
honor him!
Revere him, all you
descendants of Israel!

24 For he has not despised or
disdained
the suffering of the afflicted
one;
he has not hidden his face from
him
but has listened to his cry for
help.

25 From you comes the theme of my
praise in the great assembly;
before those who fear you*
will I fulfill my vows.

26 The poor will eat and be satisfied;
they who seek the LORD will
praise him—
may your hearts live forever!

27 All the ends of the earth
will remember and turn to
the LORD,
and all the families of the nations
will bow down before him,

28 for dominion belongs to the LORD
and he rules over the nations.

29 All the rich of the earth will
feast and worship;
all who go down to the dust
will kneel before him—
those who cannot keep
themselves alive.

30 Posterity will serve him;
future generations will be
told about the Lord.

31 They will proclaim his
righteousness
to a people yet unborn—
for he has done it.

Psalm 23
A psalm of David.

1 The LORD is my shepherd, I
shall not be in want.

2 He makes me lie down in
green pastures,
he leads me beside quiet
waters,

3 he restores my soul.
He guides me in paths of
righteousness
for his name's sake.

4 Even though I walk
through the valley of the
shadow of death,*
I will fear no evil,
for you are with me;
your rod and your staff,
they comfort me.

5 You prepare a table before me
in the presence of my
enemies.
You anoint my head with oil;
my cup overflows.

6 Surely goodness and love will
follow me
all the days of my life,
and I will dwell in the house of
the LORD
forever.

Psalm 24.
Of David. A psalm.

1 The earth is the LORD's, and
everything in it,
the world, and all who live in it;

2 for he founded it upon the seas
and established it upon the
waters.

3 Who may ascend the hill of the
LORD?
Who may stand in his holy
place?

---

r 25 Hebrew him   s 4 Or through the darkest valley

4 He who has clean hands and a
    pure heart,
  who does not lift up his soul
    to an idol
  or swear by what is false.*t*
5 He will receive blessing from
    the LORD
  and vindication from God his
    Savior.
6 Such is the generation of those
    who seek him,
  who seek your face, O God of
    Jacob.*u*   *Selah*

7 Lift up your heads, O you gates;
  be lifted up, you ancient
    doors,
  that the King of glory may
    come in.
8 Who is this King of glory?
  The LORD strong and mighty,
  the LORD mighty in battle.
9 Lift up your heads, O you gates;
  lift them up, you ancient doors,
  that the King of glory may
    come in.
10 Who is he, this King of glory?
  The LORD Almighty—
  he is the King of glory.   *Selah*

Psalm 25 *v*
Of David.

1 To you, O LORD, I lift up my soul;
2 in you I trust, O my God.
  Do not let me be put to shame,
  nor let my enemies triumph
    over me.
3 No one whose hope is in you
  will ever be put to shame,
  but they will be put to shame
  who are treacherous without
    excuse.

4 Show me your ways, O LORD,
  teach me your paths;

5 guide me in your truth and
    teach me,
  for you are God my Savior,
  and my hope is in you all day
    long.
6 Remember, O LORD, your great
    mercy and love,
  for they are from of old.
7 Remember not the sins of my
    youth
  and my rebellious ways;
  according to your love remem-
    ber me,
  for you are good, O LORD.

8 Good and upright is the LORD;
  therefore he instructs sinners
    in his ways.
9 He guides the humble in what
    is right
  and teaches them his way.
10 All the ways of the LORD are
    loving and faithful
  for those who keep the
    demands of his covenant.
11 For the sake of your name, O
    LORD,
  forgive my iniquity, though it
    is great.
12 Who, then, is the man that
    fears the LORD?
  He will instruct him in the
    way chosen for him.
13 He will spend his days in
    prosperity,
  and his descendants will
    inherit the land.
14 The LORD confides in those
    who fear him;
  he makes his covenant
    known to them.
15 My eyes are ever on the LORD,
  for only he will release my
    feet from the snare.

---

t 4 Or *swear falsely*   *u* 6 Two Hebrew manuscripts and Syriac (see also Septuagint); most
Hebrew manuscripts *face, Jacob*   *v* This psalm is an acrostic poem, the verses of which begin
with the successive letters of the Hebrew alphabet.

16 Turn to me and be gracious to me,
   for I am lonely and afflicted.
17 The troubles of my heart have
   multiplied;
   free me from my anguish.
18 Look upon my affliction and
   my distress
   and take away all my sins.
19 See how my enemies have
   increased
   and how fiercely they hate me!
20 Guard my life and rescue me;
   let me not be put to shame,
   for I take refuge in you.
21 May integrity and uprightness
   protect me,
   because my hope is in you.
22 Redeem Israel, O God,
   from all their troubles!

Psalm 26
Of David.

1 Vindicate me, O LORD,
   for I have led a blameless life;
   I have trusted in the LORD
   without wavering.
2 Test me, O LORD, and try me,
   examine my heart and my
   mind;
3 for your love is ever before me,
   and I walk continually in
   your truth.
4 I do not sit with deceitful men,
   nor do I consort with
   hypocrites;
5 I abhor the assembly of evildoers
   and refuse to sit with the
   wicked.
6 I wash my hands in innocence,
   and go about your altar, O
   LORD,
7 proclaiming aloud your praise
   and telling of all your
   wonderful deeds.
8 I love the house where you
   live, O LORD,

the place where your glory
dwells.
9 Do not take away my soul
   along with sinners,
   my life with bloodthirsty
   men,
10 in whose hands are wicked
   schemes,
   whose right hands are full
   of bribes.
11 But I lead a blameless life;
   redeem me and be merciful
   to me.
12 My feet stand on level ground;
   in the great assembly I will
   praise the LORD.

Psalm 27
Of David.

1 The LORD is my light and my
   salvation—
   whom shall I fear?
   The LORD is the stronghold of
   my life—
   of whom shall I be afraid?
2 When evil men advance
   against me
   to devour my flesh,w
   when my enemies and my foes
   attack me,
   they will stumble and fall.
3 Though an army besiege me,
   my heart will not fear;
   though war break out against me,
   even then will I be confident.
4 One thing I ask of the LORD,
   this is what I seek:
   that I may dwell in the house
   of the LORD
   all the days of my life,
   to gaze upon the beauty of the
   LORD
   and to seek him in his temple.
5 For in the day of trouble

w 2 Or to slander me

he will keep me safe in his
dwelling;
he will hide me in the shelter
of his tabernacle
and set me high upon a rock.
6 Then my head will be exalted
above the enemies who
surround me;
at his tabernacle will I sacrifice
with shouts of joy;
I will sing and make music to
the LORD.

7 Hear my voice when I call, O
LORD;
be merciful to me and answer
me.
8 My heart says of you, "Seek
hisˣ face!"
Your face, LORD, I will seek.
9 Do not hide your face from me,
do not turn your servant
away in anger;
you have been my helper.
Do not reject me or forsake me,
O God my Savior.
10 Though my father and mother
forsake me,
the LORD will receive me.
11 Teach me your way, O LORD;
lead me in a straight path
because of my oppressors.
12 Do not turn me over to the
desire of my foes,
for false witnesses rise up
against me,
breathing out violence.

13 I am still confident of this:
I will see the goodness of the
LORD
in the land of the living.
14 Wait for the LORD;
be strong and take heart
and wait for the LORD.

Psalm 28

Of David.

1 To you I call, O LORD my Rock;
do not turn a deaf ear to me.
For if you remain silent,
I will be like those who have
gone down to the pit.
2 Hear my cry for mercy
as I call to you for help,
as I lift up my hands
toward your Most Holy Place.

3 Do not drag me away with the
wicked,
with those who do evil,
who speak cordially with their
neighbors
but harbor malice in their
hearts.
4 Repay them for their deeds
and for their evil work;
repay them for what their
hands have done
and bring back upon them
what they deserve.
5 Since they show no regard for
the works of the LORD
and what his hands have done,
he will tear them down
and never build them up again.

6 Praise be to the LORD,
for he has heard my cry for
mercy.
7 The LORD is my strength and
my shield;
my heart trusts in him, and I
am helped.
My heart leaps for joy
and I will give thanks to him
in song.
8 The LORD is the strength of his
people,
a fortress of salvation for his
anointed one.

x 8 Or To you, O my heart, he has said, "Seek my

9 Save your people and bless
your inheritance;
be their shepherd and carry
them forever.

Psalm 29
A psalm of David.

1 Ascribe to the LORD, O mighty
ones,
ascribe to the LORD glory and
strength.
2 Ascribe to the LORD the glory
due his name;
worship the LORD in the
splendor of his[y] holiness.

3 The voice of the LORD is over
the waters;
the God of glory thunders,
the LORD thunders over the
mighty waters.
4 The voice of the LORD is powerful;
the voice of the LORD is
majestic.
5 The voice of the LORD breaks
the cedars;
the LORD breaks in pieces the
cedars of Lebanon.
6 He makes Lebanon skip like a
calf,
Sirion[z] like a young wild ox.
7 The voice of the LORD strikes
with flashes of lightning.
8 The voice of the LORD shakes
the desert;
the LORD shakes the Desert of
Kadesh.
9 The voice of the LORD twists
the oaks[a]
and strips the forests bare.
And in his temple all cry,
"Glory!"

10 The LORD sits[b] enthroned over
the flood;

the LORD is enthroned as
King forever.
11 The LORD gives strength to his
people;
the LORD blesses his people
with peace.

Psalm 30
A psalm. A song. For the dedication
of the temple.[c] Of David.

1 I will exalt you, O LORD,
for you lifted me out of the
depths
and did not let my enemies
gloat over me.
2 O LORD my God, I called to you
for help
and you healed me.
3 O LORD, you brought me up
from the grave[d];
you spared me from going
down into the pit.

4 Sing to the LORD, you saints of
his;
praise his holy name.
5 For his anger lasts only a
moment,
but his favor lasts a lifetime;
weeping may remain for a night,
but rejoicing comes in the
morning.

6 When I felt secure, I said,
"I will never be shaken."
7 O LORD, when you favored me,
you made my mountain[e]
stand firm;
but when you hid your face,
I was dismayed.

8 To you, O LORD, I called;
to the Lord I cried for mercy:
9 "What gain is there in my
destruction,[f]
in my going down into the pit?

---

y 2 Or LORD with the splendor of   z 6 That is, Mount Hermon   a 9 Or LORD makes the
deer give birth   b 10 Or sat   c Title: Or palace   d 3 Hebrew Sheol   e 7 Or hill country
f 9 Or there if I am silenced

Will the dust praise you?
  Will it proclaim your
    faithfulness?
10 Hear, O LORD, and be merciful
    to me;
  O LORD, be my help."

11 You turned my wailing into
    dancing;
  you removed my sackcloth
    and clothed me with joy,
12 that my heart may sing to you
    and not be silent.
  O LORD my God, I will give
    you thanks forever.

Psalm 31

For the director of music.
A psalm of David.

1 In you, O LORD, I have taken
    refuge;
  let me never be put to shame;
    deliver me in your
    righteousness.
2 Turn your ear to me,
    come quickly to my rescue;
  be my rock of refuge,
    a strong fortress to save me.
3 Since you are my rock and my
    fortress,
  for the sake of your name
    lead and guide me.
4 Free me from the trap that is
    set for me,
  for you are my refuge.
5 Into your hands I commit my
    spirit;
  redeem me, O LORD, the God
    of truth.

6 I hate those who cling to
    worthless idols;
  I trust in the LORD.
7 I will be glad and rejoice in
    your love,
  for you saw my affliction

and knew the anguish of my
    soul.
8 You have not handed me over
    to the enemy
  but have set my feet in a
    spacious place.

9 Be merciful to me, O LORD, for
    I am in distress;
  my eyes grow weak with
    sorrow,
  my soul and my body with
    grief.
10 My life is consumed by anguish
    and my years by groaning;
  my strength fails because of my
    affliction,*g*
    and my bones grow weak.
11 Because of all my enemies,
    I am the utter contempt of
    my neighbors;
  I am a dread to my friends—
    those who see me on the
    street flee from me.
12 I am forgotten by them as
    though I were dead;
  I have become like broken
    pottery.
13 For I hear the slander of many;
    there is terror on every side;
  they conspire against me
    and plot to take my life.

14 But I trust in you, O LORD;
    I say, "You are my God."
15 My times are in your hands;
    deliver me from my enemies
    and from those who pursue
    me.
16 Let your face shine on your
    servant;
  save me in your unfailing
    love.
17 Let me not be put to shame, O
    LORD,
  for I have cried out to you;

8 10 Or *guilt*

but let the wicked be put to
shame
and lie silent in the grave.*h*
18 Let their lying lips be silenced,
for with pride and contempt
they speak arrogantly against
the righteous.

19 How great is your goodness,
which you have stored up for
those who fear you,
which you bestow in the sight
of men
on those who take refuge in
you.
20 In the shelter of your presence
you hide them
from the intrigues of men;
in your dwelling you keep
them safe
from accusing tongues.

21 Praise be to the LORD,
for he showed his wonderful
love to me
when I was in a besieged city.
22 In my alarm I said,
"I am cut off from your sight!"
Yet you heard my cry for mercy
when I called to you for help.

23 Love the LORD, all his saints!
The LORD preserves the
faithful,
but the proud he pays back in
full.
24 Be strong and take heart,
all you who hope in the LORD.

Psalm 32

Of David. A *maskil.i*

1 Blessed is he
whose transgressions are
forgiven,
whose sins are covered.
2 Blessed is the man

whose sin the LORD does not
count against him
and in whose spirit is no deceit.

3 When I kept silent,
my bones wasted away
through my groaning all day
long.
4 For day and night
your hand was heavy upon
me;
my strength was sapped
as in the heat of summer.
Selah

5 Then I acknowledged my sin to
you
and did not cover up my
iniquity.
I said, "I will confess
my transgressions to the
LORD"—
and you forgave
the guilt of my sin.   *Selah*

6 Therefore let everyone who is
godly pray to you
while you may be found;
surely when the mighty waters
rise,
they will not reach him.
7 You are my hiding place;
you will protect me from
trouble
and surround me with songs
of deliverance.   *Selah*

8 I will instruct you and teach
you in the way you should
go;
I will counsel you and watch
over you.
9 Do not be like the horse or the
mule,
which have no understanding
but must be controlled by bit
and bridle
or they will not come to you.

---

h 17 Hebrew *Sheol*   *i* Title: Probably a literary or musical term

10 Many are the woes of the
    wicked,
        but the LORD's unfailing love
        surrounds the man who
        trusts in him.

11 Rejoice in the LORD and be
    glad, you righteous;
        sing, all you who are upright
        in heart!

Psalm 33

1 Sing joyfully to the LORD, you
    righteous;
        it is fitting for the upright to
        praise him.
2 Praise the LORD with the harp;
        make music to him on the
        ten-stringed lyre.
3 Sing to him a new song;
        play skillfully, and shout for
        joy.

4 For the word of the LORD is
    right and true;
        he is faithful in all he does.
5 The LORD loves righteousness
    and justice;
        the earth is full of his
        unfailing love.

6 By the word of the LORD were
    the heavens made,
        their starry host by the breath
        of his mouth.
7 He gathers the waters of the
    sea into jarsj;
        he puts the deep into
        storehouses.
8 Let all the earth fear the LORD;
        let all the people of the world
        revere him.
9 For he spoke, and it came to be;
        he commanded, and it stood
        firm.

10 The LORD foils the plans of the
    nations;
        he thwarts the purposes of
        the peoples.
11 But the plans of the LORD
    stand firm forever,
        the purposes of his heart
        through all generations.

12 Blessed is the nation whose
    God is the LORD,
        the people he chose for his
        inheritance.
13 From heaven the LORD looks
    down
        and sees all mankind;
14 from his dwelling place he
    watches
        all who live on earth—
15 he who forms the hearts of all,
        who considers everything
        they do.

16 No king is saved by the size of
    his army;
        no warrior escapes by his
        great strength.
17 A horse is a vain hope for
    deliverance;
        despite all its great strength it
        cannot save.
18 But the eyes of the LORD are on
    those who fear him,
        on those whose hope is in his
        unfailing love,
19 to deliver them from death
        and keep them alive in
        famine.

20 We wait in hope for the LORD;
        he is our help and our shield.
21 In him our hearts rejoice,
        for we trust in his holy name.
22 May your unfailing love rest
    upon us, O LORD,
        even as we put our hope in
        you.

j 7 Or *sea as into a heap*

Psalm 34 [k]

Of David. When he pretended to be
insane before Abimelech, who drove
him away, and he left.

1 I will extol the LORD at all times;
   his praise will always be on
   my lips.
2 My soul will boast in the LORD;
   let the afflicted hear and
   rejoice.
3 Glorify the LORD with me;
   let us exalt his name together.

4 I sought the LORD, and he
   answered me;
   he delivered me from all my
   fears.
5 Those who look to him are
   radiant;
   their faces are never covered
   with shame.
6 This poor man called, and the
   LORD heard him;
   he saved him out of all his
   troubles.
7 The angel of the LORD encamps
   around those who fear him,
   and he delivers them.

8 Taste and see that the LORD is
   good;
   blessed is the man who takes
   refuge in him.
9 Fear the LORD, you his saints,
   for those who fear him lack
   nothing.
10 The lions may grow weak and
   hungry,
   but those who seek the LORD
   lack no good thing.

11 Come, my children, listen to me;
   I will teach you the fear of
   the LORD.
12 Whoever of you loves life

and desires to see many good
   days,
13 keep your tongue from evil
   and your lips from speaking
   lies.
14 Turn from evil and do good;
   seek peace and pursue it.

15 The eyes of the LORD are on
   the righteous
   and his ears are attentive to
   their cry;
16 the face of the LORD is against
   those who do evil,
   to cut off the memory of
   them from the earth.

17 The righteous cry out, and the
   LORD hears them;
   he delivers them from all their
   troubles.
18 The LORD is close to the
   brokenhearted
   and saves those who are
   crushed in spirit.

19 A righteous man may have
   many troubles,
   but the LORD delivers him
   from them all;
20 he protects all his bones,
   not one of them will be broken.

21 Evil will slay the wicked;
   the foes of the righteous will
   be condemned.
22 The LORD redeems his servants;
   no one will be condemned
   who takes refuge in him.

Psalm 35

Of David.

1 Contend, O LORD, with those
   who contend with me;
   fight against those who fight
   against me.

---

[k] This psalm is an acrostic poem, the verses of which begin with the successive letters of the
Hebrew alphabet.

2 Take up shield and buckler;
   arise and come to my aid.
3 Brandish spear and javelin*l*
   against those who pursue me.
Say to my soul,
   "I am your salvation."

4 May those who seek my life
   be disgraced and put to
   shame;
   may those who plot my ruin
   be turned back in dismay.
5 May they be like chaff before
   the wind,
   with the angel of the LORD
   driving them away;
6 may their path be dark and
   slippery,
   with the angel of the LORD
   pursuing them.
7 Since they hid their net for me
   without cause
   and without cause dug a pit
   for me,
8 may ruin overtake them by
   surprise—
   may the net they hid
   entangle them,
   may they fall into the pit, to
   their ruin.
9 Then my soul will rejoice in the
   LORD
   and delight in his salvation.
10 My whole being will exclaim,
   "Who is like you, O LORD?
   You rescue the poor from those
   too strong for them,
   the poor and needy from
   those who rob them."

11 Ruthless witnesses come
   forward;
   they question me on things I
   know nothing about.
12 They repay me evil for good
   and leave my soul forlorn.

13 Yet when they were ill, I put on
   sackcloth
   and humbled myself with
   fasting.
When my prayers returned to
   me unanswered,
14 I went about mourning
   as though for my friend or
   brother.
I bowed my head in grief
   as though weeping for my
   mother.
15 But when I stumbled, they
   gathered in glee;
   attackers gathered against
   me when I was unaware.
   They slandered me without
   ceasing.
16 Like the ungodly they
   maliciously mocked*m*;
   they gnashed their teeth at me.
17 O Lord, how long will you look
   on?
   Rescue my life from their
   ravages,
   my precious life from these
   lions.
18 I will give you thanks in the
   great assembly;
   among throngs of people I
   will praise you.

19 Let not those gloat over me
   who are my enemies without
   cause;
   let not those who hate me
   without reason
   maliciously wink the eye.
20 They do not speak peaceably,
   but devise false accusations
   against those who live quietly
   in the land.
21 They gape at me and say, "Aha!
   Aha!
   With our own eyes we have
   seen it."

l 3 Or *and block the way*   *m 16* Septuagint; Hebrew may mean *ungodly circle of mockers.*

22 O LORD, you have seen this; be
   not silent.
     Do not be far from me, O
       Lord.
23 Awake, and rise to my defense!
     Contend for me, my God and
       Lord.
24 Vindicate me in your
     righteousness, O LORD my
       God;
     do not let them gloat over me.
25 Do not let them think, "Aha,
     just what we wanted!"
     or say, "We have swallowed
       him up."

26 May all who gloat over my
     distress
     be put to shame and confusion;
     may all who exalt themselves
       over me
     be clothed with shame and
       disgrace.
27 May those who delight in my
     vindication
     shout for joy and gladness;
     may they always say, "The
       LORD be exalted,
     who delights in the
       well-being of his servant."
28 My tongue will speak of your
     righteousness
     and of your praises all day
       long.

Psalm 36

For the director of music. Of David
the servant of the LORD.

1 An oracle is within my heart
   concerning the sinfulness of
   the wicked:[n]
     There is no fear of God
       before his eyes.
2 For in his own eyes he flatters
   himself

too much to detect or hate
  his sin.
3 The words of his mouth are
   wicked and deceitful;
     he has ceased to be wise and
       to do good.
4 Even on his bed he plots evil;
     he commits himself to a
       sinful course
     and does not reject what is
       wrong.

5 Your love, O LORD, reaches to
   the heavens,
     your faithfulness to the skies.
6 Your righteousness is like the
   mighty mountains,
     your justice like the great
       deep.
     O LORD, you preserve both
       man and beast.
7 How priceless is your unfailing love!
     Both high and low among men
     find[o] refuge in the shadow of
       your wings.
8 They feast on the abundance of
   your house;
     you give them drink from
       your river of delights.
9 For with you is the fountain of
   life;
     in your light we see light.

10 Continue your love to those
   who know you,
     your righteousness to the
       upright in heart.
11 May the foot of the proud not
   come against me,
     nor the hand of the wicked
       drive me away.
12 See how the evildoers lie
   fallen—
     thrown down, not able to rise!

n 1 Or heart: / Sin proceeds from the wicked.   o 7 Or love, O God / Men find; or love / Both
heavenly beings and men / find

Psalm 37 [p]
Of David.

1 Do not fret because of evil men
   or be envious of those who
      do wrong;
2 for like the grass they will soon
      wither,
   like green plants they will
      soon die away.

3 Trust in the LORD and do good;
   dwell in the land and enjoy
      safe pasture.
4 Delight yourself in the LORD
   and he will give you the
      desires of your heart.

5 Commit your way to the LORD;
   trust in him and he will do this:
6 He will make your righteousness
      shine like the dawn,
   the justice of your cause like
      the noonday sun.

7 Be still before the LORD and
      wait patiently for him;
   do not fret when men
      succeed in their ways,
   when they carry out their
      wicked schemes.

8 Refrain from anger and turn
      from wrath;
   do not fret—it leads only to
      evil.
9 For evil men will be cut off,
   but those who hope in the
      LORD will inherit the land.

10 A little while, and the wicked
       will be no more;
   though you look for them,
       they will not be found.
11 But the meek will inherit the
       land
   and enjoy great peace.

12 The wicked plot against the
       righteous
   and gnash their teeth at them;
13 but the Lord laughs at the
       wicked,
   for he knows their day is
       coming.

14 The wicked draw the sword
       and bend the bow
   to bring down the poor and
       needy,
   to slay those whose ways are
       upright.
15 But their swords will pierce
       their own hearts,
   and their bows will be broken.

16 Better the little that the
       righteous have
   than the wealth of many
       wicked;
17 for the power of the wicked
       will be broken,
   but the LORD upholds the
       righteous.

18 The days of the blameless are
       known to the LORD,
   and their inheritance will
       endure forever.
19 In times of disaster they will
       not wither;
   in days of famine they will
       enjoy plenty.

20 But the wicked will perish:
   The LORD's enemies will be
       like the beauty of the fields,
   they will vanish—vanish like
       smoke.

21 The wicked borrow and do not
       repay,
   but the righteous give
       generously;

[p] This psalm is an acrostic poem, the stanzas of which begin with the successive letters of the
Hebrew alphabet.

22 those the LORD blesses will
inherit the land,
but those he curses will be
cut off.

23 If the LORD delights in a man's
way,
he makes his steps firm;
24 though he stumble, he will not
fall,
for the LORD upholds him
with his hand.

25 I was young and now I am old,
yet I have never seen the
righteous forsaken
or their children begging bread.
26 They are always generous and
lend freely;
their children will be blessed.

27 Turn from evil and do good;
then you will dwell in the
land forever.
28 For the LORD loves the just
and will not forsake his
faithful ones.

They will be protected forever,
but the offspring of the
wicked will be cut off;
29 the righteous will inherit the
land
and dwell in it forever.

30 The mouth of the righteous
man utters wisdom,
and his tongue speaks what is
just.
31 The law of his God is in his
heart;
his feet do not slip.

32 The wicked lie in wait for the
righteous,
seeking their very lives;
33 but the LORD will not leave
them in their power

or let them be condemned
when brought to trial.

34 Wait for the LORD
and keep his way.
He will exalt you to inherit the
land;
when the wicked are cut off,
you will see it.

35 I have seen a wicked and
ruthless man
flourishing like a green tree
in its native soil,
36 but he soon passed away and
was no more;
though I looked for him, he
could not be found.

37 Consider the blameless,
observe the upright;
there is a future*q* for the man
of peace.
38 But all sinners will be destroyed;
the future*r* of the wicked will
be cut off.

39 The salvation of the righteous
comes from the LORD;
he is their stronghold in time
of trouble.
40 The LORD helps them and
delivers them;
he delivers them from the
wicked and saves them,
because they take refuge in
him.

Psalm 38
A psalm of David. A petition.

1 O LORD, do not rebuke me in
your anger
or discipline me in your
wrath.
2 For your arrows have pierced me,
and your hand has come
down upon me.

q 37 Or there will be posterity   r 38 Or posterity

3 Because of your wrath there is
no health in my body;
my bones have no soundness
because of my sin.
4 My guilt has overwhelmed me
like a burden too heavy to
bear.

5 My wounds fester and are
loathsome
because of my sinful folly.
6 I am bowed down and brought
very low;
all day long I go about
mourning.
7 My back is filled with searing
pain;
there is no health in my
body.
8 I am feeble and utterly crushed;
I groan in anguish of heart.

9 All my longings lie open before
you, O Lord;
my sighing is not hidden
from you.
10 My heart pounds, my strength
fails me;
even the light has gone from
my eyes.
11 My friends and companions
avoid me because of my
wounds;
my neighbors stay far away.
12 Those who seek my life set
their traps,
those who would harm me
talk of my ruin;
all day long they plot
deception.

13 I am like a deaf man, who
cannot hear,
like a mute, who cannot open
his mouth;
14 I have become like a man who
does not hear,
whose mouth can offer no
reply.

15 I wait for you, O LORD;
you will answer, O Lord my
God.
16 For I said, "Do not let them
gloat
or exalt themselves over me
when my foot slips."

17 For I am about to fall,
and my pain is ever with me.
18 I confess my iniquity;
I am troubled by my sin.
19 Many are those who are my
vigorous enemies;
those who hate me without
reason are numerous.
20 Those who repay my good with
evil
slander me when I pursue
what is good.

21 O LORD, do not forsake me;
be not far from me, O my
God.
22 Come quickly to help me,
O Lord my Savior.

Psalm 39

For the director of music. For Jeduthun.
A psalm of David.

1 I said, "I will watch my ways
and keep my tongue from sin;
I will put a muzzle on my mouth
as long as the wicked are in
my presence."
2 But when I was silent and still,
not even saying anything
good,
my anguish increased.
3 My heart grew hot within me,
and as I meditated, the fire
burned;
then I spoke with my tongue:

4 "Show me, O LORD, my life's
end
and the number of my days;
let me know how fleeting is
my life.

5 You have made my days a mere
    handbreadth;
  the span of my years is as
    nothing before you.
  Each man's life is but a
    breath.   *Selah*

6 Man is a mere phantom as he
    goes to and fro:
  He bustles about, but only in
    vain;
  he heaps up wealth, not
    knowing who will get it.

7 "But now, Lord, what do I look
    for?
  My hope is in you.
8 Save me from all my
    transgressions;
  do not make me the scorn of
    fools.
9 I was silent; I would not open
    my mouth,
  for you are the one who has
    done this.
10 Remove your scourge from me;
  I am overcome by the blow of
    your hand.
11 You rebuke and discipline men
    for their sin;
  you consume their wealth
    like a moth—
  each man is but a breath.   *Selah*

12 "Hear my prayer, O LORD,
  listen to my cry for help;
  be not deaf to my weeping.
  For I dwell with you as an
    alien,
  a stranger, as all my fathers
    were.
13 Look away from me, that I may
    rejoice again
  before I depart and am no
    more."

Psalm 40

For the director of music.
Of David. A psalm.

1 I waited patiently for the LORD;
  he turned to me and heard
    my cry.
2 He lifted me out of the slimy
    pit,
  out of the mud and mire;
  he set my feet on a rock
  and gave me a firm place to
    stand.
3 He put a new song in my
    mouth,
  a hymn of praise to our God.
  Many will see and fear
  and put their trust in the
    LORD.

4 Blessed is the man
  who makes the LORD his trust,
  who does not look to the proud,
  to those who turn aside to
    false gods.[s]
5 Many, O LORD my God,
  are the wonders you have
    done.
  The things you planned for us
  no one can recount to you;
  were I to speak and tell of
    them,
  they would be too many to
    declare.

6 Sacrifice and offering you did
    not desire,
  but my ears you have
    pierced[t,u];
  burnt offerings and sin offerings
  you did not require.
7 Then I said, "Here I am, I have
    come—
  it is written about me in the
    scroll.[v]

s 4 Or to falsehood   t 6 Hebrew; Septuagint but a body you have prepared for me (see also
Symmachus and Theodotion)   u 6 Or opened   v 7 Or come / with the scroll written for me

8 I desire to do your will, O my
God;
   your law is within my heart."

9 I proclaim righteousness in the
great assembly;
   I do not seal my lips,
   as you know, O LORD.
10 I do not hide your
righteousness in my heart;
   I speak of your faithfulness
   and salvation.
I do not conceal your love and
your truth
   from the great assembly.

11 Do not withhold your mercy
from me, O LORD;
   may your love and your truth
   always protect me.
12 For troubles without number
surround me;
   my sins have overtaken me,
   and I cannot see.
They are more than the hairs
of my head,
   and my heart fails within me.

13 Be pleased, O LORD, to save me;
   O LORD, come quickly to help
   me.
14 May all who seek to take my
life
   be put to shame and confusion;
   may all who desire my ruin
   be turned back in disgrace.
15 May those who say to me,
   "Aha! Aha!"
   be appalled at their own shame.
16 But may all who seek you
rejoice and be glad in you;
   may those who love your salvation always say,
   "The LORD be exalted!"

17 Yet I am poor and needy;
   may the Lord think of me.
You are my help and my
deliverer;
   O my God, do not delay.

Psalm 41
For the director of music.
A psalm of David.

1 Blessed is he who has regard
for the weak;
   the LORD delivers him in
   times of trouble.
2 The LORD will protect him and
preserve his life;
   he will bless him in the land
   and not surrender him to the
   desire of his foes.
3 The LORD will sustain him on
his sickbed
   and restore him from his bed
   of illness.

4 I said, "O LORD, have mercy on
me;
   heal me, for I have sinned
   against you."
5 My enemies say of me in
malice,
   "When will he die and his
   name perish?"
6 Whenever one comes to see me,
   he speaks falsely, while his
   heart gathers slander;
   then he goes out and spreads
   it abroad.

7 All my enemies whisper
together against me;
   they imagine the worst for
   me, saying,
8 "A vile disease has beset him;
   he will never get up from the
   place where he lies."
9 Even my close friend, whom I
trusted,
   he who shared my bread,
   has lifted up his heel against
   me.

10 But you, O LORD, have mercy
on me;
   raise me up, that I may repay
   them.

11 I know that you are pleased
    with me,
  for my enemy does not
    triumph over me.
12 In my integrity you uphold me
  and set me in your presence
    forever.

13 Praise be to the LORD, the God
    of Israel,
  from everlasting to
    everlasting.
  Amen and Amen.

BOOK II

Psalms 42-72

Psalm 42 w

For the director of music.
A *maskil* x of the Sons of Korah.

1 As the deer pants for streams
    of water,
  so my soul pants for you, O
    God.
2 My soul thirsts for God, for the
    living God.
  When can I go and meet with
    God?
3 My tears have been my food
    day and night,
  while men say to me all day long,
    "Where is your God?"
4 These things I remember
    as I pour out my soul:
  how I used to go with the mul-
    titude,
  leading the procession to the
    house of God,
  with shouts of joy and
    thanksgiving
  among the festive throng.

5 Why are you downcast, O my
    soul?

Why so disturbed within me?
  Put your hope in God,
  for I will yet praise him,
    my Savior and 6 my God.

My y soul is downcast within me;
  therefore I will remember you
  from the land of the Jordan,
    the heights of Hermon—from
    Mount Mizar.
7 Deep calls to deep
  in the roar of your waterfalls;
  all your waves and breakers
  have swept over me.

8 By day the LORD directs his love,
  at night his song is with me—
    a prayer to the God of my life.

9 I say to God my Rock,
  "Why have you forgotten me?
  Why must I go about mourning,
    oppressed by the enemy?"
10 My bones suffer mortal agony
    as my foes taunt me,
  saying to me all day long,
    "Where is your God?"

11 Why are you downcast, O my
    soul?
  Why so disturbed within me?
  Put your hope in God,
  for I will yet praise him,
    my Savior and my God.

Psalm 43 z

1 Vindicate me, O God,
  and plead my cause against
    an ungodly nation;
  rescue me from deceitful and
    wicked men.
2 You are God my stronghold.
  Why have you rejected me?
  Why must I go about mourning,
    oppressed by the enemy?

w In many Hebrew manuscripts Psalms 42 and 43 constitute one psalm.   x Title: Probably
a literary or musical term   y 5,6 A few Hebrew manuscripts, Septuagint and Syriac; most
Hebrew manuscripts *praise him for his saving help.* / 6 O my God, my   z In many Hebrew
manuscripts Psalms 42 and 43 constitute one psalm.

3 Send forth your light and your
    truth,
    let them guide me;
  let them bring me to your holy
      mountain,
  to the place where you dwell.
4 Then will I go to the altar of
    God,
  to God, my joy and my
    delight.
  I will praise you with the harp,
    O God, my God.

5 Why are you downcast, O my
    soul?
  Why so disturbed within me?
  Put your hope in God,
  for I will yet praise him,
    my Savior and my God.

Psalm 44

For the director of music.
Of the Sons of Korah. A *maskil.*[a]

1 We have heard with our ears,
    O God;
  our fathers have told us
  what you did in their days,
    in days long ago.
2 With your hand you drove out
    the nations
  and planted our fathers;
  you crushed the peoples
  and made our fathers flourish.
3 It was not by their sword that
    they won the land,
  nor did their arm bring them
    victory;
  it was your right hand, your
    arm,
  and the light of your face, for
    you loved them.

4 You are my King and my God,
  who decrees[b] victories for
    Jacob.

5 Through you we push back our
    enemies;
  through your name we
    trample our foes.
6 I do not trust in my bow,
  my sword does not bring me
    victory;
7 but you give us victory over
    our enemies,
  you put our adversaries to
    shame.
8 In God we make our boast all
    day long,
  and we will praise your name
    forever.   *Selah*

9 But now you have rejected and
    humbled us;
  you no longer go out with
    our armies.
10 You made us retreat before the
    enemy,
  and our adversaries have
    plundered us.
11 You gave us up to be devoured
    like sheep
  and have scattered us among
    the nations.
12 You sold your people for a
    pittance,
  gaining nothing from their
    sale.

13 You have made us a reproach
    to our neighbors,
  the scorn and derision of
    those around us.
14 You have made us a byword
    among the nations;
  the peoples shake their heads
    at us.
15 My disgrace is before me all
    day long,
  and my face is covered with
    shame

---

a Title: Probably a literary or musical term   *b* 4 Septuagint, Aquila and Syriac; Hebrew
King, O God; / command

16 at the taunts of those who
    reproach and revile me,
  because of the enemy, who is
    bent on revenge.

17 All this happened to us,
    though we had not forgotten
      you
  or been false to your
    covenant.
18 Our hearts had not turned
    back;
  our feet had not strayed from
    your path.
19 But you crushed us and made
    us a haunt for jackals
  and covered us over with
    deep darkness.

20 If we had forgotten the name
    of our God
  or spread out our hands to a
    foreign god,
21 would not God have discovered
    it,
  since he knows the secrets of
    the heart?
22 Yet for your sake we face death
    all day long;
  we are considered as sheep to
    be slaughtered.

23 Awake, O Lord! Why do you
    sleep?
  Rouse yourself! Do not reject
    us forever.
24 Why do you hide your face
  and forget our misery and
    oppression?

25 We are brought down to the
    dust;
  our bodies cling to the
    ground.
26 Rise up and help us;
  redeem us because of your
    unfailing love.

Psalm 45

For the director of music. To [the tune
of] "Lilies." Of the Sons of Korah.
A *maskil.c* A wedding song.

1 My heart is stirred by a noble
    theme
  as I recite my verses for the
    king;
  my tongue is the pen of a
    skillful writer.

2 You are the most excellent of
    men
  and your lips have been
    anointed with grace,
  since God has blessed you
    forever.
3 Gird your sword upon your
    side, O mighty one;
  clothe yourself with splendor
    and majesty.
4 In your majesty ride forth
    victoriously
  in behalf of truth, humility
    and righteousness;
  let your right hand display
    awesome deeds.
5 Let your sharp arrows pierce
    the hearts of the king's
    enemies;
  let the nations fall beneath
    your feet.
6 Your throne, O God, will last
    for ever and ever;
  a scepter of justice will be the
    scepter of your kingdom.
7 You love righteousness and
    hate wickedness;
  therefore God, your God, has
    set you above your
    companions
  by anointing you with the oil
    of joy.
8 All your robes are fragrant with
    myrrh and aloes and cassia;

c Title: Probably a literary or musical term

from palaces adorned with
ivory
the music of the strings
makes you glad.
9 Daughters of kings are among
your honored women;
at your right hand is the
royal bride in gold of Ophir.

10 Listen, O daughter, consider
and give ear:
Forget your people and your
father's house.
11 The king is enthralled by your
beauty;
honor him, for he is your
lord.
12 The Daughter of Tyre will
come with a gift,*d*
men of wealth will seek your
favor.

13 All glorious is the princess
within [her chamber];
her gown is interwoven with
gold.
14 In embroidered garments she is
led to the king;
her virgin companions follow
her
and are brought to you.
15 They are led in with joy and
gladness;
they enter the palace of the
king.

16 Your sons will take the place of
your fathers;
you will make them princes
throughout the land.
17 I will perpetuate your memory
through all generations;
therefore the nations will
praise you for ever and
ever.

Psalm 46

For the director of music. Of the Sons of
Korah. According to *alamoth.e* A song.

1 God is our refuge and strength,
an ever-present help in
trouble.
2 Therefore we will not fear,
though the earth give way
and the mountains fall into
the heart of the sea,
3 though its waters roar and foam
and the mountains quake
with their surging.   *Selah*

4 There is a river whose streams
make glad the city of God,
the holy place where the
Most High dwells.
5 God is within her, she will not
fall;
God will help her at break of
day.
6 Nations are in uproar,
kingdoms fall;
he lifts his voice, the earth
melts.

7 The LORD Almighty is with us;
the God of Jacob is our
fortress.   *Selah*

8 Come and see the works of the
LORD,
the desolations he has
brought on the earth.
9 He makes wars cease to the
ends of the earth;
he breaks the bow and
shatters the spear,
he burns the shields*f* with fire.
10 "Be still, and know that I am
God;
I will be exalted among the
nations,
I will be exalted in the earth."

d 12 Or A Tyrian robe is among the gifts   *e Title: Probably a musical term*   *f 9 Or chariots*

11 The LORD Almighty is with us;
   the God of Jacob is our
   fortress.   *Selah*

Psalm 47

For the director of music.
Of the Sons of Korah. A psalm.

1 Clap your hands, all you nations;
   shout to God with cries of joy.
2 How awesome is the LORD
   Most High,
   the great King over all the
   earth!
3 He subdued nations under us,
   peoples under our feet.
4 He chose our inheritance for us,
   the pride of Jacob, whom he
   loved.   *Selah*

5 God has ascended amid shouts
   of joy,
   the LORD amid the sounding
   of trumpets.
6 Sing praises to God, sing praises;
   sing praises to our King, sing
   praises.
7 For God is the King of all the
   earth;
   sing to him a psalm*g* of praise.
8 God reigns over the nations;
   God is seated on his holy
   throne.
9 The nobles of the nations
   assemble
   as the people of the God of
   Abraham,
   for the kings*h* of the earth
   belong to God;
   he is greatly exalted.

Psalm 48

A song. A psalm of the Sons of Korah.

1 Great is the LORD, and most
   worthy of praise,
   in the city of our God, his
   holy mountain.
2 It is beautiful in its loftiness,
   the joy of the whole earth.
   Like the utmost heights of
   Zaphon*i* is Mount Zion,
   the*j* city of the Great King.
3 God is in her citadels;
   he has shown himself to be
   her fortress.
4 When the kings joined forces,
   when they advanced together
5 they saw [her] and were
   astounded;
   they fled in terror.
6 Trembling seized them there,
   pain like that of a woman in
   labor.
7 You destroyed them like ships
   of Tarshish
   shattered by an east wind.
8 As we have heard,
   so have we seen
   in the city of the LORD Almighty,
   in the city of our God:
   God makes her secure forever
                                Selah

9 Within your temple, O God,
   we meditate on your
   unfailing love.
10 Like your name, O God,
   your praise reaches to the
   ends of the earth;
   your right hand is filled with
   righteousness.
11 Mount Zion rejoices,
   the villages of Judah are glad
   because of your judgments.
12 Walk about Zion, go around
   her,
   count her towers,

---

g 7 Or a maskil (probably a literary or musical term)   *h 9 Or shields*   *i 2 Zaphon* can
refer to a sacred mountain or the direction north.   *j 2 Or earth, / Mount Zion, on the
northern side / of the*

13 consider well her ramparts,
view her citadels,
that you may tell of them to
the next generation.
14 For this God is our God for ever
and ever;
he will be our guide even to
the end.

Psalm 49

For the director of music.
Of the Sons of Korah. A psalm.

1 Hear this, all you peoples;
listen, all who live in this
world,
2 both low and high,
rich and poor alike:
3 My mouth will speak words of
wisdom;
the utterance from my heart
will give understanding.
4 I will turn my ear to a proverb;
with the harp I will expound
my riddle:

5 Why should I fear when evil
days come,
when wicked deceivers
surround me—
6 those who trust in their wealth
and boast of their great riches?
7 No man can redeem the life of
another
or give to God a ransom for
him—
8 the ransom for a life is costly,
no payment is ever enough—
9 that he should live on forever
and not see decay.

10 For all can see that wise men die;
the foolish and the senseless
alike perish
and leave their wealth to
others.

11 Their tombs will remain their
houses[k] forever,
their dwellings for endless
generations,
though they had[l] named
lands after themselves.

12 But man, despite his riches,
does not endure;
he is[m] like the beasts that
perish.

13 This is the fate of those who
trust in themselves,
and of their followers, who
approve their sayings. *Selah*
14 Like sheep they are destined
for the grave,[n]
and death will feed on them.
The upright will rule over them
in the morning;
their forms will decay in the
grave,[o]
far from their princely
mansions.
15 But God will redeem my life[p]
from the grave;
he will surely take me to
himself. *Selah*

16 Do not be overawed when a
man grows rich,
when the splendor of his
house increases;
17 for he will take nothing with
him when he dies,
his splendor will not descend
with him.
18 Though while he lived he
counted himself blessed—
and men praise you when
you prosper—
19 he will join the generation of
his fathers,
who will never see the light
[of life].

---

k 11 Septuagint and Syriac; Hebrew *In their thoughts their houses will remain* l 11 Or /
for they have m 12 Hebrew; Septuagint and Syriac read verse 12 the same as verse 20.
n 14 Hebrew *Sheol*; also in verse 15 o 14 Hebrew *Sheol*; also in verse 15 p 15 Or *soul*

20 A man who has riches without
      understanding
   is like the beasts that perish.

Psalm 50
A psalm of Asaph.

1 The Mighty One, God, the LORD,
      speaks and summons the
      earth
   from the rising of the sun to
      the place where it sets.
2 From Zion, perfect in beauty,
   God shines forth.
3 Our God comes and will not be
      silent;
   a fire devours before him,
   and around him a tempest
      rages.
4 He summons the heavens
      above,
   and the earth, that he may
      judge his people:
5 "Gather to me my consecrated
      ones,
   who made a covenant with
      me by sacrifice."
6 And the heavens proclaim his
      righteousness,
   for God himself is judge.
                                    Selah

7 "Hear, O my people, and I will
      speak,
   O Israel, and I will testify
      against you:
   I am God, your God.
8 I do not rebuke you for your
      sacrifices
   or your burnt offerings,
      which are ever before me.
9 I have no need of a bull from
      your stall
   or of goats from your pens,
10 for every animal of the forest is
      mine,

   and the cattle on a thousand
      hills.
11 I know every bird in the
      mountains,
   and the creatures of the field
      are mine.
12 If I were hungry I would not
      tell you,
   for the world is mine, and all
      that is in it.
13 Do I eat the flesh of bulls
   or drink the blood of goats?
14 Sacrifice thank offerings to
      God,
   fulfill your vows to the Most
      High,
15 and call upon me in the day of
      trouble;
   I will deliver you, and you
      will honor me."

16 But to the wicked, God says:

   "What right have you to recite
      my laws
   or take my covenant on your
      lips?
17 You hate my instruction
   and cast my words behind you.
18 When you see a thief, you join
      with him;
   you throw in your lot with
      adulterers.
19 You use your mouth for evil
   and harness your tongue to
      deceit.
20 You speak continually against
      your brother
   and slander your own
      mother's son.
21 These things you have done
      and I kept silent;
   you thought I was altogether*q*
      like you.
   But I will rebuke you
   and accuse you to your face.

q 21 Or thought the 'I AM' was

22 "Consider this, you who forget
      God,
   or I will tear you to pieces,
      with none to rescue;
23 He who sacrifices thank
      offerings honors me,
   and he prepares the way
      so that I may show him[r] the
      salvation of God."

Psalm 51

For the director of music. A psalm of
David. When the prophet Nathan came
to him after David had committed
adultery with Bathsheba.

1 Have mercy on me, O God,
      according to your unfailing
      love;
   according to your great com-
      passion
      blot out my transgressions.
2 Wash away all my iniquity
   and cleanse me from my sin.

3 For I know my transgressions,
   and my sin is always before me.
4 Against you, you only, have I
      sinned
   and done what is evil in your
      sight,
   so that you are proved right
      when you speak
   and justified when you judge.
5 Surely I was sinful at birth,
   sinful from the time my
      mother conceived me.
6 Surely you desire truth in the
      inner parts[s];
   you teach[t] me wisdom in the
      inmost place.

7 Cleanse me with hyssop, and I
      will be clean;
   wash me, and I will be whiter
      than snow.

8 Let me hear joy and gladness;
   let the bones you have
      crushed rejoice.
9 Hide your face from my sins
   and blot out all my iniquity.

10 Create in me a pure heart, O
      God,
    and renew a steadfast spirit
      within me.
11 Do not cast me from your
      presence
    or take your Holy Spirit from
      me.
12 Restore to me the joy of your
      salvation
    and grant me a willing spirit,
      to sustain me.

13 Then I will teach transgressors
      your ways,
    and sinners will turn back to
      you.
14 Save me from bloodguilt, O
      God,
    the God who saves me,
    and my tongue will sing of
      your righteousness.
15 O Lord, open my lips,
    and my mouth will declare
      your praise.
16 You do not delight in sacrifice,
      or I would bring it;
    you do not take pleasure in
      burnt offerings.
17 The sacrifices of God are[u] a
      broken spirit;
    a broken and contrite heart,
    O God, you will not despise.

18 In your good pleasure make
      Zion prosper;
    build up the walls of
      Jerusalem.
19 Then there will be righteous
      sacrifices,

---

[r] 23 Or and to him who considers his way / I will show
his phrase is uncertain.   [t] 6 Or you desired...; / you taught   [u] 17 Or My sacrifice, O God, is   [s] 6 The meaning of the Hebrew for

whole burnt offerings to
delight you;
then bulls will be offered on
your altar.

Psalm 52

For the director of music. A maskil[v] of
David. When Doeg the Edomite had gone
to Saul and told him: "David has gone
to the house of Ahimelech."

1 Why do you boast of evil, you
mighty man?
Why do you boast all day
long,
you who are a disgrace in the
eyes of God?
2 Your tongue plots destruction;
it is like a sharpened razor,
you who practice deceit.
3 You love evil rather than good,
falsehood rather than
speaking the truth.   Selah
4 You love every harmful word,
O you deceitful tongue!

5 Surely God will bring you
down to everlasting ruin:
He will snatch you up and
tear you from your tent;
he will uproot you from the
land of the living.   Selah
6 The righteous will see and fear;
they will laugh at him, saying,
7 "Here now is the man
who did not make God his
stronghold
but trusted in his great wealth
and grew strong by
destroying others!"

8 But I am like an olive tree
flourishing in the house of
God;
I trust in God's unfailing love
for ever and ever.

9 I will praise you forever for
what you have done;
in your name I will hope, for
your name is good.
I will praise you in the
presence of your saints.

Psalm 53

For the director of music. According to
mahalath.[w] A maskil[x] of David.

1 The fool says in his heart,
"There is no God."
They are corrupt, and their
ways are vile;
there is no one who does good.

2 God looks down from heaven
on the sons of men
to see if there are any who understand,
any who seek God.
3 Everyone has turned away,
they have together become
corrupt;
there is no one who does good,
not even one.

4 Will the evildoers never learn—
those who devour my people
as men eat bread
and who do not call on God?
5 There they were, overwhelmed
with dread,
where there was nothing to
dread.
God scattered the bones of
those who attacked you;
you put them to shame, for
God despised them.

6 Oh, that salvation for Israel
would come out of Zion!
When God restores the
fortunes of his people,
let Jacob rejoice and Israel be
glad!

---

v Title: Probably a literary or musical term   w Title: Probably a musical term
x Title: Probably a literary or musical term

Psalm 54

For the director of music. With stringed instruments. A *maskil*[v] of David. When the Ziphites had gone to Saul and said, "Is not David hiding among us?"

1 Save me, O God, by your name;
   vindicate me by your might.
2 Hear my prayer, O God;
   listen to the words of my mouth.

3 Strangers are attacking me;
   ruthless men seek my life—
   men without regard for God.
                              Selah

4 Surely God is my help;
   the Lord is the one who sustains me.

5 Let evil recoil on those who slander me;
   in your faithfulness destroy them.

6 I will sacrifice a freewill offering to you;
   I will praise your name, O LORD,
   for it is good.
7 For he has delivered me from all my troubles,
   and my eyes have looked in triumph on my foes.

Psalm 55

For the director of music. With stringed instruments. A *maskil*[z] of David.

1 Listen to my prayer, O God,
   do not ignore my plea;
2   hear me and answer me.
   My thoughts trouble me and I am distraught
3   at the voice of the enemy,
   at the stares of the wicked;
   for they bring down suffering upon me
   and revile me in their anger.

4 My heart is in anguish within me;
   the terrors of death assail me.
5 Fear and trembling have beset me;
   horror has overwhelmed me.
6 I said, "Oh, that I had the wings of a dove!
   I would fly away and be at rest—
7 I would flee far away
   and stay in the desert;   *Selah*
8 I would hurry to my place of shelter,
   far from the tempest and storm."

9 Confuse the wicked, O Lord,
   confound their speech,
   for I see violence and strife in the city.
10 Day and night they prowl about on its walls;
   malice and abuse are within it.
11 Destructive forces are at work in the city;
   threats and lies never leave its streets.

12 If an enemy were insulting me,
   I could endure it;
   if a foe were raising himself against me,
   I could hide from him.
13 But it is you, a man like myself,
   my companion, my close friend,
14 with whom I once enjoyed sweet fellowship
   as we walked with the throng at the house of God.

---

v Title: Probably a literary or musical term   *z* Title: Probably a literary or musical term

15 Let death take my enemies by
surprise;
    let them go down alive to the
grave,*a*
    for evil finds lodging among
them.

16 But I call to God,
    and the LORD saves me.
17 Evening, morning and noon
    I cry out in distress,
    and he hears my voice.
18 He ransoms me unharmed
    from the battle waged
against me,
    even though many oppose
me.
19 God, who is enthroned forever,
    will hear them and afflict
them—   *Selah*
men who never change their
ways
    and have no fear of God.

20 My companion attacks his
friends;
    he violates his covenant.
21 His speech is smooth as butter,
    yet war is in his heart;
    his words are more soothing
than oil,
    yet they are drawn swords.

22 Cast your cares on the LORD
    and he will sustain you;
    he will never let the
righteous fall.
23 But you, O God, will bring
    down the wicked
    into the pit of corruption;
    bloodthirsty and deceitful
men
    will not live out half their
days.

    But as for me, I trust in you.

Psalm 56

For the director of music. To [the tune
of] "A Dove on Distant Oaks." Of David.
A *miktam.b* When the Philistines
    had seized him in Gath.

1 Be merciful to me, O God, for
    men hotly pursue me;
    all day long they press their
attack.
2 My slanderers pursue me all
    day long;
    many are attacking me in
    their pride.

3 When I am afraid,
    I will trust in you.
4 In God, whose word I praise,
    in God I trust; I will not be
    afraid.
    What can mortal man do to
    me?

5 All day long they twist my words;
    they are always plotting to
    harm me.
6 They conspire, they lurk,
    they watch my steps,
    eager to take my life.

7 On no account let them escape;
    in your anger, O God, bring
    down the nations.
8 Record my lament;
    list my tears on your scroll*c*—
    are they not in your record?
9 Then my enemies will turn back
    when I call for help.
    By this I will know that God
    is for me.
10 In God, whose word I praise,
    in the LORD, whose word I
    praise—
11 in God I trust; I will not be
    afraid.
    What can man do to me?

a 15 Hebrew *Sheol*   *b* Title: Probably a literary or musical term   *c 8* Or / *put my tears in
your wineskin*

12 I am under vows to you, O God;
    I will present my thank
        offerings to you.
13 For you have delivered me[d]
        from death
    and my feet from stumbling,
    that I may walk before God
        in the light of life.[e]

Psalm 57

For the director of music. [To the tune
of] "Do Not Destroy." Of David.
A *miktam.*[f] When he had fled
from Saul into the cave.

1 Have mercy on me, O God,
    have mercy on me,
    for in you my soul takes
        refuge.
    I will take refuge in the
        shadow of your wings
    until the disaster has passed.

2 I cry out to God Most High,
    to God, who fulfills [his
        purpose] for me.
3 He sends from heaven and
        saves me,
    rebuking those who hotly
        pursue me;   *Selah*
    God sends his love and his
        faithfulness.

4 I am in the midst of lions;
    I lie among ravenous beasts—
    men whose teeth are spears
        and arrows,
    whose tongues are sharp
        swords.

5 Be exalted, O God, above the
        heavens;
    let your glory be over all the
        earth.

6 They spread a net for my feet—
    I was bowed down in distress.

They dug a pit in my path—
    but they have fallen into it
        themselves.   *Selah*

7 My heart is steadfast, O God,
    my heart is steadfast;
    I will sing and make music.
8 Awake, my soul!
    Awake, harp and lyre!
    I will awaken the dawn.

9 I will praise you, O Lord,
        among the nations;
    I will sing of you among the
        peoples.
10 For great is your love, reaching
        to the heavens;
    your faithfulness reaches to
        the skies.

11 Be exalted, O God, above the
        heavens;
    let your glory be over all the
        earth.

Psalm 58

For the director of music. [To the tune
of] "Do Not Destroy." Of David.
A *miktam.*[g]

1 Do you rulers indeed speak just-
        ly?
    Do you judge uprightly
        among men?
2 No, in your heart you devise
        injustice,
    and your hands mete out
        violence on the earth.
3 Even from birth the wicked go
        astray;
    from the womb they are
        wayward and speak lies.
4 Their venom is like the venom
        of a snake,
    like that of a cobra that has
        stopped its ears,

d 13 Or my soul   e 13 Or the land of the living   f Title: Probably a literary or musical term
g Title: Probably a literary or musical term

5 that will not heed the tune of
   the charmer,
  however skillful the
    enchanter may be.

6 Break the teeth in their
   mouths, O God;
  tear out, O LORD, the fangs of
    the lions!

7 Let them vanish like water that
   flows away;
  when they draw the bow, let
    their arrows be blunted.

8 Like a slug melting away as it
   moves along,
  like a stillborn child, may
    they not see the sun.

9 Before your pots can feel [the
   heat of] the thorns—
  whether they be green or
    dry—the wicked will be
    swept away.h

10 The righteous will be glad
   when they are avenged,
  when they bathe their feet in
    the blood of the wicked.

11 Then men will say,
   "Surely the righteous still are
    rewarded;
  surely there is a God who
    judges the earth."

Psalm 59

For the director of music. [To the tune
of] "Do Not Destroy." Of David. A
miktam.i When Saul had sent men to
watch David's house in order to kill him.

1 Deliver me from my enemies,
   O God;
  protect me from those who
    rise up against me.

2 Deliver me from evildoers
   and save me from
    bloodthirsty men.

3 See how they lie in wait for me!
   Fierce men conspire against me
  for no offense or sin of mine,
    O LORD.

4 I have done no wrong, yet they
   are ready to attack me.
  Arise to help me; look on my
    plight!

5 O LORD God Almighty, the God
   of Israel,
  rouse yourself to punish all
    the nations;
  show no mercy to wicked
    traitors.   *Selah*

6 They return at evening,
   snarling like dogs,
  and prowl about the city.

7 See what they spew from their
   mouths—
  they spew out swords from
    their lips,
  and they say, "Who can hear
    us?"

8 But you, O LORD, laugh at them;
   you scoff at all those nations.

9 O my Strength, I watch for you;
   you, O God, are my fortress,
10 my loving God.

God will go before me
   and will let me gloat over
    those who slander me.

11 But do not kill them, O Lord
   our shield,j
  or my people will forget.
  In your might make them
    wander about,
  and bring them down.

12 For the sins of their mouths,
   for the words of their lips,
  let them be caught in their
    pride.
  For the curses and lies they
    utter,

---

h 9 The meaning of the Hebrew for this verse is uncertain.   i Title: Probably a literary or
musical term   j 11 Or *sovereign*

13 consume them in wrath,
consume them till they are no
more.
Then it will be known to the
ends of the earth
that God rules over
Jacob.   Selah

14 They return at evening,
snarling like dogs,
and prowl about the city.
15 They wander about for food
and howl if not satisfied.
16 But I will sing of your strength,
in the morning I will sing of
your love;
for you are my fortress,
my refuge in times of trouble.

17 O my Strength, I sing praise to
you;
you, O God, are my fortress,
my loving God.

Psalm 60

For the director of music. To [the tune
of] "The Lily of the Covenant." A
*miktam*k of David. For teaching. When he
fought Aram Naharaim*l* and Aram
Zobah,*m* and when Joab returned
and struck down twelve thousand
Edomites in the Valley of Salt.

1 You have rejected us, O God,
and burst forth upon us;
you have been angry—now
restore us!
2 You have shaken the land and
torn it open;
mend its fractures, for it is
quaking.
3 You have shown your people
desperate times;
you have given us wine that
makes us stagger.

4 But for those who fear you,
you have raised a banner
to be unfurled against the
bow.   Selah

5 Save us and help us with your
right hand,
that those you love may be
delivered.
6 God has spoken from his
sanctuary:
"In triumph I will parcel out
Shechem
and measure off the Valley of
Succoth.
7 Gilead is mine, and Manasseh
is mine;
Ephraim is my helmet,
Judah my scepter.
8 Moab is my washbasin,
upon Edom I toss my sandal;
over Philistia I shout in
triumph."

9 Who will bring me to the
fortified city?
Who will lead me to Edom?
10 Is it not you, O God, you who
have rejected us
and no longer go out with
our armies?
11 Give us aid against the enemy,
for the help of man is
worthless.
12 With God we will gain the
victory,
and he will trample down our
enemies.

Psalm 61

For the director of music. With stringed
instruments. Of David.

1 Hear my cry, O God;
listen to my prayer.

---

k Title: Probably a literary or musical term   l Title: That is, Arameans of Northwest
Mesopotamia   m Title: That is, Arameans of central Syria

2 From the ends of the earth I
  call to you,
  I call as my heart grows faint;
  lead me to the rock that is
  higher than I.
3 For you have been my refuge,
  a strong tower against the foe.

4 I long to dwell in your tent
  forever
  and take refuge in the shelter
  of your wings.   *Selah*
5 For you have heard my vows, O
  God;
  you have given me the heritage
  of those who fear your name.

6 Increase the days of the king's life,
  his years for many generations.
7 May he be enthroned in God's
  presence forever;
  appoint your love and
  faithfulness to protect him.

8 Then will I ever sing praise to
  your name
  and fulfill my vows day after
  day.

Psalm 62

For the director of music. For Jeduthun.
A psalm of David.

1 My soul finds rest in God alone;
  my salvation comes from him.
2 He alone is my rock and my
  salvation;
  he is my fortress, I will never
  be shaken.

3 How long will you assault a man?
  Would all of you throw him
  down—
  this leaning wall, this
  tottering fence?
4 They fully intend to topple him
  from his lofty place;
  they take delight in lies.

With their mouths they bless,
  but in their hearts they
  curse.   *Selah*

5 Find rest, O my soul, in God
  alone;
  my hope comes from him.
6 He alone is my rock and my
  salvation;
  he is my fortress, I will not be
  shaken.
7 My salvation and my honor
  depend on God[n];
  he is my mighty rock, my
  refuge.
8 Trust in him at all times, O
  people;
  pour out your hearts to him,
  for God is our refuge.   *Selah*

9 Lowborn men are but a breath,
  the highborn are but a lie;
  if weighed on a balance, they
  are nothing;
  together they are only a breath.
10 Do not trust in extortion
  or take pride in stolen goods;
  though your riches increase,
  do not set your heart on them.

11 One thing God has spoken,
  two things have I heard:
  that you, O God, are strong,
12 and that you, O Lord, are
  loving.
  Surely you will reward each
  person
  according to what he has done.

Psalm 63

A psalm of David. When he was in
the Desert of Judah.

1 O God, you are my God,
  earnestly I seek you;
  my soul thirsts for you,
  my body longs for you,

n 7 Or / God Most High is my salvation and my honor

in a dry and weary land
where there is no water.

2 I have seen you in the
sanctuary
and beheld your power and
your glory.
3 Because your love is better
than life,
my lips will glorify you.
4 I will praise you as long as I
live,
and in your name I will lift
up my hands.
5 My soul will be satisfied as
with the richest of foods;
with singing lips my mouth
will praise you.

6 On my bed I remember you;
I think of you through the
watches of the night.
7 Because you are my help,
I sing in the shadow of your
wings.
8 My soul clings to you;
your right hand upholds me.

9 They who seek my life will be
destroyed;
they will go down to the
depths of the earth.
10 They will be given over to the
sword
and become food for jackals.

11 But the king will rejoice in God;
all who swear by God's name
will praise him,
while the mouths of liars will
be silenced.

Psalm 64

For the director of music.
A psalm of David.

1 Hear me, O God, as I voice my
complaint;

protect my life from the
threat of the enemy.
2 Hide me from the conspiracy of
the wicked,
from that noisy crowd of
evildoers.
3 They sharpen their tongues like
swords
and aim their words like
deadly arrows.
4 They shoot from ambush at the
innocent man;
they shoot at him suddenly,
without fear.

5 They encourage each other in
evil plans,
they talk about hiding their
snares;
they say, "Who will see
them*?"
6 They plot injustice and say,
"We have devised a perfect
plan!"
Surely the mind and heart of
man are cunning.

7 But God will shoot them with
arrows;
suddenly they will be struck
down.
8 He will turn their own tongues
against them
and bring them to ruin;
all who see them will shake
their heads in scorn.

9 All mankind will fear;
they will proclaim the works
of God
and ponder what he has done.
10 Let the righteous rejoice in the
LORD
and take refuge in him;
let all the upright in heart
praise him!

---

o 5 Or *us*

Psalm 65

For the director of music.
A psalm of David. A song.

1 Praise awaits[p] you, O God, in
Zion;
to you our vows will be
fulfilled.
2 O you who hear prayer,
to you all men will come.
3 When we were overwhelmed
by sins,
you forgave[q] our
transgressions.
4 Blessed are those you choose
and bring near to live in your
courts!
We are filled with the good
things of your house,
of your holy temple.

5 You answer us with awesome
deeds of righteousness,
O God our Savior,
the hope of all the ends of the
earth
and of the farthest seas,
6 who formed the mountains by
your power,
having armed yourself with
strength,
7 who stilled the roaring of the
seas,
the roaring of their waves,
and the turmoil of the
nations.
8 Those living far away fear your
wonders;
where morning dawns and
evening fades
you call forth songs of joy.

9 You care for the land and
water it;
you enrich it abundantly.

The streams of God are filled
with water
to provide the people with
grain,
for so you have ordained it.[r]
10 You drench its furrows
and level its ridges;
you soften it with showers
and bless its crops.
11 You crown the year with your
bounty,
and your carts overflow with
abundance.
12 The grasslands of the desert
overflow;
the hills are clothed with
gladness.
13 The meadows are covered with
flocks
and the valleys are mantled
with grain;
they shout for joy and sing.

Psalm 66

For the director of music.
A song. A psalm.

1 Shout with joy to God, all the
earth!
2 Sing the glory of his name;
make his praise glorious!
3 Say to God, "How awesome are
your deeds!
So great is your power
that your enemies cringe
before you.
4 All the earth bows down to
you;
they sing praise to you,
they sing praise to your
name."   *Selah*

5 Come and see what God has
done,
how awesome his works in
man's behalf!

---

p 1 Or *befits;* the meaning of the Hebrew for this word is uncertain.   q 3 Or *made*
atonement for   r 9 Or *for that is how you prepare the land*

6 He turned the sea into dry land,
  they passed through the
      waters on foot—
  come, let us rejoice in him.
7 He rules forever by his power,
  his eyes watch the nations—
  let not the rebellious rise up
      against him.   *Selah*

8 Praise our God, O peoples,
  let the sound of his praise be
      heard;
9 he has preserved our lives
  and kept our feet from slipping.
10 For you, O God, tested us;
   you refined us like silver.
11 You brought us into prison
   and laid burdens on our backs.
12 You let men ride over our
      heads;
   we went through fire and
      water,
   but you brought us to a place
      of abundance.

13 I will come to your temple with
      burnt offerings
   and fulfill my vows to you—
14 vows my lips promised and my
      mouth spoke
   when I was in trouble.
15 I will sacrifice fat animals to you
   and an offering of rams;
   I will offer bulls and
      goats.   *Selah*

16 Come and listen, all you who
      fear God;
   let me tell you what he has
      done for me.
17 I cried out to him with my
      mouth;
   his praise was on my tongue.
18 If I had cherished sin in my
      heart,
   the Lord would not have
      listened;
19 but God has surely listened
   and heard my voice in prayer.

20 Praise be to God,
   who has not rejected my prayer
   or withheld his love from me!

Psalm 67

For the director of music. With stringed
instruments. A psalm. A song.

1 May God be gracious to us and
      bless us
  and make his face shine
      upon us,   *Selah*
2 that your ways may be known
      on earth,
  your salvation among all
      nations.

3 May the peoples praise you, O
      God;
  may all the peoples praise you.
4 May the nations be glad and
      sing for joy,
  for you rule the peoples justly
  and guide the nations of
      the earth.   *Selah*
5 May the peoples praise you, O
      God;
  may all the peoples praise
      you.

6 Then the land will yield its
      harvest,
  and God, our God, will bless
      us.
7 God will bless us,
  and all the ends of the earth
      will fear him.

Psalm 68

For the director of music. Of David.
A psalm. A song.

1 May God arise, may his
      enemies be scattered;
  may his foes flee before him.
2 As smoke is blown away by the
      wind,
  may you blow them away;
  as wax melts before the fire,
  may the wicked perish before
      God.

3 But may the righteous be glad
    and rejoice before God;
    may they be happy and joyful.

4 Sing to God, sing praise to his
    name,
    extol him who rides on the
        clouds⁵—
    his name is the LORD—
    and rejoice before him.
5 A father to the fatherless, a
    defender of widows,
    is God in his holy dwelling.
6 God sets the lonely in families,ᵗ
    he leads forth the prisoners
        with singing;
    but the rebellious live in a
        sun-scorched land.

7 When you went out before
    your people, O God,
    when you marched through
        the wasteland,   Selah
8 the earth shook,
    the heavens poured down
        rain,
    before God, the One of Sinai,
    before God, the God of Israel.
9 You gave abundant showers, O
    God;
    you refreshed your weary
        inheritance.
10 Your people settled in it,
    and from your bounty, O
        God, you provided for the
        poor.

11 The Lord announced the word,
    and great was the company
        of those who proclaimed it:
12 "Kings and armies flee in haste;
    in the camps men divide the
        plunder.
13 Even while you sleep among
    the campfires,ᵘ

the wings of [my] dove are
    sheathed with silver,
    its feathers with shining gold."
14 When the Almightyᵛ scattered
    the kings in the land,
    it was like snow fallen on
        Zalmon.
15 The mountains of Bashan are
    majestic mountains;
    rugged are the mountains of
        Bashan.
16 Why gaze in envy, O rugged
    mountains,
    at the mountain where God
        chooses to reign,
    where the LORD himself will
        dwell forever?
17 The chariots of God are tens of
    thousands
    and thousands of thousands;
    the Lord [has come] from
        Sinai into his sanctuary.
18 When you ascended on high,
    you led captives in your train;
    you received gifts from men,
    even fromʷ the rebellious—
    that you,ˣ O LORD God, might
        dwell there.

19 Praise be to the Lord, to God
    our Savior,
    who daily bears our burdens.
                                Selah
20 Our God is a God who saves;
    from the Sovereign LORD
    comes escape from death.

21 Surely God will crush the
    heads of his enemies,
    the hairy crowns of those
        who go on in their sins.
22 The Lord says, "I will bring
    them from Bashan;
    I will bring them from the
        depths of the sea,

---

⁵ 4 Or / prepare the way for him who rides through the deserts   ᵗ 6 Or the desolate in a
homeland   ᵘ 13 Or saddlebags   ᵛ 14 Hebrew Shaddai   ʷ 18 Or gifts for men, / even
ˣ 18 Or they

23 that you may plunge your feet
in the blood of your foes,
while the tongues of your
dogs have their share."

24 Your procession has come into
view, O God,
the procession of my God and
King into the sanctuary.
25 In front are the singers, after
them the musicians;
with them are the maidens
playing tambourines.
26 Praise God in the great
congregation;
praise the LORD in the
assembly of Israel.
27 There is the little tribe of
Benjamin, leading them,
there the great throng of
Judah's princes,
and there the princes of
Zebulun and of Naphtali.

28 Summon your power, O God*y*;
show us your strength, O
God, as you have done
before.
29 Because of your temple at
Jerusalem
kings will bring you gifts.
30 Rebuke the beast among the
reeds,
the herd of bulls among the
calves of the nations.
Humbled, may it bring bars of
silver.
Scatter the nations who
delight in war.
31 Envoys will come from Egypt;
Cush*z* will submit herself to
God.

32 Sing to God, O kingdoms of the
earth,
sing praise to the Lord,   *Selah*

33 to him who rides the ancient
skies above,
who thunders with mighty
voice.
34 Proclaim the power of God,
whose majesty is over Israel,
whose power is in the skies.
35 You are awesome, O God, in
your sanctuary;
the God of Israel gives power
and strength to his people.

Praise be to God!

Psalm 69

For the director of music. To [the tune
of] "Lilies." Of David.

1 Save me, O God,
for the waters have come up
to my neck.
2 I sink in the miry depths,
where there is no foothold.
I have come into the deep
waters;
the floods engulf me.
3 I am worn out calling for help;
my throat is parched.
My eyes fail,
looking for my God.
4 Those who hate me without
reason
outnumber the hairs of my
head;
many are my enemies without
cause,
those who seek to destroy me.
I am forced to restore
what I did not steal.

5 You know my folly, O God;
my guilt is not hidden from
you.

6 May those who hope in you
not be disgraced because of me,
O Lord, the LORD Almighty;

---

y 28 Many Hebrew manuscripts, Septuagint and Syriac; most Hebrew manuscripts *Your God
has summoned power for you*   *z* 31 That is, the upper Nile region

may those who seek you
   not be put to shame because
      of me,
   O God of Israel.
7 For I endure scorn for your
      sake,
   and shame covers my face.
8 I am a stranger to my brothers,
   an alien to my own mother's
      sons;
9 for zeal for your house
      consumes me,
   and the insults of those who
      insult you fall on me.
10 When I weep and fast,
   I must endure scorn;
11 when I put on sackcloth,
   people make sport of me.
12 Those who sit at the gate mock
      me,
   and I am the song of the
      drunkards.

13 But I pray to you, O LORD,
   in the time of your favor;
in your great love, O God,
   answer me with your sure
      salvation.
14 Rescue me from the mire,
   do not let me sink;
deliver me from those who
      hate me,
   from the deep waters.
15 Do not let the floodwaters
      engulf me
   or the depths swallow me up
   or the pit close its mouth
      over me.
16 Answer me, O LORD, out of the
      goodness of your love;
   in your great mercy turn to
      me.
17 Do not hide your face from
      your servant;
   answer me quickly, for I am
      in trouble.

18 Come near and rescue me;
   redeem me because of my
      foes.
19 You know how I am scorned,
      disgraced and shamed;
   all my enemies are before you.
20 Scorn has broken my heart
      and has left me helpless;
I looked for sympathy, but
      there was none,
   for comforters, but I found
      none.
21 They put gall in my food
   and gave me vinegar for my
      thirst.

22 May the table set before them
      become a snare;
   may it become retribution
      and[a] a trap.
23 May their eyes be darkened so
      they cannot see,
   and their backs be bent
      forever.
24 Pour out your wrath on them;
   let your fierce anger overtake
      them.
25 May their place be deserted;
   let there be no one to dwell
      in their tents.
26 For they persecute those you
      wound
   and talk about the pain of
      those you hurt.
27 Charge them with crime upon
      crime;
   do not let them share in your
      salvation.
28 May they be blotted out of the
      book of life
   and not be listed with the
      righteous.

29 I am in pain and distress;
   may your salvation, O God,
      protect me.

---

[a] 22 Or *snare* / *and their fellowship become*

30 I will praise God's name in song
and glorify him with
thanksgiving.
31 This will please the LORD more
than an ox,
more than a bull with its
horns and hoofs.
32 The poor will see and be glad—
you who seek God, may your
hearts live!
33 The LORD hears the needy
and does not despise his
captive people.
34 Let heaven and earth praise
him,
the seas and all that move in
them,
35 for God will save Zion
and rebuild the cities of
Judah.
Then people will settle there
and possess it;
36 the children of his servants
will inherit it,
and those who love his name
will dwell there.

Psalm 70

For the director of music.
Of David. A petition.

1 Hasten, O God, to save me;
O LORD, come quickly to help
me.
2 May those who seek my life
be put to shame and
confusion;
may all who desire my ruin
be turned back in disgrace.
3 May those who say to me,
"Aha! Aha!"
turn back because of their
shame.
4 But may all who seek you
rejoice and be glad in you;
may those who love your salvation always say,
"Let God be exalted!"

5 Yet I am poor and needy;
come quickly to me, O God.
You are my help and my
deliverer;
O LORD, do not delay.

Psalm 71

1 In you, O LORD, I have taken
refuge;
let me never be put to shame.
2 Rescue me and deliver me in
your righteousness;
turn your ear to me and save
me.
3 Be my rock of refuge,
to which I can always go;
give the command to save me,
for you are my rock and my
fortress.
4 Deliver me, O my God, from
the hand of the wicked,
from the grasp of evil and
cruel men.
5 For you have been my hope, O
Sovereign LORD,
my confidence since my
youth.
6 From birth I have relied on you;
you brought me forth from
my mother's womb.
I will ever praise you.
7 I have become like a portent to
many,
but you are my strong refuge.
8 My mouth is filled with your
praise,
declaring your splendor all
day long.
9 Do not cast me away when I
am old;
do not forsake me when my
strength is gone.
10 For my enemies speak against
me;
those who wait to kill me
conspire together.

11 They say, "God has forsaken him;
    pursue him and seize him,
    for no one will rescue him."

12 Be not far from me, O God;
    come quickly, O my God, to
    help me.

13 May my accusers perish in shame;
    may those who want to harm
    me
    be covered with scorn and
    disgrace.

14 But as for me, I will always
    have hope;
    I will praise you more and
    more.

15 My mouth will tell of your
    righteousness,
    of your salvation all day long,
    though I know not its measure.

16 I will come and proclaim your
    mighty acts, O Sovereign
    LORD;
    I will proclaim your
    righteousness, yours alone.

17 Since my youth, O God, you
    have taught me,
    and to this day I declare your
    marvelous deeds.

18 Even when I am old and gray,
    do not forsake me, O God,
    till I declare your power to the
    next generation,
    your might to all who are to
    come.

19 Your righteousness reaches to
    the skies, O God,
    you who have done great
    things.
    Who, O God, is like you?

20 Though you have made me see
    troubles, many and bitter,
    you will restore my life again;
    from the depths of the earth
    you will again bring me up.

21 You will increase my honor
    and comfort me once again.

22 I will praise you with the harp
    for your faithfulness, O my
    God;
    I will sing praise to you with
    the lyre,
    O Holy One of Israel.

23 My lips will shout for joy
    when I sing praise to you—
    I, whom you have redeemed.

24 My tongue will tell of your
    righteous acts
    all day long,
    for those who wanted to harm me
    have been put to shame and
    confusion.

Psalm 72
Of Solomon.

1 Endow the king with your jus-
    tice, O God,
    the royal son with your
    righteousness.

2 He will[b] judge your people in
    righteousness,
    your afflicted ones with justice.

3 The mountains will bring
    prosperity to the people,
    the hills the fruit of
    righteousness.

4 He will defend the afflicted
    among the people
    and save the children of the
    needy;
    he will crush the oppressor.

5 He will endure[c] as long as the
    sun,
    as long as the moon, through
    all generations.

6 He will be like rain falling on a
    mown field,
    like showers watering the
    earth.

---

b 2 Or *May he*; similarly in verses 3-11 and 17   c 5 Septuagint; Hebrew *You will be feared*

7 In his days the righteous will
       flourish;
   prosperity will abound till the
       moon is no more.

8 He will rule from sea to sea
   and from the River[d] to the
       ends of the earth.[e]
9 The desert tribes will bow
       before him
   and his enemies will lick the
       dust.
10 The kings of Tarshish and of
       distant shores
   will bring tribute to him;
   the kings of Sheba and Seba
       will present him gifts.
11 All kings will bow down to him
   and all nations will serve him.

12 For he will deliver the needy
       who cry out,
   the afflicted who have no one
       to help.
13 He will take pity on the weak
       and the needy
   and save the needy from
       death.
14 He will rescue them from
       oppression and violence,
   for precious is their blood in
       his sight.

15 Long may he live!
   May gold from Sheba be
       given him.
   May people ever pray for him
   and bless him all day long.
16 Let grain abound throughout
       the land;
   on the tops of the hills may it
       sway.
   Let its fruit flourish like
       Lebanon;
   let it thrive like the grass of
       the field.

17 May his name endure forever;
   may it continue as long as the
       sun.

   All nations will be blessed
       through him,
   and they will call him blessed.

18 Praise be to the LORD God, the
       God of Israel,
   who alone does marvelous
       deeds.
19 Praise be to his glorious name
       forever;
   may the whole earth be filled
       with his glory.
   Amen and Amen.

20 This concludes the prayers of
       David son of Jesse.

BOOK III

Psalms 73-89

Psalm 73

A psalm of Asaph.

1 Surely God is good to Israel,
   to those who are pure in
       heart.

2 But as for me, my feet had
       almost slipped;
   I had nearly lost my foothold.
3 For I envied the arrogant
   when I saw the prosperity of
       the wicked.

4 They have no struggles;
   their bodies are healthy and
       strong.[f]
5 They are free from the burdens
       common to man;
   they are not plagued by
       human ills.
6 Therefore pride is their
       necklace;

---

d 8 That is, the Euphrates   *e 8* Or *the end of the land*   *f 4* With a different word division
of the Hebrew; Masoretic Text *struggles at their death; / their bodies are healthy*

they clothe themselves with
violence.
7 From their callous hearts
comes iniquity*g*;
the evil conceits of their
minds know no limits.
8 They scoff, and speak with
malice;
in their arrogance they
threaten oppression.
9 Their mouths lay claim to heaven,
and their tongues take
possession of the earth.
10 Therefore their people turn to
them
and drink up waters in
abundance.*h*
11 They say, "How can God know?
Does the Most High have
knowledge?"

12 This is what the wicked are like—
always carefree, they increase
in wealth.

13 Surely in vain have I kept my
heart pure;
in vain have I washed my
hands in innocence.
14 All day long I have been plagued;
I have been punished every
morning.
15 If I had said, "I will speak thus,"
I would have betrayed your
children.
16 When I tried to understand all
this,
it was oppressive to me
17 till I entered the sanctuary of
God;
then I understood their final
destiny.

18 Surely you place them on
slippery ground;

you cast them down to ruin.
19 How suddenly are they
destroyed,
completely swept away by
terrors!
20 As a dream when one awakes,
so when you arise, O Lord,
you will despise them as
fantasies.

21 When my heart was grieved
and my spirit embittered,
22 I was senseless and ignorant;
I was a brute beast before you.

23 Yet I am always with you;
you hold me by my right hand.
24 You guide me with your
counsel,
and afterward you will take
me into glory.
25 Whom have I in heaven but you?
And earth has nothing I
desire besides you.
26 My flesh and my heart may fail,
but God is the strength of my
heart
and my portion forever.

27 Those who are far from you
will perish;
you destroy all who are
unfaithful to you.
28 But as for me, it is good to be
near God.
I have made the Sovereign
LORD my refuge;
I will tell of all your deeds.

Psalm 74

*A maskil**i** of Asaph.*

1 Why have you rejected us
forever, O God?
Why does your anger smolder
against the sheep of your
pasture?

---

g 7 Syriac (see also Septuagint); Hebrew *Their eyes bulge with fat*   *h* 10 The meaning of
the Hebrew for this verse is uncertain.   *i* Title: Probably a literary or musical term

2 Remember the people you
purchased of old,
the tribe of your inheritance,
whom you redeemed—
Mount Zion, where you
dwelt.
3 Turn your steps toward these
everlasting ruins,
all this destruction the enemy
has brought on the
sanctuary.

4 Your foes roared in the place
where you met with us;
they set up their standards as
signs.
5 They behaved like men
wielding axes
to cut through a thicket of
trees.
6 They smashed all the carved
paneling
with their axes and hatchets.
7 They burned your sanctuary to
the ground;
they defiled the dwelling
place of your Name.
8 They said in their hearts, "We
will crush them completely!"
They burned every place
where God was worshiped
in the land.
9 We are given no miraculous
signs;
no prophets are left,
and none of us knows how
long this will be.

10 How long will the enemy mock
you, O God?
Will the foe revile your name
forever?
11 Why do you hold back your
hand, your right hand?
Take it from the folds of your
garment and destroy them!
12 But you, O God, are my king
from of old;

you bring salvation upon the
earth.
13 It was you who split open the
sea by your power;
you broke the heads of the
monster in the waters.
14 It was you who crushed the
heads of Leviathan
and gave him as food to the
creatures of the desert.
15 It was you who opened up
springs and streams;
you dried up the ever flowing
rivers.
16 The day is yours, and yours
also the night;
you established the sun and
moon.
17 It was you who set all the
boundaries of the earth;
you made both summer and
winter.

18 Remember how the enemy has
mocked you, O LORD,
how foolish people have
reviled your name.
19 Do not hand over the life of
your dove to wild beasts;
do not forget the lives of your
afflicted people forever.
20 Have regard for your covenant,
because haunts of violence
fill the dark places of the
land.
21 Do not let the oppressed
retreat in disgrace;
may the poor and needy
praise your name.

22 Rise up, O God, and defend
your cause;
remember how fools mock
you all day long.
23 Do not ignore the clamor of
your adversaries,
the uproar of your enemies,
which rises continually.

Psalm 75

For the director of music. [To the tune
of] "Do Not Destroy."
A psalm of Asaph. A song.

1 We give thanks to you, O God,
   we give thanks, for your
   Name is near;
   men tell of your wonderful
   deeds.

2 You say, "I choose the
   appointed time;
   it is I who judge uprightly.

3 When the earth and all its
   people quake,
   it is I who hold its pillars
   firm.   *Selah*

4 To the arrogant I say, 'Boast no
   more,'
   and to the wicked, 'Do not lift
   up your horns.

5 Do not lift your horns against
   heaven;
   do not speak with
   outstretched neck.'"

6 No one from the east or the west
   or from the desert can exalt a
   man.

7 But it is God who judges:
   He brings one down, he
   exalts another.

8 In the hand of the LORD is a cup
   full of foaming wine mixed
   with spices;
   he pours it out, and all the
   wicked of the earth
   drink it down to its very dregs.

9 As for me, I will declare this
   forever;
   I will sing praise to the God
   of Jacob.

10 I will cut off the horns of all
   the wicked,

but the horns of the righteous
   will be lifted up.

Psalm 76

For the director of music. With stringed
instruments. A psalm of Asaph. A song.

1 In Judah God is known;
   his name is great in Israel.

2 His tent is in Salem,
   his dwelling place in Zion.

3 There he broke the flashing
   arrows,
   the shields and the swords,
   the weapons of war.   *Selah*

4 You are resplendent with light,
   more majestic than
   mountains rich with game.

5 Valiant men lie plundered,
   they sleep their last sleep;
   not one of the warriors
   can lift his hands.

6 At your rebuke, O God of Jacob,
   both horse and chariot lie still.

7 You alone are to be feared.
   Who can stand before you
   when you are angry?

8 From heaven you pronounced
   judgment,
   and the land feared and was
   quiet—

9 when you, O God, rose up to
   judge,
   to save all the afflicted of the
   land.   *Selah*

10 Surely your wrath against men
   brings you praise,
   and the survivors of your
   wrath are restrained.*j*

11 Make vows to the LORD your
   God and fulfill them;
   let all the neighboring lands
   bring gifts to the One to be
   feared.

j 10 Or *Surely the wrath of men brings you praise, / and with the remainder of wrath you arm
yourself*

12 He breaks the spirit of rulers;
   he is feared by the kings of
      the earth.

Psalm 77

For the director of music. For Jeduthun.
Of Asaph. A psalm.

1 I cried out to God for help;
   I cried out to God to hear me.
2 When I was in distress, I
      sought the Lord;
   at night I stretched out
      untiring hands
   and my soul refused to be
      comforted.

3 I remembered you, O God, and
      I groaned;
   I mused, and my spirit grew
      faint.   *Selah*
4 You kept my eyes from closing;
   I was too troubled to speak.
5 I thought about the former
      days,
   the years of long ago;
6 I remembered my songs in the
      night.
   My heart mused and my
      spirit inquired:

7 "Will the Lord reject forever?
   Will he never show his favor
      again?
8 Has his unfailing love vanished
      forever?
   Has his promise failed for all
      time?
9 Has God forgotten to be merciful?
   Has he in anger withheld his
      compassion?"   *Selah*

10 Then I thought, "To this I will
      appeal:
   the years of the right hand of
      the Most High."
11 I will remember the deeds of
      the LORD;

yes, I will remember your
   miracles of long ago.
12 I will meditate on all your works
   and consider all your mighty
      deeds.

13 Your ways, O God, are holy.
   What god is so great as our
      God?
14 You are the God who performs
      miracles;
   you display your power
      among the peoples.
15 With your mighty arm you
      redeemed your people,
   the descendants of Jacob and
      Joseph.   *Selah*

16 The waters saw you, O God,
   the waters saw you and
      writhed;
   the very depths were
      convulsed.
17 The clouds poured down water,
   the skies resounded with
      thunder;
   your arrows flashed back and
      forth.
18 Your thunder was heard in the
      whirlwind,
   your lightning lit up the world;
   the earth trembled and quaked.
19 Your path led through the sea,
   your way through the mighty
      waters,
   though your footprints were
      not seen.
20 You led your people like a flock
   by the hand of Moses and
      Aaron.

Psalm 78

A *maskil*[k] of Asaph.

1 O my people, hear my teaching;
   listen to the words of my
      mouth.

---

k Title: Probably a literary or musical term

2 I will open my mouth in
      parables,
   I will utter hidden things,
      things from of old—
3 what we have heard and
      known,
   what our fathers have told us.
4 We will not hide them from
      their children;
   we will tell the next
      generation
   the praiseworthy deeds of the
      LORD,
   his power, and the wonders
      he has done.
5 He decreed statutes for Jacob
   and established the law in
      Israel,
   which he commanded our
      forefathers
   to teach their children,
6 so the next generation would
      know them,
   even the children yet to be
      born,
   and they in turn would tell
      their children.
7 Then they would put their trust
      in God
   and would not forget his deeds
   but would keep his
      commands.
8 They would not be like their
      forefathers—
   a stubborn and rebellious
      generation,
   whose hearts were not loyal to
      God,
   whose spirits were not
      faithful to him.

9 The men of Ephraim, though
      armed with bows,
   turned back on the day of
      battle;
10 they did not keep God's
      covenant
   and refused to live by his law.

11 They forgot what he had done,
   the wonders he had shown
      them.
12 He did miracles in the sight of
      their fathers
   in the land of Egypt, in the
      region of Zoan.
13 He divided the sea and led
      them through;
   he made the water stand firm
      like a wall.
14 He guided them with the cloud
      by day
   and with light from the fire
      all night.
15 He split the rocks in the desert
   and gave them water as
      abundant as the seas;
16 he brought streams out of a
      rocky crag
   and made water flow down
      like rivers.

17 But they continued to sin
      against him,
   rebelling in the desert against
      the Most High.
18 They willfully put God to the test
   by demanding the food they
      craved.
19 They spoke against God, saying,
   "Can God spread a table in
      the desert?
20 When he struck the rock, water
      gushed out,
   and streams flowed
      abundantly.
   But can he also give us food?
   Can he supply meat for his
      people?"
21 When the LORD heard them, he
      was very angry;
   his fire broke out against
      Jacob,
   and his wrath rose against
      Israel,
22 for they did not believe in God
   or trust in his deliverance.

23 Yet he gave a command to the skies above
and opened the doors of the heavens;
24 he rained down manna for the people to eat,
he gave them the grain of heaven.
25 Men ate the bread of angels;
he sent them all the food they could eat.
26 He let loose the east wind from the heavens
and led forth the south wind by his power.
27 He rained meat down on them like dust,
flying birds like sand on the seashore.
28 He made them come down inside their camp,
all around their tents.
29 They ate till they had more than enough,
for he had given them what they craved.
30 But before they turned from the food they craved,
even while it was still in their mouths,
31 God's anger rose against them;
he put to death the sturdiest among them,
cutting down the young men of Israel.
32 In spite of all this, they kept on sinning;
in spite of his wonders, they did not believe.
33 So he ended their days in futility
and their years in terror.
34 Whenever God slew them, they would seek him;
they eagerly turned to him again.
35 They remembered that God was their Rock,

that God Most High was their Redeemer.
36 But then they would flatter him with their mouths,
lying to him with their tongues;
37 their hearts were not loyal to him,
they were not faithful to his covenant.
38 Yet he was merciful;
he forgave their iniquities
and did not destroy them.
Time after time he restrained his anger
and did not stir up his full wrath.
39 He remembered that they were but flesh,
a passing breeze that does not return.

40 How often they rebelled against him in the desert
and grieved him in the wasteland!
41 Again and again they put God to the test;
they vexed the Holy One of Israel.
42 They did not remember his power—
the day he redeemed them from the oppressor,
43 the day he displayed his miraculous signs in Egypt,
his wonders in the region of Zoan.
44 He turned their rivers to blood;
they could not drink from their streams.
45 He sent swarms of flies that devoured them,
and frogs that devastated them.
46 He gave their crops to the grasshopper,
their produce to the locust.

47 He destroyed their vines with
   hail
      and their sycamore-figs with
      sleet.
48 He gave over their cattle to the
   hail,
      their livestock to bolts of
      lightning.
49 He unleashed against them his
   hot anger,
      his wrath, indignation and
      hostility—
   a band of destroying angels.
50 He prepared a path for his anger;
      he did not spare them from
      death
   but gave them over to the
   plague.
51 He struck down all the
   firstborn of Egypt,
      the firstfruits of manhood in
      the tents of Ham.
52 But he brought his people out
   like a flock;
      he led them like sheep
      through the desert.
53 He guided them safely, so they
   were unafraid;
      but the sea engulfed their
      enemies.
54 Thus he brought them to the
   border of his holy land,
      to the hill country his right
      hand had taken.
55 He drove out nations before
   them
      and allotted their lands to
      them as an inheritance;
      he settled the tribes of Israel
      in their homes.

56 But they put God to the test
   and rebelled against the Most
   High;
      they did not keep his statutes.
57 Like their fathers they were
   disloyal and faithless,
      as unreliable as a faulty bow.

58 They angered him with their
   high places;
      they aroused his jealousy
      with their idols.
59 When God heard them, he was
   very angry;
      he rejected Israel completely.
60 He abandoned the tabernacle
   of Shiloh,
      the tent he had set up among
      men.
61 He sent [the ark of] his might
   into captivity,
      his splendor into the hands of
      the enemy.
62 He gave his people over to the
   sword;
      he was very angry with his
      inheritance.
63 Fire consumed their young
   men,
      and their maidens had no
      wedding songs;
64 their priests were put to the
   sword,
      and their widows could not
      weep.

65 Then the Lord awoke as from
   sleep,
      as a man wakes from the
      stupor of wine.
66 He beat back his enemies;
      he put them to everlasting
      shame.
67 Then he rejected the tents of
   Joseph,
      he did not choose the tribe of
      Ephraim;
68 but he chose the tribe of Judah,
      Mount Zion, which he loved.
69 He built his sanctuary like the
   heights,
      like the earth that he
      established forever.
70 He chose David his servant
      and took him from the sheep
      pens;

71 from tending the sheep he
brought him
to be the shepherd of his
people Jacob,
of Israel his inheritance.
72 And David shepherded them
with integrity of heart;
with skillful hands he led them.

Psalm 79
A psalm of Asaph.

1 O God, the nations have in-
vaded your inheritance;
they have defiled your holy
temple,
they have reduced Jerusalem
to rubble.
2 They have given the dead
bodies of your servants
as food to the birds of the air,
the flesh of your saints to the
beasts of the earth.
3 They have poured out blood
like water
all around Jerusalem,
and there is no one to bury
the dead.
4 We are objects of reproach to
our neighbors,
of scorn and derision to those
around us.

5 How long, O LORD? Will you be
angry forever?
How long will your jealousy
burn like fire?
6 Pour out your wrath on the
nations
that do not acknowledge you,
on the kingdoms
that do not call on your name;
7 for they have devoured Jacob
and destroyed his homeland.
8 Do not hold against us the sins
of the fathers;
may your mercy come
quickly to meet us,
for we are in desperate need.

9 Help us, O God our Savior,
for the glory of your name;
deliver us and forgive our sins
for your name's sake.
10 Why should the nations say,
"Where is their God?"
Before our eyes, make known
among the nations
that you avenge the
outpoured blood of your
servants.
11 May the groans of the
prisoners come before you;
by the strength of your arm
preserve those condemned to
die.
12 Pay back into the laps of our
neighbors seven times
the reproach they have
hurled at you, O Lord.
13 Then we your people, the
sheep of your pasture,
will praise you forever;
from generation to generation
we will recount your praise.

Psalm 80
For the director of music. To [the tune
of] "The Lilies of the Covenant."
Of Asaph. A psalm.

1 Hear us, O Shepherd of Israel,
you who lead Joseph like a
flock;
you who sit enthroned be-
tween the cherubim, shine
forth
2 before Ephraim, Benjamin
and Manasseh.
Awaken your might;
come and save us.

3 Restore us, O God;
make your face shine upon us,
that we may be saved.

4 O LORD God Almighty,
how long will your anger
smolder

against the prayers of your
people?
5 You have fed them with the
bread of tears;
you have made them drink
tears by the bowlful.
6 You have made us a source of
contention to our neighbors,
and our enemies mock us.

7 Restore us, O God Almighty;
make your face shine upon us,
that we may be saved.

8 You brought a vine out of Egypt;
you drove out the nations
and planted it.
9 You cleared the ground for it,
and it took root and filled the
land.
10 The mountains were covered
with its shade,
the mighty cedars with its
branches.
11 It sent out its boughs to the
Sea,*l*
its shoots as far as the River.*m*

12 Why have you broken down its
walls
so that all who pass by pick
its grapes?
13 Boars from the forest ravage it
and the creatures of the field
feed on it.
14 Return to us, O God Almighty!
Look down from heaven and
see!
Watch over this vine,
15   the root your right hand has
planted,
the son*n* you have raised up
for yourself.

16 Your vine is cut down, it is
burned with fire;

at your rebuke your people
perish.
17 Let your hand rest on the man
at your right hand,
the son of man you have
raised up for yourself.
18 Then we will not turn away
from you;
revive us, and we will call on
your name.

19 Restore us, O LORD God
Almighty;
make your face shine upon us,
that we may be saved.

Psalm 81

For the director of music.
According to *gittith*.*o* Of Asaph.

1 Sing for joy to God our
strength;
shout aloud to the God of
Jacob!
2 Begin the music, strike the
tambourine,
play the melodious harp and
lyre.

3 Sound the ram's horn at the
New Moon,
and when the moon is full,
on the day of our Feast;
4 this is a decree for Israel,
an ordinance of the God of
Jacob.
5 He established it as a statute
for Joseph
when he went out against
Egypt,
where we heard a language
we did not understand.*p*

6 He says, "I removed the burden
from their shoulders;
their hands were set free
from the basket.

---

l 11 Probably the Mediterranean   *m* 11 That is, the Euphrates   *n* 15 Or *branch*
o Title: Probably a musical term   *p* 5 Or / *and we heard a voice we had not known*

7 In your distress you called and
   I rescued you,
   I answered you out of a
      thundercloud;
   I tested you at the waters
      of Meribah.   *Selah*

8 "Hear, O my people, and I will
      warn you—
   if you would but listen to me,
      O Israel!
9 You shall have no foreign god
      among you;
   you shall not bow down to an
      alien god.
10 I am the LORD your God,
   who brought you up out of
      Egypt.
   Open wide your mouth and I
      will fill it.

11 "But my people would not
      listen to me;
   Israel would not submit to me.
12 So I gave them over to their
      stubborn hearts
   to follow their own devices.

13 "If my people would but listen
      to me,
   if Israel would follow my ways,
14 how quickly would I subdue
      their enemies
   and turn my hand against
      their foes!
15 Those who hate the LORD
   would cringe before him,
   and their punishment would
      last forever.
16 But you would be fed with the
      finest of wheat;
   with honey from the rock I
      would satisfy you."

Psalm 82
A psalm of Asaph.

1 God presides in the great as-
      sembly;

he gives judgment among the
      "gods":

2 "How long will you^q defend the
      unjust
   and show partiality to the
      wicked?   *Selah*
3 Defend the cause of the weak
      and fatherless;
   maintain the rights of the
      poor and oppressed.
4 Rescue the weak and needy;
   deliver them from the hand
      of the wicked.

5 "They know nothing, they
      understand nothing.
   They walk about in darkness;
   all the foundations of the
      earth are shaken.

6 "I said, 'You are "gods";
   you are all sons of the Most
      High.'
7 But you will die like mere men;
   you will fall like every other
      ruler."

8 Rise up, O God, judge the
      earth,
   for all the nations are your
      inheritance.

Psalm 83
A song. A psalm of Asaph.

1 O God, do not keep silent;
   be not quiet, O God, be not
      still.
2 See how your enemies are astir,
   how your foes rear their heads.
3 With cunning they conspire
      against your people;
   they plot against those you
      cherish.
4 "Come," they say, "let us
      destroy them as a nation,
   that the name of Israel be
      remembered no more."

q 2 The Hebrew is plural.

5 With one mind they plot
  together;
    they form an alliance against
    you—
6 the tents of Edom and the
  Ishmaelites,
    of Moab and the Hagrites,
7 Gebal,r Ammon and Amalek,
  Philistia, with the people of
  Tyre.
8 Even Assyria has joined them
  to lend strength to the
  descendants of Lot.   *Selah*

9 Do to them as you did to
  Midian,
    as you did to Sisera and Jabin
    at the river Kishon,
10 who perished at Endor
   and became like refuse on
   the ground.
11 Make their nobles like Oreb
   and Zeeb,
     all their princes like Zebah
     and Zalmunna,
12 who said, "Let us take possession
   of the pasturelands of God."

13 Make them like tumbleweed, O
   my God,
     like chaff before the wind.
14 As fire consumes the forest
   or a flame sets the mountains
   ablaze,
15 so pursue them with your
   tempest
     and terrify them with your
     storm.
16 Cover their faces with shame
   so that men will seek your
   name, O LORD.

17 May they ever be ashamed and
   dismayed;
     may they perish in disgrace.
18 Let them know that you, whose
   name is the LORD—

that you alone are the Most
High over all the earth.

Psalm 84

For the director of music. According to
gittith.s Of the Sons of Korah. A psalm.

1 How lovely is your dwelling
  place,
    O LORD Almighty!
2 My soul yearns, even faints,
  for the courts of the LORD;
    my heart and my flesh cry out
    for the living God.

3 Even the sparrow has found a
  home,
    and the swallow a nest for
    herself,
      where she may have her
      young—
  a place near your altar,
    O LORD Almighty, my King
    and my God.
4 Blessed are those who dwell in
  your house;
    they are ever praising
    you.   *Selah*

5 Blessed are those whose
  strength is in you,
    who have set their hearts on
    pilgrimage.
6 As they pass through the Valley
  of Baca,
    they make it a place of springs;
    the autumn rains also cover it
    with pools.t
7 They go from strength to
  strength,
    till each appears before God
    in Zion.

8 Hear my prayer, O LORD God
  Almighty;
    listen to me, O God of
    Jacob.   *Selah*

---

r 7 That is, Byblos   s Title: Probably a musical term   t 6 Or *blessings*

BOBBY MOTE
★ ★ ★

The first time I walked into Thomas and Mac, the first performance on Friday night before the crowd got there, just made the hair stand up on the back of my neck. I was so excited! I had a horse called Icicle, supposed to be a phenomenal horse, and I got to nod my head at the NFR! I won the first ride and I won the first go-round; this was made for me—so exciting!

Actually, I had never considered rodeoing until I was thirteen and joined my friends in Junior Rodeo. In high school my friends and I listened to Chris LeDoux, the 1976 World Champion bareback rider, who sang about the romantic side of bareback riding. I think that got me geared in the direction of riding bareback horses.

At first getting on bucking horses was kind of a scary deal. The element of fear was there every time I was about to nod my head. I grew up going to church and I knew about the Lord. I decided it would be best to get closer to God and pray each time before I got on a bucking horse. That's probably what started me working faith into my everyday life.

When I first started to rodeo professionally full-time, I traveled with Clint Cory. I learned an incredible amount from Clint and the experiences we had were terrific. In 2001 I got my priorities mixed up and was overly serious to win all the time. I pushed all my friends away without realizing why at the time. My traveling partners, Clint Cory and Jason Havens, didn't want to travel with me anymore so I went by myself.

I made the Finals and rode the first nine rounds. I thought it was a result of being so serious, taking care of business all year. I got on my horse in the 10th round and got bucked off.

It seemed like one of the toughest things in my life, at the time. Looking back, it was the best thing that could've happened because I wasn't ready to win the world title at that point. The way I'd acted and treated people was not good. I apologized to Clint and Jason and they were gracious enough to understand. In 2002, I won the World Championship. It was a terrific turnaround for me. Between 2001 and 2002 was a real learning experience.

You don't want to do things to people that you don't want done to you. It seems to me that every action has a consequence whether it's good or bad. In my opinion, the most important thing you can do is have faith in God and faith in yourself. Never give up on God and never give up on yourself, because neither one will ever let you down. If you ever give up, the party is over.

★ ★ ★

JAMES GHOLSON

★ ★ ★

Horses, cattle and ranching have been my life as long as I can remember. My first memories are being on horseback and having a strong ranching family. But things changed, and I grew up wild and a little "broncy."

The Lord chose me at an early age, and he has never forsaken me. He led me to the Matador Ranch to work, and there I met my wife and best friend of forty years. After the birth of our first son I gave up drinking, we started going to church and I found the joy and peace of my salvation.

Things changed again as I found myself out of God's will. I was really full of myself and the Lord said enough is enough. He got my full attention after a bad truck wreck and then a horse wreck. I thought I would quit drinking again and get back in church, but the Lord wanted all of me, not just part of me. After my wife, June, got really sick and I lost a very close friend all at the same time, I couldn't handle the load on my own. The Lord got me on my knees and I prayed not so much for myself, but for those I loved so much. I found peace beyond belief.

The Lord gave me two Scriptures that I go to over and over. Psalm 23 (page 366) is my mainstay. It shows me the Way.

The apostle Paul's words in Galatians (page 255) show me how I was and where I was headed: *"So I say, live by the Spirit, and you will not gratify the desires of the sinful nature. For the sinful nature desires what is contrary to the Spirit, and the Spirit what* is contrary to the sinful nature. They are in conflict with each other, so that you do not do what you want. But if you are led by the Spirit, you are not under law.

"The acts of the sinful nature are obvious: sexual immorality, impurity and debauchery; idolatry and witchcraft; hatred, discord, jealousy, fits of rage, selfish ambition, dissensions, factions and envy; drunkenness, orgies, and the like. I warn you, as I did before, that those who live like this will not inherit the kingdom of God.

"But the fruit of the Spirit is love, joy, peace, patience, kindness, goodness, faithfulness, gentleness and self-control. Against such things there is no law. Those who belong to Christ Jesus have crucified the sinful nature with its passions and desires. Since we live by the Spirit, let us keep in step with the Spirit."

★ ★ ★

© James Gholson

OLD CONCHO

I remember the day Old Concho died, I'd like to tell you
'bout it if I may.
'Cause it made me feel a little strange inside like I ain't
felt since that day.

We was alone there in the bunkhouse; he was sick and I
was achin'
From a bronc that throwed me the day before, about my
keen ridin' skills I was mistaken.

"Come over here son," he gravely said. And I listened to
his say.
'Bout all the things he'd done in life and what he'd like
to've done in his day.

He talked of open ranges. All the places that he'd
know'd.
The big outfits he'd ridden for from Montana to Old
Mexico.

He talked about the friends he'd lost in Germany in
the war.
A tear rolled down his wrinkled cheek, then he
paused and then named some more.

He asked me to read the Bible. Psalm 23 I believe.
"The Lord is my shepherd, I shall not want." And
then he took ahold of my sleeve.

And he said, "Son, let no man mock you when you pra
to Christ our Lord.
And look for all the answers in life within His holy
word."

"Oh ropin' skill and ridin's important here in this life
we live,
But as we travel this journey my son, there's something
more important to give."

"Oh, teach those skills to the young ones," he said, and
boy he'd sure taught me.
"But leave with them also the knowledge you have of
what Christ did for you and for me."

He breathed in deep a couple of times and then he sort
sighed.
Still clutchin' my arm but with a smile on his face, he
softly and quietly died.

I'll never forget the things he said and how he made m
feel that day.
And when it comes my time to cross the divide, I pray
I'll make a young puncher feel that way.

9 Look upon our shield,u O God;
   look with favor on your
   anointed one.

10 Better is one day in your courts
   than a thousand elsewhere;
   I would rather be a doorkeeper
   in the house of my God
   than dwell in the tents of the
   wicked.

11 For the LORD God is a sun and
   shield;
   the LORD bestows favor and
   honor;
   no good thing does he withhold
   from those whose walk is
   blameless.

12 O LORD Almighty,
   blessed is the man who trusts
   in you.

Psalm 85

For the director of music.
Of the Sons of Korah. A psalm.

1 You showed favor to your land,
   O LORD;
   you restored the fortunes of
   Jacob.

2 You forgave the iniquity of
   your people
   and covered all their sins.

Selah

3 You set aside all your wrath
   and turned from your fierce
   anger.

4 Restore us again, O God our
   Savior,
   and put away your
   displeasure toward us.

5 Will you be angry with us forever?
   Will you prolong your anger
   through all generations?

6 Will you not revive us again,
   that your people may rejoice
   in you?

7 Show us your unfailing love, O
   LORD,
   and grant us your salvation.

8 I will listen to what God the
   LORD will say;
   he promises peace to his
   people, his saints—
   but let them not return to
   folly.

9 Surely his salvation is near
   those who fear him,
   that his glory may dwell in
   our land.

10 Love and faithfulness meet
   together;
   righteousness and peace kiss
   each other.

11 Faithfulness springs forth from
   the earth,
   and righteousness looks
   down from heaven.

12 The LORD will indeed give
   what is good,
   and our land will yield its
   harvest.

13 Righteousness goes before him
   and prepares the way for his
   steps.

Psalm 86

A prayer of David.

1 Hear, O LORD, and answer me,
   for I am poor and needy.

2 Guard my life, for I am devoted
   to you.
   You are my God; save your
   servant
   who trusts in you.

3 Have mercy on me, O Lord,
   for I call to you all day long.

4 Bring joy to your servant,
   for to you, O Lord,
   I lift up my soul.

u 9 Or *sovereign*

5 You are forgiving and good, O
    Lord,
    abounding in love to all who
      call to you.
6 Hear my prayer, O LORD;
    listen to my cry for mercy.
7 In the day of my trouble I will
    call to you,
    for you will answer me.

8 Among the gods there is none
    like you, O Lord;
    no deeds can compare with
      yours.
9 All the nations you have made
    will come and worship before
      you, O Lord;
    they will bring glory to your
      name.
10 For you are great and do
    marvelous deeds;
    you alone are God.

11 Teach me your way, O LORD,
    and I will walk in your truth;
    give me an undivided heart,
    that I may fear your name.
12 I will praise you, O Lord my
    God, with all my heart;
    I will glorify your name
      forever.
13 For great is your love toward
    me;
    you have delivered me from
      the depths of the grave.ᵛ

14 The arrogant are attacking me,
    O God;
    a band of ruthless men seeks
      my life—
    men without regard for you.
15 But you, O Lord, are a
    compassionate and gracious
      God,
    slow to anger, abounding in
      love and faithfulness.

16 Turn to me and have mercy on
    me;
    grant your strength to your
      servant
    and save the son of your
      maidservant.ʷ
17 Give me a sign of your
    goodness,
    that my enemies may see it
    and be put to shame,
    for you, O LORD, have helped
      me and comforted me.

Psalm 87
Of the Sons of Korah. A psalm. A song.

1 He has set his foundation on
    the holy mountain;
2   the LORD loves the gates of
      Zion
    more than all the dwellings
      of Jacob.
3 Glorious things are said of you,
    O city of God: Selah
4 "I will record Rahabˣ and
      Babylon
    among those who
      acknowledge me—
    Philistia too, and Tyre, along
      with Cushʸ—
    and will say, 'Thisᶻ one was
      born in Zion.'"

5 Indeed, of Zion it will be said,
    "This one and that one were
      born in her,
    and the Most High himself
      will establish her."
6 The LORD will write in the
    register of the peoples:
    "This one was born in Zion."
                                      Selah
7 As they make music they will
    sing,
    "All my fountains are in you."

ᵛ 13 Hebrew *Sheol*   ʷ 16 Or *save your faithful son*   ˣ 4 A poetic name for Egypt
ʸ 4 *That is, the upper Nile region*   ᶻ 4 Or *"O Rahab and Babylon, / Philistia, Tyre and Cush,
/ I will record concerning those who acknowledge me: / 'This*

Psalm 88

A song. A psalm of the Sons of Korah.
For the director of music. According to
mahalath leannoth.[a] A *maskil*[b]
of Heman the Ezrahite.

1 O LORD, the God who saves me,
    day and night I cry out before
        you.
2 May my prayer come before you;
    turn your ear to my cry.

3 For my soul is full of trouble
    and my life draws near the
        grave.[c]
4 I am counted among those who
        go down to the pit;
    I am like a man without
        strength.
5 I am set apart with the dead,
    like the slain who lie in the
        grave,
    whom you remember no more,
    who are cut off from your care.

6 You have put me in the lowest
        pit,
    in the darkest depths.
7 Your wrath lies heavily upon
        me;
    you have overwhelmed me
        with all your waves.   Selah
8 You have taken from me my
        closest friends
    and have made me repulsive
        to them.
    I am confined and cannot es-
        cape;
9   my eyes are dim with grief.

    I call to you, O LORD, every day;
    I spread out my hands to you.
10 Do you show your wonders to
        the dead?
    Do those who are dead rise
        up and praise you?   Selah

11 Is your love declared in the grave,
    your faithfulness in
        Destruction[d]?
12 Are your wonders known in
        the place of darkness,
    or your righteous deeds in
        the land of oblivion?

13 But I cry to you for help, O LORD;
    in the morning my prayer
        comes before you.
14 Why, O LORD, do you reject me
    and hide your face from me?

15 From my youth I have been
        afflicted and close to death;
    I have suffered your terrors
        and am in despair.
16 Your wrath has swept over me;
    your terrors have destroyed me.
17 All day long they surround me
        like a flood;
    they have completely
        engulfed me.
18 You have taken my companions
        and loved ones from me;
    the darkness is my closest
        friend.

Psalm 89

A *maskil*[e] of Ethan the Ezrahite.

1 I will sing of the LORD's great
        love forever;
    with my mouth I will make
        your faithfulness known
        through all generations.
2 I will declare that your love
        stands firm forever,
    that you established your
        faithfulness in heaven itself.

3 You said, "I have made a
        covenant with my chosen
        one,
    I have sworn to David my
        servant,

---

[a] Title: Possibly a tune, "The Suffering of Affliction"   [b] Title: Probably a literary or
musical term   [c] 3 Hebrew *Sheol*   [d] 11 Hebrew *Abaddon*   [e] Title: Probably a literary
or musical term

4 'I will establish your line forever
    and make your throne firm
        through all generations.'"
                                    Selah

5 The heavens praise your
        wonders, O LORD,
    your faithfulness too, in the
        assembly of the holy ones.
6 For who in the skies above can
        compare with the LORD?
    Who is like the LORD among
        the heavenly beings?
7 In the council of the holy ones
        God is greatly feared;
    he is more awesome than all
        who surround him.
8 O LORD God Almighty, who is
        like you?
    You are mighty, O LORD, and
        your faithfulness surrounds
        you.

9 You rule over the surging sea;
    when its waves mount up,
        you still them.
10 You crushed Rahab like one of
        the slain;
    with your strong arm you
        scattered your enemies.
11 The heavens are yours, and
        yours also the earth;
    you founded the world and
        all that is in it.
12 You created the north and the
        south;
    Tabor and Hermon sing for
        joy at your name.
13 Your arm is endued with power;
    your hand is strong, your
        right hand exalted.

14 Righteousness and justice are the
        foundation of your throne;
    love and faithfulness go
        before you.

15 Blessed are those who have
        learned to acclaim you,
    who walk in the light of your
        presence, O LORD.
16 They rejoice in your name all
        day long;
    they exult in your
        righteousness.
17 For you are their glory and
        strength,
    and by your favor you exalt
        our horn.*f*
18 Indeed, our shield*g* belongs to
        the LORD,
    our king to the Holy One of
        Israel.

19 Once you spoke in a vision,
    to your faithful people you said:
    "I have bestowed strength on a
        warrior;
    I have exalted a young man
        from among the people.
20 I have found David my servant;
    with my sacred oil I have
        anointed him.
21 My hand will sustain him;
    surely my arm will strengthen
        him.
22 No enemy will subject him to
        tribute;
    no wicked man will oppress
        him.
23 I will crush his foes before him
    and strike down his
        adversaries.
24 My faithful love will be with
        him,
    and through my name his
        horn*h* will be exalted.
25 I will set his hand over the sea,
    his right hand over the rivers.
26 He will call out to me, 'You are
        my Father,
    my God, the Rock my Savior.'

---

f 17 *Horn* here symbolizes strong one.   *g* 18 Or *sovereign*   *h* 24 *Horn* here symbolizes
strength.

27 I will also appoint him my
   firstborn,
    the most exalted of the kings
       of the earth.
28 I will maintain my love to him
   forever,
    and my covenant with him
       will never fail.
29 I will establish his line forever,
    his throne as long as the
       heavens endure.

30 "If his sons forsake my law
    and do not follow my statutes,
31 if they violate my decrees
    and fail to keep my commands,
32 I will punish their sin with the
   rod,
    their iniquity with flogging;
33 but I will not take my love
    from him,
    nor will I ever betray my
       faithfulness.
34 I will not violate my covenant
    or alter what my lips have
       uttered.
35 Once for all, I have sworn by
    my holiness—
    and I will not lie to David—
36 that his line will continue
   forever
    and his throne endure before
       me like the sun;
37 it will be established forever
    like the moon,
    the faithful witness in the
       sky."   Selah

38 But you have rejected, you
    have spurned,
    you have been very angry
       with your anointed one.
39 You have renounced the
    covenant with your servant
    and have defiled his crown in
       the dust.

40 You have broken through all
    his walls
    and reduced his strongholds
       to ruins.
41 All who pass by have
    plundered him;
    he has become the scorn of
       his neighbors.
42 You have exalted the right
    hand of his foes;
    you have made all his
       enemies rejoice.
43 You have turned back the edge
    of his sword
    and have not supported him
       in battle.
44 You have put an end to his
    splendor
    and cast his throne to the
       ground.
45 You have cut short the days of
    his youth;
    you have covered him with a
       mantle of shame.   Selah

46 How long, O LORD? Will you
    hide yourself forever?
    How long will your wrath
       burn like fire?
47 Remember how fleeting is my
    life.
    For what futility you have
       created all men!
48 What man can live and not see
    death,
    or save himself from the
       power of the grave^i ?   Selah
49 O Lord, where is your former
    great love,
    which in your faithfulness
       you swore to David?
50 Remember, Lord, how your
    servant has^j been mocked,
    how I bear in my heart the
       taunts of all the nations,

---

i 48 Hebrew *Sheol*   *j 50* Or *your servants have*

51 the taunts with which your
enemies have mocked, O
LORD,
  with which they have mocked
  every step of your anointed
  one.

52 Praise be to the LORD forever!
Amen and Amen.

BOOK IV

Psalms 90-106

Psalm 90

A prayer of Moses the man of God.

1 Lord, you have been our dwelling place
  throughout all generations.
2 Before the mountains were born
  or you brought forth the
  earth and the world,
  from everlasting to
  everlasting you are God.

3 You turn men back to dust,
  saying, "Return to dust, O
  sons of men."
4 For a thousand years in your
sight
  are like a day that has just
  gone by,
  or like a watch in the night.
5 You sweep men away in the
sleep of death;
  they are like the new grass of
  the morning—
6 though in the morning it
springs up new,
  by evening it is dry and
  withered.

7 We are consumed by your anger
  and terrified by your
  indignation.
8 You have set our iniquities
  before you,

  our secret sins in the light of
  your presence.
9 All our days pass away under
your wrath;
  we finish our years with a
  moan.
10 The length of our days is
seventy years—
  or eighty, if we have the
  strength;
  yet their span[k] is but trouble
  and sorrow,
  for they quickly pass, and we
  fly away.

11 Who knows the power of your
anger?
  For your wrath is as great as
  the fear that is due you.
12 Teach us to number our days
aright,
  that we may gain a heart of
  wisdom.

13 Relent, O LORD! How long will
it be?
  Have compassion on your
  servants.
14 Satisfy us in the morning with
  your unfailing love,
  that we may sing for joy and
  be glad all our days.
15 Make us glad for as many days
  as you have afflicted us,
  for as many years as we have
  seen trouble.
16 May your deeds be shown to
  your servants,
  your splendor to their
  children.
17 May the favor[l] of the Lord our
God rest upon us;
  establish the work of our
  hands for us—
  yes, establish the work of our
  hands.

k 10 Or yet the best of them   l 17 Or beauty

Psalm 91

1 He who dwells in the shelter of
the Most High
will rest in the shadow of the
Almighty.[m]
2 I will say[n] of the LORD, "He is
my refuge and my fortress,
my God, in whom I trust."

3 Surely he will save you from
the fowler's snare
and from the deadly pestilence.
4 He will cover you with his
feathers,
and under his wings you will
find refuge;
his faithfulness will be your
shield and rampart.
5 You will not fear the terror of
night,
nor the arrow that flies by day,
6 nor the pestilence that stalks in
the darkness,
nor the plague that destroys
at midday.
7 A thousand may fall at your
side,
ten thousand at your right
hand,
but it will not come near you.
8 You will only observe with your
eyes
and see the punishment of
the wicked.

9 If you make the Most High
your dwelling —
even the LORD, who is my
refuge —
10 then no harm will befall you,
no disaster will come near
your tent.
11 For he will command his angels
concerning you
to guard you in all your ways;

12 they will lift you up in their
hands,
so that you will not strike
your foot against a stone.
13 You will tread upon the lion
and the cobra;
you will trample the great
lion and the serpent.

14 "Because he loves me," says the
LORD, "I will rescue him;
I will protect him, for he
acknowledges my name.
15 He will call upon me, and I will
answer him;
I will be with him in trouble,
I will deliver him and honor
him.
16 With long life will I satisfy him
and show him my salvation."

Psalm 92

A psalm. A song. For the Sabbath day.

1 It is good to praise the LORD
and make music to your
name, O Most High,
2 to proclaim your love in the
morning
and your faithfulness at night,
3 to the music of the ten-stringed
lyre
and the melody of the harp.

4 For you make me glad by your
deeds, O LORD;
I sing for joy at the works of
your hands.
5 How great are your works, O
LORD,
how profound your thoughts!
6 The senseless man does not know,
fools do not understand,
7 that though the wicked spring
up like grass
and all evildoers flourish,
they will be forever destroyed.

---

m 1 Hebrew *Shaddai*   n 2 Or *He says*

8 But you, O LORD, are exalted
forever.

9 For surely your enemies, O LORD,
surely your enemies will
perish;
all evildoers will be scattered.
10 You have exalted my horn[o] like
that of a wild ox;
fine oils have been poured
upon me.
11 My eyes have seen the defeat
of my adversaries;
my ears have heard the rout
of my wicked foes.

12 The righteous will flourish like
a palm tree,
they will grow like a cedar of
Lebanon;
13 planted in the house of the LORD,
they will flourish in the
courts of our God.
14 They will still bear fruit in old
age,
they will stay fresh and green,
15 proclaiming, "The LORD is
upright;
he is my Rock, and there is
no wickedness in him."

Psalm 93

1 The LORD reigns, he is robed in
majesty;
the LORD is robed in majesty
and is armed with strength.
The world is firmly established;
it cannot be moved.
2 Your throne was established
long ago;
you are from all eternity.

3 The seas have lifted up, O LORD,
the seas have lifted up their
voice;
the seas have lifted up their
pounding waves.

4 Mightier than the thunder of
the great waters,
mightier than the breakers of
the sea —
the LORD on high is mighty.

5 Your statutes stand firm;
holiness adorns your house
for endless days, O LORD.

Psalm 94

1 O LORD, the God who avenges,
O God who avenges, shine
forth.
2 Rise up, O Judge of the earth;
pay back to the proud what
they deserve.
3 How long will the wicked, O
LORD,
how long will the wicked be
jubilant?

4 They pour out arrogant words;
all the evildoers are full of
boasting.
5 They crush your people, O LORD;
they oppress your inheritance.
6 They slay the widow and the
alien;
they murder the fatherless.
7 They say, "The LORD does not
see;
the God of Jacob pays no
heed."

8 Take heed, you senseless ones
among the people;
you fools, when will you
become wise?
9 Does he who implanted the ear
not hear?
Does he who formed the eye
not see?
10 Does he who disciplines
nations not punish?
Does he who teaches man
lack knowledge?

---

o 10 Horn here symbolizes strength.

11 The LORD knows the thoughts
of man;
he knows that they are futile.

12 Blessed is the man you
discipline, O LORD,
the man you teach from your
law;

13 you grant him relief from days
of trouble,
till a pit is dug for the wicked.

14 For the LORD will not reject his
people;
he will never forsake his
inheritance.

15 Judgment will again be
founded on righteousness,
and all the upright in heart
will follow it.

16 Who will rise up for me against
the wicked?
Who will take a stand for me
against evildoers?

17 Unless the LORD had given me
help,
I would soon have dwelt in
the silence of death.

18 When I said, "My foot is
slipping,"
your love, O LORD, supported
me.

19 When anxiety was great within
me,
your consolation brought joy
to my soul.

20 Can a corrupt throne be allied
with you—
one that brings on misery by
its decrees?

21 They band together against the
righteous
and condemn the innocent to
death.

22 But the LORD has become my
fortress,

and my God the rock in
whom I take refuge.

23 He will repay them for their
sins
and destroy them for their
wickedness;
the LORD our God will
destroy them.

Psalm 95

1 Come, let us sing for joy to the
LORD;
let us shout aloud to the Rock
of our salvation.

2 Let us come before him with
thanksgiving
and extol him with music and
song.

3 For the LORD is the great God,
the great King above all gods.

4 In his hand are the depths of
the earth,
and the mountain peaks
belong to him.

5 The sea is his, for he made it,
and his hands formed the dry
land.

6 Come, let us bow down in
worship,
let us kneel before the LORD
our Maker;

7 for he is our God
and we are the people of his
pasture,
the flock under his care.

Today, if you hear his voice,
8 do not harden your hearts as
you did at Meribah,p
as you did that day at
Massahq in the desert,

9 where your fathers tested and
tried me,
though they had seen what I
did.

p 8 Meribah means quarreling.   q 8 Massah means testing.

10 For forty years I was angry
with that generation;
I said, "They are a people
whose hearts go astray,
and they have not known my
ways."
11 So I declared on oath in my anger,
"They shall never enter my
rest."

Psalm 96

1 Sing to the LORD a new song;
sing to the LORD, all the earth.
2 Sing to the LORD, praise his name;
proclaim his salvation day
after day.
3 Declare his glory among the
nations,
his marvelous deeds among
all peoples.

4 For great is the LORD and most
worthy of praise;
he is to be feared above all
gods.
5 For all the gods of the nations
are idols,
but the LORD made the
heavens.
6 Splendor and majesty are
before him;
strength and glory are in his
sanctuary.

7 Ascribe to the LORD, O families
of nations,
ascribe to the LORD glory and
strength.
8 Ascribe to the LORD the glory
due his name;
bring an offering and come
into his courts.
9 Worship the LORD in the
splendor of hisʳ holiness;
tremble before him, all the
earth.

10 Say among the nations, "The
LORD reigns."
The world is firmly established,
it cannot be moved;
he will judge the peoples
with equity.
11 Let the heavens rejoice, let the
earth be glad;
let the sea resound, and all
that is in it;
12 let the fields be jubilant, and
everything in them.
Then all the trees of the forest
will sing for joy;
13 they will sing before the
LORD, for he comes,
he comes to judge the earth.
He will judge the world in
righteousness
and the peoples in his truth.

Psalm 97

1 The LORD reigns, let the earth
be glad;
let the distant shores rejoice.

2 Clouds and thick darkness
surround him;
righteousness and justice are
the foundation of his throne.
3 Fire goes before him
and consumes his foes on
every side.
4 His lightning lights up the world;
the earth sees and trembles.
5 The mountains melt like wax
before the LORD,
before the Lord of all the earth.
6 The heavens proclaim his
righteousness,
and all the peoples see his glory.

7 All who worship images are
put to shame,
those who boast in idols—
worship him, all you gods!

ʳ 9 Or LORD with the splendor of

8 Zion hears and rejoices
    and the villages of Judah are
        glad
  because of your judgments, O
        LORD.
9 For you, O LORD, are the Most
        High over all the earth;
  you are exalted far above all
        gods.
10 Let those who love the LORD
        hate evil,
  for he guards the lives of his
        faithful ones
    and delivers them from the
        hand of the wicked.
11 Light is shed upon the righteous
    and joy on the upright in
        heart.
12 Rejoice in the LORD, you who
        are righteous,
    and praise his holy name.

Psalm 98
A psalm.

1 Sing to the LORD a new song,
    for he has done marvelous
        things;
  his right hand and his holy arm
    have worked salvation for him.
2 The LORD has made his
        salvation known
    and revealed his
        righteousness to the nations.
3 He has remembered his love
    and his faithfulness to the
        house of Israel;
  all the ends of the earth have
        seen
    the salvation of our God.

4 Shout for joy to the LORD, all
        the earth,
  burst into jubilant song with
        music;
5 make music to the LORD with
        the harp,
  with the harp and the sound
        of singing,

6 with trumpets and the blast of
        the ram's horn—
  shout for joy before the
        LORD, the King.

7 Let the sea resound, and
        everything in it,
    the world, and all who live in it.
8 Let the rivers clap their hands,
    let the mountains sing
        together for joy;
9 let them sing before the LORD,
    for he comes to judge the earth.
  He will judge the world in
        righteousness
    and the peoples with equity.

Psalm 99

1 The LORD reigns,
    let the nations tremble;
  he sits enthroned between the
        cherubim,
    let the earth shake.
2 Great is the LORD in Zion;
    he is exalted over all the
        nations.
3 Let them praise your great and
        awesome name—
    he is holy.

4 The King is mighty, he loves
        justice—
  you have established equity;
  in Jacob you have done
    what is just and right.
5 Exalt the LORD our God
    and worship at his footstool;
    he is holy.

6 Moses and Aaron were among
        his priests,
  Samuel was among those
        who called on his name;
  they called on the LORD
    and he answered them.
7 He spoke to them from the
        pillar of cloud;
  they kept his statutes and the
        decrees he gave them.

8 O LORD our God,
    you answered them;
    you were to Israel[s] a forgiving
        God,
    though you punished their
        misdeeds.[t]
9 Exalt the LORD our God
    and worship at his holy
        mountain,
    for the LORD our God is holy.

Psalm 100

A psalm. For giving thanks.

1 Shout for joy to the LORD, all
    the earth.
2 Worship the LORD with glad-
    ness;
    come before him with joyful
        songs.
3 Know that the LORD is God.
    It is he who made us, and we
        are his[u];
    we are his people, the sheep
        of his pasture.
4 Enter his gates with thanksgiving
    and his courts with praise;
    give thanks to him and praise
        his name.
5 For the LORD is good and his
    love endures forever;
    his faithfulness continues
        through all generations.

Psalm 101

Of David. A psalm.

1 I will sing of your love and jus-
    tice;
    to you, O LORD, I will sing
        praise.
2 I will be careful to lead a
    blameless life—
    when will you come to me?

I will walk in my house
    with blameless heart.

3 I will set before my eyes
    no vile thing.

The deeds of faithless men I hate;
    they will not cling to me.
4 Men of perverse heart shall be
    far from me;
    I will have nothing to do with
        evil.

5 Whoever slanders his neighbor
    in secret,
    him will I put to silence;
    whoever has haughty eyes and
        a proud heart,
    him will I not endure.

6 My eyes will be on the faithful
    in the land,
    that they may dwell with me;
    he whose walk is blameless
    will minister to me.

7 No one who practices deceit
    will dwell in my house;
    no one who speaks falsely
    will stand in my presence.

8 Every morning I will put to silence
    all the wicked in the land;
    I will cut off every evildoer
    from the city of the LORD.

Psalm 102

A prayer of an afflicted man. When he is
faint and pours out his lament
before the LORD.

1 Hear my prayer, O LORD;
    let my cry for help come to
        you.
2 Do not hide your face from me
    when I am in distress.
    Turn your ear to me;
    when I call, answer me quickly.
3 For my days vanish like smoke;
    my bones burn like glowing
        embers.

---

s 8 Hebrew *them* t 8 Or *I an avenger of the wrongs done to them* u 3 Or *and not we
ourselves*

4 My heart is blighted and
    withered like grass;
  I forget to eat my food.
5 Because of my loud groaning
  I am reduced to skin and
    bones.
6 I am like a desert owl,
  like an owl among the ruins.
7 I lie awake; I have become
  like a bird alone on a roof.
8 All day long my enemies taunt
    me;
  those who rail against me use
    my name as a curse.
9 For I eat ashes as my food
  and mingle my drink with
    tears
10 because of your great wrath,
  for you have taken me up
    and thrown me aside.
11 My days are like the evening
    shadow;
  I wither away like grass.

12 But you, O LORD, sit enthroned
    forever;
  your renown endures
    through all generations.
13 You will arise and have
    compassion on Zion,
  for it is time to show favor to
    her;
  the appointed time has come.
14 For her stones are dear to your
    servants;
  her very dust moves them to
    pity.
15 The nations will fear the name
    of the LORD,
  all the kings of the earth will
    revere your glory.
16 For the LORD will rebuild Zion
  and appear in his glory.
17 He will respond to the prayer
    of the destitute;
  he will not despise their plea.

18 Let this be written for a future
    generation,
  that a people not yet created
    may praise the LORD:
19 "The LORD looked down from
    his sanctuary on high,
  from heaven he viewed the
    earth,
20 to hear the groans of the
    prisoners
  and release those condemned
    to death."
21 So the name of the LORD will
    be declared in Zion
  and his praise in Jerusalem
22 when the peoples and the
    kingdoms
  assemble to worship the
    LORD.

23 In the course of my life[v] he
    broke my strength;
  he cut short my days.
24 So I said:
  "Do not take me away, O my
    God, in the midst of my
    days;
  your years go on through all
    generations.
25 In the beginning you laid the
    foundations of the earth,
  and the heavens are the work
    of your hands.
26 They will perish, but you
    remain;
  they will all wear out like a
    garment.
  Like clothing you will change
    them
  and they will be discarded.
27 But you remain the same,
  and your years will never end.
28 The children of your servants
    will live in your presence;
  their descendants will be
    established before you."

v 23 Or By his power

Psalm 103

Of David.

1 Praise the LORD, O my soul;
  all my inmost being, praise
    his holy name.
2 Praise the LORD, O my soul,
  and forget not all his benefits—
3 who forgives all your sins
  and heals all your diseases,
4 who redeems your life from the
    pit
  and crowns you with love
    and compassion,
5 who satisfies your desires with
    good things
  so that your youth is renewed
    like the eagle's.

6 The LORD works righteousness
  and justice for all the
    oppressed.

7 He made known his ways to
    Moses,
  his deeds to the people of Israel:
8 The LORD is compassionate
    and gracious,
  slow to anger, abounding in
    love.
9 He will not always accuse,
  nor will he harbor his anger
    forever;
10 he does not treat us as our sins
    deserve
  or repay us according to our
    iniquities.
11 For as high as the heavens are
    above the earth,
  so great is his love for those
    who fear him;
12 as far as the east is from the
    west,
  so far has he removed our
    transgressions from us.
13 As a father has compassion on
    his children,
  so the LORD has compassion
    on those who fear him;

14 for he knows how we are formed,
  he remembers that we are dust.
15 As for man, his days are like grass,
  he flourishes like a flower of
    the field;
16 the wind blows over it and it is
    gone,
  and its place remembers it no
    more.
17 But from everlasting to
    everlasting
  the LORD's love is with those
    who fear him,
  and his righteousness with
    their children's children—
18 with those who keep his covenant
  and remember to obey his
    precepts.

19 The LORD has established his
    throne in heaven,
  and his kingdom rules over all.

20 Praise the LORD, you his angels,
  you mighty ones who do his
    bidding,
  who obey his word.
21 Praise the LORD, all his
    heavenly hosts,
  you his servants who do his
    will.
22 Praise the LORD, all his works
  everywhere in his dominion.

  Praise the LORD, O my soul.

Psalm 104

1 Praise the LORD, O my soul.

  O LORD my God, you are very
    great;
  you are clothed with splendor
    and majesty.
2 He wraps himself in light as
    with a garment;
  he stretches out the heavens
    like a tent
3   and lays the beams of his
    upper chambers on their
    waters.

He makes the clouds his chariot
    and rides on the wings of the
    wind.
4 He makes winds his messengers,[w]
    flames of fire his servants.

5 He set the earth on its
    foundations;
    it can never be moved.
6 You covered it with the deep as
    with a garment;
    the waters stood above the
    mountains.
7 But at your rebuke the waters
    fled,
    at the sound of your thunder
    they took to flight;
8 they flowed over the mountains,
    they went down into the
    valleys,
    to the place you assigned for
    them.
9 You set a boundary they cannot
    cross;
    never again will they cover
    the earth.

10 He makes springs pour water
    into the ravines;
    it flows between the
    mountains.
11 They give water to all the
    beasts of the field;
    the wild donkeys quench
    their thirst.
12 The birds of the air nest by the
    waters;
    they sing among the branches.
13 He waters the mountains from
    his upper chambers;
    the earth is satisfied by the
    fruit of his work.
14 He makes grass grow for the
    cattle,
    and plants for man to
    cultivate—

bringing forth food from the
    earth:
15 wine that gladdens the heart of
    man,
    oil to make his face shine,
    and bread that sustains his
    heart.
16 The trees of the LORD are well
    watered,
    the cedars of Lebanon that he
    planted.
17 There the birds make their nests;
    the stork has its home in the
    pine trees.
18 The high mountains belong to
    the wild goats;
    the crags are a refuge for the
    coneys.[x]

19 The moon marks off the seasons,
    and the sun knows when to
    go down.
20 You bring darkness, it becomes
    night,
    and all the beasts of the
    forest prowl.
21 The lions roar for their prey
    and seek their food from God.
22 The sun rises, and they steal
    away;
    they return and lie down in
    their dens.
23 Then man goes out to his work,
    to his labor until evening.

24 How many are your works, O
    LORD!
    In wisdom you made them all;
    the earth is full of your
    creatures.
25 There is the sea, vast and
    spacious,
    teeming with creatures
    beyond number—
    living things both large and
    small.

w 4 Or angels   x 18 That is, the hyrax or rock badger

26 There the ships go to and fro,
and the leviathan, which you
formed to frolic there.

27 These all look to you
to give them their food at the
proper time.

28 When you give it to them,
they gather it up;
when you open your hand,
they are satisfied with good
things.

29 When you hide your face,
they are terrified;
when you take away their
breath,
they die and return to the
dust.

30 When you send your Spirit,
they are created,
and you renew the face of the
earth.

31 May the glory of the LORD
endure forever;
may the LORD rejoice in his
works—

32 he who looks at the earth, and
it trembles,
who touches the mountains,
and they smoke.

33 I will sing to the LORD all my
life;
I will sing praise to my God
as long as I live.

34 May my meditation be pleasing
to him,
as I rejoice in the LORD.

35 But may sinners vanish from
the earth
and the wicked be no more.

Praise the LORD, O my soul.

Praise the LORD.y

Psalm 105

1 Give thanks to the LORD, call on
his name;
make known among the
nations what he has done.

2 Sing to him, sing praise to him;
tell of all his wonderful acts.

3 Glory in his holy name;
let the hearts of those who
seek the LORD rejoice.

4 Look to the LORD and his
strength;
seek his face always.

5 Remember the wonders he has
done,
his miracles, and the
judgments he pronounced,

6 O descendants of Abraham his
servant,
O sons of Jacob, his chosen
ones.

7 He is the LORD our God;
his judgments are in all the
earth.

8 He remembers his covenant
forever,
the word he commanded, for
a thousand generations,

9 the covenant he made with
Abraham,
the oath he swore to Isaac.

10 He confirmed it to Jacob as a
decree,
to Israel as an everlasting
covenant:

11 "To you I will give the land of
Canaan
as the portion you will
inherit."

12 When they were but few in
number,
few indeed, and strangers in
it,

y 35 Hebrew *Hallelu Yah*; in the Septuagint this line stands at the beginning of Psalm 105.

13 they wandered from nation to
        nation,
     from one kingdom to another.
14 He allowed no one to oppress
        them;
     for their sake he rebuked
        kings:
15 "Do not touch my anointed
        ones;
     do my prophets no harm."
16 He called down famine on the
        land
     and destroyed all their
        supplies of food;
17 and he sent a man before
        them—
     Joseph, sold as a slave.
18 They bruised his feet with
        shackles,
     his neck was put in irons,
19 till what he foretold came to
        pass,
     till the word of the LORD
        proved him true.
20 The king sent and released him,
     the ruler of peoples set him
        free.
21 He made him master of his
        household,
     ruler over all he possessed,
22 to instruct his princes as he
        pleased
     and teach his elders wisdom.
23 Then Israel entered Egypt;
     Jacob lived as an alien in the
        land of Ham.
24 The LORD made his people very
        fruitful;
     he made them too numerous
        for their foes,
25 whose hearts he turned to hate
        his people,
     to conspire against his
        servants.
26 He sent Moses his servant,
     and Aaron, whom he had
        chosen.

27 They performed his miraculous
        signs among them,
     his wonders in the land of
        Ham.
28 He sent darkness and made the
        land dark—
     for had they not rebelled
        against his words?
29 He turned their waters into
        blood,
     causing their fish to die.
30 Their land teemed with frogs,
     which went up into the
        bedrooms of their rulers.
31 He spoke, and there came
        swarms of flies,
     and gnats throughout their
        country.
32 He turned their rain into hail,
     with lightning throughout
        their land;
33 he struck down their vines and
        fig trees
     and shattered the trees of
        their country.
34 He spoke, and the locusts came,
     grasshoppers without
        number;
35 they ate up every green thing
        in their land,
     ate up the produce of their
        soil.
36 Then he struck down all the
        firstborn in their land,
     the firstfruits of all their
        manhood.
37 He brought out Israel, laden
        with silver and gold,
     and from among their tribes
        no one faltered.
38 Egypt was glad when they left,
     because dread of Israel had
        fallen on them.
39 He spread out a cloud as a
        covering,
     and a fire to give light at
        night.

40 They asked, and he brought
   them quail
   and satisfied them with the
   bread of heaven.
41 He opened the rock, and water
   gushed out;
   like a river it flowed in the
   desert.

42 For he remembered his holy
   promise
   given to his servant Abraham.
43 He brought out his people with
   rejoicing,
   his chosen ones with shouts
   of joy;
44 he gave them the lands of the
   nations,
   and they fell heir to what
   others had toiled for—
45 that they might keep his precepts
   and observe his laws.

   Praise the LORD.[z]

Psalm 106

1 Praise the LORD.[a]

Give thanks to the LORD, for he
   is good;
   his love endures forever.
2 Who can proclaim the mighty
   acts of the LORD
   or fully declare his praise?
3 Blessed are they who maintain
   justice,
   who constantly do what is
   right.

4 Remember me, O LORD, when
   you show favor to your
   people,
   come to my aid when you
   save them,
5 that I may enjoy the prosperity
   of your chosen ones,

that I may share in the joy of
   your nation
   and join your inheritance in
   giving praise.

6 We have sinned, even as our
   fathers did;
   we have done wrong and
   acted wickedly.
7 When our fathers were in Egypt,
   they gave no thought to your
   miracles;
   they did not remember your
   many kindnesses,
   and they rebelled by the sea,
   the Red Sea.[b]
8 Yet he saved them for his
   name's sake,
   to make his mighty power
   known.
9 He rebuked the Red Sea, and it
   dried up;
   he led them through the
   depths as through a desert.
10 He saved them from the hand
   of the foe;
   from the hand of the enemy
   he redeemed them.
11 The waters covered their
   adversaries;
   not one of them survived.
12 Then they believed his promises
   and sang his praise.

13 But they soon forgot what he
   had done
   and did not wait for his counsel.
14 In the desert they gave in to
   their craving;
   in the wasteland they put
   God to the test.
15 So he gave them what they
   asked for,
   but sent a wasting disease
   upon them.

---

z 45 Hebrew *Hallelu Yah*   a 1 Hebrew *Hallelu Yah*; also in verse 48   b 7 Hebrew *Yam Suph*; that is, Sea of Reeds; also in verses 9 and 22

16 In the camp they grew envious of Moses
and of Aaron, who was consecrated to the LORD.
17 The earth opened up and swallowed Dathan;
it buried the company of Abiram.
18 Fire blazed among their followers;
a flame consumed the wicked.
19 At Horeb they made a calf and worshiped an idol cast from metal.
20 They exchanged their Glory for an image of a bull, which eats grass.
21 They forgot the God who saved them,
who had done great things in Egypt,
22 miracles in the land of Ham and awesome deeds by the Red Sea.
23 So he said he would destroy them—
had not Moses, his chosen one, stood in the breach before him
to keep his wrath from destroying them.
24 Then they despised the pleasant land;
they did not believe his promise.
25 They grumbled in their tents and did not obey the LORD.
26 So he swore to them with uplifted hand
that he would make them fall in the desert,
27 make their descendants fall among the nations
and scatter them throughout the lands.

28 They yoked themselves to the Baal of Peor
and ate sacrifices offered to lifeless gods;
29 they provoked the LORD to anger by their wicked deeds,
and a plague broke out among them.
30 But Phinehas stood up and intervened,
and the plague was checked.
31 This was credited to him as righteousness
for endless generations to come.
32 By the waters of Meribah they angered the LORD,
and trouble came to Moses because of them;
33 for they rebelled against the Spirit of God,
and rash words came from Moses' lips.c
34 They did not destroy the peoples as the LORD had commanded them,
35 but they mingled with the nations and adopted their customs.
36 They worshiped their idols, which became a snare to them.
37 They sacrificed their sons and their daughters to demons.
38 They shed innocent blood, the blood of their sons and daughters,
whom they sacrificed to the idols of Canaan,
and the land was desecrated by their blood.
39 They defiled themselves by what they did;
by their deeds they prostituted themselves.

---

c 33 Or against his spirit, / and rash words came from his lips

40 Therefore the LORD was angry
   with his people
   and abhorred his inheritance.
41 He handed them over to the
   nations,
   and their foes ruled over them.
42 Their enemies oppressed them
   and subjected them to their
   power.
43 Many times he delivered them,
   but they were bent on rebellion
   and they wasted away in
   their sin.

44 But he took note of their distress
   when he heard their cry;
45 for their sake he remembered
   his covenant
   and out of his great love he
   relented.
46 He caused them to be pitied
   by all who held them captive.

47 Save us, O LORD our God,
   and gather us from the nations,
   that we may give thanks to
   your holy name
   and glory in your praise.

48 Praise be to the LORD, the God
   of Israel,
   from everlasting to everlasting.
   Let all the people say, "Amen!"

   Praise the LORD.

BOOK V

Psalms 107-150

Psalm 107

1 Give thanks to the LORD, for he
  is good;
  his love endures forever.
2 Let the redeemed of the LORD
  say this—
  those he redeemed from the
  hand of the foe,

3 those he gathered from the
  lands,
  from east and west, from
  north and south.d
4 Some wandered in desert
  wastelands,
  finding no way to a city
  where they could settle.
5 They were hungry and thirsty,
  and their lives ebbed away.
6 Then they cried out to the
  LORD in their trouble,
  and he delivered them from
  their distress.
7 He led them by a straight way
  to a city where they could
  settle.
8 Let them give thanks to the
  LORD for his unfailing love
  and his wonderful deeds for
  men,
9 for he satisfies the thirsty
  and fills the hungry with
  good things.

10 Some sat in darkness and the
   deepest gloom,
   prisoners suffering in iron
   chains,
11 for they had rebelled against
   the words of God
   and despised the counsel of
   the Most High.
12 So he subjected them to bitter
   labor;
   they stumbled, and there was
   no one to help.
13 Then they cried to the LORD in
   their trouble,
   and he saved them from their
   distress.
14 He brought them out of
   darkness and the deepest
   gloom
   and broke away their chains.

d 3 Hebrew *north and the sea*

15 Let them give thanks to the
   LORD for his unfailing love
   and his wonderful deeds for
   men,
16 for he breaks down gates of
   bronze
   and cuts through bars of iron.

17 Some became fools through
   their rebellious ways
   and suffered affliction
   because of their iniquities.
18 They loathed all food
   and drew near the gates of
   death.
19 Then they cried to the LORD in
   their trouble,
   and he saved them from their
   distress.
20 He sent forth his word and
   healed them;
   he rescued them from the
   grave.
21 Let them give thanks to the
   LORD for his unfailing love
   and his wonderful deeds for
   men.
22 Let them sacrifice thank
   offerings
   and tell of his works with
   songs of joy.

23 Others went out on the sea in
   ships;
   they were merchants on the
   mighty waters.
24 They saw the works of the
   LORD,
   his wonderful deeds in the
   deep.
25 For he spoke and stirred up a
   tempest
   that lifted high the waves.
26 They mounted up to the
   heavens and went down to
   the depths;
   in their peril their courage
   melted away.

27 They reeled and staggered like
   drunken men;
   they were at their wits' end.
28 Then they cried out to the
   LORD in their trouble,
   and he brought them out of
   their distress.
29 He stilled the storm to a whisper;
   the waves of the sea were
   hushed.
30 They were glad when it grew
   calm,
   and he guided them to their
   desired haven.
31 Let them give thanks to the
   LORD for his unfailing love
   and his wonderful deeds for
   men.
32 Let them exalt him in the
   assembly of the people
   and praise him in the council
   of the elders.

33 He turned rivers into a desert,
   flowing springs into thirsty
   ground,
34 and fruitful land into a salt waste,
   because of the wickedness of
   those who lived there.
35 He turned the desert into pools
   of water
   and the parched ground into
   flowing springs;
36 there he brought the hungry to
   live,
   and they founded a city
   where they could settle.
37 They sowed fields and planted
   vineyards
   that yielded a fruitful harvest;
38 he blessed them, and their
   numbers greatly increased,
   and he did not let their herds
   diminish.

39 Then their numbers decreased,
   and they were humbled
   by oppression, calamity and
   sorrow;

40 he who pours contempt on nobles
made them wander in a
trackless waste.
41 But he lifted the needy out of
their affliction
and increased their families
like flocks.
42 The upright see and rejoice,
but all the wicked shut their
mouths.

43 Whoever is wise, let him heed
these things
and consider the great love of
the LORD.

Psalm 108

A song. A psalm of David.

1 My heart is steadfast, O God;
I will sing and make music
with all my soul.
2 Awake, harp and lyre!
I will awaken the dawn.
3 I will praise you, O LORD,
among the nations;
I will sing of you among the
peoples.
4 For great is your love, higher
than the heavens;
your faithfulness reaches to
the skies.
5 Be exalted, O God, above the
heavens,
and let your glory be over all
the earth.

6 Save us and help us with your
right hand,
that those you love may be
delivered.
7 God has spoken from his
sanctuary:
"In triumph I will parcel out
Shechem
and measure off the Valley of
Succoth.

8 Gilead is mine, Manasseh is mine;
Ephraim is my helmet,
Judah my scepter.
9 Moab is my washbasin,
upon Edom I toss my sandal;
over Philistia I shout in
triumph."

10 Who will bring me to the
fortified city?
Who will lead me to Edom?
11 Is it not you, O God, you who
have rejected us
and no longer go out with
our armies?
12 Give us aid against the enemy,
for the help of man is worthless.
13 With God we will gain the victory,
and he will trample down our
enemies.

Psalm 109

For the director of music.
Of David. A psalm.

1 O God, whom I praise,
do not remain silent,
2 for wicked and deceitful men
have opened their mouths
against me;
they have spoken against me
with lying tongues.
3 With words of hatred they
surround me;
they attack me without cause.
4 In return for my friendship
they accuse me,
but I am a man of prayer.
5 They repay me evil for good,
and hatred for my friendship.

6 Appointe an evil man/ to
oppose him;
let an accuserᵍ stand at his
right hand.
7 When he is tried, let him be
found guilty,

e 6 Or [They say:] "Appoint (with quotation marks at the end of verse 19)   f 6 Or the Evil
One   g 6 Or let Satan

and may his prayers condemn
him.

8 May his days be few;
    may another take his place of
        leadership.
9 May his children be fatherless
    and his wife a widow.
10 May his children be wandering
        beggars;
    may they be driven[h] from
        their ruined homes.
11 May a creditor seize all he has;
    may strangers plunder the
        fruits of his labor.
12 May no one extend kindness to
        him
    or take pity on his fatherless
        children.
13 May his descendants be cut off,
    their names blotted out from
        the next generation.
14 May the iniquity of his fathers be
        remembered before the LORD;
    may the sin of his mother
        never be blotted out.
15 May their sins always remain
        before the LORD,
    that he may cut off the memory
        of them from the earth.

16 For he never thought of doing
        a kindness,
    but hounded to death the poor
        and the needy and the
        brokenhearted.
17 He loved to pronounce a curse —
    may it[i] come on him;
    he found no pleasure in bless-
        ing —
    may it be[j] far from him.
18 He wore cursing as his
        garment;
    it entered into his body like
        water,
    into his bones like oil.
19 May it be like a cloak wrapped
        about him,

like a belt tied forever around
    him.
20 May this be the LORD's
        payment to my accusers,
    to those who speak evil of me.

21 But you, O Sovereign LORD,
    deal well with me for your
        name's sake;
    out of the goodness of your
        love, deliver me.
22 For I am poor and needy,
    and my heart is wounded
        within me.
23 I fade away like an evening
        shadow;
    I am shaken off like a locust.
24 My knees give way from fasting;
    my body is thin and gaunt.
25 I am an object of scorn to my
        accusers;
    when they see me, they shake
        their heads.

26 Help me, O LORD my God;
    save me in accordance with
        your love.
27 Let them know that it is your
        hand,
    that you, O LORD, have done it.
28 They may curse, but you will
        bless;
    when they attack they will be
        put to shame,
    but your servant will rejoice.
29 My accusers will be clothed
        with disgrace
    and wrapped in shame as in
        a cloak.

30 With my mouth I will greatly
        extol the LORD;
    in the great throng I will
        praise him.
31 For he stands at the right hand
        of the needy one,
    to save his life from those
        who condemn him.

h 10 Septuagint; Hebrew sought   i 17 Or curse, / and it has   j 17 Or blessing, / and it is

Psalm 110

Of David. A psalm.

1 The LORD says to my Lord:
   "Sit at my right hand
until I make your enemies
   a footstool for your feet."

2 The LORD will extend your
      mighty scepter from Zion;
   you will rule in the midst of
      your enemies.

3 Your troops will be willing
      on your day of battle.
   Arrayed in holy majesty,
      from the womb of the dawn
   you will receive the dew of
      your youth.k

4 The LORD has sworn
      and will not change his mind:
   "You are a priest forever,
      in the order of Melchizedek."

5 The Lord is at your right hand;
   he will crush kings on the day
      of his wrath.

6 He will judge the nations,
      heaping up the dead
   and crushing the rulers of the
      whole earth.

7 He will drink from a brook
      beside the way;l
   therefore he will lift up his head.

Psalm 111 m

1 Praise the LORD.n

   I will extol the LORD with all my
      heart
   in the council of the upright
      and in the assembly.

2 Great are the works of the LORD;

they are pondered by all who
      delight in them.

3 Glorious and majestic are his
      deeds,
   and his righteousness
      endures forever.

4 He has caused his wonders to
      be remembered;
   the LORD is gracious and
      compassionate.

5 He provides food for those who
      fear him;
   he remembers his covenant
      forever.

6 He has shown his people the
      power of his works,
   giving them the lands of
      other nations.

7 The works of his hands are
      faithful and just;
   all his precepts are
      trustworthy.

8 They are steadfast for ever and
      ever,
   done in faithfulness and
      uprightness.

9 He provided redemption for his
      people;
   he ordained his covenant
      forever—
   holy and awesome is his name.

10 The fear of the LORD is the
      beginning of wisdom;
   all who follow his precepts
      have good understanding.
   To him belongs eternal praise.

Psalm 112 o

1 Praise the LORD.p

   Blessed is the man who fears the
      LORD,

---

k 3 Or / your young men will come to you like the dew   l 7 Or / The One who grants
succession will set him in authority   m This psalm is an acrostic poem, the lines of which
begin with the successive letters of the Hebrew alphabet.   n 1 Hebrew Hallelu Yah   o This
psalm is an acrostic poem, the lines of which begin with the successive letters of the Hebrew
alphabet.   p 1 Hebrew Hallelu Yah

who finds great delight in his
commands.

2 His children will be mighty in
the land;
the generation of the upright
will be blessed.

3 Wealth and riches are in his
house,
and his righteousness
endures forever.

4 Even in darkness light dawns
for the upright,
for the gracious and
compassionate and
righteous man.q

5 Good will come to him who
is generous and lends
freely,
who conducts his affairs with
justice.

6 Surely he will never be shaken;
a righteous man will be
remembered forever.

7 He will have no fear of bad
news;
his heart is steadfast, trusting
in the LORD.

8 His heart is secure, he will
have no fear;
in the end he will look in
triumph on his foes.

9 He has scattered abroad his
gifts to the poor,
his righteousness endures
forever;
his hornr will be lifted high in
honor.

10 The wicked man will see and
be vexed,
he will gnash his teeth and
waste away;
the longings of the wicked
will come to nothing.

Psalm 113

1 Praise the LORD.s

Praise, O servants of the LORD,
praise the name of the LORD.

2 Let the name of the LORD be
praised,
both now and forevermore.

3 From the rising of the sun to
the place where it sets,
the name of the LORD is to be
praised.

4 The LORD is exalted over all
the nations,
his glory above the heavens.

5 Who is like the LORD our God,
the One who sits enthroned
on high,

6 who stoops down to look
on the heavens and the earth?

7 He raises the poor from the dust
and lifts the needy from the
ash heap;

8 he seats them with princes,
with the princes of their
people.

9 He settles the barren woman in
her home
as a happy mother of children.

Praise the LORD.

Psalm 114

1 When Israel came out of Egypt,
the house of Jacob from a
people of foreign tongue,

2 Judah became God's sanctuary,
Israel his dominion.

3 The sea looked and fled,
the Jordan turned back;

4 the mountains skipped like
rams,
the hills like lambs.

q 4 Or / for [the LORD] is gracious and compassionate and righteous   r 9 Horn here
symbolizes dignity.   s 1 Hebrew Hallelu Yah; also in verse 9

5 Why was it, O sea, that you
   fled,
   O Jordan, that you turned back,
6 you mountains, that you
   skipped like rams,
   you hills, like lambs?

7 Tremble, O earth, at the
   presence of the Lord,
   at the presence of the God of
   Jacob,
8 who turned the rock into a
   pool,
   the hard rock into springs of
   water.

Psalm 115

1 Not to us, O LORD, not to us
   but to your name be the glory,
   because of your love and
   faithfulness.

2 Why do the nations say,
   "Where is their God?"
3 Our God is in heaven;
   he does whatever pleases him.
4 But their idols are silver and
   gold,
   made by the hands of men.
5 They have mouths, but cannot
   speak,
   eyes, but they cannot see;
6 they have ears, but cannot hear,
   noses, but they cannot smell;
7 they have hands, but cannot
   feel,
   feet, but they cannot walk;
   nor can they utter a sound
   with their throats.
8 Those who make them will be
   like them,
   and so will all who trust in
   them.

9 O house of Israel, trust in the
   LORD—
   he is their help and shield.

10 O house of Aaron, trust in the
   LORD—
   he is their help and shield.
11 You who fear him, trust in the
   LORD—
   he is their help and shield.

12 The LORD remembers us and
   will bless us:
   He will bless the house of Israel,
   he will bless the house of
   Aaron,
13 he will bless those who fear the
   LORD—
   small and great alike.

14 May the LORD make you increase,
   both you and your children.

15 May you be blessed by the LORD,
   the Maker of heaven and
   earth.

16 The highest heavens belong to
   the LORD,
   but the earth he has given to
   man.

17 It is not the dead who praise
   the LORD,
   those who go down to silence;
18 it is we who extol the LORD,
   both now and forevermore.

Praise the LORD.*t*

Psalm 116

1 I love the LORD, for he heard
   my voice;
   he heard my cry for mercy.
2 Because he turned his ear to
   me,
   I will call on him as long as I
   live.

3 The cords of death entangled me,
   the anguish of the grave*u*
   came upon me;
   I was overcome by trouble
   and sorrow.

t 18 Hebrew *Hallelu Yah*   *u* 3 Hebrew *Sheol*

4 Then I called on the name of
the LORD:
"O LORD, save me!"

5 The LORD is gracious and
righteous;
our God is full of compassion.
6 The LORD protects the
simplehearted;
when I was in great need, he
saved me.

7 Be at rest once more, O my soul,
for the LORD has been good
to you.

8 For you, O LORD, have delivered
my soul from death,
my eyes from tears,
my feet from stumbling,
9 that I may walk before the LORD
in the land of the living.
10 I believed; therefore[v] I said,
"I am greatly afflicted."
11 And in my dismay I said,
"All men are liars."

12 How can I repay the LORD
for all his goodness to me?
13 I will lift up the cup of salvation
and call on the name of the
LORD.
14 I will fulfill my vows to the LORD
in the presence of all his
people.

15 Precious in the sight of the LORD
is the death of his saints.
16 O LORD, truly I am your servant;
I am your servant, the son of
your maidservant[w];
you have freed me from my
chains.

17 I will sacrifice a thank offering
to you
and call on the name of the
LORD.

18 I will fulfill my vows to the LORD
in the presence of all his people,
19 in the courts of the house of
the LORD—
in your midst, O Jerusalem.

Praise the LORD.[x]

Psalm 117

1 Praise the LORD, all you nations;
extol him, all you peoples.
2 For great is his love toward us,
and the faithfulness of the
LORD endures forever.

Praise the LORD.[y]

Psalm 118

1 Give thanks to the LORD, for he
is good;
his love endures forever.

2 Let Israel say:
"His love endures forever."
3 Let the house of Aaron say:
"His love endures forever."
4 Let those who fear the LORD say:
"His love endures forever."

5 In my anguish I cried to the
LORD,
and he answered by setting
me free.
6 The LORD is with me; I will not
be afraid.
What can man do to me?
7 The LORD is with me; he is my
helper.
I will look in triumph on my
enemies.

8 It is better to take refuge in the
LORD
than to trust in man.
9 It is better to take refuge in the
LORD
than to trust in princes.

v 10 Or believed even when   w 16 Or servant, your faithful son   x 19 Hebrew Hallelu Yah
y 2 Hebrew Hallelu Yah

10 All the nations surrounded me,
   but in the name of the LORD I
      cut them off.
11 They surrounded me on every
      side,
   but in the name of the LORD I
      cut them off.
12 They swarmed around me like
      bees,
   but they died out as quickly
      as burning thorns;
   in the name of the LORD I cut
      them off.
13 I was pushed back and about
      to fall,
   but the LORD helped me.
14 The LORD is my strength and
      my song;
   he has become my salvation.

15 Shouts of joy and victory
      resound in the tents of the
      righteous:
   "The LORD's right hand has
      done mighty things!
16   The LORD's right hand is
      lifted high;
   the LORD's right hand has
      done mighty things!"

17 I will not die but live,
   and will proclaim what the
      LORD has done.
18 The LORD has chastened me
      severely,
   but he has not given me over
      to death.

19 Open for me the gates of
      righteousness;
   I will enter and give thanks
      to the LORD.
20 This is the gate of the LORD
   through which the righteous
      may enter.

21 I will give you thanks, for you
      answered me;
   you have become my salvation.

22 The stone the builders rejected
      has become the capstone;
23 the LORD has done this,
   and it is marvelous in our
      eyes.
24 This is the day the LORD has
      made;
   let us rejoice and be glad in it.

25 O LORD, save us;
   O LORD, grant us success.

26 Blessed is he who comes in the
      name of the LORD.
   From the house of the LORD
      we bless you.z
27 The LORD is God,
   and he has made his light
      shine upon us.
   With boughs in hand, join in
      the festal procession
      upa to the horns of the altar.

28 You are my God, and I will give
      you thanks;
   you are my God, and I will
      exalt you.

29 Give thanks to the LORD, for he
      is good;
   his love endures forever.

Psalm 119 b

Aleph

1 Blessed are they whose ways
      are blameless,
   who walk according to the
      law of the LORD.
2 Blessed are they who keep his
      statutes
   and seek him with all their
      heart.

---

z 26 The Hebrew is plural.   a 27 Or Bind the festal sacrifice with ropes / and take it
b This psalm is an acrostic poem; the verses of each stanza begin with the same letter of the
Hebrew alphabet.

3 They do nothing wrong;
    they walk in his ways.
4 You have laid down precepts
    that are to be fully obeyed.
5 Oh, that my ways were steadfast
    in obeying your decrees!
6 Then I would not be put to
        shame
    when I consider all your
        commands.
7 I will praise you with an
        upright heart
    as I learn your righteous laws.
8 I will obey your decrees;
    do not utterly forsake me.

Beth

9 How can a young man keep his
        way pure?
    By living according to your
        word.
10 I seek you with all my heart;
    do not let me stray from your
        commands.
11 I have hidden your word in my
        heart
    that I might not sin against you.
12 Praise be to you, O LORD;
    teach me your decrees.
13 With my lips I recount
    all the laws that come from
        your mouth.
14 I rejoice in following your statutes
    as one rejoices in great riches.
15 I meditate on your precepts
    and consider your ways.
16 I delight in your decrees;
    I will not neglect your word.

Gimel

17 Do good to your servant, and I
        will live;
    I will obey your word.
18 Open my eyes that I may see
    wonderful things in your law.
19 I am a stranger on earth;
    do not hide your commands
        from me.

20 My soul is consumed with longing
    for your laws at all times.
21 You rebuke the arrogant, who
        are cursed
    and who stray from your
        commands.
22 Remove from me scorn and
        contempt,
    for I keep your statutes.
23 Though rulers sit together and
        slander me,
    your servant will meditate on
        your decrees.
24 Your statutes are my delight;
    they are my counselors.

Daleth

25 I am laid low in the dust;
    preserve my life according to
        your word.
26 I recounted my ways and you
        answered me;
    teach me your decrees.
27 Let me understand the
        teaching of your precepts;
    then I will meditate on your
        wonders.
28 My soul is weary with sorrow;
    strengthen me according to
        your word.
29 Keep me from deceitful ways;
    be gracious to me through
        your law.
30 I have chosen the way of truth;
    I have set my heart on your
        laws.
31 I hold fast to your statutes, O
        LORD;
    do not let me be put to shame.
32 I run in the path of your
        commands,
    for you have set my heart free.

He

33 Teach me, O LORD, to follow
        your decrees;
    then I will keep them to the
        end.

34 Give me understanding, and I
    will keep your law
      and obey it with all my heart.
35 Direct me in the path of your
    commands,
      for there I find delight.
36 Turn my heart toward your
    statutes
      and not toward selfish gain.
37 Turn my eyes away from
    worthless things;
      preserve my life according to
      your word.[c]
38 Fulfill your promise to your
    servant,
      so that you may be feared.
39 Take away the disgrace I dread,
      for your laws are good.
40 How I long for your precepts!
      Preserve my life in your
      righteousness.

Waw

41 May your unfailing love come
    to me, O LORD,
      your salvation according to
      your promise;
42 then I will answer the one who
    taunts me,
      for I trust in your word.
43 Do not snatch the word of
    truth from my mouth,
      for I have put my hope in
      your laws.
44 I will always obey your law,
      for ever and ever.
45 I will walk about in freedom,
      for I have sought out your
      precepts.
46 I will speak of your statutes
    before kings
      and will not be put to shame,
47 for I delight in your commands
    because I love them.

48 I lift up my hands to[d] your
    commands, which I love,
      and I meditate on your
      decrees.

Zayin

49 Remember your word to your
    servant,
      for you have given me hope.
50 My comfort in my suffering is
    this:
      Your promise preserves my
      life.
51 The arrogant mock me without
    restraint,
      but I do not turn from your law.
52 I remember your ancient laws,
    O LORD,
      and I find comfort in them.
53 Indignation grips me because
    of the wicked,
      who have forsaken your law.
54 Your decrees are the theme of
    my song
      wherever I lodge.
55 In the night I remember your
    name, O LORD,
      and I will keep your law.
56 This has been my practice:
      I obey your precepts.

Heth

57 You are my portion, O LORD;
      I have promised to obey your
      words.
58 I have sought your face with all
    my heart;
      be gracious to me according
      to your promise.
59 I have considered my ways
      and have turned my steps to
      your statutes.
60 I will hasten and not delay
      to obey your commands.

---

c 37 Two manuscripts of the Masoretic Text and Dead Sea Scrolls; most manuscripts of the
Masoretic Text *life in your way* d 48 Or *for*

61 Though the wicked bind me
     with ropes,
   I will not forget your law.
62 At midnight I rise to give you
     thanks
   for your righteous laws.
63 I am a friend to all who fear you,
   to all who follow your
     precepts.
64 The earth is filled with your
     love, O LORD;
   teach me your decrees.

Teth

65 Do good to your servant
     according to your word, O
     LORD.
66 Teach me knowledge and good
     judgment,
   for I believe in your commands.
67 Before I was afflicted I went
     astray,
   but now I obey your word.
68 You are good, and what you do
     is good;
   teach me your decrees.
69 Though the arrogant have
     smeared me with lies,
   I keep your precepts with all
     my heart.
70 Their hearts are callous and
     unfeeling,
   but I delight in your law.
71 It was good for me to be afflicted
   so that I might learn your
     decrees.
72 The law from your mouth is
     more precious to me
   than thousands of pieces of
     silver and gold.

Yodh

73 Your hands made me and
     formed me;
   give me understanding to
     learn your commands.
74 May those who fear you rejoice
     when they see me,

   for I have put my hope in
     your word.
75 I know, O LORD, that your laws
     are righteous,
   and in faithfulness you have
     afflicted me.
76 May your unfailing love be my
     comfort,
   according to your promise to
     your servant.
77 Let your compassion come to
     me that I may live,
   for your law is my delight.
78 May the arrogant be put to
     shame for wronging me
     without cause;
   but I will meditate on your
     precepts.
79 May those who fear you turn to
     me,
   those who understand your
     statutes.
80 May my heart be blameless
     toward your decrees,
   that I may not be put to shame.

Kaph

81 My soul faints with longing for
     your salvation,
   but I have put my hope in
     your word.
82 My eyes fail, looking for your
     promise;
   I say, "When will you comfort
     me?"
83 Though I am like a wineskin in
     the smoke,
   I do not forget your decrees.
84 How long must your servant
     wait?
   When will you punish my
     persecutors?
85 The arrogant dig pitfalls for me,
   contrary to your law.
86 All your commands are
     trustworthy;
   help me, for men persecute
     me without cause.

87 They almost wiped me from
the earth,
but I have not forsaken your
precepts.
88 Preserve my life according to
your love,
and I will obey the statutes of
your mouth.

Lamedh

89 Your word, O LORD, is eternal;
it stands firm in the heavens.
90 Your faithfulness continues
through all generations;
you established the earth,
and it endures.
91 Your laws endure to this day,
for all things serve you.
92 If your law had not been my
delight,
I would have perished in my
affliction.
93 I will never forget your precepts,
for by them you have
preserved my life.
94 Save me, for I am yours;
I have sought out your
precepts.
95 The wicked are waiting to
destroy me,
but I will ponder your statutes.
96 To all perfection I see a limit;
but your commands are
boundless.

Mem

97 Oh, how I love your law!
I meditate on it all day long.
98 Your commands make me
wiser than my enemies,
for they are ever with me.
99 I have more insight than all my
teachers,
for I meditate on your
statutes.
100 I have more understanding
than the elders,
for I obey your precepts.

101 I have kept my feet from every
evil path
so that I might obey your word.
102 I have not departed from your
laws,
for you yourself have taught
me.
103 How sweet are your words to
my taste,
sweeter than honey to my
mouth!
104 I gain understanding from your
precepts;
therefore I hate every wrong
path.

Nun

105 Your word is a lamp to my feet
and a light for my path.
106 I have taken an oath and
confirmed it,
that I will follow your
righteous laws.
107 I have suffered much;
preserve my life, O LORD,
according to your word.
108 Accept, O LORD, the willing
praise of my mouth,
and teach me your laws.
109 Though I constantly take my
life in my hands,
I will not forget your law.
110 The wicked have set a snare for
me,
but I have not strayed from
your precepts.
111 Your statutes are my heritage
forever;
they are the joy of my heart.
112 My heart is set on keeping your
decrees
to the very end.

Samekh

113 I hate double-minded men,
but I love your law.
114 You are my refuge and my
shield;

I have put my hope in your
word.
115 Away from me, you evildoers,
that I may keep the
commands of my God!
116 Sustain me according to your
promise, and I will live;
do not let my hopes be
dashed.
117 Uphold me, and I will be
delivered;
I will always have regard for
your decrees.
118 You reject all who stray from
your decrees,
for their deceitfulness is in
vain.
119 All the wicked of the earth you
discard like dross;
therefore I love your statutes.
120 My flesh trembles in fear of
you;
I stand in awe of your laws.

Ayin

121 I have done what is righteous
and just;
do not leave me to my
oppressors.
122 Ensure your servant's
well-being;
let not the arrogant oppress me.
123 My eyes fail, looking for your
salvation,
looking for your righteous
promise.
124 Deal with your servant
according to your love
and teach me your decrees.
125 I am your servant; give me
discernment
that I may understand your
statutes.
126 It is time for you to act, O LORD;
your law is being broken.
127 Because I love your commands
more than gold, more than
pure gold,

128 and because I consider all your
precepts right,
I hate every wrong path.

Pe

129 Your statutes are wonderful;
therefore I obey them.
130 The unfolding of your words
gives light;
it gives understanding to the
simple.
131 I open my mouth and pant,
longing for your commands.
132 Turn to me and have mercy on
me,
as you always do to those
who love your name.
133 Direct my footsteps according
to your word;
let no sin rule over me.
134 Redeem me from the
oppression of men,
that I may obey your precepts.
135 Make your face shine upon
your servant
and teach me your decrees.
136 Streams of tears flow from my
eyes,
for your law is not obeyed.

Tsadhe

137 Righteous are you, O LORD,
and your laws are right.
138 The statutes you have laid
down are righteous;
they are fully trustworthy.
139 My zeal wears me out,
for my enemies ignore your
words.
140 Your promises have been
thoroughly tested,
and your servant loves them.
141 Though I am lowly and
despised,
I do not forget your precepts.
142 Your righteousness is
everlasting
and your law is true.

143 Trouble and distress have come
      upon me,
    but your commands are my
      delight.
144 Your statutes are forever right;
    give me understanding that I
      may live.

Qoph

145 I call with all my heart; answer
      me, O LORD,
    and I will obey your decrees.
146 I call out to you; save me
    and I will keep your statutes.
147 I rise before dawn and cry for
      help;
    I have put my hope in your
      word.
148 My eyes stay open through the
      watches of the night,
    that I may meditate on your
      promises.
149 Hear my voice in accordance
      with your love;
    preserve my life, O LORD,
      according to your laws.
150 Those who devise wicked
      schemes are near,
    but they are far from your law.
151 Yet you are near, O LORD,
    and all your commands are
      true.
152 Long ago I learned from your
      statutes
    that you established them to
      last forever.

Resh

153 Look upon my suffering and
      deliver me,
    for I have not forgotten your
      law.
154 Defend my cause and redeem me;
    preserve my life according to
      your promise.
155 Salvation is far from the wicked,
    for they do not seek out your
      decrees.

156 Your compassion is great, O
      LORD;
    preserve my life according to
      your laws.
157 Many are the foes who
      persecute me,
    but I have not turned from
      your statutes.
158 I look on the faithless with
      loathing,
    for they do not obey your
      word.
159 See how I love your precepts;
    preserve my life, O LORD,
      according to your love.
160 All your words are true;
    all your righteous laws are
      eternal.

Sin and Shin

161 Rulers persecute me without
      cause,
    but my heart trembles at your
      word.
162 I rejoice in your promise
    like one who finds great spoil.
163 I hate and abhor falsehood
    but I love your law.
164 Seven times a day I praise you
    for your righteous laws.
165 Great peace have they who
      love your law,
    and nothing can make them
      stumble.
166 I wait for your salvation, O LORD,
    and I follow your commands.
167 I obey your statutes,
    for I love them greatly.
168 I obey your precepts and your
      statutes,
    for all my ways are known to
      you.

Taw

169 May my cry come before you,
      O LORD;
    give me understanding
      according to your word.

170 May my supplication come
      before you;
    deliver me according to your
      promise.
171 May my lips overflow with praise,
    for you teach me your
      decrees.
172 May my tongue sing of your
      word,
    for all your commands are
      righteous.
173 May your hand be ready to
      help me,
    for I have chosen your precepts.
174 I long for your salvation, O
      LORD,
    and your law is my delight.
175 Let me live that I may praise
      you,
    and may your laws sustain me.
176 I have strayed like a lost sheep.
    Seek your servant,
    for I have not forgotten your
      commands.

Psalm 120
A song of ascents.

1 I call on the LORD in my distress,
    and he answers me.
2 Save me, O LORD, from lying lips
    and from deceitful tongues.

3 What will he do to you,
    and what more besides, O
      deceitful tongue?
4 He will punish you with a
      warrior's sharp arrows,
    with burning coals of the
      broom tree.

5 Woe to me that I dwell in
      Meshech,
    that I live among the tents of
      Kedar!
6 Too long have I lived
    among those who hate peace.
7 I am a man of peace;
    but when I speak, they are
      for war.

Psalm 121
A song of ascents.

1 I lift up my eyes to the hills—
    where does my help come
      from?
2 My help comes from the LORD,
    the Maker of heaven and earth.

3 He will not let your foot slip—
    he who watches over you will
      not slumber;
4 indeed, he who watches over
      Israel
    will neither slumber nor sleep.

5 The LORD watches over you—
    the LORD is your shade at
      your right hand;
6 the sun will not harm you by day,
    nor the moon by night.

7 The LORD will keep you from
      all harm—
    he will watch over your life;
8 the LORD will watch over your
      coming and going
    both now and forevermore.

Psalm 122
A song of ascents. Of David.

1 I rejoiced with those who said
      to me,
    "Let us go to the house of the
      LORD."
2 Our feet are standing
    in your gates, O Jerusalem.

3 Jerusalem is built like a city
    that is closely compacted
      together.
4 That is where the tribes go up,
    the tribes of the LORD,
    to praise the name of the LORD
      according to the statute given
      to Israel.
5 There the thrones for judgment
      stand,
    the thrones of the house of
      David.

6 Pray for the peace of Jerusalem:
   "May those who love you be
      secure.
7 May there be peace within
      your walls
   and security within your
      citadels."
8 For the sake of my brothers
      and friends,
   I will say, "Peace be within you."
9 For the sake of the house of the
      LORD our God,
   I will seek your prosperity.

Psalm 123
A song of ascents.

1 I lift up my eyes to you,
   to you whose throne is in
      heaven.
2 As the eyes of slaves look to
      the hand of their master,
   as the eyes of a maid look to
      the hand of her mistress,
   so our eyes look to the LORD
      our God,
   till he shows us his mercy.

3 Have mercy on us, O LORD,
   have mercy on us,
   for we have endured much
      contempt.
4 We have endured much
      ridicule from the proud,
   much contempt from the
      arrogant.

Psalm 124
A song of ascents. Of David.

1 If the LORD had not been on our
      side—
   let Israel say—
2 if the LORD had not been on
      our side
   when men attacked us,
3 when their anger flared against
      us,
   they would have swallowed
      us alive;

4 the flood would have engulfed
      us,
   the torrent would have swept
      over us,
5 the raging waters
   would have swept us away.

6 Praise be to the LORD,
   who has not let us be torn by
      their teeth.
7 We have escaped like a bird
   out of the fowler's snare;
   the snare has been broken,
   and we have escaped.
8 Our help is in the name of the
      LORD,
   the Maker of heaven and
      earth.

Psalm 125
A song of ascents.

1 Those who trust in the LORD are
   like Mount Zion,
   which cannot be shaken but
      endures forever.
2 As the mountains surround
      Jerusalem,
   so the LORD surrounds his
      people
   both now and forevermore.

3 The scepter of the wicked will
      not remain
   over the land allotted to the
      righteous,
   for then the righteous might
      use
   their hands to do evil.

4 Do good, O LORD, to those who
      are good,
   to those who are upright in
      heart.
5 But those who turn to crooked
      ways
   the LORD will banish with the
      evildoers.

Peace be upon Israel.

Psalm 126

A song of ascents.

1 When the LORD brought back
      the captives toᵉ Zion,
   we were like men who
      dreamed.ᶠ
2 Our mouths were filled with
      laughter,
   our tongues with songs of joy.
   Then it was said among the na-
      tions,
      "The LORD has done great
         things for them."
3 The LORD has done great
      things for us,
   and we are filled with joy.

4 Restore our fortunes,ᵍ O LORD,
      like streams in the Negev.
5 Those who sow in tears
      will reap with songs of joy.
6 He who goes out weeping,
      carrying seed to sow,
   will return with songs of joy,
      carrying sheaves with him.

Psalm 127

A song of ascents. Of Solomon.

1 Unless the LORD builds the
      house,
   its builders labor in vain.
   Unless the LORD watches over
      the city,
   the watchmen stand guard in
      vain.
2 In vain you rise early
      and stay up late,
   toiling for food to eat—
   for he grants sleep toʰ those
      he loves.

3 Sons are a heritage from the
      LORD,
   children a reward from him.

4 Like arrows in the hands of a
      warrior
   are sons born in one's youth.
5 Blessed is the man
   whose quiver is full of them.
   They will not be put to shame
      when they contend with their
         enemies in the gate.

Psalm 128

A song of ascents.

1 Blessed are all who fear the
      LORD,
   who walk in his ways.
2 You will eat the fruit of your
      labor;
   blessings and prosperity will
      be yours.
3 Your wife will be like a fruitful
      vine
   within your house;
   your sons will be like olive
      shoots
   around your table.
4 Thus is the man blessed
   who fears the LORD.

5 May the LORD bless you from
      Zion
   all the days of your life;
   may you see the prosperity of
      Jerusalem,
6 and may you live to see your
      children's children.

   Peace be upon Israel.

Psalm 129

A song of ascents.

1 They have greatly oppressed
      me from my youth—
   let Israel say—
2 they have greatly oppressed
      me from my youth,

ᵉ 1 Or LORD restored the fortunes of   ᶠ 1 Or men restored to health   ᵍ 4 Or Bring back our
captives   ʰ 2 Or eat— / for while they sleep he provides for

but they have not gained the
victory over me.
3 Plowmen have plowed my back
and made their furrows long.
4 But the LORD is righteous;
he has cut me free from the
cords of the wicked.

5 May all who hate Zion
be turned back in shame.
6 May they be like grass on the roof,
which withers before it can
grow;
7 with it the reaper cannot fill
his hands,
nor the one who gathers fill
his arms.

8 May those who pass by not say,
"The blessing of the LORD be
upon you;
we bless you in the name of
the LORD."

Psalm 130
A song of ascents.

1 Out of the depths I cry to you,
O LORD;
2 O Lord, hear my voice.
Let your ears be attentive
to my cry for mercy.

3 If you, O LORD, kept a record
of sins,
O Lord, who could stand?
4 But with you there is forgiveness;
therefore you are feared.

5 I wait for the LORD, my soul waits,
and in his word I put my hope.
6 My soul waits for the Lord
more than watchmen wait for
the morning,
more than watchmen wait for
the morning.

7 O Israel, put your hope in the
LORD,

for with the LORD is unfailing
love
and with him is full
redemption.
8 He himself will redeem Israel
from all their sins.

Psalm 131
A song of ascents. Of David.

1 My heart is not proud, O LORD,
my eyes are not haughty;
I do not concern myself with
great matters
or things too wonderful for
me.
2 But I have stilled and quieted
my soul;
like a weaned child with its
mother,
like a weaned child is my
soul within me.

3 O Israel, put your hope in the
LORD
both now and forevermore.

Psalm 132
A song of ascents.

1 O LORD, remember David
and all the hardships he
endured.
2 He swore an oath to the LORD
and made a vow to the
Mighty One of Jacob:
3 "I will not enter my house
or go to my bed —
4 I will allow no sleep to my eyes,
no slumber to my eyelids,
5 till I find a place for the LORD,
a dwelling for the Mighty
One of Jacob."

6 We heard it in Ephrathah,
we came upon it in the fields
of Jaar:[j]

---

*i 6 That is, Kiriath Jearim   j 6 Or heard of it in Ephrathah, / we found it in the fields of
Jaar. (And no quotes around verses 7-9)*

7 "Let us go to his dwelling place;
   let us worship at his
      footstool—
8 arise, O LORD, and come to
   your resting place,
   you and the ark of your might.
9 May your priests be clothed
   with righteousness;
   may your saints sing for joy."

10 For the sake of David your
    servant,
   do not reject your anointed
      one.

11 The LORD swore an oath to
    David,
   a sure oath that he will not
      revoke:
"One of your own descendants
   I will place on your throne—
12 if your sons keep my covenant
   and the statutes I teach them,
then their sons will sit
   on your throne for ever and
      ever."

13 For the LORD has chosen Zion,
    he has desired it for his
      dwelling:
14 "This is my resting place for
    ever and ever;
   here I will sit enthroned, for I
      have desired it—
15 I will bless her with abundant
    provisions;
   her poor will I satisfy with
      food.
16 I will clothe her priests with
    salvation,
   and her saints will ever sing
      for joy.

17 "Here I will make a horn[k] grow
    for David
   and set up a lamp for my
      anointed one.

18 I will clothe his enemies with
    shame,
   but the crown on his head
      will be resplendent."

Psalm 133
A song of ascents. Of David.

1 How good and pleasant it is
   when brothers live together
      in unity!
2 It is like precious oil poured on
    the head,
   running down on the beard,
running down on Aaron's beard,
   down upon the collar of his
      robes.
3 It is as if the dew of Hermon
   were falling on Mount Zion.
For there the LORD bestows his
   blessing,
   even life forevermore.

Psalm 134
A song of ascents.

1 Praise the LORD, all you ser-
    vants of the LORD
   who minister by night in the
      house of the LORD.
2 Lift up your hands in the
    sanctuary
   and praise the LORD.

3 May the LORD, the Maker of
    heaven and earth,
   bless you from Zion.

Psalm 135

1 Praise the LORD.[l]

Praise the name of the LORD;
   praise him, you servants of
      the LORD,
2 you who minister in the house
    of the LORD,
   in the courts of the house of
      our God.

---

k 17 *Horn* here symbolizes strong one, that is, king.   l 1 Hebrew *Hallelu Yah*; also in verses
3 and 21

3 Praise the LORD, for the LORD
    is good;
    sing praise to his name, for
      that is pleasant.
4 For the LORD has chosen Jacob
      to be his own,
    Israel to be his treasured
      possession.

5 I know that the LORD is great,
    that our Lord is greater than
      all gods.
6 The LORD does whatever
      pleases him,
    in the heavens and on the
      earth,
    in the seas and all their depths.
7 He makes clouds rise from the
      ends of the earth;
    he sends lightning with the rain
    and brings out the wind from
      his storehouses.

8 He struck down the firstborn of
      Egypt,
    the firstborn of men and
      animals.
9 He sent his signs and wonders
      into your midst, O Egypt,
    against Pharaoh and all his
      servants.
10 He struck down many nations
    and killed mighty kings—
11 Sihon king of the Amorites,
    Og king of Bashan
    and all the kings of Canaan—
12 and he gave their land as an
      inheritance,
    an inheritance to his people
      Israel.

13 Your name, O LORD, endures
      forever,
    your renown, O LORD,
    through all generations.
14 For the LORD will vindicate his
      people
    and have compassion on his
      servants.

15 The idols of the nations are
      silver and gold,
    made by the hands of men.
16 They have mouths, but cannot
      speak,
    eyes, but they cannot see;
17 they have ears, but cannot hear
    nor is there breath in their
      mouths.
18 Those who make them will be
      like them,
    and so will all who trust in
      them.

19 O house of Israel, praise the
      LORD;
    O house of Aaron, praise the
      LORD;
20 O house of Levi, praise the
      LORD;
    you who fear him, praise the
      LORD.
21 Praise be to the LORD from
      Zion,
    to him who dwells in
      Jerusalem.

Praise the LORD.

Psalm 136

1 Give thanks to the LORD, for he
    is good.
      His love endures forever.
2 Give thanks to the God of gods.
      His love endures forever.
3 Give thanks to the Lord of lords:
      His love endures forever.

4 to him who alone does great
      wonders,
      His love endures forever.
5 who by his understanding
      made the heavens,
      His love endures forever.
6 who spread out the earth upon
      the waters,
      His love endures forever.
7 who made the great lights—
      His love endures forever.

8 the sun to govern the day,
His love endures forever.

9 the moon and stars to govern
the night;
His love endures forever.

10 to him who struck down the
firstborn of Egypt
His love endures forever.

11 and brought Israel out from
among them
His love endures forever.

12 with a mighty hand and
outstretched arm;
His love endures forever.

13 to him who divided the Red
Sea*m* asunder
His love endures forever.

14 and brought Israel through the
midst of it,
His love endures forever.

15 but swept Pharaoh and his
army into the Red Sea;
His love endures forever.

16 to him who led his people
through the desert,
His love endures forever.

17 who struck down great kings,
His love endures forever.

18 and killed mighty kings—
His love endures forever.

19 Sihon king of the Amorites
His love endures forever.

20 and Og king of Bashan—
His love endures forever.

21 and gave their land as an
inheritance,
His love endures forever.

22 an inheritance to his servant
Israel;
His love endures forever.

23 to the One who remembered
us in our low estate
His love endures forever.

24 and freed us from our enemies,
His love endures forever.

25 and who gives food to every
creature.
His love endures forever.

26 Give thanks to the God of heaven.
His love endures forever.

Psalm 137

1 By the rivers of Babylon we sat
and wept
when we remembered Zion.

2 There on the poplars
we hung our harps,

3 for there our captors asked us
for songs,
our tormentors demanded
songs of joy;
they said, "Sing us one of the
songs of Zion!"

4 How can we sing the songs of
the LORD
while in a foreign land?

5 If I forget you, O Jerusalem,
may my right hand forget [its
skill].

6 May my tongue cling to the
roof of my mouth
if I do not remember you,
if I do not consider Jerusalem
my highest joy.

7 Remember, O LORD, what the
Edomites did
on the day Jerusalem fell.
"Tear it down," they cried,
"tear it down to its
foundations!"

8 O Daughter of Babylon,
doomed to destruction,
happy is he who repays you
for what you have done to
us—

---

m 13 Hebrew *Yam Suph*; that is, Sea of Reeds; also in verse 15

9 he who seizes your infants
and dashes them against the
rocks.

Psalm 138
Of David.

1 I will praise you, O LORD, with
all my heart;
before the "gods" I will sing
your praise.
2 I will bow down toward your
holy temple
and will praise your name
for your love and your
faithfulness,
for you have exalted above all
things
your name and your word.
3 When I called, you answered
me;
you made me bold and
stouthearted.

4 May all the kings of the earth
praise you, O LORD,
when they hear the words of
your mouth.
5 May they sing of the ways of
the LORD,
for the glory of the LORD is
great.

6 Though the LORD is on high, he
looks upon the lowly,
but the proud he knows from
afar.
7 Though I walk in the midst of
trouble,
you preserve my life;
you stretch out your hand
against the anger of my foes,
with your right hand you
save me.
8 The LORD will fulfill [his
purpose] for me;

your love, O LORD, endures
forever—
do not abandon the works of
your hands.

Psalm 139
For the director of music.
Of David. A psalm.

1 O LORD, you have searched me
and you know me.
2 You know when I sit and when
I rise;
you perceive my thoughts
from afar.
3 You discern my going out and
my lying down;
you are familiar with all my
ways.
4 Before a word is on my tongue
you know it completely, O
LORD.

5 You hem me in—behind and
before;
you have laid your hand
upon me.
6 Such knowledge is too
wonderful for me,
too lofty for me to attain.

7 Where can I go from your
Spirit?
Where can I flee from your
presence?
8 If I go up to the heavens, you
are there;
if I make my bed in the
depths,[n] you are there.
9 If I rise on the wings of the
dawn,
if I settle on the far side of
the sea,
10 even there your hand will
guide me,
your right hand will hold me
fast.

n 8 Hebrew *Sheol*

11 If I say, "Surely the darkness
    will hide me
  and the light become night
    around me,"
12 even the darkness will not be
    dark to you;
  the night will shine like the day,
    for darkness is as light to you.
13 For you created my inmost being;
  you knit me together in my
    mother's womb.
14 I praise you because I am
    fearfully and wonderfully
    made;
  your works are wonderful,
    I know that full well.
15 My frame was not hidden from
    you
  when I was made in the
    secret place.
  When I was woven together in
    the depths of the earth,
16   your eyes saw my unformed
    body.
  All the days ordained for me
    were written in your book
  before one of them came to be.

17 How precious too me are your
    thoughts, O God!
  How vast is the sum of them!
18 Were I to count them,
  they would outnumber the
    grains of sand.
  When I awake,
    I am still with you.

19 If only you would slay the
    wicked, O God!
  Away from me, you
    bloodthirsty men!
20 They speak of you with evil
    intent;
  your adversaries misuse your
    name.

21 Do I not hate those who hate
    you, O LORD,
  and abhor those who rise up
    against you?
22 I have nothing but hatred for
    them;
  I count them my enemies.
23 Search me, O God, and know
    my heart;
  test me and know my anxious
    thoughts.
24 See if there is any offensive
    way in me,
  and lead me in the way
    everlasting.

Psalm 140

For the director of music.
A psalm of David.

1 Rescue me, O LORD, from evil
    men;
  protect me from men of
    violence,
2 who devise evil plans in their
    hearts
  and stir up war every day.
3 They make their tongues as
    sharp as a serpent's;
  the poison of vipers is on
    their lips.   *Selah*

4 Keep me, O LORD, from the
    hands of the wicked;
  protect me from men of
    violence
  who plan to trip my feet.
5 Proud men have hidden a
    snare for me;
  they have spread out the
    cords of their net
  and have set traps for me
    along my path.   *Selah*

6 O LORD, I say to you, "You are
    my God."

---

o 17 Or *concerning*

Hear, O LORD, my cry for
mercy.
7 O Sovereign LORD, my strong
deliverer,
who shields my head in the
day of battle—
8 do not grant the wicked their
desires, O LORD;
do not let their plans succeed,
or they will become proud.
Selah

9 Let the heads of those who
surround me
be covered with the trouble
their lips have caused.
10 Let burning coals fall upon them;
may they be thrown into the
fire,
into miry pits, never to rise.

11 Let slanderers not be
established in the land;
may disaster hunt down men
of violence.

12 I know that the LORD secures
justice for the poor
and upholds the cause of the
needy.

13 Surely the righteous will praise
your name
and the upright will live
before you.

Psalm 141
A psalm of David.

1 O LORD, I call to you; come
quickly to me.
Hear my voice when I call to
you.
2 May my prayer be set before
you like incense;
may the lifting up of my
hands be like the evening
sacrifice.

3 Set a guard over my mouth, O
LORD;
keep watch over the door of
my lips.
4 Let not my heart be drawn to
what is evil,
to take part in wicked deeds
with men who are evildoers;
let me not eat of their
delicacies.

5 Let a righteous man[p] strike
me—it is a kindness;
let him rebuke me—it is oil
on my head.
My head will not refuse it.

Yet my prayer is ever against the
deeds of evildoers;
6 their rulers will be thrown
down from the cliffs,
and the wicked will learn that
my words were well spoken.
7 [They will say,] "As one plows
and breaks up the earth,
so our bones have been
scattered at the mouth of
the grave.[q]"

8 But my eyes are fixed on you,
O Sovereign LORD;
in you I take refuge—do not
give me over to death.
9 Keep me from the snares they
have laid for me,
from the traps set by evildoers.
10 Let the wicked fall into their
own nets,
while I pass by in safety.

Psalm 142
A *maskil*[r] of David. When he was in the
cave. A prayer.

1 I cry aloud to the LORD;
I lift up my voice to the LORD
for mercy.

---

p 5 Or *Let the Righteous One*   *q* 7 Hebrew *Sheol*   *r* Title: Probably a literary or musical
term

2 I pour out my complaint before
   him;
   before him I tell my trouble.

3 When my spirit grows faint
      within me,
   it is you who know my way.
   In the path where I walk
   men have hidden a snare for
      me.

4 Look to my right and see;
   no one is concerned for me.
   I have no refuge;
   no one cares for my life.

5 I cry to you, O LORD;
   I say, "You are my refuge,
   my portion in the land of the
      living."

6 Listen to my cry,
   for I am in desperate need;
   rescue me from those who pur-
      sue me,
   for they are too strong for
      me.

7 Set me free from my prison,
   that I may praise your name.

   Then the righteous will gather
      about me
   because of your goodness to
      me.

Psalm 143
A psalm of David.

1 O LORD, hear my prayer,
   listen to my cry for mercy;
   in your faithfulness and
      righteousness
   come to my relief.

2 Do not bring your servant into
      judgment,
   for no one living is righteous
      before you.

3 The enemy pursues me,
   he crushes me to the ground;
   he makes me dwell in darkness
   like those long dead.

4 So my spirit grows faint within
      me;
   my heart within me is
      dismayed.

5 I remember the days of long
      ago;
   I meditate on all your works
   and consider what your
      hands have done.

6 I spread out my hands to you;
   my soul thirsts for you like a
      parched land.   Selah

7 Answer me quickly, O LORD;
   my spirit fails.
   Do not hide your face from me
   or I will be like those who go
      down to the pit.

8 Let the morning bring me word
   of your unfailing love,
   for I have put my trust in you.
   Show me the way I should go,
   for to you I lift up my soul.

9 Rescue me from my enemies, O
      LORD,
   for I hide myself in you.

10 Teach me to do your will,
   for you are my God;
   may your good Spirit
   lead me on level ground.

11 For your name's sake, O LORD,
   preserve my life;
   in your righteousness, bring
   me out of trouble.

12 In your unfailing love, silence
   my enemies;
   destroy all my foes,
   for I am your servant.

Psalm 144
Of David.

1 Praise be to the LORD my Rock,
   who trains my hands for
      war,
   my fingers for battle.

2 He is my loving God and my
      fortress,

my stronghold and my
deliverer,
my shield, in whom I take refuge,
who subdues peoples[s] under
me.

³ O LORD, what is man that you
care for him,
the son of man that you think
of him?
⁴ Man is like a breath;
his days are like a fleeting
shadow.

⁵ Part your heavens, O LORD,
and come down;
touch the mountains, so that
they smoke.
⁶ Send forth lightning and
scatter [the enemies];
shoot your arrows and rout
them.
⁷ Reach down your hand from
on high;
deliver me and rescue me
from the mighty waters,
from the hands of foreigners
⁸ whose mouths are full of lies,
whose right hands are
deceitful.

⁹ I will sing a new song to you, O
God;
on the ten-stringed lyre I will
make music to you,
¹⁰ to the One who gives victory to
kings,
who delivers his servant David
from the deadly sword.

¹¹ Deliver me and rescue me
from the hands of foreigners
whose mouths are full of lies,
whose right hands are
deceitful.

¹² Then our sons in their youth
will be like well-nurtured
plants,
and our daughters will be like
pillars
carved to adorn a palace.
¹³ Our barns will be filled
with every kind of provision.
Our sheep will increase by
thousands,
by tens of thousands in our
fields;
¹⁴ our oxen will draw heavy
loads.[t]
There will be no breaching of
walls,
no going into captivity,
no cry of distress in our
streets.

¹⁵ Blessed are the people of
whom this is true;
blessed are the people whose
God is the LORD.

Psalm 145 [u]
A psalm of praise. Of David.

¹ I will exalt you, my God the
King;
I will praise your name for
ever and ever.
² Every day I will praise you
and extol your name for ever
and ever.

³ Great is the LORD and most
worthy of praise;
his greatness no one can
fathom.
⁴ One generation will commend
your works to another;
they will tell of your mighty
acts.

---

[s] 2 Many manuscripts of the Masoretic Text, Dead Sea Scrolls, Aquila, Jerome and Syriac;
most manuscripts of the Masoretic Text *subdues my people*   [t] 14 Or *our chieftains will be
firmly established*   [u] This psalm is an acrostic poem, the verses of which (including verse
13b) begin with the successive letters of the Hebrew alphabet.

5 They will speak of the glorious
    splendor of your majesty,
  and I will meditate on your
    wonderful works.ᵛ
6 They will tell of the power of
    your awesome works,
  and I will proclaim your great
    deeds.
7 They will celebrate your
    abundant goodness
  and joyfully sing of your
    righteousness.

8 The LORD is gracious and
    compassionate,
  slow to anger and rich in love.
9 The LORD is good to all;
  he has compassion on all he
    has made.
10 All you have made will praise
    you, O LORD;
  your saints will extol you.
11 They will tell of the glory of
    your kingdom
  and speak of your might,
12 so that all men may know of
    your mighty acts
  and the glorious splendor of
    your kingdom.
13 Your kingdom is an everlasting
    kingdom,
  and your dominion endures
    through all generations.

  The LORD is faithful to all his
    promises
  and loving toward all he has
    made.ʷ
14 The LORD upholds all those
    who fall
  and lifts up all who are
    bowed down.
15 The eyes of all look to you,

and you give them their food
  at the proper time.
16 You open your hand
  and satisfy the desires of
    every living thing.

17 The LORD is righteous in all his
    ways
  and loving toward all he has
    made.
18 The LORD is near to all who
    call on him,
  to all who call on him in truth.
19 He fulfills the desires of those
    who fear him;
  he hears their cry and saves
    them.
20 The LORD watches over all who
    love him,
  but all the wicked he will
    destroy.

21 My mouth will speak in praise
    of the LORD.
  Let every creature praise his
    holy name
  for ever and ever.

Psalm 146

1 Praise the LORD.ˣ

  Praise the LORD, O my soul.
2   I will praise the LORD all my
      life;
  I will sing praise to my God
      as long as I live.

3 Do not put your trust in princes,
  in mortal men, who cannot
    save.
4 When their spirit departs, they
    return to the ground;
  on that very day their plans
    come to nothing.

ᵛ 5 Dead Sea Scrolls and Syriac (see also Septuagint); Masoretic Text *On the glorious
splendor of your majesty / and on your wonderful works I will meditate*   ʷ 13 One
manuscript of the Masoretic Text, Dead Sea Scrolls and Syriac (see also Septuagint); most
manuscripts of the Masoretic Text do not have the last two lines of verse 13.   ˣ 1 *Hebrew
Hallelu Yah; also in verse 10*

5 Blessed is he whose help is the
    God of Jacob,
    whose hope is in the LORD his
    God,
6 the Maker of heaven and earth,
    the sea, and everything in
    them—
    the LORD, who remains
    faithful forever.
7 He upholds the cause of the
    oppressed
    and gives food to the hungry.
    The LORD sets prisoners free,
8   the LORD gives sight to the
        blind,
    the LORD lifts up those who are
        bowed down,
    the LORD loves the righteous.
9 The LORD watches over the alien
    and sustains the fatherless
        and the widow,
    but he frustrates the ways of
        the wicked.

10 The LORD reigns forever,
    your God, O Zion, for all
        generations.

    Praise the LORD.

Psalm 147

1 Praise the LORD.y

    How good it is to sing praises to
        our God,
    how pleasant and fitting to
        praise him!

2 The LORD builds up Jerusalem;
    he gathers the exiles of Israel.
3 He heals the brokenhearted
    and binds up their wounds.
4 He determines the number of
        the stars
    and calls them each by name.

5 Great is our Lord and mighty
    in power;
    his understanding has no limit.
6 The LORD sustains the humble
    but casts the wicked to the
        ground.

7 Sing to the LORD with
        thanksgiving;
    make music to our God on
        the harp.
8 He covers the sky with clouds;
    he supplies the earth with rain
    and makes grass grow on the
        hills.
9 He provides food for the cattle
    and for the young ravens
        when they call.

10 His pleasure is not in the
        strength of the horse,
    nor his delight in the legs of a
        man;
11 the LORD delights in those who
        fear him,
    who put their hope in his
        unfailing love.

12 Extol the LORD, O Jerusalem;
    praise your God, O Zion,
13 for he strengthens the bars of
        your gates
    and blesses your people
        within you.
14 He grants peace to your borders
    and satisfies you with the
        finest of wheat.

15 He sends his command to the
        earth;
    his word runs swiftly.
16 He spreads the snow like wool
    and scatters the frost like ashes.
17 He hurls down his hail like
        pebbles.
    Who can withstand his icy
        blast?

y 1 Hebrew Hallelu Yah; also in verse 20

18 He sends his word and melts
   them;
   he stirs up his breezes, and
   the waters flow.

19 He has revealed his word to
   Jacob,
   his laws and decrees to Israel.

20 He has done this for no other
   nation;
   they do not know his laws.

   Praise the LORD.

Psalm 148

1 Praise the LORD.ᶻ

   Praise the LORD from the
   heavens,
   praise him in the heights
   above.

2 Praise him, all his angels,
   praise him, all his heavenly
   hosts.

3 Praise him, sun and moon,
   praise him, all you shining
   stars.

4 Praise him, you highest heavens
   and you waters above the
   skies.

5 Let them praise the name of
   the LORD,
   for he commanded and they
   were created.

6 He set them in place for ever
   and ever;
   he gave a decree that will
   never pass away.

7 Praise the LORD from the earth,
   you great sea creatures and
   all ocean depths,

8 lightning and hail, snow and
   clouds,
   stormy winds that do his
   bidding,

9 you mountains and all hills,
   fruit trees and all cedars,

10 wild animals and all cattle,
   small creatures and flying
   birds,

11 kings of the earth and all nations,
   you princes and all rulers on
   earth,

12 young men and maidens,
   old men and children.

13 Let them praise the name of
   the LORD,
   for his name alone is exalted;
   his splendor is above the
   earth and the heavens.

14 He has raised up for his people
   a horn,ᵃ
   the praise of all his saints,
   of Israel, the people close to
   his heart.

   Praise the LORD.

Psalm 149

1 Praise the LORD.ᵇ

   Sing to the LORD a new song,
   his praise in the assembly of
   the saints.

2 Let Israel rejoice in their Maker;
   let the people of Zion be glad
   in their King.

3 Let them praise his name with
   dancing
   and make music to him with
   tambourine and harp.

4 For the LORD takes delight in
   his people;
   he crowns the humble with
   salvation.

5 Let the saints rejoice in this honor
   and sing for joy on their beds.

6 May the praise of God be in
   their mouths

ᶻ 1 Hebrew Hallelu Yah; also in verse 14   ᵃ 14 Horn here symbolizes strong one, that is,
king.   ᵇ 1 Hebrew Hallelu Yah; also in verse 9

and a double-edged sword in
their hands,
7 to inflict vengeance on the
    nations
  and punishment on the
    peoples,
8 to bind their kings with fetters,
  their nobles with shackles of
    iron,
9 to carry out the sentence
    written against them.
  This is the glory of all his saints.

Praise the LORD.

Psalm 150

1 Praise the LORD.c

Praise God in his sanctuary;
  praise him in his mighty
    heavens.

2 Praise him for his acts of
    power;
  praise him for his surpassing
    greatness.
3 Praise him with the sounding
    of the trumpet,
  praise him with the harp and
    lyre,
4 praise him with tambourine
    and dancing,
  praise him with the strings
    and flute,
5 praise him with the clash of
    cymbals,
  praise him with resounding
    cymbals.

6 Let everything that has breath
    praise the LORD.

Praise the LORD.

---

c 1 Hebrew *Hallelu Yah*; also in verse 6

Proverbs

Prologue: Purpose and Theme

1 ¹ The proverbs of Solomon son
of David, king of Israel:

² for attaining wisdom and
    discipline;
  for understanding words of
    insight;

³ for acquiring a disciplined and
    prudent life,
  doing what is right and just
    and fair;

⁴ for giving prudence to the
    simple,
  knowledge and discretion to
    the young—

⁵ let the wise listen and add to
    their learning,
  and let the discerning get
    guidance—

⁶ for understanding proverbs and
    parables,
  the sayings and riddles of the
    wise.

⁷ The fear of the LORD is the
    beginning of knowledge,
  but fools*a* despise wisdom and
    discipline.

Exhortations to Embrace Wisdom

Warning Against Enticement

⁸ Listen, my son, to your father's
    instruction
  and do not forsake your
    mother's teaching.

⁹ They will be a garland to grace
    your head
  and a chain to adorn your
    neck.

¹⁰ My son, if sinners entice you,
   do not give in to them.

¹¹ If they say, "Come along with
    us;
  let's lie in wait for someone's
    blood,
  let's waylay some harmless
    soul;

¹² let's swallow them alive, like
    the grave,*b*
  and whole, like those who go
    down to the pit;

¹³ we will get all sorts of valuable
    things
  and fill our houses with
    plunder;

¹⁴ throw in your lot with us,
   and we will share a common
    purse"—

¹⁵ my son, do not go along with
    them,
  do not set foot on their paths;

¹⁶ for their feet rush into sin,
   they are swift to shed blood.

¹⁷ How useless to spread a net
   in full view of all the birds!

¹⁸ These men lie in wait for their
    own blood;
  they waylay only themselves!

¹⁹ Such is the end of all who go
    after ill-gotten gain;
  it takes away the lives of
    those who get it.

---

a 7 The Hebrew words rendered *fool* in Proverbs, and often elsewhere in the Old Testament,
denote one who is morally deficient.   *b 12* Hebrew *Sheol*

Warning Against Rejecting Wisdom

20 Wisdom calls aloud in the
    street,
   she raises her voice in the
    public squares;
21 at the head of the noisy streetsᶜ
    she cries out,
   in the gateways of the city she
    makes her speech:

22 "How long will you simple
    onesᵈ love your simple
    ways?
   How long will mockers
    delight in mockery
   and fools hate knowledge?
23 If you had responded to my
    rebuke,
   I would have poured out my
    heart to you
   and made my thoughts
    known to you.
24 But since you rejected me when
    I called
   and no one gave heed when I
    stretched out my hand,
25 since you ignored all my advice
   and would not accept my
    rebuke,
26 I in turn will laugh at your
    disaster;
   I will mock when calamity
    overtakes you —
27 when calamity overtakes you
    like a storm,
   when disaster sweeps over
    you like a whirlwind,
   when distress and trouble
    overwhelm you.

28 "Then they will call to me but I
    will not answer;
   they will look for me but will
    not find me.

29 Since they hated knowledge
   and did not choose to fear the
    LORD,
30 since they would not accept my
    advice
   and spurned my rebuke,
31 they will eat the fruit of their
    ways
   and be filled with the fruit of
    their schemes.
32 For the waywardness of the
    simple will kill them,
   and the complacency of fools
    will destroy them;
33 but whoever listens to me will
    live in safety
   and be at ease, without fear
    of harm."

Moral Benefits of Wisdom

2 ¹ My son, if you accept my
    words
   and store up my commands
    within you,
2 turning your ear to wisdom
   and applying your heart to
    understanding,
3 and if you call out for insight
   and cry aloud for
    understanding,
4 and if you look for it as for
    silver
   and search for it as for hidden
    treasure,
5 then you will understand the
    fear of the LORD
   and find the knowledge of
    God.
6 For the LORD gives wisdom,
   and from his mouth come
    knowledge and
    understanding.
7 He holds victory in store for the
    upright,

ᶜ *21* Hebrew; Septuagint / *on the tops of the walls*   ᵈ *22* The Hebrew word rendered
simple in Proverbs generally denotes one without moral direction and inclined to evil.

he is a shield to those whose
walk is blameless,
8 for he guards the course of the
just
and protects the way of his
faithful ones.
9 Then you will understand what
is right and just
and fair—every good path.
10 For wisdom will enter your
heart,
and knowledge will be
pleasant to your soul.
11 Discretion will protect you,
and understanding will guard
you.
12 Wisdom will save you from the
ways of wicked men,
from men whose words are
perverse,
13 who leave the straight paths
to walk in dark ways,
14 who delight in doing wrong
and rejoice in the
perverseness of evil,
15 whose paths are crooked
and who are devious in their
ways.
16 It will save you also from the
adulteress,
from the wayward wife with
her seductive words,
17 who has left the partner of her
youth
and ignored the covenant she
made before God.e
18 For her house leads down to
death
and her paths to the spirits of
the dead.
19 None who go to her return
or attain the paths of life.
20 Thus you will walk in the ways
of good men

and keep to the paths of the
righteous.
21 For the upright will live in the
land,
and the blameless will remain
in it;
22 but the wicked will be cut off
from the land,
and the unfaithful will be torn
from it.

Further Benefits of Wisdom

3 1 My son, do not forget my
teaching,
but keep my commands in
your heart,
2 for they will prolong your life
many years
and bring you prosperity.

3 Let love and faithfulness never
leave you;
bind them around your neck,
write them on the tablet of
your heart.
4 Then you will win favor and a
good name
in the sight of God and man.

5 Trust in the LORD with all your
heart
and lean not on your own
understanding;
6 in all your ways acknowledge
him,
and he will make your paths
straightf

7 Do not be wise in your own
eyes;
fear the LORD and shun evil.
8 This will bring health to your
body
and nourishment to your bones.

9 Honor the LORD with your
wealth,

e 17 Or covenant of her God   f 6 Or will direct your paths

with the firstfruits of all your
crops;

10 then your barns will be filled to
overflowing,
and your vats will brim over
with new wine.

11 My son, do not despise the
LORD's discipline
and do not resent his rebuke,

12 because the LORD disciplines
those he loves,
as a father[g] the son he
delights in.

13 Blessed is the man who finds
wisdom,
the man who gains
understanding,

14 for she is more profitable than
silver
and yields better returns than
gold.

15 She is more precious than rubies;
nothing you desire can
compare with her.

16 Long life is in her right hand;
in her left hand are riches and
honor.

17 Her ways are pleasant ways,
and all her paths are peace.

18 She is a tree of life to those
who embrace her;
those who lay hold of her will
be blessed.

19 By wisdom the LORD laid the
earth's foundations,
by understanding he set the
heavens in place;

20 by his knowledge the deeps
were divided,
and the clouds let drop the
dew.

21 My son, preserve sound
judgment and discernment,

do not let them out of your
sight;

22 they will be life for you,
an ornament to grace your
neck.

23 Then you will go on your way
in safety,
and your foot will not
stumble;

24 when you lie down, you will
not be afraid;
when you lie down, your
sleep will be sweet.

25 Have no fear of sudden disaster
or of the ruin that overtakes
the wicked,

26 for the LORD will be your
confidence
and will keep your foot from
being snared.

27 Do not withhold good from
those who deserve it,
when it is in your power to
act.

28 Do not say to your neighbor,
"Come back later; I'll give it
tomorrow"—
when you now have it with you.

29 Do not plot harm against your
neighbor,
who lives trustfully near you.

30 Do not accuse a man for no
reason—
when he has done you no
harm.

31 Do not envy a violent man
or choose any of his ways,

32 for the LORD detests a perverse
man
but takes the upright into his
confidence.

33 The LORD's curse is on the
house of the wicked,

but he blesses the home of
the righteous.
34 He mocks proud mockers
but gives grace to the humble.
35 The wise inherit honor,
but fools he holds up to shame.

Wisdom Is Supreme

4 ¹ Listen, my sons, to a father's
instruction;
pay attention and gain
understanding.
2 I give you sound learning,
so do not forsake my teaching.
3 When I was a boy in my
father's house,
still tender, and an only child
of my mother,
4 he taught me and said,
"Lay hold of my words with
all your heart;
keep my commands and you
will live.
5 Get wisdom, get understanding;
do not forget my words or
swerve from them.
6 Do not forsake wisdom, and
she will protect you;
love her, and she will watch
over you.
7 Wisdom is supreme; therefore
get wisdom.
Though it cost all you have,h
get understanding.
8 Esteem her, and she will exalt
you;
embrace her, and she will
honor you.
9 She will set a garland of grace
on your head
and present you with a crown
of splendor."

10 Listen, my son, accept what I
say,

and the years of your life will
be many.
11 I guide you in the way of wisdom
and lead you along straight
paths.
12 When you walk, your steps will
not be hampered;
when you run, you will not
stumble.
13 Hold on to instruction, do not
let it go;
guard it well, for it is your life.
14 Do not set foot on the path of
the wicked
or walk in the way of evil
men.
15 Avoid it, do not travel on it;
turn from it and go on your
way.
16 For they cannot sleep till they
do evil;
they are robbed of slumber
till they make someone
fall.
17 They eat the bread of
wickedness
and drink the wine of
violence.
18 The path of the righteous is like
the first gleam of dawn,
shining ever brighter till the
full light of day.
19 But the way of the wicked is
like deep darkness;
they do not know what makes
them stumble.

20 My son, pay attention to what I
say;
listen closely to my words.
21 Do not let them out of your
sight,
keep them within your heart;
22 for they are life to those who
find them

---

h 7 Or *Whatever else you get*

and health to a man's whole
body.
23 Above all else, guard your heart,
for it is the wellspring of life.
24 Put away perversity from your
mouth;
keep corrupt talk far from
your lips.
25 Let your eyes look straight ahead,
fix your gaze directly before
you.
26 Make level[i] paths for your feet
and take only ways that are
firm.
27 Do not swerve to the right or
the left;
keep your foot from evil.

Warning Against Adultery

5 1 My son, pay attention to my
wisdom,
listen well to my words of
insight,
2 that you may maintain discretion
and your lips may preserve
knowledge.
3 For the lips of an adulteress
drip honey,
and her speech is smoother
than oil;
4 but in the end she is bitter as
gall,
sharp as a double-edged
sword.
5 Her feet go down to death;
her steps lead straight to the
grave.[j]
6 She gives no thought to the
way of life;
her paths are crooked, but
she knows it not.

7 Now then, my sons, listen to me;
do not turn aside from what I
say.
8 Keep to a path far from her,

do not go near the door of her
house,
9 lest you give your best strength
to others
and your years to one who is
cruel,
10 lest strangers feast on your
wealth
and your toil enrich another
man's house.
11 At the end of your life you will
groan,
when your flesh and body are
spent.
12 You will say, "How I hated
discipline!
How my heart spurned
correction!
13 I would not obey my teachers
or listen to my instructors.
14 I have come to the brink of
utter ruin
in the midst of the whole
assembly."

15 Drink water from your own
cistern,
running water from your own
well.
16 Should your springs overflow in
the streets,
your streams of water in the
public squares?
17 Let them be yours alone,
never to be shared with
strangers.
18 May your fountain be blessed,
and may you rejoice in the
wife of your youth.
19 A loving doe, a graceful deer—
may her breasts satisfy you
always,
may you ever be captivated
by her love.
20 Why be captivated, my son, by
an adulteress?

i 26 Or Consider the   j 5 Hebrew Sheol

Why embrace the bosom of
another man's wife?

21 For a man's ways are in full
view of the LORD,
and he examines all his paths.

22 The evil deeds of a wicked man
ensnare him;
the cords of his sin hold him
fast.

23 He will die for lack of discipline,
led astray by his own great
folly.

Warnings Against Folly

6 **1** My son, if you have put up
security for your neighbor,
if you have struck hands in
pledge for another,

2 if you have been trapped by
what you said,
ensnared by the words of
your mouth,

3 then do this, my son, to free
yourself,
since you have fallen into
your neighbor's hands:
Go and humble yourself;
press your plea with your
neighbor!

4 Allow no sleep to your eyes,
no slumber to your eyelids.

5 Free yourself, like a gazelle
from the hand of the
hunter,
like a bird from the snare of
the fowler.

6 Go to the ant, you sluggard;
consider its ways and be wise!

7 It has no commander,
no overseer or ruler,

8 yet it stores its provisions in
summer
and gathers its food at
harvest.

9 How long will you lie there,
you sluggard?
When will you get up from
your sleep?

10 A little sleep, a little slumber,
a little folding of the hands to
rest—

11 and poverty will come on you
like a bandit
and scarcity like an armed
man.[k]

12 A scoundrel and villain,
who goes about with a
corrupt mouth,

13 who winks with his eye,
signals with his feet
and motions with his fingers,

14 who plots evil with deceit in
his heart—
he always stirs up dissension.

15 Therefore disaster will overtake
him in an instant;
he will suddenly be destroyed—
without remedy.

16 There are six things the LORD
hates,
seven that are detestable to
him:

17   haughty eyes,
a lying tongue,
hands that shed innocent
blood,

18   a heart that devises wicked
schemes,
feet that are quick to rush
into evil,

19   a false witness who pours out
lies
and a man who stirs up
dissension among brothers.

Warning Against Adultery

20 My son, keep your father's
commands

---

k 11 Or *like a vagrant / and scarcity like a beggar*

and do not forsake your
mother's teaching.
21 Bind them upon your heart
forever;
fasten them around your neck.
22 When you walk, they will guide
you;
when you sleep, they will
watch over you;
when you awake, they will
speak to you.
23 For these commands are a lamp,
this teaching is a light,
and the corrections of discipline
are the way to life,
24 keeping you from the immoral
woman,
from the smooth tongue of
the wayward wife.
25 Do not lust in your heart after
her beauty
or let her captivate you with
her eyes,
26 for the prostitute reduces you
to a loaf of bread,
and the adulteress preys upon
your very life.
27 Can a man scoop fire into his
lap
without his clothes being
burned?
28 Can a man walk on hot coals
without his feet being scorched?
29 So is he who sleeps with
another man's wife;
no one who touches her will
go unpunished.
30 Men do not despise a thief if he
steals
to satisfy his hunger when he
is starving.
31 Yet if he is caught, he must pay
sevenfold,
though it costs him all the
wealth of his house.
32 But a man who commits
adultery lacks judgment;

whoever does so destroys
himself.
33 Blows and disgrace are his lot,
and his shame will never be
wiped away;
34 for jealousy arouses a
husband's fury,
and he will show no mercy
when he takes revenge.
35 He will not accept any
compensation;
he will refuse the bribe,
however great it is.

Warning Against the Adulteress

7 1 My son, keep my words
and store up my commands
within you.
2 Keep my commands and you
will live;
guard my teachings as the
apple of your eye.
3 Bind them on your fingers;
write them on the tablet of
your heart.
4 Say to wisdom, "You are my
sister,"
and call understanding your
kinsman;
5 they will keep you from the
adulteress,
from the wayward wife with
her seductive words.

6 At the window of my house
I looked out through the
lattice.
7 I saw among the simple,
I noticed among the young
men,
a youth who lacked judgment.
8 He was going down the street
near her corner,
walking along in the direction
of her house
9 at twilight, as the day was
fading,
as the dark of night set in.

10 Then out came a woman to
     meet him,
  dressed like a prostitute and
     with crafty intent.
11 (She is loud and defiant,
  her feet never stay at home;
12 now in the street, now in the
     squares,
  at every corner she lurks.)
13 She took hold of him and
     kissed him
  and with a brazen face she said:

14 "I have fellowship offerings[l] at
     home;
  today I fulfilled my vows.
15 So I came out to meet you;
  I looked for you and have
     found you!
16 I have covered my bed
  with colored linens from Egypt.
17 I have perfumed my bed
  with myrrh, aloes and
     cinnamon.
18 Come, let's drink deep of love
     till morning;
  let's enjoy ourselves with love!
19 My husband is not at home;
  he has gone on a long journey.
20 He took his purse filled with
     money
  and will not be home till full
     moon."

21 With persuasive words she led
     him astray;
  she seduced him with her
     smooth talk.
22 All at once he followed her
  like an ox going to the
     slaughter,
  like a deer[m] stepping into a
     noose[n]
23 till an arrow pierces his liver,
  like a bird darting into a snare,

little knowing it will cost him
     his life.

24 Now then, my sons, listen to
     me;
  pay attention to what I say.
25 Do not let your heart turn to
     her ways
  or stray into her paths.
26 Many are the victims she has
     brought down;
  her slain are a mighty throng.
27 Her house is a highway to the
     grave,[o]
  leading down to the chambers
     of death.

Wisdom's Call

8 1 Does not wisdom call out?
  Does not understanding raise
     her voice?
2 On the heights along the way,
  where the paths meet, she
     takes her stand;
3 beside the gates leading into
     the city,
  at the entrances, she cries
     aloud:
4 "To you, O men, I call out;
  I raise my voice to all
     mankind.
5 You who are simple, gain
     prudence;
  you who are foolish, gain
     understanding.
6 Listen, for I have worthy things
     to say;
  I open my lips to speak what
     is right.
7 My mouth speaks what is true,
  for my lips detest wickedness.
8 All the words of my mouth are
     just;
  none of them is crooked or
     perverse.

---

l 14 Traditionally *peace offerings*   *m* 22 Syriac (see also Septuagint); Hebrew *fool*
n 22 The meaning of the Hebrew for this line is uncertain.   *o* 27 Hebrew *Sheol*

9 To the discerning all of them
     are right;
   they are faultless to those
     who have knowledge.
10 Choose my instruction instead
     of silver,
   knowledge rather than choice
     gold,
11 for wisdom is more precious
     than rubies,
   and nothing you desire can
     compare with her.

12 "I, wisdom, dwell together with
     prudence;
   I possess knowledge and
     discretion.
13 To fear the LORD is to hate evil;
   I hate pride and arrogance,
     evil behavior and perverse
     speech.
14 Counsel and sound judgment
     are mine;
   I have understanding and
     power.
15 By me kings reign
   and rulers make laws that are
     just;
16 by me princes govern,
   and all nobles who rule on
     earth.p
17 I love those who love me,
   and those who seek me find me.
18 With me are riches and honor,
   enduring wealth and prosperity.
19 My fruit is better than fine gold;
   what I yield surpasses choice
     silver.
20 I walk in the way of
     righteousness,
   along the paths of justice,
21 bestowing wealth on those who
     love me
   and making their treasuries full.

22 "The LORD brought me forth as
     the first of his works,q,r
   before his deeds of old;
23 I was appointeds from eternity,
   from the beginning, before
     the world began.
24 When there were no oceans, I
     was given birth,
   when there were no springs
     abounding with water;
25 before the mountains were
     settled in place,
   before the hills, I was given
     birth,
26 before he made the earth or its
     fields
   or any of the dust of the world.
27 I was there when he set the
     heavens in place,
   when he marked out the
     horizon on the face of the
     deep,
28 when he established the clouds
     above
   and fixed securely the
     fountains of the deep,
29 when he gave the sea its
     boundary
   so the waters would not
     overstep his command,
   and when he marked out the
     foundations of the earth.
30 Then I was the craftsman at
     his side.
   I was filled with delight day
     after day,
   rejoicing always in his
     presence,
31 rejoicing in his whole world
   and delighting in mankind.

32 "Now then, my sons, listen to me;
   blessed are those who keep
     my ways.

---

p 16 Many Hebrew manuscripts and Septuagint; most Hebrew manuscripts and nobles—all
righteous rulers   q 22 Or way; or dominion   r 22 Or The LORD possessed me at the
beginning of his work; or The LORD brought me forth at the beginning of his work   s 23 Or
fashioned

33 Listen to my instruction and be
wise;
  do not ignore it.
34 Blessed is the man who listens
to me,
  watching daily at my doors,
  waiting at my doorway.
35 For whoever finds me finds life
and receives favor from the
LORD.
36 But whoever fails to find me
harms himself;
  all who hate me love death."

Invitations of Wisdom and of Folly

9 **1** Wisdom has built her house;
  she has hewn out its seven
  pillars.
2 She has prepared her meat and
mixed her wine;
  she has also set her table.
3 She has sent out her maids,
and she calls
  from the highest point of the
  city.
4 "Let all who are simple come in
here!"
  she says to those who lack
  judgment.
5 "Come, eat my food
and drink the wine I have
mixed.
6 Leave your simple ways and
you will live;
  walk in the way of
  understanding.

7 "Whoever corrects a mocker
invites insult;
  whoever rebukes a wicked
  man incurs abuse.
8 Do not rebuke a mocker or he
will hate you;
  rebuke a wise man and he
  will love you.

9 Instruct a wise man and he will
be wiser still;
  teach a righteous man and he
  will add to his learning.

10 "The fear of the LORD is the
beginning of wisdom,
  and knowledge of the Holy
  One is understanding.
11 For through me your days will
be many,
  and years will be added to
  your life.
12 If you are wise, your wisdom
will reward you;
  if you are a mocker, you alone
  will suffer."

13 The woman Folly is loud;
  she is undisciplined and
  without knowledge.
14 She sits at the door of her house,
  on a seat at the highest point
  of the city,
15 calling out to those who pass by,
  who go straight on their way.
16 "Let all who are simple come in
here!"
  she says to those who lack
  judgment.
17 "Stolen water is sweet;
  food eaten in secret is
  delicious!"
18 But little do they know that the
dead are there,
  that her guests are in the
  depths of the grave.ᵗ

Proverbs of Solomon

10 **1** The proverbs of Solomon:
A wise son brings joy to his
father,

ᵗ *18* Hebrew *Sheol*

but a foolish son grief to his
mother.

2 Ill-gotten treasures are of no
value,
but righteousness delivers
from death.

3 The LORD does not let the
righteous go hungry
but he thwarts the craving of
the wicked.

4 Lazy hands make a man poor,
but diligent hands bring wealth.

5 He who gathers crops in
summer is a wise son,
but he who sleeps during
harvest is a disgraceful son.

6 Blessings crown the head of the
righteous,
but violence overwhelms the
mouth of the wicked.ᵘ

7 The memory of the righteous
will be a blessing,
but the name of the wicked
will rot.

8 The wise in heart accept
commands,
but a chattering fool comes to
ruin.

9 The man of integrity walks
securely,
but he who takes crooked
paths will be found out.

10 He who winks maliciously
causes grief,
and a chattering fool comes
to ruin.

11 The mouth of the righteous is a
fountain of life,
but violence overwhelms the
mouth of the wicked.

12 Hatred stirs up dissension,
but love covers over all
wrongs.

13 Wisdom is found on the lips of
the discerning,
but a rod is for the back of
him who lacks judgment.

14 Wise men store up knowledge,
but the mouth of a fool
invites ruin.

15 The wealth of the rich is their
fortified city,
but poverty is the ruin of the
poor.

16 The wages of the righteous
bring them life,
but the income of the wicked
brings them punishment.

17 He who heeds discipline shows
the way to life,
but whoever ignores
correction leads others
astray.

18 He who conceals his hatred has
lying lips,
and whoever spreads slander
is a fool.

19 When words are many, sin is
not absent,
but he who holds his tongue
is wise.

20 The tongue of the righteous is
choice silver,
but the heart of the wicked is
of little value.

21 The lips of the righteous
nourish many,
but fools die for lack of
judgment.

ᵘ 6 Or *but the mouth of the wicked conceals violence*; also in verse 11

22 The blessing of the LORD brings
wealth,
  and he adds no trouble to it.

23 A fool finds pleasure in evil
conduct,
  but a man of understanding
  delights in wisdom.

24 What the wicked dreads will
overtake him;
  what the righteous desire will
  be granted.

25 When the storm has swept by,
the wicked are gone,
  but the righteous stand firm
  forever.

26 As vinegar to the teeth and
smoke to the eyes,
  so is a sluggard to those who
  send him.

27 The fear of the LORD adds
length to life,
  but the years of the wicked
  are cut short.

28 The prospect of the righteous is
joy,
  but the hopes of the wicked
  come to nothing.

29 The way of the LORD is a refuge
for the righteous,
  but it is the ruin of those who
  do evil.

30 The righteous will never be
uprooted,
  but the wicked will not
  remain in the land.

31 The mouth of the righteous
brings forth wisdom,
  but a perverse tongue will be
  cut out.

32 The lips of the righteous know
what is fitting,
  but the mouth of the wicked
  only what is perverse.

11 1 The LORD abhors dishonest
scales,
  but accurate weights are his
  delight.

2 When pride comes, then comes
disgrace,
  but with humility comes
  wisdom.

3 The integrity of the upright
guides them,
  but the unfaithful are
  destroyed by their
  duplicity.

4 Wealth is worthless in the day
of wrath,
  but righteousness delivers
  from death.

5 The righteousness of the
blameless makes a straight
way for them,
  but the wicked are brought
  down by their own
  wickedness.

6 The righteousness of the
upright delivers them,
  but the unfaithful are trapped
  by evil desires.

7 When a wicked man dies, his
hope perishes;
  all he expected from his
  power comes to nothing.

8 The righteous man is rescued
from trouble,
  and it comes on the wicked
  instead.

9 With his mouth the godless
destroys his neighbor,
  but through knowledge the
  righteous escape.

10 When the righteous prosper,
the city rejoices;
  when the wicked perish,
  there are shouts of joy.

11 Through the blessing of the
    upright a city is exalted,
  but by the mouth of the
    wicked it is destroyed.

12 A man who lacks judgment
    derides his neighbor,
  but a man of understanding
    holds his tongue.

13 A gossip betrays a confidence,
  but a trustworthy man keeps
    a secret.

14 For lack of guidance a nation
    falls,
  but many advisers make
    victory sure.

15 He who puts up security for
    another will surely suffer,
  but whoever refuses to strike
    hands in pledge is safe.

16 A kindhearted woman gains
    respect,
  but ruthless men gain only
    wealth.

17 A kind man benefits himself,
  but a cruel man brings
    trouble on himself.

18 The wicked man earns
    deceptive wages,
  but he who sows
    righteousness reaps a sure
    reward.

19 The truly righteous man attains
    life,
  but he who pursues evil goes
    to his death.

20 The LORD detests men of
    perverse heart
  but he delights in those
    whose ways are blameless.

21 Be sure of this: The wicked will
    not go unpunished,
  but those who are righteous
    will go free.

22 Like a gold ring in a pig's snout
  is a beautiful woman who
    shows no discretion.

23 The desire of the righteous
    ends only in good,
  but the hope of the wicked
    only in wrath.

24 One man gives freely, yet gains
    even more;
  another withholds unduly, but
    comes to poverty.

25 A generous man will prosper;
  he who refreshes others will
    himself be refreshed.

26 People curse the man who
    hoards grain,
  but blessing crowns him who
    is willing to sell.

27 He who seeks good finds
    goodwill,
  but evil comes to him who
    searches for it.

28 Whoever trusts in his riches
    will fall,
  but the righteous will thrive
    like a green leaf.

29 He who brings trouble on his
    family will inherit only
    wind,
  and the fool will be servant to
    the wise.

30 The fruit of the righteous is a
    tree of life,
  and he who wins souls is wise.

31 If the righteous receive their
    due on earth,
  how much more the ungodly
    and the sinner!

12 ¹ Whoever loves discipline
    loves knowledge,
  but he who hates correction is
    stupid.

2 A good man obtains favor from the LORD,
but the LORD condemns a crafty man.

3 A man cannot be established through wickedness,
but the righteous cannot be uprooted.

4 A wife of noble character is her husband's crown,
but a disgraceful wife is like decay in his bones.

5 The plans of the righteous are just,
but the advice of the wicked is deceitful.

6 The words of the wicked lie in wait for blood,
but the speech of the upright rescues them.

7 Wicked men are overthrown and are no more,
but the house of the righteous stands firm.

8 A man is praised according to his wisdom,
but men with warped minds are despised.

9 Better to be a nobody and yet have a servant
than pretend to be somebody and have no food.

10 A righteous man cares for the needs of his animal,
but the kindest acts of the wicked are cruel.

11 He who works his land will have abundant food,
but he who chases fantasies lacks judgment.

12 The wicked desire the plunder of evil men,
but the root of the righteous flourishes.

13 An evil man is trapped by his sinful talk,
but a righteous man escapes trouble.

14 From the fruit of his lips a man is filled with good things
as surely as the work of his hands rewards him.

15 The way of a fool seems right to him,
but a wise man listens to advice.

16 A fool shows his annoyance at once,
but a prudent man overlooks an insult.

17 A truthful witness gives honest testimony,
but a false witness tells lies.

18 Reckless words pierce like a sword,
but the tongue of the wise brings healing.

19 Truthful lips endure forever,
but a lying tongue lasts only a moment.

20 There is deceit in the hearts of those who plot evil,
but joy for those who promote peace.

21 No harm befalls the righteous,
but the wicked have their fill of trouble.

22 The LORD detests lying lips,
but he delights in men who are truthful.

23 A prudent man keeps his knowledge to himself,
but the heart of fools blurts out folly.

24 Diligent hands will rule,
but laziness ends in slave labor.

25 An anxious heart weighs a man
down,
but a kind word cheers him up.

26 A righteous man is cautious in
friendship,[v]
but the way of the wicked
leads them astray.

27 The lazy man does not roast[w]
his game,
but the diligent man prizes
his possessions.

28 In the way of righteousness
there is life;
along that path is immortality.

13 1 A wise son heeds his
father's instruction,
but a mocker does not listen
to rebuke.

2 From the fruit of his lips a man
enjoys good things,
but the unfaithful have a
craving for violence.

3 He who guards his lips guards
his life,
but he who speaks rashly will
come to ruin.

4 The sluggard craves and gets
nothing,
but the desires of the diligent
are fully satisfied.

5 The righteous hate what is false,
but the wicked bring shame
and disgrace.

6 Righteousness guards the man
of integrity,
but wickedness overthrows
the sinner.

7 One man pretends to be rich,
yet has nothing;
another pretends to be poor,
yet has great wealth.

8 A man's riches may ransom his
life,
but a poor man hears no threat.

9 The light of the righteous
shines brightly,
but the lamp of the wicked is
snuffed out.

10 Pride only breeds quarrels,
but wisdom is found in those
who take advice.

11 Dishonest money dwindles away,
but he who gathers money little
by little makes it grow.

12 Hope deferred makes the heart
sick,
but a longing fulfilled is a tree
of life.

13 He who scorns instruction will
pay for it,
but he who respects a
command is rewarded.

14 The teaching of the wise is a
fountain of life,
turning a man from the
snares of death.

15 Good understanding wins favor,
but the way of the unfaithful
is hard.[x]

16 Every prudent man acts out of
knowledge,
but a fool exposes his folly.

17 A wicked messenger falls into
trouble,
but a trustworthy envoy
brings healing.

---

[v] 26 Or *man is a guide to his neighbor*   [w] 27 The meaning of the Hebrew for this word is
uncertain.   [x] 15 Or *unfaithful does not endure*

18 He who ignores discipline comes
     to poverty and shame,
   but whoever heeds correction
     is honored.

19 A longing fulfilled is sweet to
     the soul,
   but fools detest turning from
     evil.

20 He who walks with the wise
     grows wise,
   but a companion of fools
     suffers harm.

21 Misfortune pursues the sinner,
   but prosperity is the reward
     of the righteous.

22 A good man leaves an
     inheritance for his
     children's children,
   but a sinner's wealth is stored
     up for the righteous.

23 A poor man's field may produce
     abundant food,
   but injustice sweeps it away.

24 He who spares the rod hates his
     son,
   but he who loves him is
     careful to discipline him.

25 The righteous eat to their
     hearts' content,
   but the stomach of the wicked
     goes hungry.

14 1 The wise woman builds her
        house,
      but with her own hands the
        foolish one tears hers down.

2 He whose walk is upright fears
     the LORD,
   but he whose ways are
     devious despises him.

3 A fool's talk brings a rod to his
     back,
   but the lips of the wise
     protect them.

4 Where there are no oxen, the
     manger is empty,
   but from the strength of an ox
     comes an abundant harvest.

5 A truthful witness does not
     deceive,
   but a false witness pours out
     lies.

6 The mocker seeks wisdom and
     finds none,
   but knowledge comes easily
     to the discerning.

7 Stay away from a foolish man,
   for you will not find
     knowledge on his lips.

8 The wisdom of the prudent is to
     give thought to their ways,
   but the folly of fools is
     deception.

9 Fools mock at making amends
     for sin,
   but goodwill is found among
     the upright.

10 Each heart knows its own
     bitterness,
   and no one else can share its
     joy.

11 The house of the wicked will be
     destroyed,
   but the tent of the upright
     will flourish.

12 There is a way that seems right
     to a man,
   but in the end it leads to
     death.

13 Even in laughter the heart may
     ache,
   and joy may end in grief.

14 The faithless will be fully
     repaid for their ways,
   and the good man rewarded
     for his.

15 A simple man believes anything,
but a prudent man gives
thought to his steps.

16 A wise man fears the LORD and
shuns evil,
but a fool is hotheaded and
reckless.

17 A quick-tempered man does
foolish things,
and a crafty man is hated.

18 The simple inherit folly,
but the prudent are crowned
with knowledge.

19 Evil men will bow down in the
presence of the good,
and the wicked at the gates of
the righteous.

20 The poor are shunned even by
their neighbors,
but the rich have many
friends.

21 He who despises his neighbor
sins,
but blessed is he who is kind
to the needy.

22 Do not those who plot evil go
astray?
But those who plan what is
good findy love and
faithfulness.

23 All hard work brings a profit,
but mere talk leads only to
poverty.

24 The wealth of the wise is their
crown,
but the folly of fools yields
folly.

25 A truthful witness saves lives,
but a false witness is deceitful.

26 He who fears the LORD has a
secure fortress,
and for his children it will be
a refuge.

27 The fear of the LORD is a
fountain of life,
turning a man from the
snares of death.

28 A large population is a king's
glory,
but without subjects a prince
is ruined.

29 A patient man has great
understanding,
but a quick-tempered man
displays folly.

30 A heart at peace gives life to
the body,
but envy rots the bones.

31 He who oppresses the poor
shows contempt for their
Maker,
but whoever is kind to the
needy honors God.

32 When calamity comes, the
wicked are brought down,
but even in death the
righteous have a refuge.

33 Wisdom reposes in the heart of
the discerning
and even among fools she lets
herself be known.z

34 Righteousness exalts a nation,
but sin is a disgrace to any
people.

35 A king delights in a wise
servant,
but a shameful servant incurs
his wrath.

y 22 Or show   z 33 Hebrew; Septuagint and Syriac / but in the heart of fools she is not
known

15 **1** A gentle answer turns away
      wrath,
   but a harsh word stirs up
      anger.

2 The tongue of the wise
      commends knowledge,
   but the mouth of the fool
      gushes folly.

3 The eyes of the LORD are
      everywhere,
   keeping watch on the wicked
      and the good.

4 The tongue that brings healing
      is a tree of life,
   but a deceitful tongue crushes
      the spirit.

5 A fool spurns his father's
      discipline,
   but whoever heeds correction
      shows prudence.

6 The house of the righteous
      contains great treasure,
   but the income of the wicked
      brings them trouble.

7 The lips of the wise spread
      knowledge;
   not so the hearts of fools.

8 The LORD detests the sacrifice
      of the wicked,
   but the prayer of the upright
      pleases him.

9 The LORD detests the way of
      the wicked
   but he loves those who
      pursue righteousness.

10 Stern discipline awaits him
      who leaves the path;
   he who hates correction will die.

11 Death and Destruction[a] lie
      open before the LORD—

how much more the hearts of
   men!

12 A mocker resents correction;
   he will not consult the wise.

13 A happy heart makes the face
      cheerful,
   but heartache crushes the
      spirit.

14 The discerning heart seeks
      knowledge,
   but the mouth of a fool feeds
      on folly.

15 All the days of the oppressed
      are wretched,
   but the cheerful heart has a
      continual feast.

16 Better a little with the fear of
      the LORD
   than great wealth with
      turmoil.

17 Better a meal of vegetables
      where there is love
   than a fattened calf with
      hatred.

18 A hot-tempered man stirs up
      dissension,
   but a patient man calms a
      quarrel.

19 The way of the sluggard is
      blocked with thorns,
   but the path of the upright is
      a highway.

20 A wise son brings joy to his
      father,
   but a foolish man despises his
      mother.

21 Folly delights a man who lacks
      judgment,
   but a man of understanding
      keeps a straight course.

---

a 11 Hebrew *Sheol and Abaddon*

22 Plans fail for lack of counsel,
  but with many advisers they
    succeed.

23 A man finds joy in giving an apt
    reply—
  and how good is a timely word!

24 The path of life leads upward
    for the wise
  to keep him from going down
    to the grave.b

25 The LORD tears down the proud
    man's house
  but he keeps the widow's
    boundaries intact.

26 The LORD detests the thoughts
    of the wicked,
  but those of the pure are
    pleasing to him.

27 A greedy man brings trouble to
    his family,
  but he who hates bribes will live.

28 The heart of the righteous
    weighs its answers,
  but the mouth of the wicked
    gushes evil.

29 The LORD is far from the wicked
  but he hears the prayer of the
    righteous.

30 A cheerful look brings joy to
    the heart,
  and good news gives health
    to the bones.

31 He who listens to a life-giving
    rebuke
  will be at home among the
    wise.

32 He who ignores discipline
    despises himself,
  but whoever heeds correction
    gains understanding.

33 The fear of the LORD teaches a
    man wisdom,c
  and humility comes before
    honor.

16 1 To man belong the plans of
    the heart,
  but from the LORD comes the
    reply of the tongue.

2 All a man's ways seem innocent
    to him,
  but motives are weighed by
    the LORD.

3 Commit to the LORD whatever
    you do,
  and your plans will succeed.

4 The LORD works out everything
    for his own ends—
  even the wicked for a day of
    disaster.

5 The LORD detests all the proud
    of heart.
  Be sure of this: They will not
    go unpunished.

6 Through love and faithfulness
    sin is atoned for;
  through the fear of the LORD
    a man avoids evil.

7 When a man's ways are
    pleasing to the LORD,
  he makes even his enemies
    live at peace with him.

8 Better a little with righteousness
  than much gain with injustice.

9 In his heart a man plans his
    course,
  but the LORD determines his
    steps.

10 The lips of a king speak as an
    oracle,

b 24 Hebrew Sheol   c 33 Or Wisdom teaches the fear of the LORD

and his mouth should not
betray justice.

11 Honest scales and balances are
from the LORD;
all the weights in the bag are
of his making.

12 Kings detest wrongdoing,
for a throne is established
through righteousness.

13 Kings take pleasure in honest lips;
they value a man who speaks
the truth.

14 A king's wrath is a messenger
of death,
but a wise man will appease it.

15 When a king's face brightens, it
means life;
his favor is like a rain cloud in
spring.

16 How much better to get
wisdom than gold,
to choose understanding
rather than silver!

17 The highway of the upright
avoids evil;
he who guards his way
guards his life.

18 Pride goes before destruction,
a haughty spirit before a fall.

19 Better to be lowly in spirit and
among the oppressed
than to share plunder with
the proud.

20 Whoever gives heed to
instruction prospers,
and blessed is he who trusts
in the LORD.

21 The wise in heart are called
discerning,

and pleasant words promote
instruction.d

22 Understanding is a fountain of
life to those who have it,
but folly brings punishment to
fools.

23 A wise man's heart guides his
mouth,
and his lips promote
instruction.e

24 Pleasant words are a
honeycomb,
sweet to the soul and healing
to the bones.

25 There is a way that seems right
to a man,
but in the end it leads to death.

26 The laborer's appetite works for
him;
his hunger drives him on.

27 A scoundrel plots evil,
and his speech is like a
scorching fire.

28 A perverse man stirs up
dissension,
and a gossip separates close
friends.

29 A violent man entices his
neighbor
and leads him down a path
that is not good.

30 He who winks with his eye is
plotting perversity;
he who purses his lips is bent
on evil.

31 Gray hair is a crown of splendor;
it is attained by a righteous life.

32 Better a patient man than a
warrior,

d 21 Or words make a man persuasive   e 23 Or mouth / and makes his lips persuasive

a man who controls his temper
than one who takes a city.

33 The lot is cast into the lap,
but its every decision is from
the LORD.

17 **1** Better a dry crust with
peace and quiet
than a house full of feasting,*f*
with strife.

2 A wise servant will rule over a
disgraceful son,
and will share the inheritance
as one of the brothers.

3 The crucible for silver and the
furnace for gold,
but the LORD tests the heart.

4 A wicked man listens to evil
lips;
a liar pays attention to a
malicious tongue.

5 He who mocks the poor shows
contempt for their Maker;
whoever gloats over disaster
will not go unpunished.

6 Children's children are a crown
to the aged,
and parents are the pride of
their children.

7 Arrogant*g* lips are unsuited to a
fool—
how much worse lying lips to
a ruler!

8 A bribe is a charm to the one
who gives it;
wherever he turns, he
succeeds.

9 He who covers over an offense
promotes love,
but whoever repeats the matter
separates close friends.

10 A rebuke impresses a man of
discernment
more than a hundred lashes a
fool.

11 An evil man is bent only on
rebellion;
a merciless official will be
sent against him.

12 Better to meet a bear robbed of
her cubs
than a fool in his folly.

13 If a man pays back evil for
good,
evil will never leave his house.

14 Starting a quarrel is like
breaching a dam;
so drop the matter before a
dispute breaks out.

15 Acquitting the guilty and
condemning the innocent—
the LORD detests them both.

16 Of what use is money in the
hand of a fool,
since he has no desire to get
wisdom?

17 A friend loves at all times,
and a brother is born for
adversity.

18 A man lacking in judgment
strikes hands in pledge
and puts up security for his
neighbor.

19 He who loves a quarrel loves
sin;
he who builds a high gate
invites destruction.

20 A man of perverse heart does
not prosper;
he whose tongue is deceitful
falls into trouble.

f 1 Hebrew sacrifices g 7 Or Eloquent

21 To have a fool for a son brings
      grief;
   there is no joy for the father
      of a fool.

22 A cheerful heart is good
      medicine,
   but a crushed spirit dries up
      the bones.

23 A wicked man accepts a bribe
      in secret
   to pervert the course of
      justice.

24 A discerning man keeps
      wisdom in view,
   but a fool's eyes wander to
      the ends of the earth.

25 A foolish son brings grief to his
      father
   and bitterness to the one who
      bore him.

26 It is not good to punish an
      innocent man,
   or to flog officials for their
      integrity.

27 A man of knowledge uses
      words with restraint,
   and a man of understanding
      is even-tempered.

28 Even a fool is thought wise if
      he keeps silent,
   and discerning if he holds his
      tongue.

18 1 An unfriendly man pursues
      selfish ends;
   he defies all sound judgment.

2 A fool finds no pleasure in
      understanding
   but delights in airing his own
      opinions.

3 When wickedness comes, so
      does contempt,
   and with shame comes
      disgrace.

4 The words of a man's mouth
      are deep waters,
   but the fountain of wisdom is
      a bubbling brook.

5 It is not good to be partial to
      the wicked
   or to deprive the innocent of
      justice.

6 A fool's lips bring him strife,
   and his mouth invites a beating.

7 A fool's mouth is his undoing,
   and his lips are a snare to his
      soul.

8 The words of a gossip are like
      choice morsels;
   they go down to a man's
      inmost parts.

9 One who is slack in his work
   is brother to one who destroys.

10 The name of the LORD is a
      strong tower;
   the righteous run to it and
      are safe.

11 The wealth of the rich is their
      fortified city;
   they imagine it an unscalable
      wall.

12 Before his downfall a man's
      heart is proud,
   but humility comes before
      honor.

13 He who answers before
      listening—
   that is his folly and his shame.

14 A man's spirit sustains him in
      sickness,
   but a crushed spirit who can
      bear?

15 The heart of the discerning
      acquires knowledge;
   the ears of the wise seek it
      out.

16 A gift opens the way for the giver
    and ushers him into the
        presence of the great.

17 The first to present his case
        seems right,
    till another comes forward
        and questions him.

18 Casting the lot settles disputes
    and keeps strong opponents
        apart.

19 An offended brother is more
        unyielding than a fortified
        city,
    and disputes are like the
        barred gates of a citadel.

20 From the fruit of his mouth a
        man's stomach is filled;
    with the harvest from his lips
        he is satisfied.

21 The tongue has the power of
        life and death,
    and those who love it will eat
        its fruit.

22 He who finds a wife finds what
        is good
    and receives favor from the
        LORD.

23 A poor man pleads for mercy,
    but a rich man answers harshly.

24 A man of many companions
        may come to ruin,
    but there is a friend who
        sticks closer than a brother.

19 ¹ Better a poor man whose
        walk is blameless
    than a fool whose lips are
        perverse.

2 It is not good to have zeal
        without knowledge,
    nor to be hasty and miss the way.

3 A man's own folly ruins his life,
    yet his heart rages against the
        LORD.

4 Wealth brings many friends,
    but a poor man's friend
        deserts him.

5 A false witness will not go
        unpunished,
    and he who pours out lies will
        not go free.

6 Many curry favor with a ruler,
    and everyone is the friend of
        a man who gives gifts.

7 A poor man is shunned by all
        his relatives—
    how much more do his
        friends avoid him!
    Though he pursues them with
        pleading,
    they are nowhere to be
        found.ʰ

8 He who gets wisdom loves his
        own soul;
    he who cherishes
        understanding prospers.

9 A false witness will not go
        unpunished,
    and he who pours out lies will
        perish.

10 It is not fitting for a fool to live
        in luxury—
    how much worse for a slave
        to rule over princes!

11 A man's wisdom gives him
        patience;
    it is to his glory to overlook
        an offense.

12 A king's rage is like the roar of
        a lion,
    but his favor is like dew on
        the grass.

___
h 7 The meaning of the Hebrew for this sentence is uncertain.

13 A foolish son is his father's ruin,
and a quarrelsome wife is like
a constant dripping.

14 Houses and wealth are
inherited from parents,
but a prudent wife is from the
LORD.

15 Laziness brings on deep sleep,
and the shiftless man goes
hungry.

16 He who obeys instructions
guards his life,
but he who is contemptuous
of his ways will die.

17 He who is kind to the poor
lends to the LORD,
and he will reward him for
what he has done.

18 Discipline your son, for in that
there is hope;
do not be a willing party to
his death.

19 A hot-tempered man must pay
the penalty;
if you rescue him, you will
have to do it again.

20 Listen to advice and accept
instruction,
and in the end you will be
wise.

21 Many are the plans in a man's
heart,
but it is the LORD's purpose
that prevails.

22 What a man desires is unfailing
loveⁱ;
better to be poor than a liar.

23 The fear of the LORD leads to life:
Then one rests content,
untouched by trouble.

24 The sluggard buries his hand in
the dish;
he will not even bring it back
to his mouth!

25 Flog a mocker, and the simple
will learn prudence;
rebuke a discerning man, and
he will gain knowledge.

26 He who robs his father and
drives out his mother
is a son who brings shame
and disgrace.

27 Stop listening to instruction,
my son,
and you will stray from the
words of knowledge.

28 A corrupt witness mocks at
justice,
and the mouth of the wicked
gulps down evil.

29 Penalties are prepared for
mockers,
and beatings for the backs of
fools.

20 **1** Wine is a mocker and beer
a brawler;
whoever is led astray by them
is not wise.

2 A king's wrath is like the roar of
a lion;
he who angers him forfeits his
life.

3 It is to a man's honor to avoid
strife,
but every fool is quick to
quarrel.

4 A sluggard does not plow in
season;
so at harvest time he looks
but finds nothing.

ⁱ 22 Or *A man's greed is his shame*

5 The purposes of a man's heart
  are deep waters,
  but a man of understanding
    draws them out.

6 Many a man claims to have
    unfailing love,
  but a faithful man who can
    find?

7 The righteous man leads a
    blameless life;
  blessed are his children after
    him.

8 When a king sits on his throne
    to judge,
  he winnows out all evil with
    his eyes.

9 Who can say, "I have kept my
    heart pure;
  I am clean and without sin"?

10 Differing weights and differing
    measures—
  the LORD detests them both.

11 Even a child is known by his
    actions,
  by whether his conduct is
    pure and right.

12 Ears that hear and eyes that
    see—
  the LORD has made them both.

13 Do not love sleep or you will
    grow poor;
  stay awake and you will have
    food to spare.

14 "It's no good, it's no good!" says
    the buyer;
  then off he goes and boasts
    about his purchase.

15 Gold there is, and rubies in
    abundance,
  but lips that speak knowledge
    are a rare jewel.

16 Take the garment of one who
    puts up security for a
    stranger;
  hold it in pledge if he does it
    for a wayward woman.

17 Food gained by fraud tastes
    sweet to a man,
  but he ends up with a mouth
    full of gravel.

18 Make plans by seeking advice;
  if you wage war, obtain
    guidance.

19 A gossip betrays a confidence;
  so avoid a man who talks too
    much.

20 If a man curses his father or
    mother,
  his lamp will be snuffed out
    in pitch darkness.

21 An inheritance quickly gained
    at the beginning
  will not be blessed at the end.

22 Do not say, "I'll pay you back
    for this wrong!"
  Wait for the LORD, and he will
    deliver you.

23 The LORD detests differing
    weights,
  and dishonest scales do not
    please him.

24 A man's steps are directed by
    the LORD.
  How then can anyone
    understand his own way?

25 It is a trap for a man to
    dedicate something rashly
  and only later to consider his
    vows.

26 A wise king winnows out the
    wicked;
  he drives the threshing wheel
    over them.

27 The lamp of the LORD searches
   the spirit of a man*j*;
   it searches out his inmost being.

28 Love and faithfulness keep a
   king safe;
   through love his throne is
   made secure.

29 The glory of young men is their
   strength,
   gray hair the splendor of the old.

30 Blows and wounds cleanse
   away evil,
   and beatings purge the
   inmost being.

21 ¹ The king's heart is in the
    hand of the LORD;
    he directs it like a watercourse
    wherever he pleases.

² All a man's ways seem right to
  him,
  but the LORD weighs the heart.

³ To do what is right and just
  is more acceptable to the
  LORD than sacrifice.

⁴ Haughty eyes and a proud
  heart,
  the lamp of the wicked, are sin!

⁵ The plans of the diligent lead to
  profit
  as surely as haste leads to
  poverty.

⁶ A fortune made by a lying tongue
  is a fleeting vapor and a
  deadly snare.*k*

⁷ The violence of the wicked will
  drag them away,
  for they refuse to do what is
  right.

⁸ The way of the guilty is devious,

but the conduct of the
   innocent is upright.

⁹ Better to live on a corner of the
  roof
  than share a home with a
  quarrelsome wife.

10 The wicked man craves evil;
   his neighbor gets no mercy
   from him.

11 When a mocker is punished,
   the simple gain wisdom;
   when a wise man is instructed,
   he gets knowledge.

12 The Righteous One*l* takes note
   of the house of the wicked
   and brings the wicked to ruin.

13 If a man shuts his ears to the
   cry of the poor,
   he too will cry out and not be
   answered.

14 A gift given in secret soothes
   anger,
   and a bribe concealed in the
   cloak pacifies great wrath.

15 When justice is done, it brings
   joy to the righteous
   but terror to evildoers.

16 A man who strays from the
   path of understanding
   comes to rest in the company
   of the dead.

17 He who loves pleasure will
   become poor;
   whoever loves wine and oil
   will never be rich.

18 The wicked become a ransom
   for the righteous,
   and the unfaithful for the
   upright.

j 27 Or *The spirit of man is the LORD's lamp*   *k* 6 Some Hebrew manuscripts, Septuagint
and Vulgate; most Hebrew manuscripts *vapor for those who seek death*   *l* 12 Or *The
righteous man*

19 Better to live in a desert
    than with a quarrelsome and
        ill-tempered wife.

20 In the house of the wise are stores
        of choice food and oil,
    but a foolish man devours all
        he has.

21 He who pursues righteousness
        and love
    finds life, prosperity[m] and
        honor.

22 A wise man attacks the city of
        the mighty
    and pulls down the stronghold
        in which they trust.

23 He who guards his mouth and
        his tongue
    keeps himself from calamity.

24 The proud and arrogant man—
        "Mocker" is his name;
    he behaves with overweening
        pride.

25 The sluggard's craving will be
        the death of him,
    because his hands refuse to
        work.

26 All day long he craves for more,
    but the righteous give
        without sparing.

27 The sacrifice of the wicked is
        detestable—
    how much more so when
        brought with evil intent!

28 A false witness will perish,
    and whoever listens to him
        will be destroyed forever.[n]

29 A wicked man puts up a bold
        front,
    but an upright man gives
        thought to his ways.

30 There is no wisdom, no insight,
        no plan
    that can succeed against the
        LORD.

31 The horse is made ready for the
        day of battle,
    but victory rests with the LORD.

22

1 A good name is more
    desirable than great riches;
to be esteemed is better than
    silver or gold.

2 Rich and poor have this in
        common:
    The LORD is the Maker of
        them all.

3 A prudent man sees danger and
        takes refuge,
    but the simple keep going and
        suffer for it.

4 Humility and the fear of the LORD
    bring wealth and honor and life.

5 In the paths of the wicked lie
        thorns and snares,
    but he who guards his soul
        stays far from them.

6 Train[o] a child in the way he
        should go,
    and when he is old he will not
        turn from it.

7 The rich rule over the poor,
    and the borrower is servant to
        the lender.

8 He who sows wickedness reaps
        trouble,
    and the rod of his fury will be
        destroyed.

9 A generous man will himself be
        blessed,
    for he shares his food with
        the poor.

---

m 21 Or righteousness   n 28 Or / but the words of an obedient man will live on
o 6 Or Start

10 Drive out the mocker, and out
    goes strife;
    quarrels and insults are ended.

11 He who loves a pure heart and
    whose speech is gracious
    will have the king for his
    friend.

12 The eyes of the LORD keep
    watch over knowledge,
    but he frustrates the words of
    the unfaithful.

13 The sluggard says, "There is a
    lion outside!"
    or, "I will be murdered in the
    streets!"

14 The mouth of an adulteress is a
    deep pit;
    he who is under the LORD's
    wrath will fall into it.

15 Folly is bound up in the heart
    of a child,
    but the rod of discipline will
    drive it far from him.

16 He who oppresses the poor to
    increase his wealth
    and he who gives gifts to the
    rich—both come to poverty.

Sayings of the Wise

17 Pay attention and listen to the
    sayings of the wise;
    apply your heart to what I
    teach,

18 for it is pleasing when you keep
    them in your heart
    and have all of them ready on
    your lips.

19 So that your trust may be in the
    LORD,
    I teach you today, even you.

20 Have I not written thirty^p
    sayings for you,
    sayings of counsel and
    knowledge,

21 teaching you true and reliable
    words,
    so that you can give sound
    answers
    to him who sent you?

22 Do not exploit the poor because
    they are poor
    and do not crush the needy in
    court,

23 for the LORD will take up their
    case
    and will plunder those who
    plunder them.

24 Do not make friends with a hot-
    tempered man,
    do not associate with one
    easily angered.

25 or you may learn his ways
    and get yourself ensnared.

26 Do not be a man who strikes
    hands in pledge
    or puts up security for debts;

27 if you lack the means to pay,
    your very bed will be
    snatched from under you.

28 Do not move an ancient
    boundary stone
    set up by your forefathers.

29 Do you see a man skilled in his
    work?
    He will serve before kings;
    he will not serve before
    obscure men.

23 1 When you sit to dine with a
    ruler,
    note well what^q is before you,

2 and put a knife to your throat
    if you are given to gluttony.

p 20 Or *not formerly written; or not written excellent*   *q* 1 Or *who*

3 Do not crave his delicacies,
  for that food is deceptive.

4 Do not wear yourself out to get
  rich;
    have the wisdom to show
    restraint.

5 Cast but a glance at riches, and
  they are gone,
    for they will surely sprout
    wings
  and fly off to the sky like an
  eagle.

6 Do not eat the food of a stingy
  man,
    do not crave his delicacies;

7 for he is the kind of man
  who is always thinking about
  the cost.^{r}
    "Eat and drink," he says to you,
    but his heart is not with you.

8 You will vomit up the little you
  have eaten
    and will have wasted your
    compliments.

9 Do not speak to a fool,
  for he will scorn the wisdom
  of your words.

10 Do not move an ancient
   boundary stone
     or encroach on the fields of
     the fatherless,

11 for their Defender is strong;
   he will take up their case
   against you.

12 Apply your heart to instruction
   and your ears to words of
   knowledge.

13 Do not withhold discipline from
   a child;
     if you punish him with the
     rod, he will not die.

14 Punish him with the rod
   and save his soul from death.^{s}

15 My son, if your heart is wise,
   then my heart will be glad;

16 my inmost being will rejoice
   when your lips speak what is
   right.

17 Do not let your heart envy sinners,
   but always be zealous for the
   fear of the LORD.

18 There is surely a future hope
   for you,
     and your hope will not be cut
     off.

19 Listen, my son, and be wise,
   and keep your heart on the
   right path.

20 Do not join those who drink
   too much wine
     or gorge themselves on meat,

21 for drunkards and gluttons
   become poor,
     and drowsiness clothes them
     in rags.

22 Listen to your father, who gave
   you life,
     and do not despise your
     mother when she is old.

23 Buy the truth and do not sell it;
   get wisdom, discipline and
   understanding.

24 The father of a righteous man
   has great joy;
     he who has a wise son
     delights in him.

25 May your father and mother be
   glad;
     may she who gave you birth
     rejoice!

26 My son, give me your heart
   and let your eyes keep to my
   ways,

---

^{r} 7 Or *for as he thinks within himself,* / *so he is*; or *for as he puts on a feast,* / *so he is*
^{s} 14 Hebrew *Sheol*

27 for a prostitute is a deep pit
    and a wayward wife is a
        narrow well.
28 Like a bandit she lies in wait,
    and multiplies the unfaithful
        among men.

29 Who has woe? Who has sorrow?
    Who has strife? Who has
        complaints?
    Who has needless bruises?
        Who has bloodshot eyes?
30 Those who linger over wine,
    who go to sample bowls of
        mixed wine.
31 Do not gaze at wine when it is
        red,
    when it sparkles in the cup,
    when it goes down smoothly!
32 In the end it bites like a snake
    and poisons like a viper.
33 Your eyes will see strange sights
    and your mind imagine
        confusing things.
34 You will be like one sleeping on
        the high seas,
    lying on top of the rigging.
35 "They hit me," you will say,
        "but I'm not hurt!
    They beat me, but I don't feel it!
    When will I wake up
    so I can find another drink?"

24 1 Do not envy wicked men,
        do not desire their company;
2 for their hearts plot violence,
    and their lips talk about
        making trouble.

3 By wisdom a house is built,
    and through understanding it
        is established;
4 through knowledge its rooms
        are filled
    with rare and beautiful
        treasures.

5 A wise man has great power,
    and a man of knowledge
        increases strength;

6 for waging war you need
        guidance,
    and for victory many advisers.

7 Wisdom is too high for a fool;
    in the assembly at the gate he
        has nothing to say.

8 He who plots evil
    will be known as a schemer.
9 The schemes of folly are sin,
    and men detest a mocker.

10 If you falter in times of trouble,
    how small is your strength!

11 Rescue those being led away to
        death;
    hold back those staggering
        toward slaughter.
12 If you say, "But we knew
        nothing about this,"
    does not he who weighs the
        heart perceive it?
    Does not he who guards your
        life know it?
    Will he not repay each person
        according to what he has
        done?

13 Eat honey, my son, for it is
        good;
    honey from the comb is sweet
        to your taste.
14 Know also that wisdom is sweet
        to your soul;
    if you find it, there is a future
        hope for you,
    and your hope will not be cut
        off.

15 Do not lie in wait like an
        outlaw against a righteous
        man's house,
    do not raid his dwelling place;
16 for though a righteous man
        falls seven times, he rises
        again,
    but the wicked are brought
        down by calamity.

17 Do not gloat when your enemy
    falls;
  when he stumbles, do not let
    your heart rejoice,
18 or the LORD will see and
    disapprove
  and turn his wrath away from
    him.

19 Do not fret because of evil men
  or be envious of the wicked,
20 for the evil man has no future
    hope,
  and the lamp of the wicked
    will be snuffed out.

21 Fear the LORD and the king, my
    son,
  and do not join with the
    rebellious,
22 for those two will send sudden
    destruction upon them,
  and who knows what
    calamities they can bring?

Further Sayings of the Wise

23 These also are sayings of the
wise:
  To show partiality in judging is
    not good:
24 Whoever says to the guilty,
    "You are innocent"—
  peoples will curse him and
    nations denounce him.
25 But it will go well with those
    who convict the guilty,
  and rich blessing will come
    upon them.

26 An honest answer
  is like a kiss on the lips.

27 Finish your outdoor work
  and get your fields ready;
  after that, build your house.

28 Do not testify against your
    neighbor without cause,
  or use your lips to deceive.
29 Do not say, "I'll do to him as he
    has done to me;
  I'll pay that man back for
    what he did."

30 I went past the field of the
    sluggard,
  past the vineyard of the man
    who lacks judgment;
31 thorns had come up everywhere,
  the ground was covered with
    weeds,
  and the stone wall was in ruins.
32 I applied my heart to what I
    observed
  and learned a lesson from
    what I saw:
33 A little sleep, a little slumber,
  a little folding of the hands to
    rest—
34 and poverty will come on you
    like a bandit
  and scarcity like an armed man.^{t}

More Proverbs of Solomon

25 1 These are more proverbs of
Solomon, copied by the men
of Hezekiah king of Judah:
2 It is the glory of God to conceal
    a matter;
  to search out a matter is the
    glory of kings.

3 As the heavens are high and
    the earth is deep,
  so the hearts of kings are
    unsearchable.

4 Remove the dross from the
    silver,
  and out comes material for^u
    the silversmith;

t 34 Or like a vagrant / and scarcity like a beggar   u 4 Or comes a vessel from

5 remove the wicked from the
    king's presence,
  and his throne will be
    established through
    righteousness.

6 Do not exalt yourself in the
    king's presence,
  and do not claim a place
    among great men;
7 it is better for him to say to
    you, "Come up here,"
  than for him to humiliate you
    before a nobleman.

  What you have seen with your
    eyes
8   do not bring\(^v\) hastily to court,
  for what will you do in the end
    if your neighbor puts you to
    shame?

9 If you argue your case with a
    neighbor,
  do not betray another man's
    confidence,
10 or he who hears it may shame
    you
  and you will never lose your
    bad reputation.

11 A word aptly spoken
  is like apples of gold in
    settings of silver.

12 Like an earring of gold or an
    ornament of fine gold
  is a wise man's rebuke to a
    listening ear.

13 Like the coolness of snow at
    harvest time
  is a trustworthy messenger to
    those who send him;
  he refreshes the spirit of his
    masters.

14 Like clouds and wind without
    rain

is a man who boasts of gifts
  he does not give.

15 Through patience a ruler can
    be persuaded,
  and a gentle tongue can
    break a bone.

16 If you find honey, eat just
    enough—
  too much of it, and you will
    vomit.

17 Seldom set foot in your
    neighbor's house—
  too much of you, and he will
    hate you.

18 Like a club or a sword or a
    sharp arrow
  is the man who gives false
    testimony against his
    neighbor.

19 Like a bad tooth or a lame foot
  is reliance on the unfaithful in
    times of trouble.

20 Like one who takes away a
    garment on a cold day,
  or like vinegar poured on soda,
  is one who sings songs to a
    heavy heart.

21 If your enemy is hungry, give
    him food to eat;
  if he is thirsty, give him water
    to drink.
22 In doing this, you will heap
    burning coals on his head,
  and the LORD will reward you.

23 As a north wind brings rain,
  so a sly tongue brings angry
    looks.

24 Better to live on a corner of the
    roof
  than share a house with a
    quarrelsome wife.

25 Like cold water to a weary soul
is good news from a distant
land.

26 Like a muddied spring or a
polluted well
is a righteous man who gives
way to the wicked.

27 It is not good to eat too much
honey,
nor is it honorable to seek
one's own honor.

28 Like a city whose walls are
broken down
is a man who lacks self-control.

26 ¹ Like snow in summer or
rain in harvest,
honor is not fitting for a fool.

² Like a fluttering sparrow or a
darting swallow,
an undeserved curse does not
come to rest.

³ A whip for the horse, a halter
for the donkey,
and a rod for the backs of fools!

⁴ Do not answer a fool according
to his folly,
or you will be like him
yourself.

⁵ Answer a fool according to his
folly,
or he will be wise in his own
eyes.

⁶ Like cutting off one's feet or
drinking violence
is the sending of a message by
the hand of a fool.

⁷ Like a lame man's legs that
hang limp
is a proverb in the mouth of a
fool.

⁸ Like tying a stone in a sling
is the giving of honor to a fool.

⁹ Like a thornbush in a
drunkard's hand
is a proverb in the mouth of a
fool.

¹⁰ Like an archer who wounds at
random
is he who hires a fool or any
passer-by.

¹¹ As a dog returns to its vomit,
so a fool repeats his folly.

¹² Do you see a man wise in his
own eyes?
There is more hope for a fool
than for him.

¹³ The sluggard says, "There is a
lion in the road,
a fierce lion roaming the
streets!"

¹⁴ As a door turns on its hinges,
so a sluggard turns on his bed.

¹⁵ The sluggard buries his hand in
the dish;
he is too lazy to bring it back
to his mouth.

¹⁶ The sluggard is wiser in his
own eyes
than seven men who answer
discreetly.

¹⁷ Like one who seizes a dog by
the ears
is a passer-by who meddles in
a quarrel not his own.

¹⁸ Like a madman shooting
firebrands or deadly arrows

¹⁹ is a man who deceives his
neighbor
and says, "I was only joking!"

²⁰ Without wood a fire goes out;
without gossip a quarrel dies
down.

²¹ As charcoal to embers and as
wood to fire,

so is a quarrelsome man for kindling strife.

22 The words of a gossip are like choice morsels;
they go down to a man's inmost parts.

23 Like a coating of glaze[w] over earthenware
are fervent lips with an evil heart.

24 A malicious man disguises himself with his lips,
but in his heart he harbors deceit.

25 Though his speech is charming, do not believe him,
for seven abominations fill his heart.

26 His malice may be concealed by deception,
but his wickedness will be exposed in the assembly.

27 If a man digs a pit, he will fall into it;
if a man rolls a stone, it will roll back on him.

28 A lying tongue hates those it hurts,
and a flattering mouth works ruin.

27 ¹ Do not boast about tomorrow,
for you do not know what a day may bring forth.

2 Let another praise you, and not your own mouth;
someone else, and not your own lips.

3 Stone is heavy and sand a burden,
but provocation by a fool is heavier than both.

4 Anger is cruel and fury overwhelming,
but who can stand before jealousy?

5 Better is open rebuke than hidden love.

6 Wounds from a friend can be trusted,
but an enemy multiplies kisses.

7 He who is full loathes honey,
but to the hungry even what is bitter tastes sweet.

8 Like a bird that strays from its nest
is a man who strays from his home.

9 Perfume and incense bring joy to the heart,
and the pleasantness of one's friend springs from his earnest counsel.

10 Do not forsake your friend and the friend of your father,
and do not go to your brother's house when disaster strikes you—
better a neighbor nearby than a brother far away.

11 Be wise, my son, and bring joy to my heart;
then I can answer anyone who treats me with contempt.

12 The prudent see danger and take refuge,
but the simple keep going and suffer for it.

13 Take the garment of one who puts up security for a stranger;
hold it in pledge if he does it for a wayward woman.

14 If a man loudly blesses his
    neighbor early in the
    morning,
  it will be taken as a curse.

15 A quarrelsome wife is like
    a constant dripping on a rainy
    day;
16 restraining her is like
    restraining the wind
    or grasping oil with the hand.

17 As iron sharpens iron,
  so one man sharpens another.

18 He who tends a fig tree will eat
    its fruit,
  and he who looks after his
    master will be honored.

19 As water reflects a face,
  so a man's heart reflects the
    man.

20 Death and Destruction*x* are
    never satisfied,
  and neither are the eyes of man.

21 The crucible for silver and the
    furnace for gold,
  but man is tested by the
    praise he receives.

22 Though you grind a fool in a
    mortar,
  grinding him like grain with a
    pestle,
  you will not remove his folly
    from him.

23 Be sure you know the condition
    of your flocks,
  give careful attention to your
    herds;
24 for riches do not endure forever,
  and a crown is not secure for
    all generations.

25 When the hay is removed and
    new growth appears

and the grass from the hills is
    gathered in,
26 the lambs will provide you with
    clothing,
  and the goats with the price
    of a field.
27 You will have plenty of goats' milk
    to feed you and your family
  and to nourish your servant
    girls.

28 ¹ The wicked man flees
    though no one pursues,
  but the righteous are as bold
    as a lion.

2 When a country is rebellious, it
    has many rulers,
  but a man of understanding and
    knowledge maintains order.

3 A ruler*y* who oppresses the poor
    is like a driving rain that
    leaves no crops.

4 Those who forsake the law
    praise the wicked,
  but those who keep the law
    resist them.

5 Evil men do not understand
    justice,
  but those who seek the LORD
    understand it fully.

6 Better a poor man whose walk
    is blameless
  than a rich man whose ways
    are perverse.

7 He who keeps the law is a
    discerning son,
  but a companion of gluttons
    disgraces his father.

8 He who increases his wealth by
    exorbitant interest
  amasses it for another, who
    will be kind to the poor.

---

x 20 Hebrew *Sheol and Abaddon*   *y* 3 Or *A poor man*

9 If anyone turns a deaf ear to
the law,
even his prayers are
detestable.

10 He who leads the upright along
an evil path
will fall into his own trap,
but the blameless will receive
a good inheritance.

11 A rich man may be wise in his
own eyes,
but a poor man who has
discernment sees through
him.

12 When the righteous triumph,
there is great elation;
but when the wicked rise to
power, men go into hiding.

13 He who conceals his sins does
not prosper,
but whoever confesses and
renounces them finds
mercy.

14 Blessed is the man who always
fears the LORD,
but he who hardens his heart
falls into trouble.

15 Like a roaring lion or a
charging bear
is a wicked man ruling over a
helpless people.

16 A tyrannical ruler lacks
judgment,
but he who hates ill-gotten
gain will enjoy a long life.

17 A man tormented by the guilt
of murder
will be a fugitive till death;
let no one support him.

18 He whose walk is blameless is
kept safe,
but he whose ways are
perverse will suddenly fall.

19 He who works his land will
have abundant food,
but the one who chases
fantasies will have his fill
of poverty.

20 A faithful man will be richly
blessed,
but one eager to get rich will
not go unpunished.

21 To show partiality is not good—
yet a man will do wrong for a
piece of bread.

22 A stingy man is eager to get rich
and is unaware that poverty
awaits him.

23 He who rebukes a man will in
the end gain more favor
than he who has a flattering
tongue.

24 He who robs his father or
mother
and says, "It's not wrong"—
he is partner to him who
destroys.

25 A greedy man stirs up
dissension,
but he who trusts in the LORD
will prosper.

26 He who trusts in himself is a
fool,
but he who walks in wisdom
is kept safe.

27 He who gives to the poor will
lack nothing,
but he who closes his eyes to
them receives many curses.

28 When the wicked rise to power,
people go into hiding;
but when the wicked perish,
the righteous thrive.

29

1 A man who remains stiff-
necked after many rebukes
will suddenly be destroyed—
without remedy.

2 When the righteous thrive, the
people rejoice;
when the wicked rule, the
people groan.

3 A man who loves wisdom
brings joy to his father,
but a companion of prostitutes
squanders his wealth.

4 By justice a king gives a
country stability,
but one who is greedy for
bribes tears it down.

5 Whoever flatters his neighbor
is spreading a net for his feet.

6 An evil man is snared by his
own sin,
but a righteous one can sing
and be glad.

7 The righteous care about
justice for the poor,
but the wicked have no such
concern.

8 Mockers stir up a city,
but wise men turn away anger.

9 If a wise man goes to court
with a fool,
the fool rages and scoffs, and
there is no peace.

10 Bloodthirsty men hate a man of
integrity
and seek to kill the upright.

11 A fool gives full vent to his
anger,
but a wise man keeps himself
under control.

12 If a ruler listens to lies,
all his officials become wicked.

13 The poor man and the oppressor
have this in common:
The LORD gives sight to the
eyes of both.

14 If a king judges the poor with
fairness,
his throne will always be secure.

15 The rod of correction imparts
wisdom,
but a child left to himself
disgraces his mother.

16 When the wicked thrive, so
does sin,
but the righteous will see
their downfall.

17 Discipline your son, and he will
give you peace;
he will bring delight to your
soul.

18 Where there is no revelation, the
people cast off restraint;
but blessed is he who keeps
the law.

19 A servant cannot be corrected
by mere words;
though he understands, he
will not respond.

20 Do you see a man who speaks
in haste?
There is more hope for a fool
than for him.

21 If a man pampers his servant
from youth,
he will bring grief[z] in the end.

22 An angry man stirs up
dissension,
and a hot-tempered one
commits many sins.

---

[z] *21* The meaning of the Hebrew for this word is uncertain.

23 A man's pride brings him low,
   but a man of lowly spirit
      gains honor.

24 The accomplice of a thief is his
      own enemy;
   he is put under oath and dare
      not testify.

25 Fear of man will prove to be a
      snare,
   but whoever trusts in the
      LORD is kept safe.

26 Many seek an audience with a
      ruler,
   but it is from the LORD that
      man gets justice.

27 The righteous detest the
      dishonest;
   the wicked detest the upright.

Sayings of Agur

30 1 The sayings of Agur son of
   Jakeh—an oracleᵃ:

   This man declared to Ithiel,
      to Ithiel and to Ucal:ᵇ

2 "I am the most ignorant of men;
   I do not have a man's
      understanding.

3 I have not learned wisdom,
   nor have I knowledge of the
      Holy One.

4 Who has gone up to heaven
      and come down?
   Who has gathered up the
      wind in the hollow of his
      hands?
   Who has wrapped up the
      waters in his cloak?
   Who has established all the
      ends of the earth?

What is his name, and the
   name of his son?
Tell me if you know!

5 "Every word of God is flawless;
   he is a shield to those who
      take refuge in him.

6 Do not add to his words,
   or he will rebuke you and
      prove you a liar.

7 "Two things I ask of you, O LORD;
   do not refuse me before I die:

8 Keep falsehood and lies far
      from me;
   give me neither poverty nor
      riches,
   but give me only my daily
      bread.

9 Otherwise, I may have too
      much and disown you
   and say, 'Who is the LORD?'
   Or I may become poor and
      steal,
   and so dishonor the name of
      my God.

10 "Do not slander a servant to his
      master,
   or he will curse you, and you
      will pay for it.

11 "There are those who curse
      their fathers
   and do not bless their
      mothers;

12 those who are pure in their
      own eyes
   and yet are not cleansed of
      their filth;

13 those whose eyes are ever so
      haughty,
   whose glances are so disdainful;

14 those whose teeth are swords
   and whose jaws are set with
      knives

ᵃ 1 Or Jakeh of Massa   ᵇ 1 Masoretic Text; with a different word division of the Hebrew
declared, "I am weary, O God; / I am weary, O God, and faint.

to devour the poor from the
earth,
the needy from among
mankind.

15 "The leech has two daughters.
'Give! Give!' they cry.

"There are three things that are
never satisfied,
four that never say, 'Enough!':
16 the grave,c the barren womb,
land, which is never satisfied
with water,
and fire, which never says,
'Enough!'

17 "The eye that mocks a father,
that scorns obedience to a
mother,
will be pecked out by the
ravens of the valley,
will be eaten by the vultures.

18 "There are three things that are
too amazing for me,
four that I do not understand:
19 the way of an eagle in the sky,
the way of a snake on a rock,
the way of a ship on the high
seas,
and the way of a man with a
maiden.

20 "This is the way of an
adulteress:
She eats and wipes her mouth
and says, 'I've done nothing
wrong.'

21 "Under three things the earth
trembles,
under four it cannot bear up:
22 a servant who becomes king,
a fool who is full of food,

23 an unloved woman who is
married,
and a maidservant who
displaces her mistress.

24 "Four things on earth are small,
yet they are extremely wise:
25 Ants are creatures of little
strength,
yet they store up their food in
the summer;
26 coneysd are creatures of little
power,
yet they make their home in
the crags;
27 locusts have no king,
yet they advance together in
ranks;
28 a lizard can be caught with the
hand,
yet it is found in kings'
palaces.

29 "There are three things that are
stately in their stride,
four that move with stately
bearing:
30 a lion, mighty among beasts,
who retreats before nothing;
31 a strutting rooster, a he-goat,
and a king with his army
around him.e

32 "If you have played the fool
and exalted yourself,
or if you have planned evil,
clap your hand over your
mouth!
33 For as churning †he milk
produces butter,
and as twisting the nose
produces blood,
so stirring up anger produces
strife."

---

c 16 Hebrew *Sheol*   d 26 That is, the hyrax or rock badger   e 31 Or *king secure against
revolt*

Sayings of King Lemuel

31 ¹ The sayings of King Lemuel—an oracle*f* his mother taught him:

² "O my son, O son of my womb,
  O son of my vows,*g*
³ do not spend your strength on women,
  your vigor on those who ruin kings.

⁴ "It is not for kings, O Lemuel—
  not for kings to drink wine,
  not for rulers to crave beer,
⁵ lest they drink and forget what the law decrees,
  and deprive all the oppressed of their rights.
⁶ Give beer to those who are perishing,
  wine to those who are in anguish;
⁷ let them drink and forget their poverty
  and remember their misery no more.

⁸ "Speak up for those who cannot speak for themselves,
  for the rights of all who are destitute.
⁹ Speak up and judge fairly;
  defend the rights of the poor and needy."

Epilogue: The Wife of Noble Character

¹⁰ *h*A wife of noble character who can find?
  She is worth far more than rubies.
¹¹ Her husband has full confidence in her
  and lacks nothing of value.
¹² She brings him good, not harm,
  all the days of her life.
¹³ She selects wool and flax
  and works with eager hands.
¹⁴ She is like the merchant ships,
  bringing her food from afar.
¹⁵ She gets up while it is still dark;
  she provides food for her family
  and portions for her servant girls.
¹⁶ She considers a field and buys it;
  out of her earnings she plants a vineyard.
¹⁷ She sets about her work vigorously;
  her arms are strong for her tasks.
¹⁸ She sees that her trading is profitable,
  and her lamp does not go out at night.
¹⁹ In her hand she holds the distaff
  and grasps the spindle with her fingers.
²⁰ She opens her arms to the poor
  and extends her hands to the needy.
²¹ When it snows, she has no fear for her household;
  for all of them are clothed in scarlet.
²² She makes coverings for her bed;
  she is clothed in fine linen and purple.
²³ Her husband is respected at the city gate,

---

f 1 Or *of Lemuel king of Massa, which* *g* 2 Or / *the answer to my prayers* *h* 10 Verses 10-31 are an acrostic, each verse beginning with a successive letter of the Hebrew alphabet.

where he takes his seat
among the elders of the
land.

24 She makes linen garments and
sells them,
and supplies the merchants
with sashes.

25 She is clothed with strength
and dignity;
she can laugh at the days to
come.

26 She speaks with wisdom,
and faithful instruction is on
her tongue.

27 She watches over the affairs of
her household

and does not eat the bread of
idleness.

28 Her children arise and call her
blessed;
her husband also, and he
praises her:

29 "Many women do noble things,
but you surpass them all."

30 Charm is deceptive, and beauty
is fleeting;
but a woman who fears the
LORD is to be praised.

31 Give her the reward she has
earned,
and let her works bring her
praise at the city gate.

A WORD ABOUT THE NIV

This New Testament of the New International Version of the Holy
Bible is a completely new translation made by over a hundred scholars working directly from the best available Greek texts. It had its
beginning in 1965 when, after several years of exploratory study by
committees from the Christian Reformed Church and the National
Association of Evangelicals, a group of scholars met at Palos Heights,
Illinois, and concurred in the need for a new translation of the Bible
in contemporary English. This group, though not made up of official
church representatives, was transdenominational. Its conclusion was
endorsed by a large number of leaders from many denominations
who met in Chicago in 1966.

Responsibility for the new version was delegated by the Palos
Heights group to a self-governing body of fifteen, the Committee on
Bible Translation, composed for the most part of biblical scholars
from colleges, universities and seminaries. In 1967 the New York
Bible Society (now the International Bible Society) generously un-
dertook the financial sponsorship of the project—a sponsorship that
made it possible to enlist the help of many distinguished scholars.
The fact that participants from the United States, Great Britain, Can-
ada, Australia and New Zealand worked together gave the project its
international scope. That they were from many denominations—including Anglican, Assemblies of God, Baptist, Brethren, Christian
Reformed, Church of Christ, Evangelical Free, Lutheran, Methodist,
Nazarene, Presbyterian, Wesleyan and other churches—helped to
safeguard the translation from sectarian bias.

How it was made helps to give the New International Version its
distinctiveness. The translation of each book was assigned to a team
of scholars. Next, one of the Intermediate Editorial Committees revised the initial translation, with constant reference to the Hebrew,
Aramaic or Greek. Their work then went to one of the General Editorial Committees, which checked it in detail and made another thorough revision. This revision in turn was carefully reviewed by the
Committee on Bible Translation, which made further changes and

then released the final version for publication. In this way the entire Bible underwent three revisions, during each of which the translation was examined for its faithfulness to the original languages and for its English style.

All this involved many thousands of hours of research and discussion regarding the meaning of the texts and the precise way of putting them into English. It may well be that no other translation has been made by a more thorough process of review and revision from committee to committee than this one.

From the beginning of the project, the Committee on Bible Translation held to certain goals for the New International Version: that it would be an accurate translation and one that would have clarity and literary quality and so prove suitable for public and private reading, teaching, preaching, memorizing and liturgical use. The Committee also sought to preserve some measure of continuity with the long tradition of translating the Scriptures into English.

In working toward these goals, the translators were united in their commitment to the authority and infallibility of the Bible as God's Word in written form. They believe that it contains the divine answer to the deepest needs of humanity, that it sheds unique light on our path in a dark world, and that it sets forth the way to our eternal well-being.

The first concern of the translators has been the accuracy of the translation and its fidelity to the thought of the biblical writers. They have weighed the significance of the lexical and grammatical details of the Hebrew, Aramaic and Greek texts. At the same time, they have striven for more than a word-for-word translation. Because thought patterns and syntax differ from language to language, faithful communication of the meaning of the writers of the Bible demands frequent modifications in sentence structure and constant regard for the contextual meanings of words.

The Committee on Bible Translation submitted the developing version to a number of stylistic consultants. Samples of the translation were tested for clarity and ease of reading by various kinds of people—young and old, highly educated and less well educated, ministers and laymen. Concern for clear and natural English motivated the translators and consultants. In view of the international use of English, the translators sought to avoid obvious Americanisms on the one hand and obvious Anglicanism on the other. A British edition reflects the comparatively few differences of significant idiom and of spelling.

As for the traditional pronouns "thou," "thee" and "thine" in reference to the Deity, the translators judged that to use these archaisms (along with the old verb forms such as "doest," "wouldest" and "hadst") would violate accuracy in translation. Greek does not use special pronouns for the persons of the Godhead. A present-day translation is not enhanced by forms that in the time of the King James Version were used in everyday speech, whether referring to God or man.

The Greek text used in translating the New Testament was an eclectic one. No other piece of ancient literature has such an abundance of manuscript witnesses as does the New Testament. Where existing manuscripts differ, the translators made their choice of readings according to accepted principles of New Testament textual criticism. Footnotes call attention to places where there was uncertainty about what the original text was. The best current printed texts of the Greek New Testament were used.

There is a sense in which the work of translation is never wholly finished. This applies to all great literature and uniquely so to the Bible. In 1973 the New Testament in the New International Version was published. Since then, suggestions for corrections and revisions have been received from various sources. The Committee on Bible Translation carefully considered the suggestions and adopted a number of them. These were incorporated in the first printing of the entire BIble in 1978. Some additional revisions were made by the Committee on Bible Translation in 1983 and appear in printings after that date.

To achieve clarity the translators sometimes supplied words not in the original texts but required by the context. If there was uncertainty about such material, it is enclosed in brackets. Also for the sake of clarity or style, nouns, including some proper nouns, are sometimes substituted for pronouns, and vice versa. As an aid to the reader, italicized sectional headings are inserted in most of the books. They are not to be regarded as part of the NIV text, are not for oral reading, and are not intended to dictate the interpretation of the sections they head.

The footnotes in this version are of several kinds, most of which need no explanation. Those giving alternative translations begin with "Or" and generally introduce the alternative with the last word preceding it in the text, except when it is a single-word alternative; in poetry quoted in a footnote a slant mark indicates a line division. Footnotes introduced by "Or." do not have uniform significance. In some cases two possible translations were considered to have about equal validity. In other cases, though the translators were convinced that the translation in the text was correct, they judged that another interpretation was possible and of sufficient importance to be represented in a footnote. In the New Testament, footnotes that refer to uncertainty regarding the original text are introduced by "Some manuscripts" or similar expressions.

It should be noted that minerals, flora and fauna, architectural details, articles of clothing and jewelry, musical instruments and other articles cannot always be identified with precision. Also measures of capacity in the biblical period are particularly uncertain.

Like all translations of the Bible, made as they are by imperfect man, this one undoubtedly falls short of its goals. Yet we are grateful to God for the extent to which he has enabled us to realize these goals and for the strength he has given us and our colleagues to complete our task. We offer this version of the Bible to him in whose name for whose glory it has been made. We pray that it will lead many into a better understanding of the Holy Scriptures and a fuller knowledge of Jesus Christ the incarnate Word, of whom the Scriptures so faithfully testify.

The Committee on Bible Translation
June 1978
(Revised August 1983)

A COWBOY'S PRAYER

★ ★ ★

Heavenly Father,

We pause, mindful of the many blessings you have bestowed upon us. We ask that you be with us at this rodeo and we pray that you will guide us in the arena of life. We don't ask for special favors; we don't ask to draw around a chute-fightin' horse or to never break a barrier. Nor do we ask for all daylight runs or not to draw a steer that won't lay. Help us, Lord, to live our lives in such a manner that when we make that last inevitable ride to the country up there, where the grass grows lush, green and stirrup high, and the water runs cool, clear and deep, that you, as our last Judge, will tell us that our entry fees are paid.

—Clem McSpadden

This poem was inspired by W. A. Reynolds, an ordained
Baptist minister, who traveled across Texas in the early
1900s spreading the Gospel as a circuit preacher. It also
deals with the lessons of life I learned from the stories
he read to me as a child. He was my grandfather.

THE STORYBOOK

My Grandpa was a circuit preacher
   who traveled horseback across this land.
Preaching to the multitudes from
   the book he held in his hand.

It was kinda dog-eared at the corners,
   its cover smooth and worn,
With edges trimmed in faded gold,
   but not a page was torn.

He said it was his storybook,
   a truly wonderous thing.
He would read it to me for hours as a child,
   as we sat in the front porch swing.

Through those stories we traveled,
   to many a foreign land.
The things and places that we saw,
   were truly something grand.

We traveled to Jerusalem,
   and Joppa by the Great Sea.

We walked across the Holy Land,
    just Grandpa, the disciples, and me.

We saw the waters parted,
    at the edge of the Red Sea.
Then walked across high and dry,
    just Grandpa, Moses, and me.

We went to ancient Babylon,
    and the wall we did see,
Where we read the writings of God,
    just Grandpa, Daniel, and me.

We cast our nets upon the waters,
    at the shores of Galilee.
Then hauled up fishes and souls of men,
    just Grandpa, Peter, and me.

We witnessed all kinds of miracles,
    numerous wonders did we see,
As we walked across the Holy Land,
    just Grandpa, the disciples, and me.

But the greatest journey that I will make,
    is one that is yet to be,
As I travel toward the Great Beyond,
    just Grandpa, Jesus, and me.

© Grant Adkisson

FINDING THE WAY
Grant Adkisson
★ ★ ★

Is something missing in your life? Is there an emptiness inside of you that all the things you have done, all the things you own and even the reputation you've built can't really fill? No human accomplishment, no list of possessions and not even being religious can fill the void in every human life that we were created with. Only Jesus Christ fits that space! So, the "million dollar" question is, "How can I come to know Jesus personally?"

I'd like to show you the way. Not a man's opinion, not just a church's or a certain group's opinion, but what Almighty God himself said. This is not A way, it is THE way. God's way!

First, you have to look at God. In John's Gospel (page 145), Jesus said, *"I am the way and the truth and the life. No one comes to the Father except through me."* Jesus is the only way. The book of Proverbs (page 483) says, *There is a way that seems right to a man, but in the end it leads to death.* Do it God's way, not your way! You need to look at yourself. You are not the only one who has some emptiness inside or who has messed up. The book of Romans (you can read it starting on page 201) tells us how it is between God and humans: *There is no one righteous, not even one* and *For all have sinned and fall short of the glory of God.* And it goes on to say, *For the wages of sin is death.* Tell God you know you are a sinner. Tell him right now.

Then look back to God. The rest of that passage says, *...but the gift of God is eternal life in Christ Jesus our Lord.* Jesus Christ died on the cross to pay for your sins. Don't reject him.

According to the Bible, this is the true cowboy way: *Repent, then, and turn to God, so that your sins may be wiped out, that times of refreshing may come from the Lord* (see the book of Acts, page 160).

To repent means to change directions or to turn around. Only God can make a lasting change in your whole life. Ask him to. Ask him to forgive your sin, but remember this means you will turn away from it as well. True conversion means surrendering your

...fe to obey your Lord Jesus Christ. This doesn't mean you will be perfect. It just means you will be surrendered.

Many people want to receive God's gift of salvation, but they also want to keep living their own way. A prayer for salvation isn't a good luck charm. The Bible, God's Holy Word, makes it clear—without repentance you cannot be converted and receive eternal and abundant life in the meantime. If you are not willing to surrender, don't bother praying for salvation.

This may offend you, but Jesus once said, *"Not everyone who says to me, 'Lord, Lord,' will enter the kingdom of heaven, but only he who does the will of my Father who is in heaven"* (see Matthew's Gospel, page 9). Jesus wasn't saying you can be good enough to be saved. He's saying when you turn away from your sin and surrender your life to him, he will take control and do God's will through you.

Romans tells us, *If you confess with your mouth "Jesus is Lord," and believe in your heart that God raised him from the dead, you will be saved. For it is with your heart that you believe and are justified, and it is with your mouth that you confess and are saved. For "everyone who calls on the name of the Lord will be saved."*

Believing is not just putting something in your head.
It is having your head and heart together.

Are you ready?
Pray this practical, life-changing prayer:

God, I know that I am a sinner. Please forgive me of my wrongdoing. I've changed my mind on living my own way. I believe the Bible, that Jesus died on the cross to pay for my sins. I believe that he rose from the dead to forgive my sins and to give himself as the gift of eternal life. I surrender my life to you and receive you as the Lord of my life. Amen.

★ ★ ★

© Cynthia Hunter

WHAT NOW?

★ ★ ★

Becoming a new person in Jesus Christ isn't the end, it's the beginning! The story of your life is now entering a new chapter with God. Every day is full of choices. As a person in whom Jesus lives, you can either make those decisions based on your will or on God's Word. You can base what you do on the ever-changing input of our society or on the everlasting Word of God, the Bible.

1. Your identity: God's Word says when you received Jesus Christ as your Lord and Savior, you became a child of God. Now there is a change in where you will spend eternity: *"But in keeping with his promise we are looking forward to a new heaven and a new earth, the home of righteousness"* (see 2 Peter, page 318).

2. Bible reading: Let God talk with you through the Bible. Reading and obeying the Bible is where to start growing spiritually. God's Word, the Bible, will feed you and transform your life. But it will take discipline on your part to learn from it (check out the helps in the front of this book).

3. Prayer: You talk with God through prayer. One of the greatest privileges you have as a Christian is to communicate with God. Just talk with him like you would your best friend, because now he is!

Tell God every day how wonderful he is and how much you love him. That's called praise. Read the book of Psalms to look at the many different ways to pray to and praise God. Repent again daily and confess your sin to him. He is faithful to forgive that sin. Pray for the needs of others. That's called intercession. Make your personal requests known to him and leave them with him and he'll give you peace of mind and heart.

4. Ask for help: Jesus said that he would send a Helper. You can read about this Helper in John 14 & 15 (starting on page 144). That Helper is the Holy Spirit, who guides and enables you to fulfill God's will.

5. Tell others! The New Testament tells us that we are his representatives on this earth to tell others how they can receive the good news of salvation. Jesus himself tells us to go and make disciples of all nations (see Matthew's Gospel, page 45).

6. Find a church: There are no lone rangers in the Christian life. Ask the following questions:
- Was the message Bible-based, Christ-honoring, and applicable to your everyday life?
- Did the speaker have a genuine love for Jesus and for those he was addressing?
- Did the speaker call for people to make a personal commitment to Jesus Christ?
- Did the music help you praise God?
- Did the people make you feel loved and welcome?
- Did you leave wanting to be more committed to Christ?

7. Don't give up! Through perseverance and God's strength you will be a growing, productive Christian. Hang on to the Word of God!